KT-424-031

Dictionary of Media and Communication Studies

FIFTH EDITION

James Watson

and

Anne Hill

A member of the Hodder Headline Group
LONDON
Co-published in the United States of America by
Oxford University Press Inc., New York

First published in Great Britain in 1984
Second edition 1989
Third edition 1993
Fourth edition 1997
Fifth edition published in 2000 by
Arnold, a member of the Hodder Headline Group,
338 Euston Road, London NW1 3BH

http://www.arnoldpublishers.com

Co-published in the United States of America by
Oxford University Press Inc.,
198 Madison Avenue, New York NY10016

British Library Cataloguing in Publication Data
A catalogue record for this book is available from the British Library

Library of Congress Cataloging-in-Publication Data
A catalog record for this book is available from the Library of
Congress

ISBN 0 340 73205 9

2 3 4 5 6 7 8 9 10

Production Editor: Liz Gooster
Production Controller: Priya Gohil
Cover Design: Terry Griffiths

Typest in 9/11 Minion by J&L Composition Ltd, Filey, North Yorkshire
Printed and bound in India by Replika Press Pvt. Ltd. 100% EOU,
Delhi 110 040

What do you think about this book? Or any orther Arnold title?
Please send your comments to feedback.arnold@hodder.co.uk

Preface to the 5th edition

Prior to the very first edition of this dictionary, when we presented the original idea to our editor at Edward Arnold (as Arnold was then called), our aim was modest – a simple ABC of useful terms used in communication and media studies. The editor suggested, 'Perhaps you could add a little media history'. We did, and found ourselves in need of repositioning the words 'modest' and 'little'. The rest, as they say, is history; except that our new editor, conscious that the 5th edition of the *Dictionary of Media and Communication Studies* would coincide with the Millennium, ventured another modest proposal.

What better way to celebrate than to add a listing of media developments over the centuries? Duly assembled, our Chronology of Media Events is the chief addition to our overview of terms and histories (see p. 339). Once again we invite readers to peruse the contents, which we see as a first working draft, and let us know if they consider that we have made omissions.

We fully recognize that inventions emerge out of contexts, and through cultural pressures and opportunities, and that they are the product of many minds rather than solely the inspiration of individual scientists and technologists. Louis Lumière was as truthful as he was modest when, credited with the invention of the cinema, he said, 'What did I do? It was in the air'. Even so, his vision and enterprise, along with that of his brother Auguste, warrant celebration as much as Wellington's identification with Waterloo or Nye Bevan's with the National Health Service.

The second editorial suggestion for this 5th edition was the proposal that we adjust the title of the dictionary (originally the *Dictionary of Communication and Media Studies*) to acknowledge both the dominance of *media* in studies, and of media in our lives – to the point where, it might be claimed, interpersonal communication is fast becoming hijacked by IPC on the Net. (See the expanded entry on the INTERNET.) The first point is pretty much a fact, at least in education in the UK. This we consider to be a very good argument for the retention of Communication Studies with its stronger focus on developing individual powers of communication in terms of non-mediated exchange. If the second point is true then that reinforces the case for maintaining a broader-than-media alternative to study. Should the seemingly exponential rise in communicating on the Net (see BEDROOM CULTURE) threaten, if not marginalize, face-to-face communication we would expect educationalists (and indeed the community) to react with a degree of apprehension; pay close attention to the trend and consider balancing strategies – that is before VIRTUAL REALITY takes precedence over the 'real'.

The updated text of the dictionary will, we hope, keep the reader abreast of the chief issues, trends and perspectives of the study of communication as the new century succeeds the old. There is more, for example, on the ACTIVE AUDIENCE, with particular attention being paid to media by the young (see CHILDREN, YOUNG PEOPLE

AND THE CHANGING MEDIA ENVIRONMENT). Reflecting trends, 'izations' have been granted a field day with CULTURE: GLOBALIZATION, OF, NEWS: GLOBALIZATION OF, GLOBAL SCRUTINY, McWORLD VS JIHAD and of course DIGITALIZATION. Media production at the operational level receives attention in entries such as BALANCE-SHEET CULTURE, INDEPENDENT PRODUCERS and SWEETHEART DEALS.

NARRATIVE, READING and REALISM all make belated entries in their own right, as do PRIVACY, OTHER, COMMON SENSE and SELF-IDENTITY. The soft spot the authors have for models is sustained with McQUAIL'S ACCOUNTABILITY OF MEDIA MODEL, 1997 and his four stages of audience fragmentation (AUDIENCE: FRAGMENTATION OF). Derived from Mark D. Alleyne's book *News Revolution: Political and Economic Decisions about Global Information* (UK: Macmillan, 1997) is ALLEYNE'S NEWS REVOLUTION MODEL, 1997.

Other newcomers to this 5th edition are COMMUNITARIAN, 'COUPS AND EARTHQUAKES' SYNDROME, CRIME: TYPES OF CRIME ON SCREEN, FOCUS GROUPS, HYPERREALITY, INTERVENTION, iSOCIETY, LOOKISM, MARKET THRESHOLD, MEDIASPHERE, MUSIC: CENSORSHIP OF MUSIC, ORIENTALISM, PREDATORY PRICING, PRETTY GOOD PRIVACY, SEMIOTIC POWER, SLAPPS, TELEMATICS, VALIDITY EFFECT and VIDEO GAMES.

Many entries have been updated, adjusted or freshened up, including ADVERTISING, AUDIENCE, CAMERA, CASUALIZATION, CONGLOMERATES, CONVERGENCE, ELITE, GATEKEEPING, GENRE, HEGEMONY, INFORMATION BLIZZARDS, MEDIA IMPERIALISM, PERSONALIZATION, POWER, PRIOR RESTRAINT, REPRESENTATION, SCRIPTS, SOAPS, SURVEILLANCE SOCIETY, TECHNOLOGICAL DETERMINISM, VIRTUAL REALITY and WHISTLE BLOWING.

We expect once more to be scolded for underselling cinema and wish to repeat our argument made in prefaces to previous editions that libraries are already copiously stocked with excellent dictionaries on FILM (but see our generic entry and judge for yourself).

James Watson and Anne Hill

A checklist for use

- Words in SMALL CAPITALS mean that there is a separate entry.
- Source references are usually included in the text of each entry rather than presented in an end-of-dictionary bibliography.
- Use is made of an asterisk (*) at the end of some entries: here books of special interest or value for further reading on the topic are recommended.
- Traditional practice of referring to the city or town where a book was first published has been modified in this dictionary, reference being made to the country of origin (US or UK).
- In order to help the reader pursue research beyond individual entries, and to establish links between entries, the following 16 *collective entries* are included:

BBC	Language
Broadcasting	News
Commissions/Committees on the media	Press
Communication models	Radio
Culture	Technology of the media
Film	Television
Interpersonal communication	Theories and concepts of communication
Internet	Violence and the media

- Where c. is used it is an abbreviation for *century*.
- Communication models are listed using the name of the persons who conceived them (e.g. SHANNON AND WEAVER MODEL OF COMMUNICATION, 1949), and Commissions/committees on the media are referred to by the name of the chairpersons (e.g. ROSS COMMISSION REPORT ON THE PRESS, 1949).

Acknowledgements

The publishers would like to thank the following for permission to include the following copyright figures.

Basic Books, Inc. for Robert K. Merton, Leonard Broom, Leonard S. Cottrell, Jr., (eds): *Sociology Today: Problems and Prospects*, © 1959 by Basic Books, Inc. and reprinted by permission of the publisher; Hans-Bredow-Institut: *The Psychology of Mass Communication* by G. Maletzke; CBS College Publishing for Elizabeth G. Andersch, Lorin C. Staats and Robert N. Bostrom: *Communication in Everyday Use*, 3rd edition, © 1950, 1960 by Holt, Rinehart & Winston, Inc. and reprinted by permission of Holt, Rinehart & Winston, CBS College Publishing; F E X Dance for *Human Communication Theory: Original Essays*, Holt, Rinehart & Winston (NY) 1967, 288–300 © F E X Dance; *Journalism Quarterly* for B. H. Wesley and M. S. MacLean 'A conceptual model for communications research', *Journalism Quarterly* 34, 1957 and for 'Bass's 'double action' model of internal news flow', *Journalism Quarterly* 46, 1969 and for 'McNelly's model of news flow', *Journalism Quarterly* 36, 1959 and for 'White's gatekeeper model', *Journalism Quarterly* 27, 1950; Longman for three diagrams from *Communication Models for the Study of Mass Communication* by D. McQuail and S. Windahl; McGraw-Hill Publishing Company for a figure from *The Dynamics of Human Communication* by Myers and Myers; Mouton Publishers (a division of Walter de Gruyter & Co.) for Johnnye Akin, Alvin Goldberg, Gail Myers and Joseph Stewart: *Language Behaviour: A Book of Readings* in K. K. Sereno and C. D. Mortensen (eds): *Foundations of Communication Theory*; Macmillan Ltd. for the figure of the new revolution model, from Alleyne's *News Revolution: Political and Leisure Decisions about Global Information* © Macmillan 1997; Sage Publications Inc. 'A dependency model of mass media effects', *Communication Research* 3, 1976 and for Rogers and Dearing's 'Agenda Setting Model', from *Communication Yearbook Volume 11* and for the figure from McQuail's *Audience Analysis* © 1997. Reprinted by permission of Sage Publications Inc.; Sage Publications Ltd. for McQuail's accountability of media model from the *European Journal of Communication* © Sage 1997. Reprinted by permission of Sage-Publications Ltd; The University of Illinois Press for Schramm: 'How communication works', *The Process and Effects of Mass Communication* and Shannon and Weaver: *Mathematical Theory of Communication* and the University of Minnesota and Professor Samuel L. Becker for 'What rhetoric (communication theory) is relevant for contemporary speech communication?' in *The University of Minnesota Spring Symposium in Speech Communication*, 1968. Sage Publications Ltd. for Westerståhl and Johansson's 'News Factors in Foreign News Model', from *European Journal of Communication* (March 1994) and for Kepplinger and Habermeier's figure from *European Journal of Communication* (September 1995).

The authors would like to thank Rosalind Paul for informing us that *The Battle of the Somme* (see SOMME, THE BATTLE OF THE), shot and given public screenings in 1916, was the first-ever war film documentary and deserved both a mention in the Chronology and a dictionary entry.

Abbreviations: a selection

AA	Advertising Association
AAP	Australian Associated Press
ABA	Australian Broadcasting Authority
ABE	Association of British Editors
ABS	Association of Broadcasting & Allied Staffs
ACTT	Association of Cinematography, Television & Allied Technicians
ADP	Association of Directors & Producers
ADP	Automatic Data Processing
AFDC	Australian Film Development Corporation
AFP	Agence France-Presse
ALCS	Author's Lending & Copyright Society
AP	Associated Press
AR	Audience Research
ASA	Advertising Standards Authority
ATV	Associated Television (Associated Broadcasting Company)
BAFTA	British Academy of Film & TV Arts
BAPLA	British Association of Picture Libraries & Agencies
BARB	Broadcasters Audience Research Board
BBC	British Broadcasting Corporation
BBFC	British Board of Film Classification
BBS	Bulletin Board System
BCC	Broadcasting Complaints Commission
BFI	British Film Institute
bit	binary digit
BJA	Black Journalists' Association
BMWA	Black Media Workers Association
bps	bits per second
BSB	British Satellite Broadcasting
BSC	British Society of Cinematography
BSC	Broadcasting Standards Council
BT	British Telecom
CACI	Campaign Against Censorship of the Internet
CAM	Communications Advertising & Marketing Educational Foundation
CAP	Code of Advertising Practice; Campaign Against Pornography
CAR	Computer Assisted Reporting
CARM	Campaign Against Racism in the Media
CATV	Cable Antenna Television System
CCCS	Centre for Contemporary Culture Studies (University of Birmingham)
CCD	Charge-Coupled Device
CCN	Cable News Network
CD	Compact Disc

CDV	Compact Disc Video
CMCS	Computer Mediated Communication Systems
CNNI	Cable News Network International
COI	Central Office of Information
CPBF	Campaign for Press & Broadcasting Freedom
CPJ	Committee to Protect Journalists (US)
CRA	Community Radio Association
CRT	Cathode Ray Tube
DAB	Digital Audio Broadcasting
DBS	Direct Broadcasting Satellite
DIT	Digital Imaging Technology
DOS	Disc Operating System
DP	Data Processing
DTP	Desk Top Publishing
DTT	Digital Terrestrial Television
DVD	Digital Video Disc
EBU	European Broadcasting Union
EDP	Electronic Data Processing
ENG	Electronic News Gathering
ENS	Electronic Newsroom System
ESM	Experience Sampling Method
FAIR	Fairness and Accuracy in Reporting (US)
fax	facsimile
FFE	Fund for Free Expression (US)
FFE	Feminists for Free Expression
FM	Frequency Modulation
FOIA	Freedom of Information Act (US)
GBNE	Guild of British Newspaper Editors
GCHQ	Government Communications Headquarters
GIGO	Garbage In, Garbage Out (computer operator's acronym)
GII	Global Information Infrastructure
HDTV	High-Definition Television
HDVS	High-Definition Video System
HF	High Frequency
HMD	Head Mounted Display
HMSO	Her Majesty's Stationery Of ice
IAD	Internet Addiction Disord(r
IAMCR	International Association)f Mass Communication Research
IARP	Independent Association of Radio Producers
IBA	Independent Broadcasting Authority (succeeded by ITC in 1991)
IBM	International Business Machines
IBT	International Broadcasting Trust
IFEX	International Freedom of Expression Exchange
IFFI	International Foundation for Freedom of Information
IFJ	International Federation of Journalists
IFVA	Independent Film & Video Makers Association
IGC	Institute for Global Communications
ILR	Independent Local Radio
INR	Independent National Radio

In-tel-sat	International Telecommunications Satellite (Consortium)
IOJ	International Organization of Journalists
IPA	Institute of Practitioners in Advertising
IPA	International Publishers' Association
IPC	International Publishing Corporation
IPDC	International Programme for the Development of Communication
IPI	International Press Institute
IPR	Institute of Public Relations
Iras	Infra-red astronomy satellite
IRL	In Real Life
ISBN	International Standard Book Number
ISDN	Integrated Services Digital Networks
ISN	International Services Digital Networks
ISOC	Internet Society
IT	Information Technology
ITC	Independent Television Commission
ITCA	Independent TV Companies Association
ITU	International Telecommunications Union
ITV	Independent Television
IV	Interactive Video
IWF	Internet Watch Foundation
JICNAR	Joint Industrial Council for Newspaper Audience Research
JICPAR	Joint Industrial Council for Poster Audience Research
JICRAR	Joint Industrial Committee for Radio Audience Research (succeeded by RAJAR in 1992)
JICTAR	Joint Independent Committee for TV Advertising Research
LAN	Local Area Network
Laser	Light amplification by stimulated emission radiation
LED	Light Emitting Diode
LOP	Least Objectionable Programme
MBS	Mutual Broadcasting System
MDC	More Developed Country
MIS	Management Information System
MO	Mass Observation
modem	modulator-demodulator
MOMI	Museum of the Moving Image
MMX	Multi-Media Extensions
MPAA	Motion Picture Association of America
MR	Motivation Research
NAHBO	National Association of Hospital Broadcasting Organizations
NANAP	Non-Aligned News Agencies Pool
NASB	National Association of Student Broadcasting
NBC	National Broadcasting Company (US)
NCU	National Communications Union
NFA	National Film Archive
NFT	National Film Theatre
NGO	Non Government Agency
NIC	Newly Industrialized Country
NIIO	New International Information Order
NPA	Newspaper Proprietors Association (UK)

NUJ	National Union of Journalists
NVLA	National Viewers & Listeners Association
NWICO	New World Information & Communication Order
OB	Outside Broadcast
OCR	Optical Character Recognition
OFTEL	Office of Telecommunications
PA	Press Association
PC	Politically Correct; Personal Computer
PCC	Press Complaints Commission
PEN	Poets/Playwrights/Editors/Essayists/Novelists: PEN International
PII	Public Interest Immunity
PLR	Public Lending Rights
PR	Public Relations
PSI	Para-Social Interaction
PSN	Public Switched Network
RA	Radio Authority
RAJAR	Radio Joint Audience Research (succeeded JICRAR in 1992)
RDS	Radio Data System
RI	Reaction Index
RMB	Radio Marketing Bureau
RP	Received Pronunciation
rpm	revolutions per minute
RSF	Reporters Sans Frontières
RSI	Repetitive Strain Injury
RTS	Royal Television Society
SCA	Speech Communication Association (US)
SEFT	Society for Education in Film & Television
SIGINT	Signals Intelligence
SLR	Single Lens Reflex
STD	Subscriber Trunk Dialling
STV	Straight-To-Video
SYNCOM	Synchronous Communication Satellite
TAM	Television Audience Measurement
T & SG	Television & Screen Writers Guild
TASS	Telegraph Agency of the Soviet Union
TBDF	Trans-Border Data Flow
THESIS	Times Higher Education Supplement Internet Service
TNAUK	Talking Newspaper Association of the United Kingdom
TNC	Transnational Corporation
TTL	Through the Lens
UDHR	Universal Declaration of Human Rights
UHF	Ultra High Frequency
Unesco	United Nations Educational Scientific and Cultural Organization
UNO	United Nations Organization
UPI	United Press International
USP	Unique Selling Point/Property
VDU	Visual Display Unit
VES	Video Encoding Standard

VHD	Video High Density
VHF	Very High Frequency
VHS	Video Home System
VLV	Voice of the Listener & Viewer
VR	Virtual Reality

WELL	Whole Earth Lectronic Link (US)
WP	Word Processing
WPFC	World Press Freedom Committee
wpm	words per minute
WSET	Writers & Scholars Educational Trust
WWW	World Wide Web

A

AA-certificate, A-certificate See CERTIFI-
CATION OF FILMS.

ABC Trial, 1978 British journalists Crispin
Aubrey, John Berry and Duncan Campbell
(A, B, C) co-wrote an article in *Time-Out*
entitled 'The Eavesdroppers' in May 1976
which referred to the Government communications HQ at Cheltenham and its activities in electronic surveillance. The authors
were charged on nine counts under the
OFFICIAL SECRETS ACT. The court judge eventually dismissed the case in September
1978. Not to be outdone, British security
brought a case against *Peace News* which
had revealed the name of a secret witness
at the trial – Colonel 'B'. For breaching
Official Secrets (Colonel 'B' was a member
of British security, so it was forbidden to
publish his real name), *Peace News* was fined
£500. See CENSORSHIP; SECRECY.

Aberrant decoding See DECODE.

ABX model of communication See
NEWCOMB'S ABX MODEL.

Acceleration factor What results from
the speed-up of forms of transportation,
thus having far-reaching impact upon communities, nations and cultures. Marshall
McLUHAN preached that the combination of
accelerated modes of transport communication and the rapid development of electric
communication – TELEPHONE, TV – was having the effect of reducing the world to a
'global village'. 'All meaning,' says McLuhan
in *Understanding the Media* (UK: Routledge
& Kegan Paul, 1964), 'alters with acceleration, because all patterns of personal and
political interdependence change with any
acceleration of information'.

Accent The entire pattern of pronunciation typical of a particular region or social
group. Accent is a feature of DIALECT. The use
of most languages is marked by differing
dialects and their accompanying accents.

In Britain a range of regional accents still
survive and are important signs of regional
identity and affiliation. Though RECEIVED PRO-
NUNCIATION may still be regarded as the prestige accent more recently it has been argued

that Estuary English, a slightly Cockneyfied
accent, is starting to make in-roads into
the traditional social territory of RP. Many
individuals can use a range of accents and
switch from one to another depending on
the social situation. Accent is also an
aspect of NON-VERBAL COMMUNICATION. A
number of experiments have shown that
reactions to speakers can be influenced
by the accents they use. For example, in
H. Giles and P.F. Powesland's study of
responses to speakers using regional
accents, *Speech Style and Social Evaluation*
(UK: Academia Press, 1975), they found
that speakers with Scottish or Yorkshire
accents tend to be rated more favourably
than received pronunciation speakers for
qualities like personal integrity, good
humour and good-naturedness by speakers
with Scots or Yorkshire accents respectively
(See HYPERCORRECTION).

In an article entitled, 'It's not what you
say, it's the way that you say it', in the
Independent (15 October 1997), Emma
Haughton identifies RP, Refined Scots,
Welsh and Irish, Yorkshire and Estuary
English as being favourably received but
Brummie, Belfast, Glaswegian and West
Country accents as being viewed unfavour-
ably. These findings are similar to those of
Giles and Trudgill's study entitled 'Sociolinguistics and linguistic value judgements'
in Peter Trudgill, *On Dialect* (UK: Blackwell,
1983). Judgments will vary, though; an
individual with a Brummie accent may not
share the general view. Further there is evidence that among certain groups within
society, a covert prestige can be attached
to accents generally viewed as not prestigious, especially when they are part of
'non-standard' speech. Such accents and
'non-standard' speech may also be used to
convey an image of toughness and masculinity in certain situations, irrespective of the
actual social status of the speaker.

Differences in accents will often reflect
differences in the social structure of a
society, and in particular its patterns of
social stratification.

Accessed voices Within any society, these
are the people who have a ready and
privileged access to the channels of mass

communication: politicians, civil servants, industrialists, experts of various kinds, pundits, royals and celebrities; and it is their views and styles that are given voice. The term is used by John Hartley in his book *Understanding News* (UK: Methuen, 1982). Building on this idea in his *Language of News: Discourses and Ideology of the Press* (UK: Routledge, 1991), Roger Fowler writes, 'The political effect of this division between the accessed and unaccessed hardly needs stating: an imbalance between the representation of the already privileged, on the one hand, and the already unprivileged, on the other, with the views of the official, the powerful and the rich being constantly invoked to legitimate the status quo'. Imbalance of access results in partiality in both what is communicated and the way in which information is reported – the way it is shaped.

Access to government information: code of practice Government departments promised, following the coming into force of the Code of Practice on Access to Government Information in April 1994, to release information on request unless it is covered by any of the 15 powers of exemption. In 'State's open secrets' published in the *Guardian*, 24 January 1995, Maurice Frankel, director of the Campaign for Freedom of Information, writes that the code provides for the first time 'an independent avenue of appeal against officials and even ministers who withhold information'. However, the Code requires information to be provided but not copies of actual documents. 'The opportunities for selective editing,' Frankel points out, 'are vast.' Further, only the information of bodies subject to the ombudsman's jurisdiction are covered, which gives the police, for example, code exemption. There is a 'public interest' clause whereby the ombudsman could rule that the withholding of information might cause 'harm or prejudice'; however, the Code has no legal force; and the ombudsman can invite but not order Whitehall to disclose in such circumstances. See FREEDOM OF INFORMATION.

Access provider Or INTERNET service provider (ISP); company selling Internet connections, such as CompuServe, Demon, EasyNet and AOL (America On Line).

Accountability of media See McQUAIL'S ACCOUNTABILITY OF MEDIA MODEL, 1997.

Action code See CODES OF NARRATIVE.

Action research Some social science research is motivated by the desire to alter and improve a social situation. Action research aims not only to collect and analyse information but also to bring about practical social change.

Active-audience thesis See AUDIENCE: ACTIVE AUDIENCE.

Active listening See LISTENING.

Active participation Occurs in situations where media interest in a news story becomes involvement, and the story takes on a media-induced direction. An appetite for stories of scandal and sensation, and the cut-throat competition for circulation, can lead newspapers into playing the role of agent provocateur, as handy with the chequebook as the reporter's notebook.

Actuality Material from real life – the presentation in a broadcast programme of real events and people to illustrate some current theme or practice. RADIO, in parallel with film DOCUMENTARY, pioneered actuality in the 1930s. Producers such as Olive Shapley and Harry Harding were early innovators in this field. The radio programme *Time to Spare*, made in 1934, documented unemployment, broadcasting the voices of the unemployed and their families and creating an impact that was both moving and disturbing.

Actualization See MASLOW'S HIERARCHY OF NEEDS.

Adaptors See NON-VERBAL BEHAVIOUR: REPERTOIRE.

Advertising The extent of the *reliance* of all forms of mass media upon advertising can be gauged by glancing at any monthly edition of Brad, which comprises some 400 to 500 pages of information on where advertisements can be placed and how much they will cost. Everything is there – the national and local PRESS, TV and RADIO, CINEMA, POSTERS, bus shelters, parking meters, litter bins and transport advertising.

If advertising merely sold products, it would cause less critical concern than it does. But it also sells images, dreams, ideal ways of life, ideal images of self; it sells, then reinforces time and again, VALUES – those of consumerism; and it trades in stereotypes. In *The Shocking History of Advertising* (UK: Penguin, revised edition, 1965), E.S. Turner states that 'Advertising is the whip which hustles humanity up the road to the Better Mousetrap'.

Advertising has speeded the introduction of useful inventions to a wide as distinct from a select circle of consumers; it has spread markets, reduced the price of goods, accelerated turnover and kept people in employment.

For some analysts, advertising is a kind of magic. Raymond Williams in *Problems in Materialism and Culture*, (UK: Verso, 1980) argues that it has the ability to 'associate consumption with human desires to which it has no real reference. The magic obscures the real sources of general satisfaction because their discovery would involve radical change in the whole common way of life'. Judith Williamson in *Decoding Advertisements* (UK: Marion Boyars, 1978, 1998) shares a similar concern: 'Advertisements obscure and avoid the real issues of society, those relating to work, to jobs and wages and who works for whom. The basic issues in the present state of society which do concern money and how it is earned, are sublimated into 'meanings', 'images', 'lifestyles', to be bought with products not money.' Further the magic of advertising means that we may believe commodities can convey messages about ourselves; this leads to us being 'alienated from ourselves, since we have allowed objects to "speak" for us and have become identified with them'. Such alienation may well lead to feelings of fragmentation and discomfort within the self, feelings which may fuel a desire to seek solace in further consumption.

A number of critics point to the danger that advertising messages and the consumption they partly fuel may undermine and distort self-development. Anthony Giddens writes in *Modernity and Self-Identity* (UK:

Polity Press, 1991) that 'The consumption of ever-novel goods becomes a substitute for the genuine development of self: appearance replaces essence'. SELF-ACTUALIZATION is 'packaged and distributed according to market criteria. Mediated experience is centrally involved here. The mass media routinely present modes of life to which, it is implied, everyone should aspire'. For Don Slater in *Consumer Culture and Modernity* (UK: Polity Press, 1997), 'Consumer culture "technicizes" the project of self by treating all problems as solvable through various commodities'.

Not all would agree with such criticisms. Those subscribing to the doctrines of 19 c. Liberalism, for example, would argue that CONSUMER CULTURE, of which advertising is an integral element, liberates rather than oppresses, in providing the individual with many opportunities to rationally pursue his/her self-interest. The range of choices offered by consumer culture and post-traditional society is to be celebrated rather than seen as a cause for concern: to be able to choose being seen as the essence of being human. It should also be borne in mind that the messages of advertising have to compete with a range of other influences on behaviour in their battle for hearts, minds and identities.

The many modes of advertising may be categorized as follows: (1) Commercial consumer advertising, with its target the mass audience and its CHANNEL the mass media. (2) Trade and technical advertising, such as ads in specialist magazines. (3) Prestige advertising, particularly that of big business and large institutions, generally selling image and good name rather than specific products (See PR: PUBLIC RELATIONS). (4) Small ads, directly informational, which are the bedrock support of local periodicals and are the basis of the many giveaway papers which have been published in recent years. (5) Government advertising – health warnings, for example. (6) Charity advertising, seeking donations for worthwhile causes at home and abroad. (7) Advertising through sponsorship, mainly of sports, leisure and the arts. This indirect form of advertising has been a major development; its danger has been to make recipients of sponsorship come to rely more and more heavily on commercial support. Sponsors want quick publicity and prestige for their money and their loyalties to recipients are very often short-term.

The effect upon newspaper and BROAD-CASTING editorial and programme content is rarely overt; rather it is a process of media people 'internalizing' advertisers' demands. Ad-related newspaper features have grown enormously in the post-2nd World War period, especially in the 'quality Press', such as *The Times, Guardian, Independent* and *Daily Telegraph,* which derive over half their revenue from advertising. In press advertising, numbers count for less than the estimated purchasing power of the target readership. This explains why two major newspapers with big circulations – the *Daily Herald* (See MIRACLE OF FLEET STREET) and the *News Chronicle* – were closed down in the 1960s. They simply did not appeal to the advertisers.

Advertising has suffused our CULTURE and our LANGUAGE, helping to form a consumer culture. (See CULTURE: CONSUMER CULTURE). Its influence has been felt in modern art movements such as *pop art*; its snappy techniques as developed for TV have been widely adopted in the cinema. It has drawn into its service actors, celebrities, artists, photographers, writers, designers and FILM makers. It is often said that on TV the adverts are better than the programmes; there is a grain of truth here as there is in the claim that it is *because* of the adverts, and the goals of those who commission and make them, that the programmes are not better, more original or more challenging. See AIDA MODEL; CODE OF ADVERTISING STANDARDS AND PRACTICE (ITC); CULTURE: CONSUMER CULTURE; GRAPHIC REVOLUTION; HARMONIOUS INTERACTION; PRODUCT PLACEMENT; SPONSORSHIP: ITC CODE OF PROGRAMME SPONSORSHIP; SUBLIMINAL.

* Gillian Dyer, *Advertising as Communication* (UK: Methuen, 1982); Robert Goldman, *Reading Ads Socially* (UK: Routledge, 1992, reprinted 1995); Sean Brierley, *The Advertising Handbook* (UK: Routledge, 1995); Jib Fowles, *Advertising and Popular Culture* (UK: Sage, 1996); Angela Goddard, *The Language of Advertising: Written Texts* (US/UK: Routledge, 1998).

Advertising boycotts The reliance of the PRESS and of COMMERCIAL TELEVISION upon advertising for revenue indicates the important influence advertisers and their clients can wield over the media. Where a newspaper may be deemed to be publishing material or expressing views which might be detrimental to consumerist interest, companies pull out their expensive advertisement – or threaten to do so, and thus exercise CENSORSHIP.

Advertising: ambient advertising Advertisements which feature in contexts other than the printed page, on film or in BROAD-CASTING, which we encounter in everyday life situations, designed to surround and to confront the prospective customer – in the street, on bus shelters, in underground stations and trains, in airports, public lavatories and latterly in places of education; indeed wherever there is space for the advertiser to press home image and message. On London's underground trains in 1997, for example, hang-straps were embellished with anti-perspirant ads; in a hot summer the perfect ambient reminder to consider Vaseline Intensive Care.

Advertising: Code of Advertising Standards and Practice See CODE OF ADVERTISING STANDARDS AND PRACTICE (ITC).

Advertising: mainstreamers, aspirers, succeeders and reformers Target audiences for ADVERTISING have traditionally been defined along lines of social CLASS. Research into consumer habits and tastes produced, in the 1980s, a classification entitled, in the UK, the *Four Cs* (Cross-cultural consumer characterization), indicating the belief that these days we are all consumers and that class differences count less than personal aspiration. A BBC QED programme, *It's Tough Being a Dolphin* (May 1988) gave currency to this new approach to discovering and satisfying consumer needs. Adman John Banks described four categories of consumer. (1) *Mainstreamers* make up some 40% of consumers; security is what characterizes them in terms of their central needs, thus they buy well-known, tried brand names. (2) *Aspirers* are those for whom personal status is of prime importance; they go for what is smart and fashionable and is perceived to contribute towards the aspirer's image. (3) *Succeeders* have already arrived rather than being still on their way up; what characterizes them is their need for control – in their lives, their work, in their consumption. Advertisements which stress power and control are targeted at them. (4) *Reformers* are those who tend to put the quality of life before mere monetary acquisition. See HIDDEN NEEDS; MASLOW'S HIERARCHY OF NEEDS; VALS TYPOLOGY.

Advertising: 'Pester power' Exercised most potently at Christmas-time. The term was used in a *Guardian* editorial, 28 December 1998, to describe the results of Christmas-present ADVERTISING on children; the way that ads pressurize children into 'pestering' their parents for expensive gifts seen on TV. The editorial was responding to a report by David Piachaud, professor of Social Policy at the London School of Economics, who stated that the average child in the UK opened, on Christmas Day, presents worth £250; this, in the context of a society in which a third of all children – some 4 million of them – live in families on or below the European poverty line.

The *Guardian* urged government to act to control the targeting of children by the advertising fraternity, reminding the reader that a typical child sees approximately 10,000 commercials during 900 hours of viewing each year. It also points out the recommendations by the Advertising Standards Authority (that 'appeals to buy must only be made for suitable products which children could reasonably be expected to afford') 'are blatantly ignored'. The paper cited Sweden and Quebec, Canada where child-directed ads are banned, but was not sanguine about any meaningful action taken by the UK government.

Aesthetic Code See CODES.

Affect displays See NON-VERBAL BEHAVIOUR: REPERTOIRE.

Affective See COGNITIVE (AND AFFECTIVE).

Afghanistanism J.B. Lemert uses this term in *Criticizing the Media* (US: Sage, 1989) to describe the tendency of local media to give much critical attention to far-away issues and ignore conflicts close to home. See NEWS; NEWS VALUES.

Agenda setting Term used to describe the way the media set the order of importance of current ISSUES, especially in the reportage of news. Closely linked with the process of GATEKEEPING, agenda setting defines the context of transmission, establishes the terms of reference and the limits of debate. In BROADCASTING the agenda is more assertive than in newspapers where the reader can ignore the order of priorities set by the paper's editorial team and turn straight to the small ads or the sports page. Broadcasting is linear – one item following after another – and its agenda unavoidable (except by switching off). Interviewers in broadcasting are in *control* of pre-set agenda. They initiate, formulate the questions to be asked and have the chairperson's power of excluding areas of discussion. Very rarely does an interviewee break free from this form of control and succeed in widening the context of debate beyond what is 'on the agenda'. G. Ray Funkhouser and Eugene F. Shaw in 'How synthetic experience shapes social reality' in *Journal of Communication*, Spring 1990, subdivide agenda-setting into *micro-agenda-setting* and *macro-agenda-setting*. The first describes the way the mass media are able, through emphasis on content, to influence public perceptions of the relative importance of specific issues. The second they define as follows: 'The potential of electronic media to colour, distort, and perhaps even degrade an entire cultural world view, by presenting images of the world suited to the agenda of the media (in the US case, commercial interests), we might term "macro-agenda-setting"'. See McCOMBS AND SHAW AGENDA SETTING MODEL OF MEDIA EFFECTS, 1976; PROTOTYPING CONCEPT; ROGERS AND DEARING AGENDA SETTING MODEL, 1987.
* Maxwell E. McCombs and Donald L. Shaw, 'The evolution of agenda-setting research: twenty-five years in the marketplace of ideas' in *Journal of Communication*, Spring 1993; James W. Dearing and Everett M. Rogers, *Agenda-Setting* (US/UK: Sage, 1996).

Agitprop The Department of Agitation and Propaganda was created in 1920 as part of the Central Committee Secretariat of the Communist Party of the Soviet Union. Its responsibility was to use all available media – especially FILM – to disseminate information and ideas to the population of the world's first Communist state. The term agitprop has come to be used to describe any unashamedly political propagandizing.

Agora In the city states of ancient Greece the agora was the place of assembly where the free citizens debated matters of public concern; where public *opinion* was formulated and asserted. Public spaces have long been surrendered to enclosure or to shopping malls, but the concept remains; its practice continues at second remove – the media speak for the people, purporting to articulate and defend public interest in their role as WATCHDOGS, guarding the public from the abuses of state. PUBLIC SERVICE BROADCASTING is perceived as an extension of the agora; hence the concern often expressed about the PRIVATIZATION of broadcast media, that it is turning the agora into a marketplace of commodities (including COMMODITIZATION OF INFORMATION and entertainment) rather than a marketplace of ideas and debate. However, it could be claimed that a modern, and expanding, form of the agora is the INTERNET. See MEDIASPHERE; PUBLIC OPINION; SALON DISCOURSE.

AIDA model Guide to the principal stages of ADVERTISING a product or service: A – create Awareness; I – create Interest; D – promote Desire; A – stimulate Action or response.

Alexandra Palace Birthplace of TELEVISION in the United Kingdom. The first TV broadcasting took place from London's 'Ally Pally' on 2 November 1936. Initially the service reached only a few hundred privileged viewers in and around the capital. Some 400 TV sets, costing around £100 – the price of a small car – were in use. With the coming of the 2nd World War, TV broadcasts came to an abrupt end on 1 September 1939, by which time there were an estimated 20,000 TV sets in operation. The Alexandra Palace studios opened for business again on 7 June 1946 but had to briefly shut down transmission again in early 1947 because of the acute fuel crisis. The Alexandra Palace studios remained in service until 1955. See BROADCASTING; TELEVISION.

Alienation As a concept, derives largely from the work of Karl Marx (1818–83), who argued that the organization of industrial production robbed people of opportunities for meaningful and creative work, performed in cooperation with others and over which they had some control. Researchers have posed the question whether the mass character of the modern communications industry produces a sense of alienation in its own workers. Lewis Coser in *Men of Ideas* (US: Free Press, 1965) believes that the industrial mode of production within media organizations hamstrings the individual producer by denying his or her creativity in the quest for a mass CULTURE and that this results in alienation.

The term has a wider application. Alienation is seen as a socio-psychological condition which affects certain individuals. William Kornhauser in *The Politics of Mass Society* (US: Free Press, 1959) argues that the breakdown and decline of community groups and the extended family in modern society produces feelings of isolation and increases the possibility that people will be influenced by the appeals of extremist political groups. Alienation might therefore be a significant variable in determining an individual's receptivity to certain types of communication. See ANOMIE; INTERVENING VARIABLES.

Alignment See FRAMING.

Allegory A narrative which seeks to convey MEANING by representing abstract ethical concepts or historical/political events indirectly in the guise of certain characters, settings or plots. Historical allegory treats contemporary themes which may not be discussed openly, by presenting an historical work which implicitly involves the same themes. It is therefore a popular means of registering political protest in a repressive regime. Jean-Paul Sartre (1905–80), for example, re-wrote the classical legend of Orestes and Electra, which is concerned with the theme of freedom, in *Les Mouches* (The Flies), performed in 1943 whilst France was still under German occupation.

Alleyne's news revolution model, 1997

In *News Revolution: Political and Economic Decisions about Global Information* (UK: Macmillan, 1997), Mark D. Alleyne offers a model which 'is both a description of the international news system's political economy and a theory of the international relations of that system'. The Global News System located in the model's oval 'refers to the system of companies, organizations and people that produce the world's news'. Democratic necessity 'describes the body of reasons used to justify the existence of the news media' – the *political* justifications, and these Alleyne classifies as (1) WATCH-DOGS on government; (2) 'conduits for the two-way flow of information between people and their government'; and (3) 'as a source of information in the so-called marketplace of ideas'.

Along with political justification there is economic necessity: 'The press system and the economic system interact at a basic level whenever the media carry advertising. At a more sophisticated level, the media perform the information funtions needed for trade, currency, equities, and bond markets to perform.' Not the least of the factors relating to economics is the capacity of the media to attract or deter capital: 'News of political instability scares away investment. More positive news attracts them.'

The model identifies a dynamic of inter-acting and sometimes conflicting claims which often operate in a process of exchange, what Alleyne terms a 'trade in claims'. Claims at the top of the model are what the media want from structures of power and authority, while those at the bottom of the model are what the structures deem critical in the nature of information and its flow. Says Alleyne, 'Like the news media, these actors [states, companies, international organizations] like to manage what information the news media dissemi-nate about them. They do this through cen-sorship and propaganda. Like the news media, these actors seek self-preservation, and the actors operating in the market place are particularly concerned with getting information that will help them make effi-cient decisions'.

Alleyne's own claim for his model is that it 'takes us from the stage of merely describ-ing the wonders of new technologies and assuming positive political consequences

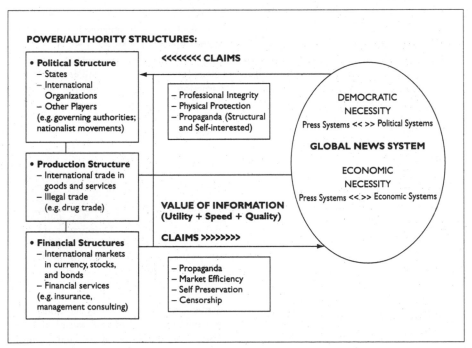

The News Revolution model

from the so-called information revolution to a clear explanation and understanding of how the news media function in international relations'.

Allness attitude Gail and Michelle Myers in *The Dynamics of Human Communication* (US: McGraw-Hill, 1985), refer to what Alfred Korzybski termed 'allness' that is the attitude that you can know or say all there is about a person, group, issue and so on. As Myers and Myers point out the *allness attitude* can constitute a considerable barrier in communication. It may mean that you communicate with certain people on the basis that you know all there is to know about them or the topic under discussion and few people take kindly to such assumptions.

The attitude may also affect how you receive messages. For example, you may believe that you already know all that you are being told or you may reject a message which contradicts what you think you know. As Myers and Myers conclude, 'The allness attitude may do much to prevent you from developing satisfying relationships with others and from communicating effectively with them'.

Alternative press See UNDERGROUND PRESS.

Amplitude See NEWS VALUES.

Analysis – modes of media analysis See DISCOURSE ANALYSIS; ETHNOGRAPHIC (APPROACH TO AUDIENCE MEASUREMENT); FUNCTIONALIST; MARXIST; SOCIAL ACTION (MODES OF MEDIA ANALYSIS).

Anamorphic lens Movie camera lens which 'squeezes' a wide picture on to standard FILM. In a projector it 'unsqueezes' the image to fill a wide screen.

Anarchist cinema Epitomized in the work of French FILM maker Jean Vigo (1905–34) who was 12 when his anarchist father, known as Miguel Almereyda, was found strangled in a French police cell in 1917. In *A propos de Nice* (1930), Vigo expressed the anarchist's views on inequality, contrasting the luxurious, suntanned life of wealthy holidaymakers with the underfed, deformed bodies of slum children. In his comic masterpiece *Zéro de Conduite*

(Nought for Conduct) produced in 1932, Vigo used anarchist friends as actors. His theme was the rebellion of schoolchildren against the rigidity of the school authorities. It was immediately banned by the French authorities. Vigo was a direct inspiration for the 'anarchistic' film of a modern, public school rebellion in Lindsay Anderson's *If*, made in 1968. (Anarchy: complete absence of law or government.)

Anchorage The part that captions play in helping to frame, or anchor, the meaning of photographic images, as reproduced in newspapers and magazines. French philospher Roland Barthes used this term to describe the way captions help 'fix' or narrow down the *choice* of meanings of the published image. He defines the caption as a 'parasitic message designed to connote the image'.

Andersch, Staats and Bostrom model of communication, 1969 Environmental or contextual factors are at the centre of the communication model devised by Elizabeth G. Andersch, Lorin C. Staats and Robert N. Bostrom and presented in *Communication in Everyday Use* (US: Holt, Rinehart & Winston).

Like BARNLUND'S TRANSACTIONAL MODEL this one stresses the *transactional* nature of the communication process, in which messages and their meanings are structured and evaluated by the Sender and subjected to reconstruction and evaluation on the part of the Receiver, all the while interacting with factors (or stimuli) in the environment. See COMMUNICATION MODELS.

Androcentric rule Term used by Jennifer Coates in *Women, Men and Language* (UK: Longman, 1993 second edition) to describe the rule by which 'Men will be seen to behave linguistically in a way that fits the writer's view of what is desirable or admirable; women on the other hand will be blamed for any linguistic state or development which is regarded by the writer as negative or reprehensible'.

Anecdote A short narrative, usually of a personal nature, used to illustrate a general issue. Anecdotes are often used in media coverage to heighten the emotional aspect

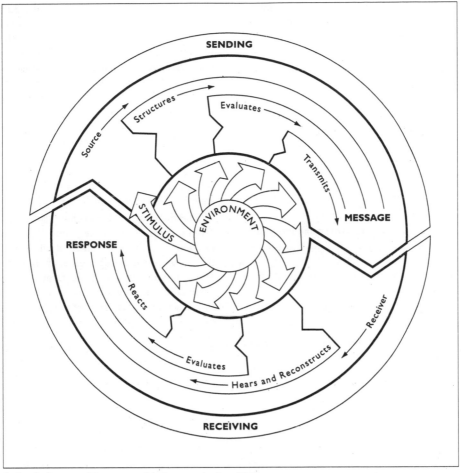

Andersch, Staats and Bostrom model of communication, 1969

of an issue. Colin Seymour-Ure in *The Political Impact of the Mass Media* (UK: Constable, 1974) recounts the use made of one such anecdote by the politician Enoch Powell in his efforts to bring the immigration issue to public attention during 1967 and 1968. Powell claimed to have received a letter from a correspondent in Northumberland expressing concern about an elderly widow in Wolverhampton who feared harassment by newly arrived immigrants in the area. This anecdote was widely reported by the PRESS, yet, despite strenuous efforts, no trace of the elderly widow could be found. The story did, however, do much to fuel the emotive manner in which the immigration issue was discussed in the popular press. See LOONY LEFTISM.

Animal communication See COMMUNICATION, ANIMAL.

Animatic Sequence of drawings representing the story of a TELEVISION advertisement, prior to filming. Another term for STORYBOARD.

Animation The process of filming still drawings, puppets, etc. in sequence to give the illusion of movement; also the actual direct drawing and painting on to positive or negative stock or on to clear celluloid itself. Long before CINEMATOGRAPHY was invented devices were in use which gave drawings the illusion of movement. By 1882 Emile Reynauld had combined his *Praxinoscope* with a projector and a decade later opened the Théâtre Optique in the Musée Grevin in Paris.

Live-action cinema became all-important once the Lumière brothers had shown its possibilities in 1895, but animation soon captured interest, from 1908 onwards, with the work of J. Stuart Blackton in the US and Emile Cohl in France. *New York Herald* cartoonist Winsor McCay made *Gertie the Dinosaur* in 1909, and in 1919 the first animated feature, *The Sinking of the Lusitania*. In November 1928 Walt Disney (1901–66) presented Mortimer, later Mickey Mouse to the world – using SYNCHRONOUS SOUND, in *Steamboat Willie*, along with his *Skeleton Dance* (1929) one of the true classics of animation film.

The laboriousness of producing thousands of drawings for filming was dramatically altered in the 1980s by the introduction to animated FILM making of COMPUTER GRAPHICS.

* Paul Wells, *Understanding Animation* (UK: Routledge, 1998).

Annan Commission Report on Broadcasting, 1977 Historian Lord Annan chaired the Royal Commission on the Future of Broadcasting whose main task was to decide what should happen to the BROADCASTING industry once the right to broadcast of the RADIO and TV companies lapsed at the end of July 1979. Also, the Annan Commission was asked to make recommendations on a fourth television channel.

Annan favoured the continuance of much of the existing broadcasting system, though the Report suggested that both the BBC and IBA should lose their local radio stations to a new Local Broadcasting Authority.

Annan also proposed a BROADCASTING COMPLAINTS COMMISSION, empowered to award costs if a complaint were upheld, and a Public Enquiry Board for Broadcasting. The task of the Board would be to hold seven-yearly public audits of the way each authority had met its responsibilities and to conduct hearings on specific ISSUES, particularly the award of FRANCHISES. A further recommendation was for an Open Broadcasting Authority to operate the fourth channel 'more as a publisher of material provided by others'.

What Annan wanted above all was a shift from DUOPOLY to a more diverse system of broadcasting in Britain: 'We want the broadcasting industry to grow. But we do not want more of the same . . . What is needed now are programmes for the different minorities which add up to make the majority.'

Annan also declared that there was 'a widely shared feeling that British broadcasting is run like a highly restricted club – managed exclusively by broadcasters according to their own criteria of what counts as good television and radio'.

The then Labour Government published a white paper, *Broadcasting* (July 1978), in response to Annan, declaring itself against the Local Broadcasting Authority and the Public Enquiry Board but in favour of the Complaints Commission and the Open Broadcasting Authority. Before there was time for legislation, the Conservatives came to power in May 1979. The Queen's Speech promised the fourth channel to COMMERCIAL TELEVISION and the proposal for an Open Broadcasting Authority was rejected. See CHANNEL FOUR; COMMISSIONS/ COMMITTEES ON THE MEDIA.

Anomie It was Emile Durkheim (1858– 1917), a French sociologist, who first used this term to describe a state of 'normlessness' in which the individual feels that there are no effective social rules governing behaviour or that those rules and VALUES to which he/she is exposed are conflicting and therefore confusing. The anomic state is most likely to occur when contact with others is limited. Durkheim linked anomie with the disturbance caused by social change and upheaval and saw it as a temporary social phenomenon. Several contemporary observers consider it a more permanent feature of modern industrial society.

MASS SOCIETY theorists have tended to view those suffering from anomie as being particularly vulnerable to over-influence by MASS COMMUNICATION. Observers have also found that some behaviour that was considered anomic was in fact SUB-CULTURAL. Another feature of anomie is that the individual may react to it by becoming ceaselessly ambitious and this in some cases can lead to severe agitation and discontent. Dissatis-fied ambition is a target for much ADVERTIS-ING and is often seen as a desirable trait in modern capitalist societies – a perspective reinforced by some of the outpourings from the mass media. A question of concern is, then, the contribution of the mass media and in particular advertising to the condi-tion of anomie. Anomie can lead to exten-sive personal as well as social breakdown, to suicide and mental illness as well as to crime, delinquency, drug addiction and alcoholism.

Anti-language Anti-languages, according to Martin Montgomery in *An Introduction to Language and Society* (UK: 1986, Methuen, reprinted 1993, Routledge) 'may be understood as extreme versions of social dialects'. Typically, anti-languages are devel-oped by sub-cultures and groups that take an antagonistic stance towards mainstream society. This stance may be general or relate to a specific area of social activity. Further, the core activities of the group, those around which the anti-language often devel-ops, may well be illegal.

The anti-language serves both to estab-lish a boundary and a degree of separateness between the group and society and to make its activities more difficult for outsiders to detect and follow. By their nature anti-languages are difficult to study but Montgomery discusses several types includ-ing those developed in Polish prisons, by the Calcutta underworld and CB Radio slang – a weak form of anti-language even when the use of CB Radio was illegal, but one with which many outsiders are now familiar.

Anti-languages are created by a process of **relexicalization** – that is, the substitution of new vocabulary for old, usually those words which refer to the activities which mark the group off from the wider commu-nity. The grammar of the parent language is often preserved. So, for example, in CB Radio slang, the phrase 'bear in the air' was used for a police helicopter. Making up new words happens frequently in anti-languages, thus making them even more difficult to penetrate.

Overlexicalization is often also a feature of anti-languages. Here a variety of new words may refer to an activity and may be used interchangeably. This makes the anti-language particularly difficult for outsiders to follow. An example, again taken from CB Radio slang, are the terms used for a police car which include 'smokey on rubber', 'jam sandwich', and 'bubble-gum machine'.

Apache silence The complex meanings of silence, as observed by the North American Apache tribes, have been tabulated by K.H. Basso in 'To give up words: silence in wes-tern Apache culture' in P. Giglioli, ed. *Lan-guage and Social Context* (UK: Penguin, 1972). Basso describes Apache silence as 'a response to uncertainty and unpredictability in social relations'. Often baffling to the out-sider, Apache silence was an important ele-ment in the courtship process; when meeting strangers; even when greeting children back from a long journey; and in the presence of other people's grief. See COMMUNICATION, NON-VERBAL.
* Adam Jaworski, *The Power of Silence: Social and Pragmatic Perspectives* (UK: Sage, 1993).

Apocryphal stories Those of doubtful origin, false or spurious. See FOLK DEVILS; LOONY LEFTISM; MYTH; RUMOUR.

Arbitrariness One of the characteristic features of human LANGUAGE is that between an object described and the word that describes it, there is a connection which is purely *arbitrary*, that is, the speech sound does not reflect features of the object denoted. For example, the word *chair* describes the object, chair, because the Eng-lish have arbitrarily decided to name it thus as a matter of convention. In contrast, ONO-MATOPOEIC expressions are *representative* rather than arbitrary in that they reflect properties of the nonlinguistic world (for example, *clatter*, *buzz*, *flap* – and *snap*, *crackle* and *pop*).

'Areopagitica' Title of a tract or pamph-let by the English poet John Milton (1608–74) in defence of the freedom of the press, published in 1644. Milton spoke out, with eloquence and courage, following the revival of censorship by parliamentary ordinance in 1643 (traditional press censorship had bro-ken down with the Long Parliament's aboli-tion of the Star Chamber in 1641). The title was taken from the Greek, *Areopagus* – the hill of Ares or Mars in Athens, where the highest judicial court held its sittings; a 'behind closed doors' court.

Milton celebrated the power and influence of the printed word: books 'do preserve, as in a vial, the purest efficacy and extraction of that living intellect that bred them. I know they are as lively, and as vigorously productive, as those fabulous dragon's teeth; and being sown up and down, may chance to spring up armed men. And yet, on the other hand, unless wariness be used, as good almost kill a man as kill a good book: who kills a man kills a resonable creature, God's image; but he who destroys a good book, kills reason itself, kills the image of God, as it were, in the eye'. See MILTON'S PARADOX.

ARTE Launched in September 1992, European TV channel broadcasting in French and German and dedicated to supporting and furthering European culture in face of a perceived American 'cultural invasion' through imported programmes.

Artefacts Things made by human workmanship; in a communication sense, the adornments which are worn which 'say something' about the wearer: dress, hairstyles, jewellery, make-up; or objects which we possess – such as motor cars or media artefacts such as a CD, newspaper or video – are indicators of our SELF-CONCEPT. See OBJECT LANGUAGE.

Article 19 This article of the European Convention for the Protection of Human Rights and Fundamental Freedom states: '(1) Everyone has the right to freedom of expression. This right shall include freedom to hold opinions and to receive and impart information and ideas without interference by public authority and regardless of frontiers . . . (2) The exercise of these freedoms, since it carries with it duties and responsibilities, may be subject to such formalities, conditions, restrictions or penalities as are prescribed by law and are necessary in a democratic society, in the interests of national security, territorial integrity or public safety . . . for preventing the disclosure of information received in confidence,

or for maintaining the authority and impartiality of the judiciary.' The upholding of the Convention is the task of the European Court of Human Rights, based in Strasbourg. The article gave birth to a pressure group, Article 19, centred in London, using electronic media to monitor state CENSORSHIP around the world. See CENSORSHIP; PRIOR RESTRAINT; SPYCATCHER CASE; THALIDOMIDE CASE.

Aspirers See ADVERTISING: MAINSTREAMERS, ASPIRERS, SUCCEEDERS, AND REFORMERS.

Assertiveness training To be assertive is to be able to communicate one's thoughts, feelings, beliefs, ATTITUDES, positions and so on in a clear, confident, honest and direct manner; it is in short to be able to stand up for oneself whilst also taking into consideration the needs and rights of other people. Being assertive differs from being aggressive in that aggressiveness involves a standing up for one's own rights and needs at the expense of others. In recent years there has been much interest in assertiveness training – that is, in enabling people to develop techniques and strategies, verbal and non-verbal, for INTERPERSONAL COMMUNICATION which will encourage them to assert themselves in social situations. The ability to be assertive is linked to self-esteem and self-confidence and thus to a positive SELF-CONCEPT. Such training provides the opportunity for considerable exploration of the relationship between the SELF-CONCEPT and interpersonal behaviour.

Attention See PERCEPTION.

Attention model of mass communication Denis McQuail in *Mass Communication Theory: An Introduction* (UK: Sage, 1987), writes that 'the essence of any market is to bring goods and services to the attention of potential customers and keep their interest'. Thus, in mass media terms, the attention model is about stimulus to buy: communication is considered to have succeeded as soon as audience attention has been won, regardless of how that attention was won. This paradigm contrasts with the TRANSMISSION MODEL OF MASS COMMUNICATION which essentially relates to notions of PUBLIC SERVICE BROADCASTING; that is, the function of communication is to deliver *messages*; to transmit information, knowledge, education and enlightment as well as to entertain. Hence public *service*. See *audience-as-public* and *audience-as-market* in the entry on AUDIENCE.

Attitudes We all hold a range of attitudes on a variety of topics and ISSUES. An attitude, according to Milton Rokeach in 'The Nature of Attitudes', *Encyclopaedia of the Social Sciences* (UK: Collier-Macmillan, 1965), is '. . . a relatively enduring organization of beliefs around an object or situation predisposing one to respond in some preferential manner'. Attitudes are learned from direct experience or through SOCIALIZATION and are capable of being changed. Attitudes may vary in their direction (that is, they may be positive, negative or neutral), their intensity and in the degree of importance attached to them. It is possible to discern three component elements of an attitude: the *cognitive* component, that is the knowledge one has, true or false, about a particular subject which may have been gathered from a wide range of sources; the *affective* component, that is, one's emotional response or feelings towards a particular subject which will be linked to one's beliefs and VALUES; and the *behaviour* component, that is, how one reacts with respect to a certain subject. Attitudes cannot be seen. Their existence can only be inferred from what people say or do. It is for this reason that accurate attitude measurement is considered to be highly problematic: people may not be that willing to communicate what they really think or feel. It is basically through communicating with others that one develops attitudes. Attitudes, once developed, influence the way in which we perceive other people and thus how we behave towards them. The mass media may shape, reinforce or challenge attitudes. For example, in conveying STEREOTYPES, mass media messages may shape people's attitudes towards GROUPS with which they have had little, if any, contact. CAMPAIGNS, such as ADVERTISING campaigns, may be designed to change people's attitudes towards a certain product. See DIFFERENTIAL PERCEPTION; DISSONANCE; NOISE; REINFORCEMENT; SELECTIVE EXPOSURE.

Attribution theory Concerned with the psychological processes by which indivi-

duals attribute causes to behaviour. Such attribution can be *dispositional* – behaviour attributed to such factors as personality and attitude – or *situational* – behaviour attributed to factors in the situation. We may, for example, blame a person's failure to gain employment on his/her laziness (dispositional attribution) or on the state of the economy (situational attribution). We tend to overestimate the influence of dispositional factors in the behaviour of other people and underestimate the influence of situational factors. They further argue that dispositional attribution can be difficult to change and that we are unwilling to discard dispositional attributions even when they are discredited. This may help explain the persistence of STEREOTYPES and PREJUDICE. Carole Wade and Carol Tavris in *Psychology* (US: HarperCollins, 1993) note that 'When it comes to explaining their *own* behaviour, most Westerners tend to choose attributes that are favourable to them . . . This self-serving bias means that people like to take credit for their good actions and let the situation account for their bad ones'.

Audience Students of media communication recognize the term *audience* as overarching all the reception processes of MESSAGE sending. Thus there is the audience for theatre, TELEVISION and cinema; there is the radio listener. There is the audience for a pop concert or at a public meeting. Communicators shape their messages to fit the perceived needs of their audience: they calculate the level of receptiveness, the degree of readiness to accept the message and the mode of delivery. Audience is readership too and the success in meeting audience/readership needs relies extensively on FEEDBACK.

Sometimes there is an extra factor in the communicator-audience situation. This might be the *client*. An advertising agency, for example, is employed by a client (a company wishing to have its products advertised) to create a commercial whose audience is the television watching public:

Of course audience needs are not the only criterion for the communicator or the client but they are central to a process which is essentially interactive and subject to a wide range of social, cultural, economic,

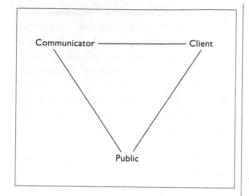

Communicator ———————— Client

Public

political and environmental influences. It might be argued that the advertiser's job is to *create* a need which his or her client's product or service will fulfil.

Increasingly during the 1980s and 1990s when DEREGULATION and PRIVATIZATION have become key ideas in the politics of BROADCASTING, and as TV has come to be seen as the most powerful means of mass communication, it has become necessary to discriminate between target audiences. Two current concepts of audience are the *audience-as-public* and the *audience-as-market*. The first stems from notions of PUBLIC SERVICE BROADCASTING, the other from COMMERCIAL (RADIO and TELEVISION) broadcasting.

Raymond Williams in *Communications* (UK: Penguin, 1976) spoke of the public service approach to broadcasting as being a 'paternal system' (SEE REITHIAN). Williams wrote of PSB as he knew it then as 'an authoritarian system with a conscience: that is to say, with values and purposes beyond the maintenance of its own power'. Though such a stance has long been open to accusations of elitism, in practical terms PSB – as represented by the BBC, for example – has been as sensitive to audience needs as its commercial rivals.

The audience-as-public relates to people as receivers of messages – information, knowledge, education, enlightenments as well as entertainment. The audience-as-market approach is less interested in the transmission of MEANING than in gaining audience attention: stimulate the costumer, then sell him a product or service. Instead of a *transmission* model of communication here we have an *attention* model. In this case

the purpose of broadcast communication is deemed effective once the audience's attention has been stimulated and held, no matter the quality of the stimulus. The difference is simple but profound: broadcasting aimed at audience-as-public defines its function as being to *serve*, audience-as-market, to *sell*.

The trend in recent times has been from one to the other, from audience-as-public to audience defined as consumers. Indeed the 1990s have seen a growing crisis in the audience-as-public paradigm as PSB has itself been dragged into the 'market' for audiences. However, in *Desperately Seeking the Audience* (UK: Routledge, 1991), Ien Ang states that the rival paradigms 'are only relatively conflicting', for both commercial and public service institutions 'cannot with their specific goals and interests in mind stop struggling to conquer audience, no matter whether audience members are identified as consumers or citizens'. In other words, commanding an audience is the prime function of both sets of institution.

John Ellis in an article 'Channel 4: Working notes' in *Screen* 24, 6 (1983), usefully discriminates between *viewers*, that is individuals, and *audience*, that is the aggregate of viewers. He writes '"audience" is a profoundly ideological concept . . . Broadcasting institutions do not seek viewers, they seek audiences'. Ang adds weight to this view: '"television audience" only exists as an imaginary entity, an abstraction constructed from the point of view of the institutions, in the interests of the institutions'. Increasingly the reality of audience as something that can be identified as well as defined and measured is problematic. With the fragmentation of audience brought about by new technologies which have considerable widened audience choice, the trend indicators suggest a shift away from *broad*cast transmission to narrowcasting which in turn confirms a new emphasis on *consumption*.

Audiences have a choice as never before, the power to switch from terrestrially produced media products to satellite, to decide when they will consume, thanks to video, or whether to direct attention to more lateral systems which cut out the major producers of media altogether – such as the Internet and World Wide Web. With the coming of digitalization, channel scarcity has rapidly given way to channel abundance. As Denis McQuail writes in *Audience Analysis* (US/ UK: Sage, 1997), audience is a single word to describe a 'diverse and complex reality'. See AUDIENCE: FRAGMENTATION OF; AUDIENCE MEASUREMENT; CATALYST EFFECT; CONTAGION EFFECT; CONTENT ANALYSIS; DECODE; DEPENDENCY THEORY; DOMINANT, SUBORDINATE, RADICAL; EXPEC- TATIONS; IDENTIFICATION; INHERITANCE FACTOR; MALETZKE'S MODEL OF THE MASS COMMUNICATION PROCESS, 1963; MOTIVATION RESEARCH (MR); OPINION POLL; PACKAGING; PARASOCIAL INTERACTION; PASSIVITY; PREFERRED READING; PR: PUBLIC RELA- TIONS; PUBLIC OPINION; RATINGS; SOCIAL ACTION (MODE OF MEDIA ANALYSIS); USES AND GRATIFICA- TIONS THEORY; WESLEY AND MACLEAN'S MODEL OF COMMUNICATION, 1957.

* Pertti Alasuutari, ed., *Rethinking the Media Audience: The New Agenda* (UK: Sage, 1999).

Audience: active audience An age-old media debate centres on the nature of audi- ence reaction to media messages. The notion of the *active* audience considers audiences proactive and independent rather than docile and accepting. The active audi- ence is seen to *use* the media rather than be used by it (See USES AND GRATIFICATIONS THE- ORY). This perception has come about sub- stantially through findings of research which has observed members of audience consum- ing media in their own homes (See ETHNO- GRAPHIC [APPROACH TO AUDIENCE MEASUREMENT]).

American analyst Herbert Schiller takes issue with the optimistic view of the active or resistive audience. In *Culture Inc. The Corporate Takeover of Public Expression* (19) (US: Oxford University Press, 1989) Schiller argues that transnational corporations have colonized culture and cultural expression, in the US and globally. He writes of 'corporate pillaging of the national information supply' and the 'proprietory control of information'. Such manifest power, he believes, calls into question the active-audience paradigm: 'A great emphasis is given to the "resistance", "subversion", and "empowerment" of the viewer. Where this resistance and subver- sion of the audience lead and what effects they have on the existing structure of power remain a mystery.' He goes on: 'It is not a matter of people being dupes, informational or cultural. It is that human beings are not equipped to deal with a pervasive disinfor- mational system – administered from the command posts of social order – that assails the senses through all cultural forms and channels.'

In turn Schiller has been criticized for underestimating the potential resistance of audience to 'corporatization'. John B. Thompson in *The Media and Modernity: A Social Theory of Media* (UK: Polity, 1995) says that 'even if one sympathises with Schiller's broad theoretical view and his cri- tical perspectives, there are many respects in which the argument is deeply unsatisfac- tory'. In particular, Thompson counters Schiller's view that American cultural imperialism has wreaked havoc with indi- genous cultures throughout the world, and that it is a seemingly unstoppable force. Thompson is of the opinion that 'Schiller . . . presents too uniform a view of American media culture . . . and of its glo- bal dominance'. See AUDIENCE: FRAGMENTATION OF; MEDIA IMPERIALISM; SELF-IDENTITY; SEMIOTIC POWER; TACTICS AND STRATEGIES.

Audience: fragmentation of In *Audience* (UK: Sage, 1997), Denis McQuail publishes the following models, with acknowledge- ment to Jan van Cuilenburg, illustrating in four succeeding stages how audiences have become fragmented since the early years of TV. The Unitary Model 'implies a single audience that is more or less coextensive with the general public'. The texts of media – BROADCASTING in particular – were shared by all, and homogenous. With the expan- sion of provision and the increase in the number of channels, diversity is shown in the Pluralist Model, representing a 'pattern of limited internal diversification'. The Core–Periphery Model 'is one in which the multiplication of channels makes possible additional and competing alternatives out- side this framework'. At this stage, says McQuail, 'It becomes possible to enjoy a television diet that differs significantly from the majority or mainstream'. The Breakup Model is characterized by 'exten- sive fragmentation and the disintegration of the central core. The audience is distributed

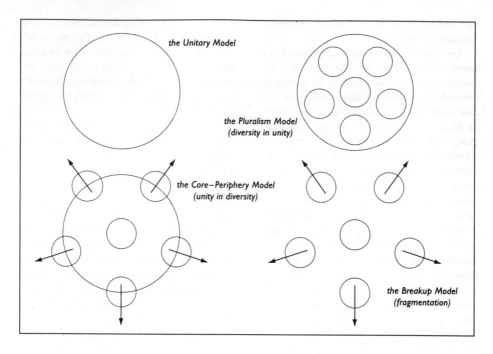

the Unitary Model

the Pluralism Model
(diversity in unity)

the Core–Periphery Model
(unity in diversity)

the Breakup Model
(fragmentation)

McQuail D., Audience Analysis, 1997, p. 138. © Reproduced by permission of Sage Publications Inc.

over many different channels in no fixed pattern, and there is only sporadically shared audience experiences'.

McQuail says that currently and for the most part, the 'core' still dominates audience use of TV: 'The reasons lie primarily in the near-universal appeal of mainstream content and the advantages to media organizations of continuing with mass provision, plus the continuing habits and patterns of social life.' The author believes that 'Media change is not enough on its own to disrupt established patterns of shared culture'. The breakup stage 'is certainly becoming more possible', but it is 'still a hypothetical pattern and has not been realised'. See DIGITALIZATION.

Audience differentiation Like the 'mass', audiences – for RADIO, TELEVISION, the cinema or readers of the PRESS – are often simplistically regarded as a homogeneous lump. It is easier to make generalizations that way; but misleading. Audience differentiation works from the premise that analysis of audience response to media messages can only be purposeful if it recognizes that the mass is a complex of individuals, differentiated by gender, age, social class, profession, education and CULTURE. See ANALYSIS – MODES OF MEDIA ANALYSIS.

Audience measurement Investigation of the size and constitution of mass media audiences has become one of the world's major service industries. Initially, audience measurement, or audience research (AR) is about number-crunching: how many readers? How many listeners or viewers? This data is then broken down along lines of class, gender, spending-power, age, occupation etc. There are two categories of measurement – quantitative and qualitative – with pressure always to translate the one into the other.

In the UK, audience measurement of one kind or another has operated since the beginning of BROADCASTING. Once the monopoly of the airwaves held by the BBC gave way to competition with the advent of COMMERCIAL TELEVISION, audience preferences became increasingly significant and audience measurement was quickly regarded as a duty and a lifeline for survival. In the UK the BBC and the ITCA (Independent TV Companies Association) share ownership of BARB (the Broadcasting Audience Research Board).

Two key terms (one might say *dread terms*, for programmes live or die by them) are *ratings* and *shares*. A rating is defined as the estimated percentage, in the case of TELEVISION, of all the 'TV households' or of all the people within a demographic group who view a specific programme or station. For example, in January 1984 there were an estimated 83,800,000 TV households in the US. A programme with a 20 rating could have been said to have reached about 16,700,000 households. A share refers to the percentage of the overall viewing figures which a particular programme commands. Thus *Hill Street Blues* 15.7/26 means a rating of 15.7% (that is of all TV households tuned to the programme) and 26% share of all viewing at the programme time. Such figures were traditionally obtained through telephone research, the use of viewing *diaries* and the *setmeter*.

In 1983, a British firm, Audit of Great Britain (AGB), entered the US audience measurement field with the so-called *People meter* (introduced into Europe as early as 1978 by Irish Television Audience Measurement and, in West Germany, by Telescopie). The people meter is designed to combine the personal element of the diary with the electronic objectivity of the setmeter. The premier US ratings company, A.C. Nielsen, responsible for the immensely influential *Nielsen ratings*, answered AGB's challenge with the *Homeunit*.

Of course the problem with the people meter has turned out to be people: they forget to switch on or to switch off and this human trait plays havoc with the accuracy of viewing figures. Also, the people meter has not proved very popular with the networks because an unexpected outcome of its use has been the registration of lower viewing figures than those denoted by traditional modes of measurement.

In *Inside Prime Time* (US: Pantheon, 1983), Todd Gitlin dubbed the obsession of the TV networks with ratings 'the fetish of immediate numerical gratification'. This fetish now extends to ways of measuring audience response using sensory devices that register viewing without buttons having to be pressed. The hunt for qualitative data arises essentially from the need of the sponsors and advertisers to have the question answered – is TV helping us to sell our products? Current research in the States is focusing on 'single-source' measurement by linking the viewing habits of specific families to their actual purchasing habits. Households are provided with an electronic 'wand' connected to the TV's people meter. With this, the household shopping is checked in, using the universal product code stamped on most packaged goods.

A major problem which has come to further haunt the already hypersensitive minds of measurers of audience is the *fragmentation* of audience through cable, video and satellite, not to mention the difficulties facing measurement with the ZAPPING and ZIPPING that goes on, facilitated by the remote control pad.

In *Desperately Seeking the Audience* (UK: Routledge, 1991), Ien Ang argues that the obsession with measurement is ultimately self-defeating: 'There is no way,' she writes, 'to foretell the ratings performance of a new programme.' There is equally no way that the networks, faced with the pressures upon them to prove that someone out there is taking notice, are going to heed Ang's conclusion: the audience must be conquered and controlled. See CUSTOM AUDIENCE RESEARCH; ETHNOGRAPHIC (APPROACH TO AUDIENCE MEASUREMENT).

* Shaun Moores, *Interpretive Audiences: The Ethnography of Media Consumption* (UK: Sage, 1993); James S. Ettema and D. Charles Whitney, eds., *Audiencemaking: How Media Create the Audience* (US: Sage, 1994); Raymond Kent, ed., *Measuring Media Audiences* (UK: Routledge, 1994); Denis McQuail, *Audience Analysis* (UK: Sage, 1997).

Audience needs See USES AND GRATIFICATIONS THEORY.

Aura That which gives art its distinctive individuality, its uniqueness, and indeed its social separateness. The age of reproduction has gone a considerable way to dismissing this aura and rendering art much more of a collective experience.

* Walter Benjamin, 'The work of art in the age of mechanical reproduction' in J. Curran, M. Gurevitch and J. Woollacott, eds., *Mass*

Communication and Society (UK: Edward Arnold, 1977).

Autocue Or teleprompt. A device which uses angled mirrors to project the words of a script on to a screen just below the lens of the TV camera. This enables a presenter to 'read' a script without looking down.

Autonomy the capacity to be self-governing, self-controlling and to be able to act in an independent manner. The term can be applied to individuals, groups or institutions. Debate normally centres on the degree of autonomy a particular individual, group or institution has; an example here would be debate about the degree to which the BBC can act independently of the government of the day. See IMPARTIALITY.

Avant-garde The innovative, advance guard in any art form; usually assaulting tradition and boundaries of acceptability. The phrase was used as early as 1845 by Gabriel-Désiré Laverdant, and the anarchist Michael Bakunin named a periodical *L'Avant-garde* in 1878.

B

'Back-bench' Journalist's slang-name, in the UK, for the night desk of a national newspaper, usually consisting of assistant editors, a night editor and the chief-sub-editor. Such a group is closest to the finished product and thus exercises a degree of power in the shaping of news. See AGENDA SETTING; GATEKEEPING; NEWS VALUES.

Bad language Andersson and Trudgill in *Bad Language* (UK: Penguin, 1990), whilst acknowledging that the term bad language is far from clear and unambiguous, refer to bad language as 'all those things (sounds, words and phrases) that may be dangerous to use. Language contains explosive totems that should be handled with care' and argue that bad language can be usefully analysed by explaining the possible explosions which may be caused by certain words, pronunciations or use of grammar. They also argue that '"Badness" is not found in the language itself but in people's views of the language'

and thus they highlight the importance of examining the values, attitudes and ideologies within societies that underpin the evaluation of some language as 'bad'. When ordinary people are asked, Andersson and Trudgill argue, '"What do you think of when you hear the phrase bad language?", most of them will certainly say "swearing"'. Whilst swearing seems to be for most people what 'bad' language is, Andersson and Trudgill point out that the term is also used to refer to the use of SLANG and JARGON, the incorrect or misuse of words, certain accents and dialects and the use of 'non-standard' English.

Several studies have shown that the evaluation of language as 'bad' in a particular instance will depend on a number of variables, which include the degree to which TABOO words or words relating to taboo behaviour are used, the social context and the social roles, age and gender of the interactors.

* Hayley Davis, 'What Makes Bad Language Bad?' in *Language and Communication*, 9.1 (1989); A. Millwood Hargrave, ed., *A Matter of Manners? The Limits of Broadcast Language* (Broadcasting Standards Council, Research Monograph Series: 3, John Libbey, 1991); Jennifer Coates in *Women, Men and Language*, (UK: Longman, 1993); Michael Rundell, 'The word on the street' in *English Today*, 11.3 (July 1995).

Back region, front region See IMPRESSION MANAGEMENT.

Bad news See GLASGOW UNIVERSITY MEDIA GROUP.

Balance See BALANCED PROGRAMMING; CONGRUENCE THEORY.

Balanced programming The PILKINGTON report, 1962, put forward three criteria for the creation of balance in TV programmes. Balance would be achieved, Pilkington stated, if channels provided the widest possible range of subject matter; if the fullest treatment was given to each subject within the range and if scheduling did not create imbalances by concentrating certain types of popular programmes at peak viewing times while relegating others, deemed less accessible, to inconvenient times. Paragraph 95 of Pilkington says, 'If service meant providing a wide enough choice of programmes of different kinds, then (it was submitted to us) there was a specially marked failure to do so in peak viewing hours'.

Balance has a more controversial, political CONNOTATION, when it is seen as a device to counter and control *bias*. More than any other MEDIUM public BROADCASTING aspires to equilibrium. Being fair to all sides can have paradoxical results: if one programme, for example, condemns the destruction of Amazon rainforests, must the balance be sustained by allowing a programme which defends that destruction? It is questionable whether fairness is actually achieved by giving air-time to ideas which flout the very principle of fairness.

Balance might ultimately mean always sitting on the fence; it may indicate a position which considers all standpoints to be tenable. Yet the balanced position - the fulcrum, as it were - from which other viewpoints are presented, has to be decided by *someone* whose IMPARTIALITY in turn might be questioned by others.

Balance-sheet culture In as yet unpublished research into the relationship between independent production companies and BROADCASTING organizations, entitled, 'What's independent about independent producers?', Anne Hill concludes that at the heart of the relationship between the broadcaster and independent producer is the contract and budget for commissioned programmes. The negotiation of these takes place in a market place variously described by the INDEPENDENT PRODUCERS and broadcasting personnel alike as a 'jungle' and 'money-driven'. The resulting financial pressures on programme-making, she concludes, produces a climate in which independent production operates within a 'balance-sheet culture', in which the harsh financial realities of programme-making seem to act as a significant constraint on the sector's ability to deliver its promise of creativity, innovation, cultural diversity and increased access to the television screen and on its actual 'independence'.

Ball-Rokeach and DeFleur's dependency model of mass communication effects, 1976 See also, DEPENDENCY THEORY.

Sandra Ball-Rokeach and Melvyn DeFleur's model poses the question, to what extent is contemporary society dependent, for information and for viewpoints, on the all-pervasive mass communication industry and, arising from this question, how far are we dependent on the media for our orientation towards the world beyond our immediate experience? In 'A dependency model of mass media effects' in *Communication Research*, 3 (1976), the authors argue that the nature and degree of dependency relate closely first to the extent to which society is subject to change, conflict or instability and second to the functions of information provision and attitude shaping of the mass media within those social structures:

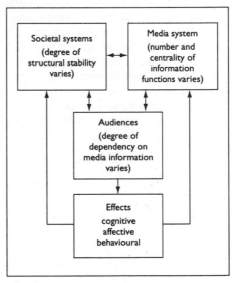

Ball–Rokeach and DeFleur's dependency model of communication effects, 1976

The model emphasizes the essentially interactive nature of the processes of media effect. The societal and media systems interact and influence audience responses which in turn influence media and society. The *cognitive* effect is that which relates to matters of the intellect and the *affective* to matters of emotion. In the cognitive area, the following areas of effect or influence are identified: creation and resolution of ambiguity; attitude formation; AGENDA SETTING; expansion of people's belief systems; value clarification. Under the affective heading, the media may be perceived as creating fear or anxiety; increasing or decreasing morale and establishing a sense of alienation. In terms of the third category, behaviour, the effects may be to activate or de-activate; formulate ISSUES and influence their resolution. They may stimulate a range of behaviours from political demonstrations to altruistic acts such as donating money to charity (see GLOBAL JUKEBOX; SOCIAL ACTION BROADCASTING). The authors cite the model as avoiding 'a seemingly untenable all-or-nothing position of saying either that the media have no significant impact on people or society, or that the media have an unbounded capacity to manipulate people and society'.

Where the model is open to most serious criticism is in its assumption that the societal structure and the media structure are independent of one another and that these are in some sort of equilibrium with audience. In many cases the media are so interlinked with power structures that a free interaction is more likely in theory than in practice. See COGNITIVE (AND AFFECTIVE); CULTURAL APPARATUS; HEGEMONY; MEDIATION; POWER ELITE.

Band-wagon effect See NOELLE-NEUMANN'S SPIRAL OF SILENCE MODEL OF PUBLIC OPINION, 1974.

Bandwidth Range of frequencies available for carrying data and expressed in hertz (cycles per second). The amount of traffic a communication CHANNEL can carry is roughly proportional to its bandwidth. A TELEPHONE system, for example, requires a bandwidth of 4 Kilohertz while a 625-line TV channel requires around 8 Megahertz.

BARB Broadcasters' Audience Research Board, limited company jointly owned by the BBC and ITCA. (Independent TV Companies Association). See AUDIENCE MEASUREMENT.

Barnlund's transactional model of communication, 1970 In 'A transactional model of communication' in K.K. Sereno and C.D. Mortensen, eds., *Foundations of Communication Theory* (US: Harper & Row, 1970), Dean C. Barnlund attempts to address the 'complexities of human communication' which present 'an unbelievably

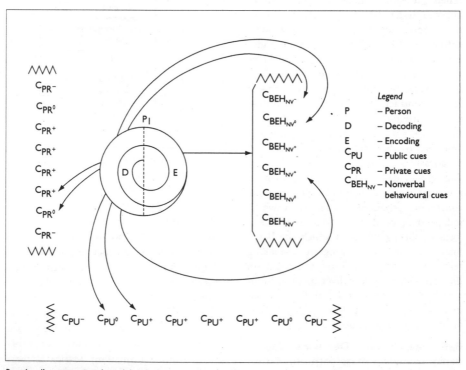

Barnlund's transactional models of communication, 1970

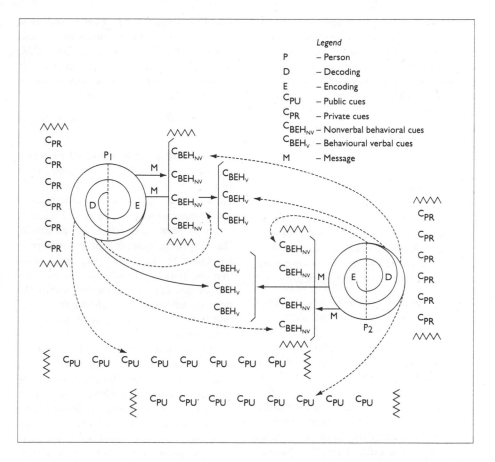

difficult challenge to the student of human affairs'. His model pays due respect to this complexity. For Barnlund communication both describes the evolution of MEANING and aims at the reduction of uncertainty. He stresses that meaning is something 'invented', 'assigned', 'given' rather than something 'received': 'Meanings may be generated while a man stands alone on a mountain trail or sits in the privacy of his study speculating about internal doubt'.

Within and around the communicant are *cues* of unlimited number, though some carrying more weight – or valence – than others at any given time. Barnlund's model indicates three sets of cues, each interacting upon one another. These are *public cues*, *private cues* and *behavioural cues*. DECODING and ENCODING are visualized as part of the same spiralling process – continuous, unrepeatable and irreversible.

Public cues Barnlund divides into *nat-*

ural – those supplied by the physical world without the intervention of people, such as atmospheric conditions, natural occurrences – and *artificial*, those resulting from people's modification and manipulation of their environment. For example, Barnlund places his communicant, Mr A, in a doctor's waiting room which contains many public artificial cues – a pile of magazines, a smell of antiseptic, a picture by Joan Miró on the wall. Private cues emanate from sources not automatically available to any other person who enters a communicative field: 'Public and private cues may be verbal or nonverbal in form, but the critical quality is that they were brought into existence and remain beyond the control of the communicants.' The third set of cues – *behavioural* – are those initiated or controlled by the communicant him/herself and in response to public and private cues, coloured by the communicant's 'sensory-motor successes and failures in the past, combined with his current appetites and needs' which will establish 'his set towards the environment'.

In the second diagram INTRAPERSONAL COMMUNICATION becomes INTERPERSONAL COMMUNICATION, with the multiplication of cues and the introduction of the MESSAGE (M).

Barnlund emphasizes the *transferability* of cues. Public cues can be transformed into private ones, private cues may be converted into public ones, while environmental and behavioural cues may merge. In short, the whole process is one of *transaction*, and few models have explored so impressively the inner dynamics of this process as Barnlund's, which also has useful application to the dynamics of MASS COMMUNICATION. See COMMUNICATION MODELS.

Barrier signals Used as personal defence mechanisms in communication situations, GESTURES such as the placing of hands and arms across the body, or folding the arms. In the business world, the classic defensive barrier is the desk. On its role in the relationship between the executive and this modern version of the old moated castle and drawbridge, much has been written – about the size and dominance of the desk, its angle to the office door, the distance between the desk and the chair placed for those who approach the boss's territory. In *Manwatching: A Field Guide to Human Behaviour* (UK: Jonathan Cape, 1977), Desmond Morris would have us believe of the executive desk that 'many a businessman would feel naked without one and hides behind it gratefully every day, wearing it like a vast wooden chastity belt'.

BART Brief Affect Recognition Test. This test was devised by P. Ekman and W.V. Friesan (1978) and discussed in Michael Argyle, *Bodily Communication* (UK: Methuen, 1988), to assess accuracy in decoding of, and individual differences in, sensitivity to facial expressions.

Basic needs See MASLOW'S HIERARCHY OF NEEDS.

Bass's 'double action' model of internal news flow, 1969 A development of two earlier classic models addressing the processes of media news production – WHITE'S GATEKEEPER MODEL, 1950 and McNELLY'S MODEL OF NEWS FLOW, 1959. In his article, 'Refining the gatekeeper concept' in *Journalism Quarterly*, 46 (1969), A.Z. Bass argues that the most important 'gates' in the exercise of GATEKEEPING are located within the news organization. Bass divides the operation into a news *gathering* stage and a news *processing* stage.

Writers, reporters and local editors are closer to the 'raw' news, the event, than those involved in Stage II of the gatekeeping process, while those involved at Stage II are closer to the power centre of the organization and therefore more subject to the organization's NORMS and VALUES and to pressures from competing stories. See MALETZKE'S MODEL OF THE MASS COMMUNICATION PROCESS, 1963.

Baton signals Chiefly manual GESTURES with which we beat time to the rhythm of spoken expression and which give emphasis and urgency. They are the stock-in-trade of declamatory communication, especially that of politicians. Not only the hands are employed in baton signals, but the head, shoulders and feet. See NON-VERBAL BEHAVIOUR: REPERTOIRE.

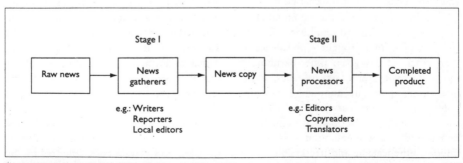

Bass's 'double action' model of internal news flow, 1969

'Battle of the Somme, The' See 'SOMME, THE BATTLE OF THE'.

BBC See BBC, ORIGINS; RADIO BROADCASTING; REITHIAN. *See also* BBC: GOVERNMENT WHITE PAPER, 1994; BROADCASTING COMPLAINTS COMMISSION; CONGLOMERATES; IMPARTIALITY; INTERNET; MONOPOLY, FOUR SCANDALS OF; PILKINGTON COMMITTEE REPORT ON BROADCASTING, 1962; PUBLIC SERVICE BROADCASTING; RADIO BALLADS, RADIO I, RADIO 2, RADIO 3, RADIO 4, RADIO 5 LIVE (BBC); RECEIVED PRONUNCIATION; SATELLITE TRANSMISSION; SCHEDULING; SELSDON COMMITTEE REPORT ON TELEVISION, 1935; ULLSWATER COMMITTEE REPORT ON BROADCASTING, 1936; WORLD REPORTER.

BBC America Launched in March 1998, BBC America comprises a BROADCASTING partnership between the BBC and the Discovery Channel of the US, issuing via cable and pay-TV channels worldwide, the 'best of the Beeb', from documentaries to *EastEnders*, from costume dramas such as *Middlemarch* to popular series such as Hamish Macbeth and *This Life*.

BBC: Government White Paper, 1994 The future of the BBC was guaranteed for another ten years by the White Paper, *The Future of the BBC: Serving the Nation, Competing Worldwide*. In renewing the corporation's charter, the White Paper confirmed that the BBC would continue as the main provider of PUBLIC SERVICE BROADCASTING (PSB). It should contribute to the growth of cable and satellite services; further develop commercial TV services; worldwide; continue to provide a broad spectrum of TV and radio programmes; guarantee special support for news, current affairs and educational programmes and cover cultural and sporting activities which 'bring the nation together'. As well as recommending giving more attention to the views of AUDIENCE on matters of taste and decency, the White Paper proposed the merger of the BROADCASTING STANDARDS COUNCIL with the BROADCASTING COMPLAINTS COMMISSION, the function of the new council to be to monitor standards and provide guidance.

BBC, origins The BBC began life as the British Broadcasting Company, incorporated on 15 December 1922 and receiving its licence to broadcast on 18 January 1923. It was a private company made up chiefly of manufacturers of BROADCASTING equipment. The Company was incorporated with 100,000 shares of stock worth £1 each. Any British wireless manufacturer could join by purchasing one or more shares, making a £50 deposit and agreeing to the terms that had been drawn up by the negotiating manufacturers and the Postmaster General.

The six largest manufacturers, in return for guaranteeing the continuing operation and financial solvency of the company, were given control. Although other manufacturers could buy stock and be admitted to membership, the principals could choose six of the Company's nine directors and these in turn had the power to select its chairman.

Each wireless set owner had to pay a 10 shilling (50p.) licence fee to the Post Office annually and the government agreed to issue licences only to people using receivers made by members of the company. Thus the manufacturers were guaranteed protection against competition.

The company was to establish eight broadcasting stations in different parts of the British Isles. Only news originating from four established NEWS AGENCIES (such as the Press Association and Reuters) could be used in broadcasting and there was to be no ADVERTISING.

By April 1923 the Postmaster General had appointed a seven-man investigating committee to review the status of the British Broadcasting Company, headed by Sir Frederick Sykes, with a mandate to consider 'broadcasting in all its aspects'. The Sykes Committee faced questions on widespread evasions of the equipment monopoly and condemnation by Beaverbrook newspapers of the control of the Six. After 34 meetings, the Committee recommended – and the government accepted – a single receiver licence of 10 shillings to cover all types of radios, and the ban was raised on foreign receivers.

Most importantly, Sykes forecast the eventual replacement of private by public operation: '. . . we consider that the control of such a potential power [of broadcasting] over public opinion and the life of the nation ought to remain with the State, and that the operation of so important a national service ought not to be allowed to become an unrestricted commercial monopoly'.

A new committee under the chairmanship of the Earl of Crawford and Balcarres, set up in 1925, led to the Charter and Licence which created the British Broadcasting Corporation and authorized it to broadcast for 10 years from 1 January 1927. It was established on three principles which were to apply to British broadcasting until the coming of COMMERCIAL TELEVISION: broadcasting became a monopoly, financed by licence fees and administered by an independent public corporation.

* Asa Briggs, *The History of Broadcasting in the United Kingdom* (UK: Oxford, vol. I 1961; vol. 2, 1965, vol. 3 1979, vol. 4 1979); Andrew Crisell, *An Introductory History of British Broadcasting* (UK: Routledge, 1997).

BBC Written Archives in the words of Paddy Scannell, in *A Social History of British Broadcasting, Vol. 1 1922–1939: Serving the Nation* (UK: Blackwell, 1991) by Scannell and David Cardiff, the archives 'must surely be one of the most important historical depositories in Britain on all aspects of 20th century British life'. They are located in the grounds of the BBC Monitoring Service at Caversham Park, Reading, and contain at least 200,000 files on all aspects of BROADCASTING from the early 1920s to the early 1960s.

Beamwidth The angular width of a RADIO or radar beam.

Becker's mosaic model of communication, 1968 Messages are rarely single, coming along one line, so the concept of a *mosaic* as a model of the communication process is a useful variant on the linear theme. S.L. Becker in 'What rhetoric (communication theory) is relevant for contemporary speech communication?' a paper presented at the University of Minnesota Spring Symposium in Speech Communication, 1968, posed the theory of a 'communication mosaic' indicating that most communicative acts link MESSAGE elements from more than the immediate social situa-

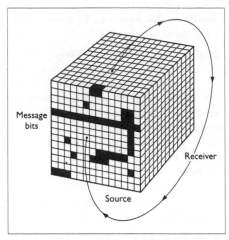

Becker's mosaic model of communication, 1968

tion – from early impressions, previous conversations, from the media, from half-forgotten comments: a mosaic of source influences.

The layers of Becker's mosaic cube correspond to layers of information. Some elements of the mosaic assert themselves, others are blocked out. The model illustrates the complexity of the many layers of the communication process and the interaction between its 'cubes' or 'tesserae' of information, showing the internal as well as the external world of communication; that which is isolated or unique, that which is recurring in a dense and ever-changing pattern. See COMMUNICATION MODELS.

Bedroom culture That which has grown up in many households in 'booted-up' nations where children and teenagers have TVs and computers in their own bedrooms. In a home-and-individualized culture young people prefer computer games and interactions on the Net to books. In a report, *Young People New Media*, based upon the first full survey of media use by children aged between 6 and 17, for 40 years, emanating from the London School of Economics and co-funded by the BROADCASTING STANDARDS COUNCIL, Sonia Livingstone presents illuminating data on young people's habits and interests in the electronic age. In the UK two thirds of under-17s have a TV in their bedroom; they spend on average five hours a day using different media. They beat their European counterparts in their adoption of what Livingstone calls 'screen entertainment culture'. Parents positively encourage their children to stay indoors, claiming they fear for their kids on the streets. Says Livingstone, 'Children are not natural couch potatoes. But for many parents a media-rich home is a response to the lack of accessible places to go out'.

Middle-class children are better provided with computer access than working-class children, though 72% of the latter have a TV-linked games machine and 71% (compared with the middle class 54%) have TVs in their bedrooms. The majority of children watch TV for up to two and a half hours a day, compared with 15 minutes reading – 18% of working-class children do not have a shelf of books in their home (compared with only 6% of middle class children).

Livingstone's report may be worrying news for reading, but she offers some assurance – her researchers found 'few if any' square-eyed children traumatized by too much TV watching. See CHILDREN, YOUNG PEOPLE AND THE CHANGING MEDIA ENVIRONMENT.

Behavioural cues See BARNLUND'S TRANSACTIONAL MODEL OF COMMUNICATION.

Behaviourism A school of psychological thought which maintains that a scientific understanding of human behaviour can only be attained from objective, observable *action*. Consciousness, feeling and other subjective aspects of human behaviour are not regarded as suitable bases for investigations.

Berlo's SMCR model of communication, 1960 David K. Berlo, who studied with Wilbur Schramm (See SCHRAMM'S MODELS OF COMMUNICATION) at the University of Illinois, produced the model below in his *The Process of Communication: An Introduction to Theory and Practice* (US: Holt, Rinehart & Winston, 1960). It is a development in a sociological direction of the SHANNON AND WEAVER MODEL OF COMMUNICATION, 1949.

Features of the process have been made explicit, due acknowledgement being made of the significance to both Source and Receiver of CULTURE and the social system in which the act of communication takes place. Berlo's model does not record the *flow* of communication, though the assumption must be that it is conceived as linear – in a line from Source to Receiver. Both FEEDBACK and the *interaction* of elements are implied rather than made explicit. In a successful act of communication, Berlo's model suggests, the skills of Source and Receiver must, to a considerable extent, *match* each other. The same may be said for attitudes or VALUES; and Knowledge must be *acknowledged*. The model rewards analysis and testing out, especially its elegant portrait of the MESSAGE. See COMMUNICATION MODELS.

Berlusconi phenomenon Term used by Gianpietro Mazzoleni in 'Towards a "Videocracy"? Italian Political Communica-

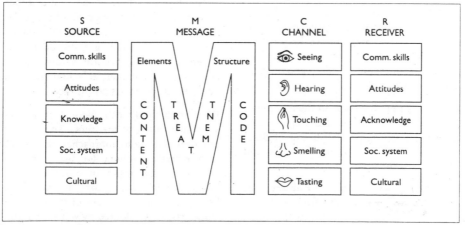

Berlo's SMCR model of communication, 1960

tion at a Turning Point' in the *European Journal of Communication*, September 1995, to describe the remarkable entry into politics, and election to prime minister of Italy in March 1994, of the media mogul Silvio Berlusconi. Mazzoleni identifies a number of interconnected factors which led to Berlusconi's success in forming a political party, Forza Italia, and in less than 50 days' electioneering, displacing the traditional duopoly of political power in Italy (the Christian Democrats and the Communists). Forza was essentially the party of commercialization and it won popularity because Berlusconi, the media man, calculated the needs of the nation's electorate-as-audience. Because of his dominant control of commercial TV in Italy, Berlusconi was able to provide himself with the kind of 'tame press' every politician dreams of.

However, Mazzoleni is of the opinion that to attribute Berlusconi's electoral success solely to his media power is a short-sighted reading of the complexity of the Berlusconi phenomenon. Rather, his message, greatly aided by the power to communicate it across the nation, 'was successful because it found several ears ready to listen to it'. Further, Berlusconi understood, perhaps more clearly than any other media mogul, that today's elections are not only fought out on the television screen, they are about grabbing popular attention by combining the emotive with the entertaining.

Though Berlusconi's triumph was short-lived – he resigned office within months – it set possible agendas for the future of political communication. In a sense he was putting into practice the principles of his own tabloid-style programmes: keep it simple, make it personal and above all ensure that it is entertaining. See MEDIATIZATION; SHOWBUSINESS, AGE OF.

Besotting peculiarities In the opinion of the *Poor Man's Guardian* of 20 August 1831, the three besotting peculiarities of Englishmen were gin-drinking, boxing matches and a veneration for titles.

Beveridge Committee Report on Broadcasting, 1950 Both from a theoretical and a practical point of view the Committee chaired by Lord Beveridge conducted the most thorough examination of BROADCASTING in Britain since its inception. Beveridge went to considerable lengths to identify and discuss the dangers of broadcasting monopoly, as then held by the BBC. Nevertheless proposals for *competitive* broadcasting were rejected on the grounds that programmes would deteriorate in quality if there were rival corporations.

Beveridge was equally firm in believing that broadcasting should be independent of government control, and declared against suggestions that the power of the BBC should be curbed through closer parliamentary supervision.

To prevent broadcasting becoming an uncontrolled bureaucracy, Beveridge recommended more active surveillance of output by the BBC's Board of Governors and a 'Public Representation Service' to bridge the gap between the BBC and the general public. Additionally, the Committee proposed regional and functional devolution of some of the corporation's activities, more comprehensive reports by the BBC on its work, and five-year reviews by small independent committees.

A major recommendation which made no headway was that the monopoly of broadcasting be extended to local authorities and universities, allowing them to operate FM RADIO stations.

Commercial broadcasting in the US style was not approved of: 'Sponsoring . . . puts the control of broadcasting ultimately in the hands of people whose interest is not broadcasting but the selling of some other goods or services or the propagation of particular ideas.' Interestingly, four of the 11 committee members (including Lord Beveridge) dissented from the majority verdict against any form of commercial ADVERTISING. See COMMISSIONS/COMMITTEES ON THE MEDIA.

Bias From the French, *biais*, slant; a one-sided inclination of the mind. The student of communication approaches this word with extreme caution, for bias generally belongs to the realm of PERCEPTION, and other people's perceptions at that: like beauty, bias lies in the eye of the beholder whose vision is coloured by VALUES and previous experience. The accusation of bias tends to be predicated on the assumption that there is an opposite – OBJECTIVITY; that there is an attainable ideal called IMPARTIALITY; that freedom from bias is not only possible but desirable. To speak, publish or broadcast without bias would imply the use of LAN-GUAGE which is *value-free*. Yet however careful we might be in what we say we disclose something of ourselves, what shaped and formed us; what counts with us, what we value. When other people appear to call that value into question, we may be tempted to classify them as biased.

* Barrie Gunter, *Measuring Bias on Television* (UK: University of Luton Press, 1997).

Bibliotherapy Or 'book therapy'; help with human problems by means of books. Used chiefly with young people, bibliotherapy has also successfully been introduced to the elderly in long-stay hospital wards or other institutions.

Bifurcation of belief See IMPARTIALITY.

Bigotry An inability and/or unwillingness to consider views, beliefs, values and opinions other than the ones you already hold. The term refers to the rigid way in which an individual may hold his/her views, beliefs and so on. Bigotry is often allied with PRE-JUDICE. Clearly bigotry is a cause of NOISE within INTERPERSONAL COMMUNICATION. As regards the process of MASS COMMUNICATION one area of debate is whether or not television programmes designed to ridicule bigotry, particularly racial bigotry, succeed in doing this among all sections of the viewing audience. Two notable examples here are *Till Death Us Do Part*, a very popular comedy in the late 1960s and early 1970s on BBC1 and its American counterpart, *All in the Family*. *Till Death Us Do Part* focuses on the bigotry of its central character, Alf Garnett. Johnny Speight who devised the programme intended to ridicule Alf Garnett's bigotry but as Angela Barry argues in 'Black mythologies: representations of black people on British television' in John Twitchin, ed., *The Black and White Media Book* (UK: Trentham Books, 1990), the overall effect of the programme was the opposite. The public airing of Alf Garnett's views gave them a real 'legitimacy'. Similar

research was done on *All in the Family* (whose leading character Archie Bunker matched Alf Garnett for bigotry) by Neil Vidmar and Milton Rokeach. Their article 'Archie Bunker's bigotry: a study in selective perception and exposure' in the *Journal of Communication*, Winter 1974, concludes that the programme whatever its intentions often reinforced the bigotry of those viewers whose prejudice it most sought to challenge. See RACISM; WEDOM, THEYDOM.

Binary opposition See POLARIZATION; SEMANTIC DIFFERENTIAL.

Bit See COMPUTERS IN COMMUNICATION.

Black Baron Unemployed Plymouth man Christopher Pile – calling himself the Black Baron – was the first person in the world to be convicted of writing and planting computer viruses, charged under the 1990 Computer Misuse Act. His actions are estimated to have cost companies over £1m, one company alone having suffered computer program damage worth £500,000.

Black English See PIDGIN.

Black English Vernacular (BEV) A term used to describe the non-standard English spoken by black people in the lowest socioeconomic groups in US urban communities. BEV is arguably significantly different from Standard American English. BEV is a variation of BLACK ENGLISH but it should be noted that, unlike BEV, some variations of Black English are fairly similar to Standard American English.

Blacklisting See HUAC: HOUSE UN-AMERICAN ACTIVITIES COMMITTEE.

Blimp A sound-proof cover fixed over a camera during shooting, to absorb running noise.

Body language See COMMUNICATION, NON-VERBAL; GESTURE; INTERPERSONAL COMMUNICATION; NON-VERBAL BEHAVIOUR: REPERTOIRE; PROXEMICS; TOUCH.

Boom A movable trolly with a telescopic arm to which a microphone is attached during BROADCASTING or FILM-making, to allow positioning of the microphone.

Boomerang effect Term used by Gail and

Michele Myers in *The Dynamics of Human Communication* (US: McGraw-Hill, 1985) to describe a situation in which a message falls within your latitude of rejection, i.e. the known views on any given issue which you do not accept. It has the effect of then shrinking or narrowing your latitude of acceptance: positions on that issue which might have been acceptable or tolerated before will now be rejected. The authors argue that messages which are very threatening to your attitudes and views may produce this effect. See LATITUDES OF ACCEPTANCE AND REJECTION.

Boomerang response Effect of a mass media MESSAGE which, in terms of audience reaction, proves to be the opposite of that which was intended. James Curran, for example, in an article entitled, 'The Boomerang Effect: the Press and the Battle for London 1981–6' in James Curran *et al.*, eds., *Impacts and Influences* (UK: Methuen, 1987), describes how a skilfully mounted public-relations campaign by Ken Livingstone in which he used the broadcast media to good effect, enabled him to counter the arguments and images advanced by the popular press in its attack on the Labour-controlled Greater London Council and himself as its leader. Interestingly a good many newspaper readers clearly adopted a stance on this issue that was contrary to that taken by the newspapers which they read. Although the GLC was abolished by the Conservative Thatcher government, Livingstone's campaign made the government look vindictive in its action.

Bowdlerize To extract from text what is deemed offensive; to expurgate. The word comes from the surname of Dr Thomas Bowdler who, in 1818, published *The Family Shakespeare* which censored 'those words and expressions which cannot with propriety be read aloud in a family'. Not only 'bad language' is bowdlerized: harmful or subversive *sentiments* can be removed or toned down, very often when a wider audience for a work is being considered. In *Subculture: The Meaning of Style* (UK/US: Methuen, 1979), Dick Hebdige observes that the original messages conveyed by early jazz music – those of anger at the negro's position in

US society, and sexual eroticism – were bowdlerized (or laundered) as jazz was fed into the mainstream popular CULTURE of the country in the 1920s and 1930s.

B-Picture In the 1940s and 1950s it was cinema practice to put on two films, the main feature – the A-Picture – and a cheaply and quickly made supporting FILM – the B-Picture. The equivalent of the 'flip-side' of a popular record, the B-Picture, or B-movie was invariably *B*udget and almost invariably *B*ad. Time, however, lends enchantment and film enthusiasts often have a soft spot for a 'GENRE' the like of which just is not made any more. Examples are Joseph H. Lewis's *Gun Crazy* (1949), Nathan Juran's *Attack of the 50 Foot Woman* (1958) and Roger Corman's *Little Shop of Horrors* (1960), which the director claimed to have made in two days.

Brainwashing Concerted effort to change attitudes using a wide range of techniques; specifically refers to the 'washing out' of political beliefs and the attempt to replace these by the political beliefs of the group, party, movement or nation responsible for the brainwashing. A similar word is *indoctrination*. It is held that brainwashing works most effectively when the subject is *isolated* and when the treatment is *intense*; collaboration is induced through systems of rewards and punishments.

Brakelight function In American communications parlance, a signal to audience that a speaker is about to conclude his or her speech. The brakelight could be a word, phrase, sentence, gesture or movement.

Breakfast-time television In the UK, the BBC was ahead of its rival, COMMERCIAL TELEVISION, when it launched its early weekday morning programme *Breakfast Time* in 1983. TV-AM, the company given the early morning FRANCHISE by the IBA followed with *Good Morning Britain*. See FRANCHISES FROM 1993.

Breakup model of audience fragmentation See AUDIENCE: FRAGMENTATION OF.

Bribery 'Subsidies' by government to British newspapers in the late 18th and early 19th c. were extensive. Sir Robert Walpole, the first 'true prime minister', who held power from 1721 to 1742, made bribery a form of government. In the last decade of his administration £50,000 was paid out in bribes to newspapers and pamphleteers in return for giving his government a quiet and supportive PRESS. Walpole's example set the tone for the future. In 1797, *The Times* with a circulation of 2000 received a government subsidy of £8112. At the same time, direct payments were made to journalists, and the government also spread its patronage by placing adverts in newspapers of which it approved. Today, bribery is a thing of the past – except for the offering of knighthoods to the editors of some newspapers, and not others. See NEWSPAPERS, ORIGINS.

Bricolage Term derived from anthropology, referring to the construction of MEANING through an improvised combination of communicative elements originating prior to their current creative use. According to John Clarke in 'Style', published in *Resistance Through Rituals: Youth Subcultures in Post-War Britain* (UK: Hutchinson, 1976), edited by Stuart Hall and Tom Jefferson, bricolage is a 'reordering and recontextualization of objects to communicate fresh meanings'. Perhaps the most famous 'bricoleurs' were the Surrealists who took familiar images and objects out of their traditional contexts and rearranged them in juxtapositions that startled and initiated new DISCOURSES. As Dick Hebdige in *Subculture: the Meaning of Style* (UK: Methuen, 1979) states, 'the teddy boy's theft and transformation of the Edwardian style revived in the early 1950s by Savile Row for wealthy young men about town can be construed as an act of bricolage'.

British Board of Film Censors Set up in 1912 to approve films for public showing. The right of local authorities to ban films had been granted in the Cinematography Act of 1909. This had resulted in a chaos of contradictory judgements. The Cinematograph Exhibitors Association and the main production companies set up their own vetting office – the BBFC. The Board consists of a president and a secretary, both appointed by the FILM industry. Like most CENSORSHIP bodies, the Board lagged behind public tastes for decades and was susceptible to influence by government. Under the more liberal regime of John Trevelyan (1958–71) the Board acquired a new image, casting off its earlier reputation for over-cautiousness. Since then the general trend of the Board's activity has been towards greater toleration while at the same time maintaining a protective attitude towards children. See CERTIFICATION OF FILMS; WILLIAMS COMMITTEE REPORT.

British Broadcasting Company See BBC, ORIGINS.

British Broadcasting Corporation See BBC; BBC, ORIGINS.

British Code of Advertising Practice Rule book of the Advertising Standards Authority, whose CAP Committee devises parameters of ethics and taste beyond which advertisers are expected not to stray. The code is spelt out in detail and responsive to evolving and changing public attitudes. For example in the sixth edition, rules governing the ADVERTISING of alcoholic drink forbid the association of drink with driving or dangerous machinery, and 'Advertisements should not encourage or appear to condone over-indulgence. Repeated buying of large rounds should not be implied'. See CODE OF ADVERTISING STANDARDS AND PRACTICE (ITC); SPONSORSHIP: ITC CODE OF PROGRAMME SPONSORSHIP.

British Film Institute An outcome of the Report of the Commission on Educational and Cultural Films, financed chiefly by the Carnegie trustees (1929–32), the BFI was set up in 1933 to foster the use of FILM for educational purposes to preserve the cultural heritage of commercial film in the vaults of the National Film Library. Today the BFI's services to film in the UK are enormous. They include: the NATIONAL FILM ARCHIVE; the National Film Theatre on London's South Bank; the financing of films by British directors; a network of regional film theatres; widening commitments to film education and the publication of works on cinema.

British Film Production Fund UK Treasury official Wilfred Eady devised this means of raising funds for FILM production in 1950. The so-called Eady Levy or Eady

Plan imposed a levy on cinema admissions to support film making. Initially a voluntary system, it became statutory under the Cinematograph Act, 1957. In 1985 the Conservative Government replaced the National Film Finance Corporation, responsible for the distribution of monies to production, with a private-sector body. State funding of £1.5m a year for five years was proposed; the private-sector body to match that for a period of three years.

Broadcast and narrowcast codes See CODES.

Broadcasting See BBC, ORIGINS; BROADCASTING ACT, 1990; CABLE TELEVISION; COMMERCIAL RADIO; COMMUNITY RADIO; PIRATE RADIO; RADIO BROADCASTING; SATELLITE TRANSMISSION; TELEVISION BROADCASTING; WIRELESS TELEGRAPHY. *See also*: ANNAN COMMISSION REPORT ON BROADCASTING, 1977; AUDIENCE MEASUREMENT; BBC: GOVERNMENT WHITE PAPER, 1994; BREAKFAST-TIME TELEVISION; BROADCASTING BILL, 1995; BROADCASTING ACT, 1980; BROADCASTING COMPLAINTS COMMISSION; BROADCASTING STANDARDS COUNCIL; CAMPAIGN FOR PRESS & BROADCASTING FREEDOM; CELLULAR RADIO; CENTURY SPEAKS, THE; CONGLOMERATES; DEVOLUTION; DIGITAL TELEVISION; FOURTEEN-DAY RULE; FRANCHISES FOR INDEPENDENT TELEVISION; FRANCHISES FROM 1993; FREQUENCY; GATEKEEPING; HUNT COMMITTEE REPORT ON CABLE TELEVISION, 1982; HYDE PARK OF THE AIR; IMPARTIALITY; INTERNET; LONGFORD COMMITTEE REPORT ON PORNOGRAPHY, 1972; MARINE BROADCASTING (OFFENCES) ACT, 1965; MINORITY REPORT OF MR SELWYN LLOYD; NETWORK; OCCUPYING POWERS; PILKINGTON COMMITTEE REPORT ON BROADCASTING, 1962; POLITICS OF ACCOMMODATION (IN THE MEDIA); PRIVATIZATION; PUBLIC SERVICE BROADCASTING; RADIO AUTHORITY PROGRAMME CODES 1 & 2; RADIO NORTHSEA; REFLECTIVE-PROJECTIVE THEORY OF BROADCASTING & MASS COMMUNICATION; REITHIAN; SANIEL PEDWAR CYMRU; SCHEDULING; SELSDON COMMITTEE REPORT ON TELEVISION, 1935; SINCERITY TEST (BY THE MEDIA); SINS OF OMISSION; SOCIAL ACTION BROADCASTING; SOUND-BITE; SOUND BROADCASTING ACT, 1972; STATUS QUO; STEREOTYPE; STUDENT RADIO; TELETEXT; TIME-SHIFT VIEWING; ULLSWATER COMMITTEE REPORT ON BROADCASTING, 1936; VIDEO; 'WAR OF THE WORLDS'; WESTMINSTER VIEW; WIRELESS TELEGRAPHY ACT, 1904.

Broadcasting Act, 1980 Receiving its Royal Assent on 13 November 1980, the Act extended the life of the IBA until the end of 1996; defined the Authority's responsibility for the new CHANNEL FOUR; set out special measures for the Fourth Channel in Wales, Saniel Pedwar Cymru (S4C) and contained a number of other important provisions relating to the future of BROADCASTING, including the establishment of a BROADCASTING COMPLAINTS COMMISSION.

Broadcasting Act, 1990 Ushered in far-reaching and controversial changes to BROADCASTING in Britain. The Act constituted a further and substantial assault on the part of government upon the traditional DUOPOLY (BBC/IBA) of broadcasting control which had prevailed since the birth of COMMERCIAL TELEVISION in the UK in 1956. The Conservative government's White Paper, *Broadcasting in the '90s: Competition, Choice and Quality* was published in 1988. The *Observer* (13 November 1988) called it 'the biggest bomb put under British TV in half-a-century'.

Announced in Parliament by the then Home Secretary, Douglas Hurd, the White Paper proposed a fifth TV channel, an expansion of Direct Satellite Broadcasting (DSB), more local TV stations, three new national RADIO networks and a growth in localized radio.

The Act of 1990 wound up the Independent Broadcasting Authority (IBA) and replaced it with a 'light-touch' Independent Television Commission (ITC), whose most important first task was to select companies for the new commercial TV franchises to operate from 1 January 1993 (See FRANCHISES FROM 1993).

Controversy raged over the manner in which the franchises were to be allocated – through secret auction. Would-be future franchise-holders were invited to put their case for selection and make a money bid, without any idea of what a reasonable bid might be. The result was regarded in many quarters as farcical: some companies bid vast amounts; others very little.

The highest monetary bidder was not automatically selected, for there was an extra qualifier, a so-called 'Quality Threshold', though at no time were the criteria for quality ever spelt out.

Prior to the announcement of the franchises by the ITC (on 16 October 1991), existing franchise-holders had tightened their financial belts – cutting back on programme investment, laying off staff – in order to have enough cash to place a winning bid. Thus, it was argued by critics, 'quality' was already being sacrificed even before the quality threshold had been crossed. There were fears that promises of quality might not, once the franchises had been won, be translated into performance.

The bids from the successful companies represented a windfall for the Treasury of over £350m a year, some £100m more than that provided by the outgoing system. Ironically, TV-am, the company believed to be the favourite of Margaret Thatcher (her daughter Carol worked for it), the prime minister who had presided over the whole franchises enterprise, was consigned to the wilderness. The franchise was awarded to Sunrise TV.

Decisions on the future of the BBC were not dealt with in the Act. See DEREGULATION; PUBLIC SERVICE BROADCASTING; PRIVATIZATION.

Broadcasting Act, 1990: radio See COMMERCIAL RADIO.

Broadcasting Bill, 1995 In December 1995 National Heritage Secretary Virginia Bottomley announced government plans for the future structuring and development of broadcasting in the UK, claiming that the bill would provide the launch pad for British companies to compete on the global stage. Existing regulations preventing independent TV companies owning more than two licences were removed, opening up the field for a new round of takeovers. However, no company would be permitted to own in excess of 15 per cent of total TV output.

Newspaper companies were permitted for the first time to control TV companies though newspapers with more than 20 per cent of national circulation were barred from owning ITV licences – a ruling directly affecting Rupert Murdoch's News International and the Mirror Group. However, the original intention, to prevent any company controlling more than 10 per cent of all-

media output was no longer part of the bill's proposals.

A central focus of the bill was the future of DIGITAL TELEVISION. Proposals for digitalization of the airways offered a prospect of many more TV channels, with the BBC being awarded its own digital TV multiplex. Classic FM and other national commercial RADIO stations were offered long-term stability if they invested in digital radio.

Broadcasting Complaints Commission In October 1971 an independent Programmes Complaints Commission was set up by the BBC, but disbanded in 1981 when the government-formed Broadcasting Complaints Commission began work under Part IV of the Broadcasting Act of 1980. Five commissioners appointed by the Secretary of State were empowered to consider and adjudicate on unjust or unfair treatment in sound or TV programmes and unwarranted infringements of privacy; consequently to oblige the offending BROADCASTING body to publicly acknowledge a proved complaint within a specified period. The Government White Paper of 1994, *The Future of the BBC: Serving the Nation, Competing Worldwide* decided on a merger of the Commission with the BROADCASTING STANDARDS COUNCIL.

Broadcasting legislation The first act of its kind in the world was the Wireless Telegraphy Act of 1904, in which the British government commanded substantial powers over the regulation of WIRELESS telegraphy. The Act gave the Postmaster General the duty to licence all wireless telegraphy apparatus. The British Broadcasting Company received its licence from the Post Office in 1923. The TELEVISION ACT, 1954 created COMMERCIAL TELEVISION in the UK with the formation of the Independent Television Authority (later the Independent Broadcasting Authority). ADVERTISING was to be kept separate from programming. Requirements were laid down to govern programming content. The Copyright Act, 1956 initiated copyright protection of broadcast material. In 1972 the Sound Broadcasting Act inaugurated commercial radio and the ITA became the IBA. The Independent Broadcasting Authority Act, 1979 empowered the

71766

IBA to create CHANNEL FOUR, while the Broadcasting Act (1980), among other regulations, created the Broadcasting Complaints Commission. In 1984 came the Video Recording Act requiring the certification of all new video releases. The Cable and Broadcasting Act of the same year set up the Cable Authority whose task was to select operators for particular areas and to oversee organizational and programming stipulations. See BROADCASTING ACT, 1990; BROADCASTING STANDARDS COUNCIL; CINEMA LEGISLATION.

Broadcasting research See AUDIENCE MEASUREMENT.

Broadcasting Standards Council Created in 1988 by the Conservative government in the UK to monitor sex and violence on British TELEVISION screens. Former editor of *The Times* and former vice-chairman of the .BBC, Sir William Rees-Mogg was appointed the Council's first chairman. According to Douglas Hurd, the Home Secretary, the initially non-statutory Council's remit would be 'taste and decency' not political censorship.

Under its first director, Roy Shaw, the BSC produced a *Code of Practice* in November 1989 and later used its modest funding to support research into broadcasting and its effects. On violence, the Code lays down the Council's principal concerns: that the regular exposure to the exhibition or reporting of violence, real or fictional, might desensitize the audience, 'making it apathetic towards the further growth of actual violence or the plight of victims'; and thus to what extent does broadcasting make a *contribution* to the incidence of violence in society? The Code acknowledges that evidence on these concerns 'is not conclusive'. In the absence of an answer, 'the Council takes the view that a society which delights in or encourages cruelty or brutality for its own sake is an ugly society, set on a path of self-destruction'. The BSC's basic attitude to the portrayal of violence, matters sexual or of doubtful taste might be summed up in the section on *Sex and Violence*: 'The borderline between sensitive observation for purposes of information and spectacle for the purposes of sensation is one to be walked with great caution'. The Council

was merged with the Broadcasting Complaints Commission following the publication of the government White Paper, *The Future of the BBC: Serving the Nation, Competing Worldwide* in 1994.

Browser Computer program facilitating, via the INTERNET, downloading and display of documents from the World Wide Web.

Brute A high-intensity spot lamp.

Butterfly In films, a net stretched over an outdoor scene to soften the sunlight.

Button apathy When a TV viewer cannot be bothered to switch off a programme, or to switch from one CHANNEL to another, he/she is probably suffering from 'button apathy'. This is a challenge to programmers to trap audience interest rapidly and early. Very often, apathy – or lethargy – does the rest, and the viewer stays loyal. See SCHEDULING.

By-line Use of the journalist's/author's name on a report or article. These are very common now in the PRESS but at one time the granting of by-lines was a rare honour, to distinguish top writers or as a reward for outstanding reportage.

C

Cable and Broadcasting Act, 1984 Drawn up by the UK Conservative government with the intention of facilitating the 'cabled society', the Act followed most of the recommendations of the HUNT COMMITTEE REPORT ON CABLE EXPANSION AND BROADCASTING POLICY, 1982, which proposed a cable network for Britain with the minimum of rules and regulations.

The Act set up a Cable Authority to select cable operators for particular areas and to maintain an overview on general matters of organization and programming. See BROADCASTING LEGISLATION.

Cable television Underground cable networks were established in the 1930s in the UK to relay RADIO broadcasts. These were later adapted to transmit TV to areas which received poor 'off-air' signals; reception problems were also the reason for the US 'cabling up' in the 1950s.

Until the election of the Conservative government in 1979, the commercial potential of cable in developing information technology had stimulated only modest interest. In March 1982 the Tory Cabinet's Information Technology Advisory Panel (ITAP), appointed in July 1981 by the prime minister Margaret Thatcher, recommended a rapid and substantial expansion of cable networks, to be established and operated by private companies, with a minimum capacity of 30 channels each. The operator of each NETWORK should, ITAP advised, be given monopoly control over the programmes transmitted. The Panel considered that it would cost some £2.5bn to wire up the homes of Britain's chief cities, the finance coming from private companies.

The HUNT REPORT was made public in September 1982, also urging the 'wiring up' of the nation, with a minimum of rules and regulations. In 1983 the Home Secretary in Mrs Thatcher's newly elected government, Leon Brittan, issued special government licences prior to a full-scale spread of cable networks.

See DIGITAL TELEVISION; OPTICAL FIBRE CABLE.

Cahiers du Cinéma French FILM magazine founded by André Bazin in 1951; associated with, and very often written by, the *Nouvelle Vague,* or New Wave directors such as Claude Chabrol and François Truffaut. The young critics of *Cahiers* reacted against the current ideological conservatism in the film world, against its reluctance to face up to or to express the facts of contemporary life.

Calcutt Committee Reports on Privacy and Related Matters, 1990 and 1993 Lawyer and Master of Magdalene College, Cambridge, David Calcutt was the government-appointed chairman in 1990 of a committee set up to examine British PRESS intrusions into personal privacy, after complaints from many quarters. Calcutt's chief recommendation was the creation of a non-statutory PRESS COMPLAINTS COMMISSION. The tenor of Calcutt's first report was a warning to the newspaper industry – either set your own house in order or it will be done for you by government legislation.

Subsequent high profile press 'intrusions' into the 'private' lives of the Royal family and of government ministers – stories which incidentally proved very popular with the newspaper-buying public – decided Calcutt that the voluntary route to better press behaviour had not worked. Calcutt's 1993 report, a solo effort, was greeted by Lord McGregor, the chairman of the PRESS COMPLAINTS COMMISSION, child of Calcutt Mark 1, as potentially 'a disaster for democracy' and 'direct CENSORSHIP for the first time in 300 years'.

Calcutt recommended: 1. A statutory code of practice for journalists and other press practitioners; 2. A press complaints tribunal comprising a judge and two lay assessors appointed by the Lord Chancellor; 3. New criminal offences to cover invasion of privacy, including bugging and the use of telephoto lenses.

Calcutt was highly critical of the performance of the Press Complaints Council, which had not been constituted, or evolved, in line with his 1990 recommendations. He dismissed the PCC as an ineffective regulator, too much in the hands of the newspaper owners.

The first government response to Calcutt Mark 2 was cool towards statutory enforcement through recommendations 1 and 2, but more persuaded concerning Calcutt's third recommendation. The theme of intrusion was at the same time being discussed by the House of Commons Heritage Committee. See DEFAMATION.

Calotype Process of photographic printmaking invented by William Henry Fox Talbot (1800–77). The Calotype method produced negatives on coated paper from which any number of paper prints could be made. Talbot celebrated his invention in his book *The Pencil of Light* (1844). See PHOTOGRAPHY, ORIGINS.

Camcorder A VIDEO camera and miniature sound recorder combined in a single unit.

Camera The first photographic camera on sale to the public was produced by London optician Francis West, for 'Photogenic Drawing' (1839). In the same year Baron Sèguier introduced a lightweight bellows camera with three 'firsts' in equipment – a darkroom tent, a photographic tripod and a ball-and-socket head. Binocular-type cameras were introduced as early as 1853, by John Benjamin Dancer of Manchester. In 1858 Thomas Skaife introduced his 'Pistolgraph': a spring shutter worked by rubber bands was released by a trigger. He once aimed his Pistolgraph at Queen Victoria and was nearly arrested for an attempt on her life. 1880 saw the first twin-reflex camera, a quarter plate with a roller-blind shutter attached to the taking lens, made by R. & J. Beck of London.

George Eastman produced the first camera incorporating roll-film, calling it the Kodak (1888). The simplicity of this camera ('Pull the string – turn the key – press the button') made mass photography possible, especially as Eastman recommended the return of the camera to the factory for development and printing.

Miniature cameras, as scientific precision instruments, were produced from 1924 (the Ermanox made by the Ernemann Works of Dresden). In 1912 George P. Smith of Missouri produced a 35mm camera taking one by one-and-a-half inch pictures on cine-FILM which was being mass produced at the time. The prototype of the Leica was constructed by Oskar Barnack in 1914; Rolleiflex was put on the market by Franke and Heidecke Braunschweig in 1947 and Voigtlander's ZOOM LENS was introduced in 1959.

In the 1960s and 1970s the application of electronics revolutionized camera and lens design. The silicon chip allowed amazing feats of miniaturization. In 1963 Eastman Kodak introduced the 126 'instant loading' cartridge, a modernization of an old idea going back to the Expo Watch camera of 1905. In 1972 they produced the pocket 110, an ultraminiature cartridge-load camera. Polaroid, in the same year, launched the SX-70 instant photo system which abandoned the method whereby a protective covering had to be peeled off the print. With SX-70, the photo image develops automatically in the light, protected by a plastic coating.

1976 saw Canon introduce its famous AE-1, a fully automatic SLR camera incorporating very advanced digital electronic technology, produced by automated methods. In the early 1980s Kodak launched its disc-camera. Three-dimensional (3-D) cameras also came on to the market at this time. An offshoot of the 35mm camera is the Advanced Photo System (APS) offering smaller, lighter cameras in which 35mm film is inserted into the camera in cassette form. However, the *digital* camera system has fast become a market leader. This requires no film. Pictures are downloaded on to a computer. Generally the digital camera works using a small card though cameras are available in which the electronic imaging device can be inserted into a 35mm camera, allowing traditional and modern uses. Digitally produced pictures can be reproduced and manipulated on-screen, issued as prints or e-mailed across the world. See PHOTOGRAPHY, ORIGINS; HIGH-SPEED PHOTOGRAPHY.

Camera cue Red light on a TV camera which is illuminated when that camera is transmitting. Known also as a 'tally light'.

Camera obscura Latin for 'dark chamber'; an early means of projecting an image – a box or room with a lens at one end and at the other a reflector which throws an external image upon a screen or table. Antonio Canaletto (1697–1768) used the *camera obscura* to considerable effect in his paintings of Venice, though the device was referred to as early as Aristotle. It was French army officer Joseph Nicèphore Nièpce (1765–1833) in 1826 who first exposed a metal plate coated with a layer of bitumen to the image in a camera obscura. The light hardened the bitumen which was washed away to reveal the fixed image. Photography,, or as Nièpce termed it, 'Heliography' – sun drawing – was born.

Where the camera obscura possessed a reflector, the **camera lucida** had a prism. When placed in front of an artist's eye the prism projects image onto paper, thus allowing accurate copying. See CAMERA, PHOTOGRAPHY, ORIGINS.

Campaign This term is most often used in the media studies context to refer to a conscious, structured and coordinated attempt at persuasion. The goals of such persuasion are varied. ADVERTISING campaigns for example aim to change people's choice of product or to persuade them to buy new products. Election campaigns aim to reinforce or change people's voting behaviour. PRESSURE GROUPS use campaigns to alert the public to a particular issue, to influence the public's opinion on that issue, to mobilize support and pressurize those in power to take some desired action. Access to the mass media is often crucial for a pressure group's successful campaign. Media personnel may also initiate campaigns to raise their audience's awareness of certain ISSUES – child abuse, for example. Indeed such campaigns can be seen as part of the mass media's AGENDA SETTING role. One focus for media research has been the measurement of how effective campaigns are.

Campaign for Press and Broadcasting Freedom UK organization founded by John Jennings in 1979 as a broad-based non-political party pressure group dedicated to making Britain's media more open, diverse and accountable. Specifically the Campaign has worked for the RIGHT OF REPLY, a Freedom of Information law and more community-based and 'alternative' newspapers. The Campaign publishes a bimonthly bulletin, *Free Press*. See JOURNALISM; PRESS.

CARAT The Communication Of Affect Recognition Ability Test developed by R. Buck (See *The Communication of Emotion*, US: Guilford, 1984), to identify individual differences in sensitivity to non-verbal communication. Unlike the PONS test, this test does not use posed emotional expressions but video tape of people in conversation about different topics.

Cards See CIGARETTE CARDS; PICTURE POST-CARDS.

Caricature A distorted representation of a person, type or action. Though we generally associate caricature with humorous CARTOONS, the process of distortion has played an important role in art. Known to the Egyptians and Greeks, caricature was revived by Italian artists of the Renaissance and developed throughout Europe in the 18th c. In England artists such as Rowland-

son (1756–1827) combined high quality draughtmanship with trenchant social and political satire. Though the most famous, *Punch* was only one among many magazines carrying cartoons in the 19th c. In England, *Vanity Fair* (founded 1868) proved a rival. In the US *Puck* (1876), in France, *Le Rire* (1894), in Germany, *Simplicissimus* (1896), made the cartoon the most impactful form of printed illustration prior to the regular use of photography. Best known of all US magazines carrying cartoons, the *New Yorker*, was founded in 1925.

Car telephone See CELLULAR RADIO.

Cartoons In fine art, a cartoon is the final preparatory drawing for a large-scale painting, tapestry or mosaic. The Leonardo cartoon in the National Gallery, London, is a notable example – ready for final working, but never completed by the artist. In modern terms, the cartoon is a humorous illustration or strip of illustrations. In 1841 a series of fine art cartoons was designed for paintings in the new Houses of Parliament in London. The satirical magazine *Punch*, founded in that year, poked fun at the drawings, with sketches entitled 'Punch's Cartoons'.

According to Alan Coren in his Foreword to W. Hewison's *The Cartoon Connection* (UK: Elm Tree Books, 1977), cartoons were born 'in the far Aurignacian days of 20,000 BC', when 'a squat, hirsute, browless man one morning dipped his stick in a dark rooty liquid, bent straight again, and, on the cave-wall of Lascaux, drew a joke about men running after buffalo'.

Hewison calls the cartoon 'drawn humour' and poses the following cartoon categories: (1) Recognition humour (where the viewer recognizes the workings of human nature); (2) Social comment (very often Recognition humour with a MESSAGE); (3) Visual puns; (4) Zany (or screw-ball); (5) Black humour (or sick, or bad taste); (6) Geometric (where, for example, lines are made to fall in love with dots); (7) Faux Naif (pretended naivety) – 'When an ideas man *can* draw but cannot develop a satisfactory comic style of *cartoon* drawing, he quite often throws in the towel and adopts a deliberately childlike style' – and (8) the

Strip cartoon the originator of which was Wilhelm Busch (1832–1904).

On the screen, Walt Disney has dominated the field of the ANIMATED cartoon but there have been many others: Paul Terry's 'Terrytoons', Pat Sulliven's Felix the Cat, Bob Cannon's Gerald McBoing-Boing, Ernest Pintoff's Human Rectangle, Flebus, Tex Avery's Chilly Willy, the endlessly warring Tom and Jerry created by William Hanna, Joe Barbera and Fred Quimby, along with countless others such as Top Cat, Scooby Doo and the Flintstones; Walter Lantz's Woody Woodpecker and Terry Gilliam's Monty Python's Flying Circus. Among those artists who have attempted to push the cartoon on FILM in an innovative direction are the Hungarian John Halas and his wife Joy Batchelor, Richard Williams and Bob Godfrey.

Casualization In the UK in the late 1980s and 1990s, the casualization of jobs by shifting full-time to part-time appointments, and the offering of short-term work contracts has been particularly prevalent in the media. For example, BBC staffing dropped by 5000 from a total of 25,000 between 1989 and 1994 and Jean Seaton writes in James Curran and Jean Seaton, *Power Without Responsibility* (UK: Routledge, 1997) that, 'By 1995 many staff were, in effect, pieceworkers or employed on short-term contracts'. One estimate by Peter Law in N. Miller and R. Allen (eds.) *Broadcasting Enters the Marketplace*, Proceedings of the 24th University of Manchester Broadcasting Symposium (UK: John Libbey, 1994) is that from 1987 to 1993, the BBC and ITV companies cut more than 14,000 jobs between them. A good many of those who left the various broadcasting organizations entered the freelance market or set up small independent production companies. More and more work traditionally done 'in house' has been offered on a freelance basis or to independent production companies many of whom also employ a significant number of workers on short-term contracts or as freelances. Fears continue to be expressed about the long-term impact of such structural changes within the TV industry in Britain, on quality and

training. However, for the broadcasting organizations the casualization of a large section of the workforce was one of the key strategies for dealing with the development of a pluralist marketplace within the industry.

The argument that this opens the field to a free market in talent has to be balanced by questions concerning who will risk the expense of training such talent. The trend has obvious implications for media training offered on degree and Higher National Diploma courses and, of course, for the future opportunities and work patterns of students on such courses.

Catalyst effect Where a book, newspaper, FILM, TV or RADIO programme has the effect of modifying a situation, or taking a *mediating* role. The actual presence of TV cameras may, it is believed, influence the course of events. The debate continues as to whether such effects are substantial or marginal, for reliable proof is hard to come by. See MEDIA-TION.

Catharsis From the Greek, 'purging', *Catharsis* is the effect upon an audience of tragedy in drama or the novel. The Greek philosopher Aristotle perceived the function of great tragedy to be the release of pent-up emotions in the audience. As a consequence, the mind is cleansed and purified. See BIBLIOTHERAPY; CATHARSIS HYPOTHESIS; COM-MUNICATION, FUNCTIONS.

Catharsis hypothesis Belief that violence and aggression on films and TV has a therapeutic effect. Exponents of this idea argue that the involvement in fantasy aggression may serve as a *displacement*, providing a harmless 'release' from hostile impulses which might otherwise be acted out. See EFFECTS OF THE MASS MEDIA.

CD – Compact disc The GRAMOPHONE equivalent of LASERVISION, the compact disc is a quarter the size of the traditional long-playing record. CDs can store an hour's music on one side, and they will never wear out and do not require painstaking cleaning. To produce such a disc, every second in a musical passage is sampled over 44,000 times, each sampling given a simple digital code which is then printed on a disc as a series of reflective pits. A small laser is beamed at the revolving disc. The code is consequently reflected back into the CD player and then converted into sound via a semiconductor chip. See SUPER DENSITY (SD) DISCS.

Ceefax Trade name of the TELETEXT service offered by the BBC since September 1974, giving viewers access to information on a wide range of services. At the push of a button appropriate information is displayed on the TV screen. Each page of information resembles a teleprinted MESSAGE and carries such items as the latest weather forecast, stock market prices and train schedules. The commercial television equivalent is Oracle. See TECHNOLOGY OF THE MEDIA.

Celebratory seeing John Corner uses this term in 'Olympic myths: the flame, the night, and the music' in Len Masterman, ed., *Television Mythologies* (UK: Comedia, 1988), to describe the perspective that results from the manner in which sporting events are portrayed on television. Corner argues that several techniques are used in the representation of such events that contribute towards this perspective; for example, repetition of exciting action highlights through action replays, close-ups, stimulating soundtracks, the exclamatory styles of the commentary, and the use of slow-motion replays. The viewer is therefore encouraged to gain intensity, excitement and a sense of celebration from viewing the events.

In the coverage of international sporting events the generation of celebratory seeing can also be used to incorporate feelings of patriotism firmly within television coverage.

Celebrity The modern version of the old hero; though while the hero was distinguished by *achievement*, the celebrity is distinguished by his/her *image*. As Daniel J. Boorstin writes in *The Image* (UK: Penguin, 1963), 'The hero was a big man; the celebrity is a big name . . . the creature of gossip, of public opinion, of magazines, and the ephemeral images of movie and television screen'. The passage of time 'creates and establishes the hero' but it 'destroys the celebrity. One is made, the other unmade, by repetition'.

Celebrity journalism See JOURNALISM: CELEBRITY JOURNALISM.

Cell Name of each of the many thousands of individual drawings which make up an ANIMATION film.

Cellular radio Comprises RADIO frequencies divided up into 'cells' of air waves facilitating, in particular, personal communications systems. For example, anyone operating a car TELEPHONE will be switched automatically from one radio frequency to another as the operator passes through the air wave cells. See MEDIA TECHNOLOGY.

Celluloid A decisive technological breakthrough for still and movie photography came in 1865 with the creation by British metallurgist Alexander Parkes of a plastic substance from nitro-cellulose, camphor and alcohol, which he named Parkesite. The material, which provides an ideal medium for carrying images, was later modified by his associate Daniel Spill and called Xylonite. An improved version – celluloid – is credited to John W. Hyatt, a printer of Albany, New York State (1869).

Censorship Pre-emptive censorship is censorship *before* the event; punitive, *after* the event. They often work in tandem: one punishment serves as a warning to others. Censorship involves the curtailment, usually by or on behalf of those in authority, of the major freedoms – of belief, expression, movement, assembly and access to information.

The most common form of censorship is that applied by the *self*. A thing is not expressed because of the risk of external censorship – from the law, from organizations and institutions, from PRESSURE GROUPS. Thus we have censorship by omission or evasion.

Few if any communities tolerate completely free expression. In the UK, for example, laws of DEFAMATION exist to protect persons against acts of communication which may offend or injure them, or their reputation in the community. Equally protective are restrictions upon material transmitted to children (see CERTIFICATION OF FILMS).

Such forms of censorship meet with general agreement, but they represent only the tip of a large legal iceberg. The UK's OFFICIAL SECRETS ACT is one of the most far-reaching weapons of legal censorship ever devised. The act (or Acts, 1911–91) makes it an offence for anyone to obtain and communicate documents and information which could be harmful to the safety and interest of the state. Such is the extent of the Official Secrets Act that, while protecting the state against the passing of crucial military secrets to the enemy, it could also prohibit the publication of the Prime Minister's lunchtime menu at Number 10 Downing Street. Employees in state services often have to sign a declaration agreeing not to disclose any information to which they have access (See LEAKS).

In addition, the state protects a commonality of interests with a wide range of laws. The Public Order Act of 1936 restricted the way we behave, or what we say, in public. If an individual uses threatening or insulting words, likely to cause a breach of the peace, this is a punishable offence. The common law offence of Sedition, of long standing, protects the sovereign, the government and its institutions from individual or groups causing intentional discontent and hatred, while the Incitement to Disaffection Act of 1934 made it an offence to try to persuade a member of the armed forces to an act of disloyalty. Equally, the Police Act of 1964 make it an offence to promote unfaithfulness by a police officer towards his duties.

It remains an offence to issue a Blasphemy – this is, to speak or communicate in writing etc. matter which may cause hatred, contempt, insult or ridicule against the Church. It is a rarely used law but a law's potency lies in its existence, in the knowledge that it can always be used when free speech appears to be getting out of hand.

Obscenity too has occupied the minds of lawmakers. Since the 17th c. certain types of indecent expression or behaviour have been subject to punishment by the law. Material considered likely to 'deprave and corrupt' has often been subject to punitive legal censorship (See OZ TRIAL). Defining what is obscene and what is liable to deprave and corrupt has proved immensely difficult. The WILLIAMS COMMITTEE REPORT ON OBSCENITY AND FILM CENSORSHIP, 1979 is probably the most level-headed attempt to resolve this problem, and to suggest what to do about censorship generally in the UK.

The targets of censorship tend to be those actions or expressions which appear to endanger by subversion, ridicule, defiance or just plain disrespect, the VALUES and value systems of the dominant HIERARCHY of society – its ESTABLISHMENT. In the UK 'sacred cows' have been the Monarchy, the Church, Nationality, the Family, Defence, each a SYMBOL in some way or other of law and order; of *control*. Censorship is a weapon to counter the ever-present threat – real or imagined – of social, and therefore political, destabilization.

To concentrate attention solely on the activities of the law in the process of censorship is to risk overlooking the immense pervasiveness of indirect censorship: 'backdoor' censorship rather than crude, head-on tactics. Indeed a regularly identifiable characteristic of censorship is the difficulty of getting to the bottom of things, that is, *who* is responsible, and *why* the censorship has taken place and what the motives behind the act of censorship are.

If seen in terms of the INTERNET and the freedom the new technology of CYBERSPACE has given to millions of users, censorship has an uncertain future. In 'Uncensorable Worlds' published in Part 3 of *Uncensored*, an *Observer* series (1994), Howard Rheingold states that, 'censorship has become much more impractical than it has ever been before. In fact, I'm beginning to think that censorship is soon going to be extinct, whether we like it or not.' Attempts by the authorities, or by organizations wishing to protect data, to censor information, expression or image-exchange on the Net will lead to re-routing and other avoidance measures. Rheingold is worried in particular about the impact of an 'uncensorable world' on the young: 'Let's face it,' he writes, 'the same wonderful technology that will connect young people to libraries and image archives will also connect them to multimedia filth and computer-assisted sexual predators.' See ABC TRIAL; 'AREOPAGITICA'; ARTICLE 19; BRAINWASHING; BROADCASTING STANDARDS COUNCIL; CALCUTT REPORTS, 1990 AND 1993; COMMERCIAL

CONFIDENTIALITY; DATA PROTECTION; DEATH ON THE ROCK; D-NOTICES; FATWA; FOURTEEN-DAY RULE; HAYS OFFICE; HUAC: HOUSE UN-AMERICAN ACTIVITIES COMMITTEE; INDEX; INTERNET: MONITORING OF CONTENT; LONGFORD COMMITTEE REPORT; LORD CHAMBERLAIN; MUSIC: CENSORSHIP OF MUSIC; SECTION 28; PAPERWORK REDUCTION ACT, 1980; SCOTT REPORT, 1996; SLAPPS; 'SOMME, THE BATTLE OF THE'; SPYCATCHER CASE; TAXES ON KNOWLEDGE; THALIDOMIDE CASE; ZIRCON AFFAIR.
* Carl Jensen, *20 Years of Censored News* (US: Seven Stories Press, 1997); David Vincent, *The Culture of Secrecy in Britain 1832–1998* (UK: Oxford University Press, 1998).

Centrality Within the communication *structure* of any social group some members will derive certain advantages or disadvantages resulting from their position in that structure; in particular, from the FREQUENCY with which they communicate with other members of the group. By using a sociogram such as that illustrated below, the *centrality* of a person within the communication structure can be measured:

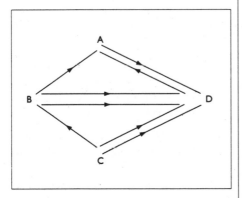

The sociogram indicates that D's *centrality index* is highest; it is arrived at by taking the total number of communication links between group members and then dividing that by the total number of such links between one member and the other members of the group. In the diagram, D's centrality may arise because of his/her status, role, articulacy, personality etc.

The concept of a centrality index enables observers to estimate quantitatively the degree of influence members of the group may have by virtue of their position in the group. The more central a member is in a communication NETWORK, the sooner he/she will be in possession of all the information at the disposal of the group. *Influence* is closely related to possession of information because the possessor has the power to choose what information to pass on, and to whom. Communication networks differ in the degree of centrality and the number of levels of centrality possible within them.

Centres for research into the media See RESEARCH CENTRES (INTO THE MEDIA).

Century Speaks, The A BBC/British Library project recording in celebration of the Millenium, the voices of the ordinary people of the UK. In preparation for *The Century Speaks* local radio stations across the country gathered nearly 10,000 hours of interviews on themes such as House and Home, Crime and the Law, Growing Up and Beliefs and Fears. Michael Green, programme director, has said that the 'aim is to make compelling radio using extraordinary people who don't happen to be famous'. The programmes were scheduled to be broadcast between August 1999 and the first months of 2000, the recordings to be housed in the Millenium Memory Bank at the British Library.

Certification of films For several years until December 1982, the BRITISH BOARD OF FILM CENSORS had the following system of certification: *X*, denoting films with high sex and violence content or other disturbing subject matter to which those under 18 were not permitted; *AA* films from which children under 14 were barred; *A* films to which children were admitted if accompanied by an adult, and *U*-certificate films admitting all. The new 1982 categories are *18* (permitting admission for those 18 and over); *15* (replacing *AA*, and raising the admission age from 14 to 15); *PG* (Parental Guidance, a symbol used in the US, and intended to show that a film contains some scenes which individual parents may feel unsuitable for children), and *U* as before. See H-CERTIFICATE.

Chamberlain, Lord See LORD CHAMBERLAIN.

Channel Each MESSAGE-carrying signal requires its route along which it is transmitted from the sender to the receiver and along which FEEDBACK may be obtained. Channels may be physical (our voices or bodies), technical (the TELEPHONE) or social (our schools, media etc.) In business organizations or institutions they may be vertical, hierarchical, formal and predominantly one-way – from the boss downwards; or horizontal, democratic, informal and two-way as between workmates and groups with common tasks, interests and sympathies. Like country paths, channels need to be kept open and frequented – and sometimes repaired – if they are to continue to be recognized as viable. See COSMOPOLITE AND LOCALITE CHANNELS; JAKOBSON'S MODEL OF COMMUNICATION 1958; PHATIC (LANGUAGE); SHANNON AND WEAVER MODEL OF COMMUNICATION, 1949.

Channel capacity C.E. Shannon and W.E. Weaver use this term to describe the upper limit of information that any communication system can handle at a given time. To discover this limit, it is first essential to know how much uncertainty – or *entropy* – a given signal will eliminate. See REDUNDANCY.

Channel 4 Under the direction of Jeremy Isaacs, in 1982, C4 became the UK's fourth TV channel; the 'quality' arm of COMMERCIAL TELEVISION. The new organization quickly became a major sponsor of independently made movies, drama series and documentaries. From the start the channel set out to challenge set ways and attitudes. Much of its programming was international in theme, whether the subject was poverty in the Third World or American football. The new channel proved the argument for *broad*casting, mixing popular viewing with minority-interest programmes and showing that the entertaining could be combined with the serious without sacrificing standards.

C4 became the first channel to provide a full hour of news daily. It was to create a high reputation for the funding of feature films, some of which, like *Four Weddings and a Funeral* (1994), proved worldwide cinema successes. The BROADCASTING ACT 1990 cleared the way for C4 to negotiate directly its own advertising revenue. The Welsh fourth channel is called Saniel Pedwar Cymru (S4C).

Channel 5 The Independent Television Commission of the UK awarded the franchise for the UK's 5th national terrestrial TV channel to Channel 5 Broadcasting in October 1995. Two other bidders, Canadian-backed UKTV and Virgin TV were turned down on the grounds that, despite its lower bid, Channel 5 Broadcasting, led by Lord Hollick and Greg Dyke, was offering more attractive and better-quality programming. The start date for broadcasting was fixed for January 1997.

Chapultepec, Declaration of, 1994 Adopted, 11 March in Mexico City by the Hemisphere Conference on Free Speech, organized by the Inter American Press Association (IAPA), the Declaration states that 'A free press enables societies to resolve their conflicts, promote their well-being and protect their liberty'. The defence of the freedom of the PRESS is absolute and unqualified: 'No law or act of government may limit freedom of expression or of the press, whatever the medium'. Chapultepec rejects prior CENSORHIP (Clause 5), licences for the importation of paper, newsgathering equipment and the assigning of RADIO frequencies (Clause 7) and asserts that no news medium nor journalist may be punished for publishing the truth for criticizing or denouncing government (Clause 10). See NEW WORLD INFORMATION ORDER; TALLOIRES DECLARATION.

Characteristics of mass communications See MASS COMMUNICATIONS: SEVEN CHARACTERISTICS.

Charter 88 Human rights movement in the UK dedicated to the creation of a Bill of Rights which would guarantee a range of civil liberties, including freedom from discrimination, and establish freedom of information and open government. The architects of the Charter argue that rights in the UK remain unformulated and conditional upon the goodwill of the government; in short that British society stands in need of a constitution which protects individual rights and the institutions of a modern pluralist democracy.

Chequebook journalism A EUPHEMISM for bribery – newspapers paying someone for exclusive rights on his or her story. The police pay their 'snouts' or 'grasses' for the common good; the PRESS pay their informants for tomorrow's headline, to serve the public's 'right to know' and to boost sales in the war of circulation.

Children's Film Foundation Set up in 1944 by J. Arthur Rank as the Children's Entertainment Films Division of the Rank Organization. The British FILM industry took over the project in 1951, naming it the CFF. In the Cinematograph Films Act of 1957, the CFF was guaranteed an annual grant from the BRITISH FILM PRODUCTION FUND. Films specially for children have been produced ever since – low-budget features, shorts and serials, shown at children's matinees and for the families of servicemen and women, never at ordinary public showings or on TV.

Children, Young People and the Changing Media Environment Title of a major research project carried out in the UK and 11 other countries during 1997–8; involving a survey of almost 15,000 children and young people. Directed by Sonia Livingstone of the Media Research Group of the London School of Economics and Political Science, in collaboration with George Gaskell and Moira Bovill, the survey's ongoing findings about how young people use the media are published in a special issue of the *European Journal of Communication* – 'Young People and the Changing Media Environment' (December 1998).

Themes addressed in the research project and summarized in the EJC are Young People's Ownership and Uses of New and Old Forms of Media in Britain and The Netherlands; Patterns of Old and New Media Use among Young People in Flanders, Germany and Sweden; Family Lifestyles and Media Use Patterns; Media Use and the Relationships of Children and Teenagers with their Peer Groups and Global Culture in Practice – a look at children and adolescents in Denmark, France and Israel.

Livingstone's introductory article, 'Mediated childhoods', explains the principles behind this ambitious and welcome scrutiny of young people and the media, and the research methods used. She points out that

'children and young people – both individually and as a market – not only respond to but also influence changes in their immediate environment, including this mediated environment'. They should be researched because 'they represent an audience neglected by the adult-centred focus on households' and 'because their uses and experiences with new media are of specific analytical relevance to media theory'.

The survey has revealed valuable data for further investigation. For example, only 64% of British children possess a shelf of books compared to 95% of the Dutch children questioned, and currently personal ownership of a computer in the UK is 48% compared with 85% in Holland. British children, however, watch more TV, the researchers explaining this as being in part due to the 'enviable reputation for producing qualilty programmes ... in Britain'. Generally, individual use of TV and computers is increasing but Dominique Pasquier and her team, analysing domestic media use among Flemish, French, Italian and Swedish children and teenagers, argues that 'collective viewing and playing are still important both with parents and siblings, and with friends' and a key adjunct to media use is *talking* about it. Thus, despite the increased privatization of media (with more and more children having their own equipment in their rooms) media use is 'still a shared experience' with other family members. It is an accompaniment to peer-group interaction, not a replacement of it. David Suess and his research team, reporting on cases in Finland, Spain and Switzerland, believe, 'Media play an important role in children's everyday lives, but they can in no way be seen to replace peer relationships or play with friends'.

Dafna Lemish and team report on interesting initial perspectives concerning young people – French, Danish and Israeli – and their mediated relations with global CULTURE. They write that 'Media seem to connect young audiences to the social "centre" of humankind', while the Internet is seen as 'another type of transnational social space'. Young people seem at ease with the *hybridity* of modern culture.

The authors talk, for instance, of 'the sense of a joint culture which is created through music, and the easy acceptance of a large diversity of musical styles, ethnic flavours, innovative appearances and marketing strategies'.

The tentative findings of Lemish and her team are that the older children become, 'the more important transnational media become' to them. Net-surfing, playing computer games, mastering English as a second language are dominant characteristics of middle- and upper-middle-class children. Home-grown media of a public service nature are seen as less 'cool' than global imports emphasizing entertainment and novelty: 'In our study we find support for . . . two parallel processes: one of adoption of a global perspective on social life, and the second of coexistence of multi-cultures, even hybrid ones in the lives of youngsters . . . What we understand from our informants is that the meeting between the global and the local can be those of coexistence and conflation, rather than assimilation vs isolationism.'

Chronology news narratives on TV are often compared to those of fictional stories (See STORYNESS) but there is obviously a number of differences, an important one of which is divergence over chronology. 'In news,' writes Allan Bell in *The Language of News Media* (UK: Blackwell, 1991), 'order is everything but chronology is nothing.' Indeed, in the news narrative the climax is reported first whereas in a story this usually comes at the end. Chronology has a low priority in the construction of news stories to the point where AUDIENCE has to be highly news-literate to follow what is going on. Bell says, 'The time structure of news stories can make the shape of a difficult film or novel look straightforward in comparison.' See AGENDA SETTING.

Cigarette cards A US company, Allen Ginter, produced the forerunner of the first British cigarette card when they packed with their Richmond Gem brand a pair of oval cards held together by a stud, one section of which was a calendar for 1884, with UK parcel postage rates on the back. By the 1890s the larger British tobacco companies were issuing cards, beginning with advertisements then progressing to series on particular themes such as soldiers, ships, royalty, sport and famous beauties.

The first company to issue photographic cigarette cards on a large scale was Ogdens who, in 1894, began their Guinea Gold and Tabs cards covering, in the next 13 years, practically every facet of life of that period. In the early 1900s there were around 50 companies issuing cards in the UK and Ireland. Reflecting the dominance of the British Empire, the cards represented many military issues, along with major inventions of the time – the motor car and the aeroplane. Exploration and discovery, and the Edwardian craze for collecting things – bird's eggs, butterflies, porcelain – were prominently reflected in the choice of subject matter as were the music hall and the scouting movement.

Early in the 1st World War (1914–18) the Wills company actually issued cards as miniature recruiting POSTERS while Gallahers put out several series of *Victoria Cross Heroes*, in 1915 and 1916. Carreras issued *Women on War Work* and *Raemaker's War Cartoons* portraying the Germans as barbarians.

Later examples of these cultural ephemera were Gallahers' *Boy Scouts, Fables and Their Morals*; Wills' *Cinema Stars* and *Radio Celebrities*. Ogdens produced a series on *Broadcasting*. With the approach of the 2nd World War (1939–45) Carreras produced *Britain's Defences* (1938), Players issued *Aircraft of the RAF* in the same year and in 1939 *Modern Naval Craft*. The most ambitious cigarette card enterprise of the period was the Imperial Tobacco Company's *Air Raid Precautions*, made available in a variety of cigarette brands.

Cigarette card production remained popular in the post-war era, though the 1960s saw a marked decline. In the 1970s came the much sought-after series from Player, *The Golden Age of Motoring*, packed in Doncella cigars. The Golden Age continued with *Steam* (1976), *Flying* (1977) and *Sail* (1978). See PICTURE POSTCARDS.

Cine-clubs Played an important role in

the development of cinema in many countries. Where, in the commercial film theatres, popular entertainment monopolized programmes, the cineclubs showed new experimental and often non-fictional work. John Grierson (1898–1972) organized the first British showing of Sergei Eisenstein's *Battleship Potemkin* at the London Film Society (formed in 1925) in 1929, along with his own seminal DOCUMENTARY *Drifters*. Minister of Propaganda in Nazi Germany, Goebbels, outlawed all cine-clubs because of their 'subversive' nature and a similar fate befell the cine-club movement in pre-2nd World War Japan.

The Depression and the failure of the media to meet head on the causes of depression, helped give belated birth to the US cine-club movement. The Workers' Film and Photo League, soon renamed the National Film and Photo League, was formed in New York in 1930. Members of the League made films as well as watched them, concentrating on filming the hunger marches and other mass protests of the time. Among their creations was a Workers' Newsreel which the League persuaded some commercial cinemas to screen.

Cinema See CINEMATOGRAPHY, ORIGINS; FILM.

Cinemacy Word coined by Thorold Dickinson to equate with literacy. His view was that education sadly neglects the cinema as a serious area of study. In the 1980s and 1990s this neglect has been redressed with the introduction into schools and colleges of communication, film and media studies, and into universities and polytechnics of many degree courses in the media field. See MEDIACY.

Cinema legislation The first legislation in the UK relating to cinema use was the Cinematograph Act of 1909. It concerned the licensing of exhibition premises and the safety of audiences. In 1922, the Celluloid and Cinematograph Film Act drew up safety rules for premises where raw CELLULOID or cinematograph film was stored and used. The Cinematograph Film Production (Special Loans) Act, 1949 established the National Film Finance Corporation and in the same year came the British Film Institute Act.

The Cinematograph Films Act, 1957 provided a statutory levy on exhibitors and exhibitions to be collected by Customs and Excise and paid to the British Film Fund Agency which would use the monies to support film production in the UK and support the Children's Film Foundation. This made the formerly voluntary levy (See BRITISH FILM PRODUCTION FUND) compulsory. The Cinematograph (Amendment) Acts of 1982 extended provision of the 1909 Act to include 'all exhibitions of moving pictures for private gain', bringing under regulation pornographic cinema and video 'clubs'. The Acts exclude from regulation *bona fide* film societies. The Films Act, 1985 abolished the Cinematograph Films Council, the Eady Levy and dissolved the National Film Finance Corporation, replacing it with the British Screen Finance Consortium. The government provided a 'starter' of £1.5m for five years to the loan fund of the BSFC whose function would be to raise funds independently of state support. See BROADCASTING LEGISLATION.

CinemaScope Wide-screen process copyrighted by 20th Century Fox in 1953 but invented much earlier by Henri Chretien. See ANAMORPHIC LENS.

Cinématographie Word first used by G. Bouly in 1892 in a French patent specification for a movie camera.

Cinematography, origins Among the earliest moving-picture inventions was the *Thaumatropical Amusement* of Englishman Henry Fitton (1826). Exploiting the phenomenon of PERSISTENCE OF VISION the Thaumatrope consisted of a round box inside of which were a number of discs each with a design on it. When the discs were twirled round, the images merged and gave the impression of a single movement.

Joseph Plateau's *Phenakistoscope* (1833), a circular design opposite a mirror, worked the same little miracle. The ZOETROPE or 'wheel of life', invented by Englishman W.G. Horner (1834) offered a revolving drum with strip sequences inside, enabling figures to jump, gallop or even do cart-wheels. Emile Renauld's *Praxinoscope* of 1877 improved on the Zoetrope by removing the slots of the drum and using mirrors to reflect the images, thus avoiding the dizziness to viewers caused by the Zoetrope; and the wonder of this device was extended with the *Projecting Praxinoscope* using a revolving disc-blade shutter to project animated images on to a screen.

The main impetus in the development of cinematography came, however, from another direction. Working in the US, English photographer Edward Muybridge (1830–1904) in the 1870s took multiple photographs of animals, birds and humans in movement. His most famous experiment was the one in which a line of cameras, using exposures of less than one thousandth of a second, 'filmed' a galloping horse. The horse triggered each camera as it passed – and proved, incidentally, that there *are* moments in a horse's movement when all its hooves are clear of the ground.

The next step was the projection of these in-sequence pictures. William Friese-Green (1855–1921) in 1890, revealed the potential of moving film when he set up a small slide projector in which the usual slide carrier had been replaced by a glass disc bearing a ring of pictures. Friese-Green's revolving disc was later demonstrated, to eager crowds, in the window of his studio in Piccadilly.

In France meanwhile Etienne Jules Marey (1830–1904) had invented a photographic 'gun' (1882) to take pictures of birds in flight and soon followed this with a camera capable of snapping 60 pictures a second on a paper-based film. In the US Thomas Alva Edison (1847–1931) produced his *Kinetograph* to take moving pictures and his KINETOSCOPE to show them. The viewer looked through a peephole in the foot-high box. The 50 feet of FILM ran for about 13 seconds. 'Kinetoscope parlours' were set up in which people could view films by putting a coin in the slot.

The most important year in the development of cinematography was 1895, with the invention of projectors in the US by Thomas Armat and Woodville Latham, in France by the Lumière brothers – Auguste

(1862–1954) and Louis (1864–1948) – and in the UK by Robert Paul. With the arrival of the Lumières on the scene, the cinema was truly born. Their vision and entrepreneurialism turned experiment into performance, private screenings into public, commercial profit. 'What did I do?' Louis Lumière is reported to have said. 'It was in the air.'

Auguste Lumière was less modest than Louis: 'My brother', he said, 'invented the cinema in one night.' On 28 December 1895, the Lumières, already highly successful in the photographic business, opened in the Salon Indien, in the Grand Café on the Boulevard des Capuchines. Seats were priced at one franc. Within weeks they were a worldwide success. Immediately the Lumières trained a brigade of cameramen-cum-projectionists and sent them abroad to several foreign countries; in quick time, some 1200 single-shot films were produced, including the Diamond Jubilee procession in London.

Cinéma vérité Or *Catalyst* cinema. DOCUMENTARY film maker Jean Rouch made the notable *Chronique d'un Été* (Chronicle of a Summer) in 1961 which pushed DIRECT CINEMA techniques into a new approach. Instead of simply being observed in their daily routines, Parisians were faced with camera and tape recorder and asked, 'Tell us, are you happy?' Rouch and co-producer Edgar Morin were suddenly on-camera participants; and so were their subjects – invited to see FILM rushes of their interviews. Their discussion of these was filmed and recorded and used as part of the end-product.

The style was named cinéma vérité in homage to the Russian movie pioneer Dziga Vertov (SEE SPINNING TOP), and translated from the term used by Vertov and his associates, *kino pravda*, film truth. Erik Barnouw in *Documentary* (UK: Oxford University Press, 1974), writes, 'The direct cinema documentarist took his camera to a situation of tension and waited hopefully for a crisis; the Rouch version of cinéma vérité tried to precipitate one. The direct cinema artist aspired to invisibility; the

Rouch cinéma vérité artist was often an avowed participant'.

Ciné-poème Dutch film maker Bert Haanstra used this expression to describe his DOCUMENTARY, *Glass* (1958), one of the most celebrated of all short films: lyrical, evocative – indeed a piece of poetry on CELLULOID. The ciné-poème was fashionable among documentary film makers in the years following the 2nd World War (1939–45).

Cinerama Extra-wide screen system invented by Fred Waller and first demonstrated in *This is Cinerama* (1952). Three projectors, electronically synchronized, created a three-section picture on the screen, giving a disturbing visual wobble at the joins. The first film story using the process was *How the West Was Won* (1962). Shortly afterwards the three-camera system was abandoned in favour of 'single-lens Cinerama', practically identical to CINEMASCOPE, though with higher definition.

Citizen Kane of the global village Description of media mogul Rupert Murdoch by Alex Brummer and Victor Keegan in a *Guardian* article (13 May 1995) entitled 'Planet Rupert takes on the galaxy'. The authors examine the growth and growth of the Murdoch global empire, referring to 'Murdoch monopolies' which are 'springing up everywhere he has a presence, having hustled out competitors', in what – thanks to digitalization – has become a 'single-product industry rather like water'. Although the authors warn that the future of mega-media services may go in different and competing directions, what we do know is that 'Mr Murdoch, by sinking billions into film libraries, newspapers, major sporting events, satellite transmission electronic networks and phone companies, is brilliantly positioned to profit from the information revolution, whatever direction it takes.' Kane was the fictional newspaper mogul in Orson Welles' film masterpiece *Citizen Kane* (1941), rather more than loosely based upon the life of the American newspaper baron, William Randolph Hearst (1863–1951) – the Rupert Murdoch of his age.

City symphonies Early FILM DOCUMENTARIES, usually Surrealist in approach, concentrating on the rhythms and patterns of city life. Walter Ruttman's *Berlin: Symphony of a City* (1927) set a fashion, taken up by many directors in the early 1930s, among whom was Jean Vigo (1905–34), who made *A propos de Nice* (On the subject of Nice) in 1929, released 1930, with Boris Kaufman, youngest brother of AVANT-GARDE documentarist Dziga Vertov. In the US Ralph Steiner and Willard Van Dyke directed *The City* (1939), a notable exposition, not of the symphony of city life, but of urban crisis.

Civil inattention Phenomenon of INTERPERSONAL COMMUNICATION observed by Erving Goffman in *Behavior in Public Places* (US: Free Press, 1963), where, after initial EYE CONTACT a person quickly withdraws visual attention from another to avoid any further recognition or need for further contact. As Goffman says, 'In performing this courtesy the eyes of the looker may pass over the eyes of the other, but no "recognition" is typically allowed'. The ritual of civil inattention Goffman says is one that 'constantly regulates the social intercourse of persons in our society'. See INDICATORS.

Clapper board See SHOT.

Claptrap See VERBAL DEVICES IN SPEECH-MAKING.

Class A factor of vital importance in the analysis of interpersonal and mass communication is the concept of *class*; and the most significant impact on the development of that concept was made by the German philosopher Karl Marx (1818–83). For him, class denoted a relationship to the *means of production* in any given society. Marx identified two main classes: the owners of the means of production (land, factories) whom he called the *bourgeoisie*, and those who were obliged to sell their labour to the owners to make a living – the *proletariat*. Although aware of other classes, he considered them of minor importance.

Marx argued that as a result of their position in the economic order, members of each class shared common experiences, lifestyles and certain political and economic interests. He believed that there was and would remain, in a capitalist society, an inevitable *conflict* between the interests of the bourgeoisie and the proletariat. He further argued that GROUP identity, class-consciousness and collective political and economic action would develop in the course of economic and political conflict. Proletarian class-consciousness was particularly likely to emerge as its members were thrown into serious difficulties and close daily associations at work.

The dominant class – the bourgeoisie – would, according to Marx, seek to impose its culture upon the rest of society. Its culture would become the *dominant* culture, its IDEOLOGY the dominant ideology. Consequently the communication systems of society would reflect the dominant culture of the bourgeoisie and also the conflict between the two classes. From a Marxist viewpoint, control of many facets of the mass media by the ownership of capital gives that class the opportunity to disseminate its own culture and ideology. Such control, in Marxist terms, plays a vital role in the maintenance of HEGEMONY.

The term is also commonly used when what is meant is *social class*. Social class membership is based, primarily, upon occupation rather than ownership or non-ownership of the means of production.

For the ADVERTISING industry and media management, social class is a significant factor in the profile of an audience. Market researchers are primarily interested in income and spending power. For those media organizations which are dependent on advertising revenue the social class composition of its audience is of obvious importance.

The inter-relationships between the social class structure and the communication processes of society are complex and research in this area is wide-ranged. Of particular concern is whether the narrowness of social class backgrounds of those who control and work in the media is reflected in its output. See ADVERTISING: MAINSTREAMERS, ASPIRERS, SUCCEEDERS AND REFORMERS; CODES; CONGLOMERATES; ELITE; ESTABLISHMENT; MARXIST (MODE OF MEDIA ANALYSIS); VALS TYPOLOGY.

Classic FM Commercial radio station broadcasting nationwide in the UK from the autumn of 1992. Its menu of popular classics presented in a lively and unpatronizing way and a policy of winning audience loyalty through competitions and sponsored musical events has proved a remarkable success.

Clause 28 See SECTION 28.

'Clean up TV' movement Brought together in Birmingham in 1963 by Mary Whitehouse and others; later called itself the National Viewers' and Listeners' Association (NVLA). Over the years the movement has succeeded in gaining access to practically every forum in which the ISSUES of BROADCASTING are discussed; additionally, the NVLA has been active as a 'morality watchdog' in other arts, especially the theatre and publishing.

The basis of NVLA thinking is that of traditional Christian ethics; the belief that the VALUES of chastity and the family underpin all that's best in western society, and that such values are constantly under threat and have to be protected.

Of equal concern to the NVLA is the increase in the display, in FILM, on TV and in the theatre, of scenes of violence. See BROADCASTING STANDARDS COUNCIL; CENSORSHIP; LONGFORD REPORT; MORAL ENTREPRENEURS.

Climax order In the process of persuading others, the *order* in which arguments and evidence are placed is of considerable importance. Research has been conducted into the *climax order* and *anti-climax order*, that is when the best point of an argument is reserved till last (climax) or used at the outset (anti-climax). The two orders have varying advantages depending on the particular conditions under which the communication is presented, including the audience's predisposition and the type of matter being transmitted. Similar concepts are the Law of PRIMACY and the Law of Recency.

Clipper chip A microchip, called the spy in the computer, the 'sleeping policeman on the superhighway of information', it was feared in the mid-1990s that it would become a compulsory element in US-made computers allowing government agencies, by means of an electronic back door, to snoop on data into and out of computers. Such was the determination of users of the INTERNET and their campaign against the clipper chip that the Clinton government temporarily retreated from its plans. However, as a V-for violence chip, it is to have a future. In February 1996 Clinton signed a Telecommunications Bill requiring that from 1998 all TV sets with a screen size of 13 inches or more should be fitted with a V-chip.

In the same month the European parliament voted in favour of a similar measure – the insertion of V-chips into every new TV set sold in Europe under the Television Without Frontiers directive. The plan to permit CENSORSHIP of violence, bad language and sexual explicitness raises the same question as the clipper chip: how, for example, might a repressive regime employ the chip to impose censorship on matters other than those it was ostensibly designed to control?

The chip is a marker of widespread concern about how much sex and violence is accessible on screen for even very young children. In April 1996 the BBC's new 10–year charter contains a clause – itself a matter of concern among broadcasters – about taste and decency.

To act on breaches of taste and decency presupposes a consensus on what they are: something difficult to reach agreement on in British culture, never mind when the cultures of 15 member states of the European Community are involved. See ENCRIPT.

Clique A close-knit group of people within a social system whose communication is largely with each other. *Clique analysis* is used to determine communication groupings within a social system and its main tool is SOCIOMETRICS.

Closed text See OPEN, CLOSED TEXTS.

Closure Occurs in a communication situation when one participant, usually the receiver of information, closes down attention, and thus deflects or refects the MESSAGE or the messenger, or terminates an encounter. The reasons for closure may relate to the unacceptability of the message: it may conflict with the attitudes, beliefs or VALUES of the receiver; it may be an 'uncomfortable truth' which causes the receiver a feeling of DISSONANCE. Also, it may have something to do with the messenger rather than the message – personal dislike of the sender on the part of the receiver or a simple unwillingness to receive *this* kind of message from *this* messenger, or it may simply reflect a wish to terminate the encounter and move on. The means of closure will involve NVC (Non-verbal communication) as well as verbal strategies. See COMMUNICATION, NON-VERBAL; PREFERRED READING.

Cocktail party problem In *On Human Communication* (US: MIT Press, 1966), Colin Cherry writes, 'One of our most important faculties is the ability to listen to, and follow, one speaker in the presence of others. This is such a common experience that we may take it for granted; we may call it "the cocktail party problem". That is, how do we filter out a barrage of communication messages, selecting one to concentrate upon?' Cherry experimented with two different taped readings being played at once, with the instruction to the subject to concentrate on one and ignore the other. Though the tapes produced a 'complete babel', and though very wide-ranging texts were used, considerable success in deciphering the MESSAGE was demonstrated, illustrating the importance of 'our ingrained speech habits at the acoustic, syllabic, or syntactic levels'. Cherry and his colleagues also experimented to see what happened when a subject was asked to read a text out loud while simultaneously listening to another one. This process, of testing the subject's ability to select from competing message channels, they called 'shadowing'.

Code of Advertising Standards and Practice (ITC) The Independent Television Commission (ITC) of the UK was empowered by the BROADCASTING ACT, 1990 to draw up and enforce a code governing standards and practice in television ADVERTISING and the sponsorship of programmes (See SPONSORSHIP: ITC CODE OF PROGRAMME SPONSORSHIP). Modelled closely on the Code of Practice issued by the IBA (Independent Broadcasting Authority, which the ITC succeeded) and the Code of the Cable

Authority, the ITC Code also had regard to the Code of Practice issued by the Broadcasting Standards Council as well as the need to fulfil requirements relating to TV advertising in the European Community Directive on Television Broadcasting (89/552/EEC) and the 1989 Council of Europe Convention on Transfrontier Television.

The ITC Code applies to all independent TV broadcasting, UK direct broadcast satellite (DBS) services and other satellite services operating out of the UK. The Code declares that television advertising 'should be legal, decent, honest and truthful'. Advertisements must at all times be distinguishable as such and recognizably separate from the programmes and they must not refer to themselves as 'programmes'. Expressions such as the term 'News flash' are not acceptable. So-called 'subliminal' advertising is prohibited: 'No advertisement may include any technical device which, by using images of very brief duration or by any other means, exploits the possibility of conveying a message to, or otherwise influencing the minds of, members of the audience without their being aware, or fully aware, of what has been done.' No advertisement of a political nature is acceptable; and none may be used in relation to an industrial dispute.

Prohibition is also extended to adverts which play upon the fears of the audience or attempt to exploit the superstitious, or which appear to discriminate on grounds of gender or race. The Code proscribes a range of products and services – breath-testing devices and products which purport to mask the effects of alcohol; the occult; betting tips and gaming, including the pools.

The Code deals with a long list of requirements concerning health and safety, protection of the environment, the use of animals in advertisements, misleadingness, price claims, comparisons and denigration. There are seven sections in the Code relating to matrimonials and introduction agencies and 13 on alcoholic drinks advertisement. Item (g) of Section 40, declares that advertisements 'must neither claim nor suggest that any drink can contribute towards sexual success or that drinking can enhance sexual attractiveness' and item (j) that no advertisement may suggest 'that

drinking is an essential attribute of masculinity'.

Appendix 1 of the Code deals with advertising and children and other appendices are: 2. financial advertising; 3. health claims, medicines and treatments; 4. charity advertising; 5. religious advertising.

Code of Programme Sponsorship
See sponsorship: ITC CODE OF PROGRAMME SPONSORSHIP.

Code of semes See CODES OF NARRATIVE.

Codes A code is generally defined as a system into which signs are organized, governed by consent. The study of codes – other than those *arbitrary* or fixed codes such as mathematics, chemical symbols, MORSE CODE, etc. – emphasizes the social dimension of communication. We have codes of conduct, ethical, aesthetic and LANGUAGE codes (See ELABORATED AND RESTRICTED CODES).

Non-verbal communication is carried on through what have been classified as **presentational codes**: GESTURE, movement of the eyes, expressions of the face, tone of voice. A **representation code** can be speech, writing, music, art, architecture, etc. Speech itself has non-verbal characteristics: **prosodic codes** affect the MEANING of the words used, through expression or pitch of voice.

The media are often referred to as employing **broadcast** and **narrowcast codes** in gearing content, level and style to expected audiences. In *Introducing Communication Studies* (UK: Methuen, 1982), John Fiske writes, 'Narrowcast codes have acquired the function in our mass society of stressing the difference between "us" (the users of the code) and "them" (the laymen, the lowbrows). Broadcast codes stress the similarities among "us" (the majority)'. In the case of TV, *Coronation Street* would represent the broadcast code and a production of Shakespeare's *King Lear* a piece of narrowcasting, though economically speaking, in terms of advertising, narrowcast may simply indicate the target audience of the advertiser.

Aesthetic codes are crucially affected by their cultural context, some of it highly conventional, some AVANT-GARDE, subject to textual rather than commonly recognized cues to meaning. Much modern art, for example, has been encoded in visual languages accessible only to a small number of people. However, over time, innovative aesthetic encoding becomes conventionalized. The obscure code has become familiar. A case in point is surrealism, whose intention was to shock cultural convention, yet whose dream symbols and often disturbing juxtapositions of objects have become a commonplace of mass advertising. What began as a code specific to itself has been transformed to one given its meaning by cultural convention. See DECODE; DOMINANT, SUBORDINATE, RADICAL; ELITE; HIGHBROW; SEMIOLOGY/SEMIOTICS.

Codes of narrative Roland Barthes in *S/Z* (UK: Basil Blackwell, 1990; translated by Richard Miller) applies a number of narrative codes in a book-length analysis, or DECONSTRUCTION, of a 23-page short story, *Sarrasine*, written by Honoré de Balzac in 1830. Barthes describes 'five major codes under which all the textual signifiers can be grouped' in a narrative. The **Proiaretic** or **Action** code (the Voice of Empirics) tells us of events – of what happens, and thus is instrumental in the sequence of the story. The code of the **seme** or sign ('semantically the unit of the signifier') refers to character and is categorized by Richard Howard in the Preface to *S/Z* as the Semantic Code (though Barthes does not actually use this term in the text). Barthes speaks of this as the Voice of the Person. Under the **Hermeneutic** or **Enigma** code (the Voice of Truth) 'we list the various (formal) terms by which an enigma can be distinguished, suggested, formulated, held in suspense and finally disclosed'. **Cultural** or **Referential** codes 'are references to a science or a body of knowledge' – 'physical, physiological, medical, psychological, literary, historical, etc.'. These are the Voice of Science. Finally there is the **Symbolic** code, the Voice of Symbol.

Barthes writes of the codes that they 'create a kind of network, a *topos* [Greek: a place, location] through which the entire text passes (or rather, in passing, becomes text)'.

This taxonomy of codes is widely used in the analysis of texts of all kinds. Nowhere, however, does Barthes suggest that such coding is prescriptive, discrete or exact. He writes 'The code is a perspective of quotations, a mirage of structures; we know only its departures and returns.' Barthes talks of a 'galaxy of signifiers, not a structure of signifieds'. For him the text 'is not unitary, architectonic, finite' and the approach to it is characterized by 'blanks and looseness of analysis'. The meaning of the 'readerly' as contrasted with the 'writerly' text is ultimately elusive. The 'blanks' and 'looseness of analysis' will be like footprints making the escape of the text'.

Codes: Programmes codes See ITC PROGRAMME CODE; RADIO AUTHORITY PROGRAMME CODES I AND 2; SPONSORSHIP: ITC CODE OF PROGRAMME SPONSORSHIP.

Cognitive (and Affective) That area or domain of human behaviour which can be described as intellectual – knowing, understanding and reasoning – is often referred to as the *cognitive*. A substantial amount of media communication is aimed at producing cognitive responses in the receiver. That area which is involved with attitudes, emotions, VALUES and feelings is termed the *affective*. Obviously the two overlap and intertwine. Whether the content of a MESSAGE is cognitive or affective in its orientations will greatly influence the mode chosen for its communication. If the content of a message is judged to be of cognitive intent, then LANGUAGE will generally be couched in neutral terms; presentation will strive after objectivity and *balance*. An affective message will be more likely to be framed in EMOTIVE LANGUAGE, its imagery directed towards emotional responses.

However, much recent media research has been directed towards a more critical analysis of the allegedly objective modes of cognitive messages. There is concern as to whether the dissemination of apparently neutral information – especially if that dissemination is of some FREQUENCY and CONSISTENCY of treatment – influences an audience's perception of national and world events. From the mass of available information, the media select and reject. They give emphasis – and legitimacy – to some issues rather than others, and they set the order of priorities (See AGENDA SETTING) as well as seeking to establish links between occurrences and their causes in the minds of the audience. If, for example, trade unions only appear in media coverage as sources of social and political conflict, both the cognitive and affective responses of audiences are likely to become unfavourable to the concept or even the existence of trade unionism. See EFFECTS OF THE MASS MEDIA; GLASGOW UNIVERSITY MEDIA GROUP.

Cognitive capture See IMPARTIALITY.

Cognitive dissonance See CONGRUENCE THEORY; DISSONANCE.

Cold media, hot media See HOT MEDIA, COLD MEDIA.

Collective representations Describe the role played by community in telling stories about itself, in particular those musical or dramatic forms, images and artefacts which speak for and about popular tastes, beliefs, values and preoccupations. At the same time the term describes the way the community may adopt images and artefacts produced for it, works of art, for example, and assigns to them significance rooted in popular needs and uses. The collective production of MEANING, says Wendy Griswold in *Cultures and Societies in a Changing World* (US: Pine Forge Press, 1994), 'tries to take away the mystery about the creation of art, ideas, beliefs, religion, and culture in general by revealing the many social activities, such as interaction, cooperation, organization, and contestation, involved in the formulation of what we designate as cultural objects'. See CULTURE: POPULAR CULTURE; EXPECTATION, HORIZONS OF.

Collocation The tendency of words to occur in regular association; words set together through customary usage such as 'fair' and 'play', 'auspicious' and 'occasion'.

Collodion or wet-plate process See PHOTOGRAPHY, ORIGINS.

Colloquialism An expression used in common, informal speech, but not as far removed from acceptable modes as SLANG. If your comments 'cut no ice' with some-body, that is a colloquialism; if you are told to 'keep yer 'air on', that is slang. It is a modest distinction, for as R. Ridout and C. Witting say in *The Facts of English* (UK: Pan Reference Books, 1973), 'the slang of yesterday becomes the colloquialism of today'. See ARGOT; DIALECT; JARGON; REGISTER.

Colonization Term used to describe the process by which various cultural material is acquired from a variety of contexts and then reassembled to construct particular messages. In this process the meaning of the original signs is often changed, if not subverted; their use may appear to celebrate differences between people but the goal to which they are put may have as its purpose the REINFORCEMENT of the DOMINANT CULTURE, and the denial of differences and the conflict which they bring.

Advertising messages contain many examples of colonization. For example, the signs and symbols widely associated with certain YOUTH CULTURES are often employed to sell goods and services to various audiences – whether young people themselves or older consumers who are presumed to identify with a particular youth culture. Ironically whilst youth cultures are often a site of resistance and challenge to the dominant culture their signs and symbols are in this way used to draw them further into the dominant culture, for instance through encouraging certain patterns of consumption and the use of financial services such as banking services.

Colour TV The first regular TV service in colour began in the US in 1954; 1960 saw the first colour service in Japan, seven years ahead of Britain. In 1969 there were 100,000 colour sets in use in the UK; by the same month in 1972 there were 1.6m and twice that 12 months later. Ferguson produced the first full-size colour receiver using transistors throughout, in 1967. Transistors consumed a quarter the power of traditional valve receivers. They ran cooler and were more reliable. Later came integrated circuits doing away with many discrete components. The surface acoustic wave (SAW) filter further refined the accuracy of colour reception as did improved shadow-mask tubes. Here stripes of colour rather than dots achieved registration of the picture's red, green and blue components without the need for any of the many correction-circuits previously required.

Comics The first newspaper comic-strip is generally considered to be that which appeared on 16 February 1896 in the *New York Sunday World*. It was a three-quarter page feature in colour called 'The Great Dog Show in M'Googan's Avenue'. Kids in the city's slum backyards were organizing their own dog show; the hero, dressed in a bright yellow nightgown, soon became the 'Yellow Kid' and 'Hogan's Alley' achieved immediate popularity as a long-running comic strip (see YELLOW KID).

The idea was not new. English cartoonist Thomas Rowlandson (1757–1827) created a comic character, Dr Syntax, who was popular with the public, and considerably earlier William Hogarth (1697–1764) included speech 'balloons' in his engravings satirizing London life.

George Orwell took comics seriously enough to write about them. In 'Boys' Weeklies' (1939), published in *Selected Essays* (UK: Penguin, 1957), Orwell analyses the social and political connotations of early publications in the GENRE.

What seems to characterize comics, in Orwell's day or our own, is their social changelessness, deep down if not in the surface detail. Orwell did find differences between the older and the new generation of weeklies, however: in the new, 'better technique, more scientific interest, more bloodshed, more leaderworship'; in 'social outlook there is hardly any advance'.

As life appears to have become more complex, and society more complicated, the STEREOTYPE of the hero has had a sustaining appeal. Picture-strip heroes such as Clark Kent, alias Superman, who first made his appearance in *Action Comics* (1938) in the US, have not only led popular (and charmed) lives on the printed paper but have translated into immensely popular FILM heroes. The debate concerning comics, and comic books, centres around the extent to which they seem to legitimize dominant social values. At the same time concern is expressed about the subversive potential of

so-called *comix* which offer a more pluralist, and sometimes radical, reading, as well as a more aesthetically conscious approach. This kind of comic also addresses adult audiences and is often anti-authority in essence. See CARTOONS.

Commanders of the social order Term used by Herbert I. Schiller in *Culture, Inc. The Corporate Takeover of Public Expression* (UK: Oxford University Press, 1989), referring to the vast transnational corporations which, he argues, have come to dominate and shape culture; establish prevailing discourses; set political, economic and cultural agendas and call the tune of mass media. Schiller talks of the PRIVATIZATION of public space: in a literal sense (public areas being transformed into privately-owned and controlled shopping malls and pleasure domes); and in an intellectual sense, through the 'corporatization' of arts, literature and media. He cites the extent to which the entire world of information (libraries, museums, universities, mass communication); and of expression (architecture, music, art); and of public spectacle (sport), have been colonized by corporations, particularly in the US, but increasingly in the rest of the world. See ACTIVE-AUDIENCE THESIS; CONSENSUS; ELITE; HEGEMONY; MANUFACTURE OF CONSENT; POWER ELITE; PRESS BARONS; PUBLIC SPHERE.

Commercial confidentiality A CENSORSHIP device employed to prevent the media transmitting, or the general public receiving, information on the grounds that such information might be commercially damaging (regardless of whether that information might be in the public interest). One particularly sensitive area of commerce which is shrouded in mystery is the arms trade. Britain is, for example, among the world's top arms-trading nations. Its government maintains an arms marketing and advisory service, the Defence Exports Services Organisation (DECO), yet this organization is notoriously secretive whenever journalists seek to find out about its work, invariably answering that information cannot be supplied for reasons of 'commercial confidentiality'.

Louis Blom-Cooper, chairman of the

Press Council in 1990 expressed the view that 'Traditional English law places a higher value on commercial interests than on the public's right to know'. See THALIDOMIDE CASE.

Commercial laissez-faire model of (media) communication In their Introduction to *The Manufacture of News* (UK: Constable, 1973) joint editors Stanley Cohen and Jock Young cite two general, and polarized, models which attempt to explain the intentions and impact of media on their audiences – the *Mass manipulative model* and the *Commercial laissez-faire model*. In the first, 'the public is seen as an atomized mass, passive receptacles of messages originating from a monolithic and powerful source'. From the perspective of the political Left it is big business – the hierarchy of capitalism – which is the seemingly all-powerful manipulator. From the perspective of the political Right, the media in this model .are seen as manipulating 'standards' by lowering them.

Drawn from the laissez-faire (leave well alone) model of the economy, the Commercial laissez-faire model mirrors the freedom of the market place where producers compete with one another to sell their products to consumers. Thus media corporations are seen as having to compete for the attention and loyalty of their consumers – the audience.

Researchers using this model tend to argue that the consumer is sovereign and that media corporations have to tailor their products to suit consumer wishes, tastes and needs. The focus of their research is, therefore, often upon the mechanisms by which such tailoring is achieved.

The Commercial laissez-faire model emerged as a critique of the mass manipulative model. It is generally the PREFERRED READING of journalists and media people themselves. Because there is competition, the argument goes, there is consequently 'variety and diversity in information and opinions presented in the mass media and that such variation minimizes the chances of manipulation'. This summary having been made in Cohen and Young's Introduction, the rest of the book's fascinating collection of reports and analyses is a remorseless

exposé of fallacies perceived in the Commercial laissez-faire model. See COMMUNICATION MODELS; EFFECTS OF THE MASS MEDIA.

Commercial radio Though PIRATE RADIO attempted to buck the BROADCASTING monopoly of the BBC during the 1960s, legitimate commercial broadcasting in the UK was not in operation till the 1970s, following the Conservative government's Sound Broadcasting Act of 1972. IBA had, by 1983, 37 commercial RADIO stations operating under licence throughout the UK and plans for over 60 commercial stations.

In the US the first commercial radio was KDKA of Pittsburg which went on the air on 2 November 1920 with a broadcast of the returns of the Harding-Cox presidential elections. In 1921 there were eight commercial radio stations, by 1922, 564. Development of radio in the US was spectacular and chaotic. In 1927 (the year that the BBC, by Royal Charter, was given a monopoly of radio broadcasting in the UK) Congress passed a Radio Act setting up the Federal Communications Commission to allocate wavelengths to broadcasters. Four radio networks were created as a hedge against monopoly – National Broadcasting Commission (NBC), Columbia Broadcasting Service (CBS), Mutual Broadcasting System (MBS) and the American Broadcasting Company (ABC), while the FCC worked towards the growth of projects of educational interest.

Despite the BBC's monopoly in the UK, commercial broadcasts in English were transmitted from abroad as early as 1925. Radio Paris, broadcasting from the Eiffel Tower, presented a fashion talk in English, sponsored by Selfridges. Only three listeners wrote to the station to say they had heard the broadcast but the commercial lobby was undaunted. In the 1930s Captain L.F. Flugge, who had arranged the fashion talk, formed and ran the International Broadcasting Company. The IBC's Radio Normandy transmitted 15–minute shows for several hours a day from 1931 and by the following year 21 British firms were paying sponsorship money for commercial broadcasting, and the UK was being beamed at commercially from The Netherlands, Spain and Luxembourg.

The IBC actually set up offices in Portland Place, London, and had its own outside broadcasting vehicles, each painted black with 'Radio Normandy 274 metres' on the side. An important part of the company's operation was the International Broadcasting Club, formed in 1932, with free membership. By 1939, the IBC had 320,000 members.

Radio Luxembourg began broadcasting on 1191 metres long wave in 1933, its first two sponsors being Zam Buk and Bile Beans. Though the Post Office conducted a sustained campaign to close down these commercial stations, it was Adolf Hitler and the 2nd World War which did the trick: many transmitters were either destroyed by the Nazis or taken over. Radio Luxembourg became Hitler's major PROPAGANDA weapon against the British. The notorious Lord Haw-Haw (William Joyce), an Irishman committed to the German cause, broadcast daily recommendations to the British to lay down their arms, from the most powerful transmitter in Europe.

Of the commercial stations, Luxembourg was the only one to start up again after the war (finally closing down in 1992). The first accredited commercial radio station on British soil was Manx Radio which began broadcasting in 1964.

With the election of the Conservatives in 1970, the Minister of Posts and Telecommunications produced a White Paper, *An Alternative Service of Broadcasting* proposing a network of about 60 commercial stations under the Independent Television Authority (to be renamed the Independent Broadcasting Authority). Opposition Spokesman Ivor Richards called it 'nothing more than the establishment of 60 pop stations'.

From the beginning, in 1972, local independent radio was to broadcast on stereo VHF as well as medium wave. The first FRANCHISES were awarded in 1973, to bring into existence the all-news London Broadcasting Company (LBC) and Capital Radio for London, with regional stations following soon afterwards.

Additional franchises were granted by the IBA in 1981. By 1988 there were 40 independent local radio stations (compared to 27 BBC local stations).

The BROADCASTING ACT, 1990 separated out the statutory overseeing of radio and television, creating for TV (in place of the IBA) the INDEPENDENT TELEVISION COMMISSION (ITC) and for radio the Radio Authority. The Radio Authority was empowered to assign frequencies, appoint licensees and to regulate programming and advertising. Also the Authority was required to draw up and periodically review codes of practice concerning programmes, advertising standards and other matters.

The Act, which came into force on 1 January 1991, with Lord Chalfont as Chairman and Peter Baldwin as Chief Executive, substantially opened up the radio airwaves to independent, commercial stations. By 1992 well over 100 commercial stations were broadcasting throughout Britain, from Breeze-AM of Cheltenham to Xtra-AM of Birmingham/Coventry. For the first time three national radio (INR) licences were offered, INR1 going to Classic FM. 1992 saw the Authority seeking applications for INR2 (broadcasting on AM) and INR3 (a speech-based service). The cost of an application for an INR licence was £10,000 and the annual licence fee £645,000.

'Special event' licences, a Home Office remit prior to the Act, became the responsibility of the Radio Authority. Licences are usually granted for 28 days and for a localized coverage area. A notable example of this kind of community-based broadcasting is Radio Cracker – run by Christian youth groups around the UK aiming to raise funds for Third World charities by broadcasting in the run-up to Christmas from 90 stations around the country. See COMMUNITY RADIO.

Commercial television Although TV in the US was commercial – relying on ADVERTISING for its revenues – from the beginning, TV in the UK was a PUBLIC SERVICE BROADCASTING monopoly until the TELEVISION ACT, 1954, which gave birth to Independent Television. The ITA's first term ran from 1954 to 1964. It became the IBA (Independent Broadcasting Authority) from 1972, when the second term lasted until 1981. The third term, from 1982, was marked by the inauguration of CHANNEL 4 and BREAKFAST TIME TELEVISION. ITV programme companies were appointed for an eight-year contract period, serving modified areas and with two fresh dual regions. In its turn the IBA was succeeded by the Independent Television Commission (ITC) on 1 January 1992. Responsibility for RADIO became that of the new Radio Authority (See BROADCASTING ACT, 1990).

The passing of the IBA represented a significant watershed in the nature of BROADCASTING in the UK. A rigorously directive body, the IBA was very much a mirror image, in terms of regulation, of its opposite number in PSB (Public Service Broadcasting), the BBC. The Conservative government of the day was committed to PRIVATIZATION and DEREGULATION and the duties of the new ITC represented a 'light-touch' approach to regulation.

The ITC is responsible for the licensing and regulating of all commercial television in the UK. In addition, it has responsibility for cable, satellite and such services as public TELETEXT. A core function of the ITC's work, as it was for the IBA, is the enforcement of a *Code of Advertising Standards and Practice.* This requires the Commission to set out advertising standards, ensure compliance with the Code and investigate complaints. It is empowered by the Control of Misleading Advertisements Regulations, 1988, to consider complaints about TV advertisements which are alleged to be misleading. The ITC's *Code of Programme Sponsorship* defines sponsorship in relation to commercial television and lays down guidelines. Rule 2 of the Code, for example, declares that 'No sponsor is permitted any influence on either the content or the scheduling of the programme he has sponsored', while Rule 7 states 'PRODUCT PLACEMENT is forbidden' (See SPONSORSHIP).

The Broadcasting Act of 1990 also made it a statutory duty to draw up a *Programme Code* governing what the Foreword of the Code calls 'due impartiality and a general code governing the portrayal of violence, appeals for donations and such other matters concerning standards and practice for programmes as the ITC considers appropriate'. The Code also gives effect in the UK to a number of requirements relating to television programmes in the European Community Directive on Television Broadcasting

on Transfrontier Television (See PROGRAMME CODE: ITC).

A significant stipulation arising from the new arrangements was that *independents,* that is independent programme-makers, must be allocated by the Channel 3 licensees a minimum of 25% of broadcasting time, the quota being based upon programmes broadcast rather than programmes commissioned.

Definition of a *large* as contrasted with a *small* licence area was specific under ITC terms. It was permitted for one body to hold a controlling interest in two regional Channel 3 licences as long as they are not both large (a limit which was raised by the BROADCASTING ACT, 1995). Of the 15 new regional channels (operational from 1 January 1993), the top nine (in terms of the share of New Advertising Revenue) are designated under Government Order as large (London Weekday, London Weekend, East, West and South Midlands, Yorkshire, North West England, South and South East England, Wales and West, and Central Scotland). Small areas are Borders and the Isle of Man, Channel Islands, North of Scotland, South West England, North East England and Northern Ireland.

Among other changes brought about following the 1990 Broadcasting Act and the allocation of new franchises (See FRANCHISES FROM 1993) was the allocating of schools broadcasting, and the funding of such broadcasting, to Channel 4. S4C, the Welsh fourth channel was directly funded by central government from 1 January 1993. The IBA's National Committees and General Advisory Council were replaced by ten regional councils, called Viewer Consultative Councils (VCCs), appointed by the ITC, to act as advisers to the ITC from the end of 1990, and these include councils for Scotland, Northern Ireland and Wales.

Commissions/committees on the media See ANNAN COMMISSION REPORT ON BROADCASTING, 1977; BEVERIDGE COMMITTEE REPORT ON BROADCASTING, 1950; BROADCASTING COMPLAINTS COMMITTEE; BROADCASTING STANDARDS COUNCIL; CALCUTT COMMITTEE ON PRIVACY & OTHER RELATED MATTERS, 1990 AND 1993; HANKEY COMMITTEE REPORT ON TELEVISION, 1943; HUNT

COMMITTEE REPORT ON CABLE EXPANSION AND BROADCASTING POLICY, 1982; LLOYD COMMITTEE REPORT, 1967; MacBRIDE COMMISSION; McGREGOR COMMISSION REPORT ON THE PRESS, 1977; PILKINGTON COMMITTEE REPORT ON BROADCASTING, 1962; ROSS COMMISSION REPORT ON THE PRESS, 1949; SELSDON COMMITTEE REPORT ON TELEVISION, 1935; SHAWCROSS COMMISSION REPORT ON THE PRESS, 1962; SYKES COMMITTEE REPORT ON BROADCASTING (SEE BBC, ORIGINS); ULLSWATER COMMITTEE REPORT ON BROADCASTING, 1936; WILLIAMS COMMITTEE REPORT ON OBSCENITY AND FILM CENSORSHIP, 1979.

Commoditization of information The notion that information is something upon which the possessor can put a price; thus information is bought and sold because it is a commodity rather than a public service. The process constitutes an important issue, and might also be termed the *privatization* of information. Herbert I. Schiller in 'Critical research in the information age', in *Journal of Communication* (Summer 1983), writes, 'The privatization of information is observable in all sectors of society . . . A new international division of labour, no less inequitable than its predecessor, is being created practically before our eyes'. Schiller refers to a 'gale of technological and industrial change whipping across the United States and other industrialized countries' which is having far-reaching effects on the way we regard, and use, information: 'In sum, long-term, deep structural forces are making communication the central process in global, national and local social organization. At the same time, the most powerful national and transnational decision-making groups are initiating and deploying new information technologies to consolidate and extend their positions.' See ELITE; HEGEMONY; INFORMATION GAPS; MEDIA IMPERIALISM; POWER; POWER ELITE; TECHNOLOGICAL DETERMINISM.

Commonality In terms of LANGUAGE, beliefs, CULTURE, general outlook, that which is *shared* within a community; that which most elements of the community have in common.

Common sense In the study of media communication and its links with culture and politics, the term 'common sense' connotes an over-readiness to believe in the apparently obvious. The Italian philosopher Antonio Gramsci (1891–1937) defined common sense as being a composite of the attitudes, beliefs and assumptions of the mass of the people, and operating within a hierarchical social order.

Common sense tends towards conformism to the IDEOLOGY of the dominant social order, and in part is the product of that ideology. It accepts 'the way things are' – the status quo – as 'the way things should be'. Indeed such structures and circumstances are so obvious (so commonsensical) that they do not warrant being questioned. Gramsci believed that what he termed the 'chaotic aggregate of disparate conceptions' comprising common sense should be challenged by intellectuals and the complacency of common sense explained and exposed.

Many commentators have focused on the role the media play in nurturing and reinforcing rather than unpacking commonsensical visions of society See EXNOMINATION; HEGEMONY.

Communication While the definitions of communication vary according to the theoretical frames of reference employed and the stress placed upon certain aspects of the total process, they all include five fundamental factors: an initiator; a recipient; a mode or vehicle; a MESSAGE and an effect. Simply expressed, the communication process begins when a *message* is conceived by a *sender*. It is then ENCODED – translated into a signal or sequence of signals – and *transmitted* via a particular MEDIUM or CHANNEL to a *receiver* who then decodes it and interprets the message, returning a signal in some way that the message has or has not been understood.

What has been termed NOISE, or interference, may impede the message. This may be internal (resistance to the message or to the sender, for example, on the part of the receiver) or external (actual noise, distraction, LANGUAGE level, etc.). During the communication process, sender, message and receiver are subject to a multitude of *cues* which influence the message, such as a person's appearance, his/her known status or the expression on his/her own face as the message is communicated or responded to (See BARNLUND'S TRANSACTIONAL MODEL).

While INTERPERSONAL COMMUNICATION is that which occurs between two or more people, INTRAPERSONAL COMMUNICATION is what you say within and to yourself. Inner thoughts, impressions, memories interact with external stimuli – the decor of a room, a painting on the wall, a beautiful landscape, a row of slum houses, a jostling crowd, a teacher at the front of the class, your friend's good or bad mood – to create a silent discourse, continuously changing and renewing itself and influencing your perceptions of self and the world.

It is important to hold in mind, as Raymond Williams points out in *Keywords* (UK: Fontana, 1976), the 'unresolved range of the original noun of action, represented at its extremes by "transmit", a one-way process, and "share" . . . a common or mutual process'. This polarity of meaning – of the one-way process as against aspects of *communion* – is fundamental to the analysis of communication, hence the attempt to generalize the distinction in such phrases as *manipulative communication* and *participative communication*.

Frank Dance in 'Toward a theory of human communication' in the book he edited, *Human Communication Theory: Original Essays* (US: Holt, Rinehart & Winston, 1967), observes that communication is something that changes even while one is in the act of examining it; it is therefore an interaction and a *transaction*. Dance and C. Larson in *The Functions of Human Communication: A Theoretical Approach* (US: Holt, Rinehart & Winston, 1976), detail their examination of 126 definitions of communication. They specify notable differences but common agreement that communication is a *process*. The authors conclude with a definition of their own: 'The production of symbolic content by an individual, according to a CODE, with anticipated consumption by other(s) according to the same code'. Or as Colin Cherry succinctly puts it in *On Human Communication* (US: MIT Press, 1957), communication is 'essentially a social affair'.

Of course a painter or a poet may quarrel with this definition. He/she might claim

that the process of communication is between artist–materials–subject-matter–artist's self or poet–words–feelings in an act of self-address, and that the eventual viewer of the painting or reader of the poem is of little account at the moment of encoding. It is open to debate whether, if the painting is stored in an attic or the poem burnt, any meaningful communication has taken place. Also, the painter or poet's work, once presented for consumption by others may be decoded – interpreted – in as many ways as there are people, each one reprocessing the work of art according to his/her own needs, NORMS, VALUES, CULTURE, EXPECTATIONS AND SOCIALIZATION.

T.R. Nilson in 'On defining communication' in *Speech Trainer*, 1957, and reprinted in K.K. Sereno and C.D. Mortensen, eds., *Foundations of Communication Theory* (US: Harper & Row, 1970), distinguishes between communication which is *instrumental*, that is intended to stimulate a response, and *situational* in which there need not be any intention of evoking a response in the transmission of stimuli.

As early as 1933, Edward Sapir differentiated between, *explicit* and *implicit* modes of communication, a perspective supported by Baker Brownell in *The Community: Its Philosophy and Practice for a Time of Crisis* (US: Harper & Bros., 1950) who speaks of *direct* and *indirect* communication. The latter Brownell defines as being a '. . . process wherein something converted into symbols is carried over from one person to another', while the former is a function of the '. . . identification of people with one another'.

A precept that few commentators would challenge is that it is *impossible not to communicate*. By saying nothing, by remaining blank-faced, by keeping our hands stiffly to our sides, we are still communicating, however negatively. We are still part of the interaction whether we like it or not. For Jurgen Ruesch, communication is 'all those processes by which people influence one another' (in 'Values, communication and culture', J. Ruesch and G. Bateson, eds., *The Social Matrix of Psychiatry* (US: W.W. Norton, 1951). At first we may resist the claim that whatever we do we are exerting an influence. Yet by trying *not* to influence we are arguably still affecting the patterns of communicative action, interaction and transaction. In our absence from the scene – from our family or work group, for example – as well as in our presence, we may still exert influence, however little, however unintended. See COMMUNICATION, FUNCTIONS; COMMUNICATION MODELS; COMMUNICATION, NON-VERBAL (NVC); MASS COMMUNICATION; SEMIOLOGY; THEORIES AND CONCEPTS OF COMMUNICATION.

* Erik Barnouw, George Gerbner, Wilbur Schramm *et al.*, *International Encyclopaedia of Communications* (UK: Oxford University Press, 4 volumes, 1989); James Watson, *Media Communication: An Introduction to Theory and Process* (UK: Macmillan, 1997); Armand and Michele Mattelart, *Theories of Communication: A Short Introduction* (UK: Sage, 1998).

Communication, functions Many and varied listings have been made by communications analysts. The following eight functions are usually quoted as being central: instrumental (to achieve or obtain something); control (to get someone to behave in a particular way); information (to find out or explain something); expression (to express one's feelings or put oneself over in a particular way); social contact (participating in company); alleviation of anxiety (to sort out a problem, ease a worry about something); stimulation (response to something of interest), and role-related (because the situation requires it). See JAKOBSON'S MODEL OF COMMUNICATION.

Communication integration See INTEGRATION.

Communication, interpersonal See INTERPERSONAL COMMUNICATION.

Communication, intrapersonal See INTRAPERSONAL COMMUNICATION.

Communication models See ALLEYNE'S NEWS REVOLUTION MODEL, 1997; ANDERSCH, STAATS AND BOSTROM MODEL OF COMMUNICATION, 1969; ATTENTION MODEL OF MASS COMMUNICATION; BALL-ROKEACH AND DEFLEUR'S DEPENDENCY MODEL OF MASS COMMUNICATION EFFECTS, 1976; BARNLUND'S TRANSACTIONAL MODEL OF COMMUNICATION, 1970; BASS'S DOUBLE ACTION MODEL OF INTERNAL NEWS FLOW, 1969; BECKER'S MOSAIC MODEL OF COMMUNICATION, 1968; COMMERCIAL LAISSEZ-FAIRE MODEL OF COMMUNICATION; DANCE'S HELICAL

MODEL OF COMMUNICATION, 1967; GALTUNG AND RUGE'S MODEL OF SELECTIVE GATEKEEPING, 1965; GERBNER'S MODEL OF COMMUNICATION, 1956; HYPODERMIC NEEDLE MODEL OF COMMUNICATION; JAKOBSON'S MODEL OF COMMUNICATION, 1958; KEPPLINGER AND HABERMEIER MODEL OF MEDIA EVENTS, 1995 (see EVENT); LASSWELL'S MODEL OF COMMUNICATION, 1948; MALETZKE'S MODEL OF THE MASS COMMUNICATION PROCESS, 1963; McCOMBS AND SHAW AGENDA SETTING MODEL OF MEDIA EFFECTS, 1976; McLEOD AND CHAFFEYS 'KITE' MODEL, 1973; McNELLY'S MODEL OF NEWS FLOW, 1959; McQUAIL'S ACCOUNTABILITY OF MEDIA MODEL, 1997; McQUAIL'S FOUR STAGES OF AUDIENCE FRAGMENTATION (see AUDIENCE: FRAGMENTATION OF); NEWCOMB'S ABX MODEL OF COMMUNICATION, 1953; NOELLE-NEUMANN'S SPIRAL OF SILENCE MODEL OF PUBLIC OPINION, 1974; ONE-STEP, TWO-STEP, MULTI-STEP FLOW MODELS OF COMMUNICATION; RILEY AND RILEY MODEL OF MASS COMMUNICATION, 1959; GRISWOLD CULTURAL DIAMOND MODEL, 1994; SCHRAMM'S MODELS OF COMMUNICATION, 1954; ROGERS AND DEARING AGENDA SETTING MODEL, 1987; SHANNON AND WEAVER MODEL OF COMMUNICATION, 1949; S-IV-R MODEL OF COMMUNICATION; TRIPOLAR MODEL OF COMPETING AGENDAS (see ROGERS AND DEARING AGENDA SETTING MODEL, 1987); WESLEY AND MACLEAN'S MODEL OF COMMUNICATION, 1957; WESTERSTÅHL AND JOHANSSON MODEL OF NEWS FACTORS IN FOREIGN NEWS, 1994; WHITE'S GATEKEEPER MODEL, 1950.

* These and other models not included in the Dictionary – such as Comstock's Psychological Model of Television Effects on Individual Behaviour, 1978, DeFleur's Model of the American Mass Media System, 1979, and Gieber and Johnson's Model of Source–Reporter Relations, 1961 – may be read about in detail in *Communication Models for the Study of Mass Communications* (UK: Longman, 5th impression, 1998) by Denis McQuail and Sven Windahl.

Communication, Non-verbal (NVC) Michael Argyle in *Bodily Communication* (UK: Methuen, 1988) identifies the main codes of NVC: TOUCH and Bodily contact; Spatial Behaviour (PROXEMICS and ORIENTATION); Appearance; FACIAL EXPRESSION; GESTURE and HEAD NODS; POSTURE; Gaze (eye movement and EYE CONTACT) and NON-VERBAL VOCALIZATIONS. Varyingly NVC conveys much of what we wish to say, and much of what we would wish to withhold. Common functions of non-verbal communication include:

the conveying of interpersonal attitudes, the display of emotional states, SELF-PRESENTATION, the regulation of interaction, the giving of meaning to verbal communication, the maintenance of interest in a communicative encounter, the provision of advance warning of the kind of verbal communication to follow and, very importantly, the provision of FEEDBACK in Communication.

Affiliation, sexual attraction, rejection, aggression, dominance, submission, appeasement, fear, grief, joy are often best expressed – and in some cases can only be expressed – through NVC. The amount of NVC in the repertoire of different peoples and nations varies considerably in range, emphasis, frequency and rules for use.

Some non-verbal signs appear to be universal, for example the eyebrow flash used in greeting. There are also many cultural difference in non-verbal communication, for example the rules regarding proximity, that is the amount of space or distance people should keep between them when communicating, are different for Middle-Eastern countries when compared with our own (see PROXEMICS).

The use of non-verbal communication may also be influenced by aspects of an individual's personality. Extroverts, for example, are thought to be more expansive in their use of gestures.

Some GENDER differences have also been noted in the use of NVC; for example, several studies have shown that women are more likely to touch each other in conversation than men are.

Certain mental illnesses may also influence a sufferer's non-verbal communicative behaviour; some people suffering schizophrenia, for example, prefer to keep a greater distance between themselves and others than is the norm for the situation.

Ambiguity often surrounds the interpretation of non-verbal signs, not least because quite a lot of body movement is not communicative in intent and it may be difficult for the receiver to know whether a particular sign was intended to communicate a message or not. For example, if the sender winks whilst talking does this suggest that the message is not to be taken seriously or that the sender has a piece of grit in his/her

eye? Judy Gahagan in *Social Interaction and its Management* (UK: Methuen, 1984) argues that the ambiguity surrounding the interpretation of non-verbal signs is essential to one of their major functions in communication – dropping hints. People may wish such messages to be open to varied interpretation so that the hint can be retracted later, if necessary. Non-verbal signs thus provide what she calls 'diplomatic flexibility'. · As Gahagan remarks, 'Non-verbal communication is a language adapted for hints and innuendo'.

See ACCENT; BART; CARAT; FACS; FAST; NON-VERBAL BEHAVIOUR: REPERTOIRE; OBJECT LANGUAGE; PONS; SILENCE.

Communication postulates See POSTULATES OF COMMUNICATION.

Communication theory See THEORIES AND CONCEPTS OF COMMUNICATION.

Communications conglomerates See CONGLOMERATES.

Communications Decency Act (US) Law passed overwhelmingly by the US Congress and signed by President Bill Clinton in February 1996, designed to ban porn on the INTERNET (See CYBERSPACE). The measure faces a number of formidable obstacles; first, the means of exercising CENSORSHIP on the Net; second, arriving at any definition of 'decency' (as compared, for example, with 'obscenity') which can win CONSENSUS in America; third, controlling indecency across frontiers (it is easy for American citizens to 'emigrate' across the Net by transmitting under the guise of 'Anonymous remailers') and fourth, persuading other nations to introduce similar legislation. Perhaps the strongest impediment to the Communications Decency Act is the United States' Constitution, the First Amendment of which prohibits Congress from 'abridging the freedom of speech'.

A coalition of 20 companies including American Online, Compuserve and the American Library Association (ALA), representing 80,000 public libraries, have, in court hearings in Philadelphia, challenged the law. Their argument has been that the Decency Act classifies on-line texts as equivalent to broadcasting (and thus BROAD-

CASTING regulation) rather than books, and narrows what is available on the Internet to what is deemed suitable for young children.

Communications gap Failure of understanding usually as a result of a lack of information, especially between different age GROUPS, economic CLASSES, political factions or cultural groups.

Communicative negligence See LAW OF THE TOTAL SITUATION.

Communicative rationality Jürgen Habermas in his vast and seminal work on communication and the public sphere, *The Theory of Communicative Action, Vol. 1: Reason and Rationalization*, (US: Beacon, 1981), and *Vol. 2: The Critique of Functionalist Reason* (UK: Polity 1983) poses the notion of communicative rationality as being characterized by truth, appropriateness and sincerity. The operation of these criteria in public life rests upon the existence of free, open and egalitarian discourse – an 'ideal speech situation' – which in turn makes understanding between elements of society more likely. Communicative rationality rests essentially on an equality of opportunity to participate in communication; still a dream aspiration as far as most societies are concerned.

Communicology The study of the nature, process and meanings sytems of all forms of communication in what Dean C. Barnlund has described as 'the totality of time, space, personality and circumstance' (in 'A transactional model of communication', K.K. Sereno and C.D. Mortensen, eds., *Foundations of Communication Theory*, US: Harper & Row, 1970).

Communitarian While the traditional liberal view of society is to emphasize the rights of the individual, the communitarian position, as the name suggests, promotes a sense of socio-cultural sharing; of community. On the downside of communitarian thinking is the risk of a forced CONSENSUS on what is the 'common good'. Fundamentalism of one kind or another emerges from this *unitary* way of defining society and the parts which comprise it. The strength of the position, and its attraction, arises from a less

integrationist viewpoint, where emphasis is upon participation in civil, political and cultural matters and thus a degree of devolution of power and decision-making.

Community radio Because RADIO BROADCASTING is the cheapest form of MASS COMMUNICATION it lends itself to 'grass roots' use by communities of interest – geographical, cultural, political. Its potential is to be run by and for local communities, special interests and followings. The development of LOCAL RADIO in the UK has made some progress towards the community ideal, but full independence, in terms of appointments, policy, financing, programming, etc. remains at levels other than the local one.

Though the term *community radio* was probably first used by Rachel Powell in a pamphlet *Possibilities for Local Radio* (UK: Centre for Contemporary Cultural Studies, University of Birmingham, December 1965), the idea goes as far back as the BEVERIDGE REPORT 1950 which proposed the use of VHF frequencies to 'establish local radio stations with independent programmes of their own. How large a scope there would be in Britain for local stations broadcasting programmes controlled by Universities or Local Authorities or public service organizations is not known, but the experiment of setting up some local stations should be tried without delay'.

In 1962 the PILKINGTON REPORT recommended that the BBC provide 'local sound broadcasting' on the basis of 'one service in some 250 localities', stations having a typical range of five miles. The 1971 government White Paper launched COMMERCIAL RADIO, but radio broadcasting through the next decade was to remain under the DUOPOLY of the BBC and IBA.

Pressure to produce a 'third' force in broadcasting in the UK, to consist of highly individual and genuinely local stations, grew in the 1980s. Throughout the country groups dedicated to the furtherance of community radio have multiplied, providing information, exerting pressure at national and local levels – and very often with transmitters at the ready (or actually broadcasting illegally).

Commutation test A useful device for

the analysis of the MEANING and impact of communication presentations such as photographs, paintings and advertisements. We may look at a newspaper picture of inner city riots. By commuting elements – images or words – in the picture, removing them and replacing them by others, how is the meaning of the picture transformed?

Compact disc See CD – COMPACT DISC.

Compassion fatigue The effect of world suffering upon mass media audiences may turn into what has been termed *compassion fatigue* in which the exposure to suffering becomes too much to take in. In an article 'Living in limbo' in the *Guardian* (21 April 1989), William Shawcross writes, 'Like Aids, Compassion Fatigue is a contemporary sickness. The symptoms are first a rush of concern for a distant and obviously suffering group, followed by tedium and a feeling of withdrawal that sometimes descends into disdain . . . Compassion Fatigue is nurtured by the speed and plethora of communications that bewilder and disorient people everywhere'. Shawcross finds this phenomenon a 'truly terrifying sickness. Those it afflicts do not waste away physically – it is their humanity that is harmed'. The compassion factor is further strained by the nature of news itself, restlessly and hungrily switching its focus of attention from one disaster to another. A classic example is the way starvation in Africa was squeezed from news pages and news bulletins by the Gulf War of 1991, only for the sufferings of the Iraqi people, including the Kurds, to be forgotten in their turn as attention focused on new issues and new tragedies.

However, John Pilger in *Hidden Agendas* (UK: Vintage, 1998) argues that 'broadcasters and journalists invented the public affliction called "compassion fatigue" which represented not the public's sentiments but conformism, long served by journalists'. A conformism that results in a reluctance, he argues, to investigate and reveal the interrelationship between western economic interests and foreign policy and its consequent effects for those living in the third world.

Competence In LINGUISTICS, a term used to describe a person's knowledge of his/her own LANGUAGE, its system of rules; his/her competence in understanding an unlimited number of sentences, in spotting grammatical errors, etc.

Completion point See VERBAL DEVICES IN SPEECH-MAKING.

Compliance, identification and internalization See INTERNALIZATION.

Complicity of users Term employed by Cees J. Hamelink to describe the reluctance of audiences to be told the truth about crises, particularly war situations but also in cases concerning government and corporate matters. In 'Ethics for media users' published in the *European Journal of Communication*, December 1995, Hamelink cites findings that indicated nearly eight out of ten Americans supporting restrictions on information imposed by the Pentagon while six out of ten said they believed the military should have exercised greater censorship. 'The [Gulf] war demonstrated that official censorship, journalistic self-censorship and the users' refusal to be informed reinforced each other.' Hamelink goes on, 'The complicity of users was an essential component in the reduction of freedom of media performance.'

Compression technology A key science in the Age of Information, in particular the era of DIGITALIZATION: the more data becomes available, the broader the available BANDWIDTH, the greater the requirement to compress information, to compact data for transmission.

Computer graphics Truly one of the wonders of the modern world: art by numbers – computer numbers – capable of feats of design of astonishing virtuosity and potential. Computer capability in the field of graphics is vast, ranging from representation of three-dimensional technical design, complete with depth cueing, to simulations of space exploration and of nuclear conflict. Computer graphics supply the visual wizardry of computer games and are also capable of producing ANIMATION in the manner of Walt Disney. In 1982, the Disney studios produced the first feature film using this technique, *Tron.* A quarter of the film is conventional live-action; the rest is computer graphics or a mixture of computer-generated images with live action. Director of *Tron*, Steven Lisburger said of animation by computer, 'It gives you a whole world, an entire geography, an entire physics, all from the mind of the computer'.

The implications of this technology do not apply merely to animation film: the computer can 'draw' backgrounds and figures so real, it can simulate everyday objects so accurately, and three-dimensionally that the movie set of the future might exist only in an electronic console. In science and medicine computer graphics are applied microscopically, simulating, for example, molecular constructs and interaction, thus opening up possibilities in the development of new drugs. Macroscopically, computer graphics have reconstructed in detail, in wire frame (line drawing), the entire city of Chicago and are serving an increasing role in space design testing. They are also opening up fresh areas of expression for artists as well as scientists. The first-ever film entirely generated by computer was the highly popular *Toy Story* (1996), from the Disney Studios.

Computers in communication Apart from chiefly military use during the 2nd World War (1939–45), computers did not begin to exert an impact upon society generally until the 1960s. An estimated 9000 computers were in operation in the world in 1960, mainly in the US. Since then the processing of information has been revolutionized. Picture a vast library of books; the data it contains can now be placed on space-saving disks which, at the touch of a button, will summon up any item of information almost instantly. What in the past might have taken a researcher weeks can now be gathered immediately, not only from one library, but from libraries all over the world. If speed of access is remarkable, *capacity* is miraculous. The personal details of an entire nation can be recorded and recalled by courtesy of the computer. The implications here for PRIVACY constitute a major issue of our time.

Paradoxically, though the computer saves time it also makes work. It colonizes, and makes formal, information which in the past would have been deemed too complicated to gather; or simply unnecessary. Where, an organization might decide it wishes to know, is a worker at any given second of his or her day, and what exactly, to the minute, is that person doing? The computer can cope. It has enlarged the definition of verifiable fact: once a single item of information is gathered on an individual, a worker, a citizen, the only limit to data recording is infinity.

Every time we use a cash card to draw money from the bank, a credit card to purchase goods from a store or even pay cash for an electronically stamped ticket for the underground, we are leaving traces of ourselves. The convenience is considerable but the intrusion is worrying.

The computer has also given birth to a new global disease – the computer virus. Just as hurricanes are given picturesque titles, so are computer viruses whose effects are similarly devastating: 'Dark Avenger', the 'Maltese Amoeba', 'Christmas Tree Worm', 'Tequila' and 'Michelangelo'. In October 1990,' for example, a Bulgarian-designed virus named 'Nomenklatura' turned the contents of computers in the UK House of Commons into a mass of jumbled characters. This was the work of a disgruntled computer-programmer, Dark Avenger.

A government-commissioned report in 1992 put the cost to British industry of computer viruses at £1 billion. The incidence of computer *fraud* is probably incalculable. The ability of individuals, often using only the simplest computer equipment, to 'hack in' to sophisticated programs – even those controling nuclear weapons – poses hair-raising questions concerning security (see HACKER).

The *displacement* of older technology by computers has been far-reaching. The newspaper industry in particular has undergone switches from mechanical, labour-intensive technology to computer-driven production which have meant very substantial cuts in the labour force. Also, traditional crafts were superseded by processes which were swifter and could be handled by unskilled or semi-skilled labour. At the same time, the computer has helped devolve the opportunity to publish, through the economies of DESK-TOP PUBLISHING (DTP), to communities, special-interest groups and educational institutions. Computer literacy has become an essential ingredient of a basic education. Software for graphics and for industrial design has become increasingly sophisticated. Computer games are a world-wide industry. Computer conferencing draws together in discussion and debate business people from all over the world, without the need for plane tickets or the risk of airport hold-ups.

The issues remain: western dominance in computer technology and know-how sustains INFORMATION GAPS between them and developing nations; the dangers, globally, of computer error; the misuses of information, indeed the inaccuracy of information which may be acted upon to the detriment of the individual; and SECRECY, for while the library has its books open for all to see on the shelves, access to computer information requires access to computers, to passwords and the ability to operate the software. See CYBERSPACE; DATA PROTECTION; INTERNET; MEDIA IMPERIALISM; TECHNOLOGICAL DETERMINISM.

Conative function of communication
See JAKOBSON'S MODEL OF COMMUNICATION, 1958.

Concurrence-seeking tendency In GROUPS, the cohesiveness of members may produce a tendency to agree at all costs, even when the decisions brought about by that unanimity may turn out to be disastrous. In *Groupthink. Psychological Studies of Policy Decisions and Fiascos* (US: Houghton Mifflin, 1972) Irving L. Janis identifies the concurrence-seeking tendency as being one which, developing unchecked in a group's decision-making processes, causes a 'deterioration of mental efficiency, reality testing, and moral judgement'.

Confederates See SLIDER.

Confirmation/disconfirmation Through communication with others we gain feedback on our SELF-CONCEPT. Several authors among them Gail Myers and Michele Myers in *The Dynamics of Human Communication* (US: McGraw-Hill, 1985) use the terms *confirmation* and *disconfirmation* to describe the kind of messages about yourself and your

view of the world you may receive in feedback. Confirming responses tend to confirm or validate the view of yourself you have put forward and/or the views you have expressed in conversation. Examples of confirming responses include direct acknowledgement of your message, agreement with the content of your message and expression of positive feelings about you.

Disconfirming responses are likely to leave you feeling confused, dissatisfied, and maybe undermined. They are not clear expressions of either approval or rejection; they are ambiguous. Such responses include the *impervious* response when the receiver gives no acknowledgement of your message; the *interrupting response* when the receiver does not let you finish your message; and the *incongruous response* when the receiver's non-verbal response is clearly contrary to the verbal response he/she is making; for example, when a fixed smile accompanies words of praise.

Conglomerates The increasing cost of entering the media market has, in part, fostered a concentration of ownership in the various sectors of the communications industry. Peter Golding and Graham Murdock in an article entitled, 'Culture, communications and political economy' in James Curran and Michael Gurevitch, eds., *Mass Media and Society* (UK: Arnold, 1996) write, 'The steadily increasing amount of cultural production accounted for by large corporations has long been a source of concern to theorists of democracy ... these longstanding worries have been reinforced in recent years by the emergence of multimedia conglomerates with significant stakes across a range of central communications sectors. ... The rise of communications conglomerates adds a new element to the old debate about the potential abuses of owner power. It is no longer a simple case of proprietors intervening in editorial decisions or firing key personnel who fall foul of their political philosophies. Cultural production is also strongly influenced by commercial strategies built around "synergies" which exploit the overlaps between the company's different media interests'.

A *communications conglomerate* is an

amalgam of corporations which operate mainly or wholly with communications or leisure interests – like the Granada group which operates the Granada TV network, a large TV rental chain and a paperback publishing company and has interests in the cinema, music publishing and numerous other entertainment outlets. Significant sectors of the communications industry are, however, part of general conglomerates whose main business concerns are outside the communications field.

The mass media can be seen as related to the industrial system in two ways: firstly they are part of it as large-scale buyers and sellers and makers of profit; secondly they are preachers of its (industry's) messages. Much of the communications industry is in the control of *multinational* or *transnational* corporations, that is companies which have large-scale investment in many different countries. John B. Thompson in *The Media and Modernity* (UK: Polity Press, 1995) notes that a handful of multinational conglomerates such as Sony, Disney, Time Warner, Bertelsmann and News Corporation own and control large numbers of the myriad operations within the media industries. Thus the multinationals keep a substantial 'finger in the pie' of these countries' information systems (See MEDIA IMPERIALISM).

The power of such conglomerates is now being extended as a result of technological CONVERGENCE. As Golding and Murdock note, 'For the first time, all forms of communications – written text, statistical data, still and moving images, music and the human voice – can be coded, stored and relayed using the same basic digital array of zeros and ones, the language of computing. As a result, the boundaries that have separated different communications sectors up until now are being rubbed away'.

The concentration of ownership, the increased potential for power which it facilitates, and the interrelationship between the communications industry and other industrial and commercial interests constitute important areas of current media research. See BERLUSCONI PHENOMENON; DIGITALIZATION; ELITE; ESTABLISHMENT; GLOBALIZATION OF MEDIA; McDONALDIZATION; NEWS AGENCIES; POWER ELITE; SOCIOMETRICS.

Congruence theory The basic premise of congruence or *balance* theory is that in the case of two people who like or dislike each other, some patterns of the relationship will be balanced – in congruence – and some will be unbalanced, as when a person dislikes the object which is liked by a liked person. You have congruence if a person you like approves of a cause or affirms a position with which you are in sympathy.

The principle of congruity as advanced by Charles Osgood and Percy Tannenbaum in 'The Principle of Congruity in the Prediction of Attitude Change', *Psychological Review* 62 (1955) holds that when change in evaluation or attitude occurs it always occurs in the direction of *increased* congruity with the prevailing frame of reference.

The opposite of cognitive balance is *cognitive dissonance*, a notion analysed by Leon Festinger in *A Theory of Cognitive Dissonance* (US: Row Peterson, 1957). The theory predicts that people will seek out information which confirms existing attitudes and views of the world or reinforces other aspects of behaviour. Similarly it predicts that people will avoid information which is likely to increase DISSONANCE. If you dislike a person, and you dislike his/her views, what he/she says is unlikely to cause cognitive dissonance, for there is a congruence here. Dissonance is acute when a liked person says something seemingly 'out of character' or fails to accord with expectations or the image held of him/her. See COGNITIVE (AND AFFECTIVE); DEFENSIVE COMMUNICATION; EFFECTS OF THE MASS MEDIA; NEWCOMB'S ABX MODEL OF COMMUNICATION, 1953; RESONANCE; SYMMETRY, STRAIN TOWARDS.

Connectivity Describes how the global web of computer information services interlink in a process of ever expanding diversification. The INTERNET, with its estimated 100 million users, provides, for example, a gigantic 'art-information exchange'. National art galleries, major museums, universities and private dealers are able to display their collections, publish catalogues, and hold on-line exhibitions in the dataspace of the Net. In its first nine months on-line, the Louvre in Paris had over a million 'visitors' on the Web site. More have visited via the Internet America's Smith-sonian Institute than have physically passed through its doors.

Roy Ascott in a talk given at London's Tate Gallery in May 1995, and published under the title of 'Aesthetics argued on a phone extension' in Multimedia Features, *Times Higher Educational Supplement*, 10 November 1995, believes, 'The Web site can be a superior kind of art magazine or cultural mail order catalogue.' The down-side 'is that questions of copyright are raised which cannot easily be resolved, and once an image is set loose in CYBERSPACE it can become anybody's possession'. Ascott, direc-tor of the Centre for Inquiry into Interactive Arts at Gwent College of Higher Education, says that on the Net 'to see is to own' and 'to see is not only to own, it is to invite trans-formation'. The Net 'enables you to enter into a process of manipulation and trans-formation of images, texts and sound' and deals 'not so much with the behaviour of forms, the aesthetic of experience, as with forms of behaviour, the aesthetic of apparition'.

Connotation Roland Barthes's second order of SIGNIFICATION in the transmission of messages. The second order comprises connotation and myth. **Denotation**, the first order of signification, is simply a process of identification. The word 'green' represents a colour; but green, at a higher level, can **connote** the countryside, permission to go ahead, the Irish, etc. Connotation is the act of adding information, insight, angle, colouration, value – MEANING, in fact, to denotation.
* R. Barthes, *Mythologies* (UK: Paladin, 1973).

Consensus That which is generally agreed; an area or basis of shared agreement among the majority. Three elements crucial to the function of consensus are: common accep-tance of laws, rules and norms; attachment to the institutions which promulgate these laws, rules and NORMS; and a widespread sense of identity or unity, of similar or iden-tical outlook. The opposite term is *dissensus*. The elements obviously vary independently, yet the strength of any one helps to strengthen the others.

Consensus, states the *International Encyclopaedia of Social Sciences* (ed. D.L. Sills; US: Macmillan and Free Press, 1968) 'operates to restrict the extension of dissen-sus and to limit conflict . . .' Beliefs about consensus 'usually concern the rightness and the qualifications of those in authority to exercise it' and thus relate to the legiti-macy of institutions, accepted standards and practices, and dominant principles. They tend to affirm existing patterns of the distribution of authority.

Consensus, therefore, is largely defined by those who have the power and the means to disseminate their definition; and the defi-nition is employed as a means of acknowl-edging and reinforcing the legitimacy of the powerful. Equally important in this context is the close affinity of outlook of the central cultural system with the central institutional system. Stuart Hood in *Hood on Television* (UK: Pluto, 1980) says 'It is the essence of the idea of consensus that it attempts, at a conscious and unconscious level, to impose the view that there is only one "right" read-ing. This assumption derives from the view that we – that is the audience and the broad-caster – are united in one nation in spite of class or political definition'. See CULTURAL APPARATUS; DISCURSIVE GAP; IMPARTIALITY; NEW-COMB'S ABX MODEL, 1953.

Consent, manufacture of The American philosopher and linguist Noam Chomsky has defined the *manufacture of consent* as a complex process whereby powerful interests inside democracies such as the US and the UK create in the public mind patterns of acceptance. In an article written for *Index on Censorship*, 1 (1987), entitled 'No anti-Israeli vendetta', Chomsky refers to 'devices of thought control' in democratic societies 'which are more pertinent for us than the crude methods of totalitarian states'. The devices arise from such aspects of the media process as control over resources and the locus of decision-making in the state and private economy. Where state policy on an issue such as the Arab-Israeli conflict, or with regard to Central American politics, is rigorously committed to one side or the other, alternative options which the public might be interested in considering, are declared out of bounds – through what

Chomsky describes as 'suppression, falsification, and Orwellian manipulation'.

* Edward S. Herman and Noam Chomsky, *Manufacturing Consent: The Political Economy of the Mass Media* (US: Pantheon, 1988).

Consistency There is general agreement among research analysts that the greater the degree of consistency in media coverage, the greater is the likelihood that audiences will absorb the projected version – adopt the PREFERRED READING – of reported situations. See EFFECTS OF THE MASS MEDIA; FREQUENCY; INTENSITY.

Consonance, hypothesis of See NEWS VALUES.

Conspiracy of silence The tacit agreement among those with significant information to keep 'mum' about it – say nothing. An early use of the phrase, perhaps even the first as far as BROADCASTING was concerned, is ascribed to the head of BBC News in 1938 at the time of the Munich crisis, when the BBC failed to broadcast any close examination of Neville Chamberlain's policy of appeasement towards Nazi Germany. See CENSORSHIP.

Conspiracy theory Not so much a theory, more a hunch or suspicion. As far as the media are concerned, the 'conspiracy' relates – in the view of those who claim it exists – to the practice of manipulating MESSAGES in order to support those who own the means of communication, their social CLASS (i.e. middle and upper) and their interests. The conspiracy theorists argue that in a capitalist society where the media are owned or strongly influenced by the capitalist ESTABLISHMENT, information is shaped to underpin existing social, economic and political conditions.

In his Introduction to the GLASGOW UNIVERSITY MEDIA GROUP publication *Bad News* (UK: Routledge & Kegan Paul, 1976), Richard Hoggart ventures to locate two levels or forms of conspiracy theory, High and Low, the one aligning with the Marxist view of media operation, the other with the generality of people who at some time or another suspect that the media project the interests and the value systems of those who own, control or run them. See HEGEMONY.

Constituency Term generally applied to an electoral area which returns a parliamentary candidate, but it is also used by researchers to refer to the readership of a newspaper and carries with it the implication that the reader's political views may be influenced by the paper's coverage of events. The notion of AUDIENCE as constituency was particularly prevalent in the age of PRESS BARONS such as Lords Northcliffe, Rothermere and Beaverbrook, who claimed access to political decision-making on the strength of the constituency of their papers' readership.

Consumerization A dominant perspective upon the last quarter of the 20th c. has been the belief that, with the global advance of transnational corporations, and their substantial buying-in to media and CULTURE generally, society has become one-dimensionalized – the consumer dimension. Instead of citizens, people have been redefined as *market*; individuals, groups, communities have been *appropriated* by market forces. Some commentators see consumption as being a modern substitute for religion, spending a substitute for praying, while the cathedrals of today are shopping malls. Big business sponsors art and thereby brings it under the wing of consumer criteria – is there a market for it and will it directly or indirectly make a profit? Big business sponsors schools and thus is in at least a poll-position to appropriate education itself. American writer Herbert J. Schiller has proved himself a scourge of corporate intrusions into the life of communities. In *Culture Inc. The Corporate Takeover of Public Expression* (UK/US: Oxford University Press, 1989), Schiller believes, 'the Corporate voice, not surprisingly, is the loudest in the land' and it also rings around the world. He believes that consumerism 'as it is propagated by the transnational corporate system and carried to the four corners of the world by new information age technologies, now seems triumphant'. He talks of 'corporate pillaging of the national information supply' and the 'proprietory control of information'.

Even the museum has 'been enlisted as a corporate instrument': history is adopted for corporate use through sponsorship. Thus eventually museums become reliant on corporate 'approval' of the past. The pressure upon them is to choose to record the kind of history that suits the corporate purpose.

Corporate power in the field of communication is so great, Schiller argues, that the active-audience paradigm is called into question: 'A great emphasis is given to the "resistance", "subversion", and "empowerment" of the viewer. Where this resistance and subversion of the audience lead and what effects they have on the existing structure of power remain a mystery.' He is of the view that 'It is not a matter of people being dupes, informational or cultural. It is that human beings are not equipped to deal with a pervasive disinformational system – administered from the command posts of social order – that assails the senses through all cultural forms and channels'.

Schiller's theme is echoed in the work of the French philosopher Jean Baudrillard whose *The Consumer Society: Myths and Structures* made its first appearance in English – translated by Chris Turner and published by Sage – in 1998. See McDONALD-IZATION.

* Jeff Hearn and Sasha Roseneil, eds., *Consuming Cultures: Power and Resistance* (UK: Macmillan, 1999).

Consumer sovereignty A phrase used in the Peacock Report, 1985, summarizing the attitude towards broadcasting of the Committee on Financing the BBC. The Committee took the market-place view that the customer knows best and that consumer tastes should be the guiding principle of RADIO and TELEVISION programming. See PUBLIC SERVICE BROADCASTING.

Consumption behaviour Term used by researchers for how audiences respond to product marketing: attitudes towards ADVERTISING, knowledge of commercials and people's buying behaviour. At the nub of market research into consumption behaviour is *motivation*. Why do people watch a TV commercial, what makes them pay attention and heed the MESSAGE? Regularly cited are three major reasons for a positive audience response: (1) *Social utility* – watching com-

mercials in order to gain information about the 'social significance' of products or brands, and the association of advertising objects with social ROLES and lifestyles; (2) *Communication utility* – watching in order to provide a basis for later INTERPERSONAL COMMUNICATION; (3) *Vicarious consumption* – participating at second-hand in desired lifestyles as a means of indirect association with those people possessing glamour or prestige. See ADVERTISING: MAINSTREAMERS, ASPIRERS, SUCCEEDERS & REFORMERS; VALS TYPOLOGY.

Contagion effect Power of the media to create a craze or even an epidemic. Examples of this are the so-called Swastika Epidemic of 1959–60 where an outbreak of swastika daubing in the US was accelerated by media coverage, and the UK Mods v. Rockers seaside battles in the 1960s. Debate continues on whether media coverage 'worsens' or prompts the street riots, often named Copycat Riots.

Stanley Cohen in 'Sensitization: the case of the Mods and Rockers' in Stanley Cohen and Jock Young, eds., *The Manufacture of News* (UK: Constable, 1973), writes, 'Constant repetition of the warring gangs' image . . . had the effect of giving these loose collections a structure they never possessed and a mythology with which to justify the structure' and the court scenes at which those arrested by the police were tried were 'arenas for acting out society's morality plays'. See EMPOWERMENT; MEDIA IMAGES; MORAL PANIC.

Contempt of Court Act, 1981 Part of the armoury of CENSORSHIP in the UK, this act restricts the reporting of court cases before they come to trial. It was first used in 1983 when several newspapers published articles on Michael Fagan, who had climbed into the Queen's bedroom at Buckingham Palace. The publishers of the *Sunday Times* and the *Daily Star* were found guilty of printing stories which ran a substantial risk of prejudicing the trial of Fagan.

The blanket and fevered coverage of the Rosemary West trial in 1995 led to defence lawyers arguing that the jury in the trial must have been influenced by media coverage of the murders committed by Frederick and Rosemary West at their Cromwell Road home, Gloucester; and that the trial had been further influenced by evidence that a number of witnesses had sold their stories to the tabloids prior to the Guilty verdict. No action was taken over the matter.

Content analysis Research into mass media content identifies, categorizes, describes and quantifies short-term and long-term trends. An early and most valuable descriptive trend study was that of Ernst Kris and Nathan Leites in 1947. In 'Trends in 20th century propaganda' in B. Berelson and M. Janowitz, eds., *Reader in Public Opinion and Communication* (US: Free Press, 1947), the authors traced the trend in propaganda from the 1st World War (1914–18) to the 2nd (1939–45), identifying a changing style towards a less emotional, less moralistic and more truthful orientation.

Content analysis serves an important function by comparing the same material as presented in different media within a nation, or between different nations; or by comparing media content with some explicit set of standards or abstract categories. On the basis of the existing body of quantitative and qualitative research, several broad generalizations may be hazarded about the content of MASS COMMUNICATION: what is communicated by the mass media is a highly selected sample of all that is available for communication; what is received and consumed by the potential audience is a highly selected sample of all that is communicated; more of what is communicated is classifiable as entertaining rather than informative or educative, and, because the mass media are aimed at the largest possible audience, most material is simple in form and uncomplicated in content. See AUDIENCE MEASUREMENT; ETHNOGRAPHIC (APPROACH TO AUDIENCE MEASUREMENT); GLASGOW UNIVERSITY MEDIA GROUP.

Control group In comparative research methods, the neutral body against which a test group is measured. Thus, in the case of AUDIENCE MEASUREMENT, the test group is exposed to a TV programme, for example, and their responses analysed against identical monitoring of the control group who have not seen the programme.

Control of the media See MEDIA CONTROL.

Conventions Established practices within a particular CULTURE or SUB-CULTURE. Conventions are identifiable in every form of communication and behaviour, some strict, like rules of grammar, others open to wider application, such as dress. Conventions are largely culture-specific and context-specific. It is an accepted convention that a candidate dress smartly for a job interview yet it would be deemed unconventional if he or she appeared on the beach clad in the same manner. Media practices have established many conventions which have become so familiar they appear 'the natural way to do things'. TELEVISION news holds to the convention of having on-screen news-readers; documentaries generally hold to the convention of having a voice-over narration. Innovators – for example in the arts – break with convention. The shock of the new often stirs among the conventional a sense of affronted VALUES. The chances of the new becoming conventionalized will depend on various factors, such as opinion LEADERS, prevalent tastes and fashions, even newsworthiness. See REDUNDANCY.

Convergence The coming together of communication devices and processes; a major feature of the development of media technology in the 1990s. In *Of Media and People* (US: Sage, 1992), Everette E. Dennis writes of forms converging 'into a single electronically based, computer-driven mode that has been described as the nearly universal integration of systems that retrieve, process, and store text, data, sound, and image', in short, *multi-media*. Dennis points out that convergence is far more than 'the stuff of hardware and software: it is the driving force that has spurred major change in the media industries and almost everywhere else'.

Convergence has operated at the technical and operational level and at the level of ownership and control. Just as individual items of hard and software have been centralized into one multi-media outfit, so media production has been centralized into fewer corporate hands, most of these transnational. With convergence has come a blurring of media functions: with the aid of a MODEM, the telephone permits us to surf the INTERNET or, regulation permitting, to summon up channels of screen entertainment. We can work from home, shop from home, summon up the world from home (if we are lucky enough to be able to pay for the technology).

A further question is whether technical and operational convergence will lead to transcultural convergence and extend the reach of what some would see as the already well-established strategy of cultural and MEDIA IMPERIALISM. For those that support this thesis, GLOBALIZATION fosters homogeneity and works in the interests of the powerful producers of cultural artefacts often located in Western countries – especially the US – whilst undermining the indigenous cultures of the less powerful receivers of such artefacts.

However such a view is seen by others as underestimating the degree to which those who receive such artefacts adapt them in the process of absorbing them into the host culture. The resultant blend may limit the degree of convergence. It should also be noted that artefacts destined for a wide market are often tailored to take account of differentiation within the market and in this process characteristics of the differing host cultures may be considered in the construction of the artefact. Moreover the flow of cultural artefacts is arguably more complex than the cultural or media imperialism thesis suggests. A number of theorists point to the essential heterogeneity of culture(s) and argue consequently that it is unlikely that cultural convergence would occur. See CYBERSPACE; DIGITALIZATION.

Conversational styles In a study of conversation among friends at dinner, entitled *Conversational Style: Analysing Talk Among Friends* (US: Ablex, 1984), Deborah Tannen identifies different conversational styles which she terms 'High Considerateness' and 'High Involvement'. Each style has different priorities. The 'High Considerateness' style places a premium on being considerate of others in conversation, of not interrupting, of listening to what someone is saying. The 'High Involvement' style on the other hand is characterized by enthusiastic involvement in a conversation and this may be at

the expense of giving sufficient space to others. One style is not necessarily better than the other but often reflects cultural differences; for example, in her study, the Briton was the most considerate of all. However, this categorization can help explain problems in INTERPERSONAL COMMUNICATION. To the highly considerate speaker the highly involved speaker may seem an exhibitionist whilst the highly involved speaker may perceive the highly considerate speaker as aloof or distant.

Co-orientation approach See McCOMBS AND SHAW AGENDA-SETTING MODEL OF MEDIA EFFECTS, 1976.

Copycat effect See CONTAGION EFFECT.

Copyrighting culture See CULTURE: COPYRIGHTING CULTURE.

Core nations, peripheral nations Cees Hamelink makes this differentiation with regard to the distribution of information in and between nations in 'Information Imbalance: Core and Periphery' in *Questioning The Media: A Critical Introduction* (UK: Sage, 1990), edited by John Downing, Ali Mohammadi and Annabelle Sreberny-Mohammadi. Hamelink argues that the transnational picture of information distribution is one of *imbalances* between core – usually industrial – nations such as the US, Canada, Western Europe, Japan and Australia and the economic periphery, predominantly rural countries such as Africa, parts of Asia and Latin America.

He cites the following examples of information imbalance: together, all the peripheral countries in 1984 owned only 4 per cent of the world's computer hardware; of the world's 700 million telephones, 75 per cent are to be found in the nine richest countries. Again, in 1984, there were 39 peripheral nations with no newspapers whatsoever, and 30 with only one, compared with Japan which had 125 dailies and the US with 168. Hamelink believes 'Information imbalance . . . undermines cultural self-determination'. Questions raised about this situation are: can imbalances be resolved through greater integration – links – between core and peripheral nation systems?; should peripheral nations bargain for 'fairer schemes and terms of trade, for cheaper transfers of technology' by pooling resources and energy? Or, more radically, should the peripherals dissociate themselves – delink – from international networks that hamper development?

Collective effort across the periphery itself, argues Hamelink, 'in itself requires the solving of many old and difficult conflicts among the poorer countries themselves'. In addition it requires 'a visionary leadership willing to forego the immediate benefits of links with the core'. In the 1990s former peripherals have moved up-league, particularly in Asia (Malaysia, South Korea, Taiwan); and in 1997 the wealth-making power of Hong Kong passed into the control of that already-advancing industrial conglomerate, China. See INFORMATION GAPS; NEW WORLD INFORMATION ORDER; YAMOUSOUKROU DECLARATION.

Corporate commitment See IMPARTIALITY.

Corporate speech Best defined in a US context: that speech which is employed in the public domain by corporations, most obviously in terms of ADVERTISING, but applicable to a whole host of discourses in which industry and commerce address the public. Corporate speech in the US is classified as having the same right as the speech of individuals and is thus protected by the First Amendment of the US Constitution, which guarantees freedom of speech. Thus, a tobacco company cannot be restrained from propagandizing, through public advertisement, its products. In such a case, corporate speech could be deemed life-threatening. Even taxes on advertising have been fought by corporations. An attempt to impose an advertising tax by the State of Florida in 1987 was repealed within six months, due to corporate pressure. According to Herbert I. Schiller in *Culture, Inc. The Corporate Takeover of Public Expression* (UK: Oxford University Press, 1989), corporations use the First Amendment to do two things: protect their profits and duck social accountability.

Cosmopolite and localite channels The situation in which the sender and receiver of a MESSAGE belong to different SOCIAL SYSTEMS or sub-systems is referred to as **cosmopolite**. Localite CHANNELS are those in which both sender and receiver belong to the same social system or sub-system.

Cosmopoliteness In most social structures there are individuals who have considerable awareness of other social situations and frequent contact with those outside their own social structure. In general the more cosmopolite an individual is the more receptive he/she is to messages containing new ideas.

Couch potato US term for confirmed and dedicated TV viewer. The expression began life among a group of friends in Los Angeles in 1976. Tongue-in-cheek publications soon followed, such as *The Official Couch Potato Handbook* (US: Migo, 1983) and *The Couch Potato Guide to Life* (US: Migo *et al.*, 1985).

Counter-culture A type of SUB-CULTURE firmly antagonistic to the dominant or prevailing CULTURE of a community. The term is generally used to describe the collection of mainly middle-class youth cultures which developed in the 1960s and whose central feature was the call for the adoption of alternative social structures and lifestyles. In 'Sub Cultures, cultures and class', John Clarke and others in Stuart Hall and Tony Jefferson, eds., *Resistance Through Rituals* (UK: Hutchinson, 1976) explore some of the distinguishing features of such a counter-culture as compared with other types of youth sub-cultures. Its opposition to the dominant cultures takes very open political and ideological forms and goes beyond the registering of complaint and resistance to the elaborate construction of alternative institutions.

Further resistance continues beyond the teenage years and its ideologies permeate all areas of life – work, home, family, school and leisure – and thus blur their boundaries, whereas in many working class youth sub-cultures such boundaries are rigorously maintained. The hippy movement, for example, embraced political protest – most notably in the form of demonstrations for peace – and developed coherent alternative philosophies; it established some alternative institutions such as an UNDERGROUND PRESS. It also proposed radical, democratic structures for the organization of work, school and the family.

More recently examples of counter-cultural protests which have received significant media attention are those surrounding ecological issues, protests which challenge many of the environmental assumptions and values of western societies. 'Eco-warriors', as the more radical of the protesters are sometimes called, may adopt a radically different lifestyle based on the principles underpinning their protest.

Although the resistance of the counter-culture is usually more open and confident than that of the sub-culture, it still contains important symbolic elements such as dress, hair STYLE and music.

Countermodernization See CULTURE: GLOBALIZATION OF.

Coups and earthquakes' syndrome Term coined by American journalist Mort Rosenblum to describe the Western attitude to NEWS emanating from 'Third World' developing nations in, for example, Africa and South America. For events in such countries to be deemed of NEWS VALUE they must come under the category of 'coups and earthquakes' – the overthrow of governments by force or natural disasters. Rosenblum wrote *Coups and Earthquakes* (US: Harper & Row) in 1979 but current practice seems not to have improved. Mark D. Alleyne in *News Revolution: Political and Economic Decisions about Global Information* (UK: Macmillan, 1997), referring to the 'coups and earthquakes' syndrome, writes, 'It sometimes seems that there is a malicious attempt to stereotype these countries, and this attitude might be propelled by various factors, including racism, political idealogy and ethnocentrism'. Alleyne believes that 'In this way, international news can be seen as a weapon of those with power in the international system, a tool to maintain the status quo, at least in regard to the inferior status of some peoples and nation-states'.

The key problem lies with prevailing news values, for the definition of news 'controls the way in which journalists decide what is important'. Yet the problem does not stop here: 'After news values are deter-mined to select what is to be news,' says Alleyne, 'journalists often use vague, short-hand terms to describe complex issues and regions.' For example, the term 'Third World' is a 'woolly generalization'.

Crab and track See SHOT.

Creole See PIDGIN.

Crime and the media An ISSUE of considerable and increasing concern is the televisualization of crime, invariably violent crime, as played out in the courts on both sides of the Atlantic. Most spectacular have been the trials of O.J. Simpson in the US and Rosemary West in the UK. In each case the media have been accused of, if not interfering with the course of justice, influencing it; taking it out of its legal framework and transforming proceedings into SOAP OPERA – titillating, often salaciously and obsessively interested in the minutae of violence.

Richard Osborn in an article 'Crime, media, violence' in *Free Press*, March–April 1996, argues that 'Crime and television are the two great cultural definers of our present era and when they are combined they are a lethal force'. Crime has NEWS VALUE aplenty: it is as Osborn puts it 'a seriously nasty business'. It is 'incredibly exciting, threatening, horrifying, fascinating and repellant all at once'. Consequently 'it makes bloody good television'. Thus TV 'wants a big slice of the action when it comes to real-life crime, and that means money, fame, news-doctoring and media trials in which the plodding business of the courts gets swamped by the video in the corner'. In Osborn's view, crime has become 'the staple diet of television' thus affecting the public's perception of crime, the 'way it thinks about crime' and the ways it responds to it. See CRIME: TYPES OF CRIME ON SCREEN; VIOLENCE AND THE MEDIA.

Crime: types of crime on screen Five types of on-screen crime are identified by Jessica Allen, Sonia Livingstone and Robert Reiner in an article 'True lies: changing images of crime in British postwar cinema' in the *European Journal of Communication*, March 1998. The authors surveyed 1461 crime-related films released between 1945 and 1991, and popular with the public, reporting that 'contrary to general beliefs about increased crime content of the media . . . our data shows a constant rate of representation, at least in the cinema over 50 years'.

The authors discuss *primary, consequential, collateral* and *contextual* crimes. To the first, that which animates the narrative, they ascribe the term McGUFFIN, borrowed from film director Alfred Hitchcock, 'to refer to the object whose pursuit provides the driving force of the narrative'. Consequential crimes are those which are committed in the course of, or in order to cover up the McGuffin, while collateral crimes are not directly related to the McGuffin though they may be committed by the central criminals. Contextual crimes may also be unrelated to the McGuffin, the primary crime, 'but portray aspects of the wider society'.

The chief McGuffin say Allen, Livingstone and Reiner is homicide, 48% of their sample films having a homicide McGuffin – contrasting substantially with crime figures in the real world, where 90% of recorded offences are property crimes. The authors noted an increase in contextual crimes during the 1960s: 'This is significant because it is contextual crime perhaps even more than the McGuffin which creates a sense of society as a whole being threatened by crime.'

The trend is linked to the 'increasing predominance of police heroes rather than amateur "sleuths"'; 'towards an increasingly graphic representation of violence in the portrayal of crime'; the degree to which crime traumatizes the victim, and the perception that crime has social origins. In their analysis, Allen, Livingstone and Reiner emphasize the complexity of the representation of crime in contexts of the 'collapse of moral certainties' in society, the dominance of Hollywood, the retreat from strict forms of CENSORSHIP and the demographic nature of AUDIENCE – largely made up of young people.
* Maggie Wykes, *News, Crime and Culture* (UK: Pluto, 1999).

Crimes of self-publicity Using violence to win media attention to publicize self or a cause (see TERRORISM AS COMMUNICATION). Term used by US novelist Don DeLillo in *The World, the Image and the Gun*, a BBC Omnibus programme (September 1991). He argues that terrorism through film and TV has displaced the novelist as narrator; that image-watchers can be their own creators of narrative through acts of violence – gunning down celebrities, for example. Delillo argues that NEWS has become 'the tragic narrative of our time'.

Crisis (definition) How do we know when a crisis is a crisis? One answer is – when the media tell us it is a crisis. Their capacity for AGENDA SETTING, of selecting the front-page headlines or the lead stories, can not only crystallize the notion of crisis in the public mind but in some cases help precipitate one, at least in the sense that people in authority – such as governments – can be forced into a crisis response to a crisis stimulus.

Critical news analysis Generic term for a wide-ranging and complex approach to the analysis of the presentation of NEWS in the mass media. Perhaps the most influential starting point for this critical analysis is the book by Stanley Cohen and Jock Young, eds., *The Manufacture of News: Social Problems, Deviance and the Mass Media* (UK: Constable, 1973). They, along with other commentators of the time, such as Professor Stuart Hall, and research teams such as the GLASGOW UNIVERSITY MEDIA GROUP, contributed to a developing awareness that the news is *socially constructed* and that it is both a social and an *ideological* construct. (See P. Berger and T. Luckmann's *The Social Construction of Reality* [UK: Penguin, 1976].) In other words, news isn't neutral. Critical news analysis focuses on content, presentation and language. Emphasizing the importance of the linguistic assembly of messages in his book *Language in the News: Discourse and Ideology and the Press* (UK: Routledge, 1991), Roger Fowler says, 'There are different ways of saying the same thing, and they are not random, accidental alternatives'; thus there can never be 'a value-free reflection of "facts"'. Two processes occur: *selection* (see AGENDA SETTING; GATEKEEPING; NEWS VALUES), followed by *transformation* according to the dictates of the medium and the influences upon all the encoders involved.

Critical news analysis is essentially a process of *decoding*. For an excellent summary of the range of approaches developed through the 1980s and into the 1990s, see Chapter 12 of Fowler, 'Conclusion: prospects for critical analysis'. See HEGEMONY; IMPARTIALITY; JOURNALISM; SAPIR-WHORF LINGUISTIC RELATIVITY HYPOTHESIS.

Cropping Photographs for publication are rarely printed up exactly as they emerge from the original negative. They are very often 'cropped', that is cut to fulfil certain objectives: the space requirements of a page; to maximize impact; to serve aesthetic or ideological criteria. Generally pictures are cropped to get rid of redundant detail which might detract from the central thrust and drama of the picture's message. See ANCHORAGE; PREFERRED READING.

Cryptography Secret LANGUAGE; the transfer of messages into secret codes. A cryptograph is anything written in *cypher*. See DATA PROTECTION.

Cues See BARNLUND'S TRANSACTIONAL MODEL OF COMMUNICATION.

Cultivation As used by US communication analyst George Gerbner, the term describes the way that the mass media system relates to the CULTURE from which it grows and which it addresses. The media 'cultivate' attitudes and VALUES in a culture. For example, audiences are cultivated into rejecting certain acts of violence while at the same time being cultivated into accepting or tolerating others. See MAINSTREAMING.

Cultivation differential The difference between the perceptions of heavy and light viewers on a particular aspect of social reality. Several researchers have focused upon the influence of TV upon an individual's perception of social reality. George Gerbner and others in 'The demonstration of power: violence profile No. 10' in *Journal of Communication*, 29 (1979), report on findings regarding the effect of TV portrayal of violence on certain viewer's perceptions of the incidence of real violence. They found that heavy viewers of TV were more likely to be influenced by, more likely to accept, the image of reality presented by TV programmes than light viewers. See EFFECTS OF THE MASS MEDIA; PORNOGRAPHY.

Cultural apparatus 'Taken as a whole', writes C. Wright Mills in *Power, Politics and People* (US: Oxford University Press, 1963), 'the cultural apparatus is the lens of mankind through which men see; the medium by which they interpret and report what they see'. It is composed of 'all the organizations and *milieux* in which artistic, intellectual and scientific work goes on, and of the means by which such work is made available to circles, publics and masses'.

The cultural apparatus features large in the process of guiding experience, defining social truths, establishing standards of credibility, image-making and opinion forming, and is 'used by dominant institutional orders'. It confers prestige and the 'prestige of culture is among the major means by which powers of decision are made to seem part of an unchallengeable authority'. Wright Mills goes on to argue that, no matter how internally free the 'cultural workman' as he names the artist or intellectual, he/she is instrinsically part of the cultural apparatus which tends in every nation to become a 'close adjunct of national authority and a leading agency of nationalist propaganda'. CULTURE and authority overlap and this overlap 'may involve the ideological use of cultural products and of cultural workmen for the legitimation of power, and the justification of decisions and policies'. See CONSENSUS; HEGEMONY; IDEOLOGICAL STATE APPARATUSES.

Cultural capital French philosopher Pierre Bourdieu makes the distinction between economic capital and cultural capital – the latter being the knowledge, tastes, attitudes, VALUES and assumptions which individuals or GROUPS possess with regard to various cultural artefacts and endeavours, in particular those of what might be termed legitimate culture – though definitions of such legitimacy are open to contest. An individual's cultural capital clearly may influence the way in which messages may be encoded or decoded. Advertisers, for example, often make assumptions about the cultural capital of the target consumer groups when constructing advertising messages. A popular late 1960s record may be used as the soundtrack in a television commercial not just because of its musical merits but because its location within a particular youth culture(s) may be felt to give the product connotational and ideological meanings related to the desire for freedom and independence. The messages may be read this way, though not necessarily accepted, by consumers familiar both with the song and the youth culture(s) but is unlikely to be read as such by someone unfamiliar with either.

The notion of cultural capital is also linked to that of CLASS, GENDER, ethnic identity and STATUS in that some cultural capital is more highly valued than others by the dominant groups within a society and indeed possession of such cultural capital is often widely taken as a sign of membership of these groups. There is among these groups a tendency to denigrate popular cultural capital. Popular cultural capital on the other hand can be seen as a rich source of responses to, including resistance to, social subordination. See CULTURE; HIGHBROW; TASTE CULTURES; YOUTH CULTURE.

* Pierre Bourdieu, *Distinction* (UK: Routledge, 1984) and *The Field of Cultural Production* (UK: Polity Press, 1993).

Cultural diamond See GRISWOLD CULTURAL DIAMOND MODEL, 1994.

Cultural Indicators research project See MAINSTREAMING.

Cultural industry See FRANKFURT SCHOOL OF THEORISTS.

Cultural studies of the media See CULTURE.

Cultural memory That which the community recalls, re-encodes in a process of making sense of the present. Cultural memory contrasts with what has been termed *instrumental* or *electronic* memory, that which can be numerically encoded and recorded, as on a computer. In *Communication, Culture and Hegemony: From the Media to Mediation* (UK: Sage, 1993), Jésus Martín-Barbero writes, 'In contrast to

instrumental memory "cultural memory" does not work with pure information or as a process of linear accumulation'; rather, it is 'articulated through experience and events. Instead of simply accumulating, it filters and weights'.

It is not, says Martín-Barbero, 'a memory we can *use*, but the memory of which we are made'. What threatens cultural memory inflicts damage on culture itself, particularly in cultures where tensions exist, dramatically, between tradition and progress. Says Martín-Barbero, a part of whose book focuses on media development in South American countries, 'In the dilemma of choice between under development and modernization, cultural memory does not count and has no place': a situation he and other scholars of cultural change view with considerable dismay.

Cultural metaphor Generally an image, or a series of images, seen to represent a culture. The expression 'An Englishman's home is his castle' attempts to classify the English – perhaps even STEREOTYPE them – by means of a dominant image or practice. In this case a number of characteristics are drawn together in the image of home as something to be defended as though it were a castle – private, self-contained, constructed to be resistant to outside intrusions and influences.

According to Martin J. Gannon and associates in *Understanding Global Cultures: Metaphorical Journeys Through 17 Countries* (US: Sage, 1994), the use of identifying metaphors can assist us in grasping the nature of our own and other cultures. Gannon confirms the saying quoted above, arguing that the dominant cultural metaphor of Britain is the house, with its solid, firm foundations, rooted in the past; a place of privacy, walls and hedges. He and his associates take the view that 'the dynamics of the culture of a particular nation can be best understood through the use of one dominant metaphor that reflects the basic values that all or most of its members accept without question or conscious thought'.

The authors cite in detailed chapters of explanation the following metaphors which represent some of the cultures on their 'metaphorical journey': American football (USA), the dance of Shiva (India), the family altar (China), the opera (Italy), wine (France), lace (Belgium), ballet (Russia), the symphony orchestra (Germany), the bullfight (Spain), the kibbutz (Israel), the garden (Japan), the *stuga* or summer home (Sweden), the market place (Nigeria) and the coffee house (Turkey). For Ireland, home of the Blarney Stone, the authors perhaps appropriately select as the country's presiding metaphor, conversation.

* Edward and Mildred Hall, *Understanding Cultural Differences* (US: Intercultural Press, 1990).

Cultural modes The *literate* mode is rooted in the written word; the *oral* mode is spoken or visual. Traditionally they have been aligned to CLASS differences; that is, the upper, better educated classes have lived by a literate mode of cultural interaction – the *dominant* CULTURE, while the more 'untutored' classes have relied upon oral modes. With the advent of electronic media the oral mode has become increasingly dominant. It is essentially the mode of FILM and TELEVISION, though both media still tend to be run by a class educated in the literate mode and whose perceptions are conditioned by such a mode. In *Culture and Society* (UK: Penguin, 1958), Raymond Williams describes the oral, working class mode as 'the basic collective idea' while the bourgeois, literate culture represents the 'basic individualist idea'. See BARDIC TELEVISION.

Cultural racism See RACISM.

Culture The sum of those characteristics which *identify* and *differentiate* human societies – a complex interweave of many factors. The culture of a nation is made up of its LANGUAGE, history, traditions, climate, geography, arts, social, economic and political NORMS, and its system of VALUES; and such a nation's size, its neighbours and its current prosperity condition the nature of its culture.

There are cultures within cultures. Thus reference is made to *working class culture or middle class culture*. Organizations and institutions can have their own cultures (See ORGANIZATION CULTURES). We refer to **cultural epochs** which are the result of developments – social, political, industrial, technological – which create cultural change.

Mass production and the mass media have contributed immensely to cultural change, giving rise to what critics have termed *mass culture* and disapprovingly portrayed as manufactured, manipulated, force-fed, marketed like soap powder and, because of its unique access to vast audiences, open to abuse of the mass by the powerful. Alan Swingewood in *The Myth of Mass Culture* (UK: Macmillan, 1977) argues, however, that there 'is no mass culture, or mass society; but there is an ideology of mass culture and mass society'. The IDEOLOGY is real enough, but the thing itself he describes as MYTH: 'If culture is the means whereby man affirms his humanity and his purposes and his aspirations to freedom and dignity then the concept and theory of mass culture are their denial and negation.'

Culture is transmitted through SOCIALIZATION to new members of a social group or society. The media play an important role in this process. A central concern of culturalist studies of the media is the degree to which the media's output may both reflect and communicate the culture of the more powerful social groups in that society at the expense of the less powerful. By asserting one culture against others, the media help to nurture a *dominant culture* and relegate rival cultures into the realms of DEVIANCE. See AGORA; ALIENATION; ALLEGORY; ANECDOTE; ANOMIE; APACHE SILENCE; ARGOT; ATTITUDES; BEDROOM CULTURE; BRICOLAGE; CELEBRATORY SEEING; CODES; COLLECTIVE REPRESENTATIONS; COLONIZATION; COMMANDERS OF THE SOCIAL ORDER; COMMUNICATIVE RATIONALITY; COMPASSION FATIGUE; CONNECTIVITY; CONSENSUAL VALIDATION; CONSENSUS; CONVERGENCE; CONSENT, MANUFACTURE OF; CONTAGION EFFECT; CONVENTIONS; COUNTER-CULTURE; CULTIVATION; CULTURAL APPARATUS; CULTURAL CAPITAL; CULTURAL MEMORY; CULTURAL METAPHOR; CULTURAL MODES; CULTURE: CONSUMER CULTURE; CULTURE: POPULAR CULTURE; DEMONIZATION; DISCOURSE; EMERGENT CULTURE; EMPOWERMENT; FOLK CULTURE; FOLK DEVILS; FRANKFURT SCHOOL OF THEORISTS; FUNCTIONALIST (MODE OF MEDIA ANALYSIS); FUNDAMENTALISM; GAMES; GENERALIZED OTHER; GESTURAL DANCE;

GOSSIP; GOSSIP NETWORKS; HE/MAN LANGUAGE; HEGEMONY; HOUSEHOLD USES OF INFORMATION AND COMMUNICATION TECHNOLOGY; HYBRID-IZATION; IDENTIFICATION; IDEOLOGICAL STATE APPARATUSES; IDEOLECT; IDEOLOGY; IMMERSION; INTER-CULTURAL INVASION (AND THE MASS MEDIA): LIFE POSITIONS; iSOCIETY; MACHINERY OF REPRESEN-TATION; MARGINALITY, MYTH OF; McDONALD-IZATION; McWORLD Vs JIHAD; MEDIASPHERE; METAMESSAGE; NEGATIVE SEMANTIC SPACE; ORALITY: PRIMARY AND SECONDARY; POLYSEMY; POSTMODERN-ISM; PROTOLANGUAGE; PUBLIC OPINION; RESISTIVE READING; RETERRITORIALIZATION: SALON DIS-COURSE; SOCIAL ANTHROPOLOGY; SOCIAL STEERAGE; SOCIALIZATION; STATUS; STREET CULTURE; SUB-CULTURE; SURVEILLANCE SOCIETY; TASTE CULTURES; TRANSCULTURATION; VALS TYPOLOGY; VISIONS OF ORDER; WEDOM, THEYDOM; YOUTH CULTURE.

* Raymond Williams, *The Long Revolution* (UK: Chatto & Windus, 1961, and Penguin, 1965) and *Culture* (UK: Fontana, 1981); Richard Hoggart, *The Uses of Literacy* (UK: Penguin, 1958); James Curran and Michael Gurevitch, *Mass Media and Society* (UK: Edward Arnold, 1991); Nick Stevenson, *Understanding Media Cultures* (UK: Sage, 1995); Colleen Roach, ed., *Communication and Culture in War and Peace* (UK: Sage, 1995); Peter Brooker, *Cultural Theory: A Glossary* (UK: Arnold, 1999); Andrew Tudor, *Decoding Culture: Theory and Method in Cultural Studies* (UK: Sage, 1999).

Culture: consumer culture Arguably consumer culture is the prevailing culture of late modernity in Western societies. Don Slater in *Consumer Culture & Modernity* (UK: Polity Press, 1997) argues that 'it is more generally bound up with central values, practices and institutions which define western modernity, such as choice, individualism and market relations'. For Slater its 'defining feature' is that it, 'denotes a social arrangement in which the relation between lived culture and social resources, between meaningful ways of life and the symbolic and material resources on which they depend, is mediated through markets'. The media and cultural industries obviously play a pivotal role in the operation of consumer culture and the nature of this relationship is the focus of much research.
* Mike Featherstone, *Consumer Culture and Postmodernism*, (UK: Sage, 1991).

Culture: copyrighting culture In the global context of communication, and in view of the open access properties of the INTERNET, a question of growing importance is – to whom does a TEXT or work belong? (See TEXT: INTEGRITY OF THE TEXT). R.V. Bettig, in *Copyrighting Culture: The Political Economy of Intellectual Property* (US/UK: Westview Press, 1996), addresses this concern, arguing that with information/knowledge becoming one of the chief commercial industries in the current age, the control of culture has fallen to a number of transnational corporations (TNCs) through their ownership of copyright. The fear of such TNCs is copyright piracy on a world scale, and their ambition is to extend, globally, measures to protect intellectual property from piracy. The Berne Convention laid initial guidelines on protection which eventually materialized in the Agreement on Trade-related Aspects of Intellectual Property Rights (TRIPS) of the World Trade Organization. This included the extension of protection to databases; computer programs being classified as literary works and therefore subject to copyright.

Texts are not only protected, their universal access – working within a global free market – is also protected; thus, for example, the attempts by one country to protect its own cultural products from cultural 'invasion' becomes an area of contention. The result, fears Bettig, threatens to be an economic domination of the information-rich nations over the information-poor. Economic dominance brings with it ideological influence. Copyright becomes a device for the COMMODITIZATION and PRIVATIZATION of knowledge where 'the views and accounts of the world held by the capitalist class and aligned class factions and groups are broadly disseminated and persistently publicized'. Global agreements, however, in practice have a mother of all battles ahead of them in the war against piracy. It has been estimated that in 1995 US trade lost over $14 billion to piracy, approximately a half of this in computer software, while in 1996 the abuse of copyright on recorded music meant, according to the International Federation of the Photographic Industry, losses of $2 billion.

Culture: globalization of Considered by many commentators as a paramount trend in the late 20th c., in which cultures and cultural practices of chiefly Western nations, America in particular, have spread through the world, dominating native, home-grown cultures. The media are seen to be the channels through which the globalizing torrent has poured; and those channels have been largely under the direction and control of transnational corporations. Under the umbrella of globalization we encounter a couple of key, linked and interactive phenomena: CONSUMERIZATION and MEDIA IMPERIALISM. With cultural dominance, fear some commentators, comes ideological dominance, and that ideology centres around the processes of production and consumption and the targeting of audiences in their role of *consumers*. Todd Gitlin in his chapter 'Prime Time Ideology: The Hegemonic Process in Television Entertainment' in *Television: The Critical View* (US/UK: Oxford University Press, 1994), edited by Horace Newcomb, believes, 'In the twentieth century, the dominant ideology has shifted toward sanctifying consumer satisfaction as the premium definition of "the pursuit of happiness"'. Corporate domination of the economy extends to corporate dominance – worldwide – of culture, at least those cultures through which profits may be obtained. It is not happiness alone that global corporatization promises but liberty, equality and fraternity: all can 'be affirmed through the existing private commodity forms, under the benign, protective eye of the national security state'.

The vision of a world dominated by American cultural products (not to mention products of other kinds, such as Coca-Cola and McDonald burgers – see McDONALIDIZATION) is challenged by observers who see in *localism* a force of resistance, or if not resistance, assimilation. Roland Robinson offers us a useful term in this respect – *glocalization* (in 'Globalization or glocalization?' in the *Journal of International Communication*, 1 (1994)), that is, the ability of people in their own cultures to deal with in their own way the cultural imports from the West, to absorb them, to adapt them – to glocalize them.

John B. Thompson in *The Media and Modernity: A Social Theory of Media* (UK: Polity, 1995) urges us to see trends of dominance within historical perspectives: 'Rather than assuming that prior to the importation of Western TV programmes etc. many Third World countries had indigenous traditions and cultural heritages which were largely unaffected by external pressures, we should see instead that the globalization of communication through electronic media is only the most recent of a series of cultural encounters, in some cases stretching back many centuries, through which values, beliefs and symbolic forms of different groups have been superimposed on one another, often in conjunction with the use of coercive, political and economic power.'

Thompson maintains that the media-imperialist position underestimates the power of audiences to make their own meanings from what they read, listen to or watch. 'Through the localized process of appropriation,' Thompson believes, 'media products are embedded in sets of practices which shape and alter their significance.'

Evidence for the process of glocalization is offered by Tamar Liebes and Elihu Katz in *The Export of Meaning: Cross Cultural Readings of Dallas* (US: Oxford University Press, 1990; UK: Polity, 1993). Their researches indicated that the American soap *Dallas* was read in quite different ways by people of different origins, cultures and outlooks. It was *Dallas* which was dominated, not the audience for *Dallas*.

Majid Tehranian in his chapter 'Ethnic discourse and the new world dysorder' in *Communication and Culture in War and Peace* (UK: Sage, 1993), edited by Colleen Roach, argues that the levelling out which is said to be a benefit of globalization is more apparent than real. In fact the 'levelling' has camouflaged 'a hegemonic project by a new modern, technocratic, internationalist elite' speaking 'the language of a new international, a new world order'. However, Tehranian perceives the 'periphery' reacting against the 'core' in a number of potentially conflictual, even explosive, ways. He speaks of *Countermodernization* as a significant contemporary trend, in which pressure groups such as some traditional religions react against modern ideas and dominant ideologies – the resurgence, for example, of fundamentalist religion in the face of scientific and technological advances; while a contrary trend, *demodernization*, is expressed by the voices of environmentalists or feminists; and by those 'localites' (as contrasted with 'cosmopolites') whose advocacy is inspired by the notion that 'Small is beautiful'.

The nature and degree of globalization of culture will continue to be fiercely debated and such debate will inevitably have to take into account inequalities of wealth, provision and media technology across nations. See NEWS: GLOBALIZATION OF; INFORMATION GAPS; SLAPPS.

* Malcolm Waters, *Globalization* (UK: Routledge, 1995); Peter Golding and Phil Harris eds., *Beyond Cultural Imperialism* (UK: Sage, 1996); Daya Kishan Thussu, ed., *Electronic Empires: Global Media and Local Resistance* (UK: Arnold, 1998); Barry Smart, ed., *Resisting McDonaldization* (UK: Sage, 1999).

Culture of deference Journalist Richard Norton-Taylor in an article 'Pressure behind the scenes' and subtitled 'A history of deference, and cosy relationships in Westminster, have made self-censorship acceptable' (UK: *Index on Censorship* 4 & 5, 1991), writes of a 'deep-seated culture of deference' existing between many British editors and journalists in their relationship with those in authority (See POWER ELITE). This, Norton-Taylor claims, arises out of an anxiety to be accepted by and be a part of the Establishment. The deference has its 'origins in the centralization of the British state and in Britain's imperial past – where there was virtually unchallenged consensus about the Empire's "civilizing mission"'. Deference, says Norton-Taylor, continues to be applied to institutions of the State such as Whitehall, the Monarchy, the courts and Parliament. This deference also helps create and supports CONSENSUS against 'enemies', against foreign rivals, in war or in business. See JOURNALISM.

Culture: popular culture Something of a redundant term in that all culture is to a degree 'popular'; otherwise if it is 'unpopu-lar', that is, if it does not attract or involve an AUDIENCE, it vanishes. The term has come to mean the culture of 'ordinary people', of the working class, the non-elite majority as contrasted with so-termed *high* or *highbrow* culture. Popular culture generally signifies *cohesion*, high culture *difference* – difference, that is, from popular culture and those with whom it is associated. Popular culture has traditionally been looked down on as something banal, trashy, unchallenging or even potentially harmful: an ELITE standpoint. In their time, theatricals, dancing, wassailing, 'pulp fiction', the PRESS, POSTERS, postcards, COMICS, SOAP OPERA, the hit-parade and the cinema have varyingly been defined as the kind of culture which contains the potential for subversion – usually of 'standards'. Popular culture tends to be controlled where it emerges from or is generated by the populace itself; promoted when it falls into the category of *transmission*, that is, created by 'culture manufacturers' for profit.

According to the French philosopher Pierre Bourdieu, popular culture is basically associated with that section of the population who lack both economical and CULTURAL CAPITAL. Since at least the 1960s popular culture has become the focus of critical attention and re-evaluation: it is *studied* – analysed, measured, in short, taken seriously.

In *Cultures and Societies in a Changing World* (US: Pine Forge Press, 1994), Wendy Griswold writes that 'Scholars examining previously despised works, genres and systems of meaning found them to contain complexities and beauties; at the same time, deconstructing previously esteemed works, genres and systems of meaning, they found widespread representations of class, hegemony, patriarchy, and illegitimate canonization.'

Culture, whether popular or 'elitist', *cultivates*, hence its fascination for researchers, commentators and students of media. What, for example, is the popular Saturday night feast of battling brawn and beauty, *Gladiators* all about? What is being *said* to us? Television, it has been claimed, has appropriated popular culture and by doing so redefined the term to mean 'that which is popular on TV'. The nature of *participation* by the populace in generating and taking part in popular culture has not been lost on TV programme makers: audience participation is the key to popular quiz and competition programmes. In *Gladiators*, for example, members of the public are invited to compete with the professionals and, worldwide, TV appears to work on the principle that culture is basically communication and that popular culture is essentially interactive.

The question remains whether, if popular culture has the genuine potential for subversion – that is, going its own ways free of hegemonic control – can TV ever be truly 'popular'? In 1995 a new cultural property was introduced into the UK with sensational popular success – the National Lottery. The BBC handed over Saturday night peak-time to the announcement of the lottery results and built an immensely popular 'entertainment' around the draw. The vast sums derived from the lottery were immediately spent on such worthy but elitists cultural enterprises as Covent Garden Opera, arguably indicating that when choices about cultural direction and cultural priorities are made, they arise not from the popular will but the preferences of the POWER ELITE. See ACTIVE-AUDIENCE THESIS; ETHNOGRAPHIC (APPROACH TO AUDIENCE MEASUREMENT); RESPONSE CODES.

Cultures of organizations See ORGANIZATION CULTURES.

Custom audience research That which is commissioned or undertaken by a company or client into AUDIENCE response to the media marketing of its product or services, generally targeting specific media outlets. Such studies produce rich, focused data while at the same time incurring doubts concerning the objectivity of that data. In contrast, *syndicated studies* are grander in scope as, like the Nielson ratings, they measure the audiences of multiple media outlets of audience response. As Peter V. Miller says in 'Made-to-order and standardized audiences: forms of reality in audience measurement' published in *Audiencemaking: How the Media Create the Audience* (US: Sage, 1994) edited by James S. Ettema and D. Charles Whitney, 'The unique, made-to-

order nature of the custom study is both its chief benefit and its major cost.' He goes on, 'The syndicated study offers comparative, longitudinal information about audiences that can be used to sell advertising space and time. Unlike the custom study, the syndicated effort provides the advertisers with a standard way to judge alternative vehicles for their messages.' See AUDIENCE MEASUREMENT.

Cut-off In INTERPERSONAL COMMUNICATION, actions which block – cut off – incoming visual signals when people are under stress: hands over eyes, deflected glance, glazed look, eyes shut, etc. See GESTURE.

Cybernetics The study of communication FEEDBACK systems in human, animal and machine. Taken from the Greek for 'Steersman', the term was the invention of American Norbert Wiener, author of *Cybernetics: or Control and Communication in the Animal and the Machine* (US: Wiley, 1949). Essentially an interdisciplinary study, Cybernetics ranges in its interest from control systems of the body to the monitoring and control of space missions. Cybernetics concerns itself with the analysis of 'whole' systems, their complexity of goals and hierarchies within contexts of perpetual change. The Greek steersman used the feedback of visual, aural and tactile indicators to chart his passage through rough seas. Today we have computers: the potential for accuracy and rapidity of feedback and control is vastly greater, and so is the potential for disaster should the feedback systems go wrong.

Cyberspace Term probably first used by William Gibson in his novel *Neuromancers* published in America by Ace Books in 1984. Gibson describes cyberspace as 'a consensual hallucination . . . [People are] creating a world. It's not really a place, it's not really space. It's notional space.' By pressing computer keys, and by grace of a modem and telephone line, the operator has access to potentially infinite information and endless exchanges with other users.

The INTERNET, with its subsidiaries and rivals, offers to the computer-explorer vast research possibilities all for a monthly rental equal to that of a TV set. We can write direct, through E-MAIL, to the President of the United States or to Bill Gates, president of Microsoft. We can call up information from the Library of Congress, check the strength of the market in Hong Kong or book a holiday in the Caribbean. We can join pressure groups and 'globalize' the issues that concern us. The Net alters for us both time and space. New York, Alaska or Alice Springs could be in the next room for all that distance counts in cyberspace; and national boundaries need no longer be barriers. Indeed, in cyberterms, national and geographical divisions are an out-of-date way of viewing the world.

According to Mark C. Taylor and Esa Saarinen in *Imagology: Media Philosophy* (UK: Routledge, 1994), itself a mercurial sortie into cybergraphics, chief among cyberspace's characteristics is *speed*. 'Power,' the authors declare, 'is speed' and the 'swift will inherit the earth.' Some commentators claim that control, traditionally exercised by governments and powerful groups such as the transnational corporations, is shifting away from centres to peripheries, from organizations to individuals forming their own, hierarchy-free associations. In a number of countries the electronic highways of information, knowledge and ideas is seen as a threat to hierarchy and authority. In India huge licence fees are levied upon electronic bulletin board owners. In Iran, Saudi Arabia, Qatar, Malaysia and Indonesia unauthorized import of satellite dishes is a criminal offence punishable by prohibitive fines.

The Net is widely envisioned in terms of new-age exploration. A Boston software computer firm has claimed in its advertising, 'Sir Francis Drake was knighted for what we do every day . . . The spirit of exploration is alive at The Computer Merchant'. In the realm of VIRTUAL REALITY imagination knows no bounds. Henry Rheingold in the book he edited on the subject, *Virtual Reality* (US: Simon & Schuster, 1991) speaks of 'my own odyssey to the outposts of a new scientific frontier . . . and an advanced glimpse of a possible new world in which reality itself might become a manufactured and metered commodity'.

By the summer of 1994 there were over 32 million users of Internet, and varyingly of World Wide Web, Cix (Compulink Information Exchange), The Well (Whole Earth 'lectronic Link) and Compuserve with its 2000 different services. Information is but a part of cyberexchange. You have personal problems – illness, sexual abuse, stuttering; is your marriage heading for the rocks? Self-help groups on the Net have proliferated as an antidote to the problems faced in the 'real' world.

Self-help suggests a degree of independence from authority and some commentators have seen in this a trend, made possible by the Net, towards the dismantling of patriarchal structures in society and existing gender relations. Is Cyberequality on its way? American academic Cheris Kramarae is not so sanguine. In 'A backstage critique of virtual reality' in *CyberSociety: Computer Mediated Communication and Community* (US: Sage, 1995) edited by Steven G. Jones, Kramarae argues that, 'Cyberspace, like earthspace, is not developed as a viable place for women.' She talks about 'malestream publications and other forums' and views 'cybersex' as something where game, play and match will continue to reflect sexist attitudes and behaviour. She notes how in many virtual reality games the essential aim of winning is control; and in some virtual reality scenarios a man may create his ideal female and then shape her responses at will. 'Sex will (has?) become another sport,' worries Kramarae, 'like hunting and shooting tanks and hostile aliens.'

Also Kramarae fears for the real ecology when we spend so much time in cyberecology. She links those fears to gender roles: 'I worry about the programs that encourage us to leave for extended periods the dirt and water of the actual places we live in . . . I can imagine the man of the house putting on his gloves and headset and visiting Costa Rica while the woman of the house stays in the real house, changing the diapers and fixing meals.' She asks whether all this means turning our backs on 'the messes we've made' in the real world.

In cyberspace, a text once issued no

longer belongs to its author: copyright becomes an impossibility. Thus there is minimum control over content which means that information exchange is as likely between Fascists as between liberals; and empowering in ways that most would consider dangerous – offering information on bomb manufacture, for example or hard porn.

There are fears that the major conglomerates, Microsoft in particular, may 'colonize' space. Already Microsoft is offering access to the Net through its software programs while at the same time opening the Net as a shop window for companies wishing to turn Cyberspace into Cybermalls. Linked with this is concern about the demography of usage. The Net has been described as 'pale and male'. The first user survey of the World Wide Web conducted by James E. Pitkow and Mimi Recker found that of 4000 respondents to the survey, over 90 per cent of users were professional, Caucasian and male. Many analysts take the view that the Net is unlikely to be a bridger of the gap between information-rich and information-poor, that it is failing to redress the balance between core and periphery; and some are of the opinion that cyberspace is largely off-limits to the poor, the ill-educated and the unemployed.

Cylinder or rotary press The most important technical development in PRINT-ING history following the invention of movable type was the steam-driven cylinder press invented by Friederich Koenig. Born in Saxony, Koenig moved to London in order to set up a works to manufacture the new machines (1812). He demonstrated that a cylinder press machine could take off impressions at the rate of over 1000 an hour. On 28 November 1814 one of the presses was used to print *The Times*. Its editor, John Walter, described the press as 'the greatest improvement connected with printing since the discovery of the art itself'. As a result of its advantage in using Koenig's press, *The Times* became the dominant and most influential newspaper of the 19th c. in the UK. See MEDIA TECHNOLOGY.

D

Daguerrotype Early photograph produced in the manner of Louis Jacques Mandé Daguerre (1789–1851) a French theatrical designer who teamed up with Joseph Nicéphore Niépce (1765–1833), a founding father of photography, in 1830. Niépce died three years later but Daguerre continued their work, fixing images on metal plates coated with silver iodide, which he treated with mercury vapour in a darkroom. Daguerre was eventually able to reduce the exposure time of a photograph from eight hours to between 20 and 30 minutes. His Daguerrotype was taken up by the French government in July 1839 and revealed to the world at a meeting of the Académies des Sciences in August. No prints could be made from a Daguerrotype; thus Daguerre's method was a cul-de-sac in photography, though a vastly successful one at the time. See PHOTOGRAPHY, ORIGINS.

Dance's helical model of communication, 1967 The earliest communication models were *linear*; their successors were *circular*, emphasizing the crucial factor of FEEDBACK in the communication process. Frank E.X. Dance in 'A helical model of communication', in the book he edited, *Human Communication Theory* (US: Holt, Rinehart & Winston, 1967), commends the circular model as an advance upon the linear one but faults it on the grounds that it suggests that communication comes back full-circle, to exactly the same point from which it started, an assumption which is 'manifestly erroneous'.

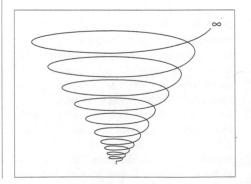

The helix or spiral, for Dance, 'combines the desirable features of the straight line and of the circle while avoiding the weaknesses of either'. He goes on, 'At any and all times, the helix gives geometric testimony to the concept that Communication while moving forward is at the same moment coming back upon itself and being affected by its past behaviour, for the coming curve of the helix is fundamentally affected by the curve from which it emerges'.

Dance's helical model parallels theories of education put forward by Jerome Bruner, and generally referred to as the *spiral curriculum*. See COMMUNICATION MODELS.

Data protection The increasing use of computers and sophisticated INFORMATION TECHNOLOGY has greatly magnified the harm to individual PRIVACY that can occur from any collection, storage or dissemination of personal information, and many countries have legislated against data abuse. Sweden, Denmark, Norway, Luxembourg, West Germany and France have all legislated to protect both the public and private sectors of society. In the US and Canada data protection legislation only applies to the public sector and compliance with it is voluntary.

In the UK, the report of the Lindop Committee (*Report of the Committee on Data Protection*, 1978) urged the need for individuals to have a right of veto on what information was passed on about them, and how this would operate in the context of 'the interests of the rest of society, which include the efficient conduct of industry, commerce and administration'. In 1984, the DATA PROTECTION ACT entered the Statute Book, and began operation in 1987 (See next entry).

CRYPTOGRAPHY, or what in modern parlance is termed *privacy transformation*, can be employed to 'scramble' data prior to storage in order to guard against accidental or deliberate disclosures of information. The problem here is how the key or code to the scrambling process is to be protected. In the US, the Hellman-Diffie method allowed for different keys for the scrambling and unscrambling processes. An alternative to this is the so-called *electronic signature* which works by reversing the roles of scrambling and unscrambling keys. Another mode is PIN – personal identity number, where everybody is issued with a personal key. PIN is already in use for the authorization of electronic funds transfers.

Data Protection Act, 1984 The purpose of the Act is 'to regulate the use of automatically processed information relating to individuals and the provision of services in respect of such information'. From 11 November 1987 the public has been able to check if any organization holds information on them; to see a copy of that information, known as personal data; to complain to the Data Protection Registrar about the way the data were collected or are being used; to have inaccurate computer records corrected or deleted in certain circumstances and to claim compensation through the courts if the 'Data subject' has suffered damage by the loss or destruction of personal data, or through an unauthorized disclosure or because of inaccuracy.

Designed to bring Britain into line with the Council of Europe Convention for the Protection of Individuals with regard to Automatic Processing of Personal Data, the Act provides for the establishment of a data watchdog, the Data Protection Registrar, and outlines eight DATA PROTECTION PRINCIPLES.

The test of any act protecting the citizen is the size and scope of the exceptions. There are three unconditional exemptions from registration: personal data required to be exempt for the purpose of safeguarding national security; data which its user is required by law to make public and personal data held by an individual and 'concerned with the management of his personal, family or household affairs or held by him only for recreational purposes'.

Subject access is barred on matters of prevention or detection of crime, the apprehension or prosecution of offenders or the assessment or collection of any tax or duty.

Data Protection Principles Listed in the DATA PROTECTION ACT, 1984 are the following eight principles governing data protection for computer users handling personal data: computer users must (1) obtain and process the information fairly and lawfully; (2)

register the purposes for which they hold the data; (3) not use or disclose the information in a way contrary to those purposes; (4) hold only information which is adequate, relevant and not excessive for the purposes; (5) hold only accurate information and, where necessary, keep it up to date; (6) not keep any information longer than is necessary; (7) give individual access to information about themselves and, where appropriate, correct or erase the information; (8) take appropriate security measures. Persons feeling that any computer user has broken one or more of the above principles may complain to the Data Protection Registrar. See PRIVACY; SECRECY.

Death on the Rock Title of a *This Week* programme put out by Thames TV and transmitted in April 1988, which provoked the ire of the Conservative government. The death was that of three members of the IRA (Sean Savage, Daniel McCann and Mairead Farrell) shot dead by members of the British government's SAS (6 March 1988); and the rock was Gibraltar. Every attempt was made by government to censor the programme yet Thames went ahead with the screening of the documentary which traced the events leading up to the killing. The editor of the programme, Roger Bolton, went into print with a book deserving to be read by every student of media, *Death on the Rock, And Other Stories* (UK: W.H. Allen, 1990). He describes the pressures he and everyone else at Thames TV were placed under as a result of the programme: it was 'the price we were having to face for questioning the Government's account of a matter of great public interest.'

The Government demanded an inquiry into the programme and the IBA (Independent Broadcasting Authority) acceded to the demand, appointing as investigators Queen's Counsel, Richard Rampton, and Lord Windlesham, member of the Tory Reform Group, former junior Conservative minister at the Home Office and Northern Ireland and a close friend of Sir Geoffrey Howe.

Contrary to the expectations of the government, and of the tabloid press, the Windlesham/Rampton Report gave *Death on the Rock* a clean bill of health, speaking of the programme-makers involved (Julian Manyon, Chris Oxley and researcher, Alison Cahn) as 'experienced, painstaking and persistent' and judging the programme as 'trenchant and avoiding triviality'.

As Bolton says, the Government was 'not a gracious loser'. Without having read the Windlesham Report, John Wakeham, leader of the Commons, said the government 'profoundly disagreed' with the findings of the Report. Most of the British Press accepted the verdict, though *The Sun*, a Murdoch paper, continued to attack the programme repeatedly: 'The verdict: Still guilty.' *Death on the Rock* went on to win the British Broadcasting Press Guild award for Best Documentary; and a similar award from the British Academy of Film & Television Arts. In September 1995 the European Court of Human Rights eventually passed judgment on the British government's conduct concerning the Gibraltar deaths. The *Guardian* headline of 28 September declared 'UK fury at SAS verdict'. By the narrowest of judicial margins (10 votes to 9), the Court ruled, in a 60-page judgment, that the shooting of the IRA terrorists by the SAS involved the use of excessive force. Cabinet minister Michael Heseltine, using what the *Guardian* leader termed a 'smokescreen of synthetic rage' attacked the ruling as 'incomprehensible', 'ludicrous' and 'extraordinary'; a response that was 'silly even from the government's point of view'. The Leader remarked on 'disturbing signs that this issue will be trampled under the stampeding hooves of Europhobia'. See CENSORSHIP; SPYCATCHER CASE.

Decency: Communications Decency Act, 1996 See COMMUNICATIONS DECENCY ACT (US).

Decipher See ENCODE; DECODE.

Decisive moment French photographer Henri Cartier-Bresson (b. 1908) used this term to describe the instant when pressing the shutter release button produced the desired image. Indeed Cartier-Bresson's timing, his ability to be at the ready when destiny appeared to be bringing highly photogenic elements together, is legendary and uncanny. Some critics claim that this instinct for the decisive moment makes Cartier-Bresson the finest of all photographers.

Declaration on the Mass Media (Unesco General Council, 1978) See MEDIA IMPERIALISM.

Decode The process of interpreting, analysing and understanding the nature of messages – written, spoken, broadcast, etc. This requires not just an understanding of the words, signs or images used but also a sharing of the VALUES and assumptions which underpin their ENCODING into a MESSAGE by the transmitter. A focus for research in communication studies is the extent to which the receiver decodes the message in the way the encoder or sender would prefer. This is an important element in the debate on the power and influence of the media.

Aberrant decoding is a term used by Umberto Eco in 'Towards a semiotic inquiry into the television message' (translation) in *Working Papers in Cultural Studies* No. 3 (UK: Birmingham University Centre for Contemporary Culture Studies, 1972) and also in *Communication Studies*, J. Corner and J. Hawthorn, eds., (UK: Edward Arnold, 1980). In this case the artist or broadcaster – the encoder – encodes a message designed to elicit an expected audience response. If the message is received by an audience which does not share the same CODES or values as the sender, it will be interpreted in an 'aberrant' way, that is, a different meaning will be assumed than that which was intended. In short, it is a difference of 'reading' the message derived from a difference of experience, perception or evaluation (See PREFERRED READING).

A simple illustration of this might be the response of an employer when a candidate arrives for a job interview in sweatshirt and jeans. The interviewee is perhaps intending to assert his individuality, his character, his attitude, whereas the employer may aberrantly decode the message as one of implied insult to the conventions of interview.

Deconstruction The process of deconstruction, as a mode of textual and inter-textual analysis is chiefly associated with the ideas of the French philosopher Jacques Derrida and his method of 'close-reading' of minute particulars in a TEXT. The search is not for an ultimate MEANING; on the contrary, Derrida sees meaning as *undecidable*: signifiers within linguistic contexts refer to further signifiers, texts to further texts in an infinite web of INTERTEXTUALITY. Deconstructors such as Derrida seek to pry behind the dominant expressions of a text, regarding these as serving to exclude subordinate terms. The technique is to *reverse* and *displace*, thus bring about an upending – an overthrow – of the hierarchies which rule all forms of expression.

In the words of Madan Sarup in *An Introductory Guide to Post-Structuralism and Postmodernism* (UK: Harvester Wheatsheaf, 1993), 'Deconstruction disarticulates traditional conceptions of the author and undermines conventional notions of reading and history . . . It kills the author, turns history and tradition into textuality and' – we must gratefully note – 'celebrates the reader'. If *self* can be constructed as a text then self is subject to deconstruction which displaces the notion of a *stable* self. The only coherence it would seem is fragmentation, leading to the conclusion that there can be no meaning, only interpretation.

Sarup's phrase 'textual undecidability' usefully sums up the position of the deconstructors as does the term 'labyrinth of deconstruction' used by Christopher Norris in *Deconstruction: Theory and Practice* (UK: Methuen, 1982).
* Jacques Derrida, *Writing and Difference* (UK: Routledge & Kegan Paul, 1976); Christopher Norris, *Derrida* (UK: Collins, 1987).

Deep Dish TV See PAPER TIGER TV.

Deep focus FILM making technique in which objects close to the camera and those far away are both in focus at the same time.

Deep structure Though the term was first used by Charles Hockett (b. 1916), the concept was given widest currency by fellow US linguist Noam Chomsky (b. 1928) in 'Current issues in linguistic theory' in J. Foder and J. Katz, eds., *The Structure of Language: Readings in the Philosophy of*

Language (US: Prentice-Hall, 1964). In its original form, *deep structure* is an underlying abstract level of sentence organization, which specifies the way a sentence should be interpreted. It is an abstract representation of SYNTAX. Surface grammar is the final stage in the syntactical representation of a sentence – the nearest one gets to the actual spoken or written form of a sentence (arrived at via the phonological – sound component – or graphological – written component – of the grammar).

The deep structure is made manifest through a process of 'transformation'. A **transformational grammar** establishes the deep and **surface structure** of a sentence and then relates these through the process of transformation. For Chomsky the deep and surface structures, and the relationship between them, provide the essential bases of LANGUAGE which, far from being merely a sequence of words strung together, is rather a series of *organized structures* (see STRUCTURALISM). This deep structure, or level, supplies information that enables the reader or listener to distinguish between alternative interpretations of sentences which have the same surface form, or sentences which have different surface forms but have the same underlying MEANING.

When, for example, a publisher replies to a budding author, 'I will waste no time in reading your manuscript', he presents a surface structure with alternative possible meanings. Yet by altering the surface structure of the sentence 'The dog chased the cat' to 'The cat was chased by the dog', the underlying idea is not altered. The transformations that might occur between deep and surface structure can be *passive* ('My father was warned by the doctor to give up smoking'), *negative* ('My father was not warned to give up smoking'), in *question* form ('Was my father warned to give up smoking?') or as an *imperative* ('Father was told – "Stop smoking!"'). There are many more possibilities.

* Noam Chomsky, *Language and Mind* (UK: Harcourt Brace Jovanovitch, 1968).

Deep throat Journalist's parlance for 'anonymous sources'. Perhaps the most famous was the unknown telephone informant calling himself 'Deep throat' who set *Washington Post* reporters Bernstein and Woodward on the trail in the WATERGATE scandal which eventually led to the resignation of President Richard Nixon. See PRESS.

Defamation Any statement made by one person which is untrue and may be considered injurious to another's reputation, causing shame, resentment, ridicule or financial loss is regarded as defamation under the Defamation Act of 1952. In permanent form, such as expressed in print, records, films, tapes, photographs, images or effigies, defamation is classed as *libel*. In temporary form such as in spoken words or gestures, defamation is classified as *slander*.

No legal aid is granted to plaintiffs or defendants in defamation cases, thus persons even with the most genuine case for grievance at reports about them in the press etc. must think twice before deciding to incur vast legal expenses in defending their reputation. The 1996 Defamation Act is, in the words of the *Guardian* Leader of 26 June, 'a generally sensitive attempt to impose practical rules upon the difficult relationship between the media and those who allege they have been defamed by them'. However, the late addition of the 'Hoffman clause' (brought by Lord Hoffman in the House of Lords and later approved by the House of Commons by a vote of 264 to 201) concerning defamation and MPs, meets with disapproval; raising 'issues of privilege which go much further than the draftsmen can ever have intended'. The clause devolves control over parliamentary privilege from the House as a whole to individual MPs, allowing them to waive parliamentary privilege in order to have the same rights as an ordinary citizen to take the media to court for alleged libel.

At first sight the amendment seems just: an MP has a right to make the media prove the truth of allegations. However, barrister Andrew Nicol, writing in the *Guardian* of 27 June 1996 states that the 'problem with such arguments is that they ignore the difference between journalistic evaluation of a story and the process of establishing the truth of a proposition in court'; in future mere doubt about whether truth can be proved in court may persuade nervous publishers to hold back on a story.

Nicol cites the 1963 decision by the US Supreme Court that if such conditions applied to public officials they would be an unconstitutional restriction on freedom of speech.

Under the Hoffman clause, if an MP waived parliamentary privilege it would mean that no source material could be accepted as evidence unless the originator appeared in court to verify that information. This could destroy at a stroke the generally honourable tradition of the media protecting its sources. 'The information,' says Nicol, 'may, for instance, come from a reliable source but one who for good reason would not wish to testify in court'. See CENSORSHIP.

Defensive communication Occurs when people hear what they do not wish to hear. DISSONANCE arises when messages cut across, or contradict, VALUES and assumptions and the reaction varies from not concentrating on the MESSAGE to deliberately misrepresenting or misunderstanding the sender's motive as well as his/her message.

Climates of threat create defensive tactics just as supportive climates help reduce them. If we know that we are being tested or evaluated, for example, our communication response will be guarded. Equally we might resort to defensive tactics if we feel the communicator of the message is intent on winning control, exerting superiority. We are less defensive in situations in which spontaneity, EMPATHY, equality and a sense of open-mindedness about the nature of the message are predominant.

Deference, culture of See CULTURE OF DEFERENCE.

Deliberative listening See LISTENING.

Demographic analysis The collection and interpretation of data about the characteristics of people other than their beliefs, VALUES and attitudes. Specifically, *demography* is the study of population, while *demology* is the theory of the origin and nature of communities.

Demonization What the media do, particularly the popular press, to those whose views they perceive to be dangerous, destabilizing, bad for business or subversive. The process of demonization begins with *personalization*, that is, focusing on the personal characteristics (invariably negative) of the leader or spokesperson advocating a cause or raising an issue, which the demonizers do not support. Having rendered the cause or issue a 'personal' matter associated with an individual, the aim of the media concerned is to destroy the credibility of the spokesperson and by doing so undermine, in the public mind, the cause for which he/she speaks. See FOLK DEVILS; LOONY LEFTISM.

Denotation See CONNOTATION.

Dependency theory The degree to which audiences are dependent upon the mass media constitutes one of the chief debates about the functions and effects of modern communication systems. In 'A dependency model of mass media effects' in G. Gumpert and R. Cathcart, eds., *Inter/Media: Interpersonal Communication in the Media* (US/UK: Oxford University Press, 1979), Sandra J. Ball-Rokeach and Melvyn DeFleur believe 'The potential for mass media messages to achieve a broad range of cognitive, affective, and behavioural effects will be increased when media systems serve many unique and central information systems'. The fewer the sources of information in a media world, the more likely the media will affect our minds and thoughts, our attitudes and how we behave. Further, that influence will have increased potential 'when there is a high degree of structural instability in the society due to conflict and change'.

However, just as the audience may be changed by information/messages it receives, in turn the media systems themselves are changed according to audience response. It is not one-way traffic. In the COGNITIVE or intellectual sphere, the authors cite the following possible media ROLES: (1) The resolution of ambiguity, and relatedly limiting the range of interpretations of situations which audiences are able to make. (2) Attitude formation. (3) AGENDA SETTING. (4) Expansion of people's systems of beliefs (for example, the tremendous growth in awareness of ecological matters).

(5) Clarification of VALUES, through the expression of *value conflicts* (See DEVIANCE; DEVIANCE AMPLIFICATION).

The authors emphasize that 'it is difficult to imagine the cognitive effect of attitude formation without accompanying affective effects', that is, emotional effects. 'In periods of intense social conflict the police may form a number of attitudes from media characterization about groups with which they have to deal', suggest Ball-Rokeach and DeFleur. 'If the media-derived attitudes contain affective elements, such as anger, hostility and frustration, it may retard the ability of the police to keep their cool when the encounter actually comes'.

The media play a significant role in the establishment and maintenance of 'we feeling', that is, communal solidarity and oneness; equally they may work towards the ALIENATION of sections of the population who are traditionally discriminated against – women, blacks, etc.

In terms of the way the media may affect audience behaviour, the authors pose the following possibilities: *activation* stimulated by media-communicated messages; or *deactivation* as a result of such messages.

Certainly at critical decision making times, such as elections, people have become increasingly dependent on the media, especially TV, for election information and guidance. Ball-Rokeach and DeFleur argue that the greater the uncertainty in society, the less clear are people's frames of reference; consequently there is greater audience dependence on media communication. See BALL-ROKEACH and DEFLEUR'S DEPENDENCY MODEL OF MASS COMMUNICATION EFFECTS, 1976; EFFECTS OF THE MASS MEDIA; THEORIES AND CONCEPTS OF COMMUNICATION.

Deregulation Describes the process whereby channels of communication, specifically RADIO and TV, are opened up beyond the existing franchise-holders. Another term in current use, 'privatization', emphasizes the practical nature of the shift, from public to commercial control, accelerated by the development of VIDEO and CABLE TELEVISION. A typical example of deregulation was the British government's decision, in 1982, to permit the private sector to compete with British Telecom in SATELLITE TRANSMISSION, in the shape of the privately-financed Mercury company.

Deregulation has profound implications for national and international communication systems. Critics fear that it will favour the powerful – companies or nations – and lead the less powerful into positions of dependence upon the powerful. See BROADCASTING; BROADCASTING ACT 1990; BROADCASTING ACT, 1995; COMMERCIAL TELEVISION.

Deregulation, Five Myths of In 'The mythology of telecommunications deregulation' (*Journal of Communication*, Winter, 1990), Vincent Mosco of Carleton University identifies five influential assumptions about the deregulation of telecommunications which he describes as myths (see here Roland Barthes' definition of MYTH): that deregulation lessens the economic role of government; benefits consumers; diminishes economic concentration; is widely supported and is inevitable. Because deregulation is clearly in the interest of the non-public sector, particularly corporations profiting from the free market, it is in the sector's interest to establish the benefits of deregulation as a natural truth: unquestionably a good thing. 'Whatever their basis in fact', writes Mosco, 'these myths continue to reflect significant political and economic interests. Moreover, they help to constitute those interests with a shared belief system . . . promoting the dismantling of a public infrastructure and massive income redistribution up the social class ladder.' Mosco goes on, 'In the long run they want to advance the transformation of information from a public resource into a marketable commodity and a form of social management control. Deregulation is more than a policy instrument; it serves as a cohesive mythology around which those who would benefit from these short- and long-run interests might rally'. At the Millennium Mosco's view is even more relevant than it was in 1990. See COMMANDERS OF THE SOCIAL ORDER; COMMODITIZATION OF INFORMATION; EXNOMINATION; HEGEMONY; INFORMATION GAPS; POWER ELITE.

Desensitization Process by which audiences are considered to be made immune, or less sensitive, to human suffering as a result of relentless exposure to such suffering in the media. A constant media diet of violence – real or fictional – is widely believed to 'harden up' people's tolerance of violence. Like the DISPLACEMENT EFFECT, the notion of desensitization remains a conjecture rather than a theory substantiated by proof. See COMPASSION FATIGUE.

Desk-Top Publishing (DTP) Word Processing (WP) combined with typographical and graphical facilities in software programs such as PageMaker (Macintosh) or PagePlus (Microsoft Windows) makes possible a wide range of professional-standard publications using the computer in combination with good-quality printers such as the laser or bubblejet. Such packages allow the operator to select page size, fonts, type sizes, employ typographical devices such as lines, boxes, shading, and to import graphics. Text can be made to flow round illustrations which can be enlarged, reduced or distorted in instants, using the miraculous mouse. See COMPUTERS IN COMMUNICATION.

Detachment, ideology of See IMPARTIALITY.

Determiner deletion A common stylistic practice of journalists where the characteristics of a person and the name are linked without use of 'the' or 'a', in the interests of verbal economy while at the same time having the effect of labelling the named person. An example might be: 'Exjailbird six-times married Joe Bloggs yesterday told the press . . .' or '"Kiss-and-tell" Minister's former live-in lover claims . . .'. Allan Bell in *The Language of News Media* (UK: Blackwell, 1991) describes this practice as a form of *titleness* which gives instant NEWS VALUE to the person being reported. See HYPHENIZED ABRIDGEMENT; LABELLING PROCESS (AND THE MEDIA).

Determinism See TECHNOLOGICAL DETERMINISM.

Developmental news That which developing nations consider will help rather than harm their prospects. 'Western news' is seen by developing nations as essentially the pursuit of 'bad' news; and bad news hurts.

The term implies government monopoly of information flow in the interests of giving a developing country a 'good name' and runs counter to Western notions of free comment. The aspirations to a reporting tradition of social responsibility rather than sensation-seeking are honourable; and the dangers – of PRESS subservience to government – obvious. See INFORMATION SOCIETY; MEDIA IMPERIALISM; NEW WORLD INFORMATION ORDER.

Deviance Social behaviour which is considered unacceptable within a social community is **deviant**; and the defining of what constitutes deviance depends upon what NORMS of conduct prevail at any given time in a society. Of primary interest in the analysis of deviance is the question – who defines deviance and why? There are two main views on this: the first maintains that the definition of what is deviant behaviour stems from a general CONSENSUS within society; the second argues that it is the most powerful groups within a society who define as deviant behaviour that which may constitute a threat to themselves or their dominant position in society. Particular interest has been focused on the role of the media in shaping definitions of deviance and then responding to those definitions (See DEVIANCE AMPLIFICATION). While from a moral standpoint the media may disapprove of deviant behaviour, there is at the same time a reliance upon it: normative behaviour rarely makes a good headline; but seaside battles between 'deviant' mods and rockers or punch-ups between 'deviant' soccer hooligans are food and drink to the press and TV. It might be argued that if deviance did not exist, it would be necessary for the media to invent it. See SENSITIZATION; SIGNIFICATION SPIRAL; STEREOTYPE.

* Richard V. Ericson, Patricia M. Baraueh and Janet B.L. Chan, *Visualizing Deviance: A Study of News Organizations* (UK: Open University, 1991).

Deviance amplification Several studies of DEVIANCE have been concerned with the role of the mass media in both the definition and amplification of deviance. Leslie Watkins first outlined the concept of deviance amplification in 'Some sociological factors in drug addiction control', D. Wilner and G. Kassebaum, eds., *Narcotics*, (US: McGraw-Hill, 1965). He argues that the way in which a society defines and reacts to deviance may in fact encourage those defined as deviant to act in a more deviant manner – this would be particularly true for deviants excluded from or restricted in participation in normal social activities. If societal reaction to deviance is strong it can lead to greater deviance which in turn may lead to stronger societal reaction and so on, establishing a **deviancy amplification spiral** in which each increase in social control is met by an increase in the level of deviancy.

Jock Young in 'The amplification of drug use', in Stanley Cohen and Jock Young, eds., *The Manufacture of News: Deviance Social Problems and the Mass Media* (UK: Constable, 1973) examines the role of the media in both precipitating and shaping such a deviancy amplification spiral. Young argues, from the evidence of this study of marijuana smoking in London's Notting Hill (1967–69), that the media can in fact play an important role in the creation of such a spiral. It is through the media that the public are alerted to the existence of certain types of deviance and if the coverage is sensational, as it was in this case, a MORAL PANIC may flare up. This results in the police and the courts being put under greater pressure to solve the problem and their attempts to do so can be, as in this case, the beginning of the spiral escalation.

Young found that the media acted as an important source of information for each group, about the other group. Also, the media's portrayal of the situation in terms of stereotypical behaviour and its sensational treatment of the problem helped to create circumstances which pushed the deviants to behave more in accordance with the STEREOTYPES provided by the media itself. See DEPENDENCY THEORY.

Deviant See SLIDER.

Devolution The spreading outwards of power and control; for example, devolving power from Whitehall to Wales or Scotland. Devolution in media terms relates to the loosening of the centralized power of, say, the BBC. See COMMERCIAL RADIO; HUNT REPORT.

Diachronic linguistics The study of LANGUAGE through the course of its history. In contrast, **synchronic liguistics** takes a fixed instant as its point of observation (chiefly a contemporary one). The distinction was first posed by Swiss linguist Ferdinand de Saussure (1857–1913).

Dialect A. dialect is usually regionally based and is a variation within a LANGUAGE which differs from the accepted *standard* in vocabulary, pronunciation and idiom. In post-war years (from 1945) regional dialects have become increasingly accepted for their own inherent value. However, according to Martin Montgomery in *An Introduction to Language and Society* (UK/US: Routledge, 1995), 'within the British Isles many of the more fundamental differences of vocabulary and sentence structure between the English dialects have become eroded. . . . Often, all that remains as a kind of historical residue of the original dialect is its distinctive mode of pronunciation – its accent'. He goes on to point out that, 'But the other kinds of dialect feature have not, of course, died out altogether'. The study of dialect further illuminates connections between CLASS background and language usage in that until recently the use of standard English was associated with an individual of high social status. Dialects, whilst adding richness and variety to a language can also, of course, form a barrier to communication. See ACCENT; COLLOQUIALISM; JARGON; REGISTER; SLANG.

Diary stories See SPOT NEWS.

Diaspora cinema Evelyn Reid uses this term 'Redefining cultural identities' in Sarah Franklin, Celia Lury and Jackie Stacey, eds., *Off-Centre: Feminism and Cultural Studies* (UK: HarperCollins Academic, 1991), to describe recent films aimed at exploring the diaspora experience of black people in Britain – 'colonization, imperialism, migration, displacement, domination, marginalization, exclusion and personal fragmentation'. Such films aim to show the diversity of these experiences. Films mentioned by Reid are: *Territories* (1984);

Passion of Remembrance (1986); and *Handsworth Songs* (1986).

Differential perception The perceptions of each individual or social group are influenced by a number of factors: knowledge, experience, social environment, and personality, for example. The precise nature of the influence these factors have varies with each individual or social group. Thus individuals and social groups are likely to perceive the same information, the same MESSAGE, quite differently. See SELECTIVE EXPOSURE.

Diffusion The process by which innovations spread to the members of a social system. Diffusion studies are concerned with messages that convey new ideas, the processes by which those ideas are conveyed and received, and the extent to which those ideas are adopted or rejected. Appropriateness of CHANNEL to MESSAGE is particularly important. For example, mass media channels are often more useful at creating awareness – knowledge – of new ideas, but interpersonal channels are considered to be more important in changing attitudes towards innovations.

The rate and success of diffusion is very much affected by the NORMS, VALUES and social structures in which the transmission of new ideas takes place. See EFFECTS OF THE MASS MEDIA.

DigiPen Institute of Technology Offered, in 1998, the world's first degree courses in video game development. Established in Redmond, Washington and backed by major games developers and manufacturers such as Nintendo, DigiPen promises not only degree-level training and qualification for would-be games creators, but masters degrees and doctorates in 3D simulation.

Digitalization The computer works digitally: information is broken down into a code of zeros and ones (bits). Today, all forms of electronic communication are converging through digital formats, and computer-mediated communication now applies to newspapers, telephone systems, BROADCASTING, film production as well as the INTERNET. Today, the TEXT of a painting in the Louvre, a song by the Spice Girls, an article in the *Journal of Communication* may be digitalized for transmission, and summoned via website 'libraries' by anyone with a personal computer, modem and telephone line (or ISDN line – Integrated Service Digital Network). Digitalization makes for profusion – of TELEVISION and RADIO channels and of fragmentation. Such are the possibilities in the 'Digital Age' that each viewer or listener ceases to be, as in the past, part of a recognizable AUDIENCE. Specialized, more targeted provision comes at an extra price. Where once the annual licence fee was the only payment for radio and TV services, now reception depends more and more on subscriptions, smartcards and digital conversion boxes. Viewing is becoming almost as expensive as a night at the opera.

Take up the new digital technology, and you pick up the cost of development and the rush for profits. Availability of what has been traditional screen fare for PUBLIC SERVICE BROADCASTING – that is, programmes available for the entire nation to watch – rapidly diminished in the last decade of the 20th c. British digital broadcasting began in 1998, with two rivals in the field, Ondigital and Sky Digital (in which News International has a 40% stake), with government insistence that they must produce compatible technology to minimize consumer confusion.

At the time of writing, the Labour government has not confirmed when the old, analogue system of broadcasting will finally be switched off in favour of digital transmission, though an estimated date is 2015. The cost of conversion or TV replacement is substantial enough to stir doubts in the industry about the future viability of multi-channel provision; and according to the European Commission, digital TV could add £15 to every electricity bill in the country as well as creating a power surge equivalent to the output of one power station.

Digitalization is the ultimate form of CONVERGENCE, technically but also in terms of *control*. All texts converge in the bit, but the investment costs of turning the electronic world digital are enormous, meaning not only that the competition is to be between media giants but that even the major operators will be continually at risk from their competitors. At the same time there are serious worries that in terms of quality of programmes and schedules more may be more of the same – an anxiety expressed by the UK's National Consumer Council. Ruth Evans, director of the Council, has been reported to say that 'Digital television will certainly change things, but only time will tell if the changes are what consumers want'.

A key question is whether segments of the population will be left behind in the new age of subscription and pay-per-view, a fear expressed by Chris Barrie, media business correspondent of the *Guardian* in an article 'Pity the new digital underclass' (6 November 1998). The poor, the elderly and the unemployed, writes Barrie, 'are in danger of being ignored at best and, at worst, run off the information highway into the gutter of technology poverty'; in other words, digitalization is feared to favour the information-rich and widen the INFORMATION GAP between them and the information-poor.

Linked to this are dark predictions about the impact of digitalization on industries and jobs. It is feared that being able to do your banking and shopping from home threatens the structures and practices of commerce and thus of those employed in the selling of goods and services. Some claim the consequences, after the inevitable trauma of change, will settle down: society will be characterized by decentralization, greater personal empowerment in which more and more people work, no longer in offices commuter journeys away, but from home.

Cees Hamelink in *World Communication: Disempowerment & Self-Empowerment* (UK/US: Zed Books, 1995) identifies four major trends in world communications, citing digitalization as the first, and interacting and interlocking with the others – consolidation, deregulation and globalization. The cost of developing digitalization leads to consolidation of ownership and control, which in turn demands the minimum of regulation in order to expand and traverse the boundaries of nation states, and in particular regulations governing and protecting public interest communication. Finally digitalization provides the technological basis for globalization 'as it facilitates the global trading of services, worldwide financial networks, and the spreading of high-technology research and development across the globe'. Preferring to use the word 'digitization', Hamelink says that 'the digital age arrives with a monumental invasion of people's privacy' through the massive collection and sale of personal data, which Hamelink considers, referring to the proliferation of electronic monitoring by employers of their employees, to be 'a fundamental violation of human rights'. He believes that digital technology is creating 'transparent societies, "glass-house" countries that are very vulnerable to external forces and to the loss of their sovereign capacities'.

He registers concern about the unreliability of technology in an age of increasing technology-dependence. 'The magnitude of possible disruptions [to society through computer error, computer breakdown or computer fraud] is mind-boggling. Software bugs, systems malfunction, computer crime and hacking can cost millions of dollars and human lives'. He talks of 'dangerous levels of vulnerability' especially for less powerful users.

Just as the modes of communication consolidate into single-system, digital operation so the institutions of communication themselves consolidate or converge in the creation of mega-companies. This is seen by many commentators to threaten comnpetition, reduce choice, restrict alternative visions and discourses; but it is also seen to put at risk freedom of expression. Hamelink asks, if a conglomerate owner of media warrants 'critical scrutiny' will it permit the media it owns to invesigate and publicize the cause of that scrutiny? He points out the extent of media ownership by companies deeply involved in the arms business: General Electric in the US owns NBC, the National Broadcasting Corporation, and fears for any meaningful debate on arms, disarmament or the arms trade.

Digitalization is seen to be both empowering (to the already powerful) and potentially disempowering (to those with less of it in the first place). In relation to the trend towards deregulation, Hamelink argues that 'tension between public good and private commodity is increasingly resolved to the latter's advantage'. Consequently the 'erosion of the public sphere by implication undermines diversity of information provision . . . everything that does not pass the market threshold because there is not a sufficiently large percentage of consumers, disappears. That may be good for markets, it may be suicidal for democratic politics and creative culture'. See DISEMPOWERMENT.

Digital retouching Or electronic retouching; process whereby laser and computer technology are combined to retouch or recreate photographs. A laser beam scans and measures images and pigmentations, then reduces them into a series of 'pixels', or minute segments. These are then recorded in digital form and stored in the computer's memory for eventual reproduction, which permits the rearrangement of the picture, a re-creation – or just plain faking.

Digital television Traditionally TV has been brought to us using standard analogue waves, but the future for both terrestrial transmission and SATELLITE TRANSMISSION will lie with binary-coded digital signals. Digital TV uses less bandwidth than the analogue mode to transmit the same amount of information, thus it offers many more channels with improved visual and sound quality. Terrestrial digital BROADCASTING will offer approximately 15 new stations, digital satellite around 200. Six frequency channels, called multiplexes, will each carry up to three TV terrestrial channels. The investment costs promise to be immense but so do the profits once the digital revolution gathers momentum. CABLE TELEVISION will also be a substantial party to the digitalization of TV transmission, especially as the UK government policy is for digitalization to apply to BBC1 and 2 and ITV, Channel 4 and Channel 5.

Digital video disc (DVD) Or digital *versatile*. One of a number of VIDEO compression systems, the size of a compact disc (CD) but holding up to 26 times more information.

The DVD allows for four full feature-length FILMS to be stored on a single disc, and permits wide-screen format. The cost of duplication is considerably less than that for VHS tape. DVDs can – unlike video tape – be encrypted, allowing the distributor to control viewing access, and in the case of parents to empower them, through the use of a program password, to restrict what their children view.

The Japanese company Sony, having pioneered the personal stereo, offered the world 'personal cinema'. The Glasstron, employing a pair of wrap-around spectacles with extra flaps, and using Dolby Surround Sound, is the first commuter-friendly cinema. It allows the viewer to watch movies on what to the brain appears to be a 52-inch screen. The DVD slots into a battery-driven, hand-held player. It provides facilities not available to the traditional filmgoer, permitting its audience of one a choice of alternative endings, along with interviews with actors and directors and supplementary film information.

Direct cinema Term used to describe the work of post-2nd World War DOCUMENTARY film makers in the US, such as Albert Maysles (*Salesman*, 1969 and *Gimme Shelter*, 1970), who coined the phrase, Stephen Leacock (*Don't Look Back*, 1968) and Frederick Wiseman (*High School*, 1968). New, lightweight equipment and improved SYNCHRONOUS SOUND recording facilities made the work of these observer-documentarists an inspiration for film makers in many other countries. Direct cinema went out into the world and recorded life as it happened, in the 'raw'. An earlier, and British, link with this mode of film making was *Free cinema*, a short-lived 'collective' of directors in London, organized by Karel Reisz (*Momma Don't Allow*, 1956) and Lindsay Anderson (*O Dreamland*, 1953). Direct cinema filmmakers had the technical edge on Free cinema because of the availability of superior sound recording. See CINÉMA VÉRITÉ.

Disconfirmation See CONFIRMATION/DISCONFIRMATION.

Discourse A form, mode or GENRE of LANGUAGE-USE. Each person has in his/her repertoire a whole range of possible discourses – the language of love, of authority, of sport, of the domestic scene. In a media sense, an example of a discourse would be the NEWS, reflecting in its choice of language and style of presentation the social, economic, political and cultural context from which the discourse emanates.

Gunther Kress in *Linguistic Processes in Sociocultural Practice* (Australia: Deakin University Press, 1985), provides the following useful explanation of discourse: 'Institutions and social groupings have specific meanings and values which are articulated in language in systematic ways. Following the work particularly of Michel Foucault, I refer to these systematically-organized modes of talking as DISCOURSE. Discourses . . . give expression to the meanings and values of an institution. Beyond that, they define, describe and delimit what is possible to say and not possible to say (and by extension what is possible to do or not to do) with respect to the area of concern of that institution, whether marginally or centrally. A discourse provides a set of possible statements about a given area, and organizes and gives structure to the manner in which a particular topic, object, process is to be talked about. In that it provides descriptions, rules, permissions and prohibitions of social and individual action.'

The analysis of discourses is central to the study of media which is essentially about how TEXTS are encoded and how the MEANING of those texts, operating within and influenced by **contexts**, is decoded. Discourses are, in the words of John Fiske, 'socially produced' and a 'socially located way of making sense of an important area of experience'. Reality is a constant part of experience – how is it reconstructed into discourse? And how is it influenced by other discourses? (See INTERTEXTUALITY.)

All discourses are framed within *narratives* of one form or another. In news, or indeed in fiction, the *story* is what happens, the discourse how the story is told and the CONNOTATIONS or meanings embedded within it – the PREFERRED READINGS. Discourses struggle for attention, some are dominant and thus hold the public key to the definition of reality. They rigorously conform to

conventions which work through mechanisms of information control (See AGENDA SETTING; CONSENSUS; GATEKEEPING) and are IDEOLOGY-driven (See CONFLICTUAL OPPOSITIONS; DEMONIZATION; PHOTO-NEGATIVIZATION; NEWS VALUES; WEDOM, THEYDOM.)

Ultimately discourse is about ruling explanations and thus contributes to the nature of MYTH. Christopher P. Campbell in *Race, Myth and the News* (US: Sage, 1995) sees myth not as the 'grand storytelling tradition associated with ancient cultures' but in the 'sense of the stories that modern societies unwittingly create to reduce life's contradictions and complexities'. This is what discourse of news does, it 'comprises continuing stories which uphold and consolidate myth which ultimately focuses on order and disorder'. Campbell argues that 'News is a way of creating order out of disorder, offering cultural meanings, resolutions and reassurances'.

Discourse serves (and services) myth and the desired end-product is COMMON SENSE; in other words a state of affairs in which that which is defined by discourses is so patently commonsensical that it cannot be seriously contradicted. Campbell identifies the divisive rather than cohesive potential of commonsensical discourse: 'The danger of the commonsense claim to truth is in its exclusion of those who live outside the familiar world it represents.' See DOMINANT DISCOURSE.
* Sue Wilkinson and Celia Kitzinger, eds., *Feminism and Discourse: Psychological Perspectives* (UK: Sage, 1995).

Discourse analysis Form of MASS COMMUNICATION analysis which concentrates upon the *ways* in which the media convey information, focusing on the LANGUAGE of presentation – linguistic patterns, word and phrase selection (lexical choices), grammatical constructions and story coherence. In particular, discourse analysis sets out to account for the textual form in which the mass media present IDEOLOGY to readership or audience. See CONTENT ANALYSIS; MODES OF MEDIA ANALYSIS.

Discourse of power The French philosopher Michel Foucault wrote that *all* arguments as to the truth are driven by the will to power, that is exert control. Clearly, in terms of the media, discourses are perceived as means of exerting influence and control over audiences. Foucault saw the field of a discourse in the same way that a physicist sees the electromagnetic field: it is defined not by its will to truth, but by its will to power. A discourse seeks power and that is what marks out its range. See HEGEMONY; IDEOLOGY.

Discursive communication Susanne Langer in *Philosophy in a New Key* (US: Harvard University Press, 1942) differentiated between what she named discursive communication – prose and logic – and non-discursive communication, such as poetry, music and ritual.

Discursive gap Professor Roger Fowler coins this phrase in his book *Language in the News: Discourse and Ideology in the Press* (UK: Routledge, 1991). The 'gap' is that which exists between the mode of address of the newspaper – formal, bureaucratic – and that of the perceived reception mode of the reader – informal and *personal*, especially readers of the popular press.

Fowler argues that 'the fundamental device in narrowing the discursive gap is the promotion of oral models within the printed newspaper text, giving an illusion of conversation in which common sense is spoken about matters on which there is consensus'. Fowler believes 'the basic task for the writer is to word institutional statements (those of the newspaper, and those of its sources) in a style appropriate to interpersonal communication, because the reader is an individual and must be addressed as such. The task is not only stylistic, but also ideological: institutional concepts have to be translated into personal thought'. In brief, the press employs a range of devices to simulate a sense of 'orality' which has the writer sitting next to the reader around the kitchen table or in the pub and joining in a process of 'co-production'; the product being CONSENSUS, an apparently shared vision of the world.

Disempowerment The taking away, from individuals, groups, communities or nations of the power to have control over their lives. In *World Communication: Disempowerment*

& Self-Empowerment (UK/US: Zed Books, 1995), Cees Hamelink describes disempowerment as 'the reduction of people's ability to define themselves and construct their own identities'. It can be the result of a deliberate strategy or the unintended outcome of developments locally, nationally or internationally. As a strategy, says Hamelink, disempowerment 'often employs the deceit of making people believe that existing conditions are desirable and preferred out of free will. The most perverse form of disempowerment makes people accept their own dependency and second rate position'. A complicating factor in the assessment of the motives lying behind disempowerment 'is the real possibility of people inviting their own disempowerment'. In communication terms, disempowerment arises from the denial of access to, or the mediated access to, information and knowledge, for dominance 'does not only operate through imposition, but also through deprivation'. The PRIVATIZATION of communications is seen as an agent of disempowerment: 'As knowledge is created and controlled as private 'property, knowledge as common good is destroyed.' For Hamelink the inherent meaning of privatization is *private = to deprive*.

It follows that if communication is a key tool in the process of empowerment it can similarly be used as a tool of empowerment. Strategies of empowerment include *regulation*, the provision of power to people through human rights legislation (such as a FREEDOM OF INFORMATION Act or laws facilitating a RIGHT OF REPLY) or public-interest regulation (such as the Charter of the BBC).

Regulation can also be seen in national press councils, usually voluntary arrangements, created to protect the public against abuses committed by newspapers and journals. The weaknesses of these forms of empowerment are many and varied: voluntary WATCHDOGS can so easily end up dogs without teeth, without the power to insist that media perform according to empowerment principles; and all of this pressupposes that the law itself is a force for equality, of access and treatment.

Another key to empowerment is education, 'the need to make people critically aware of how media are organized, how they function, and how their contents can be analysed', in other words, media education. Once again, problems abound, but the provision of media education is critical. Hamelink quotes Len Masterman in *Teaching the Media* (UK: Comedia, 1985) who believes that 'Media education is an essential step in the long march towards a truly participatory democracy, and the democratization of our institutions'.

Local action in relation to the media, local or community use of the media is a further option in the pursuit of empowerment, that is, horizontal media developments employed to counteract the vertical, hierarchical, big-business orientation currently dominant. The danger here, argues Hamelink, is that in many cases 'the alternative structures end up emulating the dominant model and seem incapable of escaping the technical and aesthetic standards of the professional community'. In any case, the possible scale of such enterprises, even with generous technical provision and support, is inevitably small. Hamelink believes that 'By and large, all efforts in technical assistance to increase the communicative power of people in the South have furthered their disempowerment through economic, technical, and cultural forms of dependency upon donor countries and institutions'.

All of these remedies lack, in Hamelink's view, a 'global dimension'. Indeed the author believes that a reversal of current domination of cultural and information processes by transnational corporations, mega-companies, 'must come from the people themselves'. He speaks of a 'duty to revolt against the worlds of Orwell and Huxley' for citizenship 'cannot be limited to a nationality, a state. People have always a double citizenship, in their state and in their world. What is needed is people's empowerment on a global scale'. See PEOPLE'S COMMUNICATION CHARTER.

Disenfranchisement (of readership)
Researchers have commented on the extent to which some newspapers reflect an assumption – possibly that of the owners and editors – that their readership is totally uninvolved and uninterested in the political processes and events of the country. It is as if the readers were politically **disenfranchised**, not able to participate in the political process, and thus news of political affairs is of no concern to them. Such papers aim to entertain, to concentrate on stories of human interest and drama rather than to inform.

Disinformation Derives from the Russian, 'Dezinformatsiya', a term especially associated with the former Soviet Union's secret service, the KGB. It applied to the use of forgery and other techniques to discredit targeted governments, persons or policies. The process of disinformation is, of course, as old as mankind, and sowing the seeds of disinformation is matched by accusing the *opposition* of spreading disinformation. See EFFECTS OF THE MASS MEDIA.

Displacement In psychological theory, Displacement is one of the major mechanisms of ego-defence identified by Freud. Displacement occurs when an individual chooses an alternative focus for the expression of feelings and emotions because he/she feels unable to express them towards their real target – the 'kick the cat' syndrome.

Displacement effect Refers to the reorganization of activities which takes place with the introduction of some new interest or attention-drawer, such as TV. Activities such as reading may be cut down, or stopped altogether, to make time for viewing. New media 'displace' or adjust the placement of other media. Cinema-going habits have been substantially affected by the introduction of TV, even more so with access to films on video.

The notion of *functional similarity* has often been applied as a yardstick to measure the extent and nature of displacement: if the new is functionally similar to the old, then the old is likely to be displaced. Functionally dissimilar activities are likely to hold their own. The difficulty is in establishing what functions a MEDIUM actually serves, which means that displacement is all the more difficult to assess. As a result of TV, do people talk less, read less, go out with friends less, socialize less? Does TV mop up marginal activities, displace real with second-hand experience; does it displace 'daydreaming'? Evidence concerning people's reactions to programmes is so open to influence from INTERVENING VARIABLES that it is difficult to use it as a basis for reliable theory. That people stay in and watch TV more instead of dining out at a restaurant may have nothing to do with TV and everything to do with financial necessity. See EFFECTS OF THE MASS MEDIA; USES AND GRATIFICATIONS THEORY.

Disqualifying communication A form of self-protection, or DEFENSIVE COMMUNICATION when, in a situation causing embarrassment, anxiety or uneasiness, people talk aimlessly about, say, the weather, or go into a variety of non-verbal responses in order to avoid direct communication. The politician's version of this is 'No comment'. See INTERPERSONAL COMMUNICATION.

Dissolve A process in camera-work by which one picture fades out and the following scene fades in on top of it. Also called a 'mix'. See SHOT.

Dissonance Occurs when two COGNITIVE inputs to our mental processes are out of line. The result is a certain amount of psychological discomfort. Action is usually taken to resolve the dissonance and restore balance. Several strategies are commonly employed in order to achieve this: downgrading the source of dissonance; compliance with rather than acceptance of new expectations and ideas; changing one's previous ideas and attitudes; and avoidance of the source of dissonance.

All MESSAGES, particularly those conveyed to a mass audience, are potentially a source of dissonance to someone. If they disturb the intended receiver(s), then they may well be ignored or rejected. The need for messages intended for a mass audience to be successful, however, ensures that such messages are often well 'laundered' in order to reduce their potential offensiveness. See CONGRUENCE THEORY; SELECTIVE EXPOSURE.

Diversification In media terms, the spread of ownership and control into a wide range of associated, and often unassociated, products and services. Thus newspapers have moved into TV share-holding; TV companies into set rentals, bingo and social clubs and motorway catering services. In parallel, great corporations have moved into media ownership – oil companies buying up newspaper chains and investing in BROADCASTING interests, book publishing and record production. The result of diversification is often, paradoxically, concentration of control, and a real danger to a newspaper, film company or publishing house of being just another 'product' on the shelf of the multi-national conglomerate whose objective is profit maximization above all other considerations. See CONGLOMERATES; DIGITALIZATION.

D-Notices Defence notices; British government memoranda requesting newspapers not to publish specific items of information considered by authority to pose a security risk if widely disseminated. Notices are issued by the Services, Press and Broadcasting Committee. They have no binding force at law, even in wartime, but a newspaper or broadcasting station defies the D-Notice at its peril.

A form of pre-emptive CENSORSHIP, the D-Notice system was most famously challenged by the *Daily Express* on 21 February 1967, with its headline story 'Cable Vetting Sensation' based upon evidence that copies of private cables were carried off for routine inspection by the security services. Colonel L.G. Logan of the D-Notice Committee had declared that publication of the information contravened the D-Notice memoranda of 1956 and 1961 against revealing 'secret intelligence or counter-intelligence methods and activities in or outside the United Kingdom'.

The then Labour government set up a Committee of privy counsellors under Lord Radcliffe to investigate. Radcliffe reported that the *Express* story was 'not inaccurate in any sense' and that no secret information had been revealed. The government took no further action except to produce a face-saving White Paper, *The D-Notice System* in June 1967. It is difficult to ascertain whether D-Notices have worked more effectively or less effectively since that time because, by the very nature of the system, we only hear about it when it breaks down. See OFFICIAL SECRETS ACT.

Documentary Any mode of communication which, in addressing an audience, **documents** events or situations – books, radio, theatre, photography, film or TV. Usually based upon recorded or observable fact, the documentary may aim for objectivity or PROPAGANDA; it may, however, in terms of *human* documentation, be highly subjective. 'Even when temperate', writes William Stott in *Documentary Expression and Thirties America* (US/UK: Oxford University Press, 1973), 'a human document carries and communicates feeling, the raw material of drama.'

British film director, producer and theorist John Grierson (1898–1972) is thought to have been first to use the word Documentary, in a New York *Sun* review (1926) of Robert Flaherty's film *Moana*, a study of the way of life of the South Seas islanders. In fact, 'documentary' is as old as the cinema itself. Louis Lumière's early short films of 1895, one showing the demolition of a wall, another of a train coming into a station, can be described as documentaries.

The founding father of documentary film making in the UK and later in Canada, Grierson never claimed scientific objectivity for such films. For him the documentary was far more than a straightforward reconstruction on film of reality. He spoke of the 'creative use of actuality' in which the director re-formed fact in order to reach towards an inner truth.

Indeed when documentarists have felt it necessary to get at the truth of a subject as they perceive it, they have not held back from fictionalization, often using actors, often turning the real-life person into an actor recreating a scene.

In the 1930s film documentary ran parallel with radio documentary – the BBC showed considerable innovative enterprise in this field, especially its Manchester studio – and, in the US, many impressive publications combined documentary evidence with outstanding photography. The themes were very often those of the Depression: concern at the plight of the poor, the unemployed, the alienated; and the mode was largely to have the people speak for themselves rather than distance the impact of their experience by using the MEDIATION of a commentator.

The documentary approach has been a recurring feature in modern theatre, especially from the 1960s. Historical or contemporary events on stage are far from new: Aeschylus dramatized the victory of Marathon (490 BC) and Shakespeare reconstructed history, often to fit the perceptions of the Tudor monarchy, in a third of his output. German dramatist Rolf Hochhuth won worldwide attention with his documentary drama *The Representative* in 1963, on the subject of the Papacy and the Jews during the 2nd World War (1939–43). He followed this up with *Soldiers* (1967) based upon the alleged involvement of British Prime Minister Winston Churchill in the wartime death of the Polish General Sikorski. In the UK, Peter Brook's highly successful *US* (1966) was an indictment of American involvement in the Vietnam war.

On-stage documentaries – in the US often termed the *Theatre of Fact* – have frequently been presented with the aid of official and press reports, original diaries, projected photographs, tape recordings and NEWSREEL films. In the case of the Royal Court production, *Falkland Sound* (1983), a moving – and damning – recollection of the Falklands War (1982) was presented through the letters home of a young naval officer killed in action.

Faction or *Dramadoc* are terms mainly associated with TV documentaries in which actors recreate historical lives, such as the BBC's *The Voyage of Charles Darwin* (1978) or play the part of famous people of the immediate past, such as Thames Television's *Edward and Mrs Simpson* (1978), Southern TV's *Winston Churchill – The Wilderness Years* (1981), and ITV's *Kennedy* (1983). To TV producers faction has come to represent an ideal synthesis of education, information and entertainment, albeit highly selective and deeply coloured by contemporary perspectives. See CINEMATOGRAPHY, ORIGINS; CINÉMA VÉRITÉ; DIRECT CINEMA; FLY ON THE WALL; RADIO BALLADS; SOAPS: DOCU-SOAPS.

Dolby system Electronic coding process originally developed to reduce unwanted sound, such as hiss, on tape recording equipment. Dolby studios expanded into cinema sound which led to the introduction of 35mm optical stereo.

Dolly A trolley on which a camera unit can be soundlessly moved about during shooting; can usually be mounted on rails. A 'crab dolly' will move in any direction.

Domestication of the foreign See NEWS: GLOBALIZATION OF.

Dominant culture See CULTURE.

Dominant discourse In a general sense, discourse is talk; converse; holding forth in speech and writing on a subject. We are referring both to the content of communicative exchanges and to the level at which those exchanges take place, and in what mode or STYLE as well as to whom the discourse is addressed. A dominant discourse is that which takes precedence over others, reducing alternative content, alternative approaches to 'holding forth' to *subordinate* discourses. All public discourse is socially and culturally based, thus it follows that the dominant discourse is usually that which emanates from those dominant in the social and cultural order:

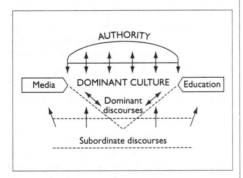

See DISCOURSE; ELITE; IDEOLOGY; HEGEMONY; POWER ELITE.

Dominant, subordinate, radical Three categories of response in terms of the *reading* of media messages on the part of audience are posed by Frank Parkin in *Class, Inequality and Political Order* (UK: Paladin, 1972). Do we accept what is told us, only half accept or substantially reject it? Parkin argues that it is our place in the social

structure which conditions our response. Stuart Hall in 'The determination of news photographs' in Stanley Cohen and Jock Young, eds., *The Manufacture of News* (UK: Constable, 1973) supports Parkin's view, with the same categories but different terminology.

The **dominant** system of response (Hall calls it a *dominant* CODE) signifies that the dominant VALUES and existing society are wholly accepted by the respondent; the **subordinate** response (Hall's *negotiated code*) indicates general acceptance of dominant values and existing social structures, but the respondent is prepared to argue that a particular group – blacks, unemployed, women – within that structure may be unfairly dealt with and that something should be done about it. The **radical** response (Hall's *oppositional code*) rejects the PREFERRED READING of the dominant code and the social VALUES that produced it.

David Morley's researches into audience response, published in *The Nationwide Audience* (UK: British Film Institute, 1980), give substance to Parkin and Hall's division of response, but also emphasize other response-conditioning factors such as education, occupation, political affiliation, geographical region, religion and family. See EFFECTS OF THE MASS MEDIA; ETHNOGRAPHIC (APPROACH TO AUDIENCE MEASUREMENT); POLYSEMY.

Double exposure Two pictures superimposed upon one another on the same piece of FILM. Like reverse motion, double exposure in filming began by being a simple visual curiosity before it became a fully fledged means of artistic expression. It was first used in still photography, where double or multiple exposure images produced what was described as 'spirit photography'. Georges Meliès (1861–1938) used it in his films from 1908. It has been used dramatically to achieve many effects, chiefly that of suggesting the supernatural and of conveying the process of thought and of spirituality.

Doughnut Principle, The See ORGANIZATION CULTURES.

Dramadoc See DOCUMENTARY.

Dress Dress is an important element of non-verbal communication and one that plays a significant role when people are forming FIRST IMPRESSIONS of one another. Generally speaking Dress refers not only to clothes but also to hairstyle, jewellery, fashion accessories and make-up. Dress can communicate many messages about personality, cultural or group identity – GENDER, CLASS, STATUS, wealth, age, roles, fashion-consciousness, STEREOTYPES, social context, historical context, to name but a few. A person may consciously or unconsciously convey messages through dress and, of course, receivers may decode these messages differently to what was intended by the sender; several receivers may decode the messages differently from each other. Dress particularly uniforms, can though convey quite clear messages. See COMMUNICATION, NON-VERBAL; OBJECT LANGUAGE.
* Dick Hebdige, *Sub-Culture: The Meaning of Style* (UK: Methuen, 1979); Ken Gelder and Sarah Thornton, eds., *The Sub-Cultures Reader* (UK: Routledge, 1997).

Dry-run TV programme rehearsal in which action, lines, cues, etc. are tried out prior to the final rehearsal.

Dub In FILM making, to blend speech, music, incidental sound and sound effects on to film or videotape. At a later stage, the LANGUAGE of the 'home' AUDIENCE may be dubbed on to the sound track in preference to subtitles.

Dubbing See POST-SYNCHRONIZATION.

Dumping World-wide practice, led by the US, of saturating foreign markets with BROADCASTING material, extremely cheap to hire in comparison with the cost of home companies making their own original programmes. See MEDIA IMPERIALISM.

Duopoly A monopoly held by two organizations rather than one. In BROADCASTING, the term is used to refer to the duopoly once held by the BBC and the IBA (Independent Broadcasting Authority; succeeded in 1991 by the ITC – Independent Television Commission). See MEDIA CONTROL.

Dyad A communication dyad consists of two persons interacting and is the elemental unit of INTERPERSONAL COMMUNICATION.

Dynamic mediation See IMPARTIALITY.

E

Eady Plan, or Eady Levy See BRITISH FILM PRODUCTION FUND.

Early Bird satellite Owned by the US Communications Satellite Corporation, Early Bird was the first of its kind to be used in the operation of long-distance inter-continental TELEPHONE services. It went into service on 28 June 1965.

Eastmancolor Colour filmstock now used universally in FILM making.

Echelon An automated global computer intelligence-gathering network run in partnership between the UK Government Communication Headquarter Agency (GCHQ) and the US National Security; using the intelligence agencies' own network of satellite and listening bases. So-termed Echelon Dictionaries search intercepted messages according to target lists of subjects and people.

Eco-horror Term sometimes used to describe a FILM or TELEVISION programme whose plot is based on the central characters' struggle for survival, usually in the wild, in the face of a variety of threats from the forces of nature. An example here is *Long Weekend* (1977).

Effects of the mass media Can be broadly defined as any change induced directly or indirectly by the recording, filming or reporting of events. Analysts of effects, or impact, are concerned with the modification of attitudes and of behaviour of individuals and GROUPS and the process of measuring these effects is immensely complicated, as the ground upon which the measurements are taken is constantly shifting.

The **actual effect** of the media on audiences, so far as it can be ascertained, is arguably less significant than the **perceived effect**. In the 19th c. those in authority were of the view that access by the mass of the population to the printed word might turn docility into uprising. The new mass MEDIUM of the cinema was similarly accused of a wide range of 'effects', while TV, in the eyes of some, is responsible for many of the ills of our time, as though such media could be somehow divorced from the social, political and cultural environment which produce them.

A few generalized hypotheses about effects can be tentatively posited: the media are probably more likely to modify and reinforce attitudes than change them; media impact will be greater among the uncommitted ('floating voters') than the committed; impact will be more influential if all the media are saying more or less the same thing at the same time (CONSISTENCY); equally, if the media are concentrating on a small rather than diverse number of stories (INTENSITY) and if they are repeating messages, images, viewpoints over and over again (FREQUENCY).

'The timing of communication processes,' writes C. Seymour-Ure in *The Political Impact of Mass Media* (UK: Constable, 1974) 'is probably one of the most important determinants of mass media effects.' If the timing is right, the media can often be the arbiters of crisis, by being in the most prominent position to define it. Because of their AGENDA SETTING capacity, the media have influence upon the criteria which, in the public domain, decide what is important and what is not, what is normal and what is DEVIANT, what is CONSENSUS and what is *dissensus*, what is significant, or newsworthy and what is marginal.

No summary of effects, however brief, should neglect the role played – some would say most powerfully – by the media in supporting, reinforcing and cementing patterns of social control, not the least by maintaining and sometimes fashioning the symbols of legitimate government. See ALIENATION EFFECT; AUDIENCE MEASUREMENT; CATALYST EFFECT; CATHARSIS HYPOTHESIS; COGNITIVE (AND AFFECTIVE); DISPLACEMENT EFFECT; FRAMING: MEDIA; FRANKFURT SCHOOL OF THEORISTS; HYPHENIZED ABRIDGEMENT; INTERCULTURAL INVASION (AND THE MASS MEDIA); INTERVENING VARIABLES (IV); LOONY LEFTISM; MAINSTREAMING; McCOMBS AND SHAW AGENDA SETTING MODE OF MEDIA EFFECTS, 1976; MEAN WORLD SYN-

DROME; MEDIATION; MULTIPLIER EFFECT; NARCOTICIZING DYSFUNCTION; PSEUDO-CONTEXT; REINFORCEMENT; RESONANCE; SLOW-DRIP; SOCIALIZATION; SOCIOMETRICS (AND MEDIA ANALYSIS); USES AND GRATIFICATIONS THEORY.

* J.M. McLeod, G.M. Kosicki and Z. Pan, 'On understanding and misunderstanding media effects,' in *Mass Media and Society*, J. Curran and M. Gurevitch, eds., (UK: Edward Arnold, 1991); Greg Philo, *Seeing and Believing: The Influence of Television* (UK: Routledge, 1990); F. Kerzenny, S. Ting-Toomey, with E. Schiff, eds., *Mass Media Effects Across Cultures* (UK: Sage, 1992); Shearon A. Lowery and Melvyn L. DeFleur, *Milestones in Mass Media Research: Media Effects* (US: Longman, 1995).

Elaborated and Restricted Codes In *Class, Codes and Control* Vol. 1 (UK: Paladin, 1971), Basil Bernstein posed a now-famous classification of language codes, the *Elaborated* and *Restricted* codes based upon researches into the language-use of children. Bernstein maintains that there are substantial differences in speech between middle CLASS and working class children, the former using the Elaborated Code, the latter the Restricted Code.

The determinant of the code in each case is the nature of the social relationships and influences to which the child is exposed. A close-knit, traditional working class community, Bernstein argues, tends to use the **Restricted Code** because a high degree of shared MEANING is assumed. In the more typically loose-knit middle class communities there are fewer grounds for making assumptions about shared meaning and therefore a more *explicit*, **Elaborated**, Code is used. This is not to say that the middle class do not possess their own Restricted codes in particular social or professional situations. The important point is that the middle classes can move with ease from a Restricted to an Elaborated code.

The Restricted Code tends to be less complex than the Elaborated, with a small vocabulary and simpler sentence structure. It tends to be spoken rather than written. It is easy to predict (high in REDUNDANCY) whereas the Elaborated Code is less easy to predict (high in ENTROPY). The Restricted Code is orientated towards social relations, towards COMMONALITY, while the Elaborated

Code represents a great emphasis on individuality and individual differences.

The one is the language of the street, the home, the playground, the pub; the other – very largely – the language of school; the language of formal education. Thus, Bernstein indicates, within the educational context, the user of the Restricted Code is placed at a disadvantage.

Bernstein does not argue that the Elaborated Code is superior to the Restricted Code, only that it is different and more useful for upward social mobility.

Bernstein's claims prompted considerable debate, some of it critical, and a number of researchers would argue that his classifcation was inflexible. Martin Montgomery, for instance, in *An Introduction to Language and Society* (UK/US: Routledge, 1995) argues that 'There is, for example, in the final analysis hardly any linguistic evidence to support the division of speech into two mutually exclusive codes or speech variants. And by the same token, Berstein's treatment of the social structure looks with hindsight somewhat rigid and schematic'.

* B. Bernstein, 'Social class, language and socialization', an extract from his major work, in J. Corner and J. Hawthorn, eds., *Communication Studies* (UK: Arnold, 1993).

Electreotactile illusion By means of VIR-TUAL REALITY technology the *feel* of something is stimulated and simulated: the touch of (virtual) sandpaper, of (virtual) skin, hair, marble, leather; usually created by data gloves installed with a tactile feedback system.

Electronic democracy See INTERACTIVE TELEVISION.

Electronic mail: E-mail The sending and receiving of E-mails – letter and memos through the 'postal' system of the computer – has become the fastest-growing means of communication in business, within institutions and between friends, families and total strangers across the world. It is possible to e-mail the President of the United States or to send a message to a colleague in the office next door or even to the person sitting right next to you, assuming, that is, that the intended receiver is actually reading his or her e-mail. E-mailing has spawned on-line love-affairs, marriages and in some cases bigamy. It has proved a useful tool in the exchange of knowledge, the provision of advice, the two-way transmission of research data and the sharing across social and national boundaries of a myriad of problems. It serves as a link between groups and communities of like interest – all at the price of a local phone-call.

It is estimated that in the US in 1998 almost 4 trillion e-mails were sent. In 1992 only 2 per cent of the American population used the e-mail service. This had risen in 1998 to 15 per cent. The rise in what has been referred to as 'computer babble' – both for business and leisure use – is such that e-mails now constitute a problem as much as an opportunity. The *Wall Street Journal* has gauged that a typical worker in a European company deals with an average 150 e-mails a day. Allowing time to read these and reply, it would take some four to five hours to process – a dramatic case of information overload. The *Journal* reported that an executive returning to the States from a business trip in Europe found 2000 e-mails waiting to be dealt with.

E-mails are also very public statements, open to the scrutiny of those not intended to read them. Then there is the growth of junk e-mails, as a *Guardian* leader of 19 January 1999 puts it, 'unsolicited e-mails from companies advertising their wares, or net nuts who believe that the whole world hangs on their thoughts'. As for ENCRYPTING messages in and out, the *Guardian* believes that 'the remedy may be worse than the disease'. As the INTERNET grows in popularity, e-mails will become INFORMATION BLIZZARDS. 'Soon,' the *Guardian* fears, 'it may be ripe to re-invent the envelope.'

Electronic newsgathering Referred to as ENG, the gathering of sound and vision news reports electronically, usually transmitted via telephone links or from transmitter vans. Much lighter and more compact than traditional film or TV cameras, electronic equipment records on to cassette, bypassing the film processing stage: pictures from the scene of action can be transmitted directly or stored electronically. EFP – Electronic Field Production is an advance on ENG, making location programmes of all kinds possible without having the cameras tied to an outside broadcasting (OB) vehicle.

Electronic newspaper At the push of a TV button – all the nation's newspapers. Already VIDEO and CABLE TELEVISION are being seen as electronic bookstalls. It is too early to predict that in future paper will stay in the trees for it will be difficult if not impossible by electronic means to create the flexibility of the newspaper in terms of *where* it can be read. See CYBERSPACE; DIGITALIZATION; INTERNET; TELETEXT; VIEWDATA.

Electronic publishing The replacement of traditional modes of PRINTING, storage and dissemination of paper by electronic means. See ELECTRONIC MAIL; VIEWDATA.

Electrophone 'Piped' entertainment through the CHANNEL of a TELEPHONE line, and thence through headphones, was available in the UK as early as 1895, 27 years before regular radio, 41 years before regular TV broadcasts, and over 80 years before cable television. The Electrophone Company of Gerrard Street, London, provided for a modest outlay a year's programmes of nightly selections of THEATRE performances, shows from the music halls and concerts, plus dozens of Sunday services.

Formed in 1894 by H.S.J. Booth, the company had 50 subscribers in London by 1896, 100 by 1919 and over 2000 by 1923. The coming of 'wireless' rendered the success of Electrophone short-lived, though transmission continued in Bournemouth till 1937.

Elite A small group within a society who may be socially acknowledged as superior in some sense and who influence or control some or all sectors of the society. Several definitions of the term elite exist and these influence the precise focus of research into the relationship between the media, elites, and society.

Early writers generally see the elite as a ruling elite or oligarchy whose power is general and affects most aspects of society. Writers, such as Vilfredo Pareto (1848–1923)

and Gaetano Mosca (1848–1941) regarded elites as being inevitable, whatever the political system.

C. Wright Mills in a study of elites in US society entitled *The Power Elite* (US: Oxford University Press, 1956) points to the similarity of backgrounds, attitudes and values, and power skills of the members of the three elites which, he argues, dominate American Society: the military, the economic and the political. He also comments on the degree of personal and family contacts between elite members and the interchangeability of personnel between top posts in the military, economic and political elites from which the 'power elite' is recruited. This concept of elite cohesion has been of interest to several media researchers who have sought to investigate links between members of economic and political elites and those who own or control the media, and the effect such links might have on media output.

The connections which run between the various elites within British society have also been explored by a number of analysts. Jeremy Paxman, for example, in *Friends in High Places: Who Runs Britain* (UK: Penguin, 1990), argues that traditionally in Britain such connections were not uncommon: 'The great institutions were run by people who had been to the same schools, spoke with the same accents, and shared the same values.' Paxman identifies in particular the public schools, Oxbridge and the Inns of Court as key institutions passed through by many who later found themselves in positions of considerable power. Whilst this connection may be weaker of late, its still-current strength should not, he argues be overlooked. Some of those enjoying powerful positions in the media also share such backgrounds.

The notion of a ruling elite or oligarchy contrasts with the Marxist concept of a ruling CLASS. Whilst elite theorists point out the necessity for the elite to recruit from outside itself, to remain accessible to the influence of the non-elite and to maintain a consensus among the non-elite which legitimates the elite's right to rule, Marxist analysis stresses the continuing and increasing *polarization* or separation of the ruling from the ruled class. Marxist analysis of the media therefore concentrates upon the role of the media in propagating the ideas of the dominant class in order to create a false consciousness, or to create HEGEMONY, which is instrumental in subjugating the rest.

The concern that the mass media are used by an elite to manipulate the masses is not only to be found in Marxist critiques of the media. Much early research into media effects centred on the notion that the media could become a powerful PROPAGANDA tool by which the few could control the socially isolated citizens of a mass society.

The liberalist–PLURALIST school of analysis sees the media as a kind of FOURTH ESTATE pressuring governing elites and reminding them of their dependency on majority opinion. Other commentators have pointed to the role social elites play in media *coverage*. Stuart Hall in 'The determination of news photographs', in Stanley Cohen and Jock Young, eds., *The Manufacture of News: Deviance, Social Problems and the Mass Media* (UK: Constable, 1973), comments that 'Newspapers are full of the actions, situations and attributes of elite persons'. Other commentators have also argued that the unequal distribution of power in Britain, and thus the eliteness of the power holder, are reflected in the degree of attention paid to such people in the media. Similarly, considerable space is devoted to the activities of elite, powerful nations.

Elite persons often serve as objects of general IDENTIFICATION; the elite can be used to say something about situations or events which affect everybody. In the UK the Royal Family are regularly used for this purpose. See COMMANDERS OF THE SOCIAL ORDER; DOMINANT DISCOURSE; ESTABLISHMENT; GUARD DOG METAPHOR; NEWS VALUES; POWER ELITE.

Ellipsis jump-cut See SOUND-BITE.

Ellul's theory of technique See TECHNIQUE: ELLUL'S THEORY OF TECHNIQUE.

E-mail See ELECTRONIC MAIL.

Emancipatory use of the media Term employed by Hans Magnus Enzensberger in 'Constituents of a theory of the media' in Denis McQuail, ed., *Sociology of Mass Communication* (UK: Penguin, 1972) to contrast with what he defines as the **Repressive use of the media**. He characterizes the Emancipatory use of the media as follows: decentralized programme (as opposed to the Repressive mode of a *centrally* controlled programme); each receiver a potential transmitter (as opposed to one transmitter, many receivers); mobilization of the masses (as opposed to immobilization of isolated individuals); interaction of those involved, and FEEDBACK (as opposed to passive consumer behaviour); a political learning process (as opposed to depoliticization); and collective production, social control by self-organization (as opposed to production by specialists, control by property owners or bureaucracy). See DOMINANT, SUBORDINATE, RADICAL.

Embargo Restriction set upon a news item, indicating when that item can be published or broadcast. A PRESS release from government or industry, for example, will be headed 'Not for publication/broadcasting until . . .' and give a specific date.

Emblem See NON-VERBAL BEHAVIOUR: REPERTOIRE.

Emergent culture Raymond Williams uses this term in *Marxism and Literature* (UK: Oxford University Press, 1977) when he argues that HEGEMONY, the state of cultural dominance of a POWER ELITE over the population, is never complete; that the DOMINANT DISCOURSES which operate in the hegemonic process are countered by alternative ways of seeing, reading and believing. Each emergent culture enters into debate or conflict with the dominant culture and is an agent for the mobilization of opposition to hegemonic control.

'No mode of production and therefore no dominant social order,' Williams writes, 'ever in reality includes or exhausts all human practice, human energy, and human intention.' There are residual VALUES and MEANINGS which represent 'areas of human experience, aspiration, and achievement which the dominant culture neglects, undervalues, opposes, represses or even cannot recognize.

Emotional dynamization Russian film

director Sergei Eisenstein (1898–1948) used this expression to describe the collision of different images and actions brought about by the editing of FILM to detonate emotional response, both in relation to the theme of the film and its cinematic or aesthetic intent. See MONTAGE.

Emotive language To describe a crowd as a 'mob' or a 'rabble' is to be emotive, to convey not only information but one's own attitude towards the crowd and one's intention of influencing the receiver's attitude towards it. Emotive LANGUAGE tells as much about the communicator as the MESSAGE. It reveals *what* he/she thinks and very often *how* he/she thinks.

IDEOLOGY is the root and inspiration of the media use of emotive language. Newspapers often use it on those they disagree with, who appear somehow to threaten what the newspapers wish to preserve. Thus, while trade unions might consider they are striking 'in defence of hard-won rights', they may be accused in banner headlines of 'holding the nation to ransom'. Here the intention of emotive language is to isolate the strikers, to establish a CONSENSUS against them and thus bring them into line. In times of national emergency such as a war, emotive language is used to whip up support and fervour for the cause and to forge a sense of national unity. During Britain's Falklands War with Argentina (1982), the *Sun* encapsulated the nature of emotive language in its infamous one-word headline. 'Gotcha!'

Empathetic listening See LISTENING.

Empathy The ability to put oneself into another person's position, into another person's shoes, and to attempt to understand his/her behaviour and perspectives without filtering them through one's own value system. It is not possible totally to avoid such filtering but to be empathetic requires that an individual makes an effort to avoid judging others on the basis of his/her own subjective experiences and perspectives, and makes an attempt to see things from the other person's point of view, whilst retaining his/her own perspectives, VALUES and so on. Clearly empathy has an impor-

tant role to play in effective interpersonal communication and in reducing barriers to communication.

Empirical Based upon *experience*. Empirical research in the social sciences centres upon fieldwork – the collection of evidence about observable human behaviour. Such enquiry usually lacks or does not make explicit the theory guiding its procedures. Its evidence may be used to establish an isolated proposition, to test certain theoretical analysis against observable behaviour, or to gain insight into certain behaviours. Such evidence may itself generate hypotheses, concepts, models, and theories.

Empowerment Giving to people, individually, as groups or communities, power over their lives, of choice and decision. The role of the media in advocating, assisting, blocking or subverting empowerment is the subject of keen debate as the media increasingly operate on a global scale. Empowerment also refers to the ways in which AUDIENCE respond to media message, the degree to which it is capable of RESISTIVE READING (See RESPONSE CODES). Those who are 'empowered' are firstly capable of interpreting for themselves the agendas and meanings of media communication. They are able to 'make use' of these agendas and meanings to further individual or communal needs, ultimately with a political purpose: the power is to change things.

In *Soap Opera and Women's Talk: The Pleasure of Resistance* (US: Sage, 1994), Mary Ellen Brown suggests that soap opera viewing 'generally considered not only apolitical but also antipolitical, can, in fact, be political and the basis for a kind of empowerment'. She argues that for women in particular, soap operas are terrain in which women's GOSSIP NETWORKS can operate in a resistive way. The very notion of empowerment in relation to the media seems to be underpinned by the idea that, without media, people are 'without power' and that with it they are in danger of being 'disempowered' (See DISEMPOWERMENT) by the distractions offered by entertainment.

Yet some of the most notable examples of people asserting their own power by challenging that of the authorities – such as the protests in the UK at motorway developments, and the mass rallies against the export of calves – indicate not only the power of values collectively expressed, but that of protesters in using the media to gain footholds on public agendas. See PEOPLE'S COMMUNICATION CHARTER.

Encipher See ENCODE.

Encode We communicate by means of a variety of visual and aural signals which are assembled according to certain rules or CODES. If Person A wishes to convey to Person B a MESSAGE which Person B is likely to understand, then the message has to be *encoded* with Person B's ability to DECODE the message-carrying signals well in mind. The MEANING of a message is something the receiver assigns in the act of decoding which is itself a part of an interaction with the encoder.

A glance at the ANDERSCH, STAATS AND BOSTROM MODEL OF COMMUNICATION, 1969 helps here. This emphasizes the stages through which the act of encoding passes. There is a stimulus to a message, which is structured – put together – and evaluated for its possible effect on the receiver before it is transmitted. The same process occurs on the part of the receiver: the message is registered; it is reconstructed according to the decoder's perception of the message and of the encoder who has delivered the message; then the response is evaluated prior to transmission.

This is only the beginning of a continuing circle of sending and receiving, encoding and decoding. Contributory to the perceptions of encoder and decoder in the process of communication are such factors as previous experience, the current and future context of the interaction and the feelings, opinions, assumptions and values of the encoder and decoder. The terms *encipher* and *decipher* are sometimes used instead of encode and decode. See DEEP STRUCTURE; ELABORATED AND RESTRICTED CODES.

Encompassing situation Term coined by W.E. Brockriede in 'Demonstrations of the concept of rhetoric', *Quarterly Journal*, 54 (1968) to describe the *context* of each and every act of communication, specifically the elaborate set of conventions and rules imposed upon an individual's behaviour in social situations.

Encrypt To 'scramble' signals – for SATELLITE TV, for example, so that non-subscribers cannot tune into programmes. Sky TV's encripting technology – VideoCrypt – relies on a *smart card* with built-in computer. Such a system could be employed by the BBC should it be obliged to become a subscription service. See CRYPTOGRAPHY.

Enfopol 19 See INTERNET: MONITORING OF CONTENT.

Enigma code See CODES OF NARRATIVE.

Enterprise fiction Term used by Estella Tincknell in an article entitled, 'Enterprise fictions: women of substance', in *Off-Centre: Feminism and Cultural Studies*, eds., Sarah Franklin, Celia Lury and Jackie Stacey (UK: HarperCollins Academic, 1991), to describe those works of fiction, written predominantly by and for women, whose central character is a woman who by dint of enterprise, energy, good looks and determination succeeds despite humble roots and early hardships in 'having it all' – wealth, power, lovers and a family. Significantly the central female characters succeed through individual endeavour working within the patriarchal STATUS QUO not by challenging and, along with other women, seeking to change it.

Tincknell comments that the success of such works in the 1980s, several of which were converted into television mini-series, was perhaps no coincidence. In many ways their central message can be read as a fictional reinforcement of the messages of right-wing political parties such as the Conservative Party in Britain or the Republican Party in the USA, which stress aspiration, and the importance of individual enterprise rather than collective action and structural change, for the success of their respective societies. Tincknell analyses in depth Barbara Taylor-Bradford's hugely successful novel, *A Women of Substance*, which she sees as a key text in relation to the 1980s. However, these fictions whilst celebrating certain aspects of femininity can be charged with undermining the feminist cause by denying the need for the collective action and structural change necessary for advancing the opportunities and rights of the majority of real-life women. See FEMINISM; GENDER.

Entropy See REDUNDANCY.

Ephemera In communications terms, publications such as CIGARETTE CARDS, PICTURE POSTCARDS and POSTERS produced for the moment, conveying information for immediate use. Ironically such ephemera are now collector's items, illuminating records of our past.

Establishing shot Opening shot or sequence showing the location of a FILM scene or a juxtaposition of characters in action to follow.

Establishment It has been argued by many political and social commentators that in the UK, among other countries, there exists a ruling ELITE known as the Establishment. This is not readily recognizable as a ruling CLASS but is composed of people who because of wealth, birth or position in government are able to exercise considerable power and influence. Generally the term is applied to those who are not directly, democratically answerable in their positions of power. See HEGEMONY.

Members of the Establishment are thought to include those in the higher echelons of the civil service, the Church, the public schools, the armed forces, Oxbridge, the Conservative Party, the judiciary and the BBC, among others. Jeremy Paxman in his exploration of the Establishment in *Friends in High Places: Who Runs Britain?* (UK: Penguin, 1990) argues that whilst the Establishment took something of a battering during the Thatcher governments (1979–90), it is far from dead.

Ethnic Term generally used in the social sciences to refer to a community of people possessing its own CULTURE. The characteristics which identify an ethnic group may include a common LANGUAGE, common customs and beliefs, and a cultural tradition. In Britain a number of languages are used which in part serve to communicate a sense

of distinct ethnic identity to the wider community. For example, Welsh, Gaelic, Punjabi, and Gujerati. Also variations of English like British Black English, serve the same purpose. A society may contain several ethnic groups some of whom, but not all, may also be racial groups. One focus of current research is an exploration of the role the media play in the construction of ethnic identities.

* Benedict Anderson, *Imagined Communities* (UK: Verso, 1984); Marie Gillespie, *Television, Ethnicity and Cultural Change*, (UK: Routledge, 1995); Bill Schwarz, 'Conservatism, nationalism and imperialism' in James Donald and Stuart Hall, eds., *Politics and Ideology* (UK: Open University Press, 1987); Stuart Hall, 'New ethnicities' in David Morley and Kuan-Hsing Chen, eds., *Stuart Hall: Critical Dialogues* (UK: Routledge, 1996).

Ethnocentrism The use of one's own CULTURE as a yardstick by which to measure, to judge, the attributes and activities of other cultures. Such judgement bears the implicit or explicit assumption that one's own culture is superior. Robert Levine and Donald Campbell in *Ethnocentrism: Theories of Conflict, Ethnic Attitudes and Group Behaviour* (US: Wiley, 1972) argue that there is a tendency for all social GROUPS and societies to be ethnocentric. If this is the case, then such a tendency could be expected to have considerable impact upon the way in which MESSAGES about other cultures are interpreted and the way in which other cultures are discussed in any one culture.

With the Civil War in Bosnia, between Serbian, Moslem and Croat ethnic groups, *ethnic cleansing*, which was long considered to be a thing of the past, was resurrected with tragic consequences: whole populations being either massacred or displaced because of their ethnic origins. Indeed, ethnic conflict, following GLASNOST in the Soviet bloc in the late 1980s, became a characteristic in the 1990s of social and cultural trends worldwide. The peace settlement in Bosnia, brokered in the autumn of 1995 by the US and enforced by NATO forces, both recognized and reinforced ethnic divisions; thus casting (perhaps unavoidably) a blight on the cause of multi-ethnic societies. See MEDIA IMPERIALISM.

Ethnographic (approach to audience measurement) An important body of cultural research into the relationship and interaction between TV texts and audience has been described as *ethnographic,* that is, describing a culture, emphasizing the native point of view. Researchers such as David Morley (see *The 'Nationwide' Audience: Structure and Decoding*) (UK: British Film Institute, 1980) have set out to discover how audiences make active use of TELEVISION as part of their own culture; as John Fiske puts it in 'British cultural studies' in *Channels of Discourse: Television and Contemporary Criticism,* ed., Robert C. Allen (UK: Methuen, 1987, reprinted by Routledge, 1990), to use television 'to make meanings that are useful to them in making sense of their own social experience and therefore themselves'. Morley and other scholars such as Dorothy Hobson (see '*Crossroads': The Drama of a Soap Opera,* UK: Methuen, 1982), went to the people, kept a low profile in terms of shaping responses – so as to avoid what has been termed 'colonial representation' – and listened, at length and over fairly extended periods, to what audience groups thought of certain programmes, their characters, their narratives, their PREFERRED READINGS.

Ethnographic studies have revealed the fact that people respond to programmes much less along lines of social class and in a much more varied way than some commentators have believed. Morley's findings indicated, for example, that the categories of textual reading by Frank Parkin (see DOMINANT, SUBORDINATE, RADICAL) and the similar reception code posed by Professor Stuart Hall, were simplistic: indeed the wide range of differing readings resisted categorization.
* Shaun Moores, *Interpreting Audiences: The Ethnography of Media Consumption* (UK: Sage, 1993); Jennifer Mason, *Qualitative Researching* (UK: Sage, 1996); Amanda Coffey, *The Ethnographic Self: Fieldwork and the Representation of Self* (UK: Sage, 1999).

Ethos In communication terms, the ethos of a communicator determines the image one has of him or her at any given time – either one person or a GROUP. In their paper 'A summary of experimental research in ethos', *Speech Monographs,* 30 (1963)

Kenneth Anderson and Theodore Clevenger Jr refer to research findings which point to two general categories of ethos: *extrinsic* and *intrinsic.* The first is the image, say, of a speaker as it exists prior to a given speech; the second is the image derived from elements during the presentation of a speech, consciously or unconsciously provided by the speaker. The final impression is a mixture of extrinsic and intrinsic factors.

The prestige of a speaker, his/her appearance, likeableness, credibility, social CLASS, voice, etc. contribute to his/her ethos. Anderson and Clevenger assert that evidence from research proves 'that the ethos of the source is related in some way to the impact of the message' and that this applies 'not only to political, social, religious and economic issues but also to matters of aesthetic judgement and personal taste'.

Euphemism In polite circles, 'belly' is not referred to, but 'stomach' is acceptable. That is a *euphemism,* the rendering of blunt, harsh or unpleasant terms in mild, inoffensive or quaint LANGUAGE. Thus 'to die' may be rendered euphemistically as 'to pass away'; a 'bookie' may prefer to seek more status by calling him/herself a 'turf accountant'. In ADVERTISING 'budget items' are preferred to 'cheap goods'. In business, people are not 'sacked' but 'the labour force is slimmed' or 'downsized'.

Some euphemism is justifiable in INTER-PERSONAL COMMUNICATION, for example at times of grief and tragedy; some are insulting to language and to human intelligence and dignity, such as the terminology of the arms race where (in so-called *Pentagon-speak*) 'demographic targeting' means the destruction of our cities by nuclear weapons; 'support structure' is civilians and 'collateral damage' is dead civilians. In the 1990s euphemism lost none of its knack of serving the dominant ideology of the moment. With the introduction of the internal market into the National Health Service, patients became *customers* unless they were dead in which case they were deemed 'negative patient episodes'. Generally in a world where *mission* substituted the aims of industry and education alike, *downsizing* or *rightsizing* became the euphemism for mass redundancies. In some educational institutions students are described as customers until they complain or cause trouble, when they revert to being students.

The Gulf War (1991) contributed to the euphemism of conflict, the sanitization of death and destruction. The bombing of the cities of Iraq was called 'denying the enemy an infrastructure'. People were 'soft targets'. Saturation bombing was 'laying down a carpet'. For a complete LOW (Lexicon of War) arising from the Gulf conflict, see Matthew d'Ancona's compilation, 'LOW warspeak' in *Index on Censorship* 4 & 5 1991. See NEWS-PEAK; NUKESPEAK.

Euronet A consortium of national computer interests in nine European countries, working towards the creation of a mutually compatible interconnection of European databases. Euronet is designed for reasons as much political as economical, as a method of ensuring that in the long term the economic control of Europe remains in European hands, and thus, inextricably, the control of information. The consortium is a defence against the computer-information HEGEMONY of the US and specifically of IBM which, by 1980, was responsible for 70 per cent of the world's computer installations.

European Community and media: 'Television without frontiers' Title of a Council of Europe directive, October 1989, the first attempt by the European Community to regulate and institutionalize BROADCASTING between member nations. The directive requires EC members to guarantee unrestricted reception for AUDIENCES across Europe and to avoid any strategies likely to limit retransmission in their territory of any EC broadcasts which meet Community conditions. The directive lays down a policy of minimum regulation, granting equal rights to commercial operators and PUBLIC SERVICE broadcasters while at the same time requiring no legal obligations to enhance public DISCOURSE.

Says Shalini S. Venturelli in 'The imagined transnational public sphere in the European Community's broadcast philosophy: implications for democracy' in the *European Journal of Communication*, December 1993, 'The European Community thus provided a continental legal framework for the expansion of a corporate vision of public communication . . . thereby undermining media policy traditions evolved under the concept of democratic public interest'. Venturelli feared a 'conversion of civil cultural tradition into commercial cultural traditions'. See DEREGULATION; FAIRNESS DOCTRINE (USA); PRIVATIZATION.

European Institute for Media Established in 1983 at the University of Manchester in partnership with the European Cultural Foundation of Amsterdam to give expression to the growing interdependence of European countries in the field of communication. In 1992 the major part of the Institution's activity in research and publication moved to Dusseldorf, leaving the Advanced Studies Unit in Manchester. Here opportunities are made available for media professionals and academics to undertake periods of study and research.

Event The occurrence which gives rise to media coverage will have fulfilled one or more, or an amalgam of NEWS VALUES. In the analysis of media, different forms of event can be identified. Primarily there is the *key event* – an air crash with the loss of many lives, a bomb explosion in the heart of a capital city. Such an event is very often the cause of, or signifier of, crisis; a threat to the smooth operation of community, national or international activity.

In 'The impact of key events on the presentation of reality' in the *European Journal of Communication*, September 1995, Hans Mathias Kepplinger and Johanna Habermeier suggest useful typology of the causes and communicative functions of events (see diagram on p. 108).

The coverage of events, especially if the topic of such events gives ground for concern about the causes and consequences of such events, stimulates the 'activities of pressure groups who see an opportunity of gaining media attention, since their concerns fit in with the established topic. The consequence is an increased number of mediated and staged events.'

Equally, such coverage tends to exert 'pressure upon decision-makers in politics, business, administration, etc.' The authors

Communicative functions	Causes		
	Genuine (independent of the media)	Mediated (influenced by the media)	Staged (for the media)
Key events			
Similar events			
Thematically related events			

Kepplinger and Habermeier model of media events, 1995

give the example of how safety rules for petrol tankers may be changed as a result of media *conjecture* about possible, rather than actual, accidents. Coverage of key events will, say Kepplinger and Habermeier, enhance the coverage of similar or related events, and add interest and urgency to events thematically linked. Of course the nature of coverage will vary between media, for example between daily and weekly newspapers or between broadsheets and tabloids.

The authors note a tendency in the reporting of key events to give the impression of an accumulation of such events (hence the sense of crisis) whereas what is actually happening is an accumulation of another kind.

Similar stories, being gathered together from the past as well as the present, are being reinvigorated and intensified as they compound information about the new key event. Key events thus trigger apparent waves of such events when in reality only one has occurred: 'Here one has to take into account that the news coverage creates a false impression that events accumulate and problems become more urgent.'

Excorporation The process by which those who are not members of the domi- nant group(s) within society, e.g. members of youth cultures and sub-cultures, utilize the material resources provided by the prevailing system to fashion cultural statements which communicate their difference from

or opposition to the dominant culture e.g. the wearing of Doc Marten boots by Skinheads. See BRICOLAGE; COUNTER-CULTURE; IDEOLOGY; STYLE; SUB-CULTURE; YOUTH CULTURE.

Exnomination Roland Barthes uses this term in *Mythologies* (UK: Paladin, 1973) to describe the assumption on the part of the communicator, usually the mass media, that certain VALUES are so basic and so widely shared, indeed so natural, that they are beyond question and need not be referred to or justified. Exnomination is integral to the working of IDEOLOGY, representing the dominant code of a society. See COMMON SENSE; DEREGULATION, FIVE MYTHS OF; HEGEMONY; MYTH.

Exotica Interest in, and commodification of, ethnic differences; most strikingly demonstrated in fashion.

Expectation, horizons of Describes the 'readiness factor' of AUDIENCE in terms of what its expectations are concerning a communicative text: is the audience well-primed for what is to come or likely to be resistant out of unawareness, ignorance, prejudice, and is audience likely to conform to the PREFERRED READING or *aberrantly* decode the text? (See DECODE). The German literary critic Hans Robert Jans uses the phrase in *Towards an Aesthetic of Reception* (US: University of Minneapolis Press, 1982), referring to each reader of a text as approaching it with horizons of expectations shaped by previous literacy, cultural and social experience. A text is interpreted on a basis of how it accords with or challenges expectations. Such expectations need to be seen in relation to, and generally arising from and interactive with COLLECTIVE REPRESENTATIONS.

Expectations People come to have a collection of ideas about what is expected of them in terms of their behaviour in certain social situations and, in turn, of what they should expect concerning the behaviour of others and of their treatment in society generally. Research into human PERCEPTION has highlighted the important influence expectations have on an individual's perception of new information. Expectations are formed from personal experience and by information received from various other sources. Information received from these other sources may modify previous expectations or play a particularly crucial role in shaping expectations about persons or social situations of which the individual has no direct experience. An item of information will be more readily accepted if it is compatible with existing ideas and expectations; if it is not then DISSONANCE may occur and the information may be rejected or ignored.

The media are an important source of information about many social and political events of which the individual has little or no first-hand experience. Several researchers have therefore sought to investigate the role played by the media in shaping audience's expectations about certain persons, social groups or social situations – those related to social unrest for example – of which the audience has little or no direct experience against which to test the validity of the media's presentation. The matter of concern here is that in such cases individuals are more than usually vulnerable to PROPAGANDA. Also of interest is the role of the media in creating STEREOTYPES by engendering a set of expectations and beliefs about particular individuals, social groups or social situations.

Experimental group A research term for the group within an experiment to whom the experimental treatment is applied (for example, the group may be asked to conform to a particularly rigorous procedure of communication whilst performing a set task). The results from this group are then compared to those from a comparable CONTROL GROUP which was not subjected to the experimental treatment. The control group provides the base-line against which the effectiveness of the treatment can be judged. Changes which take place in the behaviour of the experimental group but not the control group are likely to be seen as resulting from the treatment. See MEDIA ANALYSIS.

Exploitation A trade word covering all phases of FILM or other media-product publicity, public relations and promotion. **Exploitation pictures** are movies with little or no discernible merits apart from the capability of being sensational, very often cashing in on current trends or specific events.

Extra A crowd player in a FILM, with no lines to speak.

Extracted information See KUUKI.

Extrapersonal communication That which takes place without human involvement: machine to machine communication, for example; a major growth industry of communications with the coming of computers, increased automation and the development of robotics. See INTERPERSONAL COMMUNICATION; INTRAPERSONAL COMMUNICATION.

Eye contact Perhaps the most subtle and significant feature of non-verbal communication (See COMMUNICATION, NON-VERBAL). 'So complex is mutual eye contact,' writes C. David Mortensen in *Communication: the Study of Human Interaction* (US: McGraw-Hill, 1972), 'that a whole vocabulary is necessary to distinguish among the ways people look at each other'. We stare, glower, peep, pierce, glance, watch, gaze and scan; and we do it directly or indirectly, provocatively or furtively, confidently or nervously.

Centring is when we fix our gaze upon the eyes or face of another centrally, as an initiator of relationship. The impression of being looked at depends not simply on the directness of the eyeline but upon the relation between eye movements and that of head, facial and bodily orientation to others. Eye contact is rarely constant, nor is it necessarily mutual. It may be maintained longer when relationships are close or where there is a sustaining activity between participants. When innocuous subjects are discussed, eye contact is likely to be more prolonged than when conversation turns upon personal matters. Women, it is held, engage in more mutual glancing than men do.

Factors of psychological dominance and submissiveness are reflected in the extent and nature of eye contact. A single glance may be all that is required for an individual to assert him/herself over others, take initiative or leadership. Eye contact indicates awareness and signals interest in further contact: it can open a relationship, further it, or, by *avoidance*, close that relationship down.

Looking behaviour provides a valuable means of eliciting information from another person. As Mortensen says, 'While virtually any non-verbal cue may serve as an indicator of individual response to message cues, the fact is . . . that the area of the human eye is the *most visible* and richly revealing of all sources of expressive meaning'. See CIVIL INAT-TENTION; INDICATORS; PROXEMICS; REGULATORS.

F

Facial expression The face's main role in providing non-verbal communication lies in the expression of emotions. Michael Argyle in *Bodily Communication* (UK: Methuen, 1988) argues that the main facial expressions used to display emotion are for happiness, surprise, fear, sadness, anger, disgust, contempt, and interest. Further, several studies have suggested that the facial expressions used to display such emotions are, to quite a large extent, universal, that is, the same across different cultures.

Facial expressions play a key role in providing FEEDBACK during conversations. However, there are difficulties in accurately judging emotions from facial expressions because people often take care to conceal negative feelings and the face is thought to be more carefully controlled than other sources of non-verbal signals. In some cultures, the Japanese for example, this is particularly the case. Despite attempts to conceal one's reactions *leakage* may occur, that is some other part of the body, often in the lower half, might reveal one's true reaction. For example, whilst the face might be passive, a tapping foot might indicate that one is agitated by the message being received. See BART; COMMUNICATION, NON-VERBAL; FACS; FAST.

FACS Facial Affect Scoring System developed by Ekman and Friesen, based on small movements of the face known as Action Units. These movements are normally controlled by single facial muscles yet are observable and discrete. This system has enabled the detailed study of facial expressions and, in particular, the exploration of which aspects of the face are responsible for expressing different emotions. See COMMUNI-CATION, NON-VERBAL.

Facsimile Exact copy; today, facsimile (or fax) is the transmission of a printed or handwritten page or image by electronic means. As early as 1842 Scotsman Alexander Bain proposed the first facsimile system though it was not until the 1920s that the process was generally employed for the transmission of news, photographs, weather maps and maps for military purposes.

Newspaper editions can be transmitted across continents for simultaneous publication; the pictures of wanted criminals can be relayed instantly to practically every police force in the world while the facsimile machine can combine with the domestic TV receiver to provide a permanent record of news and other items appearing on the screen. See MEDIA TECHNOLOGY.

Faction See DOCUMENTARY.

Fade in Gradual emergence of a scene from blackness to clear, full definition. The term is used in radio as well as film and TV.

Fairness Doctrine (USA) A BROADCAST-ING regulation in the US until 1987 when the Federal Communications Commission (FCC), responsible for the observation of the regulation, abolished it. The doctrine required broadcasters to devote time to controversial issues and to air varied opposed viewpoints. In the 1980s expansion in radio and TV channels and a DOMINANT IDEOLOGY which prized the private above the public, led to pressures to DEREGULATE broadcasting. The FCC was persuaded that the broader and more diverse market-place would ensure plurality of opinion without regulation. Serious doubts have been cast upon this apparent 'guarantee', a working principle of MARKET LIBERALISM, that the market-place would ensure a 'market-place of ideas'. In *Democracy Without Citizens: Media and the Decay of American Politics* (US: Oxford University Press, 1989), Robert M. Entman voices deep scepticism about the idea of leaving controversial matters in the hands of market forces. He writes of the 'dangers of basing public policy on the assumption that the economic market inevitably nourishes journalism's contribution to democratic citizenship'; indeed, 'decisions rooted in this premise, as the FCC's elimination of the Fairness Doctrine, might actually retard progress towards a freer press and citizenship'.

Family Viewing Policy See ITC PROGRAMME CODE; VIOLENCE ON TV; CODES OF PRACTICE.

FAST Facial Affect Scoring Technique developed by Ekman, Friesen and Tomkins and discussed in Paul Ekman and Maureen O'Sullivan, 'Facial expression: methods, means and moues', in Robert S. Feldman and Bernhard Rime, eds., *Fundamentals of Nonverbal Behaviour* (France and UK: Editions de la Maison des Sciences de l'Homme and Cambridge University Press, 1991). This technique divides the face into three areas for analysis: the brows and forehead; eyes and lids; and the lower face. In combination 77 descriptors are used to record an individual's expressions: 8 of these relate to the brows and forehead; 17 to the eyes and lids and 45 to the lower face. See COMMUNICATION, NON-VERBAL.

Fatwa On St Valentine's Day 1989, Iran's Ayatollah Khomeini issued a 'fatwa', or edict, against the British novelist Salman Rushdie for his novel *Satanic Verses* (1988). The book was deemed blasphemous, guilty of containing scenes so insulting to the Islamic faith that every true Moslem had a bounden duty to kill the author. To carry out the fatwa would guaran-

tee a place in heaven. Rushdie went into hiding, with police protection. He became a Middle Eastern hostage only in his own country. The fatwa applied to all those involved in the publication of the novel. Bookshops were fire-bombed. The Japanese translator of the novel was attacked, beaten up and stabbed to death and an Italian translator stabbed.

The fatwa against Rushdie was described by the South African novelist Nadine Gordimer as 'a crime against humanity' which 'casts a shadow over the free development of literature everywhere' ('Is religious persecution once more tolerated?' in The *Guardian*, 6 February 1992). The case illustrates the profound differences in cultural expectations and practices between Western and Islamic nations; and the clash has been at its most poignant in Britain where the Moslem community is torn between the demands of their religions and the laws – and VALUES – of their adopted country. The Iranian government distanced itself from the fatwa death sentence in 1998, without actually withdrawing it officially. See CENSORSHIP.

Fax See FACSIMILE.

Federal Communications Commission (FCC) Set up by the US federal government in 1934; a body empowered to regulate interstate and foreign communications such as radio and TV – originating in America.

Federal Radio Commission Formed in the US in 1927 by government to exercise statutory authority and regulation over radio broadcasting which, until then, had been a free-for-all.

Feedback According to *Chambers Twentieth Century Dictionary* (ed. A.M. Macdonald, UK, 1972), feedback is the 'return of part of the output of a system to the input as a means towards improved quality or self-correction of error'; in *A Dictionary of New English, 1963–1972* (eds., C.L. Barnhart, S. Steinmetz and R.K. Barnhart, US/UK: Longman, 1973), feedback is 'a reciprocal effect of one person or thing upon another; a reaction or response that modifies, corrects, etc., the behaviour of that which produced the reaction or response'. Without feedback – the signal which is stimulated by an act of communication, biological, mechanical, human or animal – meaningful contact halts and cannot make progress.

Feedback is the regenerative circuit, or loop, of communication. A student who submits his/her essay to the teacher expects feedback in terms of comments and a mark. Unless this feedback occurs, the student lacks guidance for the future; more, he/she is likely to be demotivated and draw back from further communicative interaction.

When the student's essay *is* returned it may contain **positive** or **negative feedback**: harsh comments, without encouragement, and a low mark might well be more demotivating than not receiving any feedback at all. Praise and supportive criticism on the other hand are likely to produce a positive response – of greater effort and motivation.

Central to the purpose of feedback is *control*; that is, feedback enables the communicator to adjust his/her MESSAGE, or response, to that of the sender, and to the context in which the communicative activity takes place. At the interpersonal level feedback is transmitted by voice, expression, GESTURE, sight, hearing, touch, smell, etc. The greater the distance between communicators, the fewer of the 'senses' being employed to 'read' and return feedback, the more difficult it is to arrange and control, and the more difficult it is to assess its nature and meaning. See CYBERNETICS.

Feminism Though embracing different perspectives and schools of thought, fundamentally feminism is concerned with the advancement and achievement of equal social and political rights for women, and the fight against SEXISM. Feminism challenges many traditional, patriarchal, assumptions about the behavioural difference expected of men and women and the assignment of social roles and STATUS which rests on them; and what it perceives as a widespread devaluing of women's attributes, experiences and perspectives.

One focus of current research is the exploration of the ROLE that the media play both in fostering and reinforcing SEXISM and more generally notions of femininity and masculinity, and media coverage of women's rights issues and the feminist movement

and its ideas. Another important research interest is the degree to which LANGUAGE and its use reflect and perpetuate sexism and assumptions about differences between masculine and feminine behaviour. See ANDROCENTRIC RULE; ENTERPRISE FICTION; FETAL PERSONHOOD; GENDER; GENDERED GENRE; GENDERLECTS; HE/MAN LANGUAGE; HEDGES; MALE-AS-NORM; MELODRAMA; MUTED GROUPS; PLUS MALE, MINUS MALE; REPORT-TALK/RAPPORT-TALK; SECTION 28; STEREOTYPE; TAG QUESTIONS.
* Jennifer Coates, *Women, Men and Language* (UK: Longman, 1993); Liesbet van Zoonen, 'Feminist Perspectives' in James Curran and Michael Gurevitch, eds., *Mass Media and Society* (UK: Arnold, 1996); Charlotte Brunsden, Julie D'Acci and Lyn Spigel, eds., *Feminist Television Criticism* (US/UK: Clarendon Press, 1997).

Fetal personhood Particularly in the US and Britain, debate on the abortion issue has seen the emergence of what R. Petchesky in *Abortion and Women's Choice: The State, Sexuality and Reproductive Freedom* (US: Northeastern University Press, 1984) has called the 'Doctrine of fetal personhood'.

In *Off-Centre: Feminism and Cultural Studies* edited by Sarah Franklin, Celia Lury and Jackie Stacey (UK: HarperCollins Academic, 1991) a series of articles analyses the debate on the abortion issues at the time prior to and just after the introduction of the Alton Bill in the 1987/88 session of Parliament. This Bill sought to change abortion legislation and in particular to reduce the upper time limit of legal abortion to 18 weeks. It was noted that the concept of 'fetal personhood' was central to the terms of this debate. A key argument that was repeatedly put forward was that advances in medical technology meant that a foetus can have an identity and the possibility, beyond a certain time, of a life separate from that of the pregnant woman. Along with this notion of fetal personhood came the notion of fetal rights, rights which might even be in opposition to the rights of the pregnant woman. Emphasis upon the impact of medical advancement upon the sustainability of the foetus and its possible entitlement to fetal rights became the main focus for coverage of the debate in the British media. According to Tess Randles in 'The Alton Bill and the media's "consensual" position' in *Off-*

Centre, the appeal to science and technology has helped set the 'parameters for a consensual framework for understanding abortion as a moral dilemma'. The debate was thus seen as 'a means of reaching a "compromise" within the terms of a consensual framework, in which medical judgement was used as a basis for establishing the social and political parameters of the abortion question'.

Randles goes on to argue that this stance lent an air of objectivity to the anti-abortion campaign and helped marginalize the feminist perspective which saw the issue much more in terms of the argument that a woman's right to choice and to have control over her own body are important elements of sexual equality. Later the Thatcher government proposed an amendment to the upper time limit to bring it to 24 weeks and this was passed by Parliament. See Chapter 7 'In the wake of the Alton Bill: science, technology and reproductive politics' in *Off-Centre*.

Fibre-optic technology One of the wonder-products of the Information Age, fibre-optic cable is fine-spun glass, a mixture of silicon and oxygen, through which digital CODES are passed in pulsing light. Its impact on TELEPHONE technology has been immense and its potential for this, CABLE TELEVISION, and many other purposes, turns so rapidly into achievement and new possibilities that even the experts find it difficult to plan for fibre's accelerating capacity.

Fibre-optic cable can carry 10 times further than coaxial without requiring a booster. Over 7500 different channels can operate along a single pair of optical fibres, though the potential number lies in millions. Because fibre-optic transmission is free from electrical interference, cable can be cheaply laid along existing railway lines; it can follow existing electricity pylons, enclosed in the earth wire. Fibre-optic cable has already been laid across the English Channel, and 1989 saw the first submarine cable across the Atlantic. All forms of cable are limited in terms of the span of the NET-WORKS by the number of cable terminals. In contrast, SATELLITE TRANSMISSION has a global reception capacity. The future will see a closer linkage between satellite technology and fibre-optics. See TECHNOLOGY OF THE MEDIA.

Fiction values These work with and *as* NEWS VALUES. Milly Buonanno in an article 'News-values and fiction-values: news as serial device and criteria of "fictionworthiness" in Italian fiction', published in the *European Journal of Communication*, June 1993, argues that the criteria for modern TV and film fiction parallel news values. She cites, for example, the high social status of the protagonists (the *elite* value of news) and the emphasis on proximity, that which is 'happening in our own backyards' (an ethnocentric news value). She quotes Giuseppe Ferrara, Italian film and TV director, who incorporates real news dramas into his fictions, referring to these as *news pills*.

Film See ANARCHIST CINEMA; ANIMATION; BRITISH BOARD OF FILM CENSORS; BRITISH FILM INSTITUTE; BRITISH FILM PRODUCTION FUND; CATALYST EFFECT; CELLULOID; CERTIFICATION OF FILMS; CINEMATOGRAPHY, ORIGINS; CINÉMA VÉRITÉ; DIGITAL VIDEO DISC (DVD); DIRECT CINEMA; DOCUMENTARY; DOUBLE EXPOSURE; EMOTIONAL DYNAMIZATION; FILM CENSORSHIP; FILM NOIR; FLASHBACK; FLY ON THE WALL; HAYS OFFICE; HIGH-SPEED PHOTOGRAPHY; HOLLYWOOD; IMAX; KINETOSCOPE; KULESHOV EFFECT; LLOYD COMMITTEE REPORT, 1967; MARCH OF TIME; McGUFFIN; MINIMAL CINEMA; MONTAGE; MULTIPLE IMAGE; MUSICAL – FILM MUSICAL; NATIONAL FILM ARCHIVE; NEWSREEL; NEW WAVE; OMNIMAX; PARASOCIAL INTERACTION; PERSISTENCE OF VISION; PROJECTION OF PICTURES; SEMIOLOGY/SEMIOTICS; SLOW MOTION; SOVIET MANIFESTO, 1928; SOVKINO; SPAGHETTI WESTERNS; SPECIAL EFFECTS; SPINNING TOP; STORYBOARD; SUBTITLE; THAUMATROPE; TWO-REELER; VAMP; VIDEO; VISTAVISION; VITAPHONE; WESTERN; WILLIAMS COMMITTEE REPORT ON OBSCENITY AND FILM CENSORSHIP, 1979; WIPE; ZOETROPE; ZOOM LENS; ZOPRAXOGRAPHY.

Film censorship See CENSORSHIP; CERTIFICATION OF FILMS; WILLIAMS COMMITTEE REPORT ON OBSCENITY AND FILM CENSORSHIP, 1979.

Filmless camera Launched by the Japanese in 1987, the all-electronic camera is instant, avoids the need for chemical processing, can project its pictures from a standard TELEVISION monitor and even permits its images to be transmitted down a TELEPHONE line or fed into a computer for further processing. Paper pictures can be swiftly produced from VIDEO printers. However, picture quality on FILM promises to remain superior to anything produced by solid-state cameras for the foreseeable future.

Film noir Term used by French FILM critics, notably Nino Frank, to describe a particular kind of dark, suspenseful thriller. A classic of the GENRE is French director Marcel Carné's *Le Jour se Lève* (1939) – 'Day Arises', starring Jean Gabin. We see the last doomed hours of a man wanted by the police for murder. He has barred himself in his attic bedroom in an apartment block. He is totally surrounded. He has no chance; but then, Carné makes clear, the man never did have a chance. At dawn he shoots himself and, as he lies dying, his alarm clock goes off, reminding him of his otherwise intolerable life as a worker.

Described as 'symbolism with a three o'clock in the morning mood', *film noir* gained substantial currency in the US, generally thriving between the early years of the 2nd World War and the late 1950s, and ranging from John Huston's *Maltese Falcon* (1941) to Orson Welles' *Touch of Evil* (1958). Hollywood *film noir* says Michael Walker in the Introduction to *The Movie Book of Film Noir* (UK: Studio Vista, 1992), edited by Ian Cameron, features 'heroes who are frequently victims of a hostile world'. Such movies are characterized by a 'distinctive and exciting visual style, an unusual narrative complexity' and 'a generally more critical and subversive view of American ideology than the norm'.

In the view of Frank Krutnik in *A Lonely Street: Film Noir, Genre, Masculinity* (UK: Routledge, 1991), a significant proportion of such films frequently offer an engagement with problematic, even illicit potentialities within masculine identity' while at the same time drawing back from embracing or sanctioning 'such "subversive potentialities"'.

Women in *film noir*, writes E. Ann Kaplan in *Women in Film Noir* (UK: BFI, 1980), edited by Kaplan, are 'presented as desirable but dangerous to men'. They 'function as the obstacle to the male quest. The hero's success or not depends on the degree

to which he can extricate himself from the woman's manipulations.' Billy Wilder's *Double Indemnity* (1941), with Fred MacMurray as the (willingly) manipulated male victim and Barbara Stanwick as the alluring manipulator, is a classic example of the genre.

First impressions There is evidence that we tend to give too much attention to the initial information we may receive about an individual, and relatively less to later information that may be contradictory; that is, we are biased towards primacy effects. (See PRIMACY, THE LAW OF). There is some evidence that negative first impressions in particular can be resistant to change.

First impressions can clearly count in situations where most of the information is received about a person in a fairly short, discrete period of time, as in an interview. In this instance there might be little opportunity for first impressions to be modified.

In some circumstances – as when a considerable time gap intervenes between sets of information received about an individual or when there is regular, close contact with that individual – first impressions can be modified. Here the later information received may have greater impact. This is known as the *recency* effect, because it is the more recent information which is the more influential.

Fish-eye lens Camera lens of extremely short focal length and wide subject area. Some fish-eye lenses produce only a circular image; others give a full rectangular image.

Five Myths of Deregulation (See DEREGULATION, FIVE MYTHS OF).

Flashback A break in the chronology of a narrative in which events from the past are disclosed to the reader, listener or viewer, and which have a bearing on the present situation. Flashback was a device used very early in the history of the cinema. D.W. Griffith's epic *Intolerance* (1916) is made up of four flashbacks. Used with a narrator, the form achieved its greatest popularity in the cinema in the 1930s and 1940s. Orson Welles's *Citizen Kane* (1941) is made up entirely of a dazzling series of flashbacks. Equally inventive is the flashback narrative of the Ealing comedy, Robert Hamer's *Kind Hearts and Coronets* (1949). See FILM.

Flat-screen technology Called 'roll-up TV'; the late 1990s saw a race to develop flexible Liquid Crystal Display (LCD) technology which would replace bulky TV sets reliant on the cathode-ray tube, with light, high-definition screens which could be hung like paintings on a wall. Flat screens made their first appearance in early laptop computers, but these lacked colour fidelity and image resolution. The so-termed Malvern screen, developed at the Worcestershire headquarters of the imaging department of the UK's Defence Evaluation and Research Agency (Dera) employs, as later laptop computers have done, ferroelectric crystals, but operating at different voltages and alignments. When not in use the screen can be used to display works of art or photographs. Dera's prime motive in developing the Malvern screen has been to produce roll-up, animated electronic maps, or miniature screen displays built into a pilot's helmet. See TECHNOLOGY OF THE MEDIA.

Fleet Street Until the 1980s, the home of most of Britain's major national newspapers; indeed the name had become the generic term for the nation's press; a figure of speech (see METONYMY). The advent of new technology linked with the cost-cutting ambitions of newspaper owners, both of which led to bitter conflict with the PRINT UNIONS, caused an exodus from 'The Street' of all the major titles. See PRESS BARONS.
* L. Melvern, *The End of the Street* (UK: Methuen, 1986).

Floor appointment See HEAD NODS.

Flow See PROGRAMME FLOW.

Fly on the wall Popular title given to a GENRE of documentary film making, for the cinema or TV, in which the camera remains concealed, or is handled so discreetly that the subjects forget they are being filmed. Richard Denton, producer of the BBC documentary series *Kingswood: A Comprehensive School* (1982) describes the approach in 'Fly on the wall – designed to invade privacy', *Listener* (13 January, 1983) as attempting 'to remove the process of filming so far from the consciousness of the contributors that they will, in theory, forget its existence and so behave in a markedly more natural, truthful and realistic manner'. Denton speaks of two distinct problems: 'The first concerns the question of accuracy and context . . . The second, and probably more important, problem concerns privacy.' Outstanding examples of the fly-on-the-wall approach were the BBC's *Police* series (1982), the work of Roger Graef and Charles Stewart, and Channel 4's *Murder Squad* (1992). Of particular interest for fly-on-the-wall documentarists has been family interaction. First in the UK to win fame by exposing their lives to the eye of the camera were the Wilkenses of Reading, featured in the BBC series, *The Family* (1974). In 1999 Granada Television screened the lives of a mixed-race family from Leeds, in *Family Life*. See CINÉMA VÉRITÉ; DIRECT CINEMA.

Focus groups Focus groups are frequently employed in market research. Members of a group are brought together by a researcher to discuss aspects of a product, be it soap powder, a political party or a television programme. The group is often chosen to be a representative SAMPLE of all those who are thought to be the actual or potential consumers of the product. As a qualitative research method, use of focus groups allows for in-depth discussion and exploration of consumers' orientations towards and evaluations of a product.

Folk culture Term generally applied to the CULTURE of pre-industrial societies. Such societies have certain distinguishing features which are thought to affect the elements of their culture: work and leisure are undifferentiated; there is relatively little DIVISION OF LABOUR; the communities are small and social action is normally collectivist as opposed to individualist. Thus folk songs, for example, are usually firmly rooted in the everyday experience and beliefs of both the audience and the performer.

Folk devils Stanley Cohen in *Folk Devils and Moral Panics* (UK: MacGibbon & Kee, 1972), argues that societies are subject to periods of MORAL PANIC in which certain GROUPS are picked out as being a special threat to the VALUES and interests of society. The media and in particular the PRESS play an important role in transmitting this sense of outrage to the general public. These groups or individuals are usually those transgressing the values of the dominant HIERARCHY, as for example did the mods and rockers and the PUNKS. It is further argued by Cohen and others that the castigation of such groups, such folk devils, by the media is a mechanism by which adherence to dominant social norms is strengthened along with support for the forces of law and order and an extension of their powers. See LOONY LEFTISM.

* Stanley Cohen and Jock Young, eds., *The Manufacture of News: Deviance, Social Problems and the Mass Media* (UK: Constable, 1973).

Footage Length of FILM expressed in feet.

'Footprint' Term used to describe the area in which a signal from a communications satellite can be received. See SATELLITE TRANSMISSION.

Four stages in audience fragmentation See AUDIENCE: FRAGMENTATION OF.

Fourteen-Day Rule In the period after the 2nd World War (1939–45) the BBC entered into an agreement with government whereby it would not try to usurp the functions of the House of Commons as the supreme forum of the nation by BROADCASTING on ISSUES due to be debated in Parliament. An embargo was placed upon all such issues until 14 days after Parliament had debated them. It was a crippling intrusion upon the editorial rights of the corporation, and the BEVERIDGE REPORT called for the abandonment of the Rule. Nevertheless, successive governments held tenaciously to it.

In 1956 the House of Commons set up a Select Committee to investigate the workings and effects of the Rule: it recommended a reduction to seven days. Pressure from broadcasters and the PRESS continued unabated and within a year the Rule was abandoned altogether (1957). See CENSORSHIP.

Four Theories of the Press See PRESS, FOUR THEORIES OF.

Fourth estate The 18th century parliamentarian Edmund Burke (1729–97) is thought to have been the originator of this phrase describing the press and its role in society. According to Burke's definition, the other three 'Estates' were the Lords Spiritual (the church), the Lords Temporal (the judiciary) and the Commons. 'And yonder', he is believed to have said in Parliament, 'sits the Fourth Estate, more important than them all.' The implication is that the press, like the other estates, *serves* the State, as differentiable from government, and thus functions as a force for social, cultural and national cohesion. Underlying this argument is the assumption that while governments might be in error, the State is benign if not sacrosanct. A glance at states ancient and modern would suggest otherwise. The classifying of the PRESS as the Fourth Estate points up the ambivalent role of media in society: does it tell the truth, the whole truth and nothing but the truth; or because the priorities of State seem to require it, manipulate, conceal or deny that truth? See ELITE; GUARD DOG METAPHOR; MEDIA CONTROL; POWER ELITE; SPYCATCHER CASE; WATCHDOGS.

Fragmentation of audience See AUDIENCE: FRAGMENTATION OF.

Framing: interpersonal Conversations are often framed by METASIGNALS which let observers and participants know what kind of activity is going on so that they are better able to interpret the conversation. For example, is the conversation a serious argument or horseplay? Such signals also allow people to recognise what Erving Goffman in *Frame Analysis* (US: Harper & Row, 1974) terms the *alignment*, that is the relative positions with regard to status, intimacy and so on, being taken by the participants; themselves included. For example, if A explains something to B in a condescending manner, A is taking a superior alignment with regard to B. In *You Just Don't Understand: Men and Women in Conversation* (UK: Virago, 1992), Deborah Tannen argues that protective comments and gestures from men towards women 'reinforce the traditional alignment by which men protect women'. She goes on to argue that 'the act of protecting frames the protector as dominant and the protected as subordinate. However, arguably because men and women are fundamentally tuned to interpret some aspects of conversation differently, the difference in relative status signalled by such comments may be more apparent to men than women. Women may simply interpret them as indicating a desire to protect or be supportive rather than as indicative of women's traditionally sub-ordinate status in society. See GENDER; GENDERLECTS.

Framing: media The process by which the media place reality *into frame*. Framing constitues a narrative device. What is not on the page of a newspaper is 'out of frame'; what does not appear within the frame of the TV is off the public agenda. For the NEWS, there is the world – and twenty minutes to put it in the frame. Time, then – the short-ness of it – is an important deciding factor. For a soap opera, time also poses problems of framing. There are 30 minute slots to be filled, each to conclude with unfinished

business, preferably dramatic and suspense-ful, while not being so dramatically 'final' that the series cannot continue day by day, week by week. Presented with such a time-frame, soaps require many characters and many plots. To facilitate this requirement (and to capture and retain audience atten-tion) scriptwriters divide up the frame into quick-bite scenes – framing within frames.

What happens outside the creative frame – audience measurement, for example – influences the nature of the frame and what goes on inside it. Robert Entman in 'Framing: toward clarification of a fractured paradigm' in the *Journal of Communication*, 4 (1992), says that a crucial task of analysis is to show 'exactly how framing influences thinking' for 'the concept of framing con-sistently offers a way to describe the power of a communicating text'.

He argues, 'Analysis of frames illumi-nates the precise way in which influence over a human consciousness is exerted by

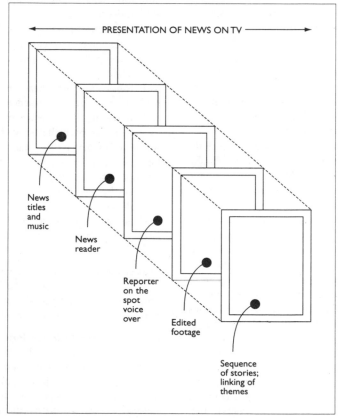

Framing reality

the transfer (or communication) of information from one location such as speech, utterance, news report, or novel – to the consciousness'. Essentially, framing constitutes *selection* and *salience* – what is perceived to be most meaningful, the one serving the other. Entman suggests that framing serves four main purposes: 1. To define problems; 2. To diagnose causes; 3. To make moral judgments and 4. To suggest remedies. These will function varyingly according to the text, but they operate in four locations in the communication process: the communicator, the text, the receiver and the culture. Communicators 'make conscious or unconscious framing judgments in deciding what to say, guided by frames (often called schemata) that organize their belief systems'. Before we frame, we are *in* a frame. The text will not only be framed by the framer within a frame it will be shaped by a number of factors – requirements concerning format and presentation, aesthetic considerations, notions of professionalism and pressures to meet the expectations of convention.

When the text comes to be 'read', the frames as presented may be at variance with the frames which guide the receiver's thinking. For Entman the culture is 'the stock of commonly invoked frames . . . exhibited in the discourse and thinking of most people in a social grouping'.

'Framing in all four locations includes similar functions: selection and highlighting, and use of the highlighting elements to construct an argument about problems and their causation, evaluation and/or solution.' This approach is useful in analysing the encoding of messages and gauging their effectiveness. It emphasizes the subjective nature of encoding by recognizing the 'invisible' schemata – psychological templates – which, however hard we try to be objective and impartial, deeply influence our actions.

For successful communication, that is, winning the interest and attention of the audience, and perhaps even going beyond that in terms of gaining the audience's assent or approval, there seems to be a need for a meeting of schemata: a common ground. The communicator selects, then attempts to give salience to those parts of the story which may fit with the existing schemata in a receiver's belief system. The power of the frame is not only in what it contains, how it emphasizes salience: there is what it leaves out. Certain themes and issues are placed in the frame, others are diminished in potential salience by being left out of the frame. The parallel with news AGENDA SETTING is strong here.

Much of what we know about the past, about history, is itself in frames – in ancient palaces and tombs, on triumphal arches, the walls and ceilings of great monasteries and cathedrals. These artefacts do not necessarily tell us what life was like in those days, rather, they tell us what was considered salient by those with power to make decisions. In *The Nature and Origins of Public Opinion* (US: Cambridge University Press, 1992), J.R. Zaller says that framing is a central power in the democratic process: it is political elites who control the framing of issues. Such framing, Zaller believes, not only influences public opinion but is capable of defining it.

At a practical level, framing is governed by professional conventions, indeed by ritual: newspapers are framed by deadlines and publication times. TV news is framed with music, graphics, headlines and news readers; each ritual presence reinforcing and increasing the salience of the frame, its dominance over alternative frames. The study of media is an example of what Entman calls *counterframing* in that it attempts to call the ritual frames into question by analysing them in the light of possible alternative frames.

* Dietram A. Scheufele, 'Framing as a theory of media effects', *Journal of Communication*, Winter 1999.

Franchise Contractual agreement; most commonly associated with the licensing to broadcast, for fixed periods, of COMMERCIAL TELEVISION and COMMERCIAL RADIO companies.

Franchises for Independent Television (UK) Royal Assent to the TELEVISION ACT, 1954 was received on 30 July and on 4 August the Independent Television Authority (later to become the Independent Broadcasting Authority) was set up by the Postmaster-General under the chairmanship of Sir

Kenneth Clark, and the first COMMERCIAL TEL-EVISION franchises were issued in 1955, with the Associated Broadcasting Company (ATV) beginning its first London transmission on 24 September 1955, and its first Midlands transmission on 17 February 1956.

The other original franchise holders were: Associated Rediffusion (broadcasting weekdays in London; starting date, 22 September 1955), Granada Television Network (weekdays, North of England; 3 May 1956), Associated British Picture Corporation (Midlands 18 February 1956 and North of England, 5 May 1956), Scottish Television (Central Scotland, 31 August 1957), TWW, Television Wales and West (South Wales and West of England; 14 January 1958), Southern Television (South of England, 30 August 1958), Tyne-Tees Television (North-East England; 15 January 1959), Anglia Television (East of England; 27 October 1959), Ulster Television (Northern Ireland; 31 October 1959), Westward Television (South-West England; 29 April 1961), Border Television (Borders, 1 September 1961 and Isle of Man, 23 March 1965), Channel Television (Channel Islands; 1 September 1962), Grampian Television (South-East Scotland; 30 September 1961) and Wales (West and North) broadcasting in Wales and North Wales from 14 September 1962. A subsidiary of ABC (Associated British Corporation), Associated British Cinemas (Television) became that franchise holder's programme contractor and in January 1964 Wales (West and North) became a subsidiary of TWW.

On 30 July 1964 all the contracts were renewed to run till 1967. Then, on 27 January 1966, it was announced that the contracts would be extended to 31 July 1968. From July 1968 some franchise areas were altered. Wales and West England – the Harlech Consortium (HTV) took in TWW. Harlech began transmissions on 4 March 1968 using TWW's schedules and eventually introduced its own programmes on 20 May 1968. New areas in 1968 were the Midlands (Associated Television Network – ATV), Lancashire (Granada Television), Yorkshire (Yorkshire Television, originally Telefusion Yorkshire and Yorkshire Inde-

pendent Television; first transmission date 29 July 1968) and two London franchises: London weekends (London Weekend Television; 2 August 1968) and London weekdays (Thames Television, including ABC Television and Rediffusion; 30 July 1968). All of these contracts were extended to run to 31 December 1981.

The IBA publicly announced its decision on new franchises on Sunday 28 December 1980, the contracts to run from 1 January 1982, for eight years. The authority, under the chairmanship of Lady Plowden, announced that Southern Television and Westward Television would lose their franchises and be replaced respectively by South and South Eastern Communications Ltd (TVS – Television South) and Television South West Ltd – TSW. Major share changes or other restructuring was insisted upon for Yorkshire Television and ATV Midlands (subsequently called Central Independent Television).

The franchise holders from 1982 were: Border Television, Scottish Television, Channel Islands Communications (Television), Central (East and West Midlands), Anglia, London Weekend, Thames, Grampian, Tyne-Tees, Granada, TVS, Television South West, Harlech, Yorkshire and Ulster. Following the UK government's White Paper, 'broadcasting in the '90s', a radical shake-up in the system of franchise allocation – by auction – was proposed, under the supervision of a new 'light touch' regulatory body, the INDEPENDENT TELEVISION COMMISSION (ITC).

Franchises from 1993 What the *Guardian* called 'the biggest shake-up in television's 36-year history', with an estimated loss of some 2500 jobs, occurred in October 1991. The Independent Television Commission (ITC) chaired by George Russell announced the winners of the 'auction' for 16 regional commercial TV franchises, including a breakfast TV licence, to extend over 10 years and commencing 1 January 1993. Four existing stations lost their renewal bids: Thames Television (replaced by Carlton Communications), Television South (Meridian Broadcasting), Television South West (Westcountry Television) and the breakfast station TV-am (Sunrise Television). The stations empowered to continued broadcasting through the 1990s were: Granada Television (for the North West), London Weekend, Yorkshire, Anglia Television, Tyne-Tees (North East), Harlech Television (Wales), Ulster Television, Channel Television (Channel Islands), Central Television (Midlands) and the Scottish channels Grampian, Border and Scottish Television. Russell declared that though the process had caused 'undoubted turmoil' within ITV, 'the quality and the viewers will win out'. This point of view was not shared by George Walden in an article 'Is this merely a lottery, or is it a serious business?' (*Daily Telegraph*, 17 October 1991). 'Sadly,' he writes, 'what has been at stake in this lottery is the quality of British television.'

The *Times* leader of 17 October called the whole affair an 'ITV auction fiasco' and said 'The government should never ask such a task again . . . auctioning terrestrial commercial television was always intended to benefit the Treasury not the television viewer. The result must be fewer resources available for programme-making and thus for competing with the cheap products on offer from the American television industry'.

The original plan of the Conservative government was to auction off the franchises to the highest bidder in a blind sale. This was later modified by the introduction of a so-called 'quality threshold'. Eight of the 16 licences did not go to the highest bidder and 13 applications were judged not to have passed the quality threshold. One notable characteristic of the new franchise winners was the declared policy of running lightly staffed publisher-broadcaster stations, on the lines of Channel 4, buying in programmes from INDEPENDENT PRODUCERS rather than the companies originating most of their own material.

Frankfurt school of theorists Founded in 1923, the Institute for Social Research in Frankfurt became the meeting point of several young Marxist intellectuals among whom were Theodor Adorno, Herbert Marcuse and Max Horkheimer. The members of the 'school' placed at the forefront of their thinking and analysis the CENTRALITY of the role of IDEOLOGY in mass communication. When Hitler came to power in 1933, the Institute moved to New York and until 1942 it was affiliated to the Sociology Department of the University of Columbia. In 1949, Horkheimer led the Institute back to Frankfurt, though Marcuse remained in America.

The Frankfurt school posed the questions: why had the prospect of radical change in society so little popular or natural support? Why was there so little consciousness of the need for politically radical change – indeed how had that sense of need been apparently eliminated from popular consciousness? Marcuse, in *One Dimensional Man* (UK: Sphere Books, 1968), contends that in advanced societies capitalism appears to have proved its worth; by 'producing the goods' it is deemed a successful system and therefore one which has rendered itself immune to criticism.

The Frankfurt school believed that CULTURE – traditionally transcendent of capitalist ethic and thus in many ways potentially subversive of it – had been harnessed by the mass media (See HEGEMONY). Classical art had been popularized, yes; but in the process of media-adoption, it had been deprived of its *oppositional* values (See DOMINANT, SUBORDINATE, RADICAL). The Frankfurt school has had considerable influence upon thinking about the media and its influence upon culture, but has been criticized for condemning existing reality without proposing how it might be changed for the better. See AUDIENCE: ACTIVE AUDIENCE; CULTIVATION; CULTURAL APPARATUS; DOMINANT DISCOURSE; HYPHENIZED ABRIDGEMENT; PSEUDOCONTEXT.

* Rolf Wiggershaus, *The Frankfurt School: Its History, Theories and Political Significance* (UK: Polity Press, paperback edition, 1995).

Freedom of information The right of access by citizens to information of public interest is enshrined in legislation in many countries, in particular the United States. In the UK in 1994 the Conservative government under John Major took a tentative step towards creating a degree of open government with its Code of Practice on Access to Government Information. In opposition, the Labour government made no secret of its intention to end secret government, the future Labour Prime Minister Tony Blair promising that a Freedom of Information Act, should Labour be elected, would 'signal a new relationship between government and people; a relationship which sees the public as legitimate stakeholders in the running of the country'. The basis of this relationship was to be freedom of information.

Not long after the massive election victory of Labour in 1997, the minister entrusted with navigating a freedom of information bill through parliament, David Clark, was sacked and responsibility for the legislation passed to the Home Office. The draft White Paper, *Your Right to Know*, was put on hold. No mention of a Freedom of Information Act was made in the Queen's Speech at the opening of Parliament, 1998, but in May 1999 Home Secretary Jack Straw broke the Government's silence on FoI (Freedom of information legislation). According to the Home Office's website Freedom of Information Unit the draft Bill was 'a major step towards implementing the Government's commitment to increasing openness in the public sector; a significant step towards involving people more in decisions which affect their lives'. The sting came in the tail: 'subject to clearly defined exemptions and conditions'.

The Bill raised the number of exemptions listed in the White Paper from seven to 21 and was generally condemned, throughout the UK press, as representing a retreat, even from Major's Code of Practice. Hugo Young, in a *Guardian* article, 25 May 1999, 'The final triumph of all the butchers and whisperers' called the Bill 'a spectacular betrayal' of the view that disclosure makes for better government decisions. 'The Bill steps far back, in areas that matter most.' The liberal and impressive White Paper 'has now, with the help of Whitehall' been 'butchered'. A key element of the White Paper is that restriction of access would only occur if an independent commissioner was satisfied that 'substantial harm' would, by revelation, be done to public interest. This condition was removed from the Bill. In an article 'Abysmal handiwork', in the

same edtion of the *Guardian*, Maurice Frankel, director of the Campaign for Freedom of Information, is equally scathing. He points out that under the proposals, 'Reports into accidents involving dangerous cars, train crashes, unsafe domestic appliances, air disasters, chemical fires or nuclear incidents will go into a permanently secret filing cabinet. The same goes for reports into risks faced by workers or the public from industrial hazards'. He asks, 'What can have blinded conscientious ministers to the abysmal nature of these proposals?' A *Daily Telegraph* leader of the same day offers an answer, stating that the proposed Bill 'will confirm the impression that no government is willing to play the political game with transparent cards'.

While signalling the appointment of a freedom of information commissioner, the Bill denies him or her independent powers, subjecting his actions to the will of government ministers. The catch-all 21 exemptions from the public's right to know are hedged, in the Bill, with further safeguards – the increase from 20 to 40 days during which the authorities must deal with information enquiries and the introduction of charges for information provided. This 'depressing damp squib' as a *Daily Mail* leader of 25 May calls it, is explained in the *Guardian*'s own leader as the result of 'Labour's weak-minded accession to the norms and prejudices of state power'.

In the summer of 1999 the *Guardian* began an intensive campaign to get the Freedom of Information Bill liberalized, marshalling the comments of scores of critics of the Bill. A *Guardian*/ICM poll rebuffed the Government's view that freedom of information was not an issue which concerned the British public. A new law giving public access to information was supported by seven out of ten people. Over 70 per cent of the population supported the principle that governments should publish all information unless its disclosure could be proved to be harmful. Sceptics believed that while public pressure might bring about modest improvements to the Bill before it became law the fear of openness among those in power would ensure that the UK remained very much what it has always been – a society dominated in its government and its institutions by secrecy.

By stark contrast, human rights legislation in the US, only part of which is the Freedom of Information Act (1966), ensures access to the most sensitive areas of government activity and also to the information of public institutions and public companies. In the US the CIA and FBI are obliged, under privacy legislation, to give access to individuals on any files held on them – though the names of informers are blanked out.

The good news for the British people is that the European Convention on Human Rights (ECHR) became part of British law in 2000. This contains rights of access to information and the protection of privacy, two potentially conflicting interests posing a dilemma for legislators, judges and the media: how might a balance be struck between the public's right to know and the individual's right to privacy? – a classic question for the student of media communication. See CENSORSHIP.

Frequency In a non-technical sense, and as used in relation to the media, *frequency* is the degree of repetition of topics of news or information in the press, on radio or TV. The more frequently a topic inhabits news headlines and news stories, the more likely it is to continue to do so; to be defined and accepted as 'important', and to have media impact.

If there were no daily reference to the doings of Parliament, for example in news columns or broadcasts, the media would be accused of neglecting their duty – that is, to reinforce through frequency the acceptance of established institutions, not the least the WESTMINSTER VIEW of British politics.

Negative frequency operates when stories are overlooked, or edged to the margins of attention. Consequently they rarely have the chance either to improve their status as news or impart the full weight of their argument. The term may also be used to refer to the way in which news items fit the frequency – the time scale – of the mode of communication. See CONSISTENCY; EFFECTS OF THE MASS MEDIA; IMMEDIACY; INTENSITY; PERIODICITY.

Front See SELF-PRESENTATION.

Front region, back region See IMPRESSION MANAGEMENT.

Functionalist (mode of media analysis) Interprets social behaviour in terms of its contribution to the assumed overall goals of society, recognizing a CONSENSUS within society of common norms and VALUES. The main focus of functionalist analysis is upon the ways in which social systems maintain *equilibrium*. A functionalist would consider any social or cultural element in relation to its contribution to the survival, integration or stability of society. The communication process features as a major component in the 'servicing' of equilibrium.

Structural functionalism, a mode of analysis developed by US sociologist Talcott Parsons, identifies common features of a complex industrial society which are central to its survival. These include the delineation and maintenance of boundaries (social, cultural, etc.); the definition of major structural units of society and the connections between them; and an overriding concern with system maintenance. This school of analysis has been particularly strong in the US.

Within the functionalist perspective, activities which contribute to the survival of a system are known as **eufunctions**; those which contribute to disturbance are known as **dysfunctions**. A distinction is also made between **manifest** and **latent functions**, the one intended and recognized by the participants, the other neither intended nor recognized.

The functionalist approach makes challengable assumptions about consensus over the goals of society, leaving untouched important questions about the *source* of these goals and the degree to which an identified source may influence the nature of the social structure and social action. Its tendency is to legitimize the status quo and to emphasize the predominance of the whole over the parts, overlooking alternative means of achieving the same or similar functions. See MARXIST; SOCIAL ACTION (MODES OF MEDIA ANALYSIS).

Functions of communication See COMMUNICATION, FUNCTIONS.

Functions of mass media See NORMATIVE THEORIES OF MASS MEDIA.

Fundamentalism Religious observation and attitudes in extreme form; current at all times, usually reactive to *modernity*, whether this is represented by alternative religions, new ideas, ways of life or change-threatening technology. Modernity, however it is defined, is regarded as a destroyer or corrupter of VALUES to the point when democracy itself is often DÉMONIZED because it appears to have failed to provide a sense of identity, of industrial and communal security in a seemingly random and chaotic world. Some commentators see fundamentalism as a reassertion of *patriarchy* in societies which are deemed to have progressed too far towards equality; some see it as a reaction to urbanization, a retreat to 'things as they used to be' – a nostalgia for a lost past.

James Davidson Hunter talks of 'culture wars' between modernists and traditionalists in *Cultural Wars: The Struggle to Define America* (US: Basic Books, 1991) and these often occur over the terrain of gender and sexual politics – over contraception, for example, and abortion, the veiling of women in Moslem states or gay rights in the American armed services. Pro-lifers in the US are 'at war' with pro-choice preferences and the battles rage across culture, in schools, in the media, in the law courts and, of course, in language itself – 'terminating a pregnancy' versus 'killing a baby'. See EXPECTATION, HORIZONS OF; POSTMODERNISM.

G

Galtung and Ruge's Model of Selective Gatekeeping, 1965 Whenever 'newsworthiness' is discussed and analysed the names of Johan Galtung and Mari Ruge are likely to be mentioned before all others. Their article, 'The structure of foreign news: The presentation of the Congo, Cuba and Cyprus crises in four foreign newspapers' in the *Journal of International Peace Research*, 1 (1965) and reprinted in *The Manufacture of News* (UK: Constable, 1973), edited by Stanley Cohen and Jock

Young, has proved a focal point for those who ask the questions, what qualifies as news? and what makes one item of news predominate over another?

The model represents the way in which events pass through the GATEKEEPING processes of the media – initially the perceptions of media people as to whether the event qualifies as news, then the selection according to a set of news criteria (I to IX) alone or in combination. For details of the criteria identified by Galtung and Ruge, see NEWS VALUES.

Games A term used in TRANSACTIONAL ANALYSIS. Eric Berne in his classic study of games entitled, *Games People Play* (UK: Penguin, 1964) describes a game as 'an ongoing series of complementary ulterior transactions progressing to a well-defined, predictable outcome.' Games are recurring sets of transactions, identifiable by their hidden motivations and the promise of psychological payoffs or gains for the game players. The victim of the game is called a *mark*, and it is a known weakness of the *mark*, known as the *gimmick*, which allows the game player to hook the victim and achieve his/her desired *payoff*. Every game, Berne believes, is essentially dishonest. Other useful terms for analysing games are *switch* which describes the point in the game where the manipulator catches out the victim and *cross up* which describes the confusion felt once the switch has taken place. A game may involve a manipulator and an unknowing victim but, of course, at times both or all the participants playing a particular game might be trying to manipulate the other(s). Game playing may often be unconscious. Game playing is often seen as a defensive strategy in communication as far as the manipulator is concerned. Berne identifies many games that are played in everyday life such as 'If It Weren't For You', 'See What You Made Me Do' and 'Harried'.

* Eric Berne, *What Do You Say After You Say Hello?* (UK: Corgi Books, 1975); Ian Stewart and Vann Joines, *TA Today* (UK: Lifespace, 1987).

Gatekeeping To reach its intended target, every MESSAGE has to pass through many 'gates'; some will be wide open, some ajar, some tightly closed. At work, the boss's

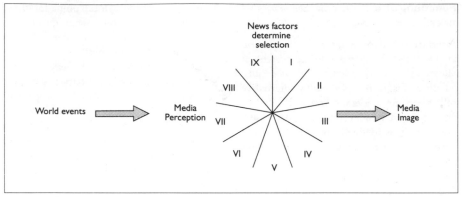

Galtung and Ruge's model of selective gatekeeping, 1965

secretary is the archetypal gatekeeper. She may be under instruction to welcome callers or delay them, by letter, by telephone or physically by 'guarding' the boss's door. Writing about **gatekeepers** in the media, Stuart Hood in 'The politics of television' in Denis McQuail, ed., *Sociology of Mass Communications* (UK: Penguin, 1972) says 'A news bulletin is the result of a number of choices by a variety of "gatekeepers". They include the editor who decides on the day's coverage, or the organizer who briefs the camera crews and reporters and allocates assignments, the film editor who selects the film to be included in the bulletin, the copy-taster who chooses the stories from the tape to accompany the film, the sub-editor who writes the story and the duty editor who supervises the compilation of the bulletin, fixes the running order of the stories and gives it its final shape'.

The selection or rejection of material is made according to a set of criteria determined by a number of factors – the gatekeeper's CLASS background, upbringing and education and his/her attitudes to the world – VALUES; plus the values, NORMS and traditional wisdom of the organization for which the gatekeeper works.

Hood believes that a substantial majority of media gatekeepers practice 'middle-class consensus politics' and it is this which colours their perceptions of news and influences the selection process. He goes on to point out that the narrow range of social background from which TV staff come, coupled with organizational pressures such

as the need to safeguard jobs and the importance of team spirit, are 'sufficient to ensure that the ground rules of consensus politics are not broken'.

The process and effect of gatekeeping in the media have undergone substantial modification in the age of electronic transmission. The age of scarcity of channels has been transformed to an age of bandwidth abundance. Consumers of communication now have at their fingertips the power to evade traditional modes of gatekeeping. Text, pictures, the latest movies, pop tunes are all becoming available on-line; and if gatekeeping has always been a process of manipulation by the communicators as well as selection, the consumer can do this too with the images and texts that he or she can summon up. As populations access the Net in increasing numbers, there is the potential for a shift of control from producer to consumer. This, at the same time, threatens to lessen the ability of governments to exercise intervention in the form of regulation and censorship. The very freedom of expression which electronic data exchange offers people worldwide will prompt governments to seek to curb this freedom – a possibility which will be made more viable once all transmission forms share the same digital network (See DIGITALIZATION).

The 21st c. holds out the prospect of a scenario in which each consumer is his or her own gatekeeper. In a networked article, 'The soul of the news machine: electronic journalism in the twenty-first century',

David Bartlett, president of the US Radio-Television News Directors Association, celebrates the potential of the new technology to 'provide the power to turn billions of digital bits into unlimited amounts of information available to all'. However, this power 'will create awesome responsibility to preserve every citizen's freedom of access to that information and the right of everyone to participate in the continuing digital conversation'.

Bartlett acknowledges a danger in this profusion of ungated information and exchange – 'it would be foolish to ignore the fact that if new technology encourages everyone to speak at the same time, nobody will be heard or understood'. See AGENDA SETTING; CONSENSUS; GALTUNG AND RUGE'S MODEL OF SELECTIVE GATEKEEPING, 1965; MR GATE; NEWS VALUES; WHITE'S GATEKEEPING MODEL, 1950.

Gender Our gender or gender identity refers to our categorization, and that of others, of ourselves as either male or female. According to Richard D. Gross in *Psychology: The Science of Mind and Behaviour* (UK: Hodder & Stoughton, 1987), gender is a cultural term and one's gender role 'refers to the behaviours, attitudes, values, beliefs and so on which a particular society expects from, or considers appropriate to, males and females on the basis of their biological sex'.

Definitions of appropriate behaviour for males and females can vary from one culture to another and, over time, within a particular culture or society. Conflict also exists within our own society regarding the precise definition of what should constitute appropriate behaviour for the different gender roles. One area of research within media studies focuses on the role that the media may play in forming or reinforcing gender STEREOTYPES and certain expectations about gender roles.

Another current focus of research interest is the degree to which a society's LANGUAGE and its use shapes and reflects notions of gender identity and gender roles. See ANDROCENTRIC RULE; FEMINISM; FRAMING; GENDERED GENRE; GENDERLECTS; HE/MAN LANGUAGE, HEDGES; MALE-AS-NORM; MELODRAMA, MUTED GROUPS; PLUS MALE/MINUS MALE; NORMS, REINFORCEMENT; SEXISM; SOAP OPERAS; TAG QUESTIONS.

Gendered genre Term used in cultural analysis to denote genres of film or television which are seen to appeal to one GENDER rather than another. For example, SOAP OPERAS are seen as primarily directed at female audiences whilst crime series appeal more to male audiences. The TEXT and its narrative patterns typically reflect such differences in audience and in part, though not uncritically, assumptions about gender roles and typical masculine and feminine behaviour. Soap operas, for instance, concentrate on the family and local neighbourhood and the interplay of interpersonal relationships within these contexts; whereas the crime series focuses on action, heroic deeds and male bonding. Some researchers have argued that the concept of gendered genre over-simplifies the potentially complex relationship between the text, its narrative form, its authors and its audience. See FEMINISM; GENRE; MELODRAMA; SEXISM.

Gendered viewing Describes the different perspectives, ways of seeing, between genders in relation to cultural, social and historical contexts. This is not simply a matter of the ways men look, or perceive, compared with the way women perceive, for as Mary Ellen Brown asserts in *Soap Opera and Women's Talk: The Pleasure of Resistance* (US: Sage, 1994), 'gender role characteristics of the one sex can be displayed by people of either sex'. Indeed, the 'simple delineations of *masculine* and *feminine* are also somewhat inappropriate because they imply masculinity as central and femininity as marginal'. Brown's book explores the ways in which women view – and use – soaps to assemble DISCOURSES of resistance through what she terms GOSSIP NETWORKS. Brown writes, 'Both soap operas and gossip claim for women a space and time in which there is freedom to play with dialogue – dialogue that does not necessarily advance the plot but is simply there for pleasure. All of these aspects fly in the face of dominant conventions'.

Genderlects In *You Just Don't Understand: Men and Women in Conversation* (UK: Virago, 1992), Deborah Tannen argues that in conversation while men 'speak and hear a language of status and independence', women 'speak' and hear a language of connection and intimacy'. These fundamentally different orientations and their influence on perception are, she argues, important factors in creating confusion and misunderstanding in conversations between men and women. These differences have led Tannen to conclude that men and women speak different *genderlects* and her book examines examples of how male and female differences in orientation and consequently in interpretation can be observed in many different contexts. See REPORT-TALK/RAPPORT-TALK.

* Mary Ellen Brown, *Soap Operas and Women's Talk: The Pleasure of Resistance* (US: Sage, 1994); Mary Crawford, *Talking Difference: On Gender and Language* (UK: Sage, 1995).

Gender signals Male and female signals in interpersonal conduct and appearance that label or place emphasis upon the sex of the signaller. See GESTURE; PROXEMICS.

Generalized other As contrasted with SIGNIFICANT OTHERS; representing society at large – the organized community or social group which, in the words of George Herbert Mead in *Mind, Self and Society From the Standpoint of a Social Behaviourist* (US: University of Chicago Press, 1934), 'gives the individual his unity of self'. Mead argues that 'it is in the form of the generalized other that the social process influences the behaviour of individuals involved in it and carrying it on'. Thus the generalized other exercises a degree of control over the conduct of its members; and its NORMS and VALUES are important determining factors in the individual's thinking. The significant other – a parent, friend, group leader or public figure – may varyingly reinforce, modify, challenge or counteract the influence of the generalized other. See SYMBOLIC INTERACTIONISM.

Genre Term deriving from the French, meaning type or classification. In literature the major classic genres were epic, tragedy, lyric, comedy and satire, eventually to be followed by the novel and short story. Genres, working at least approximately to basic ground rules of form and style, are cate-

gories to be found in all modes of artistic expression. In films there are genres of the WESTERN, gangster movies, FILM NOIR, science fiction, romantic comedy, horror, disaster, costume drama, etc. In TELEVISION there are SIT-COMS, SOAPS, detective and police series. Genres are rarely discrete or singular entities. They are subject to influence by other genres, and are often a mixture of genre elements. Indeed part of the pleasure audiences derive from genre TEXTS is their inventiveness, the way the CODES of different genres have been knowingly manipulated, sometimes to satirical effect. In short, what attracts and fascinates is their *intertextuality*. Writing in *Acts of Literature* (UK: Routledge, 1992), French philosopher Jacques Derrida is of the opinion that there is 'no genreless text'; thus the way is open to classify TV news, party political broadcasts, weather reports, quiz shows, chat shows and consumer programmes as genres.

Gerbner's model of communication, 1956 This is described by Denis McQuail in *Communication*, 2nd ed. (UK: Longman, 1993) as perhaps 'the most comprehensive attempt yet to specify all the component stages and activities of communication'. Below is a modified version of George Gerbner's model as presented in 'Towards a general model of communication', in *Audio Visual Communication Review*, 4.

M is responder to E (event) and may be human or machine (such as a microphone or camera). Gerbner's emphasis is upon the considerable *variability* in the perception of an event by a communicating agent and also in the way the MESSAGE is perceived by a receiver. He speaks of the essential 'creative, interactional nature of the perceptual process'. Equally important is the stress placed upon the importance of *context* to the 'reading' of messages, and of the *open* nature of human communication.

For Gerbner the relationship between form and context in the communication process (S = Signal) is dynamic and interactive. It is also concerned with *access* and *control*, dimensions which inevitably affect the nature and content of communication messages – their selection, shaping and distortion. At the level of the mass media this is

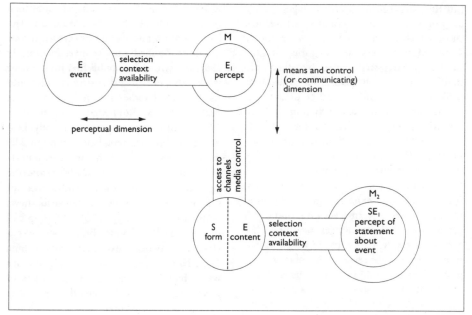

Gerbner's model of communication, 1956

obvious, but access and control also operate at the level of INTERPERSONAL communication – teachers in classrooms, for example, speakers at public meetings, parents in the home situation.

Back on the horizontal axis, Gerbner stresses the importance of *availability*. A literate electorate may have the capacity to read all the facts about a political situation, all the pros and cons of an industrial dispute but that capacity can only operate, and the pros and cons be properly weighed, if the necessary facts are made available.

What Gerbner's model does not do is address itself fully satisfactorily to the problems of how MEANING is generated. The form or CODE of the message (S) is taken for granted, whereas the advocate of SEMIOL-OGY/SEMIOTICS would argue that meaning is of the essence. See COMMUNICATION MODELS.

Gestural dance A term which has been used to describe the way in which gestures are employed to achieve interactional synchrony between participants in an encounter, e.g. the smooth handing over of the conversational floor from speaker to listener is achieved by a combination of prolonged gaze, falling intonation, returning of the hands to a rest position and possibly the

use of a gesture towards the listener to invite a contribution. The listener may have indicated a wish to speak by the use of rapid HEAD NODS.

Gestural echo See POSTURAL ECHO.

Gesture Michael Argyle in *Bodily Communication* (UK: Methuen, 1988) divides gestures and bodily movements into three main categories: Emblems, Illustrators and Self-touching. Emblems are movements, often hand movements, which can easily be translated into speech in terms of their meaning (they may often stand in for speech) within a particular group or culture. The use, in Britain, of the thumbs-up gesture to mean O.K. would be an example. Illustrators are those gestures used to illustrate or accompany speech often to aid explanation; for example, gestures used when giving directions. **Self-touching** normally indicates information about an individual's emotional state, such as the scratching of the face when anxious. In *Manwatching: A Field Guide to Human Behaviour* (UK: Jonathan Cape, 1977), Desmond Morris defines a gesture as 'any action that sends a visual signal to an onlooker'. *Incidental* gestures may be unintentional, accidental, but they still communicate messages – such as mood information. *Primary* gestures are those which are intended – a wave, a nod, a wink. Morris offers six categories of gestures: (1) *Expressive*; shared by other animals as well as humans, and including facial expression and manual gesticulations. (2) *Mimic* gestures; exclusively human, 'The essential quality of a Mimic Gesture is that it attempts to copy the thing it is trying to portray'. This category Morris subdivides into *Social* mimicry (or 'putting on a good face'); *Theatrical* mimicry; *Partial* mimicry (pretending your hand is a gun, for example); and what he terms *Vacuum* mimicry – gestures to indicate hunger or thirst. (3) *Schematic* gestures are those in which imitations become abbreviated or abridged; a gestural shorthand. (4) *Symbolic* gestures represent moods and ideas – such as the sign to indicate that you consider someone is 'round the twist'. (5) *Technical* gestures constitute specialized signal systems recognized only by those in the trade or profession, such as those employed by a TV studio manager or a fireman to his colleagues. (6) *Coded* gestures are based upon formal systems, such as Deaf-and-Dumb Sign Language, Semaphore and the Tic-tac signalling of the race course.

Many gestures carry universal MEANING but in general the gesture is critically dependent upon the cultural context in which it is made and specific contexts of timing and situation as well as the combination of gestures, for rarely do they exist alone, or without vocal accompaniment. See BARRIER SIGNALS; BATON SIGNALS; COMMUNICATION, NON-VERBAL; CUT-OFF; GENDER SIGNALS; GESTURAL DANCE; GESTURAL ECHO; GUIDE SIGNS; INSULT SIGNALS; METASIGNALS; NON-VERBAL BEHAVIOUR: REPERTOIRE; POSTURAL ECHO; PROXEMICS; RELIC GESTURES; SALUTATION DISPLAY; SHORTFALL SIGNALS; TIE-SIGNS.

Ghost-writer One who does literary work for someone else who takes the credit. The practice of publishing autobiographies and memoirs by the famous, written by ghost-writers, is widespread (not the least, it is believed, among sports persons).

Glasgow University Media Group Set up with a grant from the UK Social Science Research Council, the Group has published research findings which have won considerable attention and not unexpectedly, drawn fire from the media under investigation. By 1982, the Group had published three major works tabulating its exhaustive research into the way TV handles the news. First came *Bad News* (UK: Routledge & Kegan Paul, 1976), which exploded the generally held image of broadcasters being substantially more objective and reliable in news reporting than the press. 'Our study', wrote the eight authors of the original study, 'does not support a received view that television news is "the news as it happens".' The Group had monitored all TV news broadcasts over a six-month period, from January to June 1975. Notable among the Group's findings was a bias in TV against the activities of organized labour and a relentless emphasis upon effects rather than causes.

Later publications by the Glasgow University Media Group have been *More Bad News* (UK: Routledge & Kegan Paul, 1980), *Really Bad News* (UK: Writers and Readers' Publishing Co-operative, 1982) and *War and Peace News* (UK: Open University Press, 1985) about media coverage of the Falklands War, the Miners' Strike and Northern Ireland. The theoretical base from which the Group works may be summarized by a quotation from *More Bad News*: 'news is not a neutral and not a natural phenomenon: it is rather the manufactured production of ideology'. See RESEARCH CENTRES INTO THE MEDIA.

* John Eldridge, ed., *Getting the Message: News, Truth and Power* (UK: Routledge, 1993); Lesley Henderson, *Incest in Brookside: Audience Response to the Jordache Story* (UK: Channel 4/Glasgow University Media Group, 1996).

Glasnost Openness; Russian term for greater freedom of expression and less state SECRECY. The word became universal currency with the election to leadership in the Soviet Union of Mikhail Gorbachev, who welcomed rather than shunned world publicity and demonstrated an openness within the Russian nation and in communication with other countries not experienced since the early days of the Russian Revolution. Linked with *glasnost* has been *perestroika*, meaning reconstruction, reform in relation to government practices and expectations.

Global culture and young people See CHILDREN, YOUNG PEOPLE AND THE CHANGING MEDIA ENVIRONMENT.

Globalization of culture See CULTURE: GLOBALIZATION OF.

Globalization of media As early as the 1960s Marshall McLuhan was describing the world as an electronic village and his phrase 'global village' is now part of the language of mass communication. Certainly electronic transmission of information has become global and the institutions, the transnational corporations responsible for that transmission, are global in scale and intention. The similarity with village life is more obscure. Thanks to global transmission we are theoretically capable of knowing what is happening in backyards or back gardens world-wide. It is feared that what we may be permitted to see there will come to look more and more like what is happening in our own backyards, as familiar as American apple pie.

Globalization is also a process of *convergence*, of hardware and software, of systems of ownership and control. Globalization brings the world to our TV screens, and through the INTERNET to our computers. Information in and out converges; services, computer shopping, for example, converge with the capacity to summon up data for our individual needs. With *digitalization* of information, turning every element of data – words, pictures, sound – into digits which can be transmitted terrestrially; through the telephone line and cable, via satellite, or all of them together, the possibilities of the control of multi-media services falling into fewer and fewer corporate hands deserves to stimulate global concern.

Just as the technology of media converges, so do operation systems. Traditional regulations preventing cross-media ownership were modified or dismantled throughout the 1990s. News International, the flagship of the Murdoch dynasty (See CITIZEN KANE OF THE GLOBAL VILLAGE) operates globally in every conceivable field of mass communication, and where it does not operate alone, it is a decisive part of other conglomerate activities in the media field. For example, in May 1995 News International formed a two-billion dollar link with the American telecommunications giant, MCI, rival of the all-powerful US company AT&T. The deal put Murdoch's empire directly on to the carrier system of the superhighway, establishing Murdoch as a galactic superstar.

An observer from outer space might survey the current media scene – in which Murdoch feasts the globe with his vast library of films from the Fox archives, with US football, UK Premier League soccer and Rugby League; dominates European satellite transmission with Britain's BSkyB satellite and Asian satellite services with Star TV (not to mention his control of Australia's Channel 7 and the Delphi On-Line Internet Service) and conclude that a synonym for globalization is 'murdochization' and that the true name of McLuhan's global village is Rupertsville. See BERLUSCONI PHENOMENON; CYBERSPACE; DIGITALIZATION; DIGITAL TELEVISION; INFORMATION GAPS; McWORLD Vs JIHAD; MEDIA IMPERIALISM; NEWS: GLOBALIZATION OF.

Globalization of news See NEWS: GLOBALIZATION OF.

Global jukebox Name given to the *Live Aid* for Africa rock concert held jointly at Wembley Stadium, UK and the John F. Kennedy Stadium, Philadelphia, US on 13 July 1985. This, the first world-wide rock concert of its kind, was the brainchild of its principal organizer, rock musician Bob Geldof, and it was held to raise money for famine victims in the Sudan, Ethiopia and the Sub-Sahara.

The concert, lasting 16 hours, was transmitted by 11 satellites to an estimated television audience of between 1.5 and 2 bn people in 160 different countries – some of whom also contributed live performance and messages of support, via satellite, which were slotted into the programme.

The event, featuring some of the best known names from two generations of rock stars, vividly demonstrated the potential offered by developments in communications technology and gripped the public's imagination; it broke the largest live television audience record over 16 hours. It is estimated that the concert raised over US $100 million for famine relief by mid-1986.

Global scrutiny Describes the vastly increased *visibility* of people and events on a global scale, largely as a result of TELEVISION. John B. Thompson in *The Media and Modernity: A Social Theory of the Media* (UK: Polity, 1995) speaks of a 'regime of visibility created by an increasingly globalized system of communication'; and however, structured (See FRAMING) this power to scrutinize represents a 'significant historical development. For it means not only that political leaders must now act in an arena which is in principle open to view on a global scale, but also that recipients are able to see and experience distant individuals and events in a way that was simply not possible before'.

Global village See GLOBALIZATION; McLUHANISMS.

Glocalization See McWORLD Vs JIHAD.

Golden pen of freedom Annual award by the International Federation of Newspaper Publishers (FIEJ) based in Paris.

Gossip Traditionally gossip has been ranked as 'woman's-talk' and, within DISCOURSES and social structures which are male-dominated, given low status in the order of exchange, or even disparaged. Gossip, to outsiders, usually male, appears to be 'going nowhere', 'undirected' and ultimately pointless if not damaging. Such judgements are essentially made from ideological positions which view communication as less an exchange of experience (a cultural exchange) and more a transmission of information: in short, 'man's talk'.

Gossip deserves more serious attention than is usually given to it. In 'Gossip: notes on women's oral culture' in *Women's Studies International Quarterly*, 3 (1980), Deborah Jones defines gossip as 'a way of talking between women in their roles as women, intimate in style, personal and domestic in topic and setting, a female cultural event which springs from and perpetuates the restrictions of the female role, but also gives the comfort of validation'. Jones lists four

functions of gossip: house-talk, scandal, bitching and chatting. Such talk establishes and confirms the pleasures of interaction while at the same time working to give them value and validity. As such, it is potentially empowering.

Gossip networks A mode of resistance, by women, to male-dominated DISCOURSES. The term is used by Mary Ellen Brown in *Soap Opera and Women's Talk: The Pleasure of Resistance* (UK: Sage, 1994). Brown discusses how gossip networks arise out of viewing soap opera, and the use of such entertainment as a means of constructing alternative MEANINGS. The author asks how 'can such a trivial or even exploitative genre as soap opera be associated with the notion of empowerment for its viewers?' She responds to the question by arguing that the answer 'lies in the invisible discourse networks it plugs into and helps solidify. Such discourse networks, or gossip networks, are important for women's resistive pleasure'.

Graffiti The poor man or woman's tilt at literary immortality; writings in public but forbidden places attempting crudely or pithily or both to summarize some of life's basic truths, such as 'Suicide is the most sincere form of self-criticism', or pertinent advice, such as 'let's keep incest in the family' or even historical analysis, such as 'Emmanuel Kant but Ghengis Khan'. Ultimately, of course, 'Graffiti should be obscene and not heard', and specially-provided blank walls for graffiti writers such as Sweden has provided rob the 'art' of the thrill of doing something illegal.

Gramophone Originally the Phonograph, invented by Thomas Alva Edison (1847–1931), his first sketch of which was published in the *Scientific American*, 22 December 1877. His 'talking tinfoil' led to the creation in 1878 of the Edison Speaking Phonograph Company, and soon a single exhibition phonograph could earn as much as US $1800 a week. Concurrently, Edison designed different models, including a disc machine with a volute spiral which anticipated later developments.

Commercial recordings began in 1890,

though sound reproduction remained exceedingly poor and the wax cylinders could only play for two minutes maximum and there was no way of mass producing the cylinders. Machines were driven by cumbersome, heavy-duty batteries and were very expensive to purchase – that is until Thomas Hood Macdonald, a manager of Graphophone, rival company to Edison's, put on sale the first mechanical phonograph (1894), retailing at $75.

The Columbia company were the first to manufacture double-sided discs (1908), though the next major innovation was electrical recording, initiated by Lionel Guest and H.O. Merrimen in 1920 when they recorded, by electrical process, the Unknown Warrior burial service in Westminster Abbey. Bell Laboratories in the US proved substantial pioneers in this area, which they termed *orthophonic* recording.

The miraculous rise of the gramophone was eventually hit by the more popular mass appeal of RADIO and the 1930s were lean years, though the record industry in Europe did not plumb the depths to the extent it did in the US where, by January 1933, the record business was practically extinct. However, in September 1934, the RCA Victor sales department offered the Duo Junior, consisting of an electrically powered turntable and a magnetic pickup, primitive but popular, and by 1935 the notion of 'high-fidelity' was born. Station W2XR (later WQXR) in New York began 'high-fidelity broadcasting' in 1934, in truth, as much high publicity as hi-fi.

The 2nd World War (1939–45) cut non-military use of shellac – the material for the discs – principally imported from India, and record production was severely curtailed. 1944 saw the first examples of Decca's 'ffrr' sound reaching British ears. This was 'full frequency range reproduction' achieving standards of reproduction never previously heard.

In 1941, 127 million discs were sold; in 1947, 400 million – a year before Columbia Records in the US launched the unbreakable microgrove disc, with a playing time of 23 minutes per side. The LP (Long Playing) Record had arrived. It bore between 224

and 300 grooves per inch compared to 85 grooves on the ordinary disc; and it moved on the turntable at $33\frac{1}{3}$ rpm instead of the traditional 78. Not to be outdone, RCA Victor hit back with the 45 rpm record, thus beginning the so-called Battle of the Speeds, diminishing trade in what turned out to be a period of consumer uncertainty. It was the period too when recording by magnetic tape was rapidly expanding.

Neither ousted the other: in fact they proved complementary and expanded together in the dynamic growth period of Rock and Roll and the radio disc jockey.

Stereophonic sound, or 'two-eared listening', had been possible since the Bell Laboratories had put on binaural demonstrations at the Chicago World's Fair of 1933, and Walt Disney's film *Fantasia* (1940) showed the possibilities of multi-source music reproduction in a cinema. The stereo effect was caught first on high-quality magnetic tape. Then in 1957 the Westrex Company devised a successful method of putting two stereo channels into a single groove. By September of the following year every major record company in the US was offering stereo discs for sale.

The tape cassette emerged from Philips who demonstrated its potential at the 1963 Berlin Radio Show. They improved it substantially and in 1970 along came the DOLBY SYSTEM just at the time when tape machines were becoming popular as in-car entertainment.

An innovation in gramophone technology which has never quite caught on is Quadrophony, using four speakers rather than two, the additional channels intended to convey 'ambient' sound – fractionally delayed impulses reflected from the rear of the recording hall. Digital recording is now with us. The trusty stylus is being eased into history by the laser, and discs as we have known them banished by new developments in miniaturization. 'A partisan historian', writes Roland Gelatt of the gramophone, 'could perhaps be forgiven for claiming it as the chief marvel and solace of the century.' See CD – COMPACT DISC.

Graphic revolution Daniel Boorstin in *The Image* (UK: Penguin, 1963) uses this term to describe the accelerated importance of the visual image in the post 2nd World War period. Presented in photography and moving pictures, with all the backing of modern technological wizardry, the image has more impact in the 'graphic revolution' than the word; further, the image has become more interesting, more vivid and dramatic than the original: 'the shadow becomes the substance' and suddenly reality cannot match up to its image. See ADVERTISING; DIGITALIZATION.

Graphophone See GRAMOPHONE.

Great person orientation See GUARD DOG METAPHOR; POWER ELITE.

Grip Person in a FILM crew responsible for laying *tracks*, portable 'railway lines' for the smooth movement of the camera mounted on a DOLLY.

Griswold cultural diamond model, 1994 In *Cultures and Societies in a Changing World* (US: Pine Forge Press, 1994), Wendy Griswold offers readers the following diagram as an aid to the analysis of the cultural process:

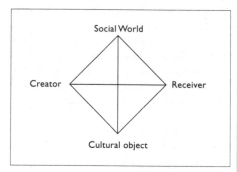

Griswold cultural diamond model, 1994

Each of the four points is linked and thus seen as interactive. Griswold admits, 'We cannot call it a theory of culture because it says nothing about how the points are related' and it is not a model 'in the strict sense because it does not indicate cause and effect'. Rather, she sees the diamond as 'an accounting device intended to encourage a fuller understanding of any cultural object's relationships to the social world'.

Groups A good deal of communication takes place within groups of one type or another. Charles H. Cooley, one of the initiators of research into group behaviour and communication, in his work, *Social Organization* (US: Scribner, 1909), classifies groups into two main types. **Primary groups** such as the family are defined as groups in which there is face-to-face communication; in which NORMS and MORES are produced; in which ROLES are allocated and in which a feeling of solidarity is enjoyed. **Secondary groups**, such as social CLASS groups, are much larger aggregates. Several researchers have sought to determine the communication processes which take place within groups and in particular the interrelationship between a group's CULTURE, roles, status structure, cohesiveness, size, and type and its communication processes.

The performance of individuals is often affected by group membership. Being in a group can enhance or inhibit individual performance depending on such factors as the nature of the task, the degree of effective leadership, the cohesiveness of the group and the flexibility of its communication networks. These factors also determine the quality of group decision-making. In certain circumstances individuals may feel they need to make less effort in a group situation and become *social loafers*; alternatively they may be motivated to work harder and become *social labourers*. At times individuals may be prepared to work harder to make up fo their less energetic group members and contribute to *social compensation*.

Certain dynamics also appear to come into play when groups make decisions. Robert A. Baron and Donn Byrne provide some examples, in *Social Psychology* (US: Allyn & Bacon, 1994 edn.), noting that, 'groups often demonstrate *group polarization*, a tendency to shift toward more extreme views. Two other potential difficulties faced by decision-making groups are *groupthink* . . . and an inability to pool unshared information'.

A small **primary group** particularly has the potential to influence the perceptions of its individual members and thus the way in which they interpret and respond to communication from sources both within and outside the group.

Secondary groups are not without influence either, in the communication process. Basil Bernstein argues, in 'Social class, language and socialization', in John Corner and Jeremy Hawthorn, eds., *Communication Studies: An Introductory Reader* (UK: Arnold, 1993), that a relationship exists between membership of a social class group and the LANGUAGE code adopted. See CONCURRENCE-SEEKING TENDENCY.

* Rupert Brown, *Group Processes* (UK/US: Blackwell, 1988).

Grub Street Description of any form of literary or journalistic drudgery. According to Dr Johnson (1709–84) Grub Street was 'originally the name of a street near Moorfields in London, much inhabited by writers of small histories, dictionaries and temporary poems, whence any mean production is called grubstreet'.

GSR Galvanic skin response: a measure of stress and emotion caused to individuals by others, especially when spatial territories have been invaded that is, someone coming too close for psychological comfort. See PROXEMICS; SPATIAL ZONES.

Guard dog metaphor A variation of the WATCHDOG metaphor representing one of the traditional functions of mass media; suggesting that the media perform as a sentry not for the community but for special interest groups which have the power and influence to establish and maintain their own security systems. In 'A guard dog perspective on the role of media' in the *Journal of Communication* Spring, 1995, George A. Donohue, Phillip J. Tichenor and Clarise N. Olien of the University of Minnesota argue that the guard dog media 'are conditioned to be suspicious of all potential intruders, and they occasionally sound the alarm for reasons that individuals in the master households, that is, the authority structure, can neither understand nor prevent. These occasions occur primarily when authority within the structure is divided'. In communities where there is no apparent conflict within power structures 'the media are sleeping guard dogs'.

The guiding principle appears to be: support the powerful unless the powerful are intruders. 'Where different local groups have conflicting interests,' say Donohue *et al.*, 'the media are more likely to reflect the views of the more powerful groups.' Consequently the guard dog role works towards internal cohesion. The metaphor contrasts with that of the media's perceived role as watchdog.

The role in this case is one of SURVEILLANCE of the powerful on behalf of and in the interests of the people. The media serve as freedom-seekers-and-defenders, hence the titles of so many early newspapers – *Sentinel, Voice of the People, Champion, Justice, Poor Man's Guardian, Observer, Enquirer* and *Advocate*.

This indicates a sharp difference with the role of guard dog media, though one which is substantially less evident in practice. The authors warn that the guard dog role should also be differentiated from the media's agenda setting capacity (See McCOMBS AND SHAW AGENDA-SETTING MODEL OF MEDIA EFFECTS, 1976 and ROGERS AND DEARING AGENDA SETTING MODEL, 1987), where the media are ascribed more independence as arbitrators of news agendas than the guard dog position can sustain. In this case it is the institutional forces, the power structures of society, which set the agenda and which the guard dog media take up and amplify.

A third 'dog' in the repertoire of the media is that of the lapdog. As Donohue *et al.* point out, 'A lapdog perspective is a total rejection of the Fourth Estate view on all counts.' The lapdog is submissive to authority and oblivious 'to all interests except those of powerful groups' and serves to frame all 'issues according to the perspectives of the highest powers in the system'.

While the guard dog is characterized by deference as contrasted with submissiveness, at least it recognizes the existence of, and gives attention to, conflict. The greater the social differentiation within a community or nation, the more extensive is the reporting of conflict. Where there is 'power uncertainty' the media are likely to 'display a tendency to concentrate on individuals while accepting the structure. In doing so, the media are reinforcing the tendency within the culture to emphasize great men and personalities rather than individuals as actors in the system who are subject to the influence of social forces and processes'.

Guide signs Actions indicating direction, sometimes called Deictic Signals: finger pointing, head pointing, eye pointing. Thumbs down and thumbs up come into this category, and all the gestures of beckoning as well as repelling. See NON-VERBAL BEHAVIOUR: REPERTOIRE.

Gum print 19th c. mode of photograph printing which made the pictures resemble oil painting.

Gutenberg Project Johan Gutenberg (1400–1468) is credited with giving the world, in 1450, the printing press and the printed word, so a project which aims to make available books of the world on the contemporary 'press' of the INTERNET is appropriately named. Originated by American Michael Hart, Project Gutenberg set out in the early 1970s to copy into digital mode the texts of some 10,000 books by the year 2001 and to distribute them at a nominal, or no, cost to the reader.

In a guest editorial for the periodical *Database* (1 December 1991), Hart envisaged the library of the future as being accessible via computer and its books being capable of being 'transmitted via disks, phone lines, or other media at a fraction of the cost in money, time, and paper as with present day paper media . . . All material will be available to all patrons from all locations at all times'. Hart's work, and that of his many volunteer helpers, enters the Internet through the computers of the University of Illinois. Because of copyright restrictions, the 'library' of Project Gutenberg is drawn essentially from the public sphere. See CYBERSPACE.

H

Hacker Just as the tomb robbers of ancient Egypt broke into seemingly impregnable pyramids and underground tombs, so the 'hacker' breaks into computer CODES and computer systems. All the hacker needs is a personal micro, know-how and persistence and some of the world's most closely

guarded information banks can be penetrated. See COMPUTERS IN COMMUNICATION.

Halo effect In initial encounters we tend to pick out one or two characteristics of a person and let these influence our general impression of him or her. For example, at an interview, it may be assumed that someone who is well qualified, neatly dressed and pleasant in manner will necessarily perform well in the job and work hard. Such generalizations from one or two characteristics are based on our implicit personality theory – that is, our basic assumptions about which characteristics go together, and how people are likely to behave.

Hammocking Strategy used by TV schedulers to boost the viewing figures of a programme by placing it between two popular programmes.

Hankey Committee Report on Television, 1943 Set up under the Coalition War Government in the UK, chaired by Lord Hankey, the committee was requested to 'prepare plans for the reinstatement and development of the television service after the War'. Hankey recommended a reopening on the 1939 basis of the 405-line system rather than wait for the development of any new, improved version. The Report was of the view that 'it is in the televising of actual events, the ability to give the viewer a front-row seat at almost every possible kind of exciting or memorable spectacle, that Television will perform its greatest service'. Hankey's general conclusion was 'that Television has come to stay . . .' See COMMISSIONS/COMMITTEES ON THE MEDIA.

Hard sell Where the advertiser goes straight for the consumer's jugular, cutting away the MYTH, the charm, the humour or the fantasy of the ADVERTISEMENT, and says bluntly, 'Buy this!' Hard sell usually indicates, on the part of the manufacturer, an impatience with his ad agency's artistry and subterfuges; or simply hard, cost-cutting times.

Hard times scenario See VALS TYPOLOGY.

Harmonious interaction Fred Inglis uses this phrase in *The Imagery of Power: A Critique of Advertising* (UK: Heinemann,

1972) to describe the friendly and mutually supportive relationship between the media and the forces of ADVERTISING. This 'harmonious interaction' of advertising and editorial styles consistently reproduces and endorses the consumer's way of life, argues Inglis.

Hays Office In the US for three decades the Hays Office meant CENSORSHIP. In 1922 leading figures in the FILM industry formed Motion Picture Producers and Distributors of America Incorporated (MPPDA) to protect their interests against a range of would-be film censors in a climate that had produced Prohibition (Volstead Act, 1919). Will H. Hays, Postmaster-General to the Harding administration, was invited to become president.

In 1930 Martin Quigley, a Chicago publisher, and Father Lord, Society of Jesus, reframed the Hays Office studio recommendations of 1927, into a Production Code (The Hays Office Code) to meet the even more restrictive demands emanating from the recently formed Legion of Decency made up of leaders of the Roman Catholic church and other religious denominations.

A Production Code Administration was prised out of the MPPDA under the direction of Roman Catholic Joseph I. Breen who, between 1934 and the anti-trust decree of 1948, supervised 95% of films made in the US. Any film released without Breen's approval was liable to a $25,000 fine and condemnation by the Legion.

Political as well as moral attitudes and behaviour were subject to severe censorship. The Legion, for example, supported the Fascists in the Spanish Civil War and generally opposed any production with Leftward leanings. The Hays Office Code remained operative until 1966. See BROADCASTING STANDARDS COUNCIL; HUAC: HOUSE UN-AMERICAN ACTIVITIES COMMITTEE.

H-certificate Category introduced by the BRITISH BOARD OF FILM CENSORS in 1930 to describe films dealing with the horrific or the supernatural and considered unsuitable for children. From 1951 the certificate was discontinued and films of this nature were included under the new X-certificate. See CERTIFICATION OF FILMS.

Head nods Head nods are an element of non-verbal communication and can be used to communicate a range of messages. They are, for example, commonly used to give positive FEEDBACK to the sender of a MESSAGE by indicating both interest and/or approval on the part of the receiver; to indicate *floor appointment*, that is to indicate whose turn it is to speak next; and to give emphasis to speech. See COMMUNICATION, NON-VERBAL.

Hearsay See RUMOUR.

Hedges According to Jennifer Coates in *Women, Men and Language* (UK: Longman, second edition, 1993) hedges are 'linguistic forms such as *I think, I'm sure, you know, sort of* and *perhaps* which express the speaker's certainty or uncertainty about the proposition under discussion'. The precise function of hedges varies with the social context and the relationship of the interactors. Coates discusses the range of uses to which hedges may be put: such as expressing confidence, suggesting uncertainty and enabling face-saving to occur when sensitive topics are being discussed. Women appear to use more hedges than men do in conversation but the precise interpretation to be placed on this is a matter for debate.

Hegemony The concept of hegemony owes much to the work of Italian political thinker Antonio Gramsci (1891–1937). A state of hegemony is achieved when a provisional alliance of certain social GROUPS exerts a CONSENSUS which makes the power of the dominant group appear both natural and legitimate.

Hegemony can, however, only be maintained by the won consent of the dominated. It is therefore, like consensus, subject to re-negotiation and ongoing redefinition. Also, the consensus may be broken as the ideologies of the *subordinate* cannot always be accommodated. Institutions such as the mass media, the family, the education system and religion, play a key role in the shaping of people's awareness and consciousness and thus can be agents through which hegemony is constructed, exercised and maintained.

The definition and workings of hegemony have obviously undergone adaptation since Gramsci's day. The power, reach and global penetration of the media as instruments of hegemony have intensified issues of control and influence.

Todd Gitlin in his chapter 'Prime time television: the hegemonic process in television entertainment' in *Television: The Critical View* (US/UK: Oxford University Press, 1994), edited by Horace Newcomb, speaks of the survival of hegemony resulting from the flexibility of its ideology: 'In the twentieth century, the dominant ideology has shifted toward sanctifying consumer satisfaction as the premium definition of "the pursuit of happiness", in this way justifying corporate domination of the economy. What is hegemonic in consumer capitalist ideology is precisely the notion that happiness, or liberty, or equality, or fraternity can be affirmed through the existing private commodity forms, under the benign, protective eye of the national security state.'

Gitlin sees rather more than pleasure on the supermarket shelf of the corporations: liberty, equality and fraternity, features of human existence not traditionally associated with getting and spending, are also for sale; or rather such qualities are *commodified*; presented in symbolic forms and promoted in commercial terms. A further strand of modern hegemony, one Gramsci would have found difficult to envisage, is the stress in modern life upon technology and the consequent socio-cultural emphasis on *efficiency* and consequently of uniformity.

If, as Jacques Ellul and a number of other commentators believe, efficiency has fast become the key determinant of human affairs in modern society (See TECHNIQUE: ELLUL'S THEORY OF TECHNIQUE), then hegemonic power, in the hands of the state and the corporate system, is likely to increase rather than diminish. See ELITE; IDEOLOGICAL STATE APPARATUSES; McDONALDIZATION.

* Jacques Ellul, *The Technological Society* (US: Knopf, 1964); Antonio Gramsci, *Selections from the Prison Notebooks* (UK: Lawrence & Wishart, 1971); Celeste Condit, 'Hegemony in a mass-mediated society: concordance about reproductive technologies' in *Critical Studies in Mass Communication*, 11 (1994); Ellul, *The Technological Bluff* (US: Eerdmans, 1990); Rick Clifton Moore, 'Hegemony, agency, and dialectical ten-

sion in Ellul's technological society' in *Journal of Communication*, Summer 1998.

Helical model of communication See DANCE'S HELICAL MODEL OF COMMUNICATION.

Helical scan See TELERECORDING.

Heliological metaphor See VISIONS OF ORDER.

He/man language Dale Spender in her book *Man Made Language* (UK: Harper-Collins, 1990 edition) refers to the principle by which for several centuries the terms *he* and *man* have been used to include women, e.g. mankind. This principle has, according to Spender, not only the effect of contributing to the perspective of MALE-AS-NORM, of males as more worthy, but also helps to construct the invisibility of women in LANGUAGE, thought and reality. Not everyone, of course, either agrees with or employs this principle, and it has become the focus of some critical scrutiny in recent decades.

Hermeneutic code See CODES OF NARRATIVE.

Hermeneutics The science of interpretations or understanding. The word is taken from the Greek, *hermeneuein*, and derives from Hermes, messenger of the gods; it means to make things clear, to announce or unveil a MESSAGE. In FILM study, a hermeneutic code, or 'code of enigma', explains by one device or another the mysteries of the plot – the situation or predicament characters find themselves in and indicates the process of resolution.

Heterophily See HOMOPHILY.

HICT Project Household Uses of Information and Communication Technology: a major research project funded by the UK's Economic and Social Research Council. Its task has been to investigate the domestic use of TV, VCR, home computer and telephone technology. It was initially carried out by a team including Andrea Dahlberg, Eric Hirsch, Sonia Livingstone, David Morley and Roger Silverstone, with the Centre for Research into Innovation, Culture and Technology at Brunel University. The researchers studied 20 families living in the south east of England, using ethnographic/participant observation methods followed up by a diversity of other approaches – time-use diaries, mental maps or brain patterns illustrating the perceived spatial location and significance of various technologies; and even scrutinizing family photo albums.

The notion of the household as a 'moral economy' is posed by the Brunel team. Are the location and use of such communication technology a reflection of the 'ordering' of the household, of relative degrees of power and status, of priorities; does it enhance or pose barriers to family interactivity; and how are differences over the uses of such technology resolved within the community of the household?

In *Consuming Technologies: Media and Information in Domestic Spaces* (UK, Routledge, 1992), edited by Silverstone, Hirsch and Morley, the authors write, 'To understand the household as a moral economy . . . is to understand the household as part of a transactional system, dynamically involved in . . . the production and exchange of commodities and meanings'. The research done by Silverstone *et al.* is one of the most far-reaching qualitative surveys of its kind, though so far not published in full.

Hidden agenda When the underlying objective of an act of communication is different from that which is stated. See IMPRESSION MANAGEMENT.

Hidden needs Vance Packhard in *The Hidden Persuaders* (UK: Penguin, 1960, with updated editions) cites eight 'hidden needs' which the adman can cater for. These are: emotional security; reassurance of worth; ego-gratification; creative outlets; love objects; a sense of power; a sense of roots; and immortality. See ADVERTISING; MASLOW'S HIERARCHY OF NEEDS; VALS TYPOLOGY.

Hierarchy Classification in graded subdivisions. The hierarchy of a company starts at the top with the chairperson or managing director; a social hierarchy is dominated by the ELITE classes who varyingly influence those CLASS divisions below them. In the media, the dominant hierarchy are the owners, top executives, major shareholders, boards of directors, etc. See CONGLOMERATES; ESTABLISHMENT; ORGANIZATIONAL CULTURES.

Highbrow Someone considered to be a member of the intellectual and cultural ELITE, whose tastes are, by definition, considered to be aesthetically superior to those of the majority, is deemed a *highbrow*. Highbrow tastes are limited to the few. The terms **middlebrow** and **lowbrow** are used to indicate a level of intellectual capacity of cultural appreciation judged against the standards of the highbrow elite.

High-definition TV 1982 saw the demonstration by Sony of Japan of 1000-line high-definition TV with picture quality indistinguishable from 35 mm film on a 2-metre screen; this, 40 years after the UK government recommendation that the BBC start on such a project. With hi-def there is none of the old flicker visible; there is detail even in shadow. Developed by NHK of Japan, hi-def TV can carry five times the information detail of a conventional screen.

High fidelity See GRAMOPHONE.

High-speed photography One of the wonders of modern technology, but a preoccupation of photographers from the earliest pioneering days, the high-speed flash process slows down, or magnifies time: the splash of a drop of water, the trajectory of a bullet, can be reduced to SLOW MOTION that permits astonishing revelations. Foremost among developers of ultra-high-speed electronic flash photography as a tool of scientific analysis was the American Harold Edgerton, inventor of the stroboscope. The term **stroboscopic photography**, or strobe photography, refers to pictures of single or multiple exposure taken by flashes of light from electrical discharges, permitting objects moving at their natural speeds to be observed in slow motion, the rate of the slow motion depending on the *frequency* of the strobe and object. When the flash frequency exactly equals that of the rotation or vibration, the object is illuminated in the same position during each cycle, and appears stationary.

Mechanical cameras such as the register-pin intermittent action camera are capable of 500 frames a second; for faster objects, there is the rotating prism camera at 1500 frames a second, slowing time down between 200 and 400 times. Even faster is the rotating mirror camera, capable of 10,000 pictures a second – a capacity which, however, is dwarfed by the image tube electronic camera which can take a million-million pictures a second.

In contrast to high-speed photography, **time-lapse photography**, by taking pictures at timed intervals of seconds, minutes, hours or days, speeds up, or telescopes time. In a few moments of film we can see the germination of a seed, the hatching of an egg or blow-fly maggots consuming a dead mouse. Audiences in the 1930s delighted in the time-lapse spectacle, in *Four Minutes to Brighton*, of travelling, via film, at 760 m.p.h. on the Brighton Belle. Apollo astronauts on the moon used time-lapse photography. Both high-speed and time-lapse photography are employed most widely to answer two questions: how is it done, and what went wrong? See PHOTOGRAPHY, ORIGINS.

Historical revisionism Term addressed specifically to attempts in the USA and Europe to write out of history the genocide of the Third Reich of Adolph Hitler; to deny that the atrocities ever took place.

Hits The number of times a website is keyed into by INTERNET visitors.

Hollywood Centre of the US film industry, located in California, providing maximum sunshine for outdoor shooting and some magnificent scenery. In 1908 *The Count of Monte Cristo*, begun in Chicago, was completed in California and the first Hollywood studio was set up in 1911. Within a year another 15 film companies had set up in business. The Hollywood studio system reached its peak in the 1930s. Its fortunes have since fluctuated, at first knocked sideways by the advent of TV, then restored by a simple philosophy of 'if you can't beat them, join them'. Today Hollywood plays a key role in the US television industries, while its film enterprises are profitably supplemented by global sales of movies on VIDEO.

* Janet Wasko, *Hollywood in the Information Age: Beyond the Silver Screen* (UK: Polity Press, 1994).

Holography With the invention of the laser in 1960 an intriguing new form of three-dimensional photography, holography, became possible. Though the theory originated with Dennis Gabor as early as 1947, development was not possible until an intense source of 'coherent' light became available, which the laser supplied. Coherent light is light of 'pure' colour containing waves of a single frequency whose wave fronts all move in perfect step.

Derived from the Greek, 'holos', or whole, and 'gram', message, the **hologram** is made without a lens by splitting a laser beam so that part of it is directed at the subject and part becomes a reference beam. When light reflected from the subject and light from the reference beam meet on the photographic plate, the wave fronts create interference patterns which contain all the visual information needed to construct a three-dimensional image of the subject, amazingly lifelike, and viewable from different angles. Recent developments have enabled holograms to be made for viewing by ordinary white light.

Holography has proved a boon to the world of business. Machine-readable reflection holograms store digital information in hundreds of layers within the emulsion of a film or plastic card. The holographed data on a credit card, passport, security access card or ticket to a high-priced event, forming a three-dimensional pattern, can be read electronically, thus providing a formidable obstacle to counterfeiting.

Holophrases In the early stages of LANGUAGE acquisition, typically from the age of 12–18 months, a child will use the limited words at its disposal to mean a number of things. Each word when used to carry a complex message is known as a holophrase. The utterance 'chips', for example, could mean 'I would like some chips', 'These are my chips' or 'Where are my chips?'. The child is at this stage very dependent on surrounding adults being able to interpret the entire message behind the word.

Home page The primary Web-site document for a person, group or organization.

Home Service Name of BBC Radio 4 founded in 1939 until the name-change in

1967. See RADIO 1; RADIO 2; RADIO 3; RADIO 4; RADIO 5 LIVE (BBC).

Homo narrans See NARRATIVE PARADIGM.

Homophily Interacting individuals who share certain attributes – beliefs, VALUES, educational background, social status – are said to be **homophilous**. Communication is commonly believed to be closer when between people who are homophilous as they are more likely to share a common LANGUAGE level and pattern of MEANING. On the other hand, **heterophily** refers to the degree to which interacting individuals differ in these attributes. Generally, heterophilic interaction is likely to cause some disturbance and confusion to the individuals concerned and thus more effort is required to make communication effective. The lack of a common language level and shared patterns of meaning which are likely to result in this situation may lead to many messages going unheeded. See CONGRUENCE THEORY.

Horizons of expectation See EXPECTATION, HORIZONS OF.

Horse opera Nickname for the WESTERN film.

Horse-race story Approach to NEWS coverage of elections anchored in the metaphor of horse racing (or any other competitive sport), in which the political party ahead in the opinion polls is 'winning at a canter' or is losing ground to the opposition which is coming up fast on the outside. Todd Gitlin in 'Bites and blips: chunk news, savvy talk and the bifurcation of American politics' in *Communication and Citizenship: Journalism and the Public Sphere* (UK: Routledge, 1991) edited by Peter Dahlgren and Colin Sparks, calls this mode of campaign journalism an 'enchantment – with means characteristic of a society which is competitive, bureaucratic, professional and technological all in one . . . This is a success culture bedazzled by sports statistics and empty of criteria for value other than numbers to answer the question, "How am I doing?" Journalists compete, news organizations compete, the channel aggression of the race is what makes their blood run'.

Hospital radio Founded in 1951. There are approximately 300 hospital radio services broadcasting music, quiz and chat shows, local news and even documentaries to 250,000 patients in some 805 of hospitals in the UK. Most of these are organized into the National Hospital Broadcasting Organization. Programmes are conveyed via cable from small studios into the bedside headphones of patients. See COMMUNITY RADIO; STUDENT RADIO.

Hot-line A direct TELEPHONE line open for instant communication between the leaders of different countries in cases of emergency.

Hot media, cold media Terms coined by Marshall McLUHAN, author of *The Gutenberg Galaxy* (Canada: University of Toronto Press, 1962) and *Understanding Media* (UK: Routledge & Kegan Paul, 1964), and forming a basic tool of his analysis of the media. For McLuhan, 'hot' media extend one sense-mode with high-definition data. Examples of 'hot' media are RADIO and FILM. 'Cold' media provide, in contrast, low-definition data, requiring much more participation by the individual. Examples are TV, TELEPHONE and CARTOONS. As Ralph Berry queries in *Communication through the Mass Media* (UK: Edward Arnold, 1971), 'All this is highly controversial . . . for example, the "hot-cold" metaphor runs speedily into difficulties (is the living theatre significantly different in the front or the rear stalls?)'.

Hotspot Or flashpoint; where activity on the INTERNET becomes so busy it resembles a major traffic jam.

Household Uses of Information and Communication Technology See HICT PROJECT.

HUAC: House Un-American Activities Committee Inspiration for Arthur Miller's play, *The Crucible*, which explored the nature of community hysteria leading to the persecution of 'suspected witches'. In the case of HUAC, set up by the US Congress in 1938 (and not wound up until February 1969), the witches were Communists, alleged Communists or Communist sympathizers. Among the witch-finders were Richard Nixon, later Republican president, and the notorious Senator Joseph McCarthy. Every section of society was scrutinized for suspects, not the least the entertainment industry. One committee member, John Rankin, a 'virulent bigot who equated Jews with Communists and Negroes with monkeys', as Godfrey Ryan describes him in his three-part series of articles, 'Un-American activities' (UK: *Index on Censorship* 1, 2 and 3, 1973), declared 'one of the most dangerous plots ever instigated for the overthrow of this government has its headquarters in Hollywood . . . The information we get is that this is the greatest hot-bed of subversive activities in the United States'.

HUAC's pursuit of 'subversives' thrived in the years of the 2nd World War and flourished even more in the years of the so-called Cold War. In *Joe McCarthy and McCarthyism: The Hate That Haunts America* (US: McGraw-Hill, 1972), Roberta Fauerlicht writes, 'Since the government had to find subversives before they could subvert, people were punished not for what they did but for what they might do. Men and women found their loyalty questioned because they liked Russian music, because they had books on Communism in their libraries, or because they believed in equality for blacks or civil liberties for Communists'. One hundred and thirty-nine government employees were fired as a result of HUAC investigations, although not a single one was found guilty of subversive acts. Hearst newspapers were prominent in applauding the work of HUAC.

Perhaps the most insidious result of HUAC activities was *blacklisting*, whereby 'suspects' – often mysteriously – failed to gain employment or were laid off from work for specious reasons. Blacklisting was keenly felt in the movie industry and in broadcasting. It is a cruel irony that where accusations were publicly proved to be fraudulent, blacklisting increased rather than decreased.

Prominent victims of HUAC scrutiny were Arthur Miller himself (he was refused a passport by the State Department in 1956), the black singer Paul Robeson, Hollywood scriptwriters Ring Lardner and Dalton Trumbo, film directors Elia Kazan and Martin Ritt (see Ritt's movie of 1976, *The Front*, on the theme of blacklisting),

writers Clifford Odets and Lillian Hellman and actors Zero Mostel (star of *The Front*) and Edward G. Robinson. During the 1960s HUAC's dominance of the hearts and minds of the American nationals was repeatedly challenged. Indeed its momentum had been seriously checked by TV commentator Edward R. Murrow who produced a *See It Now* documentary (1954) in which he suggested that McCarthy had repeatedly stepped over the fine line between investigating and persecuting.

The nightmare spell which McCarthy cast over a nation was mercifully broken when he died of liver failure in May 1957. In 1969 HUAC was reincarnated as the House Internal Security Committee which, learning the lessons of the past, opted for low-key activities, holding fewer sessions and avoiding unpleasant confrontations by not subpoenaing unfriendly witnesses.

Human Rights Watch An independent, non-governmental organization funded by private individuals and foundations worldwide, with offices in New York, Washington, Rio de Janeiro and Hong Kong. Formed in 1978, the Human Rights Watch investigates and reports on the state of human rights in Africa, the Americas, Asia, the Middle East and the signatories of the Helsinki accord on human rights, scrutinizing such matters as arms transfers, women's and children's rights and prison conditions. The organization also makes grants to writers who have suffered from political persecution.

Hunt Committee Report on Cable Expansion and Broadcasting Policy, 1982 Set up by the Conservative government, the three-man committee chaired by Lord Hunt, a former top civil servant, was required to report and make recommendations on the future of cable systems in the UK, in order to 'secure the benefits for the United Kingdom which cable technology can offer . . . in a way consistent with the wider public interest, in particular the safeguarding of public service broadcasting . . .'. In brief, the report, the result of a hurried investigation begun in March 1982 and finalized by September, recommended a future pattern of cable transmission systems marked by few regulations, many channels and as much ADVERTISING as operators could attract. The committee urged immediate expansion even before the proposed body for the supervision of FRANCHISES was created.

Pay-as-you-view TV was not given the green light by Hunt on the grounds that major national events, such as the Cup Final or Wimbledon, might be siphoned off from national access and be seen only by those on cable and able to pay. 'Cherry picking' – cabling just for the well-off suburbs of a city, for example – was also to be barred. See CABLE TELEVISION.

Hybridization Described by James Lull in *Media, Communication, Culture* (UK: Polity Press, 1995) as the 'fusing of cultural forms'. Travel and the global nature of much of the media and music industries enable a cultural form which originates in one culture to be disseminated quite quickly and easily to other cultures, where it may well be influenced by and merge with local cultural forms thus producing a cultural hybrid. Lull gives the example of rap music which has travelled widely from its roots in US inner-city ghettos and has become incorporated into other kinds of popular music in a number of other countries. See GLOBAL VILLAGE.

In particular, TELEVISION is seen as a prime agency of hybridization (or hybridity). It represents a *site of travel* in which people draw images, IDEOLOGY and visions of lifestyles other than their own. In 'travelling culture/travelling television' in *Screen*, Winter 1996, Josefa Loshitzky refers to TV as 'the new public sphere of electronic communication'. Arguments over hybridity centre on whether TV as a travelling medium creates cultural *diversity* or results in cultural *homogeneity*, or sameness.

Hypercorrection It has been noted that the attempt to use prestige pronunciation in more formal situations, by those who do not normally use it, leads to an over-correct use or exaggerated use which is sometimes termed hypercorrection. Hypercorrection seems to be more prevalent among lower middle-class women.

Hyperreality Just as hyperactivity is enhanced, or beyond-the-normal activity,

hyperreality, in the age of mass production and reproduction, offers us reality-plus. Images, simulations of reality serve to extend, to heighten the realities which they represent, to the point, in the view of some commentators, that they are more real than and preferable to actual realities. Both the French philosopher Jean Baudrillard and the Italian semiologist Umberto Eco cite Disneyland as having taken realities to a point when they achieve hyperreality, a substitute which supplants, even erases the original and replaces it with the 'reality' of simulation. In short, that which is imitating is more real, more significant, than that which is imitated.

Baudrillard, in *Selected Writings* (UK: Polity Press, 1988), edited by Mark Poster, refers to the 'society of the image' in which the real is subsumed by 'all the entanged orders of simulation'. Eco does not go so far as to say that the hyperreal supplants the real, but, in *Travels in Hyperreality* (UK: Picador, 1986) states that imitations are indeed coming to be preferred – by those who create them and those who consume them – to the original. He refers to such fakes as deriving from 'a present without depth'. He classifies Disneyland as the home of the 'total fake'. However, the real, he believes, can be reasserted through a sense of history which 'allows an escape from the temptations of hyperreality'.

'Hyperstacks' A term relating to multimedia operation, describing interactive documents which can incorporate text, graphics, animation, audio and visual data.

Hypertext Electronic text on computer, interfaced with links or pathways to other, related texts. For example the text of a novel might be the primary text while a web of supplementary texts – background notes, critiques, biographies – will be instantly available for consultation and use.

Hyphenized abridgement Herbert Marcuse uses this term in *One-Dimensional Man* (UK: Sphere Books, 1968) to describe the practice of the press of concentrating information by bringing two or more descriptive facts together by using a hyphen. Thus: 'Georgia's high-handed-lowbrowed governor . . . had the stage set for one of his wild political rallies last week.' Marcuse argues, 'The governor, his function, his physical features and his political practices are fused together into one indivisible and immutable structure' by the press employing this device 'which in its natural innocence and immediacy, overwhelms the reader's mind. The structure leaves no space for distinction . . . it moves and lives only as a whole'.

Hyphenized abridgement, used repeatedly and assertively, 'imposes *images* while discouraging on the part of the reader, conceptualization; that is, it beats him/her with images, but impedes thinking; and thus the media define for us the terms in which we are permitted to think'. See DETERMINER DELETION; EFFECTS OF MASS MEDIA; FRANKFURT SCHOOL OF THEORISTS; PSEUDO-CONTEXT; TABLOIDESE.

Hypodermic needle model of communication More a METAPHOR representing a view of the EFFECTS OF THE MASS MEDIA, the Hypodermic needle 'model' has formed a point of general reference in crediting the media with power over audiences. The basic assumption is that the mass media have a direct, immediate and influential effect upon audiences by 'injecting' information into the consciousness of the masses.

The audience is seen as impressionable and open to manipulation. Like other early models of communication flow from the media, it overlooks the possible effects of INTERVENING VARIABLES (IV) in the communication process and presents the masses as being unquestioning receptacles of media messages. This sense of the all-powerfulness of the media is a central feature of early mass society research. It is now regarded as crude and simplistic. See AUDIENCE: ACTIVE AUDIENCE; COMMERCIAL LAISSEZ-FAIRE MODEL OF (MEDIA) COMMUNICATION; COMMUNICATION MODELS; S-IV-R MODEL OF COMMUNICATION.

Hypothesis The first step of the research cycle is the formulation of an hypothesis. This will usually be based on an idea or hunch gained by the researcher from his/her own reading of earlier studies and/or from his/her own observations of society. Starting with this basic idea the researcher usually proposes a working hypothesis which will guide the research. The hypothesis proposes a relationship between certain social phenomena: for example, that people from a higher education background are more likely to read what is regarded as the quality PRESS.

Not all hypotheses are expressed as formal statements. Some can be a general collection of ideas about particular social phenomena. All hypotheses, though, must be capable of EMPIRICAL testing; that is, they must be capable of being proved or disproved by facts and argument. The hypothesis will determine the nature of the research design – the method of collecting the information which will prove or disprove the hypothesis.

Once this information has been collected and analysed the hypothesis is reviewed. It may be proved, disproved or amended. Indeed in many cases the original hypothesis may have been modified during the data collection stage of the research. Alternatively it may be decided that further evidence is required before any conclusion is reached. See MEDIA ANALYSIS.

Hypothesis of consonance See NEWS VALUES.

I

Iconic Describes a SIGN which, in some way, resembles its object; looks like it, or sounds like it. Picture-writing is iconic, as is a map. ONOMATOPOEIA (word sounds that resemble real sounds) is iconic. In SEMIOLOGY/SEMIOTICS the iconic is one of three categories of sign defined by American philosopher C.S. Peirce (1834–1914). Where the iconic describes or resembles, an *Index* is connected with its object, like smoke to fire, while the SYMBOL has no resemblance or connection, and communicates MEANING only because people agree that it shall stand for what it does. A word is a symbol. The categories are not separate and distinct. One sign may be made up of all three categories.

Ideational functions of language The use of language to explore, interpret, construct and express views about ourselves and the world. Another major function of language, the interpersonal function, is that of establishing and maintaining relationships with others. Clearly both functions are often present in communicative encounters and the two are often related.

Identification The degree to which people identify with and are influenced by characters, fictional or otherwise, in books, radio, films and TV has fascinated media analysts, especially in areas of behaviour where that identification might lead to anti-social activity such as violence. 'To identify with' has two common meanings: to participate in the situation of someone whose plight has caught one's sympathy; and to incorporate characteristics of an admired person into one's own identity by adopting that person's system of VALUES.

Identification is used in a more specific sense when we discuss the degree of influence persons, institutions and the media may have on others. In 'Processes of opinion change', *Public Opinion Quarterly*, 25 (1965), Herbert Kelman explores three basic processes of social influence with reference to opinion change and to communication. These are *compliance, identification and internalization*. The first position in this 'social influence theory' refers to the acceptance of influence in the hope of either receiving a reward or avoiding punishment. Identification in this sense occurs 'when an individual adopts behaviour derived from another person or a group because this behaviour is associated with a satisfying self-defining relationship to this person or group'. As with compliance, change or influence is reliant upon the external source and 'dependent on social support'. Internalization occurs when the proposed change, the influence, is fully believed in, accepted, taken fully on board, because the influenced person 'finds it useful for the solution of a problem or because it is congenial to his own orientation, or because it is demanded of his own values'.

Linked to the analysis of the extent to which identification takes place is the interest in *how* we identify along lines of age, CLASS or GENDER. See EFFECTS OF THE MASS MEDIA.

Idents Channel identities; snapshot films, reminding TV viewers in graphic, computer-generated form which channel they are tuned to. Idents are designed to establish an *image* of the channel, a channel *branding*. The *generic* ident is basically suitable for any programme introduction while *specific* idents create images closely reflecting the nature of particular programmes or series.

Ideological presumption Term describes the view that journalists and the news media are necessarily and unavoidably *ideologically implicated* in the MESSAGE systems and DISCOURSES to which they contribute. In *The Foucault Reader* (US: Random House, 1984) the French philosopher Michel Foucault states that the social relations of power produce and constitute knowledge, and that socio-economic power lies at the root of what we are, what we believe and what we are shown – through the media. The position locates journalists as *cultural workers*, in the service of those with power and authority.

The view is challenged by Matthew Kieron in 'News reporting and the ideological presumption' published in the *Journal of Communication*, Spring 1997. He declares that the 'presumption' is 'either false, incoherent or trivial'; it is 'overextended, misplaced and distortive'. Kieron argues that we should, in our scrutiny of journalism, acknowledge that in broadly free societies there are sufficient variables in interpretation and approach to escape the grip of the voice of authority.

Ideological state apparatuses This term derives from the work of the French philosopher Louis Althusser. Ideological state apparatuses (ISAs) are those social institutions which, according to Althusser, help shape people's consciousness in a way that secures support for the IDEOLOGY of those who control the state, that is, the dominant ideology. Such institutions include education, the family, religion, the legal system, the party-political system and the mass media. The dominant ideology is thus represented as both natural and neutral. As a result it becomes almost unseen, taken-for-granted. In contrast there is what Althusser calls the RSA (Repressive State Apparatus), the law, police, military; brought into operation – using coercion –

when the RSA is failing, through persuasion, to secure its objectives of social control. Authority relies on the media to serve as an ISA and to support situations when the RSA is brought into action. See COMMON SENSE; DISCOURSE; ELITE; HEGEMONY; MYTH; POWER ELITE.

Ideology An ideology is a system of ideas and beliefs about human conduct which has normally been simplified and manipulated in order to obtain popular support for certain actions, and which is usually emotive in its reference to social action. Karl Marx (1818–83) used the term to apply to any form of thought which underpins the social structure of a society and which consequently upholds the position of the ruling CLASS. 20th c. French philosopher Louis Althusser, drawing on the work of Marx, saw ideology as being an unconscious set of VALUES and beliefs which provide frames for our thinking which help make sense of the world.

Ideology can often be found to be hiding (or hidden) under terms such as 'common sense', the 'common sense view', which Marx would claim was merely the view of the ruling class translated by repeated usage through channels of communication into wisdom as apparently natural as fresh air – a process sometimes referred to as *mystification*. Within society there may be a variety of contending ideologies at play, representing different sets of social interests, each seeking to extend recognition and acceptance of its way of making sense of the world, its own capacity to give order and explain social existence. LANGUAGE itself may be seen not as a neutral MEDIUM but as ideological, thus in its use ensuring that ideology is present in all discourses.

Each may seek to become the dominant ideology and it can be argued that the capacity to make use of the channels of MASS COMMUNICATION is crucial to either achieving or maintaining this position. The use of the media in this respect is the focus of much media research and analysis.

German-British sociologist Karl Mannheim (1893–1947) in *Ideology and Utopia* (1936) distinguishes between ideas which defend existing interests, the STATUS

QUO, which he terms *ideologies* and ideas which seek to change the social order, which he terms *utopias*. See COMMON SENSE; CONSENSUS; CULTURAL APPARATUS; DISCOURSE; DOMINANT DISCOURSE; HEGEMONY; IDEOLOGICAL STATE APPARATUSES; MALE-AS-NORM.

* Mike Cormack, *Ideology* (UK: Batsford, 1992); Tuen A. van Dijk, *Ideology: A Multidisciplinary Approach* (UK: Sage, 1998).

Ideology of detachment See IMPARTIALITY.

Ideology of romance An aspect of HEGEMONY in which the perceptions and attitudes of women, in particular teenage girls, are 'shaped' by DOMINANT DISCOURSE into accepting the roles of wife and mother within an essentially patriarchal social structure. Wendy Halloway in 'Gender difference and the production of subjectivity' in *Changing the Subject: Psychology, Social Regulation and Subjectivity* (UK: Methuen, 1984), edited by J. Henriques *et al.*, calls this mode of communicative conditioning a 'to have and to hold' discourse which links acceptable behaviour with monogamous relationships.

The ideology of romance can be found expressed and reinforced in magazines, films, pop songs, advertising and SOAP OPERAS. It is, in the view of Mary Ellen Brown, author of *Soap Operas and Women's Talk: The Pleasures of Resistance* (UK: Sage, 1994), an ideology which 'can leave young women few options'. At the same time the ideology of romance can be seen as a rational response to, and a means of coping with, material and economic subordination, encapsulated in the song *Diamonds are a Girl's Best Friend*. Says Brown, 'Such romantic ideology positions young women in such a way that they can easily decide to buy into the system'. Most feminist writers would argue that the ideology of romance is coterminous with the notion of the *ideology of dependence*.

Ideology of silence The belief, held chiefly by governments, that the best way of 'getting things done' in, for example, attempts to win the release of political prisoners or hostages, is by secret, behind-the-scenes diplomacy. The same rule would apply in cases where one government may feel obliged, perhaps through public pressure, to protest to another country. The problem in such cases is that there is no real proof that a protest has been made and consequently no evidence as to the nature of that proof.

In an article, 'Against silence' in *Index on Censorship* (February 1987), Jacob Timerman, formerly a political prisoner in Argentina, expands on the notion of the ideology of silence and concludes that 'the only way to solve problems of decency and civilization is to speak out'.

Idiolect This is an individual's personal DIALECT which incorporates the individual variations which exist between people in their use of punctuation, grammar, vocabulary and style. No two people are likely to express themselves in exactly the same way.

Idiot salutations See PHATIC LANGUAGE.

IFEX: International Freedom of Expression Exchange A computer clearing-house formed in 1992, allowing free speech groups to cooperate and exchange information; a charter member being the UK-based human rights magazine *Index on Censorship*.

Image A likeness; a representation; a visualization. The term can have several meanings depending on the context in which it is used. It may refer to a visual representation of reality such as is seen in a photograph; it can also refer to a mental, imaginative conception of an individual, event, location or object as, for example, one conjures up an image of a character in a novel. The image does not merely reproduce, it interprets; it has added to it certain *meanings*. The writer, artist, architect, photographer and advertising image-maker all use assemblies of signs in order to represent or suggest states of mind, or abstractions. Van Dyck's equestrian portrait of Charles I shows the monarch on a noble steed against a background suffused with dramatic light. All the details of this painting converge to create an image of *kingship*, thus a process of symbolization has taken place.

The purpose of image-creation obviously varies, but all images are devised in order to evoke responses of one kind or another, usually emotional. Images often serve as psychological triggers effecting responses which are not always easy to articulate. Advertisements regale us with images of the good life; they play upon our perceived needs (See HIDDEN NEEDS; MASLOW'S HIERARCHY OF NEEDS). Image is also something we present of ourselves – our best face, the way we want the world to perceive us. Politicians work at their images more than most, and these are portrayed to fit in with the image appropriate to a public figure whose aim is to impress voters by his or her qualities of leadership and trustworthiness. Sometimes we talk of a person whose image 'has slipped', which seems to indicate the connection between image and performance (See IMPRESSION MANAGEMENT) and that it relates to an ideal. For the artist, whatever his or her MEDIUM, imagery is central to expression. It is a part of STYLE and a key to the construction of meaning. See METAPHOR.

IMAX Canadian FILM projection system developed in the 1970s, notable for the vastness of its screen for 70 mm film; installed in the UK in 1983 at the National Museum of Photography, Film and Television in Bradford; and later in London, by the Museum of the Moving Image. See OMNIMAX.

Immediacy A prime NEWS VALUE in Western newspaper, radio and television news gathering and presentation. At the centre of decision-making and of news control is the time factor, usually related to the daily cycle. In his article 'Newsmen and their time machine', in *British Journal of Sociology* (September 1977), Philip Schlesinger points out that in industrialized societies an exceptional degree of precision of timing is necessary in our working lives. 'Especially noteworthy are those who operate communication and transport systems . . . Newsmen . . . are members of a stopwatch culture.'

Immediacy shapes and structures the approach to news gathering. The report of an event must be as close to the event as possible, and ideally the event should be reported as it happens. The pure type of immediacy would be the live broadcast.

News, says Schlesinger, is 'hot' when it is most immediate. 'It is "cold", and old, when it can no longer be used during the newsday in question.' Immediacy is not only a vital factor in the selection of a story for treatment; it also helps fashion that treatment. *Pace* is what counts in presentation, especially in TV news where the priority is to keep the audience 'hooked'.

The danger with such emphasis on immediacy is that news tends to be all foreground and little background, all events and too little context, all current happening and too little concentration on the historical and cultural background to such events. Schlesinger rounds off his article by saying that it is plausible to argue 'that the more we take note of news, the less we can be aware of what lies behind it'. See EFFECTS OF THE MASS MEDIA.

Immersion The degree to which the *virtual*, the invented – as in VIRTUAL REALITY – submerges the *real* perception system of the user. The more that VR works to the exclusion of contact with the real, physical world, the more it is classified as being *immersive*. The prospect of near-total immersion, on the part of some users, is a matter of interest and concern. As Frank Biocca says in 'Communication within virtual reality: creating a space for research' in *Journal of Communication*, Autumn 1992, 'If people eventually use VR technology for the same amount of time that they spend watching television and using computers, some users could spend 20 or more years "inside" virtual reality'.

Impact of the mass media See EFFECTS OF THE MASS MEDIA.

Impartiality Just as Professor Stuart Hall doubts the existence, in media terms, of OBJECTIVITY, so Philip Schlesinger, in a remarkable study of the workings of BBC News, doubts the possibility of impartiality. Between 1972 and 1976, Schlesinger had a unique research opportunity to conduct in the newsrooms of Broadcasting House and the Television Centre, London, fieldwork which attempted 'to grasp how the world looks from the point of view of those studied' the reporters, correspondents, editors and managing editors in the most prestigious media organization in the world. He interviewed over 120 BBC news staff and spent 90 days in observation. His findings were published in *Putting 'Reality' Together. BBC News* (UK: Constable, 1978; Methuen/ University Paperback, with new Preface, 1987).

Several keywords framed the basic principles of news production: *balance, objectivity, responsibility, fairness,* freedom from *bias*; and these were, in the 'ordinary discourse of newsmen' for the most part 'interchangeable'. They could be gathered under one banner, that of *impartiality*, what Schlesinger refers to as the central mediating factor in news processing at the BBC, 'the linchpin of the BBC's ideology'. Schlesinger found this a notion 'saturated' with political and philosophical implications' and classifies the 'ideology of detachment' as in essence an example of 'latter-day Mannheimianism'. In *Ideology and Utopia* (UK: Routledge & Kegan Paul, 1936), Karl Mannheim explained how a 'socially unattached intelligentsia' could play a role in society which was *above* all conflict, capable of representing to society all relevant views. It is a theory which has regularly been condemned as an unrealistic dream but the doctrine has remained persistently attractive: by virtue of their education, argued Mannheim, the intellectuals, *déclassés*, are exposed to the 'influence of opposing tendencies in social reality'; thus theirs is the potential to improve social integration, to produce a new CONSENSUS by means of 'dynamic mediation'.

The theory implies that it is possible to view the world in a *value-free* way, and act accordingly. Schlesinger calls value-freedom 'a myth', yet one which in terms of the BBC's aspiration to impartiality, to being above the fray, 'is believed by those who propagate it' as well as being 'essential for public consumption'. Such beliefs, Schlesinger argues, 'anchor news production in the status quo'. What the BBC produces as news is 'structurally limited by the organization's place in Britain's social order' and the main consequence of that position is that 'the outputs of broadcasting are, in general, supportive of the existing social order'.

Imperialism in information systems
See MEDIA IMPERIALISM.

Implication In the production of TEXTS, particularly the NEWS, much is left implicit: assumptions about prior knowledge, expectations about response are implied rather than made manifest and this implication is generally if not always IDEOLOGICAL. As Tuen van Dijk says in 'Media contents: the interdisciplinary study of news as discourse', in *A Handbook of Qualitative Methodologies for Mass Communication Research* (UK: Routledge, 1991), edited by Klaus Bruhn Jensen and Nicholas W. Jakowsky, 'The analysis of the "unsaid" is sometimes more revealing than the study of what is actually expressed in the text'.

Impression management Technique of self-presentation defined by Erving Goffman in *The Presentation of Self in Everyday Life* (US: Anchor, 1959; UK: Penguin, 1971). Because most social interaction requires instant judgements, alignments and behaviour, the individual must be able rapidly to convey impressions of him/ herself to others, highlighting favourable aspects, concealing others. Goffman argues that impression management has the character of drama: all social ROLES, he believes, are, in a sense, *performances* in which it is important to set a scene and rehearse a role, and this means coordinating activities with others in the 'drama'. Thus we put up a *front*, 'that part of the individual's performance which regularly functions in a general and fixed fashion to define the situation for those who observe the performance'.

Our formal, public selves Goffman calls *front region* and our more informal, relaxed selves, *back region*. Indeed Goffman believes that all our roles depend upon the performer having a back region; equally all front region roles rely upon keeping the audience out of the back regions.

Teams as well as individuals operate in front and back regions: in a restaurant, for example, the front-stage conduct of the team of waiters and other staff subscribes to formal rules and rituals, even a *mystique*. Behind the scenes, however, the performers relax. The need to unify in sustaining an expected version of reality – of smartness, politeness, professionalism – gives way to a back-stage reality where individual differences can be freely aired without letting the team, or the performance, down. See SELF-PRESENTATION.

Independent producers The evolution of the independent production sector within the British television industry has been described by Kevin Robins and James Cornford in their article entitled, 'What is "flexible" about independent producers?' in *Screen*, Summer 1992, as 'One of the most significant developments in recent television history'. Their growth according to Robins and Cornford owed much to the creation of CHANNEL 4 and its launch in 1982. This launch was in itself a significant challenge to the DUOPOLY of BBC and ITV which had until then dominated TELEVISION broadcasting in Britain. Channel 4's brief was to cater for minority audiences and interests and to expand the range and diversity of programmes available to viewers. Unlike the existing companies Channel 4 was to become what Robins and Cornford describe as a 'publisher-contractor' broadcaster. Rather than make programmes of its own it commissions them from independent production companies. It was hoped that opening up programme-making to a variety of independent producers, or indies, as they are often called, would promote artistic creativity, cultural diversity and minority access to the television screen and widen the terms of political debate.

There were, however, other motives than progressive concerns behind the innovative structure of Channel 4. For the then Conservative governments the independent production sector provided a means of subjecting the duopoly to the influence of its neo-liberal, free-market philosophy. As Robins and Cornford note, 'For the Government, support for the independent producers was associated with breaking up the "cosy duopoly" and creating a new era of "flexibility" and "choice" in broadcasting'. In 1987 the government decided to encourage the independent production sector further by announcing the introduction of a quota system whereby 25% of programmes broadcast by ITV companies and the BBC had to come from independent producers – a system made statutory under the BROADCASTING ACT, 1990.

However in an industry traditionally dominated by large companies, there was enthusiastic support for the hope that independent producers could be flexible, diverse and dynamic. Robins and Cornford argue that 'There has been a surprisingly broad consensus that independent production has been a source of both cultural innovation and industrial flexibility in the television industry'. In addition to extending the diversity of programmes, the growth of the independent production sector has arguably also helped to promote change in the structure of the television industry, to a move 'from the era of "Fordism" – characterized by the dominance of large, vertically integrated corporations – to a coming "post-Fordist" era of broadcasting characterized by the vertical disintegration of large corporations and the emergence of a complex division of labour between a myriad of small and specialized firms'.

Increased financial pressures within the TV industry caused by, among other things, the franchise bids for ITV companies resulting from the 1990 Broadcasting Act, the fall in advertising revenue during the recession, an increasingly competitive market place and the need to invest in digital technology have acted to constrain the potential of independent producers. Indeed Robins and Cornford argue that, by 1992, it was already becoming apparent that there were some considerable limits to the independence of independent producers. It was evident that rather than being carriers of creativity, innovation and diversity, they were being used as 'agents of rationalization' showing the industry how it could cope with increasing financial and market pressures and reduce the cost of programme-making. They had been caught in a trap they had unwittingly helped to design. The authors quote Jonathan Davies from *TV, UK: A Special Report* (UK: Peterborough Knowledge Research, 1991) in arguing that 'the main role for the sector shifted "away from making new kinds of programmes

towards making the same kinds of programmes more cheaply"'.

Not all would share Robins and Cornford's pessimism. Denise O'Donoghue from the successful independent production company, Hat Trick Productions, in her contribution to the 24th University of Manchester Broadcasting Symposium of 1993, whilst acknowledging the financial pressures on independent producers, remained optimistic about the opportunities for enhancing creative production in the independent sector and did not see any necessary conflict between financial prudence and creative programme-making. Smaller companies may feel less optimistic.

In 1995 Price Waterhouse undertook a survey of UK independent production companies for PACT. Their report, entitled *Production '95*, was based on the 25% of usable replies received from PACT members. One of its findings was that 'The average profitability (weighed by turnover) was 6%. This is on the low side of a commercially acceptable rate. Over 14% of our sample were making losses, in the reported year'. The survey notes a clearly discernible trend towards the concentration of production in the hands of a few, large, mainly London-based, companies. John Willis in an article for the *Guardian*, 'The price of independence' (25 May 1998) has more recently pointed to concerns about the survival of the myriad of small independent production companies within the sector given the growing concentration of production.

The growth of independent production companies has helped to radically reshape the television industry but the hard-pressed financial climate in which such changes have taken place and the companies' dependent market relationship with the broadcasters, have arguably constrained their innovative, creative and radical potential. Further there are concerns not just about the pressure on quality but the lack of investment in training within the industry. See CASUALIZATION; ORGANIZATION CULTURES; PRODUCER CHOICE.

Independent Television Commission (ITC) See COMMERCIAL TELEVISION.

Independent Television Commission:

Code of Advertising Standards and Practice See CODE OF ADVERTISING STANDARDS AND PRACTICE (ITC).

Independent Television franchises See FRANCHISES FOR INDEPENDENT TELEVISION.

Index Short for Index librorum prohibitorum, a list of proscribed books. The Council of Trent, in attempting to turn the tide against the Protestant Reformation, drew up a set of rules about what Roman Catholics should, or rather should not, read. In accordance with these rules the *Index* was published by authority of Pope Paul IV in 1559. In its current form, the Index is a list not only of works prohibited in their entirety to the faithful but also of works not to be read unless or until they are corrected.

The **Index expurgatorius** of Expurgatory Index (1571), specifies passages to be expurgated in works otherwise permitted. Appropriately, the word has been used in the title of the UK magazine whose chief aim is to counter such repressions of information and expression, *Index of Censorship*.

Index as a sign See SIGN.

Indicators In INTERPERSONAL COMMUNICATION the means by which one communicator conveys his/her attitude and response to another – feelings of attraction or rejection, of evaluation or esteem of the other person. Proximity, for example, is an ideal indicator of liking (unless, of course, it becomes a GESTURE of threat or intimidation). Also important as indicators are frequent EYE CONTACT, body orientations and spontaneous gestures. See PROXEMICS.

Indies See INDEPENDENT PRODUCERS.

Inductive reasoning Involves the drawing of conclusions from collected observations and data – from evidence. The acceptability of the conclusions drawn depends upon whether or not the type and quantity of evidence can reasonably be said to support them. It is important to recognize how limited such conclusions may be. Someone unfamiliar with traffic observing the flow of traffic between 10.00 a.m. and 2.00 pm for one week, in a busy street, for example, may note that when the red traffic light is illuminated cars in front of the light stop. He/she may conclude that the illumination of the red traffic light caused the cars to stop, certainly at the times at which he/she was observing the traffic. The observer, however, could not reasonably draw conclusions about, for example, why this was the case or whether or not this occurred at times when he/she was not observing the traffic; that would require further investigation.

Deductive reasoning involves the application of an already accepted generalization or generalizations to an individual case. It is the reverse of inductive reasoning. Someone who has accepted, for example, that drinking too much alcohol before driving is dangerous might as a consequence regulate the intake of alcohol at a party if he/she were driving home – a decision based upon deductive reasoning. See EMPIRICAL; HYPOTHESIS.

Inference According to Gail Myers and Michele Myers in *The Dynamics of Human Communication* (US: McGraw-Hill, 1985), 'A statement of inference is a guess about the unknown based on the known'. We often infer, that is make assumptions, about people, events, behaviour and so on. In doing so we add these inferences to our observations. For example if we saw a young man running away from an elderly woman we might infer that he had stolen her purse but we might be quite wrong and he might be running for a bus. We automatically make inferences and in doing so rely on a range of factors such as past experiences, stereotyping, VALUES, attitudes and beliefs. Yet inferences can mislead both ourselves and others if they stray too far from our actual observations or accepted facts. Clearly, in communication we need to be careful to distinguish between statements of fact and statements of inference.

Inflection The patterns of alteration or modulation in the pitch of a person's voice.

Influence of the mass media See EFFECTS OF THE MASS MEDIA.

Infomercials Television commercials presented as programmes in their own right. A channel dedicated entirely to advertisements, Infonet, beamed to viewers by satellite, was available to American viewers in

1991. The aim of infomercials is to develop the informational and entertainment potential of traditional commercials, and extend them considerably in length. The first infomercials promoted magazines and reference books using documentary techniques.

Info-rich, info-poor See INFORMATION GAPS.

Information blizzards Traditionally, a nation's citizens have been granted too little information on which to base decisions and choices; yet in the late twentieth century that position appeared to have been reversed: nowadays there is too much information, blizzards of it, and the result is not undernourishment but confusion. John Keane in *The Media and Democracy* (UK: Polity, 1991) writes 'The world seems so full of information that what is scarce is citizens' capacities to make sense of it. The release of new opinions through the media rarely shatters unaccountable power. Publicity better resembles the throwing of snowballs into a blizzard – or the blowing of bubbles into warm summer's air'.

Keane fears that even in conditions where public service matches consumerism in media production, citizens are at risk of becoming 'trapped in a never-ending blizzard of information, without adequate free time to digest or make sense of the information flows which envelop them'. Such dangers should not, Keane believes, be exaggerated. He notes an 'increasing restiveness' in Western democracies 'about the loss of personal "privacy"' and generally 'unpredictable audience reactions' as well as pointing out that a 'growing proportion of information is never received, let alone interpreted'.

Not the least of audience's capacities to resist lies in the sustained practice, despite so many predictions of its demise, of *reading*, reflecting a 'robust yearning by large numbers of readers to exercise greater control over what they read, and to confront the world through the complexity found only in books'.

The term 'blizzard' has also been used to describe the multiple and interacting images we encounter daily, brought to us with ever-new associations by the media (See TEXT). For the French cultural critic Jean Baudrillard the sheer volume of signifiers in the contemporary world of mass communication, so readily and regularly detached from their original signification, meaning is too lost in the blizzard to be worth the trouble of attempting to define it. Consequently in this cultural blizzard anything can be made to mean anything. See Chapter 5, 'Baudrillard's Blizzards' in Nick Stephenson's *Culture, Social Theory and Mass Communication* (UK: Sage, 1995) in which Baudrillard's 'irrationalism' is challenged.

Information bomb See CYBERSPACE.

Information gaps Several researchers have been interested in the inequality in the distribution of information among different GROUPS in societies. Such inequalities are mostly the result of educational or social CLASS differences with the advantage being enjoyed by the better-educated and those in the higher-status groups. The role of the mass media in creating, widening or narrowing information gaps has been the concern of a considerable amount of research. There will be differing kinds of gaps depending on the nature of the information.

Gaps – between *information-rich* and *information-poor* – may close or widen with time. It had been thought that the increasing flow of information from the mass media might help to decrease such gaps, but the evidence here is mixed. Whilst the media may have the potential to close gaps it seems that an advantage remains with those with most communication potential and new gaps open as old ones are closed.

Whilst information gaps may exist between groups within societies, the greatest inequalities seem to be those between more developed and the less developed societies. Most of the channels of global communication are controlled by the former. This means that not only have they the potential to acquire and disseminate more information, but that also they have the potential for considerable control of the flow and content of the information going to the less developed countries.

Information gaps can also be generated, reinforced or modified through patterns of interpersonal communication. See DIFFUSION; DISCURSIVE GAP; J-CURVE; MEDIA IMPERIALISM; MIS-INFORMED SOCIETY.

Information society The Japanese were the first to apply the tag to this stage in the growth of the industrial era in which information has become the central and most significant 'commodity'. Through the development of computers and associated electronic systems, such aspects of national and international life as class relationships, government, economics and diplomacy are being visualized as functions of information transfer. Indeed we are at the point when information and wealth are practically one and the same thing. With the development of satellite surveillance it is now possible for a country highly advanced in informatics to know more about the topography of, say, a developing nation than that country's own government does. And information is power which crosses national boundaries with greater ease than invading armies.

Information is not only a commodity, but a social and cultural resource, raising questions of social allocation and control, with such associated problems as privacy, access, commercial privilege and public interest. See COMMODITIZATION OF INFORMATION; MEDIA IMPERIALISM; MISINFORMED SOCIETY.

Information suburbs See TECHNOLOGICAL DETERMINISM.

Information technology (IT) Microelectronics plus computing plus telecommunications equals IT. Its formal definition is framed as follows in a UK Department of Industry publication (1981) for Information Technology Year (1982): 'The acquisition, processing, storage and dissemination of vocal, pictorial, textual and numerical information by a micro-electronics-based combination of computing and telecommunications.'

The possibilities of IT are endless if there is the cash to pay for the hardware, the software and the service: laser beams carrying 30 channels of speech in digital form; cordless telephones; scanning devices which read the printed word out to the blind; telephones for the deaf; voice recognition; typewriters which read your typing back to you, and programmes which translate one LANGUAGE into another. See TECHNOLOGY OF THE MEDIA.

Information Technology Advisory Panel (ITAP) Report on Cable Systems See CABLE TELEVISION.

Infotainment Term used to describe the trend towards enhancing the entertainment value of factual programmes in order to increase their popularity with audiences. There are concerns, expressed by a number of analysts, that NEWS and current affairs coverage may become trivialized by such an approach. See DOCUMENTARY.
* Daniel Hallin, *We Keep America on Top of the World* (UK/US: Routledge, 1994); Jean Seaton, 'Global futures, the information society and broadcasting' in James Curran and Jean Seaton, *Power Without Responsibility* (UK: Routledge, 1997).

Infra-red photography Permits the viewer to see what the eye cannot see, in what is known as the actinic infra-red range, and is used in aerial photography, astronomy, and medical and forensic photography. See HOLOGRAPHY; ULTRA-VIOLET/FLUORESCENT PHOTOGRAPHY.

Inheritance factor The TV programme which· captures a viewer's attention paves the way for the programmes that follow it. Some commentators have complained that because certain types of programmes enjoy greater popularity than others, each channel runs the same sort of programme in the same time slot, leading to an over-standardization of programme content and form. See FORMULA BROADCASTING; BUTTON APATHY; SCHEDULING.

Inner-outer directed See VALS TYPOLOGY.

Inoculation effect In the processes of persuasion, a relative immunity in an audience may be induced by 'inoculation' prior to a concerted exercise in persuasion: if an audience is forewarned about an attempt to persuade it, when that attempt occurs, they are more capable of defence against influence.

Insert shot In FILM, close-up inserted into a dramatic scene, usually for the purpose of giving the audience a view of what the character on the screen is seeing, such as a newspaper headline, the title of a book, a cigarette, a letter, etc. See SHOT.

Institution The term institution is generally applied to patterns of behaviour which are established, approved and usually of some permanence. Such patterns of behaviour are normally rational and conscious. The term can be applied to both the abstract (e.g. religion) and the concrete (e.g. media organizations) concept of an institution. The patterns of behaviour to which this term is applied can vary, from simple routine acts to large complexes of standardized procedures governing social relationships in a large section of the population.

All institutions embody a particular complex of NORMS, VALUES, ROLES and role structures. They also, often, evolve relationships with other institutions. FUNCTIONALIST analysis tends to represent institutions as performing the functions essential to the maintenance of society and views them as being mutually sustaining. Recent research has, however, pointed to the relative autonomy of most institutions and to the often conflicting goals to be found within them. Much research into the mass media has concentrated upon their corporate role as major social institutions; upon their norms, values and relationships with other major social institutions.

Insult signals Generally defined as those signals which are *always* insulting, no matter what the context in which the signal has been made; though these do vary substantially between nationality and nationality. Such signals may communicate disinterest, boredom, superiority, contempt, impatience, rejection and mockery. **Dirt signals** appear to be universal and refer to human and animal waste products on the basis, presumably, of: cleanliness – good; filth – bad. Picking the nose with forefinger and thumb in Syria means 'Go to blazes' while in the UK a gesture of derision is to pull an imaginary lavatory chain at the same time as holding the nose. In Greece, pushing the flat of the palm towards another's face is the ultimate insult signal. Called the *moutza*, the signal represents a thrusting of filth into the opponent's face, and has ancient roots (See RELIC GESTURES).

Beyond the insult signal is the **threat signal**, an attempt to intimidate without,

necessarily, recourse to blows. Threat signals are mostly violence substitutes rather than prologues to violence, because such signals are checked, held back and distance maintained between threatener and threatened. Also, such signals are often redirected – to the insulter's own body, such as mock strangulation.

Of **obscene signals**, the phallic-displaying gesture is as old as civilized man. The Romans for example referred to the middle finger as the impudent and obscene finger. The more expressive forearm jerk is common throughout the Western world and is employed particularly in France, Italy and Spain as a threatening insult by one male towards another; however, in the UK, the signal tends to be more a crude sexual comment than a direct insult. The V-Sign, with palm facing the communicator, is the most potent gestural insult in Britain along with its single-finger variant. See COMMUNICATION, NON-VERBAL (NVC); NON-VERBAL BEHAVIOUR: REPERTOIRE.
* Desmond Morris, *Manwatching: A Field Guide to Human Behaviour* (UK: Jonathan Cape, 1977).

Integrateds See VALS TYPOLOGY.

Integration New ideas and behaviour vary in the degree to which they are incorporated into the continuing operations and way of life of members of a SOCIAL SYSTEM or subsystem. The term **communication integration** is used to describe the degree to which the members/units of a social system are interconnected by INTERPERSONAL COMMUNICATION channels.

Integrity of the text See TEXT: INTEGRITY OF THE TEXT.

Intellectual property See CULTURE: COPYRIGHTING CULTURE; TEXT: INTEGRITY OF THE TEXT.

In-tel-sat Acronym for International Telecommunications Satellite (Consortium), an organization of over 70 member nations formed to control and promote work in global communications by means of satellites. See SATELLITE TRANSMISSION.

Intensity Some news stories receive much more concentrated, more intense, coverage by the media than others, and tend to dominate or stifle competing stories. Intensity, if appropriate in terms of timing, and if given the promise of FREQUENCY, abetted by CONSISTENCY of coverage, equals *influence*, at least in the sense of making audiences aware.

General elections provide useful illustrations of the intensity of media coverage. National attention is focused on the event (usually more on personalities than ISSUES) and the legitimacy of the event is given substance and flavour. In contrast, local elections derive neither substance nor flavour from the media, who largely ignore them. See EFFECTS OF THE MASS MEDIA; NEWS VALUES.

Interaction The reciprocal action and communication, verbal or non-verbal, between two or more individuals, or two or more social GROUPS.

Successful negotiation of social interaction requires considerable mastery of the verbal and non-verbal communication deemed appropriate to the social situation and the social ROLES being performed. As Judy Gahagan comments in *Social Interaction and its Management* (UK: Methuen, 1984), 'The mere presence of others introduces a degree of control over our demeanour that we do not display when we are alone. . . . This control over demeanour suggests we follow quite strict sets of rules of conduct'. Most of these rules however are unwritten and learned, often unconsciously, through the process of SOCIALIZATION. There are arguably more ritual and rules involved in our everyday social interaction than we realize. Gahagan notes that 'We are in fact quite unaware of their existence until someone does something "odd"'. See IMPRESSION MANAGEMENT; INTERPERSONAL COMMUNICATION; SELF-MONITORING; SELF-PRESENTATION.

Interactive television Process by which TV viewers are enabled, through TELEPHONE link or cable and computer terminal, to respond to programmes and to questions put to them by programme companies.

This mode of instant FEEDBACK has immense potential and the social, political and cultural issues are far-reaching. First, only those able to afford the necessary press-button equipment will be able to register a 'vote' or opinion. Unlike the absolute secrecy of the ballot box, that vote is *record-*

able; that is, computers will be able to bank the response patterns of individuals and GROUPS.

The almost obsessive use of opinion polls in recent years will be accelerated by interactive TV: instant referendums on vital matters could become standard practice; even more intensely than at present, TV would be the central focus of election campaigns. What has been termed *electronic democracy* will have come of age.

The case *for* interactive TV is that it has potential for a more regular and sustained consultation process between the public and those who sell to them, offer them services, or govern them and thus can engender a greater sense of involvement in decision-making.

Interactivity In the simulation of VIRTUAL REALITY, interactivity describes the process by which the user exerts control over the form and content of the mediated environment.

Interception of Communications Act, 1985 A London antique dealer, James Malone, charged the British Government with unlawful PHONE-TAPPING in a case heard by the European Court of Human Rights. On 2 August 1984 the Court found in his favour, declaring that UK law covering interception was 'Obscure and open to differing interpretations'. A White Paper outlining the Government's response to the Euro court's finding was published in February 1985 and the Interception of Communications Act was on the Statute book by July. 'Intentional interception' became punishable by a maximum of two years imprisonment and a £2000 fine. However, the Act exempts official interception from prosecution provided that the Government and its agencies adhere to a set of administrative practices – in essence, the obtaining of warrants before interceptions can be made. Prevention and detection of 'serious crime' are the criteria for warrant-issue to the police and Customs and Excise. 'Interests of national security' suffice for an M15 warrant.

The European Court ruled that a system of redress be instituted for anyone subject to a phone-tap. The Act ignores the ruling: Section 9 declares inadmissible any evidence which 'tends to suggest' that a government official has been directly involved in tapping, whether lawful or not. See PRIVACY.

Internalization See IDENTIFICATION.

International Broadcasting Trust Comprises over 60 member organizations – development agencies, churches, environmental groups, trade unions, educational bodies, race and immigration bodies – whose common concern is to use TV as a means of promoting greater discussion in the UK about its relationships with developing countries and the world community. The intention is that the programmes will be an educational resource as well as informative to the general public, and the Trust publishes and distributes literature to enable educational groups using the programmes to follow up the ISSUES raised in greater depth. The Trust was formally established as an educational charity on 2 July 1982 and its launch programme was *Lucky You, Lucky Me* shown on Channel 4 in November 1982, in which Jonathan Dimbleby took a critical look at public and mass media attitudes to the developing countries.

International Commission for the Study of Communication Problems Report, 1980 See MacBRIDE COMMISSION.

International Federation of Journalists (IFJ) Organization whose testament is that 'the promotion of a new world order of information is first and foremost the business of journalists and the trade unions and not of states, governments or any pressure group of whatever kind'. The IFJ is made up of chiefly western journalists and was formed to monitor and counteract moves through Unesco to 'impose', through government, a NEW WORLD INFORMATION ORDER. See MacBRIDE COMMISSION; MEDIA IMPERIALISM; WORLD PRESS FREEDOM COMMITTEE.

International Law Enforcement Telecommunications Seminar (Ilets) See INTERNET: MONITORING OF CONTENT.

International Programme for the Development of Communication IPDC See MacBRIDE COMMISSION; MEDIA IMPERIALISM; NEW WORLD INFORMATION ORDER.

Internet Worldwide network of interlinked computer systems providing the swift exchange of digital information – texts, sounds, pictures or video. One of the few global communication systems *not* owned by the transnationals; in fact Internet is not 'owned' by anyone (yet). The Net was first established in the 1960s as an American military project, ARPANet, to link computers at research establishments and to form a network of information distribution which could survive a nuclear attack.

The information available on the Internet and its associated systems such as WWW, the World Wide Web, is immense. It includes digests of American White House briefings, university library catalogues, reproductions from the world's museums and art galleries as well as, and perhaps most importantly, offering subscribers a service of communicative *exchange* through bulletin boards and e-mail. Internet links 150 countries, though the poorest countries are predominant among those nations not yet 'wired up'.

An ICM poll published in the *Guardian*, January 1999, revealed that 29% of the UK population was now on-line, with a further 14% planning to join the Net within 12 months. The Millennium sees approximately 43% of the adult population wired up. Use of the Net, in particular e-mailing, is growing at a bewildering rate. In 1998 4 trillion e-mails were sent in the US, and that was still only representative of 15% of the population. The *Wall Street Journal* calculated that a typical worker in a European company deals with some 150 e-mails a day. Add to this the tide of junk mail which loads the Net, as a *Guardian* leader put it, 'unsolicited e-mails from companies advertising their wares or Net nuts who believe that the whole world hangs on their thoughts' and the risk of a communications 'traffic jam' of horrendous proportions is obvious.

It has been claimed for the Net – with some justification – that it is today's version of the AGORA, that open space in which public discourse can be conducted without MEDIATION of those in authority and without the GATEKEEPING and AGENDA SETTING of the mass media. Citizens speak to citizens across geographical and political boundaries; and certainly governments are worried about the freedom of access to and use of information which computer-mediated communication allows. Lin Hai, a Chinese Internet user who distributed 30,000 e-mail addresses to a democracy magazine published in the US, was jailed in 1999 for crimes against the state. His imprisonment can only be seen as a warning to others for China is estimated to have over 2 million Net surfers.

Few businesses can have grown as fast as the industry in websites. Every self-respecting company, local authority, educational establishment, human rights agency or pressure group now has its own growing website. This applies also to the media organizations such as the BBC which, according to Fletcher Research, became in 1999 the second largest among the UK's top ten websites, beaten to poll position only by Yahoo which is essentially an Internet 'gateway' to other services, while the BBC is a content provider. Thus RADIO and TELEVISION, the BBC's market specialisms, are joined to a PRESS function: the BBC puts into print, pictures and sound its vast archives of material (See CONVERGENCE). Additionally the BBC's commitment to Internet use is nurturing interest which in turn will encourage growth in the numbers of people coming on-line. See ACCESS PROVIDER; CHILDREN, YOUNG PEOPLE AND THE CHANGING MEDIA ENVIRONMENT; CYBERSPACE; DIGITALIZATION; GATEKEEPING; GUTENBERG PROJECT; HOTSPOT; HYPERREALITY; HYPERSTACKS; HYPERTEXT; INTERNET: MONITORING OF CONTENT; INTERVENTION; NEW DOCUMENT ALLIANCE; N-GEN; PORNOGRAPHY; TEXT: INTEGRITY OF THE TEXT.

Internet: monitoring of content A key feature of the development of the Internet has been the capacity of its users to evade official SURVEILLANCE; and it has been a constant challenge and provocation to those in authority that control has been so difficult to exercise. The days of freedom, at least in Europe, may be numbered. In May 1999 it was reported that European Commission ministers were planning to require manufacturers and operators to build in 'interception interfaces' to the Internet and all future digital communication systems.

Details are set out in Enfopol 19, a restricted document leaked to the Foundation for Information Policy research, based in London.

In an article 'Intercepting the Internet' in the *Guardian* (29 April 1999), freelance writer Duncan Campbell reports on plans requiring 'the installation of a network of tapping centres throughout Europe, operating almost instantly across all national boundaries, providing access to every kind of communications including the net and satellites'. According to Campbell, the plans were formulated by an organization founded in 1993 by the American FBI, the International Law Enforcement Telecommunications Seminar (Ilets), made up of police and security agents from some 20 countries. Ilets has had success in persuading the European Community to adopt its recommendations contained in a document drawn up in Bonn in 1994, the *International Requirements For Interception*. These have become law in the US. At meetings in subsequent years, Ilets has tightened further its monitoring requirements. Currently the major obstacle to the fulfilment of the demands listed in Enfopol 19 is the cost of enforcement.

Interpersonal communication Describes any mode of communication, verbal or non-verbal, between two or more people. While the term MEDIA COMMUNICATION has often been used to specify interpersonal communication at a greater than face-to-face distance, such as when the communication is by letter or TELEPHONE, it is most useful to keep the definition as wide and unprescriptive as possible.

Michele Gail Myers in *The Dynamics of Human Communication* (US: McGraw-Hill, 1985) writes 'Interpersonal communication can be defined . . . in relation to what you do with it. First, you can use communication to have an effect on your "environment", a term which means not only your immediate physical surroundings but also the psychological climate you live in, the people around you, the social interchanges you have, the information you want to get or give in order to control the questions and answers of your living. Second, you use communication to improve the predictability of your relations with all environmental forces, which act on you and on which you act to make things happen'.

A great many factors affect the sending and receiving of messages within the process of interpersonal communication, only some of which can be mentioned here. In constructing a MESSAGE the SENDER may be influenced by his/her SELF-CONCEPT and perception of the receiver(s) and the knowledge, beliefs, ATTITUDES, VALUES, assumptions and experiences on which they rest; his/her personality; the role he/she is playing at the time; the state of his/her MOTIVATION; his/her communicative competence and the context in which the communicative encounter takes place. All of these factors and others affect decisions about SELF-PRESENTATION. They also influence the receiver(s) and how he/she will interpret messages sent.

Barriers often arise in interpersonal communication and these are categorized by Richard Dimbleby and Graeme Burton in *More Than Words: An Introduction to Communication* (UK: 3rd impression, Routledge, 1997) into three main types: *technical* (these are physical barriers such as a noisy environment); *semantic* (these are barriers arising from an inability to understand the signs, verbal or non-verbal, being used by one or more of the persons involved in the transaction); and *psychological* (these barriers may be caused by a range of psychological factors, for example, the message may be perceived as a threat to one's VALUES). Common errors made in the process of SOCIAL PERCEPTION, such as stereotyping, also constitute psychological barriers to effective communication.

Speech and non-verbal communication are the main means by which messages are sent in interpersonal communication; non-verbal communication being particularly important in providing FEEDBACK and in regulating interaction. Interpersonal communication is also affected by the context in which it takes place, in GROUPS or organizations, for example, and factors found there such as NORMS, MORES, POWER relationships and so on. Good interpersonal communication skills are valued and many techniques have been developed to try to improve

them, ASSERTIVENESS TRAINING AND TRANSACTIONAL ANALYSIS being but two examples.

There is of course a rich interplay between the messages received in interpersonal and MASS COMMUNICATION and our reflection on them in the process of INTRAPERSONAL COMMUNICATION. To complicate matters further most of the factors influencing the process of interpersonal communication are formed and shaped through that process. The reader is referred to the following main entries: COMMUNICATION; COMMUNICATION, NON-VERBAL; DECODE; ENCODE; GESTURE; GROUPS; KINESICS; LANGUAGE (Collective entry); MEANING; PROXEMICS; ROLES; TOUCH. *See also*: ALLNESS ATTITUDE; APACHE SILENCE; BARNLUND'S TRANSACTIONAL MODEL OF COMMUNICATION, 1970; BARRIER SIGNALS; BATON SIGNALS; BOOMERANG EFFECT; CENTRALITY; CHANNEL; CIVIL INATTENTION; CLIQUE; COCKTAIL PARTY PROBLEM; CODES; COMMUNICATION, FUNCTIONS; CONFIRMATION/DISCONFIRMATION; CONGRUENCE THEORY; CONSUMPTION BEHAVIOUR; COSMOPOLITE AND LOCALITE CHANNELS; CUT-OFF; DEFENSIVE COMMUNICATION; DIFFERENTIAL PERCEPTION; DIFFUSION; DISCOURSE; DISQUALIFYING COMMUNICATION; DISSONANCE; DYAD; ENCOMPASSING SITUATION; ETHOS; EUPHEMISM; EYE CONTACT; FEEDBACK; GENDER SIGNALS; GSR; HOMOPHILY; IMPRESSION MANAGEMENT; INDICATORS; INSULT SIGNALS; INTERACTION; INTERVENING VARIABLES; LANGUAGE POLLUTION; LANGUE AND PAROLE; LATITUDES OF ACCEPTANCE/REJECTION; LAW OF THE TOTAL SITUATION; LEAKAGE; LEVELLING, SHARPENING, ASSIMILATION; LISTENING; LOOKING BEHAVIOUR; MESSAGE; METASIGNALS; NETWORK; NOISE; NON-VERBAL BEHAVIOUR: REPERTOIRE; NORMS; OPINION LEADER; OBJECT LANGUAGE; OVERHEARING; PARASOCIAL INTERACTION; PERSONAL SPACE; PHATIC LANGUAGE; POLARIZATION; POSTULATES OF COMMUNICATION; POSTURAL ECHO; PRAGMATICS; PRINCIPLE OF LEAST EFFORT; PRIVATE CUES; PUBLIC CUES; RELIC GESTURES; RUMOUR; SALUTATION DISPLAY; SELF-MONITORING; SHORTFALL SIGNALS; SIGNIFICANT OTHERS; SIGNIFICANT SYMBOLIZERS; SILENCE; SLIDER; SOCIOMETRICS; SPATIAL ZONES; TIE-SIGNS; ZONES.

* Michael Argyle, *The Psychology of Interpersonal Behaviour* (UK: Penguin, 1983) and *Bodily Communication* (UK: Methuen, 1975) by the same author; Richard Ellis and Ann McClintock, *If You Take My Meaning: Theory Into Practice in Human Communication* (UK: Edward Arnold, 1990); John Corner and Jeremy Hawthorn, eds.,

Communication Studies: an introductory reader (UK: Arnold, 1993); Michael Burgoon, Frank G. Hansaker and Edward Edwin J. Dawson, eds., *Human Communication* (UK: Sage, 1994).

Interpretant C.S. Peirce (1839–1914), generally regarded as the founder of the American strand of SEMIOLOGY/SEMIOTICS, used the word *interpretant* in his model defining the nature of a SIGN, which 'addresses somebody, that is, it creates in the mind of that person an equivalent sign, or perhaps a more developed sign. The sign which it creates I call the *interpretant* of the first sign. The sign stands for something, *its object*' (from J. Zeman, 'Pierce's theory of signs' in T. Sebeok ed., *A Perfusion of Signs*; US: Indiana University Press, 1977).

The *interpretant*, then, is a mental concept produced both by the sign itself and by the user's experience of the object. Peirce's sign and interpretant find a parallel in the *signifier* and *signified* of the father of the European strand of semiology, Swiss linguist Ferdinand de Saussure (1857–1913).

Intersubjectivity This term is used by Tim O'Sullivan, John Hartley, Danny Saunders and John Fiske in *Key Concepts in Communication* (UK: Methuen, 1983) to refer to those aspects of an individual's reactions to a MESSAGE which he or she shares with members of the CULTURE or SUB-CULTURE to which he or she belongs. The connotative and ideological orders of the meaning of signs are usually shared as they stem from cultural forces. See CONNOTATION; HOMOPHILY; IDEOLOGY.

Intertextuality See TEXT.

Intervening variables (IV) Those influences which come between the encoder, the MESSAGE and the decoder are referred to as *intervening variables*, mediating factors which influence the way a message is perceived and the nature and degree of its impact. Time of day, mood, state of health can all constitute intervening variables.

More importantly family, friends, peer GROUPS, respected persons, opinion leaders, etc. are capable of significant MEDIATION between what we are told and what we accept, believe or reject. Whilst people

may act as intervening variables between media messages and audience, the media may also be intervening variables between people: the TV socializes the child as do parents. It also 'comes between them' in the sense that it can stop interaction, modify it, improve it, re-channelize it (not to mention the DISSONANCE it might cause in a family when, for example, it provokes controversy). See S-IV-R MODEL OF COMMUNICATION.

Intervention Chiefly describes the policy and practice of governments to 'intervene' in, and attempt to control, the nature and flow of information. Intervention operates through laws, regulations and surveillance. From earliest times governments have, with justification, believed that communication is power – that it is an agent of change – and that such power is a threat to existing power structures. Intervention remains high on the agenda of contemporary governments apprehensive about the freedoms of access and expression brought about by on-line services. See ENCRYPT; CLIPPER CHIP.

Interviews Though there are many forms of interview and many different reasons for conducting them, the common goal is that of gaining more information from and understanding of other people, through a planned process of questions and answers. PRESS and TELEVISION journalists use interviews as a means of collecting information and opinions. Interviews can be used to provide entertainment as in chat shows; they are the most common means of selecting people for jobs or students for courses; they are a major method of data collection in the social sciences.

The kinds of questions widely used in interviews are: (1) *open* questions; these are broad, usually unstructured and often simply introduce the topic under discussion in a way that allows the interviewee a good deal of freedom in answering; (2) *closed* questions; these are restrictive, offering a fairly narrow range of answers from which the interviewee must choose; (3) *primary* questions; these introduce the subject or each new aspect of the subject under discussion; (4) *subsidiary* or *secondary* questions; these follow up the answers to primary questions; (5) *neutral* questions; these do not suggest any preferred response and (6) *leading* questions which suggest a preferred response and are not normally used in research interviews.

Intimacy at a distance See PARASOCIAL INTERACTION.

Intimization Mode of dealing with information, especially NEWS, and focusing on human interest; presented in a manner which is intimate and personal, termed 'matters of personality' by Liesbet van Zoonen in 'A tyranny of intimacy? Women, femininity and television news' in *Communication and Citizenship: Journalism and the Public Sphere* (UK: Routledge, 1991) edited by Peter Dahlgren and Colin Sparks. Van Zoonen is referring specifically to Dutch TV and argues that the increasing use of women presenters in the media is 'part and parcel of the intimization that seems to permeate most news' and risks being 'yet another articulation of traditional femininity' and what she calls 'the gendered nature of private sphere values'.

Intrapersonal communication That which takes place within ourselves: our inner monologues; our reflection upon ourselves, upon our relationships with others and with our environment. What goes on inside our heads (or hearts) is conditioned and controlled by our *self-view* and that self-view has emerged from a vast complex of past and present influences – on the view we perceive others holding about us, on our past achievements and failures, on memory-banks of good, bad and neutral actions and impressions.

Our concept of self *interacts* with our view of the world. Having been formed by experience, it is shaped and modified by subsequent experience, though rarely straightforwardly. The psychologist, for example, speaks of the *extravert* personality and the *introvert* personality. On the face of it, the extravert is characterized by a confidence in public *performance* which may indicate inner assurance, while the introvert may demonstrate a public shyness or guardedness reflective of inner uncertainty. However, the outer confidence may well be a *role*,

as in a play or performance, which may conceal an altogether different inner image or performance. The so-called introvert, on the other hand, may, through the richness or assurance of inner resources, have opted out of public role playing, or selected the role of introvert as a public defence mechanism.

Arising from both inner and outer stimuli, intrapersonal communication is a convergence, a coming-together, of both. A piece of music stirs in us, perhaps, previous memories; these memories of people or places may join with immediate impressions of events to create an ongoing DISCOURSE, between ourselves in the past, our former selves and our selves, perceiving and perceived, in the present.

Through intrapersonal communication we come to terms (or fail to come to terms) with ourselves and with others. Through it we create bridges or battlements; we make connections or we sever them; we open ourselves up or we establish self-defences.

Most of us, it is important to note, are, as it were, on our own side. We use intrapersonal communication as a means of self-assurance, of confidence-building or confidence-maintenance as well as self-discovery (or indeed self-delusion). It is what makes us unique.

Invisibility That is, invisible to the public as represented by media. The case is put by many commentators that certain sections of the population are overlooked, neglected, denied rightful attention by media, as if they did not exist. Ethnic minorities are seen to be 'invisible' or 'absent' in mainstream representations, except when they are viewed as a 'problem' in which case the spotlight of attention is trained upon them. Nations as well as individuals and groups are cloaked in invisibility, fulfilling NEWS VALUE only when there is trouble, conflict, a preceived threat to order. *Visibility* then comes at the price of STEREOTYPING and the nurturing of 'us and them' (or WEDOM/ THEYDOM attitudes). Tuen van Dijk in *Racism and the Press* (UK: Routledge, 1991) writes that 'minorities continue to be associated with a restricted number of stereotypical topics, such as immigration problems, crime, violence (especially "riots"), and ethnic relations (especially discrimination), whereas other topics, such as those in the realm of politics, social affairs and culture are under-reported'.

iSociety Term describing the dominant VALUES and desired lifestyles characteristic of people in the UK in the late 1990s. In place of the 'I'm all right' culture of the 1980s are attitudes guided by notions of individuality, independence and interactivity. In a major survey conducted by the Future Foundation it was found that the 'me culture' identified with Conservatism under Margaret Thatcher had given way to to a more ethical, tolerant and less competitive way of life, with fairer relationships between men and women. Author of the Foundation's report, Melanie Howard, told *Observer* reporter Richard Thomas ('The iSociety', 4 April 1999), 'People in the iSociety are interested in the wider impact of what they do and what they buy' and attitudes have changed in relation to jobs and careers, people defining themselves by what they do rather than by their income, prizing more and more the quality of life. Howard believes that the iGeneration in the iSociety is leaving behind the binary certainties of the past, 'Left and Right, work and home, women and men's roles'.

Readers may recognize in the criteria of the iSociety some familiar old landmarks – MASLOW'S HIERARCHY OF NEEDS, for example; in particular Maslow's idea of self-actualizing needs. An encouraging dimension of iSociety thinking is the desire to extend ethical principles governing interpersonal relationships to the workplace, both in terms of the ways employers treat those who work for them and in the social responsibility of their operations. See VALS TYPOLOGY.

Issues Those social, cultural, economic or political concerns or ideas which are, at any given time, considered important, and which are the source of debate, controversy or conflict. What is an issue for one social GROUP may not be considered such by another. Environmental issues have arguably grown out of middle CLASS concern, in particular among the younger, often college-educated members of that class.

Of vital interest to the student of communications are such questions as: how are issues disseminated? Why do some issues 'make it' to the national forum of debate while others fall by the wayside? What are the characteristics of a 'successful' issue? What prolongs an issue? What factors, other than the resolution of the issue, are involved in the decline of an issue? And, running through all these questions, what role do the processes of communication play in the definition, shaping and promoting of issues?

The media are, of course, themselves an issue, like all institutions wielding power and influence and the issues involving the role of the media in society are meat and drink for the student of communication. This has been given due acknowledgment in communication and media study syllabuses. Among the many issues of current interest involving the media are: CENSORSHIP; media ownership and control, including the role of CONGLOMERATES in world wide media activity; the part played by the media in the REINFORCEMENT of the STATUS QUO in society; in SOCIALIZATION; in their claim to represent the so-called FOURTH ESTATE; in policing the boundaries of social and political dissent and in being largely unquestioning advocates of the capitalist consumer-orientated society. See DEVIANCE AMPLIFICATION; EFFECTS OF THE MASS MEDIA; LABELLING PROCESS; McCOMBS AND SHAW AGENDA SETTING MODEL OF MEDIA EFFECTS, 1976; MEDIA CONTROL; MAINSTREAMING; MEDIA IMPERIALISM; NEWS VALUES.

ITC: Code of Advertising Standards and Practice See CODE OF ADVERTISING STANDARDS AND PRACTICE (ITC).

ITC Programme Code The Independent Television Commission succeeded the Independent Broadcasting Authority (IBA) in January 1991, consequent upon the BROADCASTING ACT, 1990 (responsibility for COMMERCIAL RADIO was transferred to the RADIO AUTHORITY). The Broadcasting Act required of both authorities the drawing up of codes of practice which would regulate all commercial broadcasting in the UK. The ITC was required to draw up and enforce a code 'governing due impartiality and a general code governing the portrayal of violence, appeals for donations and such other matters concerning standards and practice for programmes as the ITC considers appropriate'. The Code deals with bad language, sex and nudity ('Representation of sexual intercourse should be reserved until after 9pm'), bad taste in humour (i.e. jokes about personal disability and racial jokes), the portrayal of violence, scenes of extreme suffering and distress, coverage of terrorism, crime and anti-social behaviour. Much of the Code is identical to the regulations laid out in the RADIO AUTHORITY PROGRAMME CODES 1 and 2. The Family Viewing Policy warns that material 'unsuitable for children must not be broadcast at times when the largest numbers of children are viewing . . . After 9 pm and until 5.30 am, progressively less suitable (i.e. more adult) material may be shown and it may be that a programme will be acceptable, for example, at 10.30 pm which would not be suitable at 9 pm.'

J

J-Curve One focus of communications research has been the part played by personal contact in the diffusion of information about news EVENTS featured in the mass media. The assassination of President Kennedy in 1963 and the speedy diffusion of the news of the event gave an impetus to this research. The J-Curve arose from the conclusions of B.S. Greenberg and stems mainly from his work on the Kennedy assassination when he investigated the first sources of knowledge about 18 different

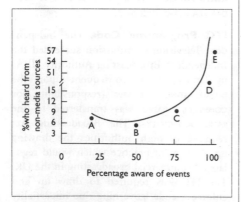

J-Curve of news diffusion

news events. It represents the relationship between the overall extent of awareness people have of such an event and the proportion of those learning of it through interpersonal sources.

Greenberg argues that news events can be divided into three groups as regards the manner of their diffusion and the involvement of personal contact in it.

Type 1 events are important to the few people who may be affected by them but are of little concern to the general public. Such events, though reported in the media, will be most generally diffused by personal contact – the announcement of an engagement, for example.

Type 2 events such as those in typical main news stories are generally regarded as important and command the attention of a large number of people. News of such events is not likely to be passed on as information through personal contact, although they may be discussed as it will be taken for granted that most people will either know of such news or that it is not of vital interest to them. An example here might be an earthquake in another country.

Type 3 events are dramatic, important and of very wide interest. Such events, like the assassination of President Kennedy or the death of Diana, Princess of Wales, get speedy and detailed coverage from the media. They also mobilize interpersonal sources and the proportion of those who learn of the events from personal sources will be considerably higher than for type 2 news items. Such events are, however, rare and are usually related to crisis situations. In the case of the Kennedy assassination, Greenberg and Parker found that the extent and speed of diffusion was amazing: 99.85% of the US population knew of the event within five hours of its occurrence. About 50% of people first heard about it through personal sources and of these a fairly high proportion were strangers – revealing the degree to which people departed from established communication patterns.

By plotting the proportion of people eventually aware of all types of events against the proportion who heard about them first from personal contacts, it was possible to group them into five categories and the line joining these five categories was J-shaped as shown in the diagram.

A is in type 1, B, C, D are in type 2 and E is in type 3. It can be seen that the size of the total audience increases progressively but the proportion of those receiving information from interpersonal sources does not; the proportion is higher for some of type 1 than for type 2 but highest for type 3.

Jakobson's model of communication, 1958 A linguist, Roman Jakobson was concerned with notions of MEANING and of the internal structure of MESSAGES. His model is a double one, involving the constitutive factors in an act of communication; each of these factors is then locked on to the function it performs. Thus the constitutive factors are:

	Context	
Addresser	*Message*	*Addressee*
	Contact	
	Code	

The functions form an identically structured model:

	Referential	
(Reality orientation of message)		
Emotive	*Poetic*	*Conative*
(Expressive)	*Phatic*	(Effect of a
	Metalingual	message on
		addressee)

Phatic here refers to the function of keeping the channels of communication open and Metalingual is the function of actually identifying the communication code which is being used. See COMMUNICATION MODELS; REDUNDANCY.

Jargon The specialist speech of groups of people with common identity – of religion, science, medicine, art, trade, profession, political party, etc. We can have educational jargon, cricket jargon, sociological jargon – that is, the in-language of people with specialist knowledge or interest. For those creating and operating jargon, it is a useful and vital means of communicating quickly between expert and expert. For those outside, jargon appears to be an unnecessarily complicated alternative to plain speaking,

and a barrier to good communication. Without the growth of jargon words and expressions in Communication and Media Studies, this dictionary would not have been deemed necessary.

JICNARS scale Administered by the Joint Industrial Committee for National Readership Surveys in the UK, JICNARS measures audience according to social class, occupation and perceived economic status: Category A (upper middle class; business and professional people, considerable private means); Category B (middle class, senior people of reasonable affluence; respectable rather than luxurious lifestyle); Category C1 (white collar workers, tradespeople, supervisory and clerical jobs), Group C2 (blue collar, skilled workers); Group D (semi-skilled or unskilled members of the 'blue collar' class) and E (those at the lowest level of subsistence, casual workers, those unemployed and/or dependent on social security schemes). This classification has come under increasing criticism over the years, especially the emphasis upon targeting the occupation of the head of a household, traditionally male. More 'with it' methods of gauging patterns of consumption have concentrated on the notion of *lifestyle* as reflected in people's aspirations. The best known of these is VALS (Values and Lifestyles). See HICT PROJECT.

Jihad Vs McWorld See McWORLD Vs JIHAD.

Jingoism Extreme and uncritical form of national patriotism. The word derives from G.W. Hunt's song, written at the time of the Russo-Turkish War (1877–78) when anti-Russian feeling in the UK was running high and Disraeli ordered the Mediterranean fleet to Constantinople: 'We don't want to fight, but by Jingo if we do/ We've got the ships, we've got the men, and got the money too'. The Falklands War of 1982 stirred up similar sentiments in Britain's popular PRESS which used language as declamatory and as sensational as anything employed during the Boer War, the two World Wars or the British invasion of Suez (1956). From the *Sun* ('The paper that supports our boys'): '74 Days That Shook the World!', 'Lions Who Did The Impossible –

By land, sea and air, our boys never faltered in their fight against tyranny' and, on the front page, in three-inch high type, 'We've Won!' (15 July 1982). With the NATO bombing of Serbia in 1999, the *Sun* showed that it had not lost its jingoist panache. Under the resounding headline 'Clobba Slobba' (referring to the Yugoslav leader Slobadan Milosevic), the paper trumpeted 'Our boys batter Serb butcher in Nato bomb blitz'. And at the foot of the page, 'We go in: See pages 2, 3, 4, 5, 6, 7 and 8'.

Johari Window The term Johari Window is derived from the first names of those who devised the model, Joseph Luft and Harrington Ingram. Effective interaction depends largely on the degree of and growth of understanding between the individuals concerned. Luft's theory of the Johari Window expounded in his work entitled *Of Human Interaction* (US: National Press Books, 1969), is a useful way in which to look at such factors of INTERPERSONAL COMMUNICATION as SELF-DISCLOSURE and FEEDBACK and the way these may influence our SELF-CONCEPT. The model, shown below, represents a way of analysing the self.

The *free area* represents the public self: information about yourself that is known to you and to others, such as your gender or race. There is a free and open exchange of information in this area.

The *blind area* contains information about yourself which is not known to you but which is known to others, such as any irritating mannerisms you might have.

The *hidden area* contains things you know about yourself but wish to keep hidden from others, such as your lack of confidence in certain situations. You normally take action to protect this area from the scrutiny of others.

The *unknown area* contains information that neither you nor others are fully conscious of but which might still be influencing your behaviour – unconscious fears, for example.

The model can be used to analyse many aspects of interpersonal behaviour. Through interpersonal communication we can come to understand ourselves better and increase the size of the free area and decrease the size of the other three. For example, self-disclosure can reduce the hidden area and increase the free area and thus enhance communication with others. Feedback from others has the potential to reduce the blind area, although possibly at some cost to SELF-ESTEEM, and further increase the free area. The degree to which we may be willing to make such changes to the relative size of the areas will of course vary with the situation and relationship. Generally speaking the greater the free area in any given situation, the easier the interaction.

Joint Committee on Censorship of the Theatre See LORD CHAMBERLAIN.

Journalese A manner of writing which employs ready-made phrases and formulas and which breeds its own short-cut language and clichés, rarely without some catchy word-rhythm: 'Tory, Tory, Hallelujah' proclaimed the *Daily Express* in 1982; in 1900, their headlines were equally ringing: 'The Boers' Last Grip Loosened'. The aim is to squeeze out the most dramatic expression with the minimum use of words. The higher the pressure on space, the more pronounced the journalese. See TABLOIDESE.

Journalism While many professions feature in the public eye, journalism can be said to *be* the public eye. Journalism reports to the public, conveying to it information, analysis, comment and entertainment while

The Johari Window

equally purporting to *represent* the public; to speak for it in the public arena.

At the same time journalism is in the business of representing to the public 'the reality out there'. It is only at first sight a curiosity that journalists refer to the reports they write, edit or present, as 'stories', yet many commentators have drawn close comparisons between journalism and fiction. In an article 'The nature of aesthetic experience' published in the *International Journal of Ethics* 36 (1926), George Herbert Mead defined two models of journalism, the *information* model and the *story* model, stating that 'the reporter is generally sent out to get a story not the facts'. Of course journalists are not always happy to be described as storytellers; after all, the job of the serious journalist is to provide information and analysis and not to turn news into entertainment. Yet subsequent commentators have confirmed Mead's definition. John Langer in 'Truly awful news on television' published in *Journalism and Popular Culture* (UK: Sage, 1992), edited by Peter Dahlgren and Colin Sparks, argues that 'serious news is also based around the story model'. However, it pretends that it is not – it declares that it is concerned with imparting the important information of the day'.

Langer is of the view that 'the world of fact and the world of fiction are bound more closely together than broadcasters are prepared to have us believe'. The implication here is that journalism has a storytelling function which has much to do with VALUES, telling stories about who we are, how we have become what we are and should become. The journalist to a degree is a maker, or at least an upholder, of MYTH in the sense that the French philosopher Roland Barthes has used the word: mythologizing is essentially a mode of explaining things, a giver of meaning albeit simplified and clarified. As Barthes puts it in *Mythologies* (UK: Paladin, 1973), myth 'abolishes the complexity of human acts'.

By a process of elimination and emphasis, the journalist *frames* MEANING (see FRAMING). In the study of media we are as interested in what does not appear in the frame as what does appear. The frame can also be seen as a set of boundaries which

journalism defines and patrols. Cultural, social or political DEVIANCE is defined and labelled by the journalist. There are those – people, movements, ideas – which are DEMONIZED, defined as dangerous to the security of the community (see LOONY LEFT-ISM). It might even be suggested that the media have a policing role in society and that journalists, at least some of them, carry out the part of 'copper's nark'.

The relationship between the role of the journalist and the exercise of power and control has been a keen focus of study. In *Visualizing Deviance: A Study of News Organizations* (UK: Open University, 1987), Richard Ericson, Patricia Baranak and Janet Chan speak of news journalists as a 'deviance-defining elite' who 'provide on-going articulation of the proper bounds to behaviour in all organized spheres of life'. American media analyst David Barsamian refers to journalists as 'stenographers of power' in *Stenographers of Power: Media and Propaganda* (US: Common Courage, 1992), meaning basically that journalists are largely servants of the state, taking down verbatim their script from the POWER ELITE. This could be described as the 'Poodle to the Powerful' model. While not being so dismissive, Alan Bell in *The Language of News Media* (UK: Blackwell, 1991) acknowledges that 'News is what an authoritative source tells a journalist . . . The more elite the source, the more newsworthy the story'. In contrast, believes Bell, 'alternative sources tend to be ignored: individuals, opposition parties, unions, minorities, fringe groups, the disadvantaged'. In certain situations, particularly of national crisis such as wartime, the editors of *Media, Crisis and Democracy: Mass Communication and the Disruption of Social Order* (UK: Sage, 1992), Marc Raboy and Bernard Dagenais argue that the media become an 'extension of the state'. They quote Anthony Lewis of the *New York Times* describing the press during the Gulf War (1991) as 'a claque applauding the American generals and politicians in charge'; while television behaved as the 'most egregious official lapdog during the war'.

The contrasting model to the Poodle is that of the Watchdog, where journalism stands guard over the public interest, a tireless terrier which snaps and snarls at injustice, corruption and abuse. Since the birth of the printed word in 1450 there have been ample cases of conformity and rebellion (if not revolution) in journalism. In the nineteenth century the courageous editors of the radical press, such as Richard Carlile and Henry Hetherington, spent many years of their lives in prison for writing about and publishing beliefs which ran counter to those of the ruling elite. In the twentieth century hundreds of journalists and news photographers have been killed while reporting events throughout the world. In 1983 at least 63 journalists were killed, world-wide, and another 124 imprisoned, according to figures issued by *Reporters Sans Frontières* and this compared with 72 killed in 1991, 61 in 1992 and 51 in 1995.

In journalism there will always be the biased and the spurious; there will continue to be invasion of privacy, nationalist hype, shameless and malicious STEREOTYPING, wallowing scandal – all 'examples' of contemporary journalism in action.

There will also continue to be high quality investigative journalism which, in the words of John Keane in 'The crisis of the sovereign state' (in Raboy and Dagenais) 'seeks to counteract the secretive and noisy arrogance of the democratic Leviathan'; which 'involves the patient investigation and exposure of political corruption and misconduct'; which sets out to 'sting political power, to tame its arrogance by extending the limits of public controversy and widening citizens' involvement in the public spheres of civil society'. See WEDOM, THEYDOM.

Journalism: celebrity journalism The preoccupation in modern print journalism with recording the activities, sayings, scandals of celebrities; described by Peter Hamill in *News Is a Verb* (US: Ballentine, 1998) as a virus, and 'the most widespread phenomena [sic] of the times'. Hamill is of the view that 'True accomplishment is marginal to the recognition factor. There is seldom any attention paid to scientists, poets, educators or archeologists'. Big names are the constant

focus of attention to the exclusion of other subjects.

Journalism: 'I-Me-My' journalism A trend as dominant in recent years as CELEBRITY JOURNALISM, of weekly columns, particularly in broadsheets, of journalists whose main interest is themselves and who recount, week in week out, personal opinion, impressions and experiences. The magazine sections of the press abound with what has been varyingly termed 'armchair punditry' and 'stocking filler' journalism.
* John Hartley, *Popular Reality: Journalism, Modernity, Popular Culture* (UK: Arnold, 1996); Beulah Ainley, *Black Journalism, White Media* (UK: Trentham Books, 1998).

Jump cut Where two scenes in a TV news report are of the same subject, taken from the same angle and distance, the 'jump cut' is to be avoided; to get round this 'jump' from one shot to virtually the same, usually of someone being interviewed, a 'cutaway' shot is inserted, that is, a reaction shot from the interviewer.

Juxtaposition jump-cut See SOUND-BITE.

K

Katz and Lazarsfeld's two-step flow model of mass communication and personal influence See ONE-STEP, TWO-STEP, MULTI-STEP FLOW MODELS OF COMMUNICATION.

Kepplinger and Habermeier Events Typology See EVENTS.

Kineme A segment or fraction of a whole communicative GESTURE; a kinetic parallel to a PHONEME (element of verbal LANGUAGE). The term was invented by Ray Birdwhistell. In *Kinesics and Context* (US: University of Philadelphia, 1970), Birdwhistell draws up a vocabulary of 60 kinemes which he found in the gestural/postural/expressive movements of American subjects. He maintains that these kinemes combine to form large units *(kinemorphs)* on the analogy of *morphemes* (or words). An example would be waving a fist or prodding the air with a finger while at the same time smiling or looking angry. See KINESICS.

Kinesics The study of communication through GESTURE, posture and body movement. In *Communication* (UK: Open University, Block 3, Units 7–10, 1975), the OU course team loosely classify *Kinesics* under five headings: (1) *Information* (indicating, for example, welcome or 'keep away'). (2) *Communication markers* (head and body movements to give emphasis to a spoken MESSAGE). (3) *Emotional state* (as expression of feeling). (4) *Expression of self* (in the way you sit or walk or hold yourself). (5) *Expression of relationship* (revealing attitude to others by how close you stand to someone, how you angle, tilt, shift your body in relationship to others or by the way hair or clothes are touched, a tie adjusted). See COMMUNICATION, NON-VERBAL; NON-VERBAL BEHAVIOUR: REPERTOIRE; PROXEMICS; TOUCH.

* Ray Birdwhistell, *Kinesics and Context* (US: University of Philadelphia, 1970).

Kinetoscope Early form of FILM projection invented in 1887 by Thomas Alva Edison (1847–1931) and his assistant K.L. Dickson. On 14 April 1894, the first Kinetoscope Parlor was opened on Broadway, New York. The Kinetoscope was a wooden cabinet furnished with a peep-slit and an inspection lens through which a single person could view the endless loop of CELLULOID film which passed below it. It was driven by a small electric motor and illuminated by an electric lamp. Edison's lasting contribution to cinematography was his use of celluloid film 35 mm wide, with four perforations for each picture, a practice that has continued to this day. See CINEMATOGRAPHY, ORIGINS.

'Kite' co-orientation approach See McCOMBS AND SHAW AGENDA-SETTING MODEL OF MEDIA EFFECTS, 1976.

Knowns, Unknowns In *Deciding What's News* (US: Pantheon, 1979) Herbert Gans says that those who are famous in society, *Knowns*, appear at least four times more frequently in TV news bulletins than unknowns. The POWER ELITE and celebrities generally tend to be both the source and subject-matter of news stories; and by being so they further qualify themselves to appear on the news as Knowns. Gans states that fewer than 50 individuals regularly appear on US news. It is not only the actions of Knowns which qualify as newsworthy, but their speech. As Allan Bell says in *The Language of News Media* (UK: Blackwell, 1991), 'Talk is news only if the right person is talking'. Meanwhile the dominance of the headlines by Knowns, by the elite, leads to other actors, other talk, being ignored. See NEWS VALUES.

Kuleshov effect Lev Kuleshov (1899–1970) was in at the sunrise of Russian cinema. He was FILM designer, film maker and film theorist. In 1920 he was given a workshop to study film methods with a group of students. His *Kuleshov effect*, demonstrated in 1922, proved how, by altering the juxtaposition of film images, their significance, for the audience, could be changed.

In 1929 he wrote 'The content of the shot in itself is not so important as the joining of two shots of different content and the method of their connection and their alternation'.

An experiment, aimed at proving his theory, showed a close-up of an actor playing a prisoner. This is linked to two different shots representing what the prisoner sees: first a bowl of soup, then the open door of freedom. Audiences were convinced that the expression on the man's face was different in each instance, though it was the same piece of film. See MONTAGE; SHOT.

Kuuki Japanese term, shared by the Chinese and Koreans, meaning a *climate of opinion requiring compliance*. In an article entitled 'The future of political communication research: a Japanese perspective' published in the *Journal of Communication* Autumn 1993, Ito Youichi explains how *kuuki* may be nurtured by the media or by those in government or by the production of what he calls *extracted information* – that which the public draws from sources other than the mass media, for example from personal experience and observation, and talking to others. The more people talk to each other, argues Youichi, the less dependent they are on the mass media. Conversely, the less they talk among themselves the more media agendas dominate the public's way of thinking and perceiving. 'If people depend heavily upon mass media for information,' writes Youichi, 'and if personal influence in political communication is weak, then the political influence of mass media may be overwhelming.' The *kuuki*, the climate of opinion requiring compliance, has been shaped by the media: the more meagre the extracted information, the weaker is the response to dominant definitions and therefore the more ready the compliance.

It is important to recognize that, at least in non-totalitarian states, the public arena is witness to competing agendas and that the agenda-setters (government, big business, the media) are often in alliance and occasionally in competition or even conflict.

Where for instance there is an alliance between the agenda of state and the public agenda, against that of big business, or the media, then we might discern *kuuki* in operation, that is a climate of opinion which may force big business or the media into line; and where the media agenda allies with public agendas against the agendas of state, government may move into line. Youichi sees the media at one point of a triangle, with government and the public making up the other two points. He concludes that 'Mass media have effects only when they stand on the majority side of the mainstream in a triadic relationship that creates and supports the kuuki that functions as a social pressure on the minority side'. See AGENDA SETTING; ROGERS AND DEARING AGENDA-SETTING MODEL, 1987; NOELLE-NEUMANN'S SPIRAL OF SILENCE MODEL OF PUBLIC OPINION, 1974.

L

Label libel A McLUHANISM. Marshall McLuhan, (1911–80) media guru of the 1960s, wrote of the way that the mass media stick labels on people, trap them in STEREOTYPES, typecast them, pigeon-hole them to the point that such generalizations become invidious and thus a mode of DEFAMATION.

Labelling process (and the media) Howard Becker in a classic study, *The Outsiders; Studies in the Sociology of Deviancy* (US: Free Press, 1963), analyses the process by which certain social actions or ideas and those who perform or express them come to be defined as DEVIANT; and which he calls 'the labelling process': 'The deviant is one to whom the label has successfully been applied; deviant behaviour is behaviour that people so label'.

Becker's work highlights the role that powerful social groups and individuals play in defining the limits of acceptable and unacceptable behaviour, through the labelling process. He argues that certain groups within society, MORAL ENTREPRENEURS, are particularly able to shape, via the mass media, new images of deviancy and new definition of social problems. See CRISIS DEFINITION; ISSUES.

LAD or Language Acquisition Device According to linguists such as Noam Chomsky, LAD is an innate device within the human mind which allows us to acquire language. The LAD is a hypothetical model of this process and is grounded in the theory that human beings are programmed to acquire and create language and thus can develop competence in any language that they are exposed to, over a period of time. See DEEP STRUCTURE.

Lame A term used by William Labov in *Language in the Inner City* (US: University of Pennsylvania Press, 1972) to describe individuals who are relatively isolated, on the margins of a group and its culture. This relatively isolated position often shows itself linguistically in that such individuals will use less the significant linguistic features of the group or culture in question.

LAN Local Area Network, a system of centralizing and coordinating the myriad forms of INFORMATION TECHNOLOGY equipment used in business; knitting together the items of office machinery which most companies have gathered piecemeal – TELEX, WORD PROCESSING, computers, VIEWDATA processes, document FACSIMILE machines, telephones.

Language See ANDROCENTRIC RULE; ANTI-LANGUAGE; APACHE SILENCE; ARBITRARINESS; BAD LANGUAGE; CENSORSHIP; CODES; COLLOQUIALISM; COMMUNICATION, NON-VERBAL; COMPETENCE; CONNOTATION; CONVERSATIONAL STYLES; CORPO-

RATE SPEECH; CULTURAL MODES; CULTURE; DEEP STRUCTURE; DIACHRONIC LINGUISTICS; DISCOURSE; DISPLACEMENT; ELABORATED AND RESTRICTED CODES; EMOTIVE LANGUAGE; EUPHEMISM; EYE CONTACT; GENDERLECTS; GESTURE; HE-MAN LANGUAGE; HEDGES; HOLOPHRASES; HOMOPHILY; IDEATIONAL FUNCTIONS OF LANGUAGE; IDIOLECT; INDICATORS; JARGON; JOURNALESE; LAD; LAME; LANGUAGE AND THOUGHT; LANGUAGE POLLUTION; LANGUE AND PAROLE; LEXIS; LINGUISTICS; LINGUISTIC DETERMINISM; MALE-AS-NORM; MEANING; METAMESSAGE; METAPHOR; METONYMY; MILITARY METAPHOR; MORPHOLOGY; MULTI-ACTUALITY; MUTED GROUPS; NEGATIVE SEMANTIC SPACE; NEOLOGISM; NEWSPEAK; ONOMATOPOEIA; OPENNESS; OVEREXTENSION; OVERLEXICALIZATION; PARADIGM; PEJORATION; PERSONAL IDIOM; PHATIC LANGUAGE; PHONEME; PHONETICS; PIDGIN; POSTULATES OF COMMUNICATION; PLUS MALE/MINUS MALE; PRAGMATICS; PROFANE LANGUAGE; PROSODIC SIGNALS; PROTOLANGUAGE; PROXEMICS; PSYCHOLINGUISTICS; RECEIVED PRONUNCIATION; REDUNDANCY; REGISTER; RELEXICALIZATION; REPORT TALK/RAPPORT TALK; RHETORIC; SAPIR-WHORF HYPOTHESIS; SEMANTIC DEROGATION OF WOMEN; SEMANTICITY; SEMANTICS; SIGN; SIGNIFICATION; SIGNIFICS; SLANG; SOCIOLINGUISTICS; STRUCTURALISM; TABOO; TABLOIDESE; TAG QUESTIONS; TELEGRAPHIC SPEECH; TOUCH; TRADITIONAL TRANSMISSION.

Language pollution According to Gail and Michele Meyers in *The Dynamics of Human Communication* (US: McGraw-Hill, 1985), this occurs 'When language is used by people to say what in fact they do not believe, when words are used, sometimes unwittingly, sometimes deliberately, to cover up rather than to explain reality, our symbolic world becomes polluted. This means that language becomes an unreliable instrument for adapting to the environment and for communicating'.

The authors identify three main types of language pollution and their common characteristics: *confusion* (unknown meanings), characterized by the use of foreign languages, unfamiliar words, technical jargon and misused terminology; *ambiguity* (too many meanings), characterized by vagueness, the use of words with multiple definitions and the use of very general imprecise statements, or terms; and *deception* (obscured meanings), characterized by

outright lies, distortion, and giving incomplete information or non-answers to questions.

Langue and Parole In his *Cours de Linguistique Générale* (1916), published after his death, Ferdinand de Saussure (1857–1914) defined *La langue*, or LANGUAGE, as a system, while *La parole* represented the actual manifestations of language in speech and writing. The former he conceived as an 'institution', a set of interpersonal rules and NORMS; the latter, events or instances, taking their meaning from, or giving MEANING to, the system.
* De Saussure, *Course in General Linguistics* (English translation; UK: Fontana/Collins, 1974).

Lapdog metaphor See GUARD DOG METAPHOR.

Lasswell's model of communication, 1948 A questioning device rather than an actual model of the communication process, Harold Lasswell's five-point approach to the analysis of the mass media has nevertheless given enduring service. It remains a useful first step in interpreting the transmission and reception of messages.

In 'The structure and function of communication in society' in Lymon Bryson, ed., *The Communication of Ideas* (US: Harper & Row, 1948) Lasswell suggests that in order to arrive at a due understanding of the MEANING systems of MASS COMMUNICATION the following sequence of questions might be put:

Who
Says *What*
In which *channel*
To *whom*
With what *effect?*

Assuming that the last question would include the notion of FEEDBACK, Lasswell's model could still do with an additional question – In what *context* (social, economic, cultural, political, aesthetic) is the communication process taking place? Also Lasswell makes no provision for INTERVENING VARIABLES, those mediating factors which have impact on the ways in which messages are received and responded to. It is useful to compare Lasswell's list to the verbal version of GERBNER'S MODEL OF COMMUNICATION, 1956. In 'Towards a general model of communication' in *Audio-Visual Communication Review*, 4 (1956), George Gerbner offers the following formula:

1 Someone
2 perceives an event
3 and reacts
4 in a situation
5 through some means
6 to make available materials
7 in some form
8 and context
9 conveying content
10 with some consequence.

See COMMUNICATION MODELS.

Latitudes of acceptance and rejection The greater the gap between an attitude a person already holds and that which another wants to persuade him/her to adopt, the less likely it is that any shift in attitude will occur. C.W. Sherif in *Attitudes and Attitude Change* (US: Greenwood Press, 1982) argues that our responses to attempts to challenge or change our attitudes are divided into three main types. (1) An individual's *latitude of acceptance* contains the opinions, ideas and so on about an issue that a person is ready to agree with or accept. (2) The *latitude of non-commitment* contains the range of opinions and ideas on the same issue that the individual is neutral about. (3) The *latitude* of *rejection* contains those ideas and opinions about an issue which the individual finds unacceptable. Further, unacceptable statements tend to be interpreted as even more hostile and unfavourable than they really are – the *contrast effect* – whilst those that are not far removed from the latitude of acceptance may gradually be incorporated into it – the *assimilation effect*. See BOOMERANG EFFECT.

Law of minimal effects Point of view that the media have little or no effect in forming or modifying the attitude of audiences. See EFFECTS OF THE MASS MEDIA.

LBC: London Broadcasting Corporation The first COMMERCIAL RADIO station to come on air in the UK, in October 1973; followed a few days later by Capital Radio.

Leadership Leaders can generally be defined as individuals within GROUPS or organizations who have influence, who provide focus, coordination and direction for the activities of the group. It may be argued that the purpose of leadership is to enable the group to function effectively and achieve its goals although in practice leadership may not always have this effect. Leadership may be and often is invested in one person but it can also be shared. Leaders may be emergent or appointed. An emergent leader is one who comes to acquire the role of leader through the process of group INTERACTION. He or she may, for example, be the person with the best ideas or communication skills. An appointed leader is one who is formally selected; leaders in work situations are often appointed to their position.

A considerable amount of research has been conducted with the aim of trying to ascertain the qualities and interpersonal skills required for effective leadership and the type of leadership needed for the optimum performance of groups or organizations. An early perspective was the *trait* approach to leadership which argues that individuals who become leaders have certain personality traits or characteristics enabling them to cope well with leadership. The suggestion is that leaders are born, not made. However, this approach has been widely criticized for being simplistic and lacking in any hard evidence to substantiate its claims.

Another approach examines the varying *styles* of leadership which may be adopted and the characteristics of each style. An example here would be represented by the work of Robert Likert. In *The Human Organization* (US: McGraw-Hill, 1967), Likert identifies four main styles of leadership: *Automatic, Persuasive, Consultative* and *Democratic*. Research into leadership styles tends to point towards the democratic leadership style as being superior to the others. However, the *situational* approach to leadership argues that different styles of leadership will be appropriate to different situations. Examples of key situational factors identified as determining suitable leadership styles include the nature of the task, the characteristics of the group and the organizational CULTURE. The *functional* approach to leadership focuses on identifying the behaviour needed from leaders so that particular groups and organizations may achieve their goals. The implication here is that individuals can improve their leadership abilities. One point all approaches are agreed on is that a good leader has to be a good communicator.

Leakage See FACIAL EXPRESSION.

Leaks A time-honoured way in which governments disseminate information, often through 'sources close to' the president or the prime minister; a way of authority manipulating the media. Leaks can always be denied. Sometimes, of course, leaks are genuine, that is they are true divulgences of information which those in authority would wish to be withheld. Here, those close to the centres of power, perhaps disagreeing with decisions about to be made or affronted at the potential mismanagement of power, disclose information with the intention of causing embarrassment and, through publicity, a change of policy. See DEEP THROAT; SECRECY.

Learned journals on communication See PERIODICALS FOR THE STUDY OF MEDIA.

Legislation See BROADCASTING LEGISLATION; CINEMA LEGISLATION.

Lexis Linguist's term to describe the vocabulary of a LANGUAGE: a unit of vocabulary is generally referred to as a **lexical** item or **lexeme**. A complete inventory of the lexical items of a language constitutes a dictionary, a **lexicon**. **Lexicography** is the overall study of the vocabulary of language, including its history.

Libel A written accusation; any malicious, defamatory publication or statement. The spoken equivalent of libel is SLANDER. Both constitute DEFAMATION and the law in the UK may impose heavy fines on those proved to have injured someone's good name. However, it is not possible to obtain legal aid in order to take, for example, a newspaper to court for libel.

Life positions In his book, *I'm O.K. You're O.K.* (US: Harper & Row, 1969), Thomas Harris identifies four Life Positions which can be used in TRANSACTIONAL ANALYSIS for exploring and examining people's feelings, attitudes or positions towards themselves and others and the way in which these influence their social interaction.

The I'm O.K. – You're O.K. position is one in which an individual believes in his/her own worth and that of others. It is a position in which we accept ourselves and others and base our transactions on this orientation. Harris argues that to reach this position requires conscious decision and effort. Harris believes many people hold an I'm not O.K. – You're O.K. position as a result of early socialization which, in attempting to shape an individual's behaviour into a pattern which is socially acceptable, contains a lot of messages critical of the individual – not O.K. messages. This position may lead to a feeling of inferiority which shows itself in defensive communication such as game playing.

Experiences in early childhood, especially abuse and neglect, may result in the individual forming the perspective that whilst he/she is O.K., other people are not. Hence the I'm O.K. – You're not O.K. position, which may show itself in a characteristically hostile, or aggressive communicative style. I'm not O.K. – You're not O.K. is the position of those who feel neither themselves nor others are O.K. This rather negative perspective may show itself through a rather despairing and resigned attitude when communicating with others.

Life positions influence the kinds of life SCRIPTS, individuals write for themselves. See GAMES.

* Ian Stewart and Vann Joines, *TA Today* (UK: Lifespace, 1987); Amy and Thomas Harris, *Staying O.K.* (UK: Arrow Books, 1995).

Lifestyle See TYPOLOGY.

Lighting cameraman In a FILM crew, the lighting cameraman or woman is responsible for the pictorial composition of the film IMAGE as well as the arrangements for lighting.

Light Programme One of three BBC RADIO channels until the introduction of Radio 1 in 1967, and a change of names for the rest: Light became Radio 2, HOME SERVICE Radio 4 and Third Programme Radio 3. The Light Programme, for general entertainment radio, was created in the year the 2nd World War ended, 1945.

Lindup Committee Report on Data Protection, 1978 See DATA PROTECTION.

Linguistic determinism The proposition that the language of a culture determines the way in which the world is perceived and thought about. Thus in acquiring a language an individual is also acquiring a particular way of thinking about the world, a particular world-view. The two linguists closely associated with this position are Benjamin Lee Whorf and Edward Sapir whose Linguistic Relativity Hypothesis helped to establish this particular view on the relationship between language and thought. Though their proposition that language actually determines thought has been much questioned, many would accept that the language at an individual's disposal influences the way he/she thinks about the world. See SAPIR-WHORF LINGUISTIC RELATIVITY HYPOTHESIS.

*Martin Montgomery, *An Introduction to Language and Society* (UK: Methuen, 1986, reprinted Routledge, 1993); Steven Pinker, *The Language Instinct* (UK: Allen Lane, 1994).

Linguistics The scientific study of LANGUAGE; a field that has seen remarkable expansion and diversification in the 20th c. particularly since the 1960s. **Diachronic** or **historical linguistics** investigates how language use has changed over time; **synchronic linguistics** is concerned with the *state* of language at any given point in time; **general linguistics** seeks to establish principles for the study of all languages; **descriptive linguistics** is concerned with the analysis of the characteristics of specific language; **contrastive linguistics** explores the contrasts between different languages or families of languages while **comparative linguistics** concentrates on common characteristics. Among a profusion of other linguistics-related studies are *anthropological linguistics, biolinguistics, psycholinguistics*

and *sociolinguistics*. See PARADIGM; SEMIOLOGY/SEMIOTICS; STRUCTURALISM.

Linotype printing Patented in 1894 by German immigrant to Baltimore, US, Ottmar Mergenthaler. The operator uses a keyboard similar to that of a TYPEWRITER. As each key is depressed a brass matrix for that particular letter drops into place. When the line is complete, the row of matrices is placed over a mould and the line of type is cast, the molten lead alloy setting almost at once. See MONOTYPE PRINTING; PRINTING.

Lip-sync Synchronization between mouth movement and the words on the FILM soundtrack.

Listening Though often taken for granted, listening is a crucial element in human communication. Gail Myers and Michele Myers in *The Dynamics of Human Communication* (US: McGraw-Hill, 1985) point out that 'Listening is often not the natural process that it is often believed to be'. Poor listening can be the cause of many breakdowns in communication. Myers and Myers go on to identify ways in which listening can be improved and communication thereby made more effective. *Active listening* reflects a certain attitude towards others. This attitude is that what others say is worth listening to and that one should attempt to imagine how what is being said makes sense to the person saying it and the feelings involved. The receiver needs to listen to the SENDER without initially passing judgement on what is being said and then mirror back to the sender what was said in order to show and to check that he/she understood the MESSAGE and the feelings that lie within it. This helps to build a supportive situation in which communication can take place. Active listening is also known as *empathetic listening*, whereas *deliberative listening* involves trying to determine, accurately, the content of the message.

Lithography PRINTING from stone, slate or a substitute such as zinc or aluminium, with greasy ink; invented in 1798 by Alois Senefelder.

Little masterpieces lasting one minute Watching a reel of British TV commercials,

Italian FILM director Federico Fellini gave them the ultimate compliment: 'How can these people produce such little master-pieces lasting one minute?' See ADVERTISING.

Little Red Schoolbook In the same year as the OZ TRIAL, 1971, Richard Handyside was taken to court for his publication *The Little Red Schoolbook*, which had originated in Denmark in 1969. Handyside's whole stock of books was sequestered by the police, and he was successfully prosecuted under the Obscene Publications Act of 1959. The subject matter concerned religious educa-tion, homework, teachers' foibles, pupils' complaints, school rules, corporal punish-ment, streaming, sex and drugs. See CENSOR-SHIP; SECTION 28.

Living newspaper A form of political PROPAGANDA drama which uses topical mate-rial and journalistic techniques in the hand-ling of current political, cultural and social ISSUES. Usually comprises short sketches on stage, or in FILM, of a satirical nature. The form originated with the Red Army of the Soviet Union during the Revolution (1917). In the US the Federal Theater Project cre-ated a Living Newspaper Unit in 1935; around the same time the living newspaper was promoted in the UK by the Unity Thea-tre in St Pancras, London. It was a left-wing amateur group and specialized in what was termed 'agitational' drama. See AGITPROP.

Lloyd Committee Report, 1967 Foll-owing a decision by the secretary of state for education and science, Anthony Cros-land, in 1965, a committee under Lord Lloyd of Hampstead was set up to enquire into the need for a National Film School in the UK. The committee's report, *National Film School*, Department of Education and Science, HMSO Code Number 27–404, recommended that a FILM school be estab-lished at the earliest possible moment and that it should provide professional training in film-making for those showing outstand-ing promise as film-makers. See NATIONAL FILM AND TELEVISION SCHOOL.

Lloyd's List The oldest international daily newspaper, founded in 1734; perhaps most noted for its role as almanac of world ship-ping movements and casualty report.

Lobbying A process in which individuals or GROUPS seek to influence those in power. Literally, the *lobby* is the passage through which MPs pass to record their votes in Parliament. Lobbying includes any device to persuade other people to give an issue their support.

Lobby Practice A book of rules of con-duct written by, and abided by, parliamen-tary Lobby correspondents who operate from offices in the House of Commons and whose access to the centres of power is highly prized. The lobby system in the British House of Commons goes as far back as 1886. Correspondents meet daily at Downing Street, the home of the prime minister, and weekly on Thursdays in the Commons for a briefing by the PM's PRESS SECRETARY.

The system has been subjected to con-siderable criticism on the grounds of its SECRECY, alleged cosiness and danger of col-lusion between government and privileged lobby correspondents. It has been varyingly called 'an instrument of closed government' and the 'real cancer of British journalism'. At the heart of the criticism is the fact that the lobby correspondents receive no more information than government wishes them to know; if they break the rules of Lobby Practice they know their privileges will be withdrawn.

Localite channel of communication See COSMOPOLITE AND LOCALITE CHANNELS.

Longford Committee Report on Por-nography, 1972 An unofficial enquiry chaired by Lord Longford arising from a debate in the House of Lords on PORNOGRA-PHY, 21 April 1971, where Longford called attention to what he considered to be mounting public concern over the great expansion of pornographic, or near porno-graphic, material. Among members of the enquiry were novelist Kingsley Amis, disc-jockey Jimmy Savile, the Archbishop of York, Lord Shawcross (see SHAWCROSS REPORT) and the then deputy editor of the *Sunday Telegraph*, Peregrine Worsthorne.

Denying that they were 'prudes or kill-joys' the committee expressed a firm belief that, in D.H. Lawrence's stark phrase, pornography 'does the dirt on sex'. The Report – *Pornography: The Longford Report* (UK: Coronet Books, 1972) declared its antipathy to pornography 'precisely because we are *for* a loving, pleasurable and satisfying sexual expression and experience as a means of enhancing the lives of men and women', and the view that 'Some liberties have to be limited if other liberties are to be enjoyed'.

The Longford enquiry was conducted amid a blaze of publicity at a time when the conflict between free expression and control was very much in the headlines (see OZ TRIAL). Perhaps above all things, the Longford Report was concerned to protect children but its desire to translate that concern into extensive legislation would, critics believed, have restrictive effects far beyond the actual dangers posed by pornography. See BROADCASTING STANDARDS COUNCIL; CENSOR-SHIP; WILLIAMS COMMITTEE REPORT ON OBSCENITY AND FILM CENSORSHIP.

Looking behaviour See CIVIL INATTENTION; EYE CONTACT.

Lookism Theory that the better looking you are the more successful you will be in life; written about at length by American psychologist Nancy Etcoff in *Survival of the Prettiest: The Science of Beauty* (US: Little, Brown, 1999). In an age of images, the image dominates our perceptions, our thoughts and our judgments. According to Etcoff even mothers love their offspring just a little bit less if they are less than handsome. In the world of work, says Dr Etcoff, 'Good looking men are more likely to get hired, at a higher salary than unattractive men'. She compares 'Looking' with sexism and racism. However these are conscious, easily recognized attitudes, while Lookism works at a subconscious level. We are largely unaware of favouring the beautiful.

Loony Leftism In the 1980s in the UK a mythology was created by local and national newspapers about the policies of Labour-led councils, particularly those in Greater London. 'Loony' became the catchword whenever councils such as Hackney, Haringey or Islington were mentioned: and the accusation arose from rumours that were simply untrue. For example, The *Daily Star* printed a headline story declaring that the Hackney council, in its attempt to stamp out racism and racist LANGUAGE in the borough, had banned the singing of 'Baa, Baa, Black Sheep' in playschools. Hackney had never considered banning the nursery rhyme; however, newspapers throughout the country and in the rest of the world picked on this example of 'Loony Leftism'. Once in print, the story gained momentum and credence. Even Labour MPs took on board the Loony Left slogan.

A study of this campaign of DISINFORMA-TION was conducted by the Goldsmith's College Media Research Group and the findings summarized in an Open Space television programme on BBC 2 (March 1988). The researchers found no substance in press allegations, yet these allegations had far-reaching effects: they coloured popular perceptions of Labour-run councils; they created out of local authority leaders a set of FOLK DEVILS and managed to sever them from their natural supporters, members of their own party and the public they were attempting to serve; and they softened the ground for central government in its onslaught on local government, particularly Metropolitan boroughs. See EFFECTS OF THE MASS MEDIA; HEGEMONY; MYTH; SECTION 28.

Lord Chamberlain Until they were abolished in 1968 the powers of the Lord Chamberlain to censor plays in the British theatre went as far back as the reign of James I, though such powers were not defined by statute until 1737. All plays, except those performed by theatre clubs, were obliged to obtain a licence from the Lord Chamberlain's office. Each script was vetted for bad LANGUAGE, subversive ideas and any criticism of monarchy, parliament, the church, etc. In 1967 a Joint Committee on Censorship of the Theatre was set up by government. This recommended freedom for the stage 'subject to the overriding requirements of the criminal law' and that managements and dramatists should be protected from 'frivolous or arbitrary' prosecutions. These recommendations formed the basis of Labour MP George Strauss's private member's bill which became law, liberating the theatre from the Lord Chamberlain in the Theatres Act of September 1968.

Lowbrow See HIGHBROW.

LP See GRAMOPHONE.

M

MacBride Commission International Commission for the Study of Communication Problems under the chairmanship of Sean MacBride, former secretary general of the International Commission of Jurists, to hear, distil and report on evidence submitted with regard to media information interaction between the Western and Third World countries. In particular, the Commission was to report on the impact of Western media technology, and the subsequent flow of Western-orientated information, upon developing nations.

Set up by Unesco in 1978 with a committee of 'fifteen wise men and one woman', including Colombian novelist Gabriel Garcia Marquez and Canadian media guru Marshall McLuhan, the Commission produced a 484 page report in 1980. This urged a strengthening of Third World independence in the field of information gathering and transmission and measures to defend national cultures against the formidable one-way flow of information and entertainment from Western capitalist nations, chiefly the US.

Successor to MacBride is the International Program for the Development of Communication (IPDC), coordinated by an intergovernmental council comprising representatives of 35 member states, elected by the General Conference of Unesco. See MEDIA IMPERIALISM; TALLOIRES DECLARATION, 1981.

Machinery of representation In modern societies, the various forms of mass media have been named the 'machinery of representation' by Professor Stuart Hall in his chapter on Media power and class power in *Bending Reality: The State of the Media* (UK: Pluto Press, 1986), edited by James Curran, Jake Ecclestone, Giles Oakley and Alan Richardson. Hall writes of the 'whole process of reporting and construction' through which reality is translated into media forms – forms which the audience is expected to recognize as reality. Yet reality, argues Hall, is not simply transcribed in 'great unassimilated lumps through our daily dose of newspapers or our nightly diet of television': 'They *all* work using language, words, text, pictures, still or moving; combining in different ways through the practices and techniques of selection, editing, montage, design, layout, format, linkage, narrative, openings, closures' – to represent the world to us'. The media exercise 'the power to represent the world in certain ways. And because there are many different and conflicting ways in which meaning about the world can be constructed, it matters profoundly what and who gets represented, *what* and *who* regularly and routinely gets left out; and *how* things, people, events, relationships are represented'. See DISCURSIVE GAP; HEGEMONY; MEANING; POWER ELITE; PREFERRED READING.

Magic system See ADVERTISING.

Magnetic tape recording Magnetic tape was invented as early as 1898 by Valdemar Poulsen in Denmark. Its possibilities were ignored for decades until developed and used by the Germans during the 2nd World War (1939–45). The impact on RADIO and FILM technology was profound.

Magnum International cooperative agency of photo-journalists, formed in 1947. Among its early members were Henri Cartier-Bresson, Robert Capa, Marc Bresson and Inge Morath; contemporaries include the Brazilian Sebastião Salgado and American Alex Webb. Magnum's objectives have been: top-quality photography, independence, objectivity and control – by the members – over the use of their pictures.
* William Manchester, *In Our Time: The World as Seen by Magnum Photographers* (UK: André Deutsch, 1989).

Mainstreamers See ADVERTISING: MAINSTREAMERS, ASPIRERS, SUCCEEDERS AND REFORMERS.

Mainstreaming Professor George Gerbner and a team of researchers at the Annenberg School of Communications, University of

Pennsylvania, conducted a massive and ongoing research project throughout the 1980s on the impact of TELEVISION on cultural attitudes and attitude formation. A process is identified which Gerbner calls *mainstreaming*, whereby television creates a coming-together, a convergence of attitude among viewers. In their article, 'The "Mainstreaming" of America: Violence Profile No. 11' in *Journal of Communication* (Summer, 1980), Gerbner, Larry Gross, Michael Morgan and Nancy Signorielli write, 'In particular, heavy viewing may serve to cultivate beliefs of otherwise disparate and divergent groups towards a more homogeneous "mainstream" view'. The authors' opinion is that TV's images 'cultivate the dominant tendencies of our culture's beliefs, ideologies, and world views' and that the 'size' of an 'effect' is far less critical 'than the direction of its steady contribution'.

The light viewer is more likely to hold divergent views and the heavy viewer more convergent views: 'For heavy viewers, television virtually monopolizes and subsumes other sources of information, ideas and consciousness'. Convergence in this sense is to the world *as shown on television*. Returning to this theme in an article for the American magazine *Et cetera* (Spring, 1987), Gerbner writes, in 'Television's Populist Brew: The Three Bs', 'The most striking political difference between light and heavy viewers in most groups is the collapse of the liberal position as the one most likely to diverge from and challenge traditional assumptions'.

The three Bs referred to in Gerbner's article are the processes by which television brings about mainstreaming. First, television *blurs* traditional social distinctions; second, it *blends* otherwise divergent GROUPS into the mainstream and thirdly *bends* 'the mainstream in the direction of the medium's interests in profit, populist politics, and power'.

In a study conducted in the UK in 1987, researchers from the Portsmouth Media Research Group, Anthony Piepe, Peter Charlton and Judy Morey (see their article 'Politics and television viewing in England: hegemony or pluralism?' in *Journal of Communication* (Winter, 1990)), found that British television 'does not cultivate a single mainstream around which a heterogenous audience converges', as in the US, but that it contains two message systems and constructs two audiences: that for essentially news-related programmes, which keep pluralist options open, and that for Soaps which do, the researchers confirm, hasten a mainstreaming tendency, particularly when heavy viewing is involved. 'Further support for this position comes from our finding that news and current affairs presenters were invariably seen [by audiences] as partisan, especially to the Right, while entertainers and soap opera characters were seen by the audience to be evenly divided among the Left, Centre and Right'. In 1994 a study of TV influence on political attitudes in Italy was published by Luca Ricolfi of the University of Turin. According to his findings summarized in 'Elections and mass media. How many votes has television moved?' (*Il Mulino*, 356) TV, public and commercial, had influenced 10 per cent of the Italian electorate and the commercial channels had significantly assisted the shift of voters from the Left and Centre to the Right.

See EFFECTS OF THE MASS MEDIA; MEAN WORLD SYNDROME; RESONANCE; SHOWBUSINESS, AGE OF.

Male-as-norm In her introduction to *Man Made Language* (UK: Routledge & Kegan Paul, 1980) Dale Spender says 'One semantic rule which we can see in operation in the language is that of the male-as-norm. At the onset it may appear to be a relatively innocuous rule for classifying the objects and events of the world, but closer examination exposes it as one of the most pervasive and pernicious rules that has been encoded'. The rules of society are manmade and so, Spender eloquently argues, is the LANGUAGE we use – the 'edification of male supremacy'. Other terms used for male-as-norm in relation to language are *Androcentralism* (male centred) and *masculist*, as well as *patriarchal*.

Spender analyses in detail other rules which establish this overall male-as-norm bias. She refers to one such rule identified by Muriel Schulz in 'The semantic derogation of women' found in Barrie Thorne and Nancy Henley (eds), *Language and Sex: Difference and Dominance* (US: Newbury

House, 1975) which is the **pejoration** of words used to describe women and their activities. It is this negative marking of words associated with women that leads, Schulz argues, to the **semantic derogation of women.** Spender goes on to discuss the work of Julia Stanley found in her article 'Gender marking in American English', A.P. Nilsen *et al., Sexism and Language* (US: NCTE, 1977) who in investigating the negative connotations associated with women argues that it is the result of the sexes being differentiated semantically in terms of plus or minus, that is plus or minus male women being marked as minus male – i.e. different from, less than the norm. Thus women are allotted a **negative semantic space** in the language. That such a rule exists, argue both Stanley and Spender, can be seen, for example, in the way that women are often described when they occupy a role traditionally occupied by a man. That they are an exception to the norm, the male-as-norm, is signalled by such adjectives as 'woman MP', 'lady judge' and so on. See ANDROCENTRIC RULE; HE/MAN LANGUAGE.

Maletzke's model of the mass communication process, 1963 What is so useful about the model constructed by German Maletzke and presented in *The Psychology of Mass Communications* (West Germany: Verlag Hans Bredow-Institut, 1963) is the

comprehensiveness of the factors operating upon the participants in the mass communication process and at the same time of the complex interaction of such factors.

The self-image of the communicator corresponds with that of the receiver: both act upon and are influenced by the MESSAGE which is itself constrained by the dictates of the MEDIUM chosen. To add to the complexity, the message is influenced by the communicator's IMAGE of the receiver and the receiver's image of the communicator. Maltetzke's is a model suggesting that in the communication process many shoulders are being looked over: the more shoulders, the more compromises, the more adjustments.

Thus not only is the communicator taking into due regard the medium and the nature of AUDIENCE, and perceiving these things through the filter of self-image and personality structure; he or she is also keenly responsive to other factors – the communication team, with its own special set of values (See NEWS VALUES) and professional practices. Beyond the team, there is the organization which in turn has to look over its shoulder towards government or the general public (See IMPARTIALITY).

Just as the communicator is a member of a team within an organizational environment, so the receiver is part of a larger context of reception: he or she is subject

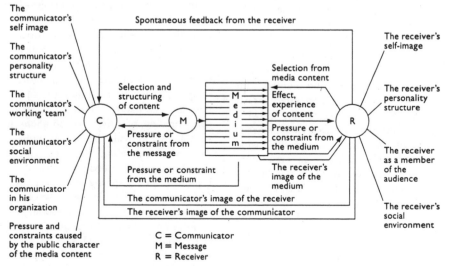

The communicator's self image

The communicator's personality structure

The communicator's working 'team'

The communicator's social environment

The communicator in his organization

Pressure and constraints caused by the public character of the media content

Spontaneous feedback from the receiver

Selection and structuring of content

Pressure or constraint from the message

Pressure or constraint from the medium

The communicator's image of the receiver

The receiver's image of the communicator

Selection from media content

Effect, experience of content

Pressure or constraint from the medium

The receiver's image of the medium

The receiver's self-image

The receiver's personality structure

The receiver as a member of the audience

The receiver's social environment

C = Communicator
M = Message
R = Receiver

Maletzke's model of the mass communication process, 1963

to influences other than the media message. Those influences may start in the living room of a family home, and the influencer's might be the viewer's or reader's family, but there are contextual influences beyond that in the pub, at work, in the community.

Maletzke's model provides students of the media with a structure for analysis. By its complexity, by suggesting an almost limitless interaction of variables, it also indicates the enormous difficulty faced by research into the EFFECTS OF THE MASS MEDIA. As Denis McQuail and Sven Windahl say in *Communication Models for the Study of Mass Communication* (UK: Longman, 5th impression, 1998), 'This complexity is, no doubt, an important reason why mass communication research has been fairly unsuccessful in explaining and predicting outcomes of the mass communication process'. See COMMUNICATION MODELS.

Manufacture of consent See CONSENT, MANUFACTURE OF.

March of Time Famous US NEWSREEL series of the 1930s, and a classic example of media interaction. Roy Larsen, one of Henry Luce's aides on *Time* magazine, had arranged to have items from the magazine broadcast on radio, and these newscasts became so popular among listeners that they were developed into a NETWORK programme, *The March of Time*. One attraction was that the programme dramatized the news; actors played 'memorable scenes from the news of the week'.

In 1934, Louis de Rochement, under Larsen's supervision, adapted the radio format to FILM which, after early uncertainties, made a notable impact. The monthly film panoramas of American and international events alerted the public to the growing menace of Fascism. They carried an Academy award winning report on life inside Nazi Germany (1938) and an even more powerful one on refugees. In 1935, 432 US cinemas were showing the *March of Time*, with its famous end-of-programme words, 'Time . . . marches on,' and by 1939 the number had trebled. The series continued till 1953. See DOCUMENTARY.

Marginality See DISPLACEMENT EFFECT.

Marginality, myth of Term applied to the practice by news media of covering events which are not traditionally given important ranking order in AGENDA SETTING; that is, they are given low or marginal status when NEWS VALUES are applied. In 'Out of bounds: the myth of marginality' published in *Television Mythologies: Stars, Shows and Signs* (UK: Comedia, 1984), edited by Len Masterman, John Hartley refers to 'that kind of thinking which makes sense of margins as irrelevant and peripheral' which 'simply "understands" that what happens at the edges either doesn't count or, worse, isn't there'. Marginalization is particularly active in the reporting of race, believes Christopher P. Campbell, writing in *Race, Myth and the News* (US: Sage, 1995): 'Because African Americans and other minorities in America often find themselves outside the periphery of mainstream society, coverage of those communities may often reflect the "marginal" interest of the news media.'

Marine Broadcasting (Offences) Act, 1965 Forbade illegal BROADCASTING and also made it an offence to supply illegal broadcasters with ADVERTISING. Effectively killed off PIRATE RADIO in and around the UK. See COMMERCIAL RADIO.

Market liberalism IDEOLOGY dominant in Western countries, adopted world-wide after the fall of Soviet communism as a normative way of state, industrial and commercial governance; its key principle – *Leave to market forces*. It is essentially the same as **capitalism** where all attempts to restrict *free enterprise* by state control or regulation generally are perceived to be ill-judged, an interference with the 'natural order of things'. Ownership of the means of production is essentially private: the 'public' denomination of private corporations has nothing to do with the public, rather, it denotes shareholding by other 'public' bodies and private individuals. Out of market liberalism has sprung the concept of the **free press**; policies urging PRIVATIZATION of all mass communication; and DEREGULATION.

John Keane in *The Media and Democracy* (UK: Polity Press, 1991) says that many market liberals 'love to talk of the need for a free communications market without censorship'. However, 'they are . . . unsympathetic or hostile to citizens' attempts to extend the role of law, to reduce the arbitrariness and secrecy of political power'. Thus two competing principles are at work. The 'free market' process coexists within 'a powerful, authoritative state which acts as an overlord of the market'. This amounts to a position where there is liberty for some but not necessarily for all.

Keane believes market liberalism 'succours the old doctrine of sovereignty of the state – permission for the state to defend itself by any means should it feel threatened, including controlling and regulating the liberties of the public'. Should there at the same time appear to be a threat to the free market, then the free market will collude with the state in seeking out and identifying 'enemies of the state'. Private sector media, in particular the press, will have taken on the role of GUARD DOG. 'Market liberalism is,' states Keane, 'a self-contradictory project . . . incapable of actualizing the "libertarian" values it affirms.' See COMMERCIAL LAISSEZ-FAIRE MODEL OF (MEDIA) COMMUNICATION; HEGEMONY.

Market threshold Decisions on media production – whether to initiate, go ahead or continue with media enterprises – depend more and more on whether there is a sufficiently large percentage of consumers to warrant investment. The market threshold is the critical point at which a media artefact justifies, financially, its existence; and the greater the competition within the market, the more critical that threshold becomes. See PRODUCER CHOICE.

Marxist (mode of media analysis) Focuses on social conflict which is seen as being essentially derived from the mode of production in capitalist societies. Karl Marx argued that the CULTURE – and communication process – of a capitalist society reflects the NORMS and VALUES of that section of the community which owns the means of production: out of the dominant CLASS springs the dominant IDEOLOGY which the media serve to disseminate and reinforce in the 'disguise' of CONSENSUS.

Marxist analysts have employed three main strategies of research (also used by other, non-Marxist commentators): *structuralist, political/economic* and *culturalist*. The structuralist approach examines the ideology embodied in media content, concentrating on 'text' and the source of the ideology. The political/economic approach investigates the location of media power within economic processes, and the structure of media production. The culturalist approach commences from the standpoint that all societies are made up of a rich variety of group cultures, but seeks to indicate that some GROUPS – therefore some cultures – receive a disproportionate representation in the media in the process of shaping and defining consensus and obscuring the roots of genuine conflict. See FUNCTIONALIST/SOCIAL ACTION (MODES OF MEDIA ANALYSIS).

Maslow's hierarchy of needs According to Abraham Maslow in his highly influential book, *Motivation and Personality* (US: Harper & Row, 1954), human behaviour reflects a range of basic needs which form a hierarchy. 'For the man who is extremely and dangerously hungry', writes Maslow, 'no other, interests exist but food.' When that need is satisfied, 'new (and still higher) needs emerge'. In what he terms a holistic-dynamic theory of MOTIVATION, Maslow cites the following basic needs: *physiological; safety* needs; *belongingness* and *loving* needs; *esteem* needs and the need for *self-actualization*. Among the physiological needs are food, water, sleep and sex. Safety needs include security, stability, protection, freedom from fear, from anxiety and from chaos; the need for structure, order, law, limits; the preference for the familiar over the unfamiliar, the known rather than the unknown; for religion.

Maslow writes that the threat of chaos or humiliation can be expected in most human beings 'to produce a regression from any higher needs to the prepotent safety needs, so that a common, almost expectable reaction, is the easier acceptance of dictatorship or of military rule' and this is 'most true of those living near the safety line'. Such people are 'particularly disturbed by threats to authority, to legality, and to the representatives of the law' (see MAINSTREAMING).

Belongingness and loving needs include

the 'deeply animal tendency to herd, to flock, to join, to belong'.

Maslow's highest-order need is self-actualization, where a person seeks and finds fulfilment: 'A musician must make music, an artist must paint if they are ultimately to be at peace with themselves'. 'What a man *can* be, he *must* be.' The term itself was coined by Kurt Goldstein in *The Organism* (US: American Book, 1939), and means in Maslow's words, 'to become everything that one is capable of becoming'. Maslow argues that the fulfilment of needs depends on essential preconditions, obviously, at the physiological level, the availability of food and water, but at the higher levels such conditions as 'freedom to speak, freedom to do what one wishes so long as no harm is done to others, freedom to express oneself, freedom to investigate and seek for information, freedom to defend oneself'. In Maslow's view 'Secrecy, censorship, dishonesty, blocking of communication threatens *all* the basis needs'.

An essential part of the process of self-actualization is the desire to know and to understand, 'to systematize, to organize, to analyse, to look for relations and meanings, to construct a system of values' and these aspects too tend towards a hierarchy: to know leads us to want to understand. Within this frame too are *aesthetic* needs. Maslow speaks of some individuals who 'get sick (in special ways) from ugliness, and are cured by beautiful surroundings'.

The hierarchy as cited by Maslow is dynamic and capable of reversal. Some people for example may go for esteem before love (though at the same time these may 'seek self-assertion for the sake of love rather than self-esteem itself'). There are artists who put creation before all else; there is the psychopathic personality suffering from a permanent loss of the love needs; and there is the potential reversal caused by the undervaluing of a long-satisfied need: 'Thus a man who has given up his job rather than lose his self-respect, and who then starves for six months or so, may be willing to take his job back even at the price of losing his self-respect.'

The hierarchy is at its most reversible in situations involving 'ideals, high social standards, high values, and the like. With such values people become martyrs'. Torture victims who defy their oppressors also confound Maslow's hierarchy. It is also acknowledged by Maslow that human behaviour is prompted by *multiple* motivations. It would be theoretically possible, he says, 'to analyse a single act of an individual and see in it the expression of his physiological needs, his safety needs, his love needs, his esteem ·needs, and self-actualization'. Equally, not all behaviour is motivated; and motivation must also be considered in the light of the 'external field', the pressures placed upon people to react in certain ways. See iSOCIETY; SELF-CONCEPT; VALS TYPOLOGY.

Mass communication Term describes institutionalized forms of public MESSAGE production and dissemination, operating on a large scale, involving a considerable division of labour in their production processes and functioning through complex mediations of print, film, recording tape and photography. John Corner and Jeremy Hawthorn point out in *Communication Studies: An Introductory Reader* (UK: Edward Arnold, 1980) that 'mass communications are *industrial* activities, produced within large organizations whose policies and professional routines are located within the political, economic and legal structures of the societies in which they operate'. Mass communication systems are deeply involved in the process of *culture production*. See CULTIVATION; CULTURAL APPARATUS; MASS COMMUNICATIONS: SEVEN CHARACTERISTICS; NORMATIVE THEORIES OF MASS MEDIA.

* Marsha and Emma Jones, *Mass Media* (UK: Macmillan, 1999).

Mass communications: seven characteristics In *Towards a Sociology of Mass Communications* (UK: Collier-Macmillan, 1969), Denis McQuail poses the following features of mass communications: (1) They normally require complex formal organizations. (2) They are directed towards large audiences. (3) They are *public* – the content is open to all and the distribution is relatively unstructured and informal. (4) Audiences are heterogeneous – of many different kinds – in composition; people living under widely different conditions in widely differing cultures. (5) The mass media can establish simultaneous contact with very large numbers of people at a distance from the source, and widely separated from one another. (6) The relationship between communicator and audience is addressed by persons known only in their public role as communicators. (7) The audience for mass communications is 'collectively unique to modern society'. It is an 'aggregate of individuals united by a common focus of interest, engaging in an identical form of behaviour, and open to activation towards common ends', yet the individuals involved 'are unknown to each other, have only a restricted amount of interaction, do not orient their actions to each other and are only loosely organized or lacking in organization'.

Massification However large the population, it is made up of individuals. Massification – a US term – is the process by which the population is regarded as, and treated as, a lumpen mass with similar if not identical tastes and attitudes. Massification serves as an excuse by society's privileged and ELITE to regard the mass as 'only capable' of benefiting from art, education, information, entertainment if it is presented in its simplest, most unchallenging form. Massification only makes headway when large numbers of people accept the image of themselves as projected by the purveyors of *mass culture*. See ADVERTISING; PUBLIC SERVICE BROADCASTING.

Mass manipulative model of (media) communication See COMMERCIAL LAISSEZ-FAIRE MODEL OF (MEDIA) COMMUNICATION.

Mass media See MASS COMMUNICATION.

Mass media effects See EFFECTS OF THE MASS MEDIA.

Mass Observation An organization founded in 1937 by Charles Madge and Tom Harrisson, with the purpose of furthering the scientific study of human behaviour in the UK. Large numbers of volunteer observers were used, recruited through advertisements in the national PRESS. At one time it is estimated that there were over 1000 such volunteers. The object of Mass Observation was ultimately the 'observation of everyone by everyone, including themselves'.

Data that has been collected is to be found in the Tom Harrisson Mass Observation Archives in the University of Sussex. See MEDIA ANALYSIS.

Mathematical theory of communication See SHANNON AND WEAVER MODEL OF COMMUNICATION, 1949.

Max Headroom The first male computer-generated TELEVISION personality; followed by Roxscene, the first female. *The Max Headroom Show* on CHANNEL 4 won the Royal Television Society's Original Programme Award in 1986.

McCombs and Shaw agenda-setting model of media effects, 1976 The process and effects of AGENDA SETTING have been a central interest for media research and study. Two important contributions to our understanding of agenda-setting theory have been articles by Maxwell E. McCombs and Donald L. Shaw – 'The agenda setting function of mass media' in *Public Opinion Quarterly*, 36 (1972) and 'Structuring the "Unseen Environment"' in the *Journal of Communication* (Spring, 1976). Shaw followed these up with 'Agenda setting and mass communication theory' in the *Gazette* XXV, 2 (1979). In their 1976 publication, the authors write, 'Audiences not only learn about public issues and other matters through the media, they also learn how much importance to attach to an issue or topic from the emphasis the mass media place upon it. For example, in reflecting what candidates are saying during a campaign, the mass media apparently determine the important issues. In other words, the mass media set the "agenda" of the campaign'. Thus in the view of McCombs and Shaw, the media are highly influential in shaping our perceptions of the world: 'This ability to affect cognitive change among individuals is one of the most important aspects of the power of mass communication' (See EFFECTS OF THE MASS MEDIA).

As the model indicates, there is a direct correlation between the amount of media exposure of X (the issue) and the degree to which the public sees X as being important. Some writers have been critical of this model for oversimplifying the process of media influence. It takes no account of influences *other* than the media in setting personal agendas in relation to public issues (See INTERVENING VARIABLES (IV); ONE-STEP, TWO-STEP, MULTI-STEP FLOW MODELS OF COMMUNICATION; SIGNIFICANT OTHERS). Another problem with the McCombs and Shaw model is highlighted by Denis McQuail and Sven Windahl in *Communication Models for the Study of Mass Communications* (UK: Longman, 5th impression, 1998). They identify not one but a range of agendas: 'We can speak of the agendas of individuals and groups or we can speak of the agendas of institutions – political parties and governments. There is an important distinction between the notion of setting personal agendas by communication directly to the public and setting an institutional agenda by influencing the politicians and decision makers'.

McQuail and Windahl perceive here a dual role for the media, influencing public opinion and influencing the ELITE: 'In reality there is a continuous interaction between elite proposals and public views, with the media acting as carrier as well as source.'

A third criticism of McComb's and Shaw's model relates to the actual intentions of the media: do they initiate and select the issues which they go on to amplify; climb aboard a 'bandwagon' of nascent public interest or respond chiefly to the promptings of the POWER ELITE? See CONSENT, MANUFACTURE OF; GUARD DOG METAPHOR; MAINSTREAMING; MEAN WORLD SYNDROME; NOELLE-NEUMANN'S SPIRAL OF SILENCE MODEL OF PUBLIC OPINION, 1974.

* McCombs and Shaw, 'The evolution of agenda setting research: twenty-five years in the marketplace of ideas', *Journal of Communication* Spring, 1993.

McDonaldization Term formulated, and introduced in his book *The McDonaldization of Society* (US: Pine Forge Press, 1992, revised edition, 1996) by George Ritzer, and with the subtitle 'An investigation into the changing character of contemporary social life'. As Ritzer points out, the book is not about the fast-food business but serves as a major 'paradigm' of a 'wide-ranging process I call *McDonaldization*', the 'process by which the principles of the fast-food restaurants are coming to dominate more and more sectors of American society as well as of the rest of the world', and these effects are felt throughout CULTURE, in 'education, work, health care, travel, leisure, dieting, politics, the family, and virtually every other aspect of society'. Ritzer sees McDonaldization as showing every sign 'of being an inexorable process by sweeping through seemingly impervious institutions and parts of

Issues	Differential media attention	Consequent public perception of issues
X_1		X_1
X_2		X_2
X_3		X_3
X_4		X_4
X_5		X_5
X_6		X_6

McCombs and Shaw's agenda-setting model of media effects, 1976

the world'. McDonalds *is* America, and wherever the Big Mac and fries are consumed, so is the American way of life, the American dream. The author analyses his subject through the frame of ideas posed by the German social theorist, Max Weber (1864–1920), on the workings of bureaucracy in the creation of an 'iron cage' of rationality, that is a bureaucratic sameness of normative behaviour impossible to escape from.

In Ritzer's view, the universalization, the rationalization of eating and other behaviours, as represented and driven by the McDonald's empire is based upon four 'alluring dimensions' of irresistibility: *efficiency* ('the optimum method for getting from one point to another'); *calculability* ('Quantity has become the equivalent to quality'); *predictability* ('There is great comfort in knowing that McDonald's offers no surprises') and *control,* a production/service discipline which applies equally to the customer as to those who serve them. Crucial in the exercise of control is the use of technology, 'the soft-drink dispenser that shuts itself off when the glass is full, the french fries machine that rings and lifts itself out of the oil when the fries are crisp'. This technology, says Ritzer, 'increases the corporation's control over workers'.

Ritzer acknowledges that McDonaldization has 'powerful advantages' but he argues that the foundations of its success mentioned above 'can be thought of as the basic components of a *rational* system' and his view is that 'rational systems inevitably spawn irrationalities' and 'irrational consequences', not the least of them matters of ecological concern. Ritzer's book focuses on the 'great costs and enormous risks of McDonaldization' and its purpose is to help alert the public to them and 'to stem its tide' while fearing that 'the future will bring with it more rather than less McDonaldization'.

* Barry Smart, *Resisting McDonaldization* (UK: Sage, 1999).

McGregor Commission Report on the Press, 1977 Under the chairmanship of Professor O.R. McGregor, the Royal Commission produced an interim report in 1976. Concerned about the shaky finances of newspapers, the Commission proposed that the State should give interest relief on loans which papers would need if they were to modernize their printing methods and cut costs. Like so many inspired ideas emerging from royal commissions, the proposal got nowhere. In its final report (1977), the Commission recognized the anti-Labour bias in most of the nation's PRESS: 'We have no doubt that over most of this century, the press had treated the beliefs and activities of the Labour movement with hostility.' The Commission recommended that the Press Council be strengthened, its influence increased; that, for example, its lay members be equal in number to its press representation. This recommendation was accepted, though the Council demurred at other advice. See COMMISSIONS/COMMITTEES ON THE MEDIA.

McGuffin FILM director Alfred Hitchcock (1899–1980) was fond of using this expression to describe any device or element of plot which captures the attention and interest of the audience, but which is intended to be, and acknowledged to be, merely a means to an end: an amiable red herring. Hitch himself described the *McGuffin* as 'that which spies are after (in films) but the audience don't care'.

McLeod and Chaffee's 'kite' model, 1973 This is best studied in conjunction with NEWCOMB'S ABX MODEL of 1953. Newcomb focuses on interpersonal links in relation to ISSUES, believing that each element (Person A and Person B) is *co-orientated* towards the other and towards X, the issue in a triangular relationship. McLeod and Chaffee take this model and apply it to mass communication. In 'Interpersonal approaches to communication research' in the *American Behavioural Scientist,* 16 (1973), they too refer to a 'co-orientational approach'. In their model there are three major 'players' – the *elite,* the *public* and, in a MEDIATING role, the *media.* The tail of the kite is current news, and issues in the news – an endless stream of new matter which the media process with the elite and public in mind, serving, as it were, both. Such a balanced, symmetrical arrangement is closer

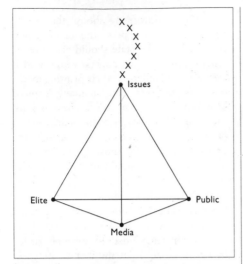

McLeod and Chaffee's 'kite' model, 1973

to the ideal than a reflection of realities, for quite clearly the elite (see POWER ELITE) have considerably more influence over media performance than the public; indeed ownership and control of media lie largely with the elite in one form or another.

To obtain a more accurate representation of the co-orientational nature of the relationship between the key players in the drama of media, it would be necessary to shift the axis a little, with the media being in much closer proximity to the elite than to the public. However, the kite metaphor remains a useful one in that the situation all the players find themselves in is unstable, and it is the stream of Xs – EVENTS, innovations, developments, changes which causes that instability. This model should also be looked at in relation to AGENDA SETTING models (See ROGERS AND DEARING AGENDA SETTING MODEL, 1987).

McLuhanism The archpriest of media analysis in the late 1960s was the Canadian professor, **Marshall McLuhan** (1911–80), creator of the Centre for Media Studies in Toronto. His headline-catching assertions and prophesies about the effect of the new media, particularly TV, on society as we know it were aided and abetted by inspired phrase-making. Described by Northrop Fry as a 'manic depressive roller-coaster of publicity', McLuhan foretold the annihilation of the printed word by the electronic

media, yet his books sold (and were read) in thousands.

The most quoted McLuhanism is his phrase, the MEDIUM IS THE MESSAGE, used as the heading of chapter 1 in *Understanding the Media* (UK: Routledge & Kegan Paul, 1964). McLuhan was convinced that with electronic transmission, especially TV, content was everywhere swamped by process. Equally he was concerned at the irresistible cultural spread which RADIO, TV and FILM made possible throughout the world, turning it into a *global village*. Radio he called the *Tribal Drum*, photography was the *Brothel-without-walls*, TV the *Timid Giant*, the motor car the *Mechanical Bride*.

Perhaps McLuhan's most valuable analysis is to be found in his examination of the impact of printing on civilization in *The Gutenberg Galaxy: The Making of Typographic Man* (UK: Routledge & Kegan Paul, 1962). See HOT MEDIA, COLD MEDIA.

McNelly's model of news flow, 1959 An improvement upon WHITE'S GATEKEEPER MODEL, 1950. In 'Intermediary communicators in the international news' in *Journalism Quarterly*, 36 (1959), J.T. McNelly identifies several intermediary stages through which a news item passes from event to presentation in mass communication form. The author follows the progress of a newsworthy event (E) taken up by a foreign correspondent (CI) and then passed through several agencies where the report of E is shaped and shortened (rather like the game of Chinese Whispers, though, hopefully, not with the same hilarious results).

McNelly illustrates a very complex process of MEDIATION which continues beyond the production/presentation stage when readers or viewers pass on the news to others by word of mouth. What the model does not do is address the criteria for news selection, the NEWS VALUES which operate the operators of the gatekeeping process. See GALTUNG AND RUGE'S MODEL OF SELECTIVE GATEKEEPING, 1965.

McQuail's accountability of media model, 1997 In a number of books and periodical articles Denis McQuail has written searchingly on the responsibilities of media to society. His model illustrating the

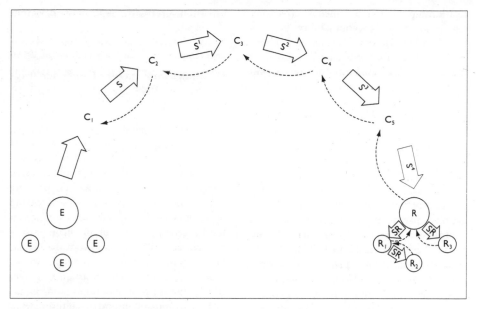

McNelly's model of intermediary communicators in news flow, showing news passing different 'gatekeepers' (after McNelly 1959)
Key to symbols in diagram:
E = Newsworthy event
C_1 = Foreign agency correspondent
C_2 = Regional bureau editor
C_3 = Agency central bureau or deskman
C_4 = National or regional home bureau editor
C_5 = Telegraph editor or radio or TV news editor
S, S^1, S^2, etc. = The report in a succession of altered (shortened) forms
R = Receiver
R_1, R_2, etc. = Family members, friends, associates, etc.
S – R = Story as modified by word of mouth transmission
Dotted line = Feedback

McNelly's model of news flow, 1959

FREE MEDIA
have
RESPONSIBILITIES
in the form of
OBLIGATIONS
which are either:

ASSIGNED   CONTRACTED   SELF-IMPOSED

for which they are held
ACCOUNTABLE
(legally, socially or morally)
either in the sense of:

LIABILITY   or   ANSWERABILITY
for harm caused   for quality of performance

McQuail's accountability of media model. McQuail D., European Journal of Communication, December 1997, p. 518. © Reprinted by permission of Sage Publications Inc.

relationship between media freedom, responsibility and accountability is published in the *European Journal of Communication*, December 1997, and analysed in the article 'Accountability of media and society: principles and means'.

The model is underpinned by principles of public service, that is, the 'best interests' of society in its broadest sense, and this framework includes people as voters and citizens as well as consumers. *Assigned* obligations may be discerned, for example, in the broadcasting charters of PSB (PUBLIC SERVICE BROADCASTING) while *contracted* obligations may relate to those bodies that commission and pay for media services. Media have responsibilities to source, to AUDIENCE, to the public at large, to minorities and obligations in relation to community and nation. *Liability* for harm caused can be seen to operate when the media are brought to court on charges of DEFAMATION, though ensuring *Answerability* in relation to quality of performance is obviously more problematic.

McQuail believes 'we face a major dilemma in reconciling the interests of society with current trends of media development'. More than ever, control over the media has become difficult to exercise, partly because of media's proliferation into many modes – brought about by new technology – and because of the transnationalization of media ownership: 'Modern mass media are less inclined to make voluntary commitments to society, less able to have any meaningful relationship with their audiences and those whom they affect, less ready to enter into dialogue.' He sees accountability as being in a state of crisis. His article examines possible ways and meanings of achieving accountability and suggests how principles and practice might cope with present and future developments.

Concluding his analysis, McQuail cautions against overstating the 'crisis of accountability'. After all, 'The performance of media reflects the imperfections of society as much as their own failings'. We must realize that 'free media have the right to be "irresponsible" and that some perceived "misuses" of autonomy will be a necessary price for potential benefits of invention, creativity, opposition, deviation and change'.
* Denis McQuail, *Media Performance: Mass Communication in the Public Interest* (UK: Sage, 1992).

McQuail's four stages of audience fragmentation, 1997 See AUDIENCE: FRAGMENTATION OF.

McWorld Vs Jihad A global conflict in cultures, represented by the transnational corporation bringing to the world 'sameness' and the counterforces of *localism*. Benjamin R. Barber in *Jihad Vs McWorld* (US: Times Books, 1995) investigates the dynamic scenario of localite resistance to the burgeoning power of all-encompassing cultures emanating chiefly from the United States (and sometimes referred to as 'Americanization'). The resistance is seen to take the form of adoption and assimilation of dominant imported cultures, what Roland Robinson has called *glocalization*, turning the global into the local. See his 'Globalization or glocalization?' in *Journal of International Communication*, 1 (1994).
* Tamar Liebes and Elihu Katz, *The Export of Meaning: Cross-Cultural Readings of Dallas* (US: Oxford University Press, 1990; UK: Polity Press, 1995).

Meaning In communication terms, a dynamic interaction between reader/viewer/listener etc. and the MESSAGE. As John Fiske put it in *Introducing Communication Studies* (UK: Methuen, 1982 and subsequent editions), 'A reader is constituted by his socio-cultural experience and thus he is the channel through which message and culture interact. This is meaning'. When we say something is 'a question of semantics', we are referring to the hazardous nature of actually pinning down, with any exactitude, the meaning of what a person says or has written. The word 'freedom' on some lips has quite a different CONNOTATION than if expressed by others.

There is a ready tendency to consider words as actually the embodiment of the meaning they attempt to describe; in fact they are approximations. Just as paper money has no intrinsic value, words have no intrinsic meaning: rather they are accredited with value or meaning by common consent. Like currency, word-meanings are subject to devaluation and manipulation. Ultimately you can paper the walls with debased currency; debased LANGUAGE becomes a weapon *against* meaning.

There is a prevalent – and understandable – assumption that an act or work of communication has to mean *something*. Thus a bemused spectator in front of, say, a work of abstract art, might declare, 'But what does it mean?' The short answer is that our spectator is unfamiliar with (or resistant to) the nature of the DISCOURSE which has, in the first instance, taken place between the artist, his/her MEDIUM and his/her environment (in place and time). Unless the spectator can 'tune in' to the signals – the CODES – operated by the artist, unless the spectator can recognize that a discourse is actually taking place, then the art he or she witnesses – for him or her, not necessarily anyone else – is meaningless. On the other hand, the spectator might instinctively warm to a work of art – be attracted by its colour, shape, texture – and still be at a loss to grasp its meaning. In this case, common ground between artist, work of art and spectator has been found. Communication has begun, and so, arguably, has meaning.

Meaning, obviously, has to be worked at. The codes or practices of specific communicative discourses have to be recognized and eventually understood, the relationship between speaker/writer/artist/musician actor/dancer, etc. and the forms and conventions of the chosen medium of communication responded to preferably sympathetically and with EMPATHY.

Meaning can be said to be in a perpetual state of re-working or re-negotiation. The artist's meaning may never be the spectator's meaning; but meaning is the property of neither. Indeed to regard meaning as something universally determinable and fixed is to create MYTH and to deal in PROPAGANDA. See DECONSTRUCTION; DEEP STRUCTURE; NEWS-PEAK; PARADIGM; POLYSEMY; PREFERRED READING; SEMIOLOGY/SEMIOTICS; SITE.

Meaning systems See DOMINANT, SUBORDI-NATE, RADICAL.

Mean world syndrome It is argued by commentators such as the American media analyst George Gerbner that the more peo-

ple watch TELEVISION, the more likely they will consider that out there is a 'mean world'. On the small screen, CONTENT ANALY-SIS tells us, crime rages about ten times more often than in real life. On TV in America – and it is little different in the UK – 55% of prime-time characters are involved in violent confrontations once a week. Heavy viewers, according to Gerbner in a series of published analyses since 1980, overestimate the statistical chance of violence in their own lives (See RESONANCE) and consequently harbour a heightened mistrust of strangers. However, Gerbner's conclusions have been challenged – in terms of reliable proof – by recent researchers. While granting that Gerbner's scenario of TV cultivating in viewers a fear of crime is interesting, Guy Cumberbatch and Dennis Howitt in *A Measure of Uncertainty. The Effects of the Mass Media* (UK: Broadcasting Standards Council/John Libbey, 1989) write, 'All in all, few empirical studies lend full support to the original Gerbner hypothesis, while there are many failures to replicate'. See EFFECTS OF THE MASS MEDIA; MAINSTREAMING.

Media accountability See McQUAIL'S ACCOUNTABILITY OF MEDIA MODEL, 1997.

Media analysis See FUNCTIONALIST/MARXIST/ SOCIAL ACTION (MODES OF MEDIA ANALYSIS).

Media control Four categories of media control are generally recognized: Authoritarian; Paternal; Commercial and Democratic. They can apply to an individual communications system, such as ownership of a newspaper, or to a state pattern of control. The first indicates a total monopoly of the means of communication and control over what is expressed. The second is what Raymond Williams in *Communication* (UK: Pelican, 1966) terms 'authoritarianism with a conscience', that is, authority with VALUES and purposes beyond those concerning the maintenance of its own power. The third relates to control by market forces: anything can be said provided that you can afford to say it and that you can say it profitably.

Democratic control is the rarest category, implying active involvement in decisions by the workforce and, indeed, the readership or audience. Control works at different levels – at the *operational* level (editors, producers, etc.), at the *allocative* level (of funds, personnel, etc.) and at the *external* level (government, advertisers, consumers).

Trends in media control have been towards greater concentration of ownership; towards ownership by CONGLOMERATE organizations and subsequently a series of over-diversifying control NETWORKS in which international finance has fingers in practically every communications pie, from newspapers to cinema, from records to satellites. Running parallel with these trends has been the development of multi-marketing of media products – books, films, TV series, video cassettes with such products being packaged for world-wide consumption; audience maximization, and therefore profit maximization being the most important driving force. See NORMATIVE THEORIES OF MASS MEDIA.

Mediacy Term first given public prominence at the 1983 British Association conference by Michael Weiss and Carol Lorac of the Communication and Social Skills Project at Brighton Polytechnic. Deemed as important, in the education curriculum of the future, as literacy and numeracy are today, mediacy is defined by Weiss and Lorac as 'the ability to understand and manipulate recorded sound and vision. Information technology and video are the machinery of mediacy: its pen and paper'.

Media effects See EFFECTS OF THE MASS MEDIA.

Media: hot and cold See HOT MEDIA, COLD MEDIA.

Media images These are the 'truths' or some would say STEREOTYPES – most certainly *conventions* – which the media operate in the definition and redefinition of CONSENSUS and by which they define, and sometimes police, the normative contours of society. As a considerable amount of our knowledge of others comes to us at second hand, through the media, the images the media use provide us with benchmarks or points of reference. Consensus is regularly defined by the media's concentration on DEVIANCE from consensus. Equally, the media stand forth as WATCHDOGS of the 'moral constituency' of

society as Howard S. Becker puts it in *Outsiders: Studies in the Sociology of Deviance* (US: Free Press, 1963); and it is their images, repeated, dramatized, often expressed in panic terms, which provide the major source of current information in society. See EFFECTS OF THE MASS MEDIA; FOLK DEVILS; MAINSTREAMING; MEAN WORLD SYNDROME; MORAL ENTREPRENEURS; MORAL PANIC.

Media imperialism Term used to describe the role Western capitalist media play in dominating Third World developing countries through communication systems. Crucial to the notion of media or cultural imperialism is the understanding of the relationship between economic, territorial, cultural and informational factors. In the age of Western economic colonialism in the 19th c. the flow of information was a vital process of growth and reinforcement. Where the trade went, so followed developing media practice and technology, reflecting the VALUES and assumptions of those who owned and manned the service.

As developing countries reached independence much concern was felt at the degree of penetration by Western media. In 1972, the General Conference of Unesco drew attention to the way the media of the richer sections of the world were a means towards 'the domination of world public opinion or a source of moral and cultural pollution'. Since then the movement towards a NEW WORLD INFORMATION order grew in vigour and strength. In 1973, in Algiers, a meeting of heads of state of non-aligned countries agreed to take concerted action to promote a fairer, more balanced exchange of information among themselves and release themselves from dependence upon the experts of the richer nations, demanding the 'reorganization of existing communication channels which are the legacy of the colonial past . . .' By 1978, the Unesco General Council agreed its new *Declaration on Mass Media* emphasizing the 'balanced' aspect of a concept of information based on the principle of 'free and balanced flow'.

Developing countries have long held a heart-felt belief that Western agencies only report the bad news of what happens in their countries and that this bad news – based upon what Anthony Smith in his book *The Geopolitics of Information* (UK: Faber, 1980) terms 'aberrational' criteria for news selection – causes serious harm, especially when such countries are in need of Western financial support and investment.

One proponent of the imperialist thesis, Herbert Schiller, in his earlier writing of the late 1960s, saw American television exports as part of an attempt by the American military industrial complex 'to subjugate the world'. He argued that the declining European empires had been replaced by an emergent US empire; one arm of this empire being the US-based, transnational communications industries which Schiller saw as working in collaboration with Western (predominantly US) political and military interests. These communications industries were for the most part funded privately by advertising revenue and were thus extensively tied to commercial interests. The cultural artefacts exported, mainly from the US, to other countries were seen as promoting the values of consumer capitalism. As such they could be seen as either reinforcing these values where they already existed, as for example in Western European countries, or as undermining traditional values and supplanting them with those of consumer capitalism in countries, such as Third World countries, where capitalist modes of production were non-existent or less developed. It was, for Schiller, a means by which the US could encourage, among other things, demand for its own products.

Schiller's thesis has met with some criticism. John B. Thompson in *The Media and Modernity* (UK: Polity Press, 1995), for example, argues that it overlooks the multipolar nature of the global economy in which Europe, Japan and South-East Asia have played an increasingly important role; the growing foreign investment in US communications such as that of Sony in Columbia, Tristar and CBS records; and the importance of other exporters of cultural artefacts such as Britain, Australia, Mexico, Brazil and India as regional producers. Thompson believes that, 'It would be quite implausible to suggest that this complex and shifting field of global power relations could be analysed in terms of the thesis of cultural imperialism. The thesis is simply too rigid and one-dimensional to do justice to a global situation which is in considerable flux'. Further, argues Thompson, the thesis tends to overlook the fact that whilst messages may be diffused on a global scale, many factors within the locale of their reception can affect the way in which they are appropriated by the audience. Both senders and receivers contribute to the construction of their meaning. Tamar Liebes and Elihu Katz, for example, in their classic study of audience reception of episodes of Dallas, *The Export of Meaning: Cross-cultural Readings of 'Dallas'* (UK: Polity Press, 1993), demonstrate the impact cultural variables can have on the reading of television texts.

Schiller has, in later writings, acknowledged these criticisms but maintains that the global domination of US culture has not significantly declined. Whatever the criticisms of the media imperialism thesis, the concentration of symbolic power mainly in the US as a result of the ongoing process of globalization of ownership within the media and cultural industries cannot be denied. (See in particular Schiller's *Culture Inc. The Corporate Takeover of Public Expression* (US: Oxford University Press, 1989).)

What is not in dispute is the ongoing North–South divide. Inequalities between nations in terms of wealth and provision have prevailed up to the Millennium and will continue for many years until the structures of deprivation are removed, worldwide. Figures quoted by Cees Hamelink in *World Communication: Disempowerment and Self Empowerment* (UK: Zed Books, 1995) indicate dramatic differences between developed and developing nations: the developing nations own only 4% of the world's computers while 75% of the world's 700 million telephones sets are to be found in the nine richest countries. Though the rich countries represent only 30% of the world's population they account for 80% of the world's press circulation. Some 1200 book titles are issued annually in Europe compared to less than 350 in African countries. In 34 periphery countries there are no TV sets at all.

It is not only the distribution which causes concern but the flow of communication. Hamelink says: 'Information flows across the globe are imbalanced, since most of the world's information moves among the countries in the North, less between the North and the South, and very little flows among the countries of the South' and this 'differential access to the management of information has put the developing countries at a serious disadvantage in the world political-economy'. This situation 'compromises their national sovereignty' and in so far as developing nations have increased 'their import capacity for communication technology, they have become more dependent upon the economic forces of the North'. See CONVERGENCE; INTER-CULTURAL INVASION; INTERNATIONAL FEDERATION OF JOURNALISTS; MACBRIDE COMMISSION; NEWS AGENCIES; NEWS AID?; NEWS VALUES; NON-ALIGNED NEWS POOL; TALLOIRES DECLARATION; WORLD PRESS FREEDOM COMMITTEE.

* Jonathan Benthall, *Disasters, Relief and the Media* (US: I.B. Tauris, 1995); James Lull, *Media, Communication, Culture: A Global Approach* (UK: Polity Press, 1995); Edward S. Herman and R.W. Chesney, *The Global Media: The New Missionaries of Corporate Capitalization* (UK/US: Cassell, 1997).

Media research centres See RESEARCH CENTRES.

Media technology See TECHNOLOGY OF THE MEDIA.

Mediation Between an event and the reporting or broadcasting of it to an audience, *mediation* occurs, that is, a process of interpretation – shaping, selecting, editing, emphasizing, de-emphasizing – according to the PERCEPTIONS, expectations and previous experience of those involved in the reporting of the event; and in accordance with the requirements and characteristics of the means of reporting. Between the *event* of a car accident or a murder and the *report* of such an event a whole series of **inter-mediating** actions take place. The event is translated into words or pictures; it is processed according to the demands of the MEDIUM – for headlines, for good pictures – and pressures such as time, space and contending messages.

Even when, in INTERPERSONAL COMMUNICA-

TION, A communicates a message to B which B conveys to C, a process of mediation inevitably takes place: B may rephrase the message, give parts of it prominence and understate other parts, supplement or distort the information.

Mediation is inescapable: much of our knowledge of life and the world comes to us at second hand, through the mediation of press and TV; our perceptions of events are coloured by the perceptions, preoccupations, VALUES, of the **mediators**.

However, the *construct* of events is far from a monopoly of the mass media; it is further **mediated**, and the process modified or altered altogether, by those around us who exert influence – friends, relatives, work colleagues etc. – and other so-called INTERVENING VARIABLES such as personal mood, time of day or state of health. See S-IV-R MODEL OF COMMUNICATION.

Media species Classification of the public in terms of their attitudes to ADVERTISING. A 1997 report drawn from research by CIA Medialab in the UK defines the following public 'species': *cynics, acquiescents, enthusiasts* and *ambivalents*. The research arm of CIA Medianetwork, Medialab conducted an 18-month survey using nationally representative focus groups. 25% of these, named cynics, resent the intrusion of national ads and feel strongly about the capacity of advertisements to subvert. Acquiescents are better news for adworld. Comprising 21% of the survey findings, they are easy-going, and they approve of ads which are funny, colourful and vivid. They do not care for national newspaper ads, or direct mail, which makes acquiescents feel vulnerable.

Enthusiasts make up 35% of respondents. They too seem unimpressed by national newspaper ads, but they enjoy TV commercials, often more than the programmes they accompany. The ambivalents are seen to be a rather inert band, resistant through being uninterested, and they take a fatalistic attitude to the effects/dangers of advertising. See VALS TYPOLOGY.

Mediasphere Term posed and defined by John Hartley in *Popular Reality: Journalism, Modernity, Popular Culture* (UK: Arnold, 1996) to describe the positioning of media, its range and breadth of influence, in relationship to the PUBLIC SPHERE, and the notion of the *Semiosphere* put forward by Yuri Lotman in *The Universe of the Mind: A Semiotic Theory of Culture* (US: University of Indiana Press, 1990). Hartley sees the semiosphere – the sphere of cultural expression and cultural MEANING – as being in a constant process of interaction with the mediasphere and public sphere. He images the relationship as resembling Russian dolls: the public sphere fits within the mediasphere which in turn fits within the semiosphere.

The most salient feature of these interlocking spheres, argues Hartley, is JOURNALISM. It was journalism which originated and nurtured concepts of freedom, of human rights, within societies. It served a key function in, and in turn was served by, the success of the American and French revolutions. The public sphere of the 19th c. was created by journalism. Hartley believes 'there would be *no* public' and consequently no progress towards the sovereignty of the people without the aid of journalistic writing, which has served, and continues to serve, as a counterforce to subordination. Indeed it is '*the* mechanism for *making* these [democratic] discourses generally available, and also for *articulating* the different forms of resistance'.

Ultimately, though, journalism's power to define and further the public sphere depends on *readership*. The changing nature of readership also alters the nature of the public and private spheres. Hartley believes that we have moved from the traditional adversarial mode of journalism, with its public, political and masculine bias to a POSTMODERNIST phase, driven in particular by popular journalism (described by Hartley as 'the textual system of modernity'). This gives emphasis not to public life 'but to private meaning'. He identifies the following shifts in the nature of readership: from male to female, from old to young, from militant to meditative, from public to private, from governmental to consumerist and from law-making to identity-forming. Hartley describes the mediasphere as 'suffused with images and issues which connect popular readerships and popular meanings together . . . the mainstream of contemporary journalism is fashion, gossip, lifestyle, consumerism and celebrity, and "news" is private, visual, narrativized and personalized'. It follows that the icon of the contemporary mediasphere is 'not the superpower but the supermodel'.

The shifts mentioned here are not, however, to be seen as having become disengaged from the past of journalism/ readership: modern journalism is populist. Yet it remains in the tradition of the radical journalism which helped give birth to the American and French revolutions.

Hartley writes that 'the radical press deserves the credit for some of the most important positive developments of modernity: for the idea of taking popular sovereignty literally, for instance; and for inventing a politicized public of citizen readers; as well as for working out in public the implications of 1789, not only for the activists in that struggle but for activists in other causes, on behalf of women and colonized peoples . . . who were able to use it as a model to argue for their own "democratic equivalence" and from previously non-politicized areas of private and personal life'. Hartley pays in turn due attention to the role played by the commercial press in the process of 'commodification of culture and language into entertainment and information' in which readership was transformed 'to circulation'.

Mediatization Process whereby political or indeed any public activity, having become reliant for its audience/electorate upon the media for its messages to be communicated, adopts the principles and methods of media communication. In particular TELEVISION has become the MEDIUM and CHANNEL of political communication. Consequently political communication pays greater attention to entertainment value as practised by TV, for example PERSONALIZATION, simplification and an emphasis on using 'media-genic' players.

In 'Towards a "videocracy"?: Italian political communication at a turning point' in the *European Journal of Communication*, September 1995, Gianpietro Mazzoleni said of the situation in Italy at the time of the 1994 elections, 'The parties are increasingly unable to bring their message to the voters and have to do it by relying on the channels of mass communication. The toll that the parties must pay is the *mediatization* of their communication activities'.

In consequence, media ceases to be the servant to and observer of political parties; and political parties become in thrall to the media, in their grip. Mazzoleni considers this a significant and far-reaching 'metamorphosis', in which the media take on the role of kingmaker – a case specifically illustrated when media mogul Silvio Berlusconi became, albeit briefly, Italy's prime minister. See BERLUSCONI PHENOMENON.

Media user ethics See TEN COMMANDMENTS FOR MEDIA CONSUMERS.

Media: uses of media by the young See CHILDREN, YOUNG PEOPLE AND THE CHANGING MEDIA ENVIRONMENT.

Media communication That mode of communication between direct, face-to-face address and MASS COMMUNICATION; into this clasification comes communication by letter or TELEPHONE.

Medium The physical or technical means of converting a communication MESSAGE into a signal capable of being transmitted along a given CHANNEL. TV for example is a medium which employs the channels of vision and sound. John Fiske in *Introduction to Communication Studies* (UK: Methuen, 1982), divides media into three categories: (1) The **presentational media**: the voice, face, body; the spoken word, GESTURE; where the medium is actually the communicator. (2) **Representational media**: books, paintings, photographs, etc., using cultural and aesthetic conventions 'to create a "text" of some sort'; they become independent of the communicator, being *works* of communication (whereas presentational media are *acts* of communication). (3) **Mechanical media** TELEPHONE, RADIO, TV, FILM, etc., and they are transmitters of 1 and 2.

The properties of the medium determine the range of codes which it can transmit; and considerably affect the nature of the message and its reception.

Medium is the message One of the clas-sic quotes of media literature and perhaps the best-known of Marshall McLUHAN (1911–80). *The medium is the message* is the first chapter heading in *Understanding Media: the Extensions of Man* (UK: Routledge & Kegan Paul, 1964). *What* is said, McLuhan believes, is deeply conditioned by the MEDIUM through which it said. The particular attributes of any medium help to determine the meaning of the communication, and no medium is neutral.

Melodrama Term first used to describe a certain type of 19th c. stage play which often included music and which was typically characterized by sensational and romantic plots, strong and often violent appeals to the audience's emotions, extravagant staging, exaggerated characters and happy endings with virtue triumphant. More recently it has been employed to describe a GENRE of 1950s Hollywood films, such as *Sunset Boulevard*, and certain kinds of television programme most notably SOAP OPERAS, such as *EastEnders*, both of which display many if not all of the original characteristics found in the stage plays, though not usually happy endings and the triumph of virtue. Such films and programmes are thought to appeal more to female audiences and thus can be seen as a *gendered* genre. As such they have become a focus of interest for FEMINIST research into the media; one current, interesting debate concerns whether or not they may be read as radical texts.

Message That which an act, or work, of communication is *about*. For purposes of definition and analysis it is sometimes necessary to treat the message as something separable from the *process* of communication; but ultimately a message can only meaningfully be examined in the context of other elements all of which are interlinked and interacting.

It is important to distinguish between the actual signal which carries the message and the message itself: a wink is a signal but what is its message? The answer depends on many factors – for example, who is winking, to whom and in what context? While message-signals, in the form of visual or aural CODES may be sent, the message may well not be understood. Thus an ambiguous smile may represent the signal that a message is being conveyed, but the receiver may fail to understand the message while recognizing the signal.

The message may draw its initial shape or purpose from the Sender or Communicator: it will be similarly influenced by the nature of the medium in which it is sent. The Receiver of a message may be close at hand, in sight of the Communicator, or some distance away. If the message involves INTRAPERSONAL COMMUNICATION, the Communicator and the Receiver may be one and the same. Both the signal and the intended message may encounter NOISE – that is, physical or psychological interference which will affect its meaningfulness. The message may elicit FEEDBACK which will further modify the message and indeed create a new communication situation and new signals and messages.

Denis McQuail in *Communication* (UK: Longman, 1975) writes that the simplest way of regarding human communication is 'to consider it as the sending from one person to another of meaningful messages'. We can rarely if ever be certain of how other people will interpret our signals, or whether we will 'get our message across'; thus the message sent may be quite different from the message received, and while we think we are communicating a single message we may, unconsciously, be putting across all sorts of other messages too.

We are selecting in and selecting out a barrage of message-carrying signals all the time. We give attention to them if we are *motivated* to do so. Thus a teacher's signals and messages may run into a thicket of difficulties: he/she is boring, has just offended the class in some way, they are distracted by the basketball match outside or Wallace on the back row has just let off a stink bomb.

The effectiveness of a message depends, at a basic, instrumental level, on the weight it carries in competition with other signals and messages but equally it depends upon the significance attached to it by the receivers. This in turn depends upon the 'set' or preparedness, of the receivers for the Sender/Message/Medium. The message of a satirical cartoon, for example, might be completely lost if the reader knows nothing about the particular circumstances to which the cartoon refers. Even a knowledge of the facts may not be enough to facilitate the intended interpretation, because this may only occur if the reader shares the social, political or cultural VALUES of the cartoonist. The CHANNEL too may affect interpretation. The fact that, say, an anti-Tory cartoon appears in the *Guardian* gives rise to a host of contextual meanings which would be modified at the very least if the same cartoon appeared in the *Daily Mail*. In short, whether we 'get our message across' depends partly upon the context in which it is received; and the values, attitudes, perceptions and knowledge of the receiver at a crucial part of that context. See DOMINANT, SUBORDINATE, RADICAL; INTERVENING VARIABLES; METAMESSAGE; POLYSEMY; PREFERRED READING.

Metalingual function of communication See JAKOBSON'S MODEL OF COMMUNICATION, 1958.

Metamessage The underlying MESSAGE in a communicative act. This may differ from what on the surface appears to be the message. The metamessage is conveyed both verbally and, often more crucially, nonverbally. The metamessage carries information about the relationships of those involved in an encounter and the attitudes they have towards each other and the topic in question. The interpretation of the metamessage is usually influenced by the way in which the message is communicated and non-verbal communication thus plays a vital role in the sending and receiving of metamessages. A simple question such as 'May I help you?' asked by someone in a higher-status ROLE, for example, can be interpreted as a friendly gesture or as an accusation of incompetence depending, in part, on the tone of voice adopted.

Metamessages can also help to frame a conversation as they help to define the nature of the encounter, for example, by defining the seriousness of the conversation and the relationships of those taking part.

Metaphor A figure of speech or a visual device which works by transporting qualities from one plane of reality to another: 'the camel is the ship of the desert'; 'life for Mary was a bed of roses'. Without metaphor there would be no scope for the development of either visual or verbal LANGUAGE; it would remain clinical and colourless.

Metaphor is not merely an expressive device but an integral part of the function of language as a *definer* as well as a reflector of reality. As a rhetorical device metaphor is central to the way media define reality, structure, maintain and monitor DISCOURSE, uphold (and sometimes challenge) hierarchies, service (and sometimes undermine) HEGEMONY. Metaphor provides us with the pictures by which we *envision* the world: we define time by metaphor ('time is money'); we view the public as inhabiting a 'space' (see AGORA); we define public argument and debate using metaphors of conflict and the notion of argument as 'war' is built into the culture we inhabit. Even where peace is being referred to, the media are more than likely to express it in military terms: 'War breaks out over classroom peace plans'. Press language is riddled with the bombast of conflict – things are axed, chopped, smashed, slashed; knives are constantly out; prime ministers stick to their guns, oppositions are routed.

We use metaphor to define the nature of communication: communication as *transmission* or communication as *ritual*. We talk of *homo narrens* (See NARRATIVE PARADIGM), casting the human being as the storytelling animal; or, with Erving Goffman, we may use the *dramaturgical* model, the metaphor of life as a stage.

In *An Introductory Guide to Post-Structuralism and Postmodernism* (UK: Harvester Wheatsheaf, 1993), Madan Sarap states 'that metaphors determine to a large extent what we think in any field. Metaphors are not idle flourishes – they shape what we do. They can help make, and defend a world view.' As well as being 'productive of insights and fresh illuminations', metaphors, according to Sarap, 'can encapsulate and put forward proposals for another way of looking at things'. They can serve as agents of change as well as weapons of reinforcement (See STEREOTYPE). 'Through metaphor,' says Sarap, 'we can have increased awareness of alternative possible worlds.'

The so-called **mixed metaphor**, beloved of politicians seeking by their RHETORIC to attract media attention, contains in a statement two or more ineptly linked images: 'Lame ducks will be barking up the wrong tree if they think government is going to bail them out every time profits take a hammering.' Though the metaphorical allusions may be all over the place, the statement's underlying IDEOLOGY is, however, crystal clear. See EUPHEMISM; METONYMY; VISIONS OF ORDER.

Metasignals A metasignal is a signal that makes a comment about a signal, or a set of signals: it directs us to the accurate meaning of the signals. For example, two people appear to exchange blows: is the fight real or make-believe? Their smiling faces form the metasignal which indicates that, at least on the surface, what we are seeing is a play-fight.

Body posture is among the chief metasignals. Equally, uniform serves effectively in this capacity. We react differently to the policeman in uniform than we might to the same person in off-duty jeans and tee-shirt. Desmond Morris in *Manwatching: A Field Guide to Human Behaviour* (UK: Jonathan Cape, 1977) says that 'In a sense the whole world of entertainment presents a non-stop Metasignal, in the form of the proscenium arch around the stage of a theatre, or the edge of the cinema or TV screen'. Audiences, he believes, can tolerate – and gain entertainment from – films and plays featuring dollops of death and mayhem because of the metasignals which indicate 'this isn't real'. Morris argues that though the actors may aim at maximum reality in their dark deeds, 'no matter how convincing they are, we still carry at the back of our minds (even as we gasp when the knife plunges home) the Metasignal of the "edge" of their stage'.

Metonymy A figure of speech in which the thing meant is represented by something which is an attribute of the original. When we talk of the newspaper business, we refer to the press – something that stands for the whole. As far as images are concerned, the metonym is a selection of one of those available to represent the whole; and from that selection flows our interpretation or understanding of the whole. Thus the selection of a piece of film of young people lounging at a street corner, or pickets in combat with the police, acts as the 'trigger of meaning' for the way the teenager or the striker is defined. For this reason, metonyms are powerful conveyors of reality, indeed so powerful that they can come to be accepted as actually *being* reality, the way things really are.

The selection of the image to serve as a metonym does not of course take place arbitrarily or in a vacuum. It is conditioned by NEWS VALUES and MYTH, that is, the dominant beliefs, cultural interpretations and explanations of reality which have come to have common currency. Pickets struggling with the police clearly fulfil a dominant myth about striking pickets; and the dominant myth is the criterion for selecting one image rather than another (for example, of peaceful, orderly pickets). Metonym and myth, therefore, are powerful agents in exploiting the 'truth factor', so it is essential to bear in mind that they are approximations and very often simulations: that is, 'constructed truth'.

Micro-myth, macro-myth Philip Schlesinger in *Putting 'Reality' Together. BBC News* (UK: Constable, 1978; Methuen/ University Paperback, 1987) examines the BBC NEWS machine at work, and identifies what in his view are two myths entertained by those who work in BBC news: the micro-myth that production staff are permitted autonomy within the organization; the macro-myth, that the BBC is an independent organization, largely socially unattached. See IMPARTIALITY.

Middlebrow See HIGHBROW.

Milieu The social environment of the individual, GROUP, CULTURE or nation.

Military metaphor See METAPHOR.

Milton's paradox On the one hand the English poet John Milton (1608–74) is famous for his stalwart defence of the freedom of expression (See AEREOPAGITICA); on the other Milton did not entirely practise what he preached. Dominant in Milton's own life was anti-Catholicism. The paradox

arises from the difference between principle and practice: during the period of the Interregnum, 1649–60 – the Commonwealth of Oliver Cromwell – Milton was an official censor, though apologists argue that the poet was less involved in CENSORSHIP than in editing and supervision. In 'Milton's paradox: the market-place of ideas in post-Communist Bulgaria', in the *European Journal of Communication*, September 1997, Ekaterina Ognianova and Byron Scott believe that 'in a simplistic way at least, Milton represents a perennial conflict between general beliefs and specific behaviour, between concepts and practice when it comes to the question of how much freedom to permit'.

Mimetic/semiosic planes In narrative, the *mimetic* is the plane of representation, the *semiosic* the plane of meaning production. See CODES OF NARRATIVE; CONNOTATION; NARRATIVE PARADIGM; PROPP'S PEOPLE; SEMIOLOGY; STORYNESS.

Minneapolis City Council enquiry into pornography See PORNOGRAPHY.

Minority Report of Mr Selwyn Lloyd This was attached to the majority BEVERIDGE COMMITTEE REPORT ON BROADCASTING, 1950, and, contrary to Beveridge who supported a continued monopoly of BROADCASTING for the BBC, argued that independent – and commercial – competition would be a good thing. Author of the Minority Report was Conservative MP Selwyn Lloyd who produced a scheme for a Commission for British Broadcasting to be set up which would licence a number of rival broadcasting stations. Lloyd wrote, 'Having considered these arguments put forward by the BBC on behalf of monopoly, I am of the opinion that independent competition will be healthy for broadcasting'. His view had considerable support in the Tory party and in the business world: commercial broadcasting in the UK was on the horizon. See COMMERCIAL RADIO; COMMERCIAL TELEVISION; MONOPOLY, FOUR SCANDALS OF.

Miracle of Fleet Street Description by Lord Northcliffe (1865–1922) of the redoubtable *Daily Herald* (1912–64), a sometimes swashbuckling radical paper which, despite having a substantial circulation and vast readership, received little advertising as a result partly of its left-wing views but perhaps more importantly because of its insistence on thorough reporting of political issues, appealed, at that time, more generally to male readers. When other national popular papers were priced at one penny, the *Daily Herald* was forced to charge two pence. Yet it lost very little in circulation, due to the energy and leadership of its greatest editor, George Lansbury, MP (1859–1940).

The *Herald* was the first newspaper in the world to reach a circulation of 2 million – in mid-1933 – though it was soon overtaken by Beaverbrook's *Daily Express.* By the time the *Herald* had reached its peak circulation of 2.1 million in 1947, the *Daily Mirror* and *Daily Express* were pushing 4 million and by 1960, sales had tumbled to 1.6 million. The *Herald* struggled on until 14 September 1964. See PRESS.

Misinformed society As the means of communication expand, the assumption that more and diverse information equates with better-informed citizens has been challenged by many commentators. In asking the question 'How far have media succeeded/failed to provide information for citizenship?', Peter Golding argues that the so-termed INFORMATION SOCIETY 'is a myth'. In 'Telling stories: sociology, journalism and the informed citizen' in the *European Journal of Communication* (December 1994), Golding believes 'We live in a media society, in which information is available at a price, or not at all' and that a more accurate term for today would be the *mis*informed society: 'Wherever we look, in coverage of race, industrial relations, welfare, foreign relations, or electoral politics, the media have failed democracy. We live in a society in blinkers.'

For Golding the 'information age' constitutes not a devolution of the message systems reaching ever wider into every part of society but a scene made up of media monoliths and a society which has become increasingly centralized in terms of decision-making and the 'reach' of vital information (See GLOBALIZATION OF MEDIA; INFORMATION BLIZZARDS; PRIVATIZATION; SURVEIL-LANCE SOCIETY). Golding's misinformed society is marked by a diminishing range of media ownership and the CASUALIZATION of labour in the media industry – BBC staff dropped by 5,000 from 25,000 between 1989 and 1994 and this policy of downsizing the labour force continues apace.

In terms of programming, Golding warns of the marginalization of serious information programmes on TV and an obsession with maximizing ratings which threaten the range and diversity of broadcasting. He sees the current flow and quality of information as fragmenting rather than unifying society, furthering not equality but inequality. The media of today render a 'flawed account of social reality' and shirk the abiding principle of a self-respecting media, 'to tell the truth and make things better'.

* Danny Schechter, *The More You Watch, The Less You Know* (US: Seven Stories Press, 1996).

Mix In FILM making a gradual transition between two shots where one dissolves into another. It is a soft fade, often used to denote the passage of time. See MONTAGE; SHOT; WIPE.

Mixing In FILM making, the process of re-recording all original dialogue, music and sound effects on to a single master sound track. See SYNCHRONOUS SOUND.

Modality The use of the words 'may' or 'might' are referred to by linguists as 'modal auxiliaries', part of the *modal system* of LANGUAGE. Modality serves to insert 'yes but' into definitions, for example of truth or reality. Modality can be confirming or disconfirming by means of its degree of affinity with that which is described, within the system or contexts in which it is described. Thus affinity between a speaker and a listener will condition the degree of modality: they may agree, 'This is true' or 'This is real' and agreement gives both a sense of security and status.

Robert Hodge and Gunther Kress in *Social Semiotics* (UK: Polity Press, 1988) write that 'A high degree of affinity indicates the expression of solidarity between participants'. The authors define affinity as 'an indicator of relations of solidarity or of power: that is, relations orientated towards the expression of solidarity or of power (difference)'. Thus 'Modality points to the social construction or contestation of knowledge-systems'. Agreement confirms the status of 'truth' and 'reality', disagreement disconfirms or undermines that status. 'Modality is consequently one of the crucial indicators of political struggle. It is a central means of contestations, and the site of the working out, whether by negotiation or imposition, of ideological systems.'

Model In social science research, a model is a tentative description of what a social process, say the communication process, or system might be like. It is a tool of explanation and analysis – very often in diagrammatic form – which attempts to show how the various elements of a situation being studied relate to each other. Models are not statements of reality; only after much further research and testing would the model be considered viable. It could then develop into a theory.

The term can also refer to a familiar process or object which is used as a point of reference when an attempt to explain the unknown is being made. An analogy is made showing the similarities between the phenomenon to be explained and one which is well known i.e. the model.

Additionally, a model can be a person whose behaviour others wish to imitate, on whom they wish to *model* themselves. The desire to model oneself on other persons is particularly strong in one's teenage years; the mass media play a significant role in presenting teenagers with a variety of such models. See COMMUNICATION MODELS; HYPOTHESIS; IDENTIFICATION.

Models of audience fragmentation See AUDIENCE: FRAGMENTATION OF.

Models of communication See COMMUNICATION MODELS.

Modem Device for converting analogue signals to digital signals and from digital to analogue. Modem is short for *mod*ulator/ *dem*odulator.

Modes of media analysis See FUNCTIONAL-IST/MARXIST/SOCIAL ACTION (MODES OF MEDIA ANALYSIS).

Monofunctional In a media sense, the term ascribing to a work – of literature, RADIO, FILM, TV – a single function; for example, to entertain. Research findings over the years have seriously challenged assumptions that particular forms of content are monofunctional. Adults declare a considerable interest in news programmes, yet functional studies have shown that for many viewers, the primary function of news is not informational. The news broadcast is, apparently, more closely related to habit; and it also affords the individual feelings of security and of social contact. See EFFECTS OF THE MASS MEDIA.

Monomorphic opinion leadership See OPINION LEADER.

Monopoly, four scandals of According to the BEVERIDGE COMMITTEE REPORT ON BROADCAST-ING. 1950, these were 'bureaucracy, complacency, favouritism and inefficiency', indicators which the Committee saw in the performance of the BBC as monopoly-holder of British airwaves. Nevertheless, Beveridge recommended the Corporation's licence be renewed because the alternative, US-style commercial TV, promised a system which was considered to be much worse. See COM-MERCIAL RADIO; COMMERCIAL TELEVISION; MINORITY REPORT OF MR SELWYN LLOYD.

Monotype printing Invented in 1889 by American Tolbert Lanston. The machine is in two parts. The first, operated by the keyboard, punches coded holes into a paper tape; the second has the tape fed into it and the code controls the casting operation. In monotype casting, unlike LINOTYPE PRINT-ING, every letter and space is cast separately.

Monroe motivated sequence Five-step sequence advocated by American Professor Alan Monroe in *Principles of Speech Communication* by Douglas Ehninger, Bruce E. Cronbach and Monroe (USA: Scott, Foresman, 1984) for use in organizing speeches, especially those with an intent to persuade. First stage, *Attention*, commanding and maintaining audience attention by some eye or ear-catching device (such as a lively story, anecdote or dramatic set of statistics).

Second, *Need*, in which the speech is made to appear relevant to audience needs. These needs are then met in step three of the sequence, *Satisfaction*, where solutions are proposed and examined. The speaker then proceeds to *Visualization*, where the audience is persuaded to see more clearly how the speaker's informaton or ideas will help them. Finally, *Action*, a plea for response, for the taking-up of the speaker's points.

Montage From the French, 'monter', to assemble; the process of cutting up FILM and arranging – editing – it into the screened sequence. Sergei Eisenstein (1898–1948) explained montage as putting together camera shots which, in combination, made a greater impact than did the sum of the parts – a creative juxtaposition. Separate elements combine to produce a new MEANING. Montage is the synthesis which gives film its unique character.

Montage is used as a *narrative* device and an *expressive* device, the one concerned with sequencing, ensuring the smooth continuity of action, the other with the intention of producing a particular effect by the clash, comparison or contrast of two or more images, often symbolic or metaphoric in meaning. This use of montage is often compared with collage in art in that it draws attention to itself as an exercise in construction: it says, Look at me as film, not reality. See ALIENATION EFFECT; KULESHOV EFFECT; SHOT.

Moral economy See HICT PROJECT.

Moral entrepreneurs Howard Becker first used this term in *Outsiders: Studies in the Sociology of Deviance* (US: Free Press, 1963) to describe those members of the community who take upon themselves the role of watchdog, vigilant against alleged attempts to subvert public morals. Such individuals often try, sometimes with success, to use the media to gain public support for their views. The letters columns of the various newspapers can be a particular vehicle for the expression of their views. Such entrepreneurs can play an important role in the development of a MORAL PANIC.

Moral panic Individuals and social GROUPS can by their activities emerge as a focus for outrage expressed by influential members of society who perceive these activities as seriously subverting the MORES and interests of the dominant CULTURE. Such reactions are, says Stanley Cohen in *Folk Devils and Moral Panics* (UK: MacGibbon & Kee, 1972 and subsequent editions), disseminated by the mass media usually in an hysterical, stylized, and stereotypical manner thus engendering a sense of moral panic. Dick Hebdige argues in *Subculture: the Meaning of Style* (UK: Methuen, 1979), that media coverage of the emergence of the punk youth culture, for example, displayed all the classic symptoms of a moral panic.

Stuart Hall, in 'Racism and reaction' in *Five Views of Multi-racial Britain* (UK: CRE, 1980), argues that racism in the British media has often assumed the form of a moral panic. The arguably media-generated moral panic over mugging in the early 1970s and the consequent association made between this crime and black youth is a well-documented case in point.

Moral rights (in a text) See TEXT: INTEGRITY OF THE TEXT.

Mores Those social rules concerning acceptable behaviour which it is considered wrong to break. Such rules play an important part in the maintenance of social order and cohesion; consequently breaches of mores usually meet with the imposition of sanctions by society – formally through laws, informally through, for example, social rejection.

Some mores are particular to a specific society, others can be found in most societies. A majority of societies respects the sanctity of human life, though this is varyingly weighed against the sanctity of social order. Also, within a society different social GROUPS may have different mores. Traditionally it is against the unwritten law of school life for pupils to tell tales to teacher. The sanction against those who do may be their temporary isolation or ejection from the group – or reprisals after school.

Mores may often prescribe both the tone and content of communication. Differences in sexual mores, for example, underpin many of the arguments about the dissemination of PORNOGRAPHY.

Morphing In film and video, seamlessly joining together different images; special effects most notably used in horror movies, when images – faces, for example – 'meta-morphose' into one another or change dramatically in appearance. Also employed in popular music videos such as Michael Jackson's *Black or White*.

Morphology Study of the structure or forms of words, traditionally distinguished from SYNTAX which deals with the rules governing the combination of words in sentences. Generally morphology divides into two fields: the study of inflections and of word-formation. See LANGUAGE.

Morse Code Devised by Samuel Morse (1791–1872), American artist and sculptor, and one of the great pioneers of TELEGRAPHY, the Morse Code is a binary code made up of dots and dashes to represent letters of the alphabet, numbers 0 to 9 and punctuation marks. By 1838 Morse had developed his code using from one to four bits (binary digits) to encode letters of the alphabet, five bits for each number and six bits for punctuation. Thus A = · -; the number one = · - - - -; a question mark = · · - - · · while the vital SOS (Save Our Souls) = · · · - - - · · ·

Subsequently modified to suit newer operations, the Morse Code – now the International Morse Code – continues in use.

Motivation Ernest R. Hilgard, Richard C. Atkinson and Rita L. Atkinson in *Introduction to Psychology* (US: Harcourt Brace Jovanovich, 1975) define motivation as 'A general term referring to the regulation of need-satisfying and goal-seeking behaviour'. The sources of motivation are varied and complex. There is general agreement that motivation arises from the desire to satisfy many needs, but there are different theories about the nature of such needs and the relative importance attached by different individuals to them.

The concept of motivation is relevant to several areas of communication and media studies. Motivation theories, for example, can help to provide a range of ideas about why people want to communicate. Of relevance here is William Schutz's theory of interpersonal needs. Schutz, in his book entitled *The Interpersonal World* (US: Science and Behaviour Books, 1966), identifies three basic interpersonal needs which he argues underlie most interpersonal behaviour: the need for *inclusion*, the need for *control* and the need for *affection*. These then are the needs one might wish to have satisfied in INTERPERSONAL COMMUNICATION. Situations in which others satisfy one or more of your needs are likely to be valued; those situations in which your needs are not met may well be avoided.

Another example of the use made of the concept of motivation is in the consideration of why and how people might be influenced or persuaded to act in certain ways, by certain messages. Much effort is expended in the ADVERTISING and public relations industries trying to devise strategies for selling products, services or people, by appealing to what are thought to be the motivations of the general public. See HIDDEN NEEDS; MASLOW'S HIERARCHY OF NEEDS; MOTIVATION RESEARCH (MR); VALS TYPOLOGY.

Motivation research (MR) The post-2nd World War period saw a boom in the US in studies which sought to understand the social psychology of audience exposure to advertising. What influences people to purchase? How can such influences be transformed into a reliable system by the advertiser? In his classic analysis of the US world of advertising, *The Hidden Persuaders* (UK: Longmans, Green, 1957; Penguin, 1960, revised and reprinted, 1981), Vance Packard describes a range of HIDDEN NEEDS identified by motivation research for the advertiser to satisfy. These include emotional security, reassurance of worth and what Packard terms ego gratification.

MR has sharpened and sophisticated its tools of measurement over the years. We now have the pupilometer to measure respondents' eye movements and the degree of 'stopping power' of the adverts under scrutiny. There are machines which offer voice-pitch analysis; machines to tabulate brain waves. Not only is psychology wheeled into action in the service of MR but so are the findings of psycholinguists, who study the mental processes governing the learning and use of language. See MEDIA ANALYSIS.

Motivation theory See MASLOW'S HIERARCHY OF NEEDS.

Mouse The computer 'mouse' is a hand-held device with a metal or rubber ball protruding from its base, used to give computer instructions without recourse to the computer keyboard.

Mr Gate American media analyst David Manning White in 1950 investigated the process of GATEKEEPING by studying the editing selections by a copy-editor – 'Mr Gate' – from the (then) three major American NEWS AGENCIES on a 30,000-circulation daily newspaper in the midwest. 'Mr Gate' in one week used 1297 column inches – about one-tenth of the 11,910 column inches supplied. 'Mr Gate' confessed to a few prejudices which might well cause him to put items on the SPIKE (reject them), and to a preference: 'I go for human interest stories in a big way'; but White also perceived how important the pressure of time was on the selection process. The nearer the next edition of the newspaper came, the stronger in NEWS VALUE a story had to be not to be rejected. See WHITE'S GATEKEEPER MODEL, 1950.

MTV Music Television; world-wide popular music VIDEO broadcasting service created by Robert Pittman in the US, to take advantage of initially free programming provided by popular video. Transmitted via SATELLITE and CABLE TELEVISION, MTV is financed by ADVERTISING (90 per cent) and sponsorship. The launch of MTV took place in August 1981. From 1.5m North American subscribers the reach of MTV has become global. In 1991 there were 201m householders in 77 countries in 5 continents subscribing to the service. Since MTV Australian was launched in 1987, MTV has extended into Brazil and Asia (where 31 countries receive MTV, transmitted from Hong Kong). MTV Europe, with its headquarters in Camden, London, dates from 1987.

It is difficult to exaggerate the cultural impact of MTV broadcasting popular music, in English, to practically every corner of the world. Corinna Sturmer in 'MTV Europe. An imaginary continent?' in *Channels of Resistance: Global Television and Local Empowerment* (UK: British Film Institute/ Channel 4 TV, 1993), edited by Tony Dowmunt, refers to 'a MTV generation'. At first sight it would seem that 'national culture is ruptured along the age faultline' with the teenage-plus age group having, through the enculturalizing impact of MTV, more in common with teenage-plus in other countries than with their own older generations.

However, as Sturmer says, 'The key problem for MTV E [Europe] is that European youth is not a homogeneous entity, and its aim must therefore be to combine global marketing with targeted regional consumers'. MTV's burgeoning success raises a number of questions about cultural dominance. For example, is American pop about to the rule the world (if it does not do so already) and by becoming so, demolish all locally created rivals? There are anomalies too, as Corinna Sturmer points out: 'In the political climate of the post-communist world, MTV's Janus-faced nature comes to light. While constructing its appeal around the rebellious image and anti-authoritarian values of rock-'n'-roll, at the same time it typifies and exists to serve the interests of advanced consumer capital.'

Multi-actuality The MEANING of communication signs – LANGUAGE – is not fixed but subject to differing interpretations according to context. The term originated with Valentin Volosinov in *Marxism and the Philosophy of Language* (US: Seminar Press, 1973; first published in Russian, 1929–30) who argued that the prevailing meaning of a word or expression – such as democracy or freedom, for example – works towards the suppression of multi-actuality, except in terms of 'social crises or revolutionary changes'. In other words, the dominant HIERARCHY will strive to impose its own meaning – *one* meaning as opposed to many. Signs, therefore, Volosinov believes, may become the 'arena for the class struggle' as the dominant group of interpreters of meaning strive to eradicate alternative meanings. See HEGEMONY; IDEOLOGY; METAPHOR.

Multimedia Combination in one system of a range of facilities: text display, sound, animated graphics, moving video; available through compact disc, described by Nolan Bushnell of Commodore (whose Dynamic

Total Vision System was first on the market, in 1991) as 'the Trojan Horse for the computer revolution', transforming TV 'from a passive to an active medium'. As with the old view format war, between Betamax and VHS, there is aggressive competition between multimedia formats.

Multiplane Walt Disney (1901–66) used this word to explain an innovation in the process of ANIMATION, illustrated in *Fantasia* (1940). Instead of building up a drawing by laying 'cells' one directly on top of the other, an illusion of depth was achieved by a space being left between the CELLULOID images of foreground, background and principal figures.

Multiple image A number of images printed beside each other on the same FILM frame, often showing different camera angles of the same action, or separate actions. Abel Gance (1889–1981) used this device with stunning effect in his masterpiece of 1926, *Napoleon*.

Multiplier effect Where CULTURE as a commodity – usually in the form of films and TV programmes – exported to other countries, opens up markets for other goods. James Monaco in 'Images and sounds as cultural commodities' in *Sight & Sound*, Autumn 1980, quotes American professor Dallas Smythe: 'The distribution of television programmes around the world from the United States . . . has the double purpose of making money for itself and serving as the front runner for the industry of the country which produced it. It is a form of advertisement; it is like the battleships, gunboats, which used to show the flag.' See MEDIA IMPERIALISM.

Musical – film musical Essentially the invention and hallmark of the US, and of Broadway, New York, in particular. Though *The Jazz Singer* (1927) was not by any means the first FILM to be accompanied by music, it is nevertheless classified as the first film musical as well as the 'talkie' which made the break-through for SYNCHRONOUS SOUND. The first all-talking, all-singing, all-dancing film was *The Broadway Melody* (1929). Colour in musicals was used with earliest success in *The Wizard of Oz* (1939).

The hey-day of the musical stretched glitteringly from the 1930s to the end of the 1950s when vastly increased production costs and the decline in mass audiences made musicals uneconomical. They were replaced in their extravagance with musical stories such as *Oklahoma!* (1955), *West Side Story* (1961) and *My Fair Lady* (1965), with *The Sound of Music* (1965) capping all at the box-office. Imitations failed, though *Cabaret* (1972) proved that old forms and old patterns could be creatively extended.

Music: censorship of music The entire edition of *Index on Censorship*, 6, 1998, was given over to a survey, worldwide, of the CENSORSHIP of music. In an editorial, Ursula Owen, Marie Korpe and Ole Reitov state that 'Music is probably the most censored art form' and that its subversive nature 'has long been recognized by rulers, religions and moralists'. Music has been censored throughout history but music censorship has flourished most extensively in the 20th c., most notably in the Third Reich of Hitler's Germany and the USSR under the tyranny of Josef Stalin. Banning the performance of music, or its broadcasting, is only one mode of censorship. When the generals seized power in Chile in 1976, the popular folk singer Victor Jara was 'silenced' for ever by being tortured and beaten to death. In Somalia in the 1980s, opera star Maryam Mursal was arrested, sacked from the National Opera, forbidden to perform and eventually forced into exile for her song 'Ulimada', a critique of the regime of General Mohammed Siyed Barre. In the UK in 1997 dance culture was criminalized through the Criminal Justice Act. In Algeria in 1998, the singer Lounès Matoub, outspoken defender of Berber culture, was murdered.

Music speaks to the heart; it is not socially or culturally exclusive, it evokes deep feelings in groups and communities as well as individuals. It has the power to unite, to bond. Where it has served as an instrument of popular protest it has been seen by those in authority as a danger to the order of things, moral, cultural, political. BROADCASTING in particular has been subject to pressures to censor, especially in times of civil or military conflict.

The BBC in the UK has long exercised music censorship. Events in Northern Ireland prompted the BBC to refuse airtime to Wings' 'Give Ireland Back to the Irish' and, during the Gulf War of 1991, the BBC Radio Training Unit compiled a list of records it considered should be treated with caution during the war. For an informative introduction to music censorship, see Julian Petley's article in *Index* 6, 1998 'Smashed Hits: An Overview'.

* Martin Cloonan, *Banned! – Censorship of Popular Music in Britain: 1967–92* (UK: Arena, 1996).

Music Television See MTV.

Muted groups A term used by Shirley and Edwin Ardener in Shirley Ardener (ed.) *Perceiving Women* (UK: Mallory Press, 1975) to refer to a group within a society whose mode of expression is not that of the dominant group(s). In order to be heard and taken notice of by the dominant group(s) members of the muted group have to express themselves in the dominant mode of expression. This may well be difficult as, for example, they may be unfamiliar with the REGISTER used by the dominant group. There may be conventions which restrict the freedom of expression of a muted group. Such disadvantages render them, therefore, relatively mute. In some cases members of the muted group may be required, by the dominant group, to be silent in certain contexts.

Women have, arguably, often found themselves in this position. Dale Spender, for example, in *Man-Made Language* (UK: HarperCollins, 1990 edition) argues that 'when women do not speak in terms that are acceptable to men, they do not get a proper hearing'. As a result, Spender goes on to argue, women often react in a protective manner by 'retreating into silence' thus reinforcing 'their own muted position'. Groups that are relatively mute are much less likely to get their arguments, experiences and perspectives acknowledged in the public arena.

* Deborah Cameron, 'Beyond alienation: an integrational approach to women and language', in John Corner and Jeremy Hawthorn, eds., *Communication Studies: An Introductory Reader* (UK: Edward Arnold, 1993).

Mystification See HEGEMONY.

Myth The generally accepted meaning of myth is of a fictitious (primitive) tale usually involving supernatural characters embodying some popular idea concerning natural or historical phenomena, often symbolizing virtues or other timeless qualities. In everyday parlance, a myth is something invented, not true. For analysts of the communication process, myth has more specific connotations. Myth is an interpretation of the way things are; a justification, a 'charter' as Bronislaw Malinowski (1884–1942) put it. For Claude Lévi-Strauss myth is a force generated to overcome contradictions. Either way, at the heart of myth is IDEOLOGY, chiefly the value-system of those at the top of society.

The French philosopher Roland Barthes (1915–80) ascribes myth to the second order of SIGNIFICATION, that is, CONNOTATION, but connotation with a very special task – to distort, to become a charter, yes, but also an *alibi*. The way Barthes defines it, myth is a weapon of the bourgeoisie which it uses to regenerate its cultural dominance.

In *Mythologies* (UK: Paladin, 1973), Barthes writes, 'Myth does not deny things, on the contrary, its function is to talk about them; simply, it purifies them, it makes them innocent, it gives them a natural and eternal justification, it gives them a clarity which is not that of an explanation but that of a statement of fact'. Myth defines 'eternal verities' which may neither be eternal nor verities. And myth acts economically, 'it abolishes the complexity of human acts, it gives them the simplicity of essences, it does away with all the dialectics, without any going back beyond what is immediately visible, it organizes a world which is without contradictions because it is without depth, a world wide open and wallowing in the evident, it establishes a blissful clarity: things appear to mean something by themselves'.

Statistically, Barthes believes, myth is on the political Right, and one of its chief inspirations is *order*, its communication mode, RHETORIC. See SEMIOLOGY/SEMIOTICS.

* J. Cuffer, *Barthes* (UK: Fontana, 1983).

Myth of marginality See MARGINALITY, MYTH OF.

Myths of Deregulation See DEREGULATION, FIVE MYTHS OF.

N

Narcotizing dysfunction One of the chief social consequences of the mass media upon AUDIENCES, in the view of P.H. Lazarsfeld and R. Merton in 'Communication, taste and social action' in L. Bryson (ed.), *The Communication of Ideas* (US: Harper & Row, 1948). This rather awful sounding affliction, of first being subdued, or 'drugged', and then put out of action by exposure to the media, comes about, believe the authors, because audiences are reduced to 'mass apathy' by a heroic effort to keep up with the vast amount of information placed before them. 'Mass communications may be included among the most respectable and efficient of social narcotics . . . increasing dosages of mass communications may be inadvertently transforming the energies of men from active participation into passive knowledge.' See COMPASSION FATIGUE; EFFECTS OF THE MASS MEDIA; USES AND GRATIFICATIONS THEORY; MAINSTREAMING.

Narration In, for example, a TELEVISION documentary, what the narrator or the voice-over tells the AUDIENCE helps structure both programme and response. Narration is the intermediary between 'raw information' and the ordered discourse or TEXT. In his monograph *Television Discourse and History* (UK: British Film Institute, 1980), Colin McArthur argues that the 'central ideological function of narration is to confer *authority* on, and to elide *contradictions* in, the discourse'. Narration, therefore, serves to identify and help further an ideological base.

Narration is as much a technical convenience as an ideological mechanism. It is a time-saver; permits summary; allows for efficient transition; it is custom-built for an expensive, time-conscious MEDIUM. Given creative independence, many programme producers have reduced the dominance of narrative or done away with it altogether, as much as possible letting the world 'speak for itself' by using sound and vision without comment; allowing camera and microphone to eavesdrop on activities free from a framing narrative. Of course the process of MEDIATION is ultimately unavoidable – cameras have to be set up in one place or another; pointed in one direction rather than another; decisions have to be made about long-shot and close-up and finally the FILM has to be edited: even without a narrator, a story has been told; reality has been reconstructed. See CODES OF NARRATIVE; NARRATIVE PARADIGM; SYMBOLIC CONVERGENCE THEORY.

Narrative In *Narratives in Popular Culture, Media, and Everyday Life* (UK: Sage, 1997) Arthur Asa Berger defines narrative as 'a story, and stories tell about things that have happened or are happening, to people, animals, aliens from outer space, insects – whatever. That is, a story contains a sequence of events, which means that narratives take place within or over, to be more precise, some kind of time period. This time period can be very short, as in a nursery tale, or very long, as in some novels and epics'. As Berger picturesquely puts it, our lives are 'immersed in narratives. Every day we swim in a sea of stories and tales . . . from our earliest days to our deaths'. Inevitably, then, the study of communication is very much concerned with the study of narratives – how they are put together, what their functions are and what uses are made of them by those who read, listen to or watch stories. In the view of Michel de Certeau in *The Practice of Everyday Life* (US: University of California, 1984), narratives 'articulate our existences'; indeed we as social, communal animals, are 'defined by stories'.

At the level of denotation narratives tell us what happened to whom and in what circumstances; at the CONNOTATIONAL level we enter the realm of MEANING, of signification: what is the story really about? This applies as much to NEWS stories as to fictional stories; indeed the news can be classified as a GENRE, that is, a mode of narratives which conforms (for the most part) to a set of particular rules.

In 1926 George Herbert Mead (in 'The

nature of aesthetic experience in the *International Journal of Ethics*, 36) defined two models of journalism, the *information* model and the *story* model, stating that 'the reporter is generally sent out to get a story not the facts'. The storyness theme is taken up by Peter Dahlgren in his Introduction to *Journalism and Popular Culture* (UK: Sage, 1992, edited by Dahlgren and Colin Sparks). He writes that 'Storytelling . . . is a key link which unites journalism and popular culture . . . narrative is a way of knowing the world'. He goes on: 'Journalism officially aims to inform about events in the world – analytical mode – and does this most often in the story mode' which both 'enhances and delimits the likely range of meanings'. Above all, like social rituals generally, the story mode has the power to bring about a sense of shared experience and of shared values. This, it might be said, is the 'story' of news, its connotational function: it is about cohesion-making as much as it is about information-transmission (See STRUC-TURE OF NEWS: REASSURANCE).

In this multi-media age narratives more than ever before interact and overlap but for convenience – of analysis and study – they continue to be classified under the heading of genres, each with its own narrative rules and traditions, each with recognizable FRAM-ING devices. In some genres the frame is tight, highly restrictive to the point of being ritualistic. Other genres have 'flexible' framing and offer the potential for change and development. SOAP OPERAS have this potential, sit-coms less so, contends Jasper Rees in the *Independent*, reviewing the second festival of sit-coms run by the UK's Channel 4. In his article 'Slap "n" Tickle', 30 July 1996, Rees says, 'In a play, events take place which irrepressibly alter the relationship between the characters. Whatever happens in a sit-com, you always go back to square one at the start of a fresh episode; the idea of stasis is built into the design. No doubt sooner or later a writer will come along and create a sitcom which breaks new ground, though this will depend as much upon external framing mechanisms such as programming and popularity as the nature of the genre itself'.

Each genre contains a range of signifiers, of conventions which audiences recognize and come to expect while at the same time readily accepting experiment with those conventions. Knowledge of the conventions on the part of audience, and recognition when convention is flouted, suggests an active 'union' between the encoder and the decoder. Audience, as it were, is 'let in on the act'; and this 'knowingness' is an important part of the enjoyment of narrative genres. When the hero in a Western chooses not to wear a gun (a great rarity), audience (because we are familiar with tradition) recognizes the salience of this decision. Such recognition could be said to constitute a form of participation.

We use our familiarity with old 'routines' as a frame for reading this new twist of narrative. We wonder whether convention will be flouted altogether as the story proceeds or whether the rules of the genre will be reasserted by the hero taking up the gun to bring about a resolution to the story. For a soap opera *time* is a key element in the framing process. There are 30-minute slots to be filled, each to conclude with unfinished business, preferably dramatic and suspenseful, while not being so dramatically 'final' that the series cannot continue into an indefinite future.

Soap narratives need time to bed down, unfold, and in their own time they reflect the timescales of audience. In some cases, the time-frame *of* the soap is as important as the time-frames *within* it. The soap 'frame', thus amply provided with time, requires many characters and many plots. The narrative template or mould out of which soaps emerge is, give or take an adjustment, the same or similar to that which produces popular narratives of all kinds, including the news. They must attract and hold attention. They must gratify both COGNITIVE (intellectual) AND AFFECTIVE (emotional) needs. They must facilitate IDENTIFICATION, *personal reference* as well as *diversion* (See USES AND GRATI-FICATIONS THEORY). They must meet the needs of a certain type of audience at a certain time of day while at the same time fulfilling such criteria as commercial viability which in turn is conditional upon ratings and audience share.

Another key element of narratives is what is termed *binary framing*, that is the story being structured in terms of opposites – heroes–villains; good–evil; kind–cruel; tolerant–intolerant; beautiful–ugly. In *Narratives* Asa Berger talks of 'central oppositions'. Stories are built around protagonists who are archetypal, with character-traits which are readily recognized – heroes, heroines, villains and victims (See PROPP'S PEOPLE). Something happens, an event producing a state of *disequilibrium*, of imbalance, which has to be corrected or resolved; and in the resolution we may read a message, a moral – about valour or self-sacrifice.

Robert C. Allen, writing in *Channels of Discourse: Television and Contemporary Criticism* (UK: Routledge, 1987, edited by Allen), differentiates between what he calls the *Hollywood narrative mode* and the *Rhetorical mode*. The first hides the means by which the text is created. It invites audience to believe that what they are seeing is real: one is absorbed into the text without being, as it were, addressed by it. In contrast, the rhetorical mode directly addresses the viewer. The news, Allen sees presented in this way – the news reader looks directly out at us; and similar formats can be recognized in cooking, sports and gardening programmes on TV: 'The texts are not only presented for us, but directed out at us.'

Asa Berger concludes his book by affirming the importance of narrative analysis in the study of communication: 'We used to think of the stories we read, listen to, and watch as little more than trivial amusements to "kill time". Now we know that people learn from stories, are emotionally affected by them, and actually need stories to lend colour and interest to their everyday lives.' See CODES OF NARRATIVE; NARRATIVE PARADIGM; SYMBOLIC CONVERGENCE THEORY.

* Nick Lacey, *Narrative and Genre: Key Concepts in Media Studies* (UK: Macmillan, 1999).

Narrative codes See CODES OF NARRATIVE.

Narrative paradigm Theory that sees people as essentially storytellers, defining humankind as *homo narrans*. A substantial section of the Autumn 1985 edition of the *Journal of Communication* was devoted to an analysis, by a variety of contributors, of the notion that if storytelling is central to human DISCOURSE and INTERACTION, then the paradigm provides an important METAPHOR for communications research which has its own story – its own narrative-base – rooted in beliefs about truth and falsehood, fact and fiction and the nature of reason.

Walter R. Fisher, Professor of Communication Arts and Sciences at the University of Southern California, in 'The narrative paradigm: in the beginning', believes that rationality in humans is determined by the nature of persons as narrative beings, by 'their inherent awareness of *narrative probability*, what constitutes a coherent story, and their constant habit of testing *narrative fidelity*, whether the stories they experience ring true with stories they know in their lives'. He goes on, 'the world is a set of stories which must be chosen among to live the good life in a process of continual recreation'.

The narrative paradigm differs from *dramatism*, or the 'dramatic paradigm' which sees humans as playing parts – prescribed ROLES – in scripts provided by existing situations, cultural patterns, institutions.

In the same issue of the *Journal*, Thomas B. Farrell, in 'Narrative in natural discourse: on conversation and rhetoric', offers a cautious qualification: 'The question, bluntly put, is whether we can be actors in and authors of the same unfinished story without doing damage to the one indispensable outcome of successful narrative: character.' Rather than narrative being the 'primary art form of everyday life', Farrell opts for RHETORIC and conversation. See CODES OF NARRATIVE; SYMBOLIC CONVERGENCE THEORY; THEORIES AND CONCEPTS OF COMMUNICATION.

Narratives: grand narratives See POSTMODERNISM.

Narrowcasting As contrasted with *broadcasting*; JARGON word to describe the process whereby advertisers, programme makers, video marketeers and producers aim at specialized-interest audiences, from gardening to golf, from astronomy to cookery; or at special *levels* of AUDIENCE distinguished by, for example, social CLASS, education or spending power.

Nasties See VIDEO NASTIES.

National Film and Television School (UK) The LLOYD COMMITTEE REPORT, 1967, had recommended that a National Film School should be established to provide professional training.

Located at Beaconsfield Studios, working under the authority of the Films Act, 1970 and funded by a direct grant from the Treasury on the Arts Vote, in association with the Office of Arts and Libraries, the National Film and Television School has produced many graduates who have made notable contributions to British cinema and television.

National Film Archive Founded in May 1935, the NFA is the largest division of the BRITISH FILM INSTITUTE. Its role is to acquire, preserve and make available for study a collection of films and TV programmes of all kinds exhibited or transmitted in the UK from any source and of any nationality. Particular emphasis is placed on British productions, which may have lasting value as works of art, examples of film or TV history or as valuable records of past and present contemporary behaviour. The Archive contains over 80,000 titles, going back as early as 1895.

National Viewers' and Listeners' Association (NVLA) See 'CLEAN UP TV' MOVEMENT.

Naturalistic illusion (of television) The visual qualities of TV can lead to the assumption that it is merely a window on the world, showing life as it really is. Stuart Hall in 'The rediscovery of "ideology"', in M. Gurevitch, T. Bennett, J. Curran, and J. Woollacott, eds., *Culture, Society and the Media* (UK: Methuen, 1982), refers to this phenomenon as the 'naturalistic illusion'. TV programmes are in fact the result of considerable planning and research.

Elaborate procedures of framing, editing and the matching of images with dialogue have to be undertaken in order to present an exposition. During these procedures decisions are taken which may significantly affect the finished presentation. Different impressions can be given, for example, of a demonstration depending upon when or where the film is taken and how it is edited.

Necessity, supervening social necessity (technology) See SUPERVENING SOCIAL NECESSITY.

Needs See MASLOW'S HIERARCHY OF NEEDS.

Negative frequency See FREQUENCY.

Negative news See NEWS VALUES.

Negative semantic space See MALE-AS-NORM.

Negativization See VISIONS OF ORDER.

Negotiated code See DOMINANT, SUBORDINATE, RADICAL.

Neologism The invention or usage of a new word, or giving an old word a new MEANING, such as 'viewer' from the French 'voyeur' to indicate someone who views other people's sometimes illicit activities. Examples: summit conference; hi-fi; motel; tailback; motorcade; pot.

Net See INTERNET.

Network Channels of communications which are interconnected are termed networks, to be found in all communication in which numbers of people are involved, such as GROUPS and organizations. Basically a communication network consists of linked dyads in which the *receiver* in one DYAD is the *source* in the next. Such networks will vary in size and not all members of the network will necessarily have equal access to information or participation. A *communication structure* is a network in which some channels are systematically neglected. Generally speaking the greater the number of links between members, and the closer the distance between them, the more likely it is that information is distributed equally; assuming all members communicate through all the links at their disposal. In a network with a high level of CENTRALITY it is likely that some members will possess more information than others. Communication networks may take several forms, such as the two illustrated here.

Networks may vary as to the ease with which individual members can be isolated from fellow members and some networks will suffer more than others from the removal of a member or a link. If a member or link is missing from a *chain* network, for

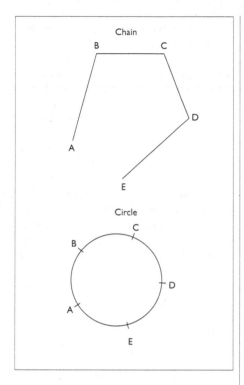

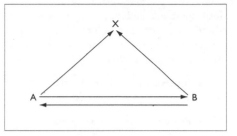

Newcomb's ABX model

A and B are communicators and X is the situation or social *context* in which the communication takes place. Both the individuals are orientated to each other and to X, and communication is conceived of as the process which supports this orientational structure. Symmetry or balance is maintained between the three elements by the transmission of information about any change in circumstance or relationship, thus allowing adjustment to take place.

For Newcomb, the process of communication is one of the interdependent factors maintaining *equilibrium,* or as Newcomb himself puts it in 'An approach to the study of communicative acts' in *Psychological Review,* 60 (1953) 'communication among human beings performs the essential functions of enabling two or more individuals to maintain simultaneous orientation to each other *and* towards objects of an external environment'. See COMMUNICATION MODELS; CONGRUENCE THEORY; McCOMBS AND SHAW AGENDA SETTING MODEL OF MEDIA EFFECTS, 1976; McCLEOD AND CHAFFEE'S 'KITE' MODEL, 1973; WESLEY AND MACLEAN'S MODEL OF COMMUNICATION, 1957.

example, the effect is likely to be more serious than if either were missing from a *circle* network. A network may also spawn a sub-network: a sub-network can be said to exist when the number of links between certain members is greater than the number of links between these members and others.

The term network is used in BROADCASTING to describe the pattern of connection of the broadcasting stations of a broadcasting company or companies. Such a connection allows the simultaneous broadcast of the same programme. To **network** a programme means to broadcast it to the widest number of TV/radio stations both within one network and in other networks. In the US, the term is used more specifically: the Networks are those companies which commission programmes and programme series.

Newcomb's ABX model of communication, 1953 In contrast to the linear structure of the SHANNON AND WEAVER MODEL OF COMMUNICATION, 1949, Theodore H. Newcomb's model is triangular in shape, and is the first to introduce as a factor the role of communication in a society or a social relationship.

New Document Alliance World-wide association of media corporations to make literary and informational texts available, by digital means, via global computer networks. The Alliance includes the Xerox Corporation, AT&T, Sun Microsystems and Microsoft: the target, the libraries of the world instantly available, from St Augustine to Jeffrey Archer. Reporting from New York for the *Observer* on 24 April 1994 ('Host books haunt the superhighway'), Robin McKie says 'books of the future may well exist as ghostly electronic entities on the Internet, or any other superhighway network, until they are summoned and turned into solid ink and paper at a local print shop'. Such texts can be provided in whole or in part. See CYBERSPACE; CONNECTIVITY; INTERNET; PROJECT GUTENBERG.

New International Information Order
See NEW WORLD INFORMATION ORDER.

New Populism See MAINSTREAMING.

News The study of news is central to most if not all courses in communication and media studies. Like information itself, the news is a vital component of the life of individuals, groups, communities and nations. News brings us information, several times daily, often on the hour. Whether it is in print or broadcast form, the news *represents* to us the world – reality; and every student soon learns that the news is a *process*, or rather an amalgam of many processes, which mediate information select it, edit it, emphasize some parts of it, distort it, even manipulate it. News, that is, the raw information which is eventually *constructed* as news is turned into NARRATIVE, a mode of storytelling, which by the application of certain professional practices – *conventions* – establishes what has come to be termed news DISCOURSE.

In this sense, news can actually be described as 'olds': what has by precedent been counted as news continues to be classified and used as news. We become acutely aware of the selective nature of news, of the fact that, for example, the elite – persons, societies, nations – appear more often in the news than ordinary people or less prestigious societies and nations. And there is a reciprocal nature about inclusion in the news: if you are important, the news covers what you do or say; if the news covers what you do or say, what you do or say becomes better known. You become a Known instead of an Unknown.

The focus of study will shift from the analysis of news *sources*, to the predisposition, reportorial approach, and the constraints upon that approach, of the *practitioners* of news; and their activities will be examined in micro and macro situations. At the micro level we would scrutinize the relationship of a practitioner to the organization which employs him/her and

thus directs and influences his or her professional activities.

At the macro level we would study the influences from outside the organization, from society itself: what part in shaping news content and presentation does big business have, or government, or the law? What social, cultural, economic or political pressures are brought to bear on news production which will influence the shape and tenor of it as it reaches the audience?

We would be equally interested in how the news was put together, how decisions were made about what was important, what less important. This would lead us into an investigation of AGENDA SETTING which will have proved a useful guide to the processes of GATEKEEPING. The agenda controls the gate; but what controls the agenda? We would need to explore the basic principles of what information, at any given time, is considered *newsworthy*. In short, we would study the news VALUES which both practitioners and media analysts have identified as influencing decision-making.

Not least of all, we would be interested in investigating how news is *received* by the audience. We would attempt to discover how audiences actually *use* the news; how far it actually does inform them, and whether it influences them. We soon understand that news reconstructs the world according to the perceptions of those who produce the news, and those who employ or influence the news producers; and we would be interested in discovering to what extent audiences take on board the 'reality' presented by news.

In examining the approaches to news production and presentation we would be alert to the capacity of audience to choose alternative readings to the realities with which they are being presented. We will most certainly have noted how news presentation has developed over the years, that it is more lively than ever before in style and content; that it is more *entertaining*. We might need to ask whether such developments have increased or decreased audience comprehension of the matters being presented: how much of what is read or seen on TV news is fully grasped, contextualized; indeed, how much of it has been retained as meaningful information?

No form of public communication has a higher profile than news production and management and issues relating to this concern a number of high aspirations – *objectivity, balance* and *impartiality* – each difficult to define both in theory and practice. Many commentators would argue that a more pressing issue is the nature of *ownership and control* and whether, in any given society, there is a *plurality* in the ways information and opinion are presented. Finally, news and news production have to be seen in relation to trends – the impact of new media technologies, the transnationalization of media ownership, the privatization of public media services and the globalization of message/meaning systems. See ANCHORAGE; AUDIENCE; AUDIENCE MEASUREMENT; BASS'S 'DOUBLE ACTION' MODEL OF INTERNAL NEWS FLOW, 1968; BIAS; CENTRALITY; CHRONOLOGY, CONGRUENCE THEORY; CONNOTATION; CRISIS (DEFINITION); CRITICAL NEWS ANALYSIS; DEVELOPMENTAL NEWS; DISINFORMATION; EFFECTS OF THE MASS MEDIA; ELECTRONIC NEWSGATHERING; EMBARGO; FLEET STREET; HORSE-RACE STORY; FOURTEEN-DAY RULE; FREQUENCY; FRAMING: MEDIA; GALTUNG AND RUGE'S MODEL OF SELECTIVE GATEKEEPING, 1965; GLASGOW UNIVERSITY MEDIA GROUP; IMPARTIALITY; INTERVENING VARIABLES (IV); INTIMIZATION; J-CURVE; KNOWNS, UNKNOWNS; LOBBY PRACTICE; MAINSTREAMING; MARGINALIZATION, MYTH OF; McCOMBS AND SHAW AGENDA-SETTING MODEL OF MEDIA EFFECT, 1976; McNELLYS MODEL OF NEWS FLOW, 1959; MEDIATION; NARRATIVE; NEWS AGENCIES; NEWS FRAMEWORKS; NEWS: GLOBALIZATION OF; NEWS MANAGEMENT; NEWS: STRUCTURE OF REASSURANCE; NEWS VALUES; NEW WORLD INFORMATION ORDER; NON-ALIGNED NEWS POOL; NORMATIVE THEORIES OF MASS MEDIA; OBJECTIVITY; ONE-STEP, TWO-STEP, MULTI-STEP FLOW MODELS OF COMMUNICATION; PHOTO-JOURNALISM; POOL SYSTEM; PREFFERED READING; PRESS BARONS; PROTOTYPING CONCEPT; PUBLIC SPHERE; SOUND-BITE; SPOT NEWS; TELEVISION NEWS: INHERENT LIMITATIONS: USES AND GRATIFICATIONS THEORY; WATCHDOGS; WESTERSTÅHL AND JOHANSSON MODEL OF NEWS FACTORS IN FOREIGN NEWS, 1994; WHITE'S GATEKEEPER MODEL, 1950.

News agencies 'The invention of the news agency', writes Anthony Smith in *The Geopolitics of Information* (UK: Faber, 1980)

'was the most important single development in the newspaper industry in the early 1800s, apart from the rotary press'. The early agencies – Reuter, Havas and Wolff – carved up the world into spheres of activity in much the same way as imperialist nations parcelled out Third World territories between them.

In 1869 the major agencies signed an Agency Alliance Treaty. Reuter was 'granted' the British Empire and the whole of the Far East; Havas – a French agency – was granted Italy, Spain, France and the Portuguese empire and the Germany-based Wolff received Austria, Scandinavia and Russia. America was awarded jointly to Havas and Reuter.

Over 60 syndicates are listed in the annual *Writers' and Artists' Yearbook* (UK: A&C Black). The biggest agencies are The Associated Press (AP), the Press Association (PA, created as early as 1868), Reuters and the United Press International.

Out of the traditional, print-centred news agencies have developed international television news agencies such as Visnews (owned by Reuters, the BBC and NBC), WTN and Worldwide Television News (owned by Independent Television News and United Press International) distributing TV news material around the clock, both 'raw' footage and complete news stories ready for transmission.

Concern has focused on the role of international news agencies in providing many of the items which find their way into domestic news coverage and this concern forms part of the argument found within the MEDIA IMPERIALISM thesis. Of the four main agencies which dominate international news flow, Jeremy Tunstall in *The Media Are American* (UK: Constable, 1994) argues that the British and two US agencies '. . . have acquired special international legitimacy' due to the widespread perception that their news is more neutral and accurate than alternatives. According to Tunstall, 'These agencies have largely shaped the presentation of international news in all countries around the world; these agencies do not merely play a major part in establishing the international political agenda, but they have done so now for a hundred years. And for a hundred years they have been the main definers of world "news values", of what sort of things have become news'. Their tendency to give two sides of the argument can be seen as a hallmark of the pluralistic values typical of Western capitalist societies, but as Tunstall points out this actually also makes it easy for other users to edit out an ideologically unwelcome perspective.

Further, 'The Anglo-American video news agencies provide the core of material for the Eurovision daily news exchange' and 'Eurovision has the most significant and long established daily news exchange in the world'. The same news item and footage can be used in many different ways to proffer a number of meanings; however, their concentration at source points to the long arm of imperialism both past and present. The relatively influential role that Britain plays in the flow of international news mainly stems, argues Tunstall, from its imperial past and the worldwide reputation of the BBC. See MEDIA IMPERIALISM; NEW WORLD INFORMATION ORDER; NON-ALIGNED NEWS POOL.

News Aid? Paul Harrison and Robin Palmer use this term in their book *News Out of Africa: Biafra to Band Aid* (UK: Hilary Shipman, 1986), to illustrate the ambivalent relationship between the media's coverage of the dramatic and distressing effects of famine in the Third World, particularly Africa. The authors note the media's long-term reticence, in news or current affairs programmes, to participate in a DISCOURSE about the underlying causes of such famine and ways in which famines might be prevented. Such reticence begs the question of whether or not coverage of the effects of famine, however galvanizing of public opinion and action in the short term, really aids finding a solution to the problem.

Indeed some commentators argue that the media's tendency to concentrate reporting of Third World countries, like Africa, around issues of natural disasters or conflict leads to the perpetuation of negative and stereotypical images of Third World citizens. Liam Kane in 'Media Studies and images of the "Third World"', *Media Education*, Spring 1990, comments that '"Third World" people tend to be portrayed very negatively, as passive victims of an unexplained poverty'. The consequence, he goes on to argue, is that we can 'easily blame poverty on a combination of "natural disasters" and the supposed ignorance, laziness or backwardness of Asians, Africans, and Latin Americans'.

What are often overlooked are the structural causes of these problems which lie in both national and international inequalities in the distribution of resources and power and the resilience and achievement of Third World citizens despite their often formidably adverse circumstances.

Another fear is of course that concentration on the symptoms rather than the causes of disasters, like famine, may lead ultimately to a dulling of the audience's sensibility to them. See COMPASSION FATIGUE; GLOBAL JUKEBOX; RACISM.

News consensus See CONSISTENCY.

News frameworks Consist of a shared set of assumptions by reporters and editors about what is newsworthy. These assumptions influence the selection of items for investigation and reporting and to some extent how they will be presented. This set of assumptions also enables journalists and editors to relate news items to an image of society in order to give them MEANING. Thus the framework can provide a 'ready reckoner' for constructing as well as selecting news which allows deadlines to be met. See NEWS VALUES.

News: globalization of SATELLITE technology coupled with trends in transnational media ownership and control have created global patterns of information transmission characterized by both CONVERGENCE and diversity. TV news services world-wide show marked similarities of content and NARRATIVE approach when stories of international dimensions are being reported. In contrast, diversity is maintained when national and local stories are dealt with. In 'The global newsroom: convergences and diversities in the globalization of television news' in *Communication and Citizenship: Journalism and the Public Sphere* (UK: Routledge, 1991) edited by Peter Dahlgren and Colin Sparks, Michael Gurevitch, Mark R. Levy and Itzhak Roeh write that convergence is in part predicated by the availability, world-wide, of pictures and reinforces what the authors term a measure of 'shared professional culture', a certain 'commonality in NEWS VALUES and news judgments, across all services'.

However, diversity asserts itself in 'lesser items' suggesting 'that this sharing of news values is not complete and that national social and political differences, as well as journalistic norms between nations, also play a part in shaping patterns of news coverage'.

Further, examples are cited of how globally available film footage is actually harnessed to national MEANINGS – same pictures, different *reading*. This in the opinion of the authors is a practice offering 'an important antidote to "naive universalism" – that is, to the assumption that events reported in the news carry their own meanings, and that the meanings embedded in news stories produced in one country can therefore be generalized to news stories told in other societies'. Gurevitch *et al.* identify what they call the 'domestication of the foreign', that is, foreign stories are 'told in ways which render them more familiar, more comprehensive and more compatible for consumption by different national audiences'. TV news then, anchored as it generally tends to be 'in narrative frameworks that are already familiar to and recognizable by news men as well as by audiences situated in particular cultures', 'simultaneously maintains both global and culturally specific orientations'. The domestication of the foreign serves as a 'countervailing force to the pull of globalization'.

* Oliver Boyd Barrett and Tehri Rautanen, eds., *The Globalization of News* (UK: Sage, 1998).

News-literate Term used by John Hartley in *Understanding News* (UK: Methuen, 1982) to describe the ability of a reader, listener or viewer to comprehend the NORMS, CODES and conventions of news programmes; to intelligently scan the news, 'recognize its familiar cast of characters and events' and to be able to spontaneously 'interpret the world at large in terms of the codes we have learnt from the news'. See NEWS VALUES.

News management Refers to the tactics employed by those – usually in government or important positions in society – who wish to shape the news to their own advantage, or to control events in such a way as to win favourable publicity. See CULTURAL APPARATUS; ELITE; NEWS VALUES; SCOTT REPORT, 1996; SOUND-BITES.

Newspaper price wars See PREDATORY PRICING.

Newspapers, origins The earliest newspapers in Britain were far more internationalist in outlook and interest than they tend to be today. The reason for this was the extensive CENSORSHIP of home news by monarch and council. As early as the 17th c. there was the so-called *Relation*, the publication of a single news story, usually related long after the events. The *Coranto* served to join individual Relations into a continuity, though still not appearing regularly. The *Diurnall* was a step forward, providing a weekly account of occurrences over several days. Like the others before it, the *Mercury* appeared in book-like form, but bore more prominently the individual stamp of writers and tended to be more immediate and more diverse. During the Civil War (1642–46) Mercuries appeared in great abundance, even on Sundays.

Contemporaneous with the *Mercury* was the *Intelligencer*, usually more formal, aspiring to be 'official'. A notable example was *The Publick Intelligencer* published with the blessing of Protector Oliver Cromwell. Indeed the street journalism of all kinds which emerged in the heady days of the English Civil War laid the basis for the popular journalism we recognize today. In the 20 years between 1640 and the restoration of the monarchy under Charles II, 30,000 news publications and pamphlets emerged in London alone.

The date usually cited for London's first regular daily paper is 1702. The intention of Samuel Buckley's *Daily Courant* was 'to give news, give it daily and impartially', and it continued for 6000 editions. By 1750 London had five daily papers, six thrice-weeklies, five weeklies and several other periodicals, all amounting to a circulation of 100,000 copies a week.

The Stamp Act of 1712 heralded over a century of increasing concern on the part of the authorities about the proliferation and influence of newspapers. Government agents reported on the contents of newspapers and there was a bristling array of laws to use against the press, such as seditious libel and profanation. Of dubious legality but considerable effectiveness was the general warrant enabling arrests and seizures of unnamed persons to be made by the King's Messengers, practically at their discretion. Though several warrants were no longer legal after 1766, the STAMP DUTY and other TAXES ON KNOWLEDGE were burgeoning until the middle of the 19th c. when massive and sustained press and popular pressure led to the reduction and eventual abolition of the duties.

New technology, the growth of ADVERTISING and a more literate general public contributed to a massive expansion of newspapers in the latter half of the 19th c. In 1821 there had been 267 newspapers, including weeklies, in the UK and by 1861, 1102. Newspaper trains which began running in 1876 meant that the London papers could reach all parts of the country, while TELEGRAPHY speeded news, increasingly provided by the NEWS AGENCIES (Paul Julius Reuter opened his London office in 1851). By 1880 London had 18 dailies; in the English provinces there were 96 dailies, four in Wales, 21 in Scotland and 17 in Ireland.

The most dramatic example of the rise in the popularity of newspapers was the boom in Sunday papers, whose audience, writes Anthony Smith in *The Newspaper: An International History* (UK: Thames & Hudson, 1979) 'came increasingly to consist of the newly literate who could not afford six papers a week and were interested in non-political news. The Sunday journals traded in horrible murders, ghastly seductions and lurid rapes, but they were combined with a distinct brand of radicalism'. Edward Lloyd's *Weekly News*, founded in 1842, was the first periodical to reach a circulation of a million, leaving the highest selling daily paper, the *Daily Telegraph*, with a 200,000 circulation, well behind.

The pattern for the future was set: new technology facilitated (and made economically necessary) massive print runs; journalism targeted itself for vast readerships; advertising became more and more the staple financial support of the press; ownership rested with very rich individuals or joint stock companies; readership patterns hardened along lines of social class – and competition became increasingly desperate. See ELECTRONIC NEWSPAPER; NORTHCLIFFE REVOLUTION; PHOTO-JOURNALISM; PRESS BARONS.

Newspeak As opposed to Oldspeak in George Orwell's novel *Nineteen Eighty-Four* (1949), where private thought and individual LANGUAGE were crimes against the totalitarian state of Oceania, and where the TV screen could actually hear what viewers were saying and see whether they were indulging in one of the worst of all crimes – private reading. Guardian of Newspeak – the official language divested of all superfluities by the MEANING defined by the State, was the Ministry of Truth (which, incidentally, had a sub-section called *Pornsoc*).

Orwell's Appendix to the novel, *The Principles of Newspeak*, explains that Newspeak was 'not only to provide a medium of expression for the world-view and mental habits proper to the devotees of Ingsoc (English Socialism), but to make all other modes of thought impossible'. Though the word 'free' would be retained in Newspeak, its meaning applied in the sense of 'This dog is free from lice'.

Newsreel The Lumière brothers fathered newsreel FILM at the birth of the cinema, from 1895, but the first regular newsreel, *Pathé Journal*, began in 1908, and French influence upon news on film was considerable for many years.

The 1st World War (1914–18) gave impetus to newsreel especially in Germany, and with the Revolution in Russia (1917) propaganda-newsreel (see AGITPROP) was regarded by the Communist government as being of vital importance in the war for hearts and minds. Dziga Vertov's *Kino-Pravda* newsreel series ran from 1922 to 1925.

Companies in the US were the first to add sound to newsreels and in the UK *British Movietone* was the first to adopt sound (1928). In the 1930s the outstanding newsreel in the US was the MARCH OF TIME series. News on TV eventually put an end to cinema newsreels. See CINEMATOGRAPHY, ORIGINS; DOCUMENTARY.

News selection See AGENDA SETTING; EVENT; GALTUNG AND RUGE'S MODEL OF SELECTIVE GATE-KEEPING, 1965; NEWS VALUES; PROTOTYPING CONCEPT; ROGERS AND DEARING AGENDA SETTING MODEL, 1987.

News: structure of reassurance In *Representing Order: Crime, Law And Justice in the News Media* (UK: Open University Press, 1991), Richard Ericson, Patricia M. Barnek and Janet B.L. Chan argue that in the construction of reality in news production a guiding function of the journalist and editor is to render things 'plausible' and thus 'provide a familiar discourse, based in common sense and precedent'. This plausibility 'in turn provides a structure of reassurance, a tool of acknowledging the familiar': by asserting the plausible-become-familiar the news construction process silences alternative definitions.

News: the 'maleness' of news If the news is to be ascribed a gender classification, some commentators argue that it is essentially 'male': male-orientated in terms of decisions over content, over NEWS VALUES and in the practical matter of who gathers, reports, edits and presents the news. In *Feminist Media Studies* (UK: Sage, 1994), Lisbet van Zoonen argues that women journalists are often expected, by male colleagues and by the organizations employing them, to perform professionally in a manner different from men; to subscribe to expectations of 'femininity': 'Women', writes van Zoonen, 'are confronted by social and cultural expectations of femininity and at the same time are expected to meet criteria of professionalism,' yet there is no evidence that women constitute a different group of professionals from their male colleagues. Van Zoonen refers to her own research in the Netherlands: two thirds of the women journalists she talked to did believe that 'women journalists pay more attention to background information and are more willing to look for spokeswomen instead of spokesmen' than their male counterparts

but there was no difference 'in the actual selection of topics or issues'.

Sue Curry Jansen in 'Beaches without bases: the gender order' published in *Invisible Crises: What Conglomerate Control of the Media Means for America and the World* (US: Westview Press, 1996), edited by George Gerbner, Hamid Mowlana and Herbert I. Schiller, states that conditions and prospects for women are equally disadvantaged in the United States. For Jansen, the news generally, and international news in particular, needs to be viewed through the 'prism of gender'.

She talks of an institutionalized bias towards maleness: 'In the United States men write most of the front-page newspaper stories. They are the subject of most of those stories – 85 per cent of the references and 66 per cent of the photos in 1993. They also dominate electronic media, accounting for 86 per cent of the correspondents and 75 per cent of the sources for US network television evening programmes.'

Women's issues and problems are not newsworthy unless they can be classified in accordance with traditional female roles – wife, mother, daughter. 'Men are typically assigned to *hard* news, news that has significant public implications. Women, in contrast, cover *soft* news stories and stories related to topics traditionally associated with female responsibilities.' In international news coverage, 'women not only are marginal but also normally absent'. Jansen says, 'Under the present global gender order, policymakers and journalists find it more *manly* to deal with guns, missiles, and violent conflicts than with matters like female infanticide in China, the increased trade in children in the sex markets of Manila and Bangkok in the wake of the AIDS epidemic, the impact of the intifada on Palestinian women, or the political activism of groups such as Women in Black, Israeli women who support the intifada'.

Jansen's views receive support from data published in April 1997 by the UK Fawcett Society. During a week's monitoring of election coverage during main news bulletins on the BBC, ITN and Channel 4, it was found that 80 per cent of news gathering and presentation was carried out by male journalists;

and the number of women featured as spokespersons in the news was similarly in a minority. Of 26 government officials asked for their views, none was a woman.

It is perhaps encouraging that the number of women MPs returned to parliament in New Labour's landslide election victory on 1 May 1997 significantly increased, from 62 under the Tories to 120, 100 of whom were Labour, including journalist Sally Keeble and former *Guardian* journalist Ruth Kelly.

News values According to the former editor of *The Sunday Times* and *The Times*, Harold Evans, in his book *The Practice of Journalism* (UK: Heinemann, 1963), 'News is people'. Long-time journalist Denis MacShane in *Using the Media* (UK: Pluto Press, 1979) sums up what journalists are on the look out for with five tenets: conflict; hardship and danger to the community; the unusual (oddity, novelty); scandal; and individualism. He quotes Lord Northcliffe (1869–1922), one of the original PRESS BARONS, who once declared, 'News is what somebody somewhere wants to suppress; all the rest is advertising'. Stuart Hood in *Hood on Television* (UK: Pluto Press, 1980), refers to *news sense* as 'the ability to judge the language and attitudes permissible within the opinion-forming organization of our society'; well within CONSENSUS thinking.

One of the most succinct explanations of news values is that of Johan Galtung and Mari Ruge in 'Structuring and selecting news' in Stanley Cohen and Jock Young, eds., *The Manufacture of News* (UK: Constable, 1973). Events will be more likely to be reported if they fulfil any, some or several of the following criteria: (1) *Frequency*: if the event takes a time approximate to the FREQUENCY of the MEDIUM. A murder, for example, is more newsworthy than the slow progress of a Third World country. (2) *Amplitude*: the bigger, the better, the more dramatic – the greater is the likelihood of the story achieving what the authors call 'threshold value'. (3) *Unambiguity*: the more clear-cut, uncomplicated the events, the more they will be noticed and reported. (4) *Familiarity*: that which is ethnocentric, of cultural proximity, and that which is

relevant; so things close to home matter most, unless things close to home are affected by far away events. (5) *Correspondence*: that is, the degree to which the events meet with our expectations, our predictions, even. In this case, say Galtung and Ruge, 'news' is actually 'olds'. They term this the 'hypothesis of consonance' – that which is familiar is registered, that which is unfamiliar is less likely to be registered. (6) *Surprise*: 'this forms an antidote in terms of criteria to (4) and (5), and works to the benefit of *good* news: 'Events have to be unexpected or rare, or preferably both, to become good news.' (7) *Continuity*: that which has been defined as news – which has hit the headlines – will continue to be newsworthy even if amplitude is reduced. (8) *Composition*: the need for a 'balance' in a news-spread leads the producer or editor to feed in contrasting elements – some home news if the predominant stories have been foreign; a little good news if the news has generally been gloomy.

Galtung and Ruge draw the following generalizations: the more events concern ELITE nations or elite people, the more events can be seen in personal terms and the more *negative* the event is in its consequences, the greater is the likelihood of selection. Consequently, once a news item has been selected, what makes it newsworthy will be accentuated (the authors call this stage 'Distortion'). *Selection* and distortion will, it is argued, take place at all steps in the chain from event to reader ('Replication').

Although Galtung and Ruge's study deals only with newspaper content, Jeremy Tunstall in *Journalists at Work* (UK: Constable, 1971), referring to the Galtung and Ruge article which had first been published in the *Journal of International Peace Research* (1965), adapts the scheme to TV news values. He itemizes four points of difference: (1) In TV the visual is given pre-eminence. The possession of new film will often increase the prominence given to a news story. (2) News items which include film of 'our own reporters' interviewing or commentating on a story are preferred. (3) TV makes use of a small fraction of the *number* of stories the newspapers carry, and even major TV items are short compared with newspaper coverage. (4) There is preference for 'hard' stories or actuality on TV news.

In 'The global newsroom: convergences and diversities in the globalization of television news' published in *Communication and Citizenship: Journalism and the Public Sphere* (UK: Routledge, 1991), edited by Peter Dahlgren and Colin Sparks, Michael Gurevitch, Mark R. Levy and Itzhak Roeh write that 'in a pictures-driven medium, the availability of dramatic pictures competes with, and often supersedes other news considerations'. They also argue that for an event to be judged newsworthy 'it must be anchored in narrative frameworks that are already familiar to and recognizable by news men as well as by audiences situated in particular cultures'; for 'different societies tell themselves – on television and elsewhere – different stories'.

The operation of such news values can be seen in the initial difficulties that can be encountered in getting airtime for stories about famine; some of which have been documented by Paul Harrison and Robert Palmer in their book, *News Out of Africa: Biafra to Band Aid* (UK: Hilary Shipman, 1986). According to Harrison and Palmer even the world-famous, harrowing 1984 footage from Korem in Ethiopia by Mohammed Amin of Visnews and Michael Buerk of the BBC was turned down for transmission by Eurovision and met initial resistance at the US network, NBC, on the grounds that there was a more important domestic crisis to cover. Even the BBC ran the item as the fourth story on the 9 o'clock edition of the television news on the day the story broke. However, the BBC did keep the story running in the following weeks and months to keep concern focused.

Once shown, the film galvanized worldwide support to aid Ethiopia. One result of the widespread shocked reaction to this footage was the formation of Band Aid and Live Aid which ultimately demonstrated the power of television in raising funds. Harrison and Palmer comment that there were no major news stories in Europe at the time and that had there been, the famine footage might never have been screened at all. Indeed the build-up to a more recent

crisis in Ethiopia, Sudan, Somalia and Mozambique received little media attention because of the preoccupation with the Gulf War. This is despite estimates that between 18 and 30 million people faced starvation at this time. The media are even less interested in reporting on the underlying causes of famine. See GALTUNG AND RUGE'S MODEL OF SELECTIVE GATEKEEPING, 1965; GLOBAL JUKEBOX; IMMEDIACY; IMPARTIALITY.

New Wave In the year 1959–60 an astonishing 67 new directors made their FILM debut in France: this was the *nouvelle vague* as Françoise-Giroud described it. At the crest of the wave were critics writing for the film magazine *Cahiers du Cinéma*, including Francoise Truffaut (1932–84), Jean-Luc Godard (b. 1930) and Claude Chabrol (b. 1930). Their films were made cheaply, often with unknown actors, improvisation, handheld cameras, location shooting and without huge teams of technicians.

The New Wave were always a loose-knit grouping of individual directors, and it was individualism – the belief in the film director as *auteur* – which was their common characteristic. They reacted against the studio product and produced films of extraordinary richness and variety.

Others in the Wave have been Alain Resnais, Chris Marker, Eric Rohmer, Jacques Rivette, Louis Malle, Roger Vadim and Agnès Varda.

New World Information Order Unesco-sponsored campaign to counter MEDIA IMPERIALISM by creating an information order that gives a more balanced view of developing countries than has been generally presented by western capitalist press coverage. The intentions of Unesco, with its International Programme for the Development of Communication (IPDC), have been interpreted as a means of exerting greater national control over access to and use of information. This, allege the critics of the Programme, would constitute a dangerous form of CENSORSHIP.

In 1981 the US Congress directed the Reagan administration to withdraw its contribution to Unesco – a quarter of its budget – if measures were taken to restrict the free flow of information. The US withdrew effectively from Unesco on 31 December, 1984 and was joined in its move by the UK. See INTER-NATIONAL FEDERATION OF JOURNALISTS; MACBRIDE COMMISSION; NON-ALIGNED NEWS POOL; TALLOIRES DECLARATION; WORLD PRESS FREEDOM COMMITTEE.

N-Gen Sort for Net-Generation, a term describing young people familiar with, and users of the INTERNET and digital technology in general. The 'N-Geners' are characterized by a level of MEDIACY which marks them out from their parents' generation. See CHILDREN, YOUNG PEOPLE AND THE CHANGING MEDIA ENVIRON-MENT; VIDEO GAMES.

* Douglas Rushkoff, *Playing the Future: How Kids' Culture Can Teach Us to Thrive in an Age of Chaos* (US: HarperCollins, 1997).

'Niche' audiences With the growth of SATELLITE TRANSMISSION, audiences have become more fragmented and consequently advertisers have to target them more precisely. Not only have they to reach the right 'niche' in terms of the age, social class, spending power, cultural attitudes and education of the TV viewer, but they have to identify the best times of day or night when the appropriate niche audience might be tuned in.

Nickelodeon An early and primitive form of cinema, of immense popularity in the US by 1905, usually consisting of a long, narrow room furnished with wooden bench seats and very basic equipment for film projection; frequently converted from a shop or store. The term is thought to have been used by showman John P. Harris, combining the Greek for theatre with the slang expression for the five cents charged for admission. The English equivalent was the *penny gaf.* Soon the Nickelodeon gave way to the more stately film-houses. In 1913, Mitchell L. Mark bought the Strand Theatre, a 3000-seater on Broadway, New York, and set in motion a fashion for neo-Baroque splendour. The movies had moved up market.

Much later, the jukebox got referred to as the nickelodeon; a translation in meaning testified in the post-2nd World War hit song, 'Put another nickel in/In the Nickelodeon . . .'

Nielsen ratings Audience measurement figures produced by the US company A.C. Nielsen, the best-known and most influential ratings information business. See AUDIENCE; RATINGS AND SHARE.

Nine American lifestyles See VALS TYPOLOGY.

Noelle-Neumann's spiral of silence model of public opinion, 1974 In her paper, 'The spiral of silence: a theory of public opinion' published in the *Journal of Communication*, 24 (1974), German professor of communications research Elisabeth Noelle-Neumann examines the interplay between three communicative factors: the mass media, INTERPERSONAL COMMUNICATION and an individual's PERCEPTION of his or her own standpoint in relation to others in society. The model is based upon the belief that people are uneasy – suffer DISSONANCE – if they feel themselves to be *isolates* with regard to general opinion and attitude: that they are the odd one out. In response to a situation, we tend to ask, what do other people think; what is the majority or dominant opinion?

A person may find 'that the views he holds are losing ground; the more this appears to be so, the more uncertain he will become of himself, and the less he will be inclined to express his opinion'. This is the spiral of silence.

The dominant view which the mass media express (See ELITE; HEGEMONY; POWER ELITE) exerts pressure to conform, to step into line; and the more this view is expressed, the more the dominant view is reinforced; the more dominant it appears, the more difficult it becomes to hold a contrary view. In a sense, Noelle-Neumann's model is a spiral within a spiral, the one an assertion, the other a withdrawal into a silence as the assertion grows stronger. In particular, note the arrows at the right hand side of the model. In relation to others around them, those holding 'different' opinions and ATTITUDES grow more and more isolated. Thus a spiral of silence on the part of individual members of the public reflect the spiral of dominance represented by the media.

Professor Noelle-Neumann's definition of public opinion is that 'which can be voiced in public without fear of sanctions

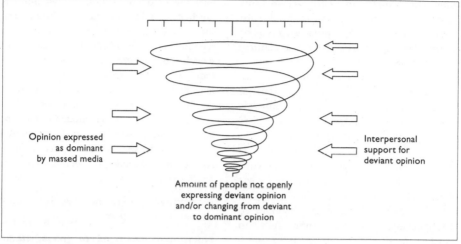

Noelle-Neumann's spiral of silence model of public opinion, 1974

and upon which action in public can be based . . . voicing opposite opinions, or acting in public accordingly, incurs the danger of isolation'. The model prompts the query whether the public merely holds back from expressing diverging or contrary views, but continues to hold them, or whether attitudes have actually been changed as a result of dominant media voices. See COMMUNICATION MODELS.

Noise Impedance or barrier between the sending and receiving of communication signals. C.E. Shannon and W. Weaver in *The Mathematical Theory of Communication* (US: University of Illinois Press, 1949) posit two levels of noise problems: level A, **engineering noise** and, at the higher level B, **semantic noise**. Level A is physical and technical and is defined as any distortion of MEANING occurring in the communication process which is not intended by the source, but which affects the reception of the MESSAGE-carrying signals and their clarity. The semantic level is 'noise' or impedance in terms of codes – linguistic, personal, psychological, cultural, etc. Later writers have identified *psychological noise* as a category in its own right. See COMMUNICATION MODELS.

Non-Aligned News Pool World-wide, non-profit-making news agency brought into existence by a decision of the Fifth Non-Aligned Summit Conference in Colombo, August 1976. 85 nations undertook to share information from their respective news gathering agencies with the aim of achieving greater balance in the reporting of events and development in non-aligned countries. The News Pool has been useful, but its potential has been limited by the competition offered by major NEWS AGENCIES and by the political situation in many countries where governments censor the free flow of information. See MEDIA IMPERIALISM.

Non-verbal behaviour: repertoire A useful classification scheme for the repertoire of non-verbal behaviour is suggested by American authors Paul Ekman and Wallace V. Friesen in 'The repertoire of nonverbal behaviour: categories, origins, usage and coding' in *Semiotica* 1 (1969). Their five categories of non-verbal movement are: emblem, illustrators, affect displays, regulators and adaptors.

Emblems are non-verbal behaviours which directly suggest specific words or phrases, usually without vocal accompaniment. Thus the beckoning first finger is the emblem for 'Come here'. Emblems are short-cut communication signals useful in many ways, especially where verbal communication is difficult or inappropriate, for example when a person is thumbing a lift.

Illustrators accompany and reinforce verbal messages – the nod of the head, a supportive smile, leaning forward to show interest, sketching something in the air with finger or hand, to give a point emphasis or clarity. Illustrators tend to be less culture-specific than emblems.

Affect displays are movements of the face and body which hold emotional MEANING: disappointment, rage, happiness, hopeful-ness, shock, etc.; indeed our whole *body language* constitutes affect displays.

For Ekman and Friesen, *regulators* are non-verbal actions which monitor and con-trol the communication of another indivi-dual. These can take the form of encouragement of the other person to go on speaking, to explain more fully, to quicken up, slow down, or get to the point. Here we use nods, smiles, grunts, ah-ha's; we shake our heads, we glance away, blink, pucker lips. Equally we can employ regula-tors in a negative sense by using non-verbal behaviours to discourage the other person from talking.

Adaptors are generally habitual beha-viours used to make a person feel more at ease in communication interactions: twist-ing a lock of hair, scratching, stroking (the hair, the chin, etc.), wringing hands, turning a ring round the finger, fiddling with jew-ellery, playing with matches – actions which are more private than public and are likely to undergo some modification when the private actions extends into a public domain. See COMMUNICATION, ·NON-VERBAL; GESTURE; PROXEMICS.

Non-verbal communication See COMMU-NICATION, NON-VERBAL.

Non-verbal vocalizations In communi-cation a number of sounds are used that are not speech but which convey important information contributing to the overall meaning of the message being conveyed. At times these sounds communicate a message without the need for accompanying speech.

Michael Argyle in *Bodily Communication* (UK: Methuen, 1988) identifies some of the main non-verbal vocalizations. There are those linked to speech which aid the under-standing and regulating of speech. These include prosodic signals, like the raising of pitch to indicate that what is being said is a question; synchronizing signals, such as the

lowering of pitch to indicate that one has finished speaking for the time being; and speech disturbances such as stutters and repetitions. Some are more independent of speech but communicate emotions, atti-tudes or other social information which may affect the encoding and decoding of the message. These include emotional noises such as cries and laughter; paralin-guistic noises which convey emotional information by such means as pitch, volume and speed; and aspects of the personal voice quality and ACCENT.

Normative acceptance See ACCEPTANCE: NORMATIVE AND PRAGMATIC.

Normative theories of mass media Building on an early work by American media analysts G.F. Siebert, T. Peterson and Wilbur Schramm, *Four Theories of the Press* (US: University of Illinois Press, 1956), Denis McQuail posits six normative theories of the mass media. In *Mass Communication Theory: An Introduction* (UK: Sage, 1983), McQuail lists (1) Authoritarian Theory; (2) Free Press Theory; (3) Social Responsibility Theory; (4) Soviet Media Theory; (5) Devel-opment Media Theory and (6) Democratic-Participant Theory.

By normative, we mean how the media *should* be, what is to be expected of them rather than what necessarily happens in practice; and it is out of the political, cul-tural and economic context that the norma-tive principles arise. Central to the normative theory is the way the media 'behave' in relation to the state, and the dominant expectations that the state has of the role of the media. The Authoritarian Theory thus appertains in a state in which PRESS or BROADCASTING freedoms not only do not exist but are not considered – by those in power, or those who support them in power – desirable even as ideals.

What Siebert *et al.* call 'Libertarian theory' McQuail terms the Free Press Theory, which is considered the chief legit-imating principle for the print media in liberal democracies. Free and public expres-sion is, implies this theory, the best way to arrive at the truth and expose error. It is a principle enshrined in the First Amendment of the American Constitution. This states that 'Congress shall make no law . . . abridging the freedom of speech of the press'. McQuail's analysis of this principle in practice is well worth noting, for he asks searching questions about *whose* freedom; about monopoly tendencies; about the close identification of notions of freedom with profit and private ownership.

The Social Responsibility Theory believes in freedom so long as it is harnessed to responsibility. Independence is desirable only so long as it is reconcilable with an obligation to society. In this sense, the media are perceived as fulfilling a role of public stewardship. They are the watchdogs of the common good against government or private abuse of power or corruption. There is an emphasis on neutrality and balance; most of all, a belief in media *accountability* to society.

Soviet Media Theory (worth noting even though the Soviet system has passed away) derives from the postulates of Marx, Engels and Lenin. Here, the media serve the interests of the socialist state, the state being an embodiment of all the members of a classless society. Because the media are *of* the people, they belong *to* the people. In practice, of course, they belong to the people's LEADERSHIP. The tasks of media are to socialize the people into desirable NORMS as defined in Marxist doctrine; to educate, inform, motivate and mobilize in the aims and aspirations of a socialist society.

Development Media Theory has arisen out of special needs in the Third World developing nations (See MacBRIDE COMMISSION; MEDIA IMPERIALISM; NEW WORLD INFORMATION ORDER). This theory eschews *bad news* theory and favours positive reporting on the grounds that for developing nations, often struggling for economic survival in competition with Western industrialized countries, reporting of disasters and setbacks can substantially injure the process of nation building.

The Democratic-Participant Media Theory emphasises the individual rights of access, of citizen and minority GROUPS, to the media, in fact the right *to* communicate; to be served by the media according to a more democratic determination of need. Thus the theory opposes the concentration of ownership and rejects the role of AUDIENCE as tame receiver. Media should be answerable, free of government or big-business intervention, small-scale, interactive and participative (See CAMPAIGN FOR PRESS AND BROADCASTING FREEDOM; COMMUNITY RADIO; RIGHT OF REPLY).

In a later publication, 'Mass media in the public interest: towards a framework of norms for media performance' in *Mass Media and Society*, eds. James Curran and Michael Gurevitch (UK: Edward Arnold, 1991), McQuail re-examines the validity of normative models because 'attempts to formulate consistent "theories" of the press' become increasingly difficult to sustain 'when media technologies and distribution systems are multiplying and when there is less consensus about basic values than in the past'. The dissolution of the Soviet Union is a case in point, though it is arguable that the 'Marxist' Media Theory might continue to apply in China and Cuba.

McQuail proffers a set of defining *principles* by which media *performance* can be judged, and these relate to community VALUES. He cites the following as *Public Communication Values*: (1) **Freedom**, acquiring its public definition through the independent status of the media, public access to channels and diversity of supply; (2) **Equality**, which concerns openness, access and objectivity (characterized by neutrality, fairness and truth); and (3) **Order**, a classification relating both to order in the sense of solidarity and in the sense of control (the one operating bottom upwards, as it were, the other top downwards). The principles interrelate, interact and are obviously in constant conflict with one another. McQuail acknowledges 'deep fissures and inconsistencies, depending on how they [the principles] are interpreted'.

However, the application of these principles to the changing patterns of media operation provide 'the essential building blocks for a quite comprehensive, flexible and changing "social theory of media", relevant to our times and of practical value in the ever widening circle of public discussion of the role of mass media in society'. See McQUAIL'S ACCOUNTABILITY OF MEDIA MODEL, 1997.

Norms Shared expectations or standards of behaviour within a particular social group or society. Any type of established group will have norms, both peculiar to itself and shared with the wider community. Of those norms widely accepted in a society, some will operate on a high, some on a low CONSENSUS. Any individual's perception and interpretation of experience will be influenced by the norms of the social groups and society to which he/she belongs. Individuals generally take such norms for granted. Communication between individuals likewise reflects certain norms, such as those of grammar and style of writing or norms of conduct which guide social INTERACTION.

Norms arise from such interaction between various individuals and social groups. Once developed, they are passed on through SOCIALIZATION to new members. Norms are not static: they are subject to renegotiation. They play a significant part in maintaining the social position of particular groups and individuals and constitute an influential agent of informal social control.

The media, as agents of communication and socialization, are in a position to both reinforce general societal norms and express the norms of certain social groups. In addition, the media have the potential to *shape* expectations of behaviour, particularly with regard to individuals or groups with whom the viewer, listener or reader is unfamiliar. It is this potential that has aroused considerable research interest. See CULTURE; MALE-AS-NORM; VALUES.

Northcliffe revolution New schooling in the late 19th c. in the UK following the Foster Education Act of 1870 created a rapidly expanding readership of literature and news. Alfred Charles William Harmsworth (1865–1922), later Lord Northcliffe, perhaps the most dynamic and extraordinary of the PRESS barons, built a press empire on the new flood-tide of literacy. Creator of the *Daily Mail* (1896) and the *Daily Mirror* (1903), Northcliffe combined a marked 'popular-educator' emphasis with a marketing sense which was energetic, imaginative, daring and ruthless. Northcliffe represents the funda-mental shift towards the exploitation of, and increasing dependence upon, ADVERTIS-ING as a means of newspaper finance.

Publicity was everything. Rivalry between papers, in terms of sensation-seeking and attention-grabbing stunts resembled – as it continues to do today – the Battle of the Titans. Raymond Williams in *The Long Revolution* (UK: Chatto & Windus, 1961) says, 'The true "Northcliffe Revolution" is less an innovation in actual journalism than a radical change in the economic basis of newspapers, tied to the new kind of advertising'.

By 1908 Northcliffe's press empire included the *Mail*, the *Mirror*, *The Times*, two Sunday papers (*Observer* and *Dispatch*) and an evening paper (*News*) plus a host of periodicals such as *Tit-Bits* and *Answers* (whose circulation had leapt from 12,000 at its inception to 352,000 two years later).

Though the so-called Northcliffe revolution was chiefly characterized by the employment of new technology, the drive for mass circulations and the wholesale reliance on advertising as the prime source of press revenue, the 'flavour' of that revolution must not be overlooked – that is, the STYLE and content emanating from the Press Barons themselves. James Curran and Jean Seaton in *Power Without Responsibility: The Press and Broadcasting in Britain* (UK: 5th edition, Routledge, 1997), write 'Northcliffe and Beaverbrook shaped the entire content of their favourite papers, including their layout'. When *The Times* changed the place in the paper of the weather report, Northcliffe raged '. . . if it's moved again, whoever does it is fired'. Curran and Seaton speak of how the personal tastes of the Barons influenced the popular journalism of the time: 'Northcliffe had a lifelong obsession with torture and death: he even kept an aquarium containing a goldfish and a pike, with a dividing partition, which he would lift up when he was in need of diversion.' He told staff of the *Daily Mail* to find 'one murder a day'.

Meddling with the content by newspaper proprietors was not, of course, new. It had gone on throughout the 19th c., but then interference had focused mainly upon political matters. What was different with Northcliffe and his ilk was that the new proprietors meddled in *everything*. See NEWSPAPERS, ORIGINS.

NVC See COMMUNICATION, NON-VERBAL (NVC).

Object See SIGN.

Objectivity Professor Stuart Hall has expressed the view that objectivity, 'like impartiality, is an operational fiction' (in 'Media power: the double bind', *Journal of Communication*, Autumn 1984). In examining the media, analysts encounter the Famous Four: balance, CONSENSUS, IMPARTIALITY and objectivity, upon which all good reporting is said to be based. The questions arising from this precept are: balance between what and what? consensus among whom? Impartiality in what sense? Objectivity in whose eyes? Considering the complex processes of MEDIATION between an event and its report in media form, is it possible to have value-free information?

'All edited or manipulated symbolic reality', says Hall, 'is impregnated with values, viewpoints, implicit theorizings, commonsense assumptions.' When there are differences between what is objective and what is not, whose opinion wins the day? Hall says of consensus that it is 'structured dominance', that is, the prevailing definition usually rests with the POWER ELITE, the 'power-ideology complex' in any society whose control of and influence upon the media gives them a greater say in the definitions of objectivity. See CULTURAL APPARATUS; DIFFERENTIAL PERCEPTION; ELITE; HEGEMONY; MACHINERY OF REPRESENTATION.

Object language According to Gail and Michele Myers in *The Dynamics of Human Communication* (US: McGraw-Hill, 1985) this term refers to 'the meanings you attribute to objects with which you surround yourself'. These objects might be items of DRESS, e.g. clothes, hairstyle, fashion accessories; your house; your furniture and so on. These and many other objects may say something about you to others: they can all be part of your SELF-PRESENTATION. These objects may not of course always convey to

others the message you wish them to. Others may not be aware of the symbolic value of the objects or simply read into them different meanings than the ones intended. You may of course be unaware yourself of messages that you may be sending to others through the objects you have. Object language may be particularly important when people are forming FIRST IMPRESSIONS of one another. A great deal of advertising certainly works on the assumption that consumer objects have as their main appeal a symbolic rather than a purely functional value.

In their book *Understanding and Sharing: An Introduction to Speech Communication* (US: Brown, 1979, reprinted 1985), authors Judy Cornelia Pearson, Paul Edward Nelson and Donald Yoder use the term **objectics**, the study of 'clothing, adornments, hairstyles, cosmetics and other artefacts that we carry with us or possess'. Object language conveys information about our age, sex, status, role, personality, relationships with groups and with other people, psychological and emotional state, self-concept, and the 'physical climate in which we live'. See COMMUNICATION, NON-VERBAL (NVC); SELF-CONCEPT.

Obscene signals See INSULT SIGNALS.

Obscenity and film censorship See WILLIAMS COMMITTEE REPORT ON OBSCENITY AND FILM CENSORSHIP, 1979.

Obsolescence Generally, anything passing out of date or out of use. In a communications sense, it refers to the link between social habits and media-using habits. Obsolescence can be defined as the abandoning of formerly institutionalized modes of conduct related to some established cultural activity.

Occupying powers In August 1993 TV playwright Dennis Potter, dying of cancer, delivered his valediction on the trends in UK media, and in particular, BROADCASTING, in the James MacTaggart Lecture at the Edinburgh International Festival. His theme centred around what he termed 'occupying powers' that is, managers of media driven by the criteria of the marketplace, where notions of aesthetic quality or public service were secondary to the tyranny of accountancy. With special focus on the management imperatives at the BBC, Potter spoke of 'strange new generations of broadcasting managements and their proprietors' responsible for a 'one-way system of communication' in which management 'trims down its staff as fast as it loses viewers'.

Potter said this new management culture can be seen as 'a model for the wider society in which all of us live'.

The Occupying Powers, at the BBC and in all other areas of society where the service ethic has been overhauled and diminished, have created a 'near-fatal crisis' of 'palpable ambivalence and doubt, where you pretend to be the commercial business you cannot be'. 'Our television has been ripped apart and falteringly re-assembled by politicians who believe that value is a monetary term only, and that a cost-accountant is thereby the most suitable adjudicator of what can and cannot be seen on our screens. And these accountants or their near-clones are employed by new kinds of Media Owners who try to gobble up everything in their path.'

Œuvre French for 'work', generally the complete works of an artist, writer, composer, etc. The word refers to the work of the mind as well as of hand and eye. Thus we may refer to the *œuvre* of Pablo Picasso (1891–1973) and mean not only the items of his work – paintings, sculpture, pottery – but, by implication, the nature or character of that work. See OPUS.

Official Secrets Act Born in a spy scare during the Agadir crisis of 1911, reinforced in 1920 during the Troubles in Ireland, given further power as war broke out in 1939, the Act censors information – access to it, and expression of it – which might be of use to the nation's enemies. It is easier to define what the Act does not cover rather than what it does. Without question, it is the single most comprehensive weapon of CENSORSHIP with regard to the activities of government in the UK, and has few parallels in the 'Free' world.

In January 1988 Conservative MP Richard Shepherd introduced a private member's bill into the House of Commons designed to reform Section 2 of the Act. Shepherd's Protection of Official Information Bill, while confirming present provisions protecting defence and natural security secrets, would have reduced the catch-all powers exercised by government under Section 2. Ministers would no longer have the exclusive right to decide that disclosure of information would damage the national interest. The government proved adamant: secrets were government business. A three-line whip was placed on the vote – at which more than 70 Tory MPs refused to vote as instructed. The bill was killed by a narrow majority of 37. Tory rebel MP and former Prime Minister Edward Heath called it a 'tarnished victory'.

In June of the same year, the government White Paper, *Reform of Section 2 of the Official Secrets Act, 1911*, was published, with the declared intention of trimming the areas defined as secret under Section 2 and clarifying what constitutes a breach of secrecy. Home Secretary Douglas Hurd claimed a 'liberalizing' of the law. However, critics, including MPs on both sides of the House, judged the new provisions to be potentially more draconian than the ones they were to replace. In particular, the new Official Secrets Act of 1990 rejects *public interest defence*, even in cases where the information concerns corruption or other forms of criminality. Brian Raymond, solicitor to civil servant Clive Ponting who was unsuccessfully prosecuted under the Act for revealing information about the sinking of the *Belgrano* during the Falklands War, said 'The obliteration of the public interest defence . . . amounts to a licence to cover up Government wrong-doing'. See D-NOTICES; SECRECY; FREEDOM OF INFORMATION; SPYCATCHER AFFAIR.

Oligopolization Oligarchy is government by a small exclusive CLASS or GROUP; in media terms, *oligopolization* is the process of communication systems falling into the hands of a small exclusive group of owners or corporations.

Omnimax Spectator-surrounding FILM projection technique developed, like IMAX, in Canada from a system invented by an Australian, Ron James. Though there are several Omnimax screens in North America, the first in Europe – and the largest screen in the world – operates at the 55 hectare Paris exhibition complex, Cité des Sciences et de L'Industrie at Porte La Villette, which opened in 1986.

La Gèode offers a projection screen covering 10,000 square feet and surrounds the spectators with a complete hemisphere, exceeding the normal field of vision. Like Imax, Omnimax uses 70 mm film which passes through the camera horizontally producing a 5 × 7 cm film image – approximately nine times the image area on ordinary cinema film. Camera and projector use a 25 mm fish-eye lens with a scope of 172 degrees. A massive light source is required to project such a gigantic picture and Omnimax has a 15 kW water-cooled xenon lamp. See TECHNOLOGY OF THE MEDIA.

One-step, two-step, multi-step flow models of communication Basically these are refinements of the HYPODERMIC NEEDLE MODEL OF COMMUNICATION. The one-step model ignores the role of the OPINION LEADER in the flow of communication and presents the view that the mass media communicate directly to a mass audience. There is no suggestion, however, that the messages reach all receivers equally or that they have the same effect on each individual in the audience. The model takes into account the influence of an individual's perception, memory and SELECTIVE EXPOSURE on his/her particular interpretation of a message. SALIENCE – or the factor of prominence – is also considered to be an important variable in the model.

A study conducted by Paul Lazarsfeld and others of the 1940 presidential election in the US threw doubt on the validity of the one-step theory. Reporting in *The People's Choice* (US: Duell, Sloan & Pearce, 1944), the authors found little evidence of the direct influence of the media; indeed people seemed more influenced by face-to-face contact with others. Lazarsfeld and his fellow researchers suggested that the flow of communication to the individual is often directed through an opinion leader who plays a vital role in both spreading and interpreting the information. They thus

proposed a **two-step model** of communication flow which later research has found to be generally useful. In highlighting the importance of the *social context* of the receiver in the process of the interpretation of mass communication messages this model differs significantly from earlier ones. It presents the mass audience as being composed of interacting and responsive individuals rather than of the socially isolated, passive atoms of earlier theories.

The **multi-step model** is a development of the other two, allowing for the sequential relaying of a MESSAGE. It is not specific about the number of steps there will be in the relaying process nor does it specify that messages must originate from a source and then pass straight through the agencies of the mass media. The model suggests a variable number of relays in the communication process and that the receivers may receive the message at various stages along the relay NETWORK. The exact number of steps in the process depends upon the following: (1) the intentions of the source; (2) the availability of the mass media; (3) the extent of audience exposure to agencies of communication; (4) the nature of the message; (5) the importance of the message to the audience.

The model has often been used in recent research. Its advantage is that it allows the researcher to account for different variables in different communication situations. See COMMUNICATION MODELS.

Onomatopoeia Words which imitate actual sounds are *onomatopoeic*, such as *bang, thud, crackle, hiss, quack* and *twitter*. They are mostly invented words. The first ever attempts at spoken LANGUAGE were very probably onomatopoeic and such words continue to be invented, not a few of them (*zap*, for example) starting life in COMICS and CARTOONS.

Open, closed texts Italian semiologist Umberto Eco has made this useful separation between texts which are varyingly shaped – to permit little interpretation on the part of audience (*closed* texts) or allow plenty of room for interpretation (*open* texts). A work of art – a poem, a painting, a piece of sculpture, for example – would represent an open text in that the intention of the writer, painter or sculptor is to express ideas or feelings which may be interpreted in different ways and at different levels.

The open text invites a sense of participation in the reader or viewer and the interaction which occurs between creator, creation and audience is one in which 'right answers' are less important than the possibility of a *proactive* response; and this may be subject to flux in differing instances and at varying times. PROPAGANDA would constitute closed text in that there is a rigorously *preferred reading*: the decoder is expected to receive the message, and register its MEANING as intended by the communicator. Any divergence from acceptance would, to quote another term of Eco's, represent ABERRANT DECODING. See ANCHORAGE.

Opera omnia Latin for 'All his works', the term denotes a total ban on an author's writings imposed by the Roman Catholic *Index Librorum Prohibitorum*, first issued in 1559. A few such prohibited writers have been David Hume, Emile Zola, Jean-Paul Sartre and Alberto Moravia. See CENSORSHIP; INDEX.

Opinion leader Someone able to influence informally other individuals' attitudes and/or behaviour in a desired way with relative frequency. He/she is a type of informal leader. Opinion leadership is earned and maintained by the individual's technical competence, sociability and conformity to the NORMS of the SOCIAL SYSTEM. When such leaders are compared to their followers several characteristics are of note: opinion leaders are more exposed to all forms of external communication; more COSMOPOLITE; of a higher social status; and more innovative. Opinion leaders are widely thought to play a vital role in the spreading of new ideas, VALUES and beliefs.

An opinion leader whose range of influence is limited to one specific topic exercises **Monomorphic opinion leadership**. This type of leadership is thought to be typical of modern, industrial societies as the complex technological base of such societies results in a sophisticated division of labour and considerable specialization of ROLES. An opinion leader whose influence

covers a wide range of topics exercises **Polymorphic opinion leadership**. This is generally thought to be more common in traditional societies. A respected, elderly member of a village, for example, might be consulted on a variety of matters ranging from marriage problems to methods of harvesting.

Opinion poll The increasing reportage of opinion poll findings after the 1945 general election in the UK was a noticeable innovation in the media's coverage of political ISSUES, and in particular in its coverage of election campaigns. Typically, such a poll is designed to illustrate 'public opinion' on a topical issue and consists of a breakdown of responses, from a SAMPLE to pre-set questions. During election campaigns polls are used primarily for forecasting the results. Some researchers have expressed the view that polls may also *influence* the outcome of a campaign, especially when their findings are well publicized. The publication of poll findings is also thought to influence opinions on specific political issues, particularly if the findings suggest a CONSENSUS of opinion.

Oppositional code See DOMINANT, SUBORDINATE, RADICAL; POLYSEMY.

Optical fibre cable See FIBRE-OPTIC TECHNOLOGY.

Opus Latin for 'work', a term most often applied to musical compositions in order of their creation (e.g. Beethoven's 9th Symphony is Opus 125).

Oral culture An oral CULTURE or SUB-CULTURE is one in which essentially most communication is by word of mouth. Pictures may also be used as a supplement but reading and writing play a minor role in the communication process.

Orality: primary and secondary In *Orality and the Technology of the Word* (US: Cornell University Press, 1982) Walter Ong in investigating the nature of the shift between oral and literate cultures differentiates between 'primary' and 'secondary' orality. The first refers to and describes pre-literate societies, the second results from the introduction of electronic media into literate societies.

Order, visions of See VISIONS OF ORDER.

Organization cultures In examining the NORMS, VALUES and practices of business organizations in his *Understanding Organizations* (UK: Penguin, 1993 edition). Charles B. Handy identifies four forms of organizational CULTURE that affect the nature or 'profile' of the organization and its patterns of communication. Each culture has, according to Handy, its own presiding deity. These are: (1) The **power culture**. This depends upon a central power source, with 'rays of power and influence' (and communication) spreading out from a central figure. Zeus, the chief of the gods of ancient Greece, who ruled by 'whim and impulse, by thunderbolt and shower of gold' is seen as the patron god of this culture. An example of such a culture is the self-made business person running his/her own company. Without such a 'spider', the web structure of the culture would collapse.

(2) The **role culture**. This is the classic bureaucracy, its model like a Greek temple, with the leadership – directors, governors, etc. represented by the pediment, the various organizational departments, the pillars of the temple and the workers at the base. Here, plainly, the communication process, following lines of authority, is vertical and chiefly one-way. Apollo, the god of reason, is seen as the patron god of this organization whose culture values logic and rationality.

(3) The **task culture**. This is a skills or ability orientated culture in which *what* an employee is capable of doing is more important than *who* he/she is in terms of position or role. The model is net-shaped, made up of interdependent strands; leadership is exchangeable according to the task in hand. This culture which is centred on task completion is not seen by Handy as having any one overall presiding deity but Athena, the warrior goddess, and Odysseus, the champion of commando leaders, would best reflect its ethos. This so-called *matrix* structure is characterized by very flexible channels of communication, horizontal rather than vertical in direction, and is responsive to change.

(4) The **person culture**. In terms of business organizations the rarest of the four. Here the organization exists only to serve the individuals within it. The model is of a cluster, a galaxy of individual stars, without hierarchical structures, constantly interchanging in form. Dionysus, the god of the 'self-oriented individual' is its ruling deity. As Handy says, 'Clearly not many organizations can exist with this sort of culture, since organizations tend to have objectives over and above the collective objectives of those who comprise them'. In its purest form, the *kibbutz* (small egalitarian Israeli community) is an example of the person culture. The *factors* Handy cites as influencing organizations cultures are: history and ownership; size; technology; goals and objectives; the environment and the people.

In *The Empty Raincoat* (UK: Arrow Books, 1995) Handy discusses a new model for organizations, based on the **Doughnut principle**, which he argues reflects the way in which the traditional models and cultures have changed and will continue to change in order to survive changes in the technological and economic environment.

The doughnut consists of a core surrounded by bounded space. It is 'an inside-out doughnut, one with the hole on the outside and the dough in the middle'. It is a 'conceptual doughnut, one for thinking with, not eating'. The core contains 'necessary jobs and necessary people'. These full-time employees often organize the activities of the bounded space which contains many other people working for the organization as flexible workers tied to the organization by flexible and often short-term contracts. Thus organizations will become much smaller in terms of the number of people they directly employ; consequently it is likely that more people will be self-employed or freelance workers. Within the television industry, for example, this method of working is now well established. See CASUALIZATION; PRODUCER CHOICE.

Orientalism Concept posed by Edward Said describing the STEREOTYPICAL image of Asia held by those in European cultures. Representation of the Orient arises from ETHNOCENTRIC attitudes with an imperialist ancestry, and results in a projected image of Asia and Asians as being exotic ('the lure of the Orient'), indolent, untrustworthy and devious; in short a misrepresentation by Western commentators and analysts, of OTHER. In *Orientalism* (UK: Routledge, 1978), Said raises the question whether anything can be truly or objectively represented. See also Said's *Culture and Imperialism* (UK: Chatto & Windus, 1993).

Orientation Orientation is an element of non-verbal communication and refers to the angle at which people sit or stand in relation to one another. Orientation can be used to convey a range of messages about relationships, mood, personality and social context. For example, if people are in a potentially hostile or competitive situation they usually face each other head on. See COMMUNICATION, NON-VERBAL.
* Cynthia Stohl, *Organizational Communication: Connectedness in Action* (US: Sage, 1995).

Other A person, persons, group, social class, community, race or nation who are not 'us' and who are defined by their difference from us; yet who by that difference contribute to our concept of self, as individuals, members of groups etc. There is the ranking of *generalized* other, as illustrated by the statement, 'Other people might like to shop on a Sunday, but for me it is still a day of rest'. Also, there are SIGNIFICANT OTHERS. These may be people, or types of people, whom we respect and whose opinions carry weight with us. They count in our lives, and they may be real or fictitious. They are often, or have the potential to be, ROLE models.

'Other' in general media use represents, by and large, those of whom we disapprove, dislike, fear; and the popular media use of Other works in *binary* fashion (See WEDOM, THEY-DOM). In everyday communication, Other plays a key role in jokes – Irish jokes, Scottish jokes, etc. – each one relying for its effect upon a CONSENSUS about the negative qualities of the butt of that joke. In TABLOID press headlines name-calling is a favourite device to put down Other and consequently boost the sense of superiority of Us over Them. When Other is perceived as a threat, the demarcation lines become more forcible; and of course in sport, Other is always the opposition – at which

point Germans become 'Krauts' and the French become 'Frogs'.

Other, then, is almost invariably those in opposition, those who are different in appearance or CULTURE and are seen in some way as a challenge to 'our' ways.

Outer-inner directed See VALS TYPOLOGY.

Out-take Piece of FILM which is not actually used in the completed version.

Overhearing Kurt H. Wolff in *The Sociology of Georg Simmel* (US: Free Press, 1950) uses this expression to describe how recipients of messages may proceed, usually below the level of awareness, to select certain parts for special attention, often distorting them, while at the same time overlooking ('overhearing') other parts entirely. In short, the human organism perceives to a considerable degree what it wants to perceive. See COCKTAIL PARTY PROBLEM; DIFFERENTIAL PERCEPTION; PERCEPTION; SELECTIVE EXPOSURE.

Overkill signals See SHORTFALL SIGNALS.

Ownership and control of mass media See MEDIA CONTROL; PRESS BARONS; OCCUPYING POWERS.

Oz Trial The longest-ever obscenity trial in the UK, lasting 26 days in the summer of 1971, centred on the *Oz School Kids Issue* (*Oz* 28). The three editors, Richard Neville, Felix Dennis and Jim Anderson were eventually acquitted on the most serious charge – that of conspiring to corrupt the morals of children, but a majority of ten to one of the trial jury found *Oz* guilty of publishing an obscene article, sending such articles through the post and having such articles for profit and gain.

Oz Publications Ink Ltd. received a total fine of £1000 with £1250 costs. Neville got a 15-month jail sentence and a recommendation that he be deported (he was Australian). Anderson received 12 months and Dennis nine. See CENSORSHIP; LITTLE RED SCHOOLBOOK; SPYCATCHER CASE.

Packaging The STYLE and the framework within which TV programmes are presented on our screens: good-looking announcers or interviewers, titling, music, the tailoring of programmes to suitable lengths, indeed any form of image-making for a media product. The word gives emphasis to the connection between the manufacture and sale of goods and the making and presentation of media products. Stuart Hood in *Hood on Television* (UK: Pluto Press, 1980) refers to TV announcers as the 'sales people of the air'.

Panopticon See SURVEILLANCE SOCIETY.

Paparazzo Aggressive, prying and often unscrupulous freelance photographer who specializes in taking pictures of celebrities; pursuing them wherever they go, armed with thick skin and zoom lenses. The word is an Italian – Calabrian – surname. It was suggested by writer Ennio Flaiano as a name for a character in Federico Fellini's *La Dolce Vita* (The Sweet Life), made in 1960.

Paparazzi were accused of hounding Diana, Princess of Wales, to her death in 1997 and the PRESS at that time made a number of resolutions to curb the use of 'intrusive' pictures.

Paper Tiger TV Media collective based in New York from 1981; an example of 'action' or 'alternative' media; a networking system of access and production, generally run on a volunteer basis, it aims to encourage grass-roots resistance to the dominance of the media industry. In 1995 Paper Tiger received a grant to distribute programming by SATELLITE to public access centres around the US. Deep Dish TV has become a nation-wide organization with a steering committee and small full-time staff. Among programmes transmitted by Deep Dish TV are *Green Screen: Grassroots Views of the Environmental Crisis*, *Behind Censorship: The Assault on Civil Liberties* and *Water, Oil and Power*.

* Tony Dowmunt (ed.), *Channels of Resistance: Global Television and Local Empowerment* (UK: BFI/Channel 4, 1993).

Paperwork Reduction Act, 1980 On the face of it, a welcome onslaught on the overproduction of bureaucratic paperwork; yet critics of this piece of American legislation view it with a degree of cynicism. In

'The tug-of-war over the First Am ment' published in *Questioning The M A Critical Introduction* (UK: Sage, 1990), edited by John Downing, Ali Mohammadi and Annabelle Sreberny-Mohammadi, Donna A. Demac and John Downing write that the Act was 'promptly used to curtail public access to government information'; in short, backdoor CENSORSHIP. Supervised and guided by the Office of Management and Budget, government agencies have used the Act to transfer the management of key information programmes to the private sector, thus furthering the retreat from public to private of information services.

Demac and Downing say that by 1985 'one-fourth of all government information was made available only in computer tapes, which put its utilization out of the financial and technical reach of the vast majority of citizens'.

Paradigm (paradigmic) Commonly used in the social sciences, the term refers to a framework of explanation within which theories from various schools of thought in a discipline are located and from which research operates. For example, James Curran in 'Rethinking the media as a public sphere' in Peter Dahlgren and Colin Sparks, eds. *Communication and Citizenship* (UK: Routledge, 1991) has identified three such paradigms which seek to explain the relationship between the mass media and the POWER structure of societies in which they operate: the Marxist or Neo-Marxist, the Liberal-Pluralist and the Radical Democratic.

Those of the Marxist or Neo-Marxist school tend to argue that it is those who own and control economic capital who are at the heart of a society's power structure and that such a position allows them to exercise power over cultural institutions, such as the mass media, in order to better pursue their economic goals. Media professionals may view themselves as autonomous but, it is argued, they have been socialized into and have internalized the norms and values of the dominant class. Thus from this perspective, a key ideological contribution made by the mass media is that it provides the AUDIENCE with frameworks for interpreting messages which encourage it to construct readings that are consistent with the interests of the dominant class. Critics of this tradition have argued, though, that it overlooks the degree of leeway which does exist for journalists to ask awkward questions and the need to consider the audience and the audience's role in constructing the meaning of mass media messages.

A competing paradigm is that offered by the Liberal-Pluralist tradition of media research, which argues that the mass media is and should be composed, rightly, of a number of competing groups operating within a free market, though subject to state intervention when this is deemed in the public interest. Groups within the mass media tend to be seen as in competition for power and influence within society. Media professionals, such as journalists, are seen to enjoy a considerable degree of autonomy over the production of media artefacts. Within this tradition some perceive the media to have a responsibility within society to behave as a WATCHDOG whose role it is to provide an arena for wide public debate about civil issues, facilitating the articulation of a plurality of views and values and in so doing to allow private individuals to exercise a form of informal control over the state. This tradition has, however, been subject to much criticism for its failure to address the narrow social base from which media professionals are often drawn resulting in women and those from working-class and/or ethnic backgrounds being under-represented; and the degree to which the political economy of media ownership, the culture of media organizations and the place of these organizations in the political economy of a society, influence the content and reading of media artefacts.

The Radical Democratic paradigm, according to James Curran, offers a synthesis between the other two paradigms. Whilst this paradigm acknowledges the links between the ownership and control of media institutions and that of other key institutions and that the free market tends to be skewed in favour of the dominant class, it does not perceive the links to be

so close that the media could be conceived as an arm of the ruling class. Rather the media is seen as, 'caught in the crossfire' providing 'a battleground between contending forces. The way in which the media responds to and mediates this conflict affects the balance of social forces and, ultimately, the distribution of rewards within society'. Journalists and media professionals are viewed as having day-to-day autonomy which allows them to make a difference and opens up the possibility for the committed radical journalism which would allow the media to act as a countervailing force and to further the cause of the less powerful. It also recognizes that not all journalists and media professionals work in media organizations which have one dominant owner and argues that those working in broadcasting and in commercial media where ownership is dispersed among a number of shareholders, may enjoy considerable freedom to criticize the powerful. The structure of the media, however, is seen as being in need of reform if it is to achieve its potential for providing diverse debate within a democratic society.

In LINGUISTICS, paradigm describes the set of relationships a linguistic unit – such as a letter or a word – has with other units in a specific context. The word is applicable in all SIGN systems, verbal, numerical, musical, etc. The alphabet is a paradigm, or set of signs, from which a choice is made to formulate the MESSAGE. A **syntagm** is a combination of the chosen signs, a chain that amounts to MEANING. In LANGUAGE we can describe the vocabulary we use as **paradigmic**, and the sentence that vocabulary is formed into, **syntagmic**.

All messages, therefore, involve *selection* from a paradigm and *combination* into a syntagm. All the units in a paradigm must share characteristics that determine the membership of that paradigm, thus letters in the alphabetic paradigm, numbers in the numerical paradigm, notes in the musical paradigm. Each unit within the paradigm must be clearly differentiable from other units; it must be characterized by *distinctive features*. Just as the paradigm is governed by shared characteristics and distinctive features, the syntagm is determined by rules or conventions by which the combination of paradigms is made – rules of grammar and syntax or, in music, rules of harmony. See SEMIOLOGY/SEMIOTICS.

Paralanguage See NON-VERBAL VOCALIZATIONS.

Parallel processing Our visual capacity allows us to process many images simultaneously – in parallel; to record both foreground and background actions. In contrast, speech capacity depends upon *serial processing*: we hear one word or phrase at a time and process it before proceeding to subsequent data.

Paraproxemics Term used to classify the way TV handles the space between people in its programmes, echoing and simulating the real-life use of space (see PROXEMICS) by individuals – for example, the close-up, medium range and distance camera shots paralleling the SPATIAL ZONES of intimate, personal and social space. Joshua Meyrowitz in 'Television and interpersonal behaviour: codes of perception and response' in G. Gumpert and R. Cathcart, eds., *Inter/Media: Interpersonal Communication in a Media World* (US/UK: Oxford University Press, 1979) writes, 'the way in which a person is framed' [by the TV camera] may suggest an interpersonal distance between that person and the viewer'. Distance, in fact, shapes viewer response, with the TV screen becoming 'a kind of "extended retina" for the viewer'.

Parasocial identification See PARASOCIAL INTERACTION.

Parasocial interaction The illusion, contributed to both by the performer and the audience in mass media communication, especially radio, TV and film, of an *interpersonal relationship* existing betwen them, free of MEDIATION. Characters (or persona) on air or film, actual or fictional, are often cited as being more 'real' to audiences than the real people they know.

In 'Mass communication and parasocial interaction: observation on intimacy at a distance', *Journal of Psychiatry*, 19 (1956), D. Horton and R.R. Wohl write, 'The persona offers, above all, a continuing relationship. His appearance is a regular and dependable event, to be counted on,

planned for, and integrated into the routines of daily life' and may be considered by his audience as 'a friend, counsellor, comforter, and model', but unlike all those real people around him, the persona is *changeless*. 'Typically, there are no challenges to a spectator's self . . . that cannot be met comfortably'.

Arguably the strongest relationship or interaction is that between audiences and fictitious characters, especially those in long-running series such as BBC Radio's *The Archers*, BBC TV's *EastEnders* or *Coronation Street* from Granada TV. Indeed, on occasion, what happens in these series, though entirely fictional, becomes a matter for national attention. Half the nation grieved – and a great many protested most passionately – when Grace Archer was burnt to death; and when that beloved villain of soap opera, JR of *Dallas* was shot, the incident was reported on BBC News. See BIBLIOTHERAPY.

Parental Guidance (PG) See CERTIFICATION OF FILMS.

Participant observation Some research evidence is collected by the researcher becoming a member of the group or social situation under observation. The researcher participates fully in the situation and those being observed may be unaware that he/she is a researcher. The advantage of this method of data collection is that the greater involvement of the researcher may facilitate an increased insight into and greater understanding of the behaviour being investigated. See ETHNOGRAPHIC (APPROACH TO AUDIENCE MEASUREMENT).

Partisan An adherent of a particular party or cause. The term is also used to describe actions as well as allegiances. Within media studies, much research has focused upon the political partisanship of the press and TV companies, that is, upon the degree to which they may support one or other political party or faction, and colour their political coverage accordingly. If such coverage gives space to the views of two factions or parties it is generally described as being **bipartisan**; if its tone is one of general disinterest, of being above party politics, it is described as being **anti-partisan**. Partisan perspectives may not, though, permeate political coverage only; they may pervade media presentations generally. See EFFECTS OF THE MASS MEDIA.

Passivity A long and widely held view of mass audiences is that they are lumpen, unreflective and essentially passive. There is little evidence for this, though assumptions carry weight, and are reflected in content selection and approach, regardless of evidence. The PILKINGTON REPORT 1962 indicated a crude view of audience response particularly to TV programmes, and it is difficult not to believe that *some* programmers regard their audiences as fields of turnips.

Modern media commentators insist on the diversity of response of audiences. James Curran and Jean Seaton in *Power Without Responsibility* (UK: Routledge, 5th edition, 1997) believe 'The public is not a passive empty box merely waiting to be filled with the injunctions of advertisers. How people react to what they see is determined by their class, age and the beliefs they already hold'. See AUDIENCE: ACTIVE AUDIENCE; AUDIENCE MEASUREMENT; EFFECTS OF THE MASS MEDIA; EMPOWERMENT; INTERACTIVITY; PLEASURE: ACTIVE AND REACTIVE; RESISTIVE READING.

Patriarchy Society ruled by or dominated by men; *patriarch* means father, thus patriarchal relates to a CULTURE shaped and governed in the interests of men, with women in a subordinate, and in some cases, subject, role. Patriarchy is reflected in customs, NORMS and VALUES, the law, education, commerce, industry, the arts, sport and, not least, LANGUAGE. Many commentators have also identified patriarchy as being assertively alive in the media, though at least at the operative (rather than managerial) level substantial advances have been made by women in journalism and broadcasting. While making it on to the media scene is a heartening challenge to male dominance, that, for women, is not the end of discrimination.

Liesbet van Zoonen in *Feminist Media Studies* (UK: Sage, 1994) refers to 'Gruesome anecdotes of women encountering blatant sexism'. Van Zoonen believes that whatever particular cultural form they may take, discriminatory attitudes towards women on the workfloor are common practice in media production world-wide.

Women's domestic and parental responsibilities prove to be tough obstacles to career progress – 'media work and motherhood have been made notoriously difficult to combine due to a lack of provision at the work place and to social values and beliefs'. See NEWS: THE 'MALENESS' OF NEWS.

Paternity of the text See TEXT: INTEGRITY OF THE TEXT.

Pauper press See UNDERGROUND PRESS.

PeaceNet See TELEDEMOCRACY.

Pejoration See MALE-AS-NORM.

'Pencil of Nature' Title of the first book ever illustrated with photographs, published in England in 1844, the work of William Henry Fox Talbot (1800–77), inventor of the CALOTYPE process of photo-printing. The range of photographs pasted into *The Pencil of Nature* was extraordinary and included intimate, informal studies of Talbot's household at his home, Laycock Abbey. See PHOTOGRAPHY, ORIGINS.

People meter Electronic recording device used to measure individual TV viewing habits. Each member of a family has a portable keypad very like the TV's remote control device. Linked to the home by telephone lines, the system's central computer correlates each viewer's number with demographical data already on record.

People's Communication Charter Proposed by Cees Hamelink in *World Communication: Disempowerment and Self-Empowerment* (UK: Zed Books, 1995) in the light of his vision that the globalization of communication threatens to further divide the information-rich from the information-poor, at the personal, community and national levels. The Charter provides a valuable text in which issues are highlighted, rights and responsibilities spelt out. The Preamble to the Charter opens with the affirmation that 'communication is basic to the life of individuals and peoples and that communication is crucial in the issues and crises which affect all members of the world community'. It is mindful 'that communication can be used to support the powerful and to victimize the powerless and that communication is fundamental to the shaping of the cultural environment of every society'.

Disempowerment is seen as a major trend; and it occurs through the 'withholding of information, by distorting information, by overwhelming people with overloads of information, or by obstructing people's access to communication channels'. In consequence the Charter urges support to enable people to develop their own communication channels through which they can speak for themselves. Under General Standards, Article 1 declares the 'conviction that all people are entitled to the respect of their dignity, integrity, equality, and liberty'. Article 2 asserts freedom of expression but aligned with that 'there should be free and independent channels of communication' on the basis that 'Free media are pluralist media'.

Article 3 speaks of the right to receive information 'about matters of public interest' and 'This includes the right to receive information which is independent of commercial and political interests'. Article 7 concerns the RIGHT OF REPLY, Article 8 speaks of the need to nurture a 'diversity of languages' and the need to 'create provisions for minority languages in the media'. Article 9 argues for the protection of people's cultural identity. In an Annexe to the fourth draft of the Charter Hamelink acknowledges contributions made by Howard Frederick, George Gerbner, David Goldberg, Wolfgang Kleinwächter, Kaarle Nordenstreng and students from Ohio State University, the American University at Washington, the University of Amsterdam and the Institute of Social Studies at the Hague. The author invites all further contributions on e-mail hamelink@antenna.nl.

Perception The process of becoming aware and making sense of the stimuli received from our environment by the senses: sight, hearing, smell, taste, and TOUCH. **Social perception** refers to the application of this process to our attempts to explain, understand, make judgments

about and predict the behaviour of other people.

Perception is selective. We are surrounded by many sensations but we tend to direct our attention to only a few of these. Our decision as to what to attend to can be influenced by environmental and personal factors: for example, *environmental* factors can include the intensity, size, motion or novelty of the stimuli whilst *personal* factors can include present needs and drives, physiological features, past experiences and learning – perceptual set – and personality. The influence of personal factors explains why individuals may pay attention to different stimuli, to different messages or parts of a message. See ATTITUDES; CULTURE; DIFFERENTIAL PERCEPTION; EMPATHY; EXPECTATIONS; FIRST IMPRESSIONS; HALO EFFECT; LABELLING PROCESS (AND THE MEDIA); MALE-AS-NORM; MORES; MOTIVATION; NORMS; PROJECTION; SAPIR-WHORF HYPOTHESIS; SELECTIVE EXPOSURE; SELF-CONCEPT; SELF-FULFILLING PROPHECY; STEREOTYPE; SUB-CULTURE; VALUES.

Performance See SELF-PRESENTATION.

Performatives Action words which indicate the nature of action through talk: *announce, insist, declare* or *denounce*. In the reporting of speech in NEWS, performatives often embody evaluative connotations, indicating approval on the part of the encoder or disapproval. 'The Minister *declined* to comment' carries with it marginally less disapproval than the statement 'The Prime Minister *refused* to comment'. The word *say* may be classified as a neutral performative unless it is contrasted with a performative used disapprovingly; thus 'The Management *say* their pay-offer is final, while the unions *claim* their actions will bring about further concessions'.

Periodicals for the study of media For the serious study of communication students have a right to expect college or university libraries to stock the US-based, but international publication, the *Journal of Communication* and the *European Journal of Communication*, both essential for the latest thinking and findings on all aspects of communication. The best-funded libraries will also stock *Communication Research, Discourse Studies, European Journal of*

Cultural Studies, International Journal of Cultural Studies, Journalism, Media, Culture and Society, and *New Media & Society,* all from the Sage Publications stable.

Periodicity Describes the time-scale of the schedules of news organizations; thus a daily newspaper has a 24-hour periodicity. The more the time-scale of a potential item of news coincides with the periodicity of the news organization, the more likely it is that the story will 'make the headlines'. Graham Murdock in 'Political deviance: the press presentation of a militant mass demonstration' in Stanley Cohen and Jock Young, eds., *The Manufacture of News* (UK: Constable, 1973 and subsequent editions), speaks of the 'event-orientation' of the daily newspaper – information which can be gathered, processed and dramatized within a 24-hour cycle (such as assassinations, clashes with the police, the speeches of politicians), stands a better chance of breaking through the news threshold than news which is gradual and undramatic. See NEWS VALUES.

Persistence of vision The realization that the eye retains an image for a split second after the object has passed gave birth to the cinema. The principle was first illustrated, and proved marketable, with toys of the 19th c. such as the THAUMATROPE – a disc with images on each side; when the disc was spun round the images merged into a single action. The ZOETROPE was a drum with illustrations of figures inside which, when spun round, conveyed the impression of movement. See CINEMATOGRAPHY, ORIGINS.

Persona See SELF-PRESENTATION.

Personal idiom Or idiosyncratic LANGUAGE; occurring in interpersonal relationships; serves the function of building relationship cohesiveness. Results of research into the use of personal idiom were published in an article 'Couples' personal idioms: exploring intimate talk' in the *Journal of Communication* (Winter, 1981) by Robert Hopper, Mark L. Knapp and Lorel Scott. Such idioms, they found, take the form of a range of idiomatic exchanges: partner nicknames: expressions of affection; labels for others outside the relationship; for use in confrontations; to deal with requests and routines;

sexual references and EUPHEMISMS; sexual invitations and teasing insults (or 'kidding').

Personalization One of the chief conventions of media reportage. Where a potential news item can be personalized it has a greater chance of being included than if it is difficult to translate into personality terms. The preference is for elite personalities. See NEWS VALUES.

John Lloyd in an article entitled 'The death of privacy: j'accuse !' (*New Statesman,* 5 March 1999) argues that this emphasis on the personal, evident for example in the media treatment of the relationship between the US President Clinton and Monica Lewinsky, a White House intern, has been at the expense of an exploration of policy and issues. He acknowledges that within TV news and current affairs it is, 'a received wisdom that only by personalizing a story can it be given meaning for a mass audience. Thus a story about public spending must find someone in pain on a hospital waiting list'. Lloyd warns 'the hazard of such stories is that the feeling swamps the understanding'.

Personalizing transformation Stuart Hall in 'The determination of news photographs' in Stanley Cohen and Jock Young, eds., *The Manufacture of News: Social Problems, Deviance and the Mass Media* (UK: Constable, 1981), discusses the way television news is *skewed* by the search for an angle from which to cover a story on the basis of available footage. One effect of this process is that television news tends to be person-orientated at the cost of giving focus to the underlying structural content of the news item, through what Hall termed a picture's 'personalizing transformation'. That is, the audience are deflected from considering the issues involved by their responses to the people they see in the coverage of the item on screen.

Personal space That which every individual feels easy in and which, if encroached upon, causes anxiety, tension or resistance. Personal space is fluid, and mobile, whereas **territorial space** tends to be stationary. S. Lyman and M. Scott in 'Territoriality: a neglected social dimension' in *Social*

Problems, 15 (1967) refer to personal space as 'the most private and inviolate of territories belonging to an individual'. See PROXEMICS.

Pester power See ADVERTISING: PESTER POWER.

Phatic (language) Derives from the Greek, 'phasis', utterance; a term finding its modern CONNOTATION in the phrase 'phatic communion ' coined by anthropologist Bronislaw Malinowski (1884–1942), meaning that part of communication which is used for establishing an atmosphere or maintaining social contact rather than for exchanging information or ideas. Phatic words and phrases have been called 'idiot salutations' and, when they comprise dialogue, 'two-stroke conversations'. Comments about the weather, enquiries about health, everyday exchanges, including nods, smiles, waves, are part of the phatic communion essential for 'oiling' or maintaining channels of communication.

Phatic LANGUAGE is central to human relationships; its significance can be best noted by its absence: you give a cheery 'hello' to a friend passing in the street to be greeted by stony silence; you halt your car to permit another motorist to go ahead of you, and he/she does not acknowledge your GESTURE. The response to such phatic neglect can be considerable. See JAKOBSON'S MODEL OF COMMUNICATION.

Phoneme The smallest unit in the sound system of a LANGUAGE. Each language can be shown to operate with a relatively small number of phonemes, some having as few as 15, others as many as 50. **Phonemics** is the study of the basic sounds of language.

Phone-tapping See PRIVACY.

Phonetics The science of human sound-making, especially sounds used in speech. Phonetics includes the study of articulation, acoustics or perception of speech, and the properties of specific languages.

Phonodisc First-ever VIDEO recording, developed by John Logie Baird (1888–1946) in 1928. This was a 10 inch 78 rpm record, in every way similar to the acoustic discs already being produced for conventional sound recording. Despite its novelty, the Phonodisc, coming so early in the age of

the development of TV, failed to succeed commercially.

Phonograph See GRAMOPHONE.

Phonology A branch of LINGUISTICS which studies the sound systems of languages. Its aim is to demonstrate the patterns of distinctive sound in spoken LANGUAGE and to make as general statements as possible about the nature of sound systems in languages throughout the world.

Photographic negativization See VISIONS OF ORDER.

Photography, origins Joseph Nicéphore Niépce (1765–1833) and his brother Claude were the first to fix images of the CAMERA OBSCURA by chemical·means in 1793, though the light sensitivity of silver nitrate had been known and written about as early as 1727 when Johann Heinrich Schulze, professor of anatomy at the University of Altdorf, published a paper indicating that the darkening of silver salts was due not to heat but to light.

1826 is generally recognized as the year in which the first photographic image was captured. Joseph Niépce's reproduction of a roof-top scene, on a pewter plate, he called Héliographie – sun drawing. In 1830 he teamed up with Louis Daguerre (1789–1851), theatrical designer and. co-inventor of the diorama. The death. of Niépce three years later left Daguerre to lead the field in France. He discovered that an almost invisible latent image could be developed using mercury vapour, thus reducing exposure time from around eight hours to between 20 and 30 minutes.

His DAGUERROTYPE was taken up by the French government in 1839, and elicited from Paul Delaroche the immortal line, 'from today, painting is dead!' In the UK astronomer Sir John Herschel (1792–1871) read a paper 'On the Art of Photography' to the Royal Society, accompanied by 23 photographs. He was the first to use the verb *to photograph* and the adjective *photographic*, in 1840 to identify *negative* and *positive* and 20 years later to use the term *snap-shot*.

William Henry Fox Talbot (1800–77) won fame and fortune with his CALOTYPE

(1841), the true technical base of photography because, unlike the Daguerrotype, its negative/positive principle made possible the making of prints from the original photographs. The inventions and discoveries which followed helped to improve the effectiveness of the photographic process. Frederick Scott Archer's *collodion* or wet-plate process, details of which were published in 1851, greatly increased sensitivity; the use of gelatine silver bromide emulsion, invented in 1871 by Dr Richard Leach Maddox, and later improved upon by John Burgess, Richard Kennett and Charles Bennett, proved a considerable advance on the collodion method, and ushered in the modern era of factory-produced photographic material, freeing the photographer from the necessity of preparing his/her own plates.

CELLULOID was invented by Alexander Parkes in 1861 and roll film made from celluloid was produced by the Eastman Company in the US from 1889. By 1902, Eastman, manufacturers of Kodak, were producing between 80% and 90% of the world's output. Very swiftly photography became the hobby of the man in the street. Every tenth person in the UK – 4 million people – was estimated to own a camera by 1900.

Colour film photography hit many technical snags in its development. A colour screen process was patented as early as 1904 by the Lumière brothers. They commercially introduced their Autochrome plates in 1907 when good panchromatic emulsion was available. However, exposure was about 40 times longer than that for black and white film. Modern methods based on multiple-layer film and coupling components were simultaneously introduced by Kodak and Agfa. In 1935, Kodachrome, created by two American amateurs, Leopold Godowsky and Leopold Mannes, was marketed, a year ahead of Agfacolor. In both, transparencies were obtained suitable for projection as well as reproduction. Electronic flash was invented in 1931 by Harold E. Egerton. See CAMERA, ORIGINS; FILMLESS CAMERA; HIGH-SPEED PHOTOGRAPHY; PHOTO-JOURNALISM; PHOTOMONTAGE; TIME-LAPSE PHOTOGRAPHY.

* Liz Wells, ed., *Photography: A Critical Introduction* (UK: Routledge, 1996).

Photogravure Engraving by photography, for purposes of PRINTING, was invented by Englishman William Henry Fox Talbot (1800–77) in 1852. It was not until 1947 that the first machine to do a complete typesetting job by means of photography was invented.

Photo-journalism Despite the popularity of photography among the general public, the press were curiously slow to realize the possibilities of photographs. The *Daily Mirror* was first in the field in the UK at the turn of the 20th c., but the use of photographs did not become commonplace till the end of the 1st World War (1914–18). In June 1919, the New York *Illustrated Daily News* at last fully acknowledged a vital means of communication – 39 years after the feasibility of printing a half-tone block (reproducing light and shade by dots of different sizes and densities) alongside type had been demonstrated by Stephen H. Horgan in the New York *Daily Graphic*. Even during the 1st World War (1914–18) press photographs were rare, and photo-reportage in the modern sense only began in the mid-1920s with the introduction of the Ermanox camera and ultra-rapid plates.

Among the fathers of modern photojournalism were Erich Saloman (1886–1944), Felix H. Man and Wolfgang Weber. With a camera hidden in his top hat, Arthur Barrett secretly took court photographs of the suffragettes, and, in February 1928, Saloman took sensational pictures of a Coburg murder trial. Man pioneered the *picture story* in, for example, *A Day in the Life of Mussolini*, 1934, and it was Man who founded *Weekly Illustrated* in the same year. He became chief photographer for *Picture Post*, founded 1938, a position he held until 1945.

Photo-journalism was given increasing status over the years by many outstanding photographers: Henri Cartier-Bresson (b. 1908) photo-reported visits to Spain (1933) and Mexico (1934); Robert Capa (1913–54) won undying fame with his war photography, especially his pictures taken during the Spanish Civil War; Bill Brandt

(1905–83) photographed the English at Home (1936) while Margaret Bowke-White, in *You Have Seen Their Faces* (1937) portrayed the conditions in the South of the US, in particular the negro chain-gangs.

Suppression of the photo-reportage of Bert Hardy from the Korean War by the proprietors of *Picture Post* led to the resignation of the magazine's outstanding editor, Tom Hopkinson.

Talented, fearless and concerned photo-journalists continue to the present, even in the age of TV and the closure of photo-papers. Don McCullin has photo-reported war, oppression, hardship and carnage all over the world in a vast array of unforgettable images. He was, incidentally, one of the photographers *not* given permission by the Ministry of Defence to cover the Falklands War (1982).

In *A Concise History of Photography* (UK: Thames & Hudson, 1965, 3rd edition by Helmet, 1986), Helmet and Alison Gernsheim write, 'No other medium can bring life and reality so close as does photography and it is in the fields of reportage and documentation that photography's most important contribution lies in modern times'. Not the least of its achievements, photography and photo-journalism have proved powerful agents in the awakening of social conscience. See DOCUMENTARY; MEDIASPHERE.
* John Hartley, *The Politics of Pictures: The Creation of the Public in the Age of Popular Media* (UK: Routledge, 1992).

Photomontage Process of mounting, superimposing, one photograph on top of another; a method almost as old as photography itself. The dadaists and surrealists experimented with Photomontage to produce visionary pictures. Laslo Moholy-Nagy (1895–1946) combined several picture components in the production of a new work and termed his approach 'photo-lastics'. Malik of Berlin were the first publishers to use photomontage for book jackets. Most extensively, the process has been employed in ADVERTISING. See PICTURE POSTCARDS.

Phototypesetting Method that bypassed the traditional metal type stage of print production by PRINTING type photographi-

cally from an optical or electric store of individual characters. Though the first photocomposing machine was created as early as 1894, it was not until it could be 'manned' by computers, in the 1960s, that the process became widespread. Modern typesetting allows operators to lay out pages on VDUs. This means that the same person can enter copy, make up the pages, check errors; then, one touch of a button and a high-quality proof is produced.

Picture postcards German Heinrich von Stephan is generally considered to have thought up the idea of a postcard, in 1865, though Emmanuel Hermann ran him close, persuading the director-general of the Austrian Post to issue the first government postcard, in 1869. It was called a 'Correspondence Card'. In 1870 the first government postcard was issued in the UK; 70 m such cards were sold in the first year. The US government followed suit in 1872.

Since then the picture postcard has provided a treasure house for the analysis of contemporary interests and attitudes: art, fashion, new technology, warfare, royalty, exploration, history, travel; ideas of patriotism and Empire, of family, entertainment, comedy, etc. The title *Mail art* has been given to a practice widespread in the late 1970s and 1980s of artists exchanging visual ideas by postcard. During the same period the postcard became popular in a propagandist role, especially among protest groups of the Left. A classic piece of PHOTOMONTAGE in postcard form is Peter Kennard's version of the Constable painting. *The Haywain*, in which the artist has superimposed cruise missiles on the 19th c. rural tranquillity of Suffolk. Such cards use CARTOONS, photographs, photograffiti and quotations.

Inevitably cards of past ages have become collectors' items; the word *Deltiology* (from the Greek, *deltion*, small picture) was coined by American Randall Rhoades for picture postcard collecting and study. See CIGARETTE CARDS; POSTERS.

Pidgin In trading and doing business with the English in the Far East, the Chinese and other peoples such as the Malays communicated in a very basic, utilitarian mode of half-English. *Pidgin* is a Chinese corruption of the word 'business'. The term is, however, more widely used. According to Elizabeth Closs Traugott and Mary Louise Pratt in *Linguistics* (US: Harcourt Brace Jovanovitch, Inc., 1980), a pidgin may be 'roughly defined as a language that is nobody's native language'. Pidgins are developed in situations where people with differing native languages are brought together, normally in a relatively powerless position, and have to communicate.

During the period of the slave trade, for example, West African slaves destined for a particular area like the Caribbean, were deliberately taken from groups which had different languages, so that it would be difficult for them to communicate and organize resistance. These people had, however, to communicate in order to survive and therefore developed a LANGUAGE which was a mixture of the prestige slaveholders' language from which they borrowed vocabulary and the grammar of the original West African languages.

Pidgins, though, tend to meet only the basic needs of communication and are very reliant on the accompanying use of NON-VERBAL COMMUNICATION for their effectiveness. Creoles are normally developed by the children of pidgin speakers and these are more complex and more flexible languages. A Creole is then a pidgin which becomes the first language of a group. In the Caribbean which saw many colonizing powers, there developed Creoles reflecting the influences of French, Dutch and Portuguese languages as well as Jamaican Creole with its close ties to English.

Over time, through the process of **Decreolization**, a Creole often changes to resemble more closely the predominant or prestige language which was its base, if this language is also used in the area. This was the case with Jamaican Creole. **Black English** derives historically from a Caribbean Creole.

In Britain, British Black English, derived largely from Jamaican Creole, is widely used by those with Afro-Caribbean origins as a linguistic marker of ETHNIC identity, and typically is part of a linguistic repertoire that also includes other varieties of English. The facility with which speakers will be able to use either British Black English or other varieties of English will depend on a number of variables, e.g. degree of exposure to either British Black or other varieties of English, social class, generation, length of time in Britain and age. The Rastafarian sub-culture has developed a variation of Creole which is overlaid with its own particular idiom and vocabulary, and more difficult for outsiders to understand, thus serving as a clear marker of distance between the sub-culture and the wider community.

* Martin Montgomery, *An Introduction to Language and Society* (UK: Methuen 1986, reprinted 1993, Routledge).

Pilkington Committee Report on Broadcasting, 1962

Set up under the chairmanship of Sir Harry Pilkington in 1960, the Committee's chief concern in a 297-page strongly worded deposition, was the nation's cultural and intellectual life and the effect upon these of BROADCASTING now that COMMERCIAL TELEVISION had been on the scene since 1954: 'Our conclusion,' declared the Committee, 'is that where it prevails it operates to lower general standards of enjoyment and understanding.'

The BBC emerged unscathed, and not a little praised, from the Committee Report: 'The BBC knows good broadcasting and by and large they are providing it.' The 'villain' of the scenario was ITV. So dissatisfied with ITV programmes were the Committee that one of their recommendations (never put into practice) was that the IBA take on responsibility for the planning of programmes.

Pilkington expressed disquiet at the portrayal of physical violence in TV programmes and of a 'comprehensive carelessness about moral standards generally'. 'From the representations which have been put to us, this is the underlying cause of the disquiet about television: the belief, deeply felt, that the way television has portrayed human behaviour and treated moral issues has already done something and will in time do much to worsen the moral climate of the country.'

Most of the recommendations of Pilkington were ignored. Only minor recommendations made any immediate progress – the right to party political broadcasts was extended; ADVERTISING magazines disappeared. Yet the Report did have its effect. It gave the BBC, staggering from the impact of ITV competition, a shot in the arm. And it was through Pilkington that the BBC was the first to receive a second channel (BBC2, 1964). ITV should receive such a channel, Pilkington recommended, only when it had been reformed.

John Whale in *The Politics of the Media* (UK: Fontana, 1977) says Pilkington 'aimed at large effects and missed them'. Nevertheless, Pilkington established a set of judgmental criteria, albeit elitist-cultural, which have formed a rallying point ever since for broadcasting reformers. See COMMISSIONS/ COMMITTEES ON THE MEDIA.

Pilot study A preliminary testing or 'experimental experiment' in which the researcher seeks to try out a new idea, system or approach; to determine whether an intended study is feasible, to clarify assumptions and improve instruments of measurement.

Pirate radio The monopoly of RADIO BROADCASTING held in the UK by the BBC was colourfully challenged in the 1960s by 'pirate' stations BROADCASTING from ancient forts and ships anchored in the North Sea. They played nonstop popular music, collected ADVERTISING revenues, paid no royalties on the music they played and thus made substantial profits. In 1964, Radio Caroline, from a ship called *Caroline*, took the air on 28 March, one of a long line of Pirates. Ronan O'Rahilly, founder of Caroline, received over 20,000 letters in the first 10 days of broadcasting. The Duke of Bedford was the first advertiser, for Woburn Abbey – an advertisement that brought in 4500 people the next day.

By the end of 1965 some 15 million listeners were tuning in regularly to pirate radio, and the pirates were making a lot of money until the Labour government put paid to existing and further development with the Marine, etc. Broadcasting (Offences) Act which became law in 1967.

Pirates appealed to a generation of teenagers – an audience the BBC later tried to win over with the creation of Radio 1. War on the pirates was initially conducted in the Council of Europe which drew up The European Agreement for the Prevention of Broadcasts transmitted outside National Territories, which member states signed in Strasbourg in 1965 and which the UK government presented to Parliament in the same year.

Among sections of the broadcasting and political establishment there was fear that the pirates might not only undermine existing systems of broadcasting but have an 'undesirable' cultural and even political impact. The Labour government's Marine Broadcasting (Offences) Act made it an offence to direct broadcasts into the UK which were unlicensed and made it an offence to buy advertising time on illegal channels. With the apparent defeat of the pirates, and the dismantling of their stations, there was clearly a gap to be filled in the pattern of official broadcasting services. At the end of 1966 the Labour government issued a White Paper containing proposals which opened the way for the creation of Radio 1.'

That was not the end of pirate radio. A widespread enthusiasm for radio broadcasting independent of the DUOPOLY was sustained through the 1970s, and in the 1980s pirates began popping up all over – making illegal broadcasts from unlicensed transmitters in woodlands, on hilltops, in back bedrooms, in garages or even on the move. Pirate *television* made its appearance by 1986, with Network 21, broadcasting to over 50,000 viewers throughout London, screening half-hour programmes on Fridays at midnight, thus bringing upon it the wrath of the Department of Trade and the full weight of the law. See COMMERCIAL RADIO; COMMUNITY RADIO; RADIO.

Pistolgraph See CAMERA, ORIGINS.

Pitch The highness or lowness of a speaker's voice. Technically, pitch is the frequency of sound made by the vocal cords.

Plagiarism From the Latin, 'plagiarius', kidnapper; the act of stealing from others their thoughts or their writings and claiming them for one's own.

Play theory of mass communication

In *The Play Theory of Mass Communication* (US: University of Chicago Press, 1967), William Stephenson counters those who speak of the harmful EFFECTS OF THE MASS MEDIA by arguing that first and foremost the media serve audiences as play-experiences. Even newspapers, says Stephenson, are read for pleasure rather than information and enlightenment. He sees the media as 'a buffer against conditions which would otherwise be anxiety producing'. The media provide *communication-pleasure*. Stephenson argues that what is most required by people within a national CULTURE is something for everyone to talk about. For him mass communication 'should serve two purposes. It should suggest how best to maximize the communication-pleasure in the world. It should also show how far autonomy for the individual can be achieved in spite of the weight of social controls against him'. See THEORIES AND CONCEPTS OF COMMUNICATION.

Pleasure: active and reactive Mary Ellen Brown in *Soap Opera and Women's Talk* (UK: Sage, 1994) speaks of the *active* and *reactive* pleasure of women viewers of soap operas. She argues that 'active pleasure for women in soap opera groups affirms their connection to a woman's culture that operates in subtle opposition to dominant culture'. It is this 'cult of the home and of women's concerns,' says Brown, 'recognized but devalued in patriarchal terms, that provides a notion of identity that values women's traditional expertise'.

On the other hand, *reactive* pleasure, 'while not rejecting the connection women often feel towards women's cultural networks and concerns, also recognizes that these concerns often arise out of women's inability to completely control their own lives'. Consequently they are able to 'recognize and to feel at an emotional level the price of oppression'. Key to resistive soap opera groups is *talking*, the very act of which 'indicates the importance of connectedness to others'. Brown acknowledges that soaps are a GENRE 'designed and developed to appeal to women's place in society' and largely to keep her in that place, yet 'Although soap operas work at isolating women in their homes and keeping them busy buying household products, in fact many observations indicate that they actually bring women together'; thus, it would seem, paradoxically undermining HEGEMONY while aiming to underpin it.

Pluralism The view that modern industrial societies have populations which are increasingly heterogeneous that is, different in kind – divided by such factors as ethnic, religious, regional and CLASS differences. Such heterogeneity, it is argued, produces a diversity of VALUES, NORMS, interests, and so on within such societies. Technological developments, such as those fostered by the digital revolution, make it increasingly possible for the media and cultural industries to address and access the heterogeneous nature of audiences – niche advertising being but one example of this. It can also be argued that a plurality of groups compete for power and influence within society. Power is seen, therefore, as being increasingly diffuse in terms of its distribution within these societies. This perspective is not without its critics. Some groups are likely to have more power than others and will be in a better position to impose their perspectives, values, and so on upon other groups. As far as the field of media studies is concerned, recent concentrations in media ownership throw some doubt on the degree to which power is becoming more diffuse in its distribution. The proliferation of media outlets has not, in the view of some commentators, guaranteed for audiences a broader choice of programmes; indeed in the 'age of DIGITALIZATION' there is the fear that *more* may prove to be *less*, and that consumerist criteria may reduce pluralism rather than extend it. See ELITE; SOCIAL ACTION (MODE OF MEDIA ANALYSIS).

Pluralist Many modes, many alternatives; in media terms, *diversity* – of ownership, STYLE, content and standpoint. A pluralist society is one in which there are many choices and many interpretations of MEANING.

Plus Male, Minus Male See MALE-AS-NORM.

Polarization Refers to the tendency to think and speak in terms of opposites (See WEDOM, THEYDOM) or what have been termed *binary oppositions.* The English language abounds with terms denoting oppostion. Reality, however, is more complex, and arguably few things can be seen meaningfully in terms of polar opposites. Our LANGUAGE then may tempt us into misleadingly simple perspectives. As Gail and Michele Myers in *The Dynamics of Human Communication* (US: McGraw-Hill, 1985) argue, 'Our language supports dividing the world into false opposites. Polarization consists of evaluating what you perceive by placing it at one end of a two-pole continuum and making the two poles appear to be mutually exclusive. . . . If you are honest, you cannot be dishonest'.

Whilst there are situations in which genuine opposites are found, what we should be wary of is applying this perspective when it is not appropriate and in so doing denying the complexities of a situation, or debate, and the range of alternatives that can or may exist. See VISIONS OF ORDER.

Politics of accommodation (in the media) Potential conflict between various individuals and GROUPS within media corporations and between these corporations and a central social authority is seen by some commentators to be *mediated* by what Tom Burns in *The BBC: Public Institution and Private World* (UK: Macmillan, 1977) calls a 'politics of accommodation'. This is a *negotiated compromise* in which notions such as professional standards and the public interest are used as trading pieces. Negotiations of this type can be conducted at several levels: between the professionals and the management, between one corporation and another and between a corporation and the government. See CONSENSUS; ELITE; ESTABLISHMENT; HEGEMONY; MEDIA CONTROL; MEDIATION.

Polysemy Many meanings; broadly used, the term describes the potential for many MEANINGS in media TEXTS, or the capacity of AUDIENCE to read into such texts their own meanings rather than merely the PREFERRED READING of the communicators. For some commentators, audience is the 'victim' of media messages; for others, it is perceived as being capable of making its own diverse responses (See AUDIENCE: ACTIVE AUDIENCE;

DOMINANT, SUBORDINATE, RADICAL). There is consensus among researchers that the extent of polysemy is to be viewed with caution.

As Celeste Michelle Condit writes in 'The rhetorical limits of polysemy' in *Television: The Critical View* (US: Oxford University Press, 1994), edited by Horace Newcomb, 'It is clear that there are substantial limits to the polysemic potential of texts and of decodings'. She recommends that we differentiate between the polysemy of texts and their interpretation by audience and suggests the term 'polyvalence' to describe the meanings ascribed to texts by audience: 'Polyvalence occurs,' says Condit, 'when audience members share understandings of the denotation of a text but disagree about the evaluation of those denotations to such a degree that they produce notably different interpretations.' It is different from polysemy in that it reflects 'not a multiplicity or instability of textual meanings but rather a difference in audience evaluations of shared denotations'.

Condit describes her research findings based upon the response of two students to an episode of the American TV cop series *Cagney & Lacey* (11 November 1985) in which the issue of abortion is dealt with. 'Jack', a pro-lifer, and 'Jill', pro-choice, had no difficulty understanding the denotational aspects of the episode. Where they took diametrically opposite viewpoints was in their response to the programme which had a pro-choice message; their CONNOTATIONAL reading. See OPEN, CLOSED TEXTS; OPINION LEADER; SIGNIFICANT OTHERS.

Polyvalence See POLYSEMY.

Pool system Practice, particularly in wartime, of governments chanelling media access to news through a regulated 'pool' of reporters; and consequently the 'pooling' of information for publication or broadcasting. This strategy of NEWS MANAGEMENT effectively censors journalists by coralling them, while at the same time claiming to offer prompt and reliable information on events. The Gulf War of 1991 offers a classic example of control through pooling.

Poor Man's Guardian Perhaps the most influential radical newspaper in Britain during the 19th c., edited by Bronterre O'Brien, published by Henry Hetherington. It appeared between 1831 and 1835, and was described by George Jacob Holyoake, a campaigner against the TAXES ON KNOWLEDGE levied by government on the PRESS, as 'the first messenger of popular and political intelligence which reached the working classes'. Other radical papers of this turbulent period were Richard Carlile's *Gauntlet* (1833–34), Robert Owen's *Crisis* (1832–34), James Watson's *Working Man's Friend* (1832–33) and Fergus O'Connor's *Northern Star* (1837–52), principal organ of the Chartist movement. See STAMP DUTY; UNDERGROUND PRESS.

Popular culture See CULTURE; POPULAR CULTURE.

Populism According to MASS SOCIETY theorists one of the distinguishing features of a mass society is its **populist** nature. Legitimacy is given to those persons, ideas or actions which are thought to best express the popular will or meet the most widely shared EXPECTATIONS. One result, such theorists claim, is that a premium is placed upon the capacity of those in leadership positions, to both create and placate popular opinion. The mass media tend to be seen as the agents through which such leaders control and exploit the masses.

Pornography Word originates from the Greek, 'writing of harlots'. Two sorts of pornography are usually differentiated, *erotica* – concentrating on physical aspects of heterosexual activity; and *exotica* – focusing on abnormal or deviationist sexual activity. Attitudes to pornography reflect a society's permissiveness, its current 'tolerance threshold' and also cast a light on prevailing social VALUES.

Tolerance of pornography only makes sense if there is no *felt* risk; if pornography is thought to be linked with the abuse of women and children and the degradation of human relationships and family life, pornography will be fought against whether the link is proved or not. In any case, pornography itself often makes the link between sexuality and violence: *hard porn* is, by general definition, a DISCOURSE in violence

which, at the very least, poses examples of possible behaviour. Of interest and concern is the indisputable fact that in many countries, including the UK, pornography is big business. Civic concern about the possible link between porn and violence was registered by the Minneapolis City Council in 1983. Exhaustive public hearings took place to provide a basis of information for a decision whether or not to add pornography as a 'discrimination against women' to existing civil rights legislation. The transcript of the Minneapolis hearings was published in 1988. Quoting evidence from academic and clinical research on the effect of pornography on ordinary men, the report stated that, exposed to pornography, men become desensitized; they seem themselves more likely to commit rape, less likely to respond sympathetically to women who are victims of rape or more likely to be lenient in their response to men who commit rape. According to the Minneapolis transcript, pornography which portrays women enjoying rape or violence or humiliation is most damaging.

As a result of the hearings the City Council passed a civil rights law enabling women victims of pornography to bring civil rights actions against the pornographers. However, the law was vetoed by the mayor and never implemented. A similar situation arose in Indianapolis where pornographers claimed they were being denied their constitutional right to free speech (under the First Amendment). Thus, in the courts, free speech took precedence over women's equality and safety from violence.

In a *New Scientist* article, 'Flesh and blood' (5 May 1990), on the effects on men of pornography, Mike Baxter writes, 'The weight of evidence is accumulating that intensive exposure to soft-core pornography desensitizes men's attitudes to rape, increases sexual callousness and shifts their preferences towards hard-core pornography. Similarly, the evidence is now strong that exposure to violent pornography increases men's acceptance of rape myths and of violence against women. . . . Many sex offenders claim they used pornography to stimulate themselves before committing their crimes'.

The arrival and expansion of the INTER-NET, with its relative freedom from control and overview, offer global opportunities for pornography, along with the pornography of race hatred (See CYBERSPACE). Any system which combines the privacy of output and input with potentially universal access will be abused. It has been argued that for women exercising their right to explore the Net there is as much danger from pre-dators as there is on the streets at night. See CENSORSHIP; DESENSITIZATION; STEREOTYPE; VIDEO NASTIES; WILLIAMS COMMITTEE REPORT ON OBSCEN-ITY AND FILM CENSORSHIP, 1979.

* Andrea Dworkin, *Pornography: Men Possessing Women* (UK: Women's Press, 1981); N. M. Mala-mud and E. M. Donnerstein, eds., *Pornography and Sexual Aggression* (US: Academic Press, 1984); D. Zillman and J. Bryant, 'Pornography, sexual callousness and the trivialization of rape' in *Journal of Communication*, Autumn, 1982. 'Pornography and Sexual Violence: Evidence of the Links (UK: *Every Woman Magazine* 1988); Catherine Itzin, 'Pornography and civil liberties' in *Index on Censorship*, 9/1990; and Itzin's book, *The Case Against Pornography: Sex Discrimination, Sexual Violence and Civil Discrimination* (UK: Grafton, 1991); Pamela Church Gibson and Roma Gibson, eds., *Women, Pornography, Power* (UK: BFI, 1993).

Portunus The Roman god of communica-tion, from *portus*, harbour, and *porta* gate. Portunus' festival day was 17 August.

Postcards See PICTURE POSTCARDS.

Posters Printed posters have had a short but vivid history, dating from the 1870s when the perfection of techniques in colour LITHOGRAPHY first made mass production possible. Posters have been described as the art gallery of the street and indeed the form has appealed to many artists, such as Henri Toulouse-Lautrec (1864–1901), members of the Art Nouveau move-ment and the graphic designers of the Bauhaus and the De Stijl group. Posters have served every mode of PROPAGANDA – social, political, religious, commercial. The arresting clarity of their images, combined with words used dramatically, emotively, humorously have often continued to

impress long after the ideas, events or products they relate to have faded from attention.

So immediate and memorable are pos-ters, and so widely recognized, that they have formed a regular inspiration for ser-ious artists: imitated, reproduced, turned into cult objects, transmuted into other meanings. Many different uses have been made, for example, of Alfred Leete's famour poster (1914) 'Your Country Needs You', in which Lord Kitchener, with sweeping mous-tache, points out towards the audience, offering a formidable challenge to all those who have not yet volunteered for the 1st World War.

In peacetime, between elections, ADVER-TISING dominates the poster contents of the billboards – sometimes with bold, witty and memorable images such as the Guinness adverts or Benetton's striking socio-political images. Posters come into their own in time of protest or revolution. Some of the finest posters were designed and printed during and after the Russian Revolution of 1917, while the Spanish Civil War (1936–38) stimulated the production of hundreds of hard-hitting, passionate and often tragic images.

Postmodernism Term referring to cul-tural, social and political attitudes and expression characteristic of the 1980s and 1990s, following the *modernist* period of psycholanalysis, functional, clean-line, machine-inspired architecture, abstract art and stream-of-consciousness fiction. Wendy Griswold in *Cultures and Societies in a Changing World* (US: Pine Forge Press, 1994), writes 'Many people believe that society has entered this new stage beyond modernity, a postindustrial stage of social development dominated by media images, in which people are connected with other places and times through proliferating channels of information'.

If hope and anxiety were features of modernism, says Griswold, 'the postmodern person is characterized by a cool absence of illusion. Modern minds were sceptical, Post-modern minds are cynical'. The prevailing cynicism is wary of traditional attempts at explaining the evolution of society. It discards the affirming or 'grand narratives' (metanarratives) of the past which subscribed to the view of the inevitability of human progress – what might be described as the Enlightenment position. Reality itself is an uncertainty: being a creation of LANGUAGE and existing in socially produced DISCOURSE, it represents an infinitely movable feast.

Marxism has been rejected by postmodernist thinkers such as Michel Foucault, Jacques Derrida, Jean-François Lyotard and Jean Baudrillard as having 'totalizing ambitions', that is, offering grandiose explanations of reality which cannot be sustained. They therefore reject the central tenet of Marxism, its belief in the emancipation of humanity.

The postmodernist position derives much of its vision from the German philosopher Friedrich Nietzsche (1844–1900), in particular his profound antipathy to any system and his rejection of the view expressed by an earlier German thinker, Georg Wilhelm Friedrich Hegel (1770–1831), of history as progress.

Instead of such totalizing, postmodernism embraces fragmentation (and this includes views on the fragmentation of time itself and therefore of concepts of the past and present). It hones in on micro-situations. The stress is on the local. Taking a deeply Rightist position, postmodernists declare that progress is a myth. If there are no unities, then nothing *figures*; if nothing figures, nothing *matters* and if nothing matters then *anything* goes.

Thus in architecture postmodernism scorns traditional forms while unapologetically plagiarizing them. It has varyingly been described as a culture of surfaces, of self-aware superficiality characterized by the ephemeral and discontinuity.

In the postmodernist approach, writes Norman K. Denzen in a review, 'Messy methods of communication research' in the *Journal of Communication* (Spring, 1995), all 'criteria are doubted, no position is privileged'. Taken to a logical conclusion such a standpoint facilitates cultural freedom and unshackled pluralism; it could also unhinge freedom from responsibility on the ground that a definition of respon-

sibility could only be arrived at on a personal, micro-level, hence the accusation made in some quarters that postmodernism is the cultural arm of the commoditization of information and knowledge.

Madan Sarup in *An Introductory Guide to Post-Structuralism and Postmodernism* (UK: Harvester Wheatsheaf, 1993) says of Baudrillard, 'Personally I find many of his insights stimulating and provocative but, generally, his position is deplorable. In Baudrillard's world truth and falsity are wholly indistinguishable, a position which I find leads to moral and political nihilism'. The danger for a postmodernist world resides in a view expressed by Lyotard, that *power* has increasingly become the criterion of – the synomym for – truth. See DECONSTRUCTION; MEDIASPHERE.

* David Harvey, *The Condition of Postmodernity: An Inquiry into the Origins of Cultural Change* (UK: Blackwell, 1990); J.F. Lyotard, *The Postmodern Condition* (UK: Manchester University Press, 1984); Frederic Jameson, *Postmodernism, or, The Cultural Logic of Late Capitalism* (UK: Verso, 1991); Christopher Norris, *Uncritical Theory: Postmodernism, Intellectuals and the Gulf War* (UK: Lawrence & Wishart, 1992); John Hartley, *Popular Reality: Journalism, Modernity, Popular Culture* (UK: Arnold, 1996).

Post-synchronization Or *dubbing*. In FILM making, the process of adding new or altered dialogue in the original language to the sound track of a film after it has been shot. See SYNCHRONOUS SOUND.

Postulates of communication To define the fundamental *attributes* of the communication process is possibly a more fruitful area of analysis than struggling for an all-embracing and acceptable *definition* of communication. C.D. Mortensen in *Communication: the Study of Human Interaction* (US: McGraw-Hill, 1972), poses a single, basic postulate, that 'Communication occurs whenever persons attribute significance to message-related behaviour'; and then follows this up with five secondary postulates. These are: (1) Communication is *dynamic*. (2) Communication is *irreversible*. (3) Communication is *proactive* (as opposed to *reactive*). Mortensen says here, 'The notion of man as a detached bystander, an objective and dispassionate reader of the environment, is nothing more than a convenient artefact. Among living creatures man is the most spectacular example of an agent who amplifies his environment'. We are *shapers*, not mere recipients. (4) Communication is *interactive*. (5) Communication is *contextual*. See COMMUNICATION MODELS; THEORIES AND CONCEPTS OF COMMUNICATION.

Postural echo Occurs when people – friends, lovers, etc. – unconsciously imitate or 'echo' each other's GESTURES and postures; this Desmond Morris in *Manwatching: A Field Guide to Human Behaviour* (UK: Jonathan Cape, 1977) describes as 'part of a natural body display of companionship'. He writes, 'Because acting in unison spells equal-status friendship, it can be used by dominant individuals to put subordinates at their ease'. See TIE-SIGNS.

Posture An element of non-verbal communication, a person's posture can be used or taken to indicate a range of aspects of behaviour. For instance, people often make judgments about others' states of mind from their body posture and certain postures do seem to communicate something of the way a person feels. Optimism, confidence and dominance, for example, are often associated with an upright posture whereas depression tends to be associated with a slouching, shrinking posture. Posture can be used to provide a variety of messages in FEEDBACK and can also be used to communicate our attitude to others.

Positive feelings towards others are often shown, in part, by a leaning forward posture in conversation, and by POSTURAL ECHO. Conversely, negative feelings can be indicated by leaning back from others. High STATUS can be signalled by an upright posture. Aggressive attitudes towards others can be demonstrated by a progressively more exaggerated exhibition of high status or dominant behaviour. Shifts in posture can be used to mark stages in a conversation. See COMMUNICATION, NON-VERBAL.

Power Power has been defined by a number of theorists but a good working definition is that provided by John B. Thompson in *The Media and Modernity: A Social Theory of the Media* (UK: Polity Press,

1995): power is 'the ability to act in pursuit of one's aims and interests, the ability to intervene in the course of events and to affect their outcome. In exercising power, individuals employ the resources available to them; resources are the means which enable them to pursue their aims and interests effectively'. Whilst the individual may be the basic building block of the power structure of any society, some blocks are arguably a lot bigger than others as some individuals have personally considerably more resources than others. Further, as Thompson argues, 'While resources can be built up personally, they are also commonly accumulated within the framework of institutions, which are important bases for the exercise of power. Individuals who occupy dominant positions within large institutions may have vast resources at their disposal, enabling them to make decisions and pursue objectives which have far-reaching consequences'.

A concept closely related to that of power is influence. Charles B. Handy in *Understanding Organizations* (UK: Penguin, 1993) describes the relationship between power and influence thus: 'Influence is the process whereby A modifies the attitudes and behaviour of B. Power is that which enables him to do it.' The exercise of power it would seem requires resources or what French and Raven term a 'power base' (quoted in B. Raven and J. Rubin, *Social Psychology*, US: John Wiley, 1983) but it also requires the selection of a method(s) of influence and arguably to some extent the acquiescence of the recipient(s). The exercise of power can then be conceptualized as a two way process in which the receiver is, to some extent, prepared to be involved. Power may be exercised in many diverse social situations, at many levels and to varying degrees; indeed it could be argued that few social encounters do not contain a power dimension, are not in some way influenced by the power relationships of those involved.

Power can also be conceived of as taking a number of forms. Thompson offers a distinction between the differing sources of power and categorizes them into four main types: economic, political, coercive and symbolic. Of course these often overlap and the way in which they do so is in itself an indication of the often complex and at times mutually supportive relationships which exist within the overall power structure. Varying forms of power are often concentrated in institutions. Economic power is based in ownership or control of those resources required for the productive activity involved in transforming human, material and financial resources into goods and services, for sale or exchange in a market in order to generate a means of subsistence; examples of economic institutions would include the stock market in Britain and media CONGLOMERATES.

Political power stems from the authority to organize the activities of individuals, groups or organizations and to control, to some extent, these activities. Institutions that are primarily concerned with exercising political power in contemporary Britain include parliament, the civil service and local authorities. Coercion or the use of force can be found in a diverse range of power relationships. Most states, for example, whatever their form of government, have resources which underscore their political power with the ability to coerce or use physical force if necessary. In present-day Britain examples of institutions which can and do exercise such power on behalf of the state include the police, the armed forces and NATO.

Very different but not necessarily less effective is symbolic power, which Thompson defines as stemming from 'the activity of producing, transmitting and receiving meaningful symbolic forms'. He sees such activity as being 'a fundamental feature of social life. . . . Individuals are constantly engaged in the activity of expressing themselves in symbolic forms and in interpreting the expressions of others; they are constantly involved in communicating with one another and exchanging information and symbolic content'. To do so, individuals draw upon the various 'means of information and communication' such as access to the channels of communications, communicative competence, knowledge and acknowledged expertise in areas of symbolic exchange. Institutions in which significant symbolic power resides would include the mass media.

Whilst institutions may be usefully perceived, for the purposes of analysis, as possessing primarily one form of power, in reality most institutions employ a number of forms of power in influencing the behaviour of others, that is they have access to resources that provide them with a complex and diverse power base. Mass media institutions, for example, have a number of aims, one of which is undoubtedly to communicate a wide range of messages to a mass audience but others would also include, for most media institutions, the need to run as a successful commercial company and to play a role within the political processes of at least one if not several countries.

The pivotal role that the mass media play in transmitting information about politics and politicians to a wide audience has resulted in media commonly being referred to as the 'FOURTH ESTATE' – a phrase originally thought to have been used by Edmund Burke when referring to the 18 c. British press. The mass media also provide audiences with many messages about the nature, distribution and location of power; of interest also are the power relationships they choose *not* to cast light on.

Power and power relationships provide an important focus for analysis of mass, organizational, group, interpersonal or intrapersonal communication. The exploration of the exercise of power gives rise to many areas of investigation which include the political economy of the mass media, power bases, factors which predispose individuals to be influenced, methods of influence, the effect of social context upon the influence process and the degree to which people may be influenced. See CONGLOMERATES; EFFECTS OF THE MASS MEDIA; ELITE; ESTABLISHMENT; MEDIA IMPERIALISM.

Power elite Term used by C. Wright Mills in his seminal analysis *Power, Politics and People* (US: Oxford University Press, 1963) to describe those members of a society who combine social and political privilege with power and influence. See CULTURAL APPARATUS; ELITE; HEGEMONY.

Power uncertainty See GUARD DOG METAPHOR.

PR See PR: PUBLIC RELATIONS.

Pragmatic acceptance See ACCEPTANCE: NORMATIVE AND PRAGMATIC.

Pragmatics The study of LANGUAGE from the viewpoint of the user, especially the choices he/she makes, the constraints he/she meets with in employing language in social situations, and the effects the use of this language has upon others in the communication situation.

Predatory pricing In relation to the PRESS, reduction in the price of a newspaper in order to undercut the competition, and in the long-run put the competition out of business. The most notable example of predatory pricing in the UK has been the reduction in price of *The Times*, part of Rupert Murdoch's News International group, on Mondays and Saturdays at an estimated cost to the company of £300m over a period of five years. The aim of such reductions has been to draw readers from *The Independent*, the *Daily Telegraph* and the *Guardian* who do not have substantial profits from TV, or satellite services to help exercise their own price reductions.

High hopes of the new Labour government banning predatory pricing were dashed when a House of Lords amendment to the Competition Bill, moving through parliament in 1998, was blocked in the House of Commons. The amendment would have made predatory pricing illegal. Allegations were made at the time that Prime Minister Tony Blair's link with Murdoch, and Labour's indebtedness to the support it received in the 1997 election from Murdoch's flagship tabloid, the *Sun*, had influenced government action. Other arguments were put that under prevailing free-market practices to outlaw price-reduction would be an unacceptable restraint upon commerce, particularly as there was clear benefit for readers of *The Times* and members of the public who could not afford – or did not wish – to pay the higher prices of its competitors.

Preferred reading Stuart Hall poses this concept in 'The determination of news photographs' in Stanley Cohen and Jock Young, eds., *The Manufacture of News* (UK: Constable, 1973). Here the preferred reading of a photograph – preferred, that is, by the transmitter of the photograph – is one, Hall believes, which guides us to an interpretation that lies within the traditional social, political and cultural VALUES of the time, symbolizing and reinforced by the interests of the dominant HIERARCHY. The framing, cropping, captioning and juxtaposition of the photograph with text all serve to close off the reader from lateral, or independent, interpretations of the photography; from ABERRANT DECODING of the MESSAGE. Thus CLOSURE is achieved. The term has come to be applied to message systems generally. See DOMINANT, SUBORDINATE, RADICAL; POLYSEMY.

Prejudice Ernest R. Hilgard, Richard C. Hilgard and Rita L. Hilgard in *Introduction to Psychology* (US: Harcourt Brace Jovanovich, 1975) define prejudice as 'an attitude that is firmly fixed, not open to free and rational discussion and resistant to change'. Such an attitude may be directed towards ideas, objects, situations or people and may be positive or negative. Prejudice is arguably of greatest concern when it is negative and directed towards other people. In this instance prejudice is often accompanied by negative stereotypes of its targets. The targets of prejudice tend to be those who are the relatively powerless members of GROUPS, organizations, or societies as well as those who are perceived as being deviant. It is of course possible to be both. The term *discrimination* is normally used to describe the acting out of prejudice.

See DEVIANCE; LABELLING PROCESS (AND THE MEDIA); NORMS; STEREOTYPE.

Press See JOURNALISM; NEWSPAPERS: ORIGINS; NEWS VALUES; NORTHCLIFFE REVOLUTION; PRESS BARONS; UNDERGROUND PRESS. *See also*: BERLUSCONI PHENOMENON; BY-LINE; CALCUTT REPORTS 1990 AND 1993; CHEQUEBOOK JOURNALISM; CONGLOMERATES; DEVELOPMENTAL NEWS; DISINFORMATION; FOLK DEVILS; FOURTEEN-DAY RULE; FOURTH ESTATE; FREQUENCY; HARMONIOUS INTERACTION; HEGEMONY; JINGOISM; LOBBY PRACTICE; McGREGOR COMMISSION REPORT ON THE PRESS, 1977; MEDIASPHERE; MEDIATION;

MR GATE; NEWS AGENCIES; NEWS FRAMEWORKS; NEWS-LITERATE; NEW WORLD INFORMATION ORDER; NON-ALIGNED NEWS POOL; OZ TRIAL; PAPARAZZO; PERIODICITY; PHOTO-JOURNALISM; PHOTOTYPESET-TING; POOR MAN'S GUARDIAN; PRESS COMPLAINTS COMMISSION; PRESS CONFERENCE; PRESS, FOUR THE-ORIES OF; PRINT UNIONS; RHETORIC; RIGHT OF REPLY; ROSS COMMISSION REPORT ON THE PRESS, 1949; SHAW-CROSS COMMISSION REPORT ON THE PRESS, 1962; SHOCK ISSUES; SHOTGUN APPROACH (TO NEWS COVERAGE); SIGNIFICATION SPIRAL; SPIKE; SPOILER; STAMP DUTY; STEREOTYPE; TABLOID; TABLOIDESE; TABLOIDIZATION; TALLOIRES DECLARATION, 1981; TAXES ON KNOWL-EDGE; TERRORISM AS COMMUNICATION; THESIS JOUR-NALISM; TOKENISM; VICTIM FUNDS; WATCHDOGS; WATERGATE; WESTMINSTER VIEW; WORLD PRESS FREE-DOM COMMITTEE; YELLOW KID; YELLOW JOURNALISM; ZINOVIEV LETTER 1924.

Press barons As early as 1884 Scots-American steel magnate Andrew Carnegie headed a syndicate which controlled eight daily papers and ten weeklies. In the UK Edward Lloyd owned the mass circulation *Daily Chronicle* and the blockbuster Sunday paper, *Lloyd's Weekly*, the first periodical to sell a million copies. As the costs of found-ing and running newspapers grew, leaving ownership a privilege of none but the very rich, or joint stock companies, the trend towards chain ownership accelerated.

By 1921, Lord Northcliffe (1865–1922) controlled *The Times*, the *Daily Mail*, the *Weekly Despatch* (later a Sunday paper) and the *London Evening News*. His brother Harold, later Lord Rothermere, controlled the *Daily Mirror*, the *Sunday Pictorial*, the *Daily Record* and several other papers. Together they owned the large magazine group Amalgamated Press while brother number three, Sir Lester Harmsworth, owned a string of papers in the southwest of England. Between them these baronial brothers owned papers with an aggregate circulation of over six million. Though con-trolling only a modest four papers – one of which, the *Daily Express*, led all its compe-titors in the late 1930s – Lord Beaverbrook (1879–1964) reached a joint circulation of 4.1 million by 1937.

Regional newspaper chains displayed similar baronialist tendencies. The Berry brothers, Lords Camrose and Kemsley,

pushed their tally from four daily and Sunday papers in 1921 to 20 daily and Sunday papers by the outbreak of the 2nd World War in 1939. As newspapers fell into fewer hands, circulation expanded dramati-cally. Between 1920 and 1939 the circulation of national dailies went from 5.4 m to 10.6 m while Sunday paper circulations rose from 13.5 m to 16 m.

Though the leading Sunday paper own-ers, Kemsley, Beaverbrook and Camrose, controlled 59% of national sales in 1937, it was 8% less than the control exercised in 1910 by lesser-known barons, Dalzil, Riddell and Lloyd. Equally the control exercised over daily circulation in 1937 by Rothermere, Beaverbrook and Cadbury fell 7% below that exercised by Pearson, Cadbury and Northcliffe in 1910. As James Curran and Jean Seaton say in *Power Without Responsi-bility* (UK: Routledge, 5th edition, 1997), 'The press magnates' hegemony over the press was, in fact, waning during the period celebrated for their ascendancy'.

Almost to a man, the press barons were autocratic, eccentric and immensely ambi-tious, exerting far-reaching editorial control and involving themselves minutely in the day-to-day running of a newspaper busi-ness. Competition was savage and unrelent-ing. It was necessary for the press barons to attract readership with special offers, life insurance, attention-catching competitions, and to fill their pages with stories their read-ers were interested in – which meant, as a *News Chronicle* survey of readers' responses in 1933 indicated, more stories about acci-dents, crime, divorce and human interest (and less 'serious' matters such as politics and world events).

Politics were important, but profits came first. In fact the British political establish-ment viewed the press barons with dislike and suspicion, for they were not so easily 'bought' or persuaded as their predecessors had been. Of course this did not stop them meddling in politics. Between 1919 and 1922 Rothermere and Northcliffe put all their press backing behind policies advocat-ing public spending cuts. Their Anti-Waste League won three parliamentary by-elections in 1921.

Beaverbrook and Rothermere formed

the United Empire Party in 1930 aimed at creating a tariff wall around the British Empire, and an election victory was achieved on the issue at Paddington in October 1930. Prime Minister Stanley Baldwin fought back – on the issue of who rules, government or press? – and won the Westminster St George's by-election comfortably.

During the 1930s Rothermere's papers the *Daily Mirror* and *Daily Mail* supported the British Union of Fascists for a brief period and were rabidly anti-Red. The record of press persuasion on single ISSUES is, however, less significant than the longer-term influence the popular press had at this time. According to Curran and Seaton this demonstrated itself in 'the consolidation of public opinion, particularly amongst the middle class, against change': 'The papers controlled by the press barons conjured up imaginary folk devils that served to strengthen commitment to dominant political norms and to unite the centre and the right against a common enemy', that is, socialism and Marxism; the so-called 'Red peril'. (See FOLK DEVILS.)

Patriotism, a deep emotional attachment to Empire, ill-concealed racialism, hatred of foreigners, these – along with their inveterate antisocialism – characterized the 'voice' of press baronage in the inter-war years.

The post-war period saw new styles of press leadership as the one-product newspaper tycoons gave way to multi-marketing trends, conglomerate owernship and more self-effacing, though no less far-reaching control. However, the 1980s have not been without baronialism in the old style. Australian Rupert Murdoch owns *The Times*, *Sunday Times*, the *Sun* and the *News of the World* along with powerful newspapers in the US and Australia. In addition, Murdoch has control of FILM studios and TELEVISION stations in the US and his media interests in Britain include BSky Television. A rival baron emerged in the mid-1980s: Robert Maxwell acquired the Mirror group, the *Daily Mirror* becoming, in the words of journalist John Pilger, 'something approaching a family album'.

The mysterious death by drowning of Maxwell in 1991 was followed by revelations of fraud on a massive scale – not the least the misappropriation by Maxwell of the *Daily Mirror* Pensions Fund. The Maxwell case exemplifies for the student of media vital issues concerning ownership and control. It raises questions about the role of financial organizations in the high-risk activities of entrepreneurs and the ease with which, seemingly, gambling with other people's money, creaming-off profits, running 'tax haven' and tax-avoiding companies and doctoring accounts, can systematically escape official redress.

It is not as if the business record of Robert Maxwell was a secret prior to the revelations of 1991. A Department of Trade and Industry investigation of Maxwell's business practices reported, in four volumes, in 1974. The DTI inspectors ended their report with these damning words: 'We regret having to conclude that, notwithstanding Mr. Maxwell's acknowledged abilities and energy, he is not in our opinion a person who can be relied on to exercise proper stewardship of a publicly quoted company.'

Such a judgment did not deter bankers subsequently from lending Maxwell £3 billion. In a *New Statement* article, 'Not a fit person' (13 December 1991), Thomas Clarke writes, 'The signal failure of any major British institution – the stock exchange, the law, the government – to do anything about it [Maxwell's "plunder of other people's lives and money"], reveals the dubious standards applied in the British business community'.

That Maxwell's business dealings were not better known is because of his tenacious use of the LIBEL laws to keep such things from public scrutiny. Clarke states: 'The fact that Maxwell successfully abused the law of libel to intimidate and gag anyone who attempted to reveal his criminal acts shows how the law of libel protects the rich at the expense of ordinary people.' See COMMANDERS OF THE SOCIAL ORDER; COMMERCIAL CONFIDENTIALITY; CONGLOMERATES; CULTURE OF DEFERENCE; MEDIA CONTROL; NEWSPAPERS: ORIGINS.

* Nicholas Coleridge, *Paper Tigers* (UK: Heinemann, 1993); Roy Greenslade, *Maxwell's Fall* (US: Simon & Shuster, 1992); Tom Bowyer, *Maxwell: The Final Verdict* (UK: HarperCollins, 1996).

Press commissions See COMMISSIONS/COM-MITTEES ON THE MEDIA.

Press Complaints Commission Body created by the UK newspaper industry, beginning its duties on 1 January 1991, and replacing the Press Council; Lord McGregor being appointed the Commission's first chairman. The PCC operates on the basis of a Code of Practice, the 'five commandments' of which concern privacy, opportunity for reply, prompt correction and appropriate prominence, the conduct of journalists and the treatment of race. The Code warns newspapers against publishing 'inaccurate, misleading or distorting material' as well as recommending them 'to distinguish clearly between comment, conjecture and fact'. See CALCUTT COMMITTEE ON PRIVACY AND RELATED MATTERS, 1990.

Press conference The use of press conferences was established in the UK by the Labour Party during the 1959 election campaign. They are held when public figures, often leading politicians, wish to relay a particular MESSAGE to the general public and to use the press as a MEDIUM for it. Such conferences have become a particular feature of general elections campaigns since the late 1960s and they are now covered on TV as well as in the press. They do facilitate an economical and efficient media coverage of such campaigns. Most importantly, press conferences are a mechanism by which the agenda can be established of issues on which the campaign will be fought. See AGENDA SETTING.

Press, four theories of So termed by F.S. Sibert, T. Peterson and W. Schramm in *Four Theories of the Press* (US: University of Illinois Press, 1956), these are the *libertarian, communist, authoritarian* and *social responsibility* traditions. See NORMATIVE THEORIES OF THE MEDIA.

Pressure groups Also known as interest groups or lobbies, pressure groups aim to influence central and local government and its actions in certain, limited areas of policy. They do not usually seek formal political office although some pressure groups do sponsor individual MPs. Pressure groups can be usefully divided into two main types:

those which act to protect their members' interests and those which are concerned to promote a cause which they believe will be in the general interests of society.

Pressure groups vary not only in the focus of their concern but more crucially in the degree of influence they have. In some cases a government may consult relevant pressure groups before introducing or amending legislation or policies and some groups enjoy relatively easy access to government.

To be successful, pressure groups need well-planned strategies of communication, or CAMPAIGNS. The methods used here vary but include letter-writing, gaining INTERVIEWS on local or national RADIO, using radio 'phone-in' slots, the distribution of literature, advertisements, demonstrations and gaining TELEVISION coverage. The mass media clearly play an important role in attempts to gain widespread public support. See LOBBYING.

Prestel See VIEWDATA.

Pretty Good Privacy Title of a computer software program designed to protect computer data from intrusion; an ENCRYPTING process created by American Phil Zimmerman, who in 1998 received the Life Achievement Award from *Secure Computing Magazine*. Governments have proved less welcoming to PGP, seeing it as a barrier to their systems of surveillance.

Price wars See PREDATORY PRICING.

Primacy, the law of The view that whichever side of a case or argument is presented first will have greater impact on an audience than anything which follows. F.H. Lund is considered to have been the first to advance this theory in 'The psychology of belief' in the *Journal of Abnormal and Social Psychology* (1925). There are those, however, who espouse the law of *recency*, asserting that that which is most recent is the more likely to have greatest impact and retention. Primacy puts its faith in first impressions, recency in last impressions; both are marginal factors in the real context of debate where *who* goes first or last, and *what* is said first or last, in what *situation* and by what *means*, are more fundamental criteria.

Primary, consequential, collateral and consequential types of crime on screen See CRIME: TYPES OF CRIME ON SCREEN.

Primary groups See GROUPS.

Primary, secondary definers In relation to EVENTS, primary definers are those such as the police who are in a position to speak authoritatively in matters of crime and public order; who are structurally dominant in terms of their potential for defining reality. The media are secondary definers, either representing, interpreting or rejecting the dominant definition. The position becomes complicated when the field of definition is occupied by rival definers – such as when employers and unions are in conflict.

Primary, secondary texts See TERTIARY TEXT; TEXT.

Prime time US term to describe the peak viewing period of TV viewing: generally between 8pm and 11pm.

Principle of least effort Posed by G.K. Zipf in *Human Behaviour and the Principle of Least Effort* (US: Addison-Wesley, 1949). Zipf believed that the human communicator minimizes wherever possible the 'probable average rate of work required' in any given situation. This Zipf describes as *effort*. The communicator needs to be understood but his/her desire, Zipf argues, is to be brief. For a full explanation, see Colin Cherry's *On Human Communication* (US: MIT Press, 1966), Chapter 3, 'On signs, language, and communication'.

Printing The system of printing used by John of Gutenberg in the 15th c., and still widely practised today, works by the application of ink, and subsequently paper, to a raised surface. This is known as *relief printing*. Other methods are *planographic* and *intaglio* or *gravure*. With the former, the design to be printed and its background are in one flat surface; in intaglio printing the part to be printed is etched or cut into the plate – the exact reverse of relief printing.

Bavarian actor/playwright Alois Senefelder in 1798 found that some kinds of stone absorb both oil and water. He drew on the stone with a greasy crayon and then dampened the stone which absorbed the water only where there was no crayon design. He then made an ink of wax, soap and lampblack which stuck to the crayon and came off on paper, producing a print. *Lithography* from the Greek 'lithos', stone, was born. Today zinc or aluminium sheets are used and the design to be printed is applied to the plates by a photographic process.

Off-set lithography, the main process of planographic printing employed today, came about as a result of an accident by American printer Ira W. Rubel who had allowed the rubber covering of the impress cylinder to become inked. He discovered that the perfect impression it transferred to the sheet of paper was of better quality than that produced by direct contact with the plate. The first patent for a system of printing using *photocomposition* was taken out by William Friese-Greene in 1895, though typesetting by photography was not in commercial use till the early 1950s. Modern photocomposition is computer-controlled. See CYLINDER PRESS; LINOTYPE PRINT-ING; MONOTYPE PRINTING.

Print unions The introduction of new technology throughout the 1980s in the UK print industry led to considerable reductions in the labour force, and consequently in the number of print unions. In 1960 14 unions represented printing and allied workers. By 1980 there were five – and reducing. SLADE (the Society of Lithographic Artists, Designers and Engravers) amalgamated with the NGA (the National Graphical Association), while SOGAT (the Society of Graphical and Allied Trades) combined with NATSOPA (the National Society of Operative Printers, Graphical and Media Personnel) to form SOGAT 82. Soon SOGAT 82 was gearing up to unite with the NGA to create the largest printing union of its kind in Europe, the GPMU (the Graphical, Paper and Media Union). On the ownership/management side of the newspaper industry there is the NPA (the National Proprietors Association) formed in 1906. For journalists, the chief trade unions is the NUJ (the National Union of Journalists).

Prior restraint Legal term describing the rights in some countries for CENSORSHIP to be exercised before publication. In the United States, where the 2nd Amendment of the Constitution protects freedom of speech, there is no such thing as *prior restraint*. In the UK, however, it was prior restraint, on the grounds of confidentiality, which prevented the publication of Peter Wright's book, *Spycatcher* (See SPYCATCHER CASE). The *Guardian, Observer* and *Sunday Times* newspapers challenged the action of the United Kingdom government at the European Court of Human Rights in Strasbourg. In November 1991 the court, while unanimously holding that the papers had been denied their right to freedom of expression when they were prevented from publishing extracts from *Spycatcher* after the book had been published widely elsewhere, nevertheless affirmed, by a vote of 14 to 10, the right to prior restraint.

The *Guardian* deemed this a step back in terms of press liberties, especially as the same court had ruled out prior restraint in the THALIDOMIDE CASE. The Court did accept that prior restraint would not be permissible if the information had been published overseas. The dissenting minority of the Euro-judges struck a more encouraging note for civil liberties, declaring that, 'in a free and democratic society there can be no room, in time of peace, for restrictions of that kind, and particularly not if these are resorted to, as they were in the present case, for governmental suppression of embarrassing information'.

In February 1999 Labour's Home Secretary Jack Straw attempted to impose prior restraint on the *Sunday Telegraph* when he received information that the paper intended to publish extracts, three days before its official release, of the Macpherson Report into police conduct in the case of the murdered teenager, Stephen Lawrence. Justice Rix at first imposed a court order then 24 hours later removed it again. A *Guardian* leader, headed 'A very British farce', declared prior restraint 'as fundamentally inimical to free speech'.

Privacy A keenly debated issue of our time is the perceived threat to, or indeed loss of, individual privacy. Our privacy is at risk from those in authority who hold informa-

tion on us, and from the media, part of whose mission is to make the private public, to uncover dark secrets, to bring illumination to facts held from view. The right to privacy obviously clashes with the right to know; where there is debate is on just how much is rightly private, and how much of public interest. Should, for example, the president of the United States have a right to protection in matters which, on the face of it, are not connected with 'public virtues' or the qualities for which the president was elected? On the other hand, is the separation between public and private personas viable – if a president deceives his wife, will he not also deceive his nation?

This issue can affect all of us at some time or another, if we do something *newsworthy*, which will invite the interest of the media; but for the most part the privacy of ordinary citizens is more at risk from surveillance on the part of those who hold data on us (See SURVEILLANCE SOCIETY). Details about ourselves as citizens, voters and consumers have, thanks to computer technology, become a commodity accessed with ease and often if not always without our knowledge. Each time we draw out money, pay for goods, order tickets for a pop concert using our switchcard, the all-seeing, all-remembering computer eye adds to its already teeming bank of information about us.

What is more, as some commentators have pointed out, we do not seem to mind; indeed many of us are happy to deliver up our privacy in return for being able to conduct our transactions more speedily. In other words, we enter into a state of complicity in the erosion of our privacy.

The French philosopher Michel Foucault, in *Discipline and Punish* (US: Pantheon, 1990), refers to 'technologies of power' which reach into the very hearts of our lives; while Mark Poster in *The Mode of Information: Poststructuralism and Social Context* (UK: Polity, 1990) fears that the 'populace has been disciplined to surveillance and to participating in the process' willingly, without coercion: 'Social security cards, drivers' licences, credit cards, library cards and the like – the individual must apply for them, have them ready at all times, use them continuously. Each transaction is recorded, encoded and added to databases. Individuals themselves in many cases fill out the forms; they are at once the source of information and the recorder of the information.'

Home networking constitutes 'the streamlined culmination of this phenomenon: the consumer, by ordering products through a modem connected to the producer's database, enters data about himself or herself directly into the producer's database in the very act of purchase'. In this sense, the population participates in 'the disciplining and surveillance of themselves as consumers'.

Less discussed than computer access to our private lives, but no less intrusive, is the practice, world-wide, with ever-increasing sophistication, of phone-tapping, and the inadequate legal protection against this form of surveillance. See *Stranger on the Line: The Secret History of Phone Tapping* (UK: Bodley Head, 1987) by Patrick Fitzgerald and Mark Leopold and *Privacy on the Line: The Politics of Wiretapping and Encryption* (UK: PIT Press, 1998) by Whitfield Diffie and Susan Landen.

It must be acknowledged that surveillance and the loss of privacy are not entirely one-way. The performance of a nation's leaders, civil servants, business people – whose activities have traditionally been shielded from public gaze – are now more *visible* to the public than ever before. John Thompson in *The Media and Modernity: A Social Theory of the Media* (UK: Polity, 1995) says that 'the development of communication media provides a means by which many people can gather information about a few and, at the same time, a few can appear before many; thanks to the media, it is primarily those who exercise power, rather than those over whom power is exercised, who are subjected to a certain kind of visibility'.

We as the public may, through the computer data systems which threaten our privacy, feel vulnerable, but, Thompson believes, the visibility made possible by communication media makes it 'more difficult for those who exercise political power to do so secretively, furtively, behind closed doors'. What Thompson refers to as the 'uncontrollable character of mediated visi-

bility' gives rise to 'a new kind of *fragility* in the political sphere'.

Scandal and sleaze bedeck the front pages of the press; on our TV screens we watch our leaders wriggle and squirm. Thompson believes that such visibility does not further conditions which encourage decisive political leadership. On the contrary, such conditions 'may lead to weakened government and political paralysis, and which may nourish the suspicion and cynicism which many people feel towards politicians and political institutions'. See CALCUTT COMMITTEE REPORTS ON PRIVACY AND RELATED MATTERS; CENSORSHIP; DATA PROTECTION ACT, 1984.

Privacy: Press Complaint's Commission Code of Practice, 1997 Following the death of Diana, Princess of Wales in a car crash in Paris, and the widespread belief that this had been caused in part by the hounding of her by PAPARAZZI, the Press Complaints Commission issued in December 1997 a code of practice concerning privacy and PRESS harassment. Clause 3 of the code declares that 'Everyone is entitled to respect for his or her privacy and family life, home, health and correspondence. A publication will be expected to justify intrusion into any individual's life without consent'. Taking pictures of people 'in private places without their consent is wholly unacceptable', a private place being 'public or private property where there is a reasonable expectation of privacy'.

On harassment, Clause 4 urges that journalists and photographers 'must neither obtain nor seek to obtain information or pictures through intimidation, harassment or persisent pursuit' and this extends to 'telephoning, questioning, pursuing or photographing individuals after having been asked to desist'. The Code also sets out rules concerning intrusion into the lives of children, banning press payment to minors. Public interest is acknowledged as well as private interest: 'game' for press enquiry include crime and serious misdemeanour and matters relating to health and public safety.

The Code is self-regulatory, without the power of law, being the creation of the newspaper industry. It draws upon the European Convention for the Protection of Human Rights and Fundamental Freedoms, Article 8 of which, having asserted the right of the citizen to respect for his or her privacy and family, home and correspondence, then lists the exceptions to the rule of personal privacy: 'There shall be no interference by a public authority with the exercise of this right except such as is in accordance with the law or is necessary . . . in the interests of national security, public safety or the economic well-being of the country, for the prevention of disorder or crime, for the protection of health or morals, or for the protection of the rights and freedoms of others.'

Private cues See BARNLUND'S TRANSACTIONAL MODEL OF COMMUNICATION.

Privatization Dominant trend in media organization throughout the 1980s and 1990s, in which public-owned media utilities were sold off into private hands; specifically into those of the great transnational companies; and with it the privatization of information itself; or as some commentators have put it, the COMMODITIZATION OF INFORMATION. In fact the process commenced with the expansionism of multi-national, multi-product corporations after the 2nd World War. It was soon perceived that in the developing Age of Information, information was profitable. Corporations which were not already owners of media, bought into media. Private ownership and its dominance of cultural and social expression – whether in the arts, education, the museums service, libraries, sport or entertainment generally – came up against a major competitor: the public sector. In this domain, information was treated as a public right available to all rather than essentially a saleable commodity.

Such rivalry in an increasingly competitive world was deemed bad for private business. It became, then, corporate policy to pressurize governments into dismantling the public sector. Rightist governments in the 1980s and 1990s (the US under Reagan and Bush, the UK under Thatcher and Major) made privatization the driving-force of political and cultural change. Notions of 'public good' or 'public interest' were to become conditional upon the requirements of 'market forces'; as was social responsibility. See COMMANDERS OF THE SOCIAL ORDER; ELITE; DEREGULATION, FIVE MYTHS OF; MANUFACTURE OF CONSENT; POWER ELITE; PUBLIC SERVICE BROADCASTING (PSB); PUBLIC SPHERE; REGULATORY FAVOURS.

Pro-con, Con-pro In capturing the attention of an audience, is it best to put good news, or good points (pro) before the bad (con), or after them? Researchers have indicated that pro-con generally works best. See PRIMACY, THE LAW OF.

Producer choice The term used to describe the operation of an internal market system within the BBC for the purchase of the services and facilities needed in programme making. Since 1993 producers have had control over their budgets and have been free to buy the services and facilities they need, e.g. post-production, from the most cost-effective provider. The BBC's previous in-house providers of such services and facilities thus have to compete with other providers for contracts from programme makers. The designer of the scheme, Sir John Birt, argued that the system would create a more cost-effective and less bureaucratic organization and thus enable more resources to be channelled into creative areas. Criticisms of the system are that it has contributed to a reduction in staffing levels; that it has accelerated the trend, partly attributable to the increasing use of independent producers, towards freelancing and casualization of employment in the TV industry; that it threatens the long-term prospects of in-house providers and thus ultimately of the BBC itself as an organization concerned with making programmes as opposed to commissioning them; and that it may eventually result in a considerable loss of expertise within the BBC and thus a lowering of standards in programme making. Further, the procedures and paperwork involved in operating such a system may mean that it proves to be even more bureaucratic than that which it replaced.

Jean Seaton in James Curran and Jean Seaton's *Power Without Responsibility* (UK: Routledge, 1997) argues that the motives behind producer choice were not entirely financial. The resulting structure left the upper hierarchies that survived 'with hugely increased powers'. Ruthlessly carried out, these changes disempowered many of those involved in programme-making and 'By 1995 many staff were, in effect, pieceworkers or employed on short-term contracts'. See CASUALIZATION; INDEPENDENT PRODUCERS; DOUGHNUT PRINCIPLE.

Product placement A branch of modern ADVERTISING, especially in the US, where agencies place, in films and TV programmes, the products of clients – brightly lit, facing camera and in clear focus – and pay programme-makers considerable sums for the privilege of doing it. In the movie *Days of Thunder* (1990), Tom Cruise wore black Levi 501s throughout and sales of the garment went up considerably. Once an artefact is featured 'in shot', the company then draws further publicity by advertising the fact in its commercials. As the worlds of big business and entertainment grow closer and interlock and as budgets for films and TV grow tighter, product placement threatens to become more assertive throughout the media.

The position of the Independent Television Commission (ITC) concerning product placement is clear: it is not allowed. The Commission's *Code of Programme Sponsorship* (See SPONSORSHIP: ITC CODE OF PROGRAMME SPONSORSHIP) defines product placement as '. . . the inclusion of, or reference to, a product or service within the programme-maker or ITC licensee (or any representative of either). This is prohibited'. However, 'When a product or service is an essential element within a programme, the programme-maker may, exceptionally, acquire a product or service at no, or less than full, cost. This is not product placement. It is acceptable providing no undue prominence is given to the product or service in question'. This is conditional upon Rule 11 being fulfilled: 'There must be no promotional reference within the programme itself to the sponsor or to any of his products or services.'

Profane language The Latin derivation of profane is *pro fana*, meaning outside the temple. Profanity referred to anyone refusing to be initiated into the ways of the temple, thus showing a contempt for that which is sacred. Profane LANGUAGE takes three main forms: religious, excretory or sexual; and the questions asked about such language are, why do people use profanities and what are the effects upon listeners – upon AUDIENCE – of the use of profanity?

J.D. Rothwell in 'Verbal obscenity: time for second thoughts' in *Western Speech*, 35 (1971) listed five reasons for using profane language: (1) to create attention; (2) to discredit someone or something; (3) to provoke confrontations; (4) to provide a type of CATHARSIS or emotional release for the user and (5) to establish interpersonal IDENTIFICATION. Profanity depends for its impact on who is actually using it and in what circumstances.

In 'The effects of three type of profane language in persuasion messages?' in the *Journal of Communication* (December 1973) Robert N. Bostrom, John R. Baseheart and Charles M. Rossiter Jr write of research which indicates that where profanity is used, 'greater attitude change can be expected to occur if the communicator is female, in any of the three categories (religious, excretory, sexual). Bostrom *et al.* also reach the general conclusion that profanity has a detrimental effect on the perceived credibility of the communicator.

Programme codes See ITC PROGRAMME CODE; RADIO AUTHORITY PROGRAMME CODES 1 AND 2; SPONSORSHIP: ITC CODE OF PROGRAMME SPONSORSHIP.

Programme flow 'In all developed broadcasting systems,' writes Raymond Williams in *Television: Technology and Cultural Form* (UK: Fontana, 1974), 'the characteristic organization, and therefore the characteristic experience, is one of sequence or flow.' Williams believes that flow is a chief principle of programming; the process of organizing a pattern of programmes, each one leading on to the next; each one being a 'tempter' for the audience to stay tuned to a particular CHANNEL. Programme boundaries, says Williams, are constantly being obscured by advertisements and/or trailers for other programmes, to counteract the itchy finger on the remote control button, and the much-feared viewer indulgence in ZAPPING.

Programme sponsorship See SPONSOR-SHIP: ITC CODE OF PROGRAMME SPONSORSHIP.

Proiaretic code See CODES OF NARRATIVE.

Projection A throwing outwards or forwards; term commonly used within several areas of communication and media studies. The ability to project oneself is an important communication skill. Here projection has been achieved when a person, in giving a talk, making a speech or acting a part on stage has reached the whole audience both with words and his/her personality. Voice, posture, EYE CONTACT, facial expression, GESTURE combine in creating effective projection.

The term can be used in a psychological sense: when people tend to project certain of their motives for behaviour, in particular those which cannot be gratified or which are regarded as unacceptable, on to other people; that is, to assume that these others share the same motives. We may be more inclined to make such assumptions about those we like and perceive as being similar to ourselves. Clearly projection can lead to errors in PERCEPTION and to misunderstandings in the communication process.

Projection of pictures A German Jesuit, Athanasius Kircher (1601–80), professor of mathematics at the Collegio Romano in Rome, is generally thought to be the first person to project a picture on to a screen. His apparatus was crude but effective, containing all the essentials – a source of light with a reflector behind it and a lens in front, a painted glass slide and a screen. Kircher's astonished audience spoke of black magic. Undaunted, the inventor published a description of his findings. The projection of moving pictures was first demonstrated by Baron Von Uchatius (1811–81) in 1853. He used a rotating glass slide, a rotating shutter and a fixed lens. An improved version contained a rotating light source, fixed slides and a series of slightly inclined lenses whose optical axes met on the centre of the screen. See CINEMATOGRAPHY, ORIGINS.

Project Mercury See SATELLITE TRANSMISSION.

Project of self See SELF-IDENTITY;

Prolefeed The rubbishy entertainment and spurious news piped to the proletariat by the Party in George Orwell's novel *Nineteen Eighty-Four* (1949).

Propaganda Usually deliberate manipulation by means of SYMBOLS (words, gestures, images, flags, monuments, music, etc.) of other people's thoughts, behaviour, attitudes and beliefs. The word originates with the Roman Catholic Congregation for the Propagation of the Faith, a committee of cardinals in charge of missionary activities of the church since 1622. See ADVERTISING; BRAINWASHING; ADVERTISING: 'PESTER POWER'; EFFECTS OF THE MASS MEDIA; LOBBYING; RHETORIC.
* Garth J. Jowett and Victoria O'Donnell, *Propaganda and Persuasion* (US: Sage, 1992); Rita Kirk Whillock and David Stayden, eds., *Hate Speech* (US: Sage, 1995).

Property: intellectual property See CULTURE: COPYRIGHTING CULTURE.

Propinquity A significant determinant of group membership, propinquity is liking through proximity; when people are close together physically there is a strain towards amicability which aids group formation, more reliably than with physically distant persons. See GROUPS.

Propp's people In a study of Russian folk tales, Vladimir Propp classified a range of stock characters identifiable in most stories (See his *Morphology of the Folk Tale* published in 1968 by the University of Texas Press). These may be individualized by being given distinguishing character traits but they are essentially *functionaries* enabling the story to unfold. Propp describes a number of archetypal story features: the *hero/subject* whose function is to seek; the *object* that is sought; the *donor* of the object; the *receiver*, where it is sent; the *helper* who aids the action and the *villain* who blocks the action. Thus in one of the world's best-known folk tales, Red Riding Hood (heroine) is sent by her mother (donor) with a basket of provisions (object) to her sick granny (receiver) who lives in the forest. She encounters the wolf (villain) and is rescued from his clutches – and his teeth – by the woodman (helper).

This formula can be added to and manipulated in line with the requirements of the genre, but it does allow us to differentiate between *story level* and *meaning level*, between the *denotive* and the *connotive*, between the so-termed *mimetic plane* (the plane of representation) and the *semiosic plane* (the plane of meaning production). See NARRATIVE.

Prosodic signals Timing, pitch and stress of utterances to convey MEANING.

Protolanguage A term used for the stage in LANGUAGE development at which the child has developed a primitive system of connecting sounds with meanings in order to communicate and consists of protoforms of the child's own creation. The protolanguage is then extended and developed through interaction with parents and others until it is gradually replaced by adult language. A child's protolanguage is thought to be an important basis for the acquisition of the language of its own culture.

Prototyping concept Relates to EVENTS, specifically *key events*, which by their occurrence and their reporting by JOURNALISTS shape subsequent coverage. The prototyping concept is posed by Hans-Bernard Brosius and Peter Eps in 'Prototyping through key events: news selection in the case of violence against aliens and asylum seekers in Germany' in the *European Journal of Communication*, September 1995. Key events, in the words of the authors, 'most often relate to especially severe catastrophes and accidents' which because of their 'outstanding nature . . . confront journalists as well as recipients with a relatively unknown situation which is difficult to evaluate and classify'. In this sense, the key event is not easily classifiable according to traditional criteria of GATEKEEPING or NEWS VALUES.

In the view of Brosius and Eps key events 'play the role of prototypes that come to mind most easily when one talks or write about an issue. Subsequent events sharing similar attributes will be more readily connected to and regarded as typical, of the issue'. It follows that the prototype serves as a 'stabilizing element that makes media content resistant to change and promotes a consistent view of the world in the recipients'. However, as key events are generally unpredictable, the news supply is changed after their occurrence, thus indicating 'an interactionist view of news selection'.

The authors admit the difficulty of identifying – aside from coverage – 'objective criteria for classifying such events as key events', though a dominant characteristic is violence and/or damage.

Proxemics The study of the way people approach others or keep their distance from others: the analysis of what we do with space as a dimension of non-verbal communication (See COMMUNICATION, NON-VERBAL). There appear to be definite features that mark the distance people observe between each other in communication situations. Within three feet is intimate; up to about eight feet is personal; over that distance is semi-public or social. The proximity between communicators differs, obviously, according to the nature of the MESSAGE and varies between cultures, classes and nations. The personal but not intimate distance of Arabs, for example, can be as little as 18 inches – intimidating for an English listener. Middle-class distances tend, it has been found, to be slightly greater than those maintained between working-class communicators. Proxemics extends to the way we allocate space to those extensions of ourselves – rooms, houses, towns, cities – and the manner in which we occupy those extensions. See DEFENSIBLE SPACE; PARAPROXEMICS.

* Edward T. Hall, *The Hidden Dimension: Man's Use of Space in Public and Private* (UK: Bodley Head, 1966); A. Fry, *Safe Space* (UK: J. M. Dent, 1987).

PR: Public relations In *Advertising as Communication* (UK: Methuen, 1982), Gillian Dyer cites the aim of PR as being 'to promote positive and favourable images of people or firms in public life, without actually appearing to do so'. Most companies have PR departments dedicated to creating and sustaining a good image with the general public. PR has also grown big in the service of politicians and political parties. As Dyer says, 'The "publicity boys" rehearse politicians before they go in front of the camera . . . they stage-manage walkabouts . . . kissing babies, all for the benefit of the mass media. Politicians and campaigns are marketed like soap'. Quentin Bell, *The PR Business* (UK: Kogan Page, 1991).

Pseudo-context In his sharply critical assessment of the impact of TELEVISION on society, in *Amusing Ourselves to Death* (UK: Methuen, 1986), American author and communications professor Neil Postman says of a pseudo-context that it is 'a structure invented to give fragmented and irrelevant information a seeming use'. However, the pseudo-context offers us no useful function for the information in terms of action, problem-solving or change. TV is the culprit in this fragmenting process. All that is left for what Postman calls the 'decontextualization of fact' by the non-print media, particularly TV, is to amuse. All knowledge, having been fragmented, is reduced to a trivial pursuit. See EFFECTS OF THE MASS MEDIA.

PSI Para-social identification; that is, members of an audience associate with fictitious characters as portrayed in the media, or with well-known personalities whom they regularly 'meet' through the MEDIATION of radio, TV, etc. See PARASOCIAL INTERACTION.

Psycholinguistics The study of the interplay between LANGUAGE acquisition, development and use and other aspects of the human mind.

Psychology This discipline seeks to explore the way in which individual behaviours are linked together to form a 'personality'. Its focus is upon the experience and behaviour of the individual, upon the individual's reaction to certain physiological and/or social conditions.

Some areas of *social* psychology are concerned with the behaviour of individuals in small GROUPS or crowds; here there is some overlap between this discipline and that of SOCIOLOGY.

* Valerie Walkerdine and Lisa Blackman, *Pyschology and the Media* (UK: Macmillan, 1999).

Public communication Alternative term to *mass media* or *mass communication* and one preferred by some writers; among them, Raymond Williams.

Public communication values See NORMATIVE THEORIES OF MASS MEDIA.

Public cues See BARNLUND'S TRANSACTIONAL MODEL OF COMMUNICATION, 1970.

Public data access See TELEDEMOCRACY.

Public interest immunity (PII) See SCOTT REPORT, 1996.

Public Interest Disclosure Act (UK), 1999 See WHISTLE BLOWING.

Public Occurrences Both Foreign and Domestic Title of the first American newspaper, founded in Boston on 25 September 1690 by Benjamin Harris. The paper survived one issue only, being immediately suppressed by the Governor and Council of the then British colony.

Public opinion Its origins are traditionally traced back to the Greek AGORA, an open space where free citizens gathered to discuss and ideally shape the affairs of state. By its nature public opinion lacks the structure of, for example, ELITE opinion and there are difficulties both of definition and identification. The modern-day opinion poll tests samples of the whole public; market and audience research have pursued increasingly sophisticated, technology-aided modes of opinion measurement. For such research, measurement is of tastes, expectations, needs, values and behaviour as well as opinions. For the student of media, the public is examined from the point of view of how the media represent public opinion, purport to speak for it, indeed, to define it; and to shape it especially in the light of perhaps the most important and specific expression of public opinion voting.

Susan Herbst and James R. Beniger in 'The changing infrastructure of public opinion' published in *Audiencemaking: How the Media Create the Audience* (US: Sage, 1994), edited by James S. Ettema and D. Charles Whitney, explore the connections between the concept of public opinion and the means by which public opinion is measured, the one being influenced by the other; thus *what* public opinion is in any situation is to a degree defined by *how* it is defined and measured. The authors say that 'both polling and voting embrace a conception of public opinion as the aggregation of individual opinions and both provide means for elite management of those opinions'.

They identify three phases in the evolution of public opinion infrastructures. The first is located in the *salons* of mid-eighteenth-century France (See SALON DISCOURSE). Here the political and intellectual elite gathered socially to discuss all matters from art to philosophy, not the least the affairs of state and the nature of government. This *elite model* of public opinion found a modestly downmarket parallel in the coffee houses of London presided over by such 'agorans' as Dr Samuel Johnson (1709–84). These 'spaces' for discourse were only one aspect of the infrastructure; what formed an extension of them were the writings of those novelists, poets, scientists and philosophers who attended the salons or met in the coffee houses.

Towards the middle of the nineteenth century the press became the dominant residence of public opinion, but the newspapers were reflecting, both in the UK and USA, the development of political parties. Herbst and Beniger believe that 'In concert with the newspapers that shared their ideologies, political parties were a critical component of the late-nineteenth century American infrastructure of public opinion expression and assessment'. In fact pressure groups of all kinds, including trade unions, contributed to the *group-based model* of public opinion.

New media technology such as RADIO and more efficient measurement practices contributed to what Herbst and Beniger term 'a shift from publics to audiences'. What had, until the emergence of audience-measurement techniques (such as the Audimeter-based Nielson ratings in the States), been an *aggregate* of opinions, was now a profile of differences – leading to what in advertising terms was to become *segmentation*. The ability to discriminate between shades of opinion as far as this *audience model* is concerned indicates advancing

degrees of rationalization, and this, state Herbst and Beniger, 'works best for those at the top of a given system'. See MEDIASPHERE.

Public radio Term used in Australia to refer to COMMUNITY RADIO.

Public relations See PR: PUBLIC RELATIONS.

Public service broadcasting (PSB) Term refers to any BROADCASTING system whose first duty is to a public within a democracy, serving to inform, educate and entertain, and to regard AUDIENCE as constituting citizens, members of communities and individuals rather than merely as consumers. Throughout world broadcasting in the 1990s PSB has suffered diminishment in the face of commercial competition, greater diversity of provision brought about by new technology and dominant ideologies working towards the PRIVATIZATION of the airways.

The BBC represents, for many, the classic example of public service broadcasting. To survive, it too has had to enter the 'market place' and compete for audiences in an age of DEREGULATION. Indeed *regulation* is a characteristic of PSB and it has applied in a substantially similar manner to COMMERCIAL TELEVISION in the UK. The Independent Broadcasting Authority (IBA) – succeeded by the ITC (Independent Television Commission) in 1991 – was subject to regulation through Parliament. For example, it has been an obligation to screen each week programmes of a serious nature, such as documentaries – programmes which would not be deemed viable if the criteria were solely financial.

Another regulation has been the obligation to strive for *balance* in terms of programme balance and in terms of eschewing biased reporting. In an age when a prime minister could declare that 'there is no such thing as society', the tenets of broadcasting as a service in the interests of the public have inevitably suffered. Not the least of these tenets has been the commitment to universal and equal provision – a direct contradiction of the principles of the market.

Peter Golding and Graham Murdock in 'Culture, communications, and political economy' in *Mass Media and Society* (UK:

Edward Arnold, 1991), edited by James Curran and Michael Gurevitch, write that assaults on PSB are 'part of a wider historical process whereby the state in capitalist societies has increasingly assumed a greater role in managing communicative activity'. This process has occurred hand in glove with big business: modern communication media are significant for their 'growing incorporation into a capitalist economic system'. See BROADCASTING ACT, 1990; COMMANDERS OF THE SOCIAL ORDER; DEREGULATION, FIVE MYTHS OF; McQUAIL'S ACCOUNTABILITY OF MEDIA MODEL, 1997; MEDIASPHERE; PUBLIC SPHERE; REITHIAN; SALON DISCOURSE.
* Denis McQuail, *Media Performance: Mass Communication and the Public Interest* (UK: Sage, 1992); John Keane, *The Media and Democracy* (UK: Polity Press, 1991).

Public sphere With the development of capitalism in the mid-17th century, argues Jürgen Habermas, a public sphere of debate and communicative interchange was opened up – mainly among the bourgeoisie – in Western society. Economic independence provided by private property, the expansion of published literature such as novels which encouraged critical reflection, and the growth of a market-based press created a new public awareness of politics and involvement in public debate. The public sphere existed between the economy and the state and represented a nascent form of *supervision* of government. However, Habermas believed that from the middle of the 19th century the public sphere came to be dominated by the expanded state and organized economic interests. The media ceased to be an agency of *empowerment*, surrendered much of its role as a WATCHDOG and became a further means by which the public were sidelined, and public opinion manipulated. According to Habermas, the public sphere ceased to be a 'neutral zone'. See MEDIASPHERE.
* Jürgen Habermas, *Communication and the Evolution of Society* (US: Beacon, 1979); Habermas, *The Structural Transformation of the Public Sphere* (UK: Polity, 1989); Peter Dahlgren and Colin Sparks, eds., *Communication and Citizenship: Journalism and the Public Sphere* (UK: Routledge, 1993); John Hartley, *Popular Reality: Journalism, Modernity, Popular Culture* (UK: Arnold, 1996).

Pulitzer Prize for journalism American award created by Joseph Pulitzer, Hungarian-born newspaper proprietor and rival of William Randolph Hearst (model for Orson Welles' film *Citizen Kane*, 1943). Along with Pulitzers for journalism, there are prizes for music and literature. Originating in 1947, the Pulitzer prizes are awarded annually.

Q

Quadrophony See GRAMOPHONE.

Quadruplex technique See TELERECORDING.

Qube See INTERACTIVE TELEVISION.

Questionnaires A popular method of data collection, a questionnaire basically consists of a series of questions designed to obtain factual information and/or information about people's attitudes, VALUES, opinions, or BELIEFS about a particular subject or issue. A questionnaire can also be constructed so as to contain questions about a *range* of topics or issues. They are regularly used as a tool of market research; and are central to AUDIENCE measurement.

It is not usually possible to give a questionnaire to all those who make up the group in which you are interested and so questionnaires are normally given to a sample (See SAMPLING); care needs to be taken to ensure that the sample represents the total population, that is the total number of people in that group in all significant respects.

Questionnaires are useful for gathering large amounts of data but may be less useful for investigating an issue in depth; here PARTICIPANT OBSERVATION or INTERVIEWS may be more useful. Further, constructing an unambiguous, unbiased and productive questionnaire is not easy – nor is the impartial analysis of the responses collected.

Quotas Limits placed upon the import of foreign printing, FILM and broadcast material to protect indigenous, home-grown media products. Quotas are immensely difficult to establish and sustain and, with the modern shift of emphasis from producers to consumers (through the availability of VIDEO, CABLE TRANSMISSION and SATELLITE TRANSMISSION) import controls will be even less effective. For quotas to work, it would be necessary to rival the attraction-value of the materials available – cheap, packaged, of proven success with audiences. See MEDIA IMPERIALISM.

Quota sample See sampling.

QWERTY Arrangement of letters on the traditional TYPEWRITER keyboard, devised in 1873 to overcome jamming problems on the world's first production machine, a Remington.

R

Racism Discrimination against individuals or GROUPS of people on the basis of assumed racial differences. The term is problematic in that there is some argument as to whether the concept of race is useful anyway in describing biological differences between people. Racism, though, rests on the belief that different races with specific characteristics can be meaningfully identified. At an individual level such discrimination takes the form of PREJUDICE, whereas the term racism is often used to describe the way in which such discrimination is embedded into the structure of a society.

Cultural racism refers to the perpetuation, consciously or unconsciously, of such discrimination and the beliefs and VALUES on which it rests through the cultural institutions of a society, e.g. education and the mass media. As Stuart Hall notes in 'The whites of their eyes: Racist ideologies and the media', in Manuel Alvarado and John O. Thompson, eds., *The Media Reader* (UK: BFI Publishing, 1990), 'the media are . . . part of the dominant means of ideological production. What they "produce" is precisely representations of the social world, images, descriptions, explanations and frames for understanding how the world is and why it works as it is said and shown to work. And, amongst other kinds of ideological labour, the media construct for us a definition of what race is, what meaning the imagery of race carries, and what the "problem of race" is understood to be. They help to classify out the world in terms of the categories of race'.

One important focus of current media research is the role that the media play in shaping and perpetuating racism and racist STEREOTYPES. Research suggests that negative and stereotypical images of black people abound and present an image of them as inferior, marginal and a potential source of social problems. For instance, Manuel Alvarado, Robin Gutch and Tana Wollen argue in *Learning the Media* (UK: Macmillan, 1987) that the portrayal of black people on television largely falls into four main categories: the exotic, for example coverage of tribal dancing used to welcome members of the Royal Family when visiting various Commonwealth countries; the *dangerous*, for example coverage of immigration as an issue which presents coloured immigrants as a threat; the *humorous*, for example situation comedies such as *In Sickness and in Health* where the humour may well serve to reinforce notions of racial differences to the detriment of coloured people; and the *pitied*, for example media coverage of famines in Africa and of Western attempts to provide aid which tend to represent famine as resulting from the inadequacies of the people and their governments rather than as a legacy of Western colonialism. See BIGOTRY; MEDIA IMPERIALISM; NEWS AID?

* Phil Cohen and Carl Gardner, eds., *It Ain't Half Racist Mum* (UK: Comedia, 1983); John Twitham, ed., *The Black and White Media Book* (UK: Trentham Books, 1990); Tuen van Dujk, *Racism and the Press* (UK: Routledge, 1992); Karen Ross, *Black and White Media: Black Imagery in Popular Films and Television* (UK: Polity, 1996); Oscar H. Gandy Jnr., *Communication and Race: A Structural Perspective* (UK: Arnold, 1998); Steve Fenton, *Racism, Class and Culture* (UK: Macmillan, 1999).

Radcliffe Committee Report, 1967 See D-NOTICES.

Radical Press See UNDERGROUND PRESS.

Radical suppression of potential (technology) See SUPERVENING SOCIAL NECESSITY.

Radio See RADIO BROADCASTING. Also: BROADCASTING ACT, 1990; CELLULAR RADIO; CENTURY SPEAKS, THE; COMMERCIAL RADIO; COMMUNITY RADIO; DOCUMENTARY; FEDERAL RADIO COMMISSION; FOURTEEN-DAY RULE; HOME SERVICE; HOSPITAL RADIO; LIGHT PROGRAMME; MARCH OF TIME; NETWORK; PIRATE RADIO; RADIO BALLADS; RADIO DEATH; RADIO DRAMA; RADIO 1; RADIO 2; RADIO

3; RADIO 4; RADIO 5 LIVE (BBC); 'WAR OF THE WORLDS; WIRELESS TELEGRAPHY; WIRELESS TELE-GRAPHY ACT, 1964.

Radio Authority See COMMERCIAL RADIO.

Radio Authority Programme Code 1
The Radio Authority took over supervision of independent commercial radio (see COMMERCIAL RADIO) from the IBA on 1 January 1991. As well as being empowered to assign frequencies and appoint licensees, the Authority was required to publish codes to which licensees must adhere. Code 1 on *News Programmes and Coverage of Matters of Political or Industrial Controversy or Relating to Current Public Policy* is based on the requirements of sections 90 and 107 of the BROADCASTING ACT, 1990. The Code insists on IMPARTIALITY in news, current affairs and documentary programmes. Notes on the Code state that the rules 'do not mean that "balance" is required in any simple mathematical sense of equal time or an equal number of lines being given to each relevant viewpoint'.

'Personal view' programmes or features on political matters must not be scheduled at times when UK and European Parliamentary or local government elections are pending. Corrections of factual errors should be broadcast, states the Code, 'as soon as is sensibly possible after the original error'. 'Licence Holders must not broadcast fiction or drama designed to commend one side or the other in a matter of political or industrial controversy unless a further drama or fictional broadcast is planned to occur within three months which commends an opposing view.' The Code acknowledges that the 'due impartiality required of a piece of fiction or drama by an independent writer is not identical to that required of a current affairs programme produced by a Licence Holder'.

Radio Authority Programme Code 2
Deals with *Violence, Sex, Taste and Decency, Children and Young People, Appeals for Donations, Religion and Other Matters* and is based on the requirements of sections 90 and 91 of the BROADCASTING ACT, 1990. Bad language is dealt with in the first paragraph of the code, sex in the second and bad taste

in humour in the third. 'The gratuitous use of language likely to offend'; 'Smut, titillation, crudity and sexual stereotyping must be avoided'; and jokes about disability or based on different racial characteristics must be 'considered with great care on every occasion'. The guidenotes on paragraph 1.2 Sex, acknowledge that much of the world's greatest drama, music and fiction 'has been concerned with love and passion, and it would be wrong (if not impossible) to require writers or lyricists to renounce all intention to shock and disturb: but the aim should be to move, not offend'.

On violence the Code states 'Licence Holders should note that there is no evidence that the portrayal of violence which is shown to have good or "legitimate" ends is less likely to be harmful to the individual, or to society, than the portrayal of violence for evil ends'. They must ensure that 'the degree of violence portrayed and described is essential to the integrity and completeness of the programme'.

The utmost care is to be taken concerning the young and the vulnerable. The Code is of the opinion that insecurity 'is less tolerable for a child – particularly an emotionally unstable child – than for a mature adult. Violence, menace and threats can take many forms – emotional, physical and verbal . . . Research evidence shows that those who are socially or emotionally insecure, particularly if adolescent, are especially vulnerable'. The Code declares that while imagination, creativity or realism on radio 'cannot be constrained to such an extent that the legitimate service to the majority is always subordinated to the constraints for a minority', nevertheless 'a civilized society pays special attention to its weaker members'.

The Code deals with a very wide range of matters – hypnotism, horoscopes, accuracy of news, PRIVACY and information gathering, crime, terrorists, defamation, smoking and drinking, drug-taking and solvent abuse, D-NOTICES and the OFFICIAL SECRETS ACT.

Radio ballads Form of musical DOCUMENTARY inspired by RADIO producer Charles Parker, and compiled by folk-singers Ewan McColl and Peggy Seeger, beginning in 1958 with *The Ballad of John Axon*. The introduction of high-quality portable taperecorders to the BBC enabled Parker and his team to create new patterns of vocal sound, interlaced with sound effects (real, not studio-simulated) which served as an 'impressionistic' means of describing the lives and work of ordinary people. John Axon was a train driver, killed in a crash, and the nature of his life was recreated in ballad and recollection. *Singing the Fishing* (1960), taking for its theme the hard life of the North Sea fisherman, won the Italia Press award. The BBC withdrew financial support from this pioneering team in 1964. See RADIO DRAMA.

Radio broadcasting The 1st World War (1914–18) had given impetus to the development of radio for military purposes, and the training of wireless operators. Visionaries of the age saw the possibility of wireless programmes as an exciting extension of wireless messages – a 'household utility' which would create a world of sound, of voices and music; that would annihilate distance and offer undreamed-of opportunities for CULTURE, entertainment and information. With the ending of the war, crystal sets tuned in by their 'cat's whisker' became immensely popular. The valve, called the 'magic lantern of radio', developed between 1904 and 1914, soon usurped the place of the crystal.

The first 'broadcast' of music and speech was made by an American R.A. Fissenden in 1906. The American Radio and Research Company was broadcasting concerts twice and three times a week as early as 1916, though KDKA of Pittsburg won the earliest renown as a pioneer in the field (on air, 1920).

A ban imposed on 'amateur' radio in Britain at the outbreak of the 1st World War was not lifted until 1919, but in February 1920 the Marconi Company in the UK began broadcasting from Writtle/Chelmsford, though later in the year the Post Office withdrew permission for these broadcasts. However, on 14 February 1922 the first regular broadcasting service in Britain was again beamed from Writtle, organized by the Experimental Section of the Designs Department of Marconi. Their

London station, 2LO, began broadcasting on 11 May of the same year.

The Post Office, faced with nearly 100 applications from manufacturers who wanted to set up broadcasting stations, and realizing the need to have some sort of control of the airways, proposed a consortium of companies to centralize broadcasting activity: the British Broadcasting Company was born, and John Reith appointed its managing director (See BBC ORIGINS). The BBC, set up by Royal Charter, came into existence 1 January 1927. It was to hold a monopoly of broadcasting in the UK until COMMERCIAL RADIO was legalized in the SOUND BROADCASTING ACT 1972.

From its beginning, radio broadcasting in the US was financed by ADVERTISING; from its beginning, radio broadcasting in the UK was free of advertising; the one was predominantly local, the other a national public service and eventually a national institution. No study of the evolution of broadcasting in the UK can avoid also being an analysis of the philosophy, vision and practices of the BBC's managing director and later director general John (later Sir John) Reith. Varyingly called the Napoleon of Broadcasting, and Prospero, the all-powerful magician, Reith disliked politics and politicians, viewed commerce with disdain (and commercialism with contempt). He forged a definition of PUBLIC SERVICE BROADCASTING that dominated broadcasting – both radio and TV – for generations and, even in the age of the dispersal of control, affects us still.

Radio news readers wore dinner jackets and bow ties to read the news, a symbol of the aloofness and distancing characteristic of Reith and much of the output of the BBC. There was even a Pronunciation Committee. Yet the Corporation resisted criticisms from the popular press that its tastes were too elitist. It was to give drama and classical music – as well as many other forms of music – a new structure and a new popularity. Equally, there was room for developing the special potentials of radio – in outside broadcasts, drama DOCUMENTARY, discussion programmes, and fireside talks.

The greatest fear of the broadcasters was – and continues to be – of government interference. Reith's caution was as monumental as the extent of his control. His desire to render the BBC beyond political reproach led to the Corporation often censoring itself so as to be one step ahead of being censored. The risks to the BBC were not imagined. During the General Strike of 1926 Winston Churchill wanted the government to commandeer the Corporation, a move Reith managed to resist – but at a price: during the strike no representative of organized labour was permitted to broadcast, and the Leader of the Opposition, Ramsay MacDonald, was also banned.

* A. Briggs, *The History of Broadcasting in the United Kingdom* (UK: Oxford University Press, four volumes, 1961, 1965 and, volumes 3 and 4, 1979); P.M. Lewis and J. Booth, *The Invisible Medium: Public Commercial and Community Radio* (UK: Macmillan, 1989); Paddy Scannell and David Cardiff, *A Social History of British Broadcasting: Vol. 1 1922–1939: Serving the Nation* (UK: Blackwell, 1991).

Radio Cracker See COMMERCIAL RADIO.

Radio Death Or Hate Radio; nickname given to Rwanda's Radio Television Libre des Milles Collines (Thousand Hills Television Radio) which, following the assassination of President Juvenal Habyarimana, conducted an intensive campaign of hatred against the minority tribe, the Tutsis (9 per cent of the population as against 90 per cent Hutu). RTLM proved the power of radio in a land almost without TV and with an illiteracy rate of over 50 per cent of the population. A broadcast in April 1994 claimed that 'by the 5th May the elimination of the Tutsis should be finished'. In an International Media Report (unpublished, 1995) for their BA degree in Media and Communication (West Kent College with the University of Greenwich), Wendy Green and Heather Williams write that the relentless propaganda of hatred 'has been blamed for 200,000 dying in the three weeks following the President's murder and hundreds of thousands more being butchered as Hutu militia combed the countryside'.

In 1995 Reporters Sans Frontières initiated a civil law suit in Paris against the founders and organizers of Radio Death alleging their responsibility for genocide, violation of humanitarian law and crimes against humanity.

In response to the torrents of hatred emerging from RTLM, Radio Gatashya was formed and appeared on air for the first time in August 1994 in Goma, its own nickname, Humanitarian Radio, providing an information service of help and support for the thousands of refugees. Sanctioned by the United Nations High Commissioner for Refugees, Radio Death's rival became, in the words of Green and Williams, 'the lone voice of humanity in the radio waves war of propaganda and hatred'.

In a BBC Radio 4 documentary *War Radio* broadcast in December 1998 journalist Micha Glenny compares the propagandist radio of Rwanda with that of local stations in Bosnia during the late 1990s, emphasizing that as LANGUAGE is the essence of radio's power, so it is the essence of ethnic and other differences. Listeners learn how ethnic groups previously sharing a common language began – through radio – to introduce words and terms that served as markers of difference. The antidote to a medium which lies as it dominates is not, Glenny concludes, to shut it down but to match it with rival radio which is professional and a respecter of the truth. It is argued that all United Nations peacekeeping enterprises should be supported by a radio service which from the beginning of UN activity is 'on air' in the battle for hearts and minds.

Radio drama The first ever radio play was Richard Hughes' *Danger* (1923), about a couple trapped in a mine, but the play which appears to have had the most substantial impact as a work in a new medium was Reginald Berkeley's *The White Château*, broadcast by the BBC to an audience of over 12m on Armistice Day, 1925 and telling an extremely harrowing story of the trench-war. Since that time hundreds of writers have been given a start in their professional lives by radio, one of whose many virtues is cheapness: today, a 30-minute radio play requires one day's studio time; an hour-long play, two days. The radio playwright need not concern him/herself with the massive costs of scene-changes; there is little need to keep costs down by writing plays for two people and an armchair. The whole world of time and space is at the writer's command.

Most importantly, there is the awaiting *imagination* of the listener. The best radio plays take the listener on a journey into his/her imagination, where the play is given its own unique setting, the characters a unique appearance – all with the help of voices, sound effects and silence; an art form, as the poet W.H. Auden once said, which is 'not spoiled by any collision with visual reality'.

Radio drama possesses the characteristic of intimacy – it has made the interior monologue, the soliloquy, a dramatic device perhaps more convincingly acceptable than on the stage; at the same time, because its stage is contained by no proscenium arch or screen-frame, because its 'stage-set' is actually the mind of the listener, radio also lends itself successfully to epic drama: Shakespeare can be marvellous on radio.

Among writers who took an early interest in radio as a serious art form was the Irish poet Louis MacNeice (1907–65). His verse plays broadcast during and after the 2nd World War, such as *The Story of My Death* (1943) and *The Dark Tower* (1946) impressively explored the potential of radio, while in 1953 another poet, Welshman Dylan Thomas (1914–53), gave to the world one of the best known and most loved plays for radio, *Under Milk Wood*. The play was first broadcast on 25 January 1954, with a distinguished all-Welsh cast and produced by Douglas Cleverdon.

For 30 years Val Gielgud as Head of Radio Drama at the BBC guided the evolution of the radio play, himself producing and writing. Throughout its history, radio drama has witnessed a strong tradition of able producers – such as Cleverdon, Lancelot Sieveking, Donald McWinnie and Alfred Bradley – nurturing writers who later became famous: Harold Pinter, Stan Barstow, Giles Cooper, Allan Prior, Alun Owen, William Trevor, Henry Livings, Peter Terson, Alan Plater, David Rudkin and Tom Stoppard.

Despite its creative potential, radio as a dramatic medium has acquired less *status*, and been paid less attention than other – more glamorous – media; and less than it deserves. However, the BBC continues to broadcast between 200 and 300 radio plays a year, classical drama as well as new works. See TELEVISION DRAMA.

Radio: Independent radio See COMMERCIAL RADIO.

Radio Luxembourg See COMMERCIAL RADIO.

Radio Normandy See COMMERCIAL RADIO.

Radio Northsea PIRATE RADIO station which began broadcasting off the coast of Essex immediately prior to the General Election of 1970. Mindful of the Labour Government's antipathy to COMMERCIAL RADIO and the Conservatives' support for it, Radio Northsea broadcast pro-Tory PROPAGANDA at an election in which the 18–21 age group were voting for the first time.

Many constituencies in London and the south-east were marginal seats. Labour lost the election; in the constituencies nearest Radio Northsea, the swing against Labour was greatest. At the Royal Opening of Parliament on 2 July 1970, the Queen's Speech confirmed that legislation would be introduced for local radio stations 'under the general supervision of an independent broadcasting authority'.

Radio 1, Radio 2, Radio 3, Radio 4, Radio 5 Live (BBC) Radios 1 to 4 have broadcast in their present form from 1967; Radio 5 took to the air in August, 1990, to be revamped into Radio 5 Live in March 1994. Prior to 1967 there was the Home Service, catering for news, plays, talks, comedy shows and magazine programmes – the *Talk* channel; the Light Programme, largely for popular music and entertainment; and the Third Programme serving the world of classical music and drama. During the 1960s PIRATE RADIO invaded the airways with pop music which attracted large audiences. The Marine Broadcasting (offenders) Act, 1967 made such stations illegal. BBC's Radio 1 was created to meet the new demand and continued through the 1990s to vie with COMMERCIAL RADIO stations for the attention of popular music fans.

Radio 2 took on a similar if not

identical role to that of the Light Programme, Radio 3 that of the Third Programme and Radio 4 became Britain's premier talk radio channel. For its richness, diversity and sheer quality of output, Radio 4 must rank among the world's finest radio services. Faced with competition from CLASSIC FM radio, Radio 3 has proved itself responsive to audience needs without sacrificing (too much) quality.

Radio 5 was to be a speech-led service catering for the needs of children and young people, sharing airtime with news and sport. Just when this pioneering new channel was beginning to win listeners and to produce programmes of originality, the BBC abandoned the adventure of, in the words of the Controller of Radio 5 Pat Ewing, introducing 'a new generation to speech radio', and opted for Radio 5 Live, more general in orientation, often crossing lines with Radio 4 but in terms of its sports coverage, unexcelled.

Random sample See SAMPLING.

Ratings See AUDIENCE MEASUREMENT.

Reaction shot When a person is being interviewed on TELEVISION there are regular in-cuts where the viewer is offered a glimpse of the reactions of the reporter or interviewer – nodding, smiling, acknowledging. When interviews take place on location rather than in the studio, such reaction shots are usually filmed separately and edited in later. See SHOT.

Readership See MEDIASPHERE.

Reading Just as, in modern usage, we refer to TEXT as any human-made artefact, rather than merely a printed text, so we refer to *reading* as a process which is a response to all texts. Use of this term suggests a more positive, attentive and interpretative reaction to a text rather than merely looking. We read critically; we analyse, while at the same time modern usage accepts the more open nature of 'readings' – their POLYSEMY (or many-meaningness). A *work*, as Roland Barthes has defined it, emanates from a creator, an encoder – writer, artist, composer, for example – but the *text* belongs in the sphere of reading and thus becomes, as it were, the property of the decoder.

It does not necessarily follow that all readings are of equal value, for inevitably there are informed as contrasted with uninformed readings. Recognition of *competence* has to be considered, and this would involve what Noam Chomsky has termed 'linguistic competence', as well as knowledge, experience, training and a degree of EMPATHY. The study of media communication is largely about learning to read competently, with perception and understanding.

Realism That which is portrayed as 'reality' in art, literature, theatre, film fiction or documentary and photography. It constitutes an imitation of perceived reality, a simulation. Because it is the result of a range of choices concerning subject-matter and aesthetics, realism is a *construct* of reality rather than a reproduction of it, influenced by VALUE and IDEOLOGY and convention. Socialist realism in Russian cinema, for instance, focuses on the realities of the lives of workers, on the land or in factories, but such portraits of reality are highly charged with the ideology of the Soviet system in the ways that labour is idealized rather than portrayed by means of a critical READING of the system.

Susan Strehle in *Fiction in the Quantum Universe* (US/UK: University of Carolina Press, 1992) suggests the use of the term 'actualism' rather than 'the old mechanistic reality' because it has 'its roots not in things [or facts] but in acts, relations and motions'. The term corresponds to ACTUALITY, an approach pioneered by early RADIO documentary makers to allow real situations to be communicated with a minimum of intervention from the programme-maker. Yet however absent seems to be the hand of MEDIATION it is (in actuality) ever-present.

Peter Dahlgren in *Television and the Public Sphere: Citizenship, Democracy and the Media* (UK: Sage, 1995) says of TELEVISION texts that 'realism' (his inverted commas) is a 'very central feature' but one which is highly problematical. We should remind ourselves, Dahlgren believes, that 'all representation involves construction'. In discussing TV the author talks of the 'pleasure of verisimilitude'.

Essentially TV is 'mimetic', it imitates reality rather more than it interprets it. In Dahlgren's view this limits the potential TV has for POLYSEMY (many meanings) and thus in this context, the representation of alternative realities.

Reassurance, structure of See NEWS: STRUCTURE OF REASSURANCE.

Received pronunciation (RP) That mode of pronunciation in English which is free of regional ACCENT and aspires to a generally accepted standard; derives from the speech of the court and of public schools; traditionally the 'vocal sign' of the educated person, adopted as the norm for BBC broadcasters, and eventually being termed 'BBC English'. RP no longer has the prestigious status or the dominance it once had. Regional accents have been 'in' since the 1960s, though RP has retained a substantial foothold in national broadcasting.

Receiver See SENDER/RECEIVER.

Recency effect See FIRST IMPRESSIONS; PRIMACY, LAW OF.

Reception studies In recent years particular research emphasis has been placed upon the ways that AUDIENCES *receive* media messages; how they react to their reading, listening and viewing; and what audiences *do* with that experience, what *meanings* they make of it. Such reception studies have, as far as TELEVISION is concerned, shifted from a prime focus on audience response to news and current affairs to the investigation of audience reception of popular genres, such as soaps. See AUDIENCE MEASUREMENT.
* Tony Wilson, *Watching Television: Hermeneutics, Reception and Popular Culture* (UK: Polity Press, 1995); Sonia Livingstone, *Making Sense of Television: The Psychology of Audience Interpretation* (UK: Routledge paperback, 1998).

Record player See GRAMOPHONE.

Redundancy In communication terms, that which is conventional or predictable in any message. Its opposite is **Entropy**, that which is unexpected and surprising, of low predictability. John Fiske in *Introduction*

to Communication Studies (UK: Methuen, 1982) says 'The English language is about 50% redundant. This means we can delete about 50% of any utterance and still have a usable language capable of transmitting understandable messages'. Redundancy is established through frequent use until it becomes a CONVENTION, both technical, in terms of correctness, and social, in terms of general acceptability. It is essential if the MEANING of messages is to have wide currency and be 'on wave-length' with the CODES and reference tables of the receiver.

The **Entropic** challenges these codes and reference tables with novelty – new expression, new thought, overturning predictability and probability. The art of the AVANT-GARDE is entropic; at least in its initial phase, it speaks in a LANGUAGE the general public find difficult to understand, and often provocative. Of course the shock of the new passes: yesterday's outrage is today's fashion, yesterday's entropy is today's redundancy. A scan of the popular arts reveals their reliance on the conventional forms and practice which make up redundancy – the predictable rhymes and metres of pop songs, for example, the repetitive refrains of folk songs. Fiske writes, 'Redundancy is generally a force for the status quo and against change. Entropy is less comfortable, more stimulating, more shocking perhaps, but harder to communicate effectively'. See PHATIC LANGUAGE.

Referent The actual object, entity in the external world to which a SIGN or linguistic expression **refers**. The referent of the word *table* is the object 'table'.

Referential code See CODES OF NARRATIVE.

Reflective-projective theory of broadcasting and mass communication Posed by Lee Loevinger in 'The ambiguous mirror: the reflective-projective theory of broadcasting and mass communication' in G. Gumpert and R. Cathcart, eds., *Inter/Media: Interpersonal Communication in a Media World* (US/UK: Oxford University Press, 1979). Loevinger states 'that mass communications are best understood as mirrors of society that reflect an ambiguous image in which each observer projects or sees his own vision of himself and society'. The media reflect images of society but not of the individual.

'While the mirror can pick out points and aspects of society, it cannot create a culture or project an image that does not reflect something already existing in some form in society.' BROADCASTING can clarify or distort images of society; it can focus broadly or narrowly. According to the theory, the media 'are most unlikely to become instruments of social reform or great public enlightenment'. Thus violence on TV reflects the existence of and tolerance of violence in society.

Loevinger emphasizes the point that the image is perceived *individually* by each member of the media audience who projects or sees in the media his/her own visions or images: 'broadcasting is an electronic mirror reflecting an ambiguous image of its environment in which the audience sees its vision of society.' See THEORIES AND CONCEPTS OF COMMUNICATION.

Reflexivity Self-monitoring in terms of COGNITIVE practice; but more significantly for the analysis of the individual's self-positioning within a fast-changing society in which NORMS, VALUES and practices are rendered less certain, less distinct. Reflexivity is central to the construction of identity. It operates intuitively and aesthetically as well as cognitively and mass communication is seen to be an agency in the control of or liberation of self-interpretation in relation to the READING of and reaction to media TEXTS. Reflexivity makes critical use of NARRATIVES, personal and collective, through which sense is forged out of experience. See SELF-IDENTITY.

Reformers See ADVERTISING: MAINSTREAMERS, ASPIRERS, SUCCEEDERS AND REFORMERS.

Refutation The employment of counter-arguments, evidence and proof to dispute the arguments of another person. Strictly speaking, to disprove allegations.

Register Term describing the compass of a voice or instrument, the range of sound tones produced in a particular manner. The soprano and the bass sing in different *registers*. The word also describes the structures of LANGUAGE used in varying social contexts: its levels of vocabulary, sentence construction, tones and inflexions. Thus the register adopted by an infant school teacher in his/her class will differ from the register selected for the staff room, just as a scientist will adjust his/her register between conversations held with scientific colleagues and with casual acquaintances in the local pub. In PRINTING, register refers to the exact adjustment of position, as of colours in a picture, or letterpress on opposite sides of the page.

Regulatory favours In an age when multinational corporations have acquired local, national and global *voice* by investing in media, it comes as no surprise to observe them using that voice to promote corporate interests, to employ those media to pressurize government to grant them favours. Jeremy Tunstall and Michael Parker in *Media Moguls* (UK: Routledge, 1991) use the term *regulatory favours* which governments cede to big media-owning companies in return for a 'good press'. These favours principally constitute the abolition or waiving of media regulations which might hinder expansionist interests. See CONGLOMERATES; DEREGULATION; PRIVATIZATION.

Reinforcement There has been much argument over the role of the mass media in reinforcing, in underpinning, certain social and political VALUES and structures. Considerable attention has been given to two areas: the media's portrayal of violence and the role of the mass media in political communications.

There are those who claim that the frequent incidence of violence in the media has contributed to an alleged increase in acts of violence in society. Research evidence, however, gives few clear pointers as to the nature or extent of any media influence. One school of thought rejects the notion that the media directly encourage violent behaviour in all viewers but argues that the media violence may reinforce already existing tendencies to violence in some viewers. This position is not without its critics. James Halloran in an essay entitled 'The effects of the media portrayal of violence and aggression' in J. Tunstall, ed., *Media Sociology*

(UK: Constable, 1970), points to several research projects which have indicated that the media may play a more direct and general role in shaping the audience's attitude towards violence.

P.F. Lazarsfeld, B. Berelson and H. Gaudet in a classic study of the effects of political communication by the mass media on voting behaviour, *The People's Choice* (US: Columbia University Press, 1948), comment that the media's main effect is to reinforce existing political preferences. The notions of *selective perception*, SELECTIVE EXPOSURE and *selective recall* are used to explain how the same output can reinforce the diverse views, values and beliefs of a mass audience. It is suggested that the audiences, rather than being passive receptacles for media output, select from the output those messages which are in accordance with their own prior dispositions and give attention to these (see AUDIENCE: ACTIVE AUDIENCE).

The close links between media organizations and other dominant social and political institutions have led researchers to investigate the degree to which the mass media reinforce prevailing social and political hierarchies. Michael Tracey in *The Production of Political Television* (UK: Routledge & Kegan Paul, 1978) argues that as regards BROADCASTING the relationship between the media and dominant institutions tends to be complex and to have been characterized by 'alternate moments of apparent autonomy and real subjection'.

Researchers analysing the media's treatment of women have noted the way the media have reinforced the traditional, limited role of women in society. In this respect the media would appear by and large to back up the patriarchalism of contemporary British social and political hierarchies. There is also concern that some media representations of ethnic minorities reinforces negative stereotyping of members of these groups. See EFFECTS OF THE MASS MEDIA; POLITICS OF ACCOMMODATION (IN THE MEDIA); RESONANCE.

Reithian Attitudes to BROADCASTING as typified by the first Director General of the BBC, Sir John Reith (1889–1971), who dominated the rise of broadcasting in the UK like a colossus. Dour, high-principled, autocratic, paternalist and a Scottish Presbyterian to boot, Reith was appointed General Manager of the newly formed British Broadcasting Company in December 1922. 'Some might call it luck', writes Ronald Blythe in *The Age of Illusion: England in the Twenties and Thirties 1919–40* (UK: Penguin, 1964), 'he called it Providence. The microphone was born and John Reith was there to suckle it, to guide its infant lispings, to wean it from the pap of the first years, to train it, lecture it, cherish it, and protect it from the tycoons, sometimes to spank it, but finally to see it take its place authoritatively among the most ancient institutions in the country. And all in less than a decade'.

Reith's philosophy was that broadcasting was a heaven-sent opportunity to educate and enlighten the people in the ways of quality, and that 'giving the people what they wanted' was the way to perdition. This 'Tsar of Savoy Hill' as the PRESS called him, believed 'in the medicinal effects of education – a cultural dictatorship' said the *New Statesman* on Armistice Day, 1933. Though George Lansbury MP said of Reith, 'I have always felt that Sir John Reith would have made a very excellent Hitler for this country', Clement Attlee saw advantages: 'He puts up a splendid resistance to vested interests of all kinds.' Elitist, imperious and sabbatarian, Reith nevertheless created in the BBC an organization resistant to commercialism, favouring the arts, serious debate and notions of public responsibility. Reith strove for IMPARTIALITY but never achieved balance: coverage of Royal activities in the 1920s and 1930s was not in any way matched by coverage of the activities of the Labour movement and the unions and, during the General Strike of 1926, the BBC remained strictly 'neutral': it stayed silent. Reith, the Napoleon of Broadcasting, as Colonel Moore Brabazon called him, resigned as 'DG' (director general), as his own staff spoke of him, in 1937. See BBC, ORIGINS.

Relic gestures Those physical *gestures* which have outlived their original situation, yet continue to be used to effect even though their derivation is no longer obvious or explicable. Such gestures survive not only from historical past but from a human's infantile past. For example, the rocking to and fro of disaster victims in the face of intolerable grief.

Repertoire of non-verbal behaviour - See NON-VERBAL BEHAVIOUR: REPERTOIRE.

Repetitive strain injury (RSI) Brought on by regular and intensive use of computer keyboards and thus the 'Disease of journalists' as well as secretaries; resulting in severe pain in the hands, arm, neck and back. Once RSI has taken hold it is difficult and sometimes impossible for the sufferer to carry on working. It was reported in 1991 that a third of the journalists on the *Financial Times* were affected by RSI.

Reporters Sans Frontières Montpellier-based group of journalists set up in 1987 to defend PRESS freedom worldwide, and journalists in trouble.

Report-talk rapport-talk This is one way in which men and women's conversational style differs according to Deborah Tannen in her *You Just Don't Understand Me: Women and Men in Conversation* (UK: Virago Press, 1992). Men, she argues, are confident with public speech or what she calls *report-talk*, whether this be in a formal or an informal situation where several people are in conversation. In these situations, when the company is mixed, men typically participate more in conversation than women and in part their performance may be a way of establishing status and control. In a more private setting though, this difference in the participation rate between men and women may change or even reverse. Here *rapport-talk* with which women, Tannen argues, are more comfortable is more appropriate. Rapport-talk is used for establishing and reinforcing intimacy. These differences reflect the different GENDERLECTS that Tannen argues men and women use, which in turn reflect one main difference in their use of conversation: men using conversation to establish status and control, women to establish intimacy.

Representation A core function of media is to *re*-present to AUDIENCES the realities of 'the world out there'. Most of our knowledge of that world – its realities – is brought to us via the media; and our perception of reality is MEDIATED by newspapers, TV, advertisments, films, etc. The media *image* the world for us. They do this by means of selection and interpretation which operate through GATEKEEPING and according to AGENDAS which are suffused by IDEOLOGY. The media represent to us the past as well as the present, and representations – or interpretations – of the past affect our perceptions of the present. Out of such representations arise issues – concerning the representation of women, for example, of race, poverty, minorities. What we as audience know of Africa and Africans, of Serbs and Albanians, of Israelis and Arabs is what we have experienced through the reports and pictures brought to us by the media. The study of media representation, therefore, is central to cultural, media and communication studies. Because it is impossible to represent the world in all its massive complexity, media representation has to be viewed as a 'version' of reality, in which FRAMING has taken place according to criteria such as NEWS VALUES or pressures to propagandize, sensationalize, binarize (that is, divide 'us' from 'them' – See WEDOM/THEYDOM) or seek to impose MEANING upon webs of complexity. Representation is essentially about *definition*, and media representation tends to be about imposing certain definitions, and therefore meanings, over others; thus endeavouring to affect the preferences of the public. See DISCOURSE.
* Nick Lacey, *Image and Representation: Key Concepts in Media Studies* (UK: Macmillan, 1998).

Representation, machinery of See MACHINERY OF REPRESENTATION.

Representation of crime on screen See CRIME: TYPES OF CRIME ON SCREEN.

Representative sample See SAMPLING.

Repressive state apparatus See IDEOLOGICAL STATE APPARATUSES.

Repressive use of the media See EMANCIPATORY USE OF THE MEDIA.

Re-regulation The notion that DEREGULATION of media – essentially BROADCASTING –

has actually meant fewer regulations and more freedom is challenged by Karen Siune and Wolfgang Truetzschler in *Dynamics of Media Politics* (UK: Sage, 1992). The authors write 'What has frequently been referred to as deregulation has turned out to be regulation in another form, and the concept of "re-regulation" is much more appropriate'. The more systems are fragmented, the authors argue, the more detailed rules are created concerning minor – but still significant – aspects of media structure; in contrast to the former overall framework 'that provides only vague outlines'.

Research centres (into the media) In the UK there are centres of research into CULTURE and the media at the universities of Birmingham, Glasgow, Leeds, Leicester, London, Loughborough, Portsmouth and Sheffield. At Birmingham there is the Centre for Contemporary Cultural Studies; at Glasgow the GLASGOW UNIVERSITY MEDIA GROUP; at Leeds the Centre for Television Research; at Leicester the Centre for Mass Communication; at Loughborough the Communication Research Centre; at Portsmouth, the Media Research Group; at Sheffield the Centre for English Cultural Tradition; and in London the Media Research Groups at Goldsmith's College and the London School of Economics and Political Science.

Resistance (of audience to media) See DOMINANT, SUBORDINATE, RADICAL; POLYSEMY.

Resistive reading Occurs when AUDIENCE chooses not to accept without question the PREFERRED READING of media messages. Considerable research has been conducted into the capacity of audiences, and of segments of audiences such as women, to react independently to DOMINANT DISCOURSES: hence the active-audience thesis. See AUDIENCE: ACTIVE AUDIENCE; EMPOWERMENT; RESPONSE CODES.

Resonance Term used by George Gerbner and fellow researchers at the Annenberg School of Communications, University of Pennsylvania, Philadelphia, to describe a condition experienced by TELEVISION viewers when what they see matches their expectations. If what they see confirms their vision of the world, of reality, that vision *resonates*. It is reinforced. More, for in 'The "main-streaming" of America: violence profile no. 11' (*Journal of Communication,* Summer 1980) Gerbner, Larry Gross, Michael Morgan and Nancy Signorielli state that where TV reality and a person's experience or PERCEPTION of reality are in alignment, 'the combination may result in a coherent and powerful "double dose" of the television message'. For example, city dwellers living in centres of high crime will find TV's violent imagery congruent with their experience. 'These people receive a "double dose" of messages that the world is violent, and consequently show the strongest associations between viewing and fear'. See EFFECTS OF THE MASS MEDIA; MAINSTREAMING; MEAN WORLD SYNDROME.

Response Reaction to a stimulus or stimuli which may or may not result in observable behaviour. In the context of communication and media studies, the term usually refers to an individual or audience's reaction to messages received. See AUDIENCE.

Response codes See DOMINANT, SUBORDINATE, RADICAL; POLYSEMY.

Restricted code See ELABORATED AND RESTRICTED CODES.

Reterritorialization According to James Lull in *Media, Communication and Culture* (UK: Polity Press, 1995), reterritorialization means '. . . first that the foundations of cultural territory – ways of life, artifacts, symbols and contexts – are all open to new interpretations and understandings', and secondly, 'implies that culture is constantly reconstituted through social interaction, sometimes by creative uses of personal communications technology and the mass media'. Thus cultural territory is potentially dynamic and changing, so re-shaping is constantly possible.

Revisionism See HISTORICAL REVISIONISM.

Rhetoric Traditionally, the theory and practice of eloquence, whether spoken or written; the use of LANGUAGE so as to persuade others. The word is almost always used today as a term of criticism: rhetoric is the style in which bare-faced persuasion – politicking – is used. It is emotive; it belongs to speeches and while it is very often resounding it is rarely eloquent because it trades in empty phrases and endless repetitions. It is essentially REDUNDANT in that it tells supporters what they already know and antagonists what they know and don't want to hear. Rhetoric is the stock-in-trade of the PRESS, and of the popular press in particular. Practically every front-page headline is rhetorical in that it is soaked through with the ideological attitudes of the newspaper, not the least the belief in what sells newspapers, what commands attention, what readers want to be told.

Indeed it might be said that one of the prime functions the popular press sets itself is to translate actuality into rhetoric: complex issues are translated into the simplifying mode of MYTH, of WEDOM, THEYDOM, Militant and Moderate, Order and Disorder, Black and White, Management and Unions, Dries and Wets. See NEWS VALUES.

Rhetoric of numbers Phrase used by Itzhak Roeh and Saul F. Feldman to describe how the PRESS, the popular press in particular, use numbers and amounts for rhetorical rather than factual purposes. The authors' analysis of the headlines of two Hebrew dailies, one elite, one popular, is reported on in 'The rhetoric of numbers in front-page journalism: how numbers contribute to the melodramatic in the popular press', published in *Text* 4/4 (1984).

Rhyming slang See SLANG.

Rhythms of reception Term used by Tania Modleski in *Living with a Vengence: Mass Produced Fantasies for Women* (UK: Methuen, 1982), to refer to the relationship between women's daytime viewing patterns for SOAP OPERAS and the performance of housework tasks. This relationship, Modleski argues, extends to the relationship between the viewer's work in the home and the narrative offered by soap operas with their emphasis on the domestic, neighbourhood characters and family dilemmas. Arguably it also tends to locate the viewer as a housewife and mother.

Right of reply A long-established practice in continental countries, the right of reply in the UK press has been argued for long, hard and generally unsuccessfully. Such a right would require newspaper editors to publish within a given time the replies of individuals or organizations who allege serious PRESS misrepresentation, or face a special court and a fine if found to be in error. It is argued that such a right would act as a deterrent to editorial bias and unethical practices. Newspapers *do* publish apologies but these are usually for printing factual errors which might land them with LIBEL actions. See CAMPAIGN FOR PRESS AND BROADCASTING FREEDOM; PEOPLE'S COMMUNICATION CHARTER.

Riley and Riley model of mass, communication, 1959 John W. Riley Jr and Matilda White Riley in 'Mass communication and the social system', in R.K. Merton, L. Broom and L.S. Cottrell Jr, eds., *Sociology Today: Problems and Prospects* (US: Basic

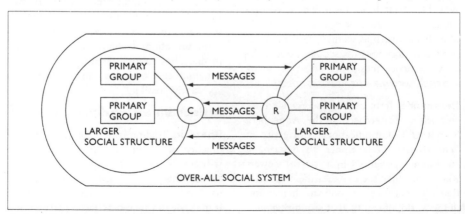

Riley and Riley model of mass communication, 1959

Books, 1959; Harper Torch Books, vol. 2, 1965) pose a model in which the process of communication is an integral part of the SOCIAL SYSTEM.

For Riley and Riley, both the Communicator (C) and the Recipient (R) are affected in the message process of sending, receiving, reciprocating, by the three social orders: the primary group or groups of which C and R are members; the larger social structure, that is the immediate community – social, cultural, industrial – to which they belong, and the overall social system. All of these are in dynamic interaction, with messages flowing multi-directionally.

The mass media audience Riley and Riley perceive as being neither impassive nor isolated but 'a composite of recipients who are related to one another, and whose responses are patterned in terms of these relationships'. See COMMUNICATION MODELS; NETWORK.

Ritual, rites of passage A ritual can be seen as a carefully constructed act of communication, a focused organization of SYM-BOLS, loaded with a range of meanings significant for the individuals or social GROUPS concerned. Some rituals involve a great deal of ceremonial activity whilst those of everyday life may be fairly simple. Rituals can be religious or secular. They operate to give individuals or groups a sense of collective identity and security.

Rites of passage is a term used to refer to those rituals which mark transition from one status, stage or state to another either by the whole community or, more commonly, by individuals. The ceremonies which mark such changes provide a symbolic confirmation of the change of social identity involved: a wedding ceremony would be an example of one such ceremony.

Rogers and Dearing agenda setting model, 1987 Published in the *Communication Yearbook 11* (US: Sage, 1987) and examined in *Communication Models for the Study of Mass Communication*, McQuail and Windahl eds. (UK: Longman, 5th impression, 1998), this development by E.M. Rogers and J.W. Dearing of previous AGENDA SETTING models is a welcome acknowledgement of the *competing* agendas in the public sphere.

In their Yearbook article, 'Agenda-setting, where has it been, where is it going?' the authors see the public agenda as existing separately, though locked between, the policy agenda, of the state, of government, and

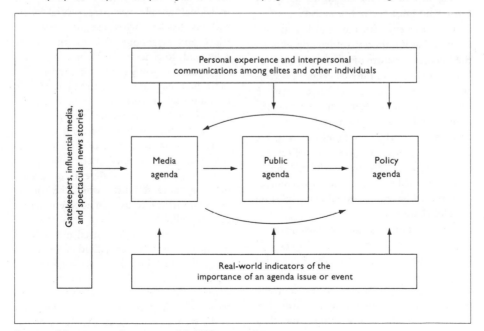

Rogers and Dearing agenda setting model, 1987

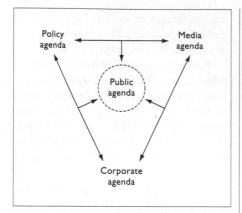

Tripolar model of competing agendas

the media, each subject to influence by the others.

The triad of agendas is itself influenced by a number of contextual factors 'out there', for example, spectacular news stories. There are substantial factors which shape one, two or all agendas but which may also temper, or restrict, the effectiveness of those agendas, such as personal experience or what Rogers and Dearing call 'real world indicators' of the importance of an agenda issue. In this sense, reality remains something other than what is constructed in the media, or 'fed to' the public as reality by those who forge the policy agenda.

One problem with the model is its *linearity* in that it does not sufficiently indicate the interactive nature of competing agendas. It also presents the public agenda (presumably the agenda of the public) as being in the same league, in terms of power, as the other agendas. Lastly, the model could arguably have a fourth agenda added to it, the *corporate* agenda, in order to reflect the increasingly prominent role in all aspects of policy, public debate and media operation, played by transnational companies on the global stage.

The Dictionary's authors would pose here a modest alternative to Rogers and Dearing, which emphasizes the interactive nature of the dominant agendas while shifting the public agenda into no less central a position, but one which is by its nature less defined, inevitably more diffuse and thus more open to influence.

Roles A social role consists of the expected behaviour associated with a particular social position. Thus the social position of a 'journalist' identifies a body of behaviours expected of a journalist, that is the role of the journalist in society. Role is a relational term. People play roles within a context in which other people are also playing roles. Roles within society or a social group carry with them responsibilities, obligations and rights. There is some evidence that the role a person or GROUP occupies within a given social context can influence the pattern of communication adopted. Basil Bernstein, for example, argues in 'Social class, language and socialization' in P.P. Giglioli, ed., *Language and Social Context* (UK: Penguin, 1972) that selective access to the Elaborated LANGUAGE code may well result from the fact that there is selective access to the social roles which require its use (see ELABORATED AND RESTRICTED CODES).

Behaviour identified with a role is not necessarily rigidly prescribed. Through INTERACTION with others, individuals can change the expectations which determine a particular role. To some extent roles can be *negotiated* within a social context; within small, informal groups roles are often arrived at through interaction alone. An individual usually performs several roles, such as teacher, wife, daughter, mother, friend and neighbour. This multiplicity of roles tends to generate problems of conflicting demands, known as **role strain**. The individual may often have to adjust his/her communication pattern – non-verbal as well as verbal – to suit each particular role. Role strain occurs when our communication patterns cut across each other; when unexpected encounters take place between people from different role situations or, more seriously, when the role is deeply unnatural to us – an apparent denial of 'true' self.

The concept of role is used not only to describe the position of individuals within a social structure but also that of groups or organizations. In this sense commentators write of the role – or roles – of the mass media in society; hence the so-claimed role of the PRESS AS WATCHDOGS, defenders of the public good.

* Erving Goffman, *The Presentation of Self in Everyday Life* (UK: Penguin, 1959).

Roll film The first roll film for use in cameras was introduced by A.J. Melhuish and J.B. Spencer in 1854, though roll film cameras were not marketed until the Kodak of 1888.

Romance: ideology of See IDEOLOGY OF ROMANCE.

Ross Commission Report on the Press, 1949 Under the chairmanship of Sir David Ross, the Commission followed from an initial debate on the press in the House of Commons. It worked for two years before producing its report (1949). Ross's main conclusions were that there was nothing approaching a monopoly of ownership of the UK press, and that the existing concentration of ownership was not so great as to prejudice the free expression of opinion or the accurate presentation of news.

However, Ross was not so optimistic about standards of quality and OBJECTIVITY: 'all the popular papers and certain of the quality fall short of the standards achieved by the best, either through excessive partisanship or through distortion for the sake of news values'. The Report proposed the formation of a General Council of the Press to encourage the growth of public responsibility and public service on the part of journalists.

It took four years for the newspaper industry to respond positively to this proposal. The Council, later named the Press Council (1964–91), made its first pronouncement in July 1953 concerning a *Daily Mirror* poll on whether Princess Margaret should marry her father's equerry, Group Captain Peter Townsend. See COMMISSIONS/COMMITTEES ON THE MEDIA.

Rostrum camera In TV, a film camera fixed in position over a table and used to take still photographs.

Rotary press See CYLINDER PRESS.

Royal Commissions on the media See COMMISSIONS/COMMITTEES ON THE MEDIA.

Rumour Indirect and unsubstantiated information; hearsay; transmitted along informal channels by word of mouth. Rumour has the following characteristic features: it can rarely if ever be traced back to its origin; it can spread (almost) at the speed of light; it will only spread if the rumour has the momentum of credibility (even if this credibility is only the size of a pinch of salt), and it thrives in close-knit communities which have either no regular or formal channels of communication or channels which are inefficient or not recognized as important.

A process of MEDIATION occurs at most or all points of telling, the original narrative being exaggerated and usually decorated with envy, spite or resentment. Good news rarely travels as quickly as bad news. In organizations, rumour often circulates most strongly in sub-cultures of those people generally well down in the HIERARCHY and who tend to be last in the queue when information is passed through formal channels.

The only antidote to rumour is efficient, full and open, participative communication, with strong lines of horizontal as well as vertical communication. The impact of rumour is rarely beneficial; in the main, rumour is corrosive of relationships, fuels suspicion and bad feeling. Its favourite habitat is a communication vacuum. One dubious compensation is that the subjects, or 'victims', of rumour are generally the last to hear of it; unless, of course, they started the rumour themselves. See INTERPERSONAL COMMUNICATIONS; LEVELLING, SHARPENING, ASSIMILATION; LOONY LEFTISM.

Running story See SPOT NEWS.

Rushdie affair See FATWA.

Rushes In FILM-making, prints of 'takes' that are made immediately after a day's shooting; these are examined by the film team, led by the director, before the next day's shooting. Produced at a 'rush' from negative, they are also known as 'dailies'.

S

Salience All messages are not given equal attention by the receiver; some messages, or parts of a MESSAGE, appear more prominent, more **salient,** to the receiver. This predisposition towards certain messages, or parts of a message, can be the result of a complex of factors such as life experience, attitudes, VALUES and interests. There has been considerable research into the role of the media in the formation of salience, particularly in the field of current affairs. The focus of investigation here is the extent to which extensive media coverage of certain issues leads the audience to perceive those issues as being politically significant. See AGENDA SETTING; McCOMBS AND SHAW AGENDA SETTING MODEL OF MEDIA EFFECTS, 1976.

Salon discourse According to Susan Herbst and James R. Beniger in 'The changing infrastructure of public opinion' in *Audiencemaking: How Media Create the Audience* (US: Sage, 1994), edited by James S. Ettema and D. Charles Whitney, the first use of the term *public opinion* was made by Jacques Necker, the finance minister to the French King Louis XIV (1638–1715). Necker was referring specifically to the *salons* of the day, generally if not always presided over by women of high birth and attended by intellectuals, poets, statesmen and philosophers. Here, among many things, matters of state were freely discussed and later diffused by the writings of those who attended the salons. Herbst and Beniger refer to this as the *elite model* of public opinion infrastructure: 'The public in the model is composed only of the most highly educated and influential members of society, while the bulk of the people are purposely excluded because their opinion is thought to be uninformed, and are in any case irrelevant – most people have no political power.'·The authors argue that this model of public opinion held sway until the American and French revolutions.

Salutation display Means by which we demonstrate that we wish someone well, or at the very least do not ostensibly wish them harm – greeting when we meet and when we part company. Salutation display varies according to such factors as the nature of our relationship with the greeted person, the context of the encounter and

the length of prior separation. See GESTURE; SHORTFALL SIGNALS.

Samizdat Russian, meaning 'self-published', a secret publication during the Soviet-Communist era, circulated by hand, usually printed on a duplicator or simply on a TYPE-WRITER with carbon copies, by dissident writers, at great personal risk of reprisals by the authorities. *The First Circle* (1968) by Russian novelist Alexander Solzhenitsyn began life in Samizdat. The word **Tamizdat** described work produced by Russians in the west, published there and then smuggled into the Soviet Union. *Dr Zhivago* (1957) by Boris Pasternak (1890–1960) is an example of this. See GLASNOST.

Sampling A statistical method of selecting a group for analysis, from a larger social group known as the *population*, the statistical term for all those persons, events or entities that are relevant to the subject of the enquiry. The aim of sampling is to be able to use what is discovered about the **sample** group as a basis for inference about the behaviour of the population. The reliability of such inferences depends upon how far the sample is representative of the population. A **representative sample** is constructed in such a way that it contains members of various significant categories and classifications in the same proportion as they appear in the population.

Not all samples are representative, or *quota* samples: random sampling techniques are also used. A **random sample** is selected in such a way that every member of the population has an equal chance of being chosen. Such a sample is used when it is felt that the population is not divided into particularly significant categories or classifications.

Saniel Pedwar Cymru See S4C.

Sapir-Whorf linguistic relativity hypothesis Developed by two notable linguists, Edward Sapir (1884–1939) and Benjamin Lee Whorf (1897–1941). Succinctly stated, it proposes that ways of thinking and patterns of CULTURE (and also to some extent social structure), are determined by the structure of the LANGUAGE used in a particular culture. An individual's or group's thought and DISCOURSE about life generally can only be expressed in language and are thus constrained by the language structure available. See POSTMODERNISM.

Satellite transmission There are three main types of satellite: (1) weather and observational satellites; (2) communications satellites and (3) space probes. Sputnik in 1957 was the first observational satellite; *Telstar*, in 1962, the first communications satellite. Working off solar-powered batteries, satellites have equipment for monitoring the conditions in and around themselves and sending data back to earth for control purposes. Also, they carry reception equipment for control signals from earth for correction of orbital travel etc. Satellites orbiting the earth have generally given way to geo-stationary operation, that is satellites stationed some 23,000 miles out in space at a constant altitude and keeping pace with the revolutions of the earth.

Signals from ground stations are beamed to the geo-stationary communications satellites and reflected by them to receiving stations which then relay the signals by cable for recording or transmission, or to receiving 'dishes' or antennae. Most communication satellites receive and transmit simultaneously from a number of earth stations.

TV pictures were first transmitted via satellite on 10 July 1962 when *Telstar* was launched at Cape Canaveral, US, and circled the earth every 157.8 minutes, enabling live TV pictures transmitted from Andover, Maine, to be received at Goonhilly Down, Cornwall and in Brittany (11 July). In 1964 the unmanned *Syncom* relayed pictures of the Olympic Games from Tokyo. The first commercial communications satellite was *Early Bird* which marked the beginning of regular TV transmission via satellite (2 May 1965).

The UK franchise for a three-transponder direct-broadcast satellite (DBS) was granted in 1986, with a start date of 1990. After financial and investment doubts which led to early backers – such as the BBC – withdrawing from DBS plans, the contract for Britain's first two DBS channels was awarded to British Satellite Broadcasting (BSB). Rupert Murdoch's Sky Satellite arrived ahead of BSB, beginning programme transmission in the UK in March 1989.

Between them, the rival companies estimated to have spent £1.25 billion, yet by October 1990, such were the colossal start-up expenses, that British Satellite Broadcasting was forced into a merger with Sky. The 'squarial' dish, created to bring BSB programmes into the home suddenly became scrap. The founding principle of the free market – that competition is the basic dynamic of success – was itself 'squarialized'. Sky took on the initials of BSB, becoming British Sky Television. Corporate monopoly of satellite transmission joined that of those other 'free enterprise' industries in the UK, gas and electricity.

Murdoch's ambition to make News Corp a global provider of TV programming was marked in the 1990s with the acquisition of Star Television in Asia. In November 1995 News Corp joined with the Globo Organization of Brazil, Grupo Televisa of Mexico and Telecommunications Inc. of the US to set up a satellite TV service for Latin American and Caribbean markets with estimated total launch costs of 500m dollars.

Scanner Mobile control room used in outside TV broadcasts.

Scheduling Process by which programmes or types of programme are 'timetabled' in order to attract maximum audiences, and to keep them attracted in the face of competition from rival programmes. The aim of the programme scheduler is to minimize the danger of audiences switching off, or even worse, over. Michael Pilsworth in '"An imperfect art" – TV scheduling in Britain' in *Sight and Sound*, Autumn 1980, describes the 'art' as building 'towards a climax, the audience peak, little by little as the evening progresses. Peaks and troughs are to be avoided'. Low-appeal programmes are usually placed against weak opposition, or they are 'hammocked', that is, placed in between 'bankers', trusting to the INHERITANCE FACTOR. Conversely there is the so-called 'pre-echo' effect where anticipation of a really popular programme can induce viewers to switch on earlier – and thus watch a programme with less popular appeal.

Scheduling techniques assume a high degree of passivity on the part of an audience, and might be said seriously to underestimate audience potential for variety and challenge. Competitive scheduling above all reduces the range of choice open to the viewer simply by making risk-taking more difficult.

Schema (plural, schemata). A schema is basically a framework or pattern, stored in the memory, which preserves and organizes information about some event or concept. The framework may be expanded as new information about the event or concept is acquired. It is argued by several researchers concerned with learning and memory, that existing schemata affect our PERCEPTION of new information and that there is a tendency for us to try and fit new information into our existing frameworks – at least initially.

Schemata themselves can form cross-linkages to provide a wider mental or conceptual map of an area of knowledge or experience. This perspective on the way in which we receive and process information has important implications for the analysis of the way in which we send and receive messages in the communication process.

Schramm's models of communication, 1954 Wilbur Schramm built on the SHANNON AND WEAVER MODEL OF COMMUNICATION, 1949 (The Mathematical Theory of Communication), but was more interested in mass communication than in the technology of communication transmission. In 'How communication works' in W. Schramm, ed., *The Process and Effects of Mass Communication* (US: University of Illinois Press, 1954) the author poses three models (see figure).

Shannon and Weaver's 'Transmitter' and 'Receiver' become 'ENCODER' and 'DECODER', and their essentially linear model is restructured in Schramm's second model to demonstrate the overlapping, interactive nature of the communication process and the importance of what the Encoder and Decoder bring with them to the communication situation, their 'Field of Experience'; where that field of experience overlaps is the signal, Schramm's third model emphasizes

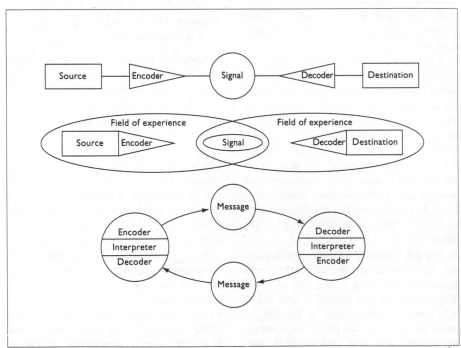

Schramm's models of communication, 1954

FEEDBACK, and in doing so points up the *circularity* of the communication process. See COMMUNICATION MODELS.

Scott Report, 1996 The five-volume *Report on the Inquiry into the Export of Defence Equipment and Dual-Use Goods to Iraq and Related Prosecutions* by the Right Honourable Sir Richard Scott was published in February 1996. So sensitive about its contents was the Conservative government of John Major that access to the report was denied to the Opposition until half-an-hour before the Report was due to be debated in Parliament. This meant that government ministers and their Whitehall teams were given eight days in which to prepare their defence.

The response to the report was, in the view of many commentators as well as a substantial section of the public, as shameful as the behaviour the Scott inquiry delved in to. Indeed, the way that the government machine, prior to the publication of the report, attempted to rubbish it, and then when it had been published, distort its findings by selection and evasion, ought to be a case study for communication students everywhere (See CENSORSHIP; NEWS MANAGEMENT).

Basically (forgive the distortion through selection) the story is as follows: arms sales to Iraq immediately prior to the invasion by Saddam of Kuwait were banned. This was government policy. What actually was occurring was that arms-making equipment continued to be exported to Iraq, and this matter was known to ministers. The 'conspiracy' did not, however, include HM Customs and Excise who brought a case against the directors of the arms-machinery exporting company, Matrix Churchill.

Evidence which could have at least clarified the company's position, and headed off both court case and possible prison sentences was in the hands of ministers, namely William Waldegrave, the Treasury chief secretary, and Sir Nicholas Lyell, the Attorney-General. Yet the evidence which could have cleared Matrix Churchill was withheld using PIIs, Public Interest Immunity certificates; in common parlance, 'gagging orders', signed by ministers. These,

originating as 2nd World War emergency powers, 'should be reviewed' Scott urged in his report, for they have been a 'reprehensible abuse of executive power by successive administrations'.

The key accusation concerned ministerial accountability to Parliament; the key issue, whether ministers had knowingly lied to Parliament over the Iraq – Matrix Churchill affair. In such matters, what you see (or read in this case) is what you perceive: the government claimed 'No cover-up!', the Opposition parties 'read' Scott as saying otherwise.

The vote in the Commons following a debate on Scott (26 February 1996) was won by the government by one vote (320 to 319) in what Donald Macintyre of the *Independent* called 'a high wire drama' and the *Sun* a 'Commons mauling' and the *Daily Mirror* 'the hollowest of victories'. Though the *Mirror* demanded on its front page 'Now Go!' there were no government resignations.

Screen entertainment culture See BEDROOM CULTURE.

Scripts These are described by Eric Berne in *What Do You Say After You Say Hello?* (UK: Corgi Books, 1975) as 'a preconscious life plan' by which an individual structures 'longer periods of time – months, years or his whole life'. Scripts are developed in our early years but then have the capacity to influence and shape our transactions with others. A script contains within it an individual's self-concept and his/her general perception of and orientation towards other people and the world. It thus forms a basis for action. Berne identifies a number of possible scripts individuals may have as a result of their early experiences. One example is the 'You Can't Trust Anybody' script. An individual with this script would obviously be suspicious and distrustful of others and act accordingly; such a script has obvious implications for communication with others. Berne argues that individuals tend to seek proof that their scripts are valid, by behaving in a way or interpreting behaviour in a manner that will reinforce them. So to a greater or lesser extent behaviour might be script-driven. Scripts can obviously be limiting but can, of course, be changed.

In *TA Today* (UK: Lifespace, 1987) Ian Stewart and Vann Joines discuss three main types of script: Winning, Losing or Hamartic and Non-winning or Banal scripts. A 'winner' is an individual who achieves the goals he/she has set for him/herself. It is also implied that these are met, 'comfortably, happily and smoothly'. A loser does not achieve set goals or does but is unhappy or damaged as a result. The authors write that 'Losing scripts can be broadly classified as first-, second- and third-degree, according to the severity of the payoff. .... A third-degree losing script culminates in death, serious injury or illness or a legal crisis'. Third-degree losing scripts may be defined as *hamartic* – a word 'derived from the Ancient Greek hamartia meaning "a basic flaw". It reflects the way in which a losing script, like an Ancient Greek drama, seems to lead inexorably from the early negative decision to the tragic final scene'. A non-winning or banal script is one focused on playing safe and not taking risks. It may result in small gains and losses but the individual will remain a 'non-winner'. It seems that many people have a mixture of scripts: winning in some aspects of life whilst losing in others. However, Stewart and Joines argue, 'Most important of all is to realize that *any script can be changed*'. See GAMES, TRANSACTIONAL ANALYSIS.

Secondary groups See GROUPS.

Secondary viewing Term describing the circumstances in which TV viewing forms an accompaniment to other activities such as homework and reading.

Secrecy In a *Guardian* review, 'Whitehall secrets farce' of David Hooper's *Official Secrets: The Use and Abuse of the Act* (UK: Secker, 1987), former civil servant Clive Ponting writes that secrecy 'is deeply embedded in the British political and administrative structure and the ethos of the ruling class. We desperately need a democratic revolution and a massive increase in government accountability'. In the 1980s and 1990s in Britain secrecy became a way of government perhaps even

more intensely than in the past. But it has been selective secrecy. Ponting himself was unsuccessfully prosecuted for divulging information about the sinking of the Belgrano during the Falklands War (1982). His argument in defence was that he had a public duty which in certain circumstances should always override confidentiality. However, he states that when ministers rather than their servants 'leaked' damaging information, 'instead of the police the Cabinet Secretary was called in to conduct a discreet enquiry and the Attorney-General handed out immunity from prosecution'. 'In 75 years,' says Ponting, 'not a single Minister or ex-Minister has ever been prosecuted despite the most flagrant breaches of the law'. See CENSORSHIP; ELITE; FREEDOM OF IN-FORMATION; HEGEMONY; OFFICIAL SECRETS ACT; PRIVACY; SPYCATCHER CASE; ZIRCON AFFAIR.

Section 28 Local government legislation introduced by the Tory government in 1988 included a clause, section 28, banning the 'promotion of homosexuality' by local authorities.

Jackie Stacey in 'Promoting normality: Section 28 and the regulation of sexuality' in *Off-Centre: Feminism and Cultural Studies* (UK: HarperCollins Academic, 1991) explores the way in which the debate was conducted on Section 28, a debate in which the media obviously played a key role. She argues the focus of the debate was the need to protect the nuclear family against what the Thatcher government presented as attacks from, in the main, lesbians and gay men and their alternative concepts of sexuality and definitions of the family. Lesbians and gay men were portrayed as powerful threats whereas in reality, Stacey argues, they were relatively powerless groups within society.

However, their representation as being powerful helped the government, aided by certain sections of the media, to legitimate attacks against them and their rights. Indeed some coverage in the press argued that lesbian and gay men had gone too far in their pursuance of equal rights and had only themselves to blame if they became victims of a backlash. In this debate little mention was made of the threat heterosexual men can pose to family life in terms of wife- or child-abuse. Stacey argues that 'Heterosexual men are in fact the group in this society which has proved most threatening to children. Yet Section 28 was consistently legitimized by the claim that children need protection from lesbians and gay men who threaten them with corruption, if not implicit seduction'. Indeed the debate at times was conducted in the tunes of a classic MORAL PANIC. The introduction of Section 28 met with considerable opposition.

Segmentation Term generally used to describe the constituent nature of TELEVISION – chopped up into segments, of news, comedy, drama, commercial, documentary, quiz shows etc. John Fiske in 'Moments of television', in Ellen Seiter *et al.*, *Remote Control: Television, Audience and Cultural Power* (UK: Routledge, 1989), writes, 'Segmented texts are marked by abrupt transformations from segment to segment that require active, experienced, televisionally literate viewers to negotiate'.

In a broader sense and in relation to ADVERTISING and the targeting of audiences for the sale of goods and services (not to mention the marketing of images, ideas, ideologies, political parties, etc.), segmentation relates to current practices dividing consumers into life-style categories. Segmentation indicates a recognition that audiences are heterogeneous rather than homogeneous. Classification of audience into socio-economic groupings has become an industry in its own right. See VALS TYPOLOGY.

Selective exposure Individuals have a tendency to attend to, **expose** themselves to, messages that are consistent with their existing attitudes and beliefs. Equally they practise *selective perception* – reading messages in accordance with their existing attitudes. Thus they may either ignore or misinterpret those messages, or parts of a MESSAGE, which conflict with or are dissimilar to held attitudes and expectations. Sometimes also referred to as *selective negligence*. See DIFFERENTIAL PERCEPTION; DISSONANCE; REINFORCEMENT.

Self-actualization See MASLOW'S HIERARCHY OF NEEDS.

Self-concept A person's self-concept is the total view that person has of him or herself. It includes such elements as an individual's PERCEPTION of his or her character, body image, abilities, emotions, qualities and relationships with others. The self-concept is commonly seen as being composed of the self-image and self-esteem. The self-image can be seen as the descriptive part of the self-concept. It is the picture we have of ourselves. Self-esteem, on the other hand is the evaluative part – it is how we feel about ourselves.

The self-image can be further divided into three elements: the self as I think I am, the self as I think others see me and the self I would like to be (the ideal self-image). Discrepancies between the ideal self-image and the self as I think I am can result in a low level of self-esteem as our self-esteem is usually based on our perceived successes and failures in life. Other people are clearly very influential in shaping any individual's conception of self, as in part an individual's self-concept depends upon his/her perception of the ideas others have about him/her. Individuals also attempt to influence the ideas others have, through controlling the impressions they create in self-presentation. The FEEDBACK received from self-presentation enables the individual both to evaluate and shape his/her self-image. Paul Watzlawick, Janet Helmick Beavin and Don. D. Jackson have suggested in *Pragmatics of Human Communication: A Study of Interactional Patterns, Pathologies and Paradoxes* (US: W.W. Norton, 1967), that others respond to us in three distinct ways and that these include *confirmation*, *rejection* and *disconfirmation*. Confirmation takes place when others affirm our self-view; rejection when others do not treat us in a manner consistent with our self-view and disconfirmation when others fail to respond to our view of self or when others respond in a neutral manner.

Messages concerning the self abound in the content of INTERPERSONAL COMMUNICATION, whilst INTRAPERSONAL COMMUNICATION also plays a vital role not only in the generation of ideas about ourselves, some of which we may incorporate into the self which we present to others for feedback, but also in the decoding and evaluating of messages which we receive from others and in deciding whether to or how to act on them.

How we see ourselves affects the way we communicate. If, for example, we see ourselves as popular and sociable we are likely to be confident and outgoing in our communication with others. Excessive concern over self-esteem can lead to self-consciousness. People who are self-conscious are often shy, easily embarrassed and anxious in the presence of other people.

It should be remembered that the self-concept is not fixed but subject to continuing modification and change; it can change according to the situations we are in, the people we are with and over time and may also be found in MASS COMMUNI-CATION, for example in images of ideal women found in advertisements. See ASSER-TIVENESS TRAINING; CONFIRMATION/DISCONFIRMA-TION; DEVIANCE AMPLIFICATION; IMPRESSION MANAGEMENT; JOHARI WINDOW; LABELLING PRO-CESS (AND THE MEDIA) SELF-FULFILLING PROPHECY; SELF-MONITORING; SELF-PRESENTATION.

* Brian Morris, *Anthropology of The Self: The Individual in Cultural Perspective* (UK: Pluto 1994).

Self-disclosure statements, verbal and non-verbal, that we make intentionally about ourselves which give others previously unknown information. See JOHARI WINDOW.

Self-disclosure is based on honest, open INTERACTION between people. Usually when we self-disclose to others, they reciprocate and in this way a deeper understanding and relationship may develop. Of course we have to make careful choices in the first place about those to whom we will self-disclose, at what rate, to what extent, on what topics and in what situations. Self-disclosure involves an element of risk; an error of choice, for example if we self-disclose too much too soon in a relationship, may result in a rebuff.

Through self-disclosure we not only learn more about others but also more about ourselves in that others' disclosures can contain views about ourselves. It is also a means by which we can come to terms with the positive and negative aspects of our self-image.

Self-fulfilling prophecy This effect occurs when the act of predicting that certain behaviour will take place helps cause that behaviour to occur and the prediction or prophecy is fulfilled. The expectations people have of an individual's behaviour can, if communicated to the individual, help create a situation in which the individual conforms to the expectations and fulfils the prophecy. There is a clear link between LABELLING and the self-fulfilling prophecy effect in that the act of applying a label can be the first step in ensuring a self-fulfilling prophecy.

The effect may be found particularly in situations where individuals have differing amounts of power and where one or more individuals are involved in the evaluating of others.

Clearly the message contained in INTER-PERSONAL and MASS COMMUNICATION may often carry labels and thus have the potential for triggering self-fulfilling prophecy effects, but it is largely through intrapersonal communication that an individual decides whether or not to conform to the expectations of others. Further, the self-fulfilling prophecy effect is only one of many influences on our behaviour and it may not be relevant in all cases. See DEVIANCE AMPLI-FICATION; LABELLING PROCESS (AND THE MEDIA); SELF-CONCEPT.

Self-Identity In his book *Modernity and Self-Identity* (UK: Polity Press, 1991) Anthony Giddens defines self-identity in the conditions of late modernity as 'the self as reflexively understood by the person in terms of his or her biography'. Whilst self-identity is seen as normally having a degree of continuity it is 'such continuity as interpreted reflexively by the agent'. Self-identity also involves cognitive awareness of the self: 'To be a "person" is not just to be a reflexive actor, but to have a concept of a person.' Self-identity is an integral element of the SELF-CONCEPT.

Giddens further argues that although concepts of what a 'person' is may vary across cultures, 'The capacity to use "I" in shifting contexts, characteristic of every known culture, is the most elemental feature of reflexive conceptions of personhood'. Self-identity, Giddens argues, requires self-conscious thought and action; it is not 'something that is just given . . . but something that has to be routinely created and sustained in the reflexive activities of the individual'. It is an ongoing project, for in the conditions of late modernity self-identity has to be explored, developed and modified against a background of changing circumstances.

Giddens identifies four influences evident in the structure of post-traditional societies which create the plurality of choices that make difficult the struggle of maintaining a coherent self-identity and which make necessary a *project of self*. Identities can only be achieved through choice – 'we have no choice but to choose' – given that much of the tradition which allowed them to be ascribed or indicated has lost its hold. Individuals inhabit a 'pluralization of lifeworlds' in which they have to present a number of different identities as they move from one social sphere to another, often negotiating differing expectations of their behaviour as they do so. What Giddens terms 'methodological doubt' is yet another feature of late modernity; certainty is seen as fragile as truth is seen as contextual and authority and reason provisional. 'Mediated experience' is seen to be at the heart of social life. Through the mass media and travel a vast range of 'lifeworlds' are presented to audiences, thus increasing the range of options available in the construction of identities. Further, such identities have to be adjusted to cope with the range of changes that an individual is likely to encounter in such a society; the change to self-identity that usually accompanies a divorce being but one example. Giddens argues that little help is available to individuals in making such choices, although artefacts within consumer CULTURE may promise guidance – self-help manuals, for example. The ability to control SELF-PRESENTATION and in doing this to actively construct and reconstruct bodily appearance is seen by Giddens as essential to maintaining a coherent self-identity.

Don Slater notes in *Consumer Culture & Modernity* (UK: Polity Press, 1997) that another influence on late modernity – 'commercialization' – has resulted in 'a greater fluidity in the use of goods to construct identities and lifestyles'. It has also resulted, arguably, in individuals perceiving themselves, in part, as consumers – a perception which would reinforce the notion that individuals must make choices. There are, of course, innumerable attempts to appeal to aspects of the self in ADVERTISING and marketing. The danger, warns Giddens, is that 'the project of self becomes translated into one of possession of desired goods and the pursuit of artificially framed styles of life . . . The consumption of ever-novel goods becomes a substitute for the genuine development of self'. For Slater, 'Consumer culture "technicizes" the project of self by treating all problems as solvable through various commodities'. Further, 'identity can be seen as a saleable commodity'. Individuals may feel under pressure to 'sell' themselves in various social situations. Arguably many commodities are promoted on the grounds of their value to the individual in his/her task of constructing and maintaining self-identity. See IMPRESSION MANAGEMENT; MASLOW'S HIERARCHY OF NEEDS; SELF-CONCEPT; SELF-MONITORING.

Self-image See SELF-CONCEPT.

Self-monitoring This term refers to the degree to which people are sensitive to and able to respond to the demands of social situations with regard to their own behaviour. Richard D. Gross in *Psychology: the Science of Mind and Behaviour* (UK: Hodder & Stoughton, 1986) identifies high and low self-monitors. High self-monitors are motivated to and able to assess the demands of different situations and adjust their SELF-PRESENTATION and general behaviour accordingly. Low self-monitors on the other hand tend to behave in a similar fashion regardless of the situation, and their behaviour is more likely to be influenced by their own internal states. High self-monitors appear much more able to conceal their own moods, feelings and so on. Evidence suggests that high self-monitors have better social skills; for example, they can interpret non-verbal communication more accurately than low self-monitors.

Self-presentation Term used to describe the way in which we behave and communicate in differing social situations. It carries with it the implication that to some degree we consciously present ourselves to others in any given situation. The FEEDBACK we gain from self-presentation plays a role in shaping and changing our SELF-CONCEPT.

Erving Goffman in *The Presentation of Self in Everyday Life* (US: Anchor, 1959; UK: Penguin, 1971) employs the dramaturgical perspective to analyse social interaction. Goffman writes, 'life itself is a dramatically enacted thing. All the world is not, of course a stage, but the crucial ways in which it is not are not easy to specify . . . In short, we all act better than we know how'.

Goffman puts forward several useful concepts which have become influential in analysing self-presentation. A key concept is that of *persona*. The persona is the character we take on to play a part in a particular social situation. Different situations will usually require us to play different parts and therefore adopt different personas. So, for example, the persona an individual would adopt when visiting a folk festival with friends might be very different from the persona he/she would adopt in carrying out his/her work role as a High Court Judge.

The persona is part of our way of dealing with different people and the demands of different social situations. Once chosen for a particular situation it influences how we communicate in that situation. The ability to choose an appropriate persona for a situation and communicate accordingly can be seen as an important communication skill, as can the ability to shift from one persona to another as situations demand it. Further, it is likely that the ROLE a person is playing may dictate the kinds of persona it would be appropriate to adopt in any given situation.

Goffman uses the term *performance* to describe the act of self-presentation and in many cases these performances can be seen as *staged*. In staging a performance in everyday life we would use props just as actors would on a theatre stage; obvious examples here are DRESS, cars and furnishings. A well-established pattern of action which may be

used as part of a performance is known as a *routine*. An example here would be a characteristic display of temper.

According to Goffman we also perform from behind a *front* which he defines as 'that part of the individual's performance which regularly functions in a general and fixed fashion to define the situation for those who observe the performance'. Standard parts of the front are the *setting*, e.g. one's home and the *personal front*, e.g. age, DRESS, sex. See CONFIRMATION/DISCONFIRMATION; IMPRESSION MANAGEMENT; SELF-MONITORING.

Self-regulation Although BROADCASTING in the UK has traditionally been regulated by acts of Parliament and governing charters, the PRESS has been self-regulating. The Press Council was an *advisory* body, set up by the newspaper industry; its successor, the PRESS COMPLAINTS COMMISSION, which started work 1 January 1991, has similarly no statutory powers. The question often asked is whether the press, dominated by a handful of media barons, can be left to regulate itself – that is, be judge of its own malpractices. A negative view of self-regulation has been taken by the CAMPAIGN FOR PRESS & BROADCASTING FREEDOM in its publication, *Free Press*. The June 1991 issue declared 'The CPBF is sceptical that the PCC will take any meaningful steps to redress press abuses'. See CALCUTT COMMITTEE ON PRIVACY AND RELATED MATTERS, 1990.

Self-serving bias See ATTRIBUTION THEORY.

Self-touching See GESTURE.

Selsdon Committee Report on Television 1935 The task of Lord Selsdon's Committee was 'to consider the development of Television and advise the Postmaster-General on the relative merits of several systems and on the conditions under which any public television should be provided'. The Report recommended that the BBC be made the initiating body, and that the cost of TV broadcasting be borne from the revenue derived from the existing 10 shilling RADIO licence fee. See COMMISSIONS/COMMITTEES ON THE MEDIA.

Semantic code See CODES OF NARRATIVE.

Semantic derogation of women See MALE-AS-NORM.

Semantic differential The analysis of *semantic differential* is one of three traditional empirical methods of measuring audience response to the media, the others being CONTENT ANALYSIS and the investigation of USES AND GRATIFICATIONS. In exploring semantic – or MEANING – differentials, analysts concentrate on people's attitudes, feelings and emotions towards certain concepts and VALUES as actuated by media performance. The values under scrutiny are presented in preliminary form by words or statements. These are then selected and expressed as binarily opposed concepts (Offensive – Not Offensive, for example) on a five or seven point scale. Binary opposition is the most extreme form of significant difference possible. A sample audience, or selected group, is tested on the scale or scales, and the results averaged. The method was given currency by Charles Osgood in *The Measurement of Meaning* (US: University of Illinois Press, 1967).

Semantics A major branch of linguistics in which the MEANING of LANGUAGE is analysed. The study of the origins of the form and meaning of words is *Etymology*, a branch of Semantics. The crucial point about the study of Semantics is that it is an exploration of change – how the context of usage, historical, social, cultural, etc. – alters the meanings of words and expressions used. When King James II observed that the new St Paul's Cathedral was *amusing, awful* and *artificial* he did not intend to be derogatory about Sir Christopher Wren's masterpiece; rather he meant that it was 'pleasing, awe-inspiring, and skilfully achieved'.

The differences are, of course, far from merely evolutionary. What, for example, is the meaning of the word *equality*? Its definition is modified by the perceptions and VALUES of all those who use it, and the situation in which it is used. As Simeon Potter points out in *Our Language* (UK: Penguin, 1950), 'Men frequently find themselves at cross-purposes with one another because they persist in using words in different senses. Their long arguments emit more heat than light because their conceptions of the point at issue, whether Marxism,

democracy, capitalism, the good life, western civilization, culture, art, internationalism, freedom of the individual, equality of opportunity, redistribution of wealth, social security, progress, or what not, are by no means identical. From heedless sloth, or sheer lack of intelligence men do not trouble to clarify their conceptions'. Semantics, therefore, must lie at the heart of any serious study of communication processes. See SEMANTIC DIFFERENTIAL.

Semiology/Semiotics Word derives from the Greek, 'semeion', sign, and Semiology is the general science of sign systems and their role in the construction and reconstruction of MEANING. All social life, indeed every facet of social practice, is mediated by LANGUAGE – conceived as a system of signs and representations, arranged by CODES and articulated through various DISCOURSES. Sign systems, believes the Semiologist, have no fixed meaning. The perception of the sign system rests upon the social context of the participants and the interaction between them.

Semiology examines the SIGN itself, the codes or systems into which the signs are organized and the CULTURE within which these codes and signs operate. The primary focus of Semiology is upon the text, thus differentiating such an approach from the *process* models of communication which regard the text – the MESSAGE – as only one element of several in the communication process. For example, the Semiologist prefers the term 'reader' (even of a painting, photograph or film) to receiver because it implies a greater degree of activity, and that the process of reading is socially and culturally conditioned. The reader helps to create the meaning and significance of the text by bringing to it his/her experience, VALUES and emotional responses.

There is special emphasis on the link between the 'reading' and the IDEOLOGY of the reader. 'Wherever a sign is present,' writes V.N. Volosinov in *Marxism and the Philosophy of Language* (US: Seminar, 1973), 'ideology is present too. Everything ideological possesses a semiotic value'; or as Umberto Eco says, 'Semiology shows us the universe of ideologies arranged in codes and sub-codes within the universe of signs' (in 'Articulations of the cinematic code' in *Cinematics* 1, undated).

The theories of Swiss linguist Ferdinand de Saussure (1857–1913) provided the foundation stone of Semiology. His lectures, *Cours de Linguistique Générale* (1916) were published after his death by two pupils, Charles Bally and Albert Sechehaye. De Saussure set out to demonstrate that speech is not merely a linear sequence like beads on a string but a *system* and *structure* where points on the string relate to other points on the string in various ways (the so-called *syntagmic* structure) and operate in a network of relationships with other possible points which could substitute for it (the *paradigmic* structure).

The American logician and philosopher C.S. Peirce (1834–1914) approached the structure of language with a wider-angle lens, conceiving semiotics (the term preferred in the US) as being an interdisciplinary science in which sign systems manifested in structures and levels could be analysed from philosophical, psychological and sociological as well as linguistic points of view.

Peirce and other philosophers such as Charles Morris and Rudolph Carnap saw the field as divisible into three areas: SEMANTICS, the study of the links between linguistic expressions and the objects in the world to which they refer or which they describe; SYNTACTICS, the study of the relation of these expressions to each other; and PRAGMATICS, the study of the dependence of the meaning of these expressions on their users (including the social context in which they are used).

The terminology of Semiology/Semiotics is complex and daunting, but the names Peirce gave to his categories are worth quoting here: the sign he called an ICON resembles the object it wishes to describe, like a photograph; an *index* establishes a direct link between the sign and its object (smoke is an index to fire); finally, the SYMBOL where there is neither connection nor resemblance between sign and object. A symbol communicates only because there is agreement among people that it shall stand for what it does (letters combined into words are symbols).

Semiology has come to apply, as a system of analysis, to every aspect of communication. There is practically nothing which is not a sign capable of meaning, or SIGNIFICATION. The work of the French philosopher Roland Barthes (1915–80) has exercised particular influence on our understanding of areas such as music, eating, clothes and dance as well as language. See PARADIGM; MYTH.

Semiosic plane See MIMETIC/SEMIOSIC PLANES.

Semiotic power The power, by members of the public – audience, consumers – to turn the consumerist signs and symbols which dominate contemporary life to their own uses. The case is put by John Fiske who, while acknowledging the power of ADVERTISING and consumerist PROPAGANDA generally, gives substantial credit to individuals to exercise a 'semiotic power' – resistance – of their own. Our initial impression of the public flocking, for example, to an enticing new shopping mall might be to see it as a clear indicator of corporate influence at work. However, Fiske argues in his chapter 'Shopping for pleasure' in *Reading the Popular* (US: Unwin Hyman, 1989) that 'the department store was the first public space legitimately available to women' and the 'fashionable commodities it offers provide a legitimated public identity and a means of participating in the ideology of progress'.

For Fiske 'the meanings of commodities do not lie in themselves as objects, and are not determined by their conditions of production and distribution, but are produced finally by the way they are consumed'. While he readily agrees that resistance from the bottom up in society is difficult and rarely likely to be effective beyond the micro-level of everyday life, this is not a reason to deny its existence. He writes, 'Scholarship that neglects or devalues these practices seems to me to be guilty of a disrespect for the weak that is politically reprehensible'.

Big companies may *make* style, in clothes or more broadly in lifestyle, but such styles are not followed slavishly. Rather they are *appropriated*: 'Women, despite the wide variety of social formations to which they belong, all share the experience of subordination under patriarchy and have evolved a variety of tactical responses that enable them to deal with it on a day-to-day level. So, too, other subordinated groups, however defined – by class, race, age, religion, or whatever – have evolved everyday practices that enable them to live within and against the forces that subordinate them.'

Fiske refers to people as forging their own meanings out of the signifiers available to them, exerting semiotic power, and though working only at the micro-level of society 'may well act as a constant erosive force upon the macro, weakening the system from within so that it is more amenable to change at the structural level'. See AUDIENCE: ACTIVE AUDIENCE.

Sender/receiver General terms often used in linear models of communication to denote the beginning and end of the communication process. Tim O'Sullivan, John Hartley, Danny Saunders and John Fiske in *Key Concepts of Communication* (UK: Methuen, 1994) draw some comparisons between the usage of these terms and others marking the same positions in the communication process.

Research with a technical or process-centred orientation tends to employ the terms *transmitter* and *receiver* to mark these key positions in the communication process, as is the case for example in the SHANNON AND WEAVER MODEL OF COMMUNICATION, 1949.

The terms *encoder* and *decoder* imply that communication involves coding processes and they are commonly used in research analysing such processes; an example here is SCHRAMM'S MODELS OF COMMUNICATION, 1954.

Addresser and *Addressee* are the terms used in JAKOBSON'S MODEL OF COMMUNICATION, 1958 and they imply that certain modes of address are appropriate to each position.

The terms *author* and *reader* tend to be used in the semiotic school of thought. Research here concentrates on the TEXT and the process by which its MEANING is generated. In this process the reader, as well as the author, is accorded an active role through, for example, the personal and cultural experiences he or she brings to the reading

of the text. The author may and often will, in constructing the text, try to guide the reader towards a PREFERRED READING, a preferred interpretation, but cannot actually determine exactly how the reader will interpret the text. See DECODE; ENCODE; SEMIOLOGY/SEMIOTICS.

Sensitization The process by which the media can alert the public, and specific social groups, to the fact that certain social actions are taking place, or to the possibility that certain social actions might take place. Stanley Cohen, for example, concludes in 'Sensitization: the case of the Mods and Rockers', in Stanley Cohen and Jock Young, eds., *The Manufacture of News: Deviance, Social Problems and the Mass Media* (UK: Constable, 1973 and subsequent editions) that media coverage of the Bank Holiday activities of the Mods and Rockers gangs, at certain southern holiday resorts in the mid-1960s, played a significant role in 'Reinforcing and magnifying a predisposition to expect trouble: "Something's going to happen"'.

Cohen argues that once this perception had been established there was a tendency to interpret new, similar incidents in the same manner and fairly trivial events, normally overlooked, received media attention. Thus, 'Through the process of sensitization, incidents which would not have been defined as unusual or worthy of attention . . . acquired a new meaning'. In this particular case sensitization was the first step in a process of media coverage which, Cohen argues, significantly affected the course of real events. See LOONY LEFTISM; MEDIA IMAGES.

Sentence meaning, utterance meaning In his two-volume work, *Semantics* (UK: Cambridge University Press, 1977), John Lyons makes a useful distinction in the matter of 'meaning' versus 'use' in our employment of LANGUAGE. *Sentence* meaning is directly related to the grammatical and lexical (choice of words) meaning of a sentence, while *utterance* meaning includes all 'secondary' aspects of meaning, particularly those related to the context in which a linguistic exchange takes place. It is this distinction, between sentence and utterance meaning which allows a person to say one thing and actually *mean* something else.

Serial processing See PARALLEL PROCESSING.

Set A state of mental expectancy which is grounded in pre-formed ideas about some future event. The impact of a MESSAGE is always influenced, to some extent, by the mental set of the receiver.

Seven characteristics of mass communications See MASS COMMUNICATIONS, SEVEN CHARACTERISTICS.

Sexism Discrimination against people on the grounds of assumed differences in their qualities, behaviours and characteristics resulting from their sex. Such discrimination may be targeted against men as well as women, but generally women are seen as its main victims. Sexism may manifest itself in an individual as a form of PREJUDICE or BIGOTRY, but more fundamentally concern focuses on the degree to which such discrimination is embedded within the structure and LANGUAGE of a society. In this respect the role that the media may play in generating or perpetuating this discrimination has been a theme of considerable recent research. See FEMINISM; GENDER; MALE-AS-NORM; STEREOTYPE.

S4C The Welsh counterpart of CHANNEL 4 – *Saniel Pedwar Cymru.* Approximately half the channel's output is in Welsh to serve the 500,000 Welsh-speakers in Wales.

Shadowing See COCKTAIL PARTY PROBLEM.

Shannon and Weaver model of communication, 1949 Developed by C.E. Shannon and W. Weaver to assist the construction of a mathematical theory of communication which could be applied in a wide variety of information transfer situations, whether by humans, machines or other systems. It is essentially a linear, process-centred model.

Shannon and Weaver were engineers working for the Bell Telephone Laboratories in the US and their objective was to ensure maximum efficiency of the *channels* of communication, in their case TELEPHONE cable and RADIO wave. However, in *Mathematical Theory of Communication* (US: University of Illinois Press, 1949), they claim for their theory a much wider application to human communication than solely the technical one. Within the framework of their model of transmission, the authors identify three levels of problems in the analysis of communication: Level A (technical), Level B (semantic – the MEANING as emanating from the Transmitter's mode of address) and Level C (effectiveness in terms of reception or understanding on the part of the Receiver). Shannon and Weaver's model was constructed mainly to tackle Level A problems, and the assumption seems to be that to sort out the technical problems by improving ENCODING will, almost automatically, lead to improvements at Levels B and C.

In the Shannon and Weaver model, no provision has been made for FEEDBACK and the fact that feedback modifies both the MESSAGE and the communication situation; nor is there any acknowledgment of the importance of *context* – social, political, cultural – in influencing all stages of the communication process. Nevertheless, the Shannon and Weaver model arguably gave birth to what has come to be termed Communication

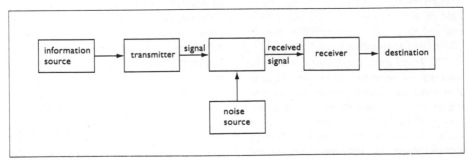

Shannon and Weaver model of communication

Studies. See CHANNEL CAPACITY; COMMUNICA-TION STUDIES; CYBERNETICS: REDUNDANCY.

Shawcross Commission Report on the Press, 1962 The five-member Commission chaired by Lord Shawcross, lawyer and former Labour minister, declared that the real enemy of good-quality newspapers was competition; and competition threatened diversity. 'Within any class of competitive newspapers', said the Report, 'the economies of large-scale operation provide a natural tendency for a newspaper which already has a large circulation to flourish, and to attract still more readers, whilst a newspaper which has a small circulation is likely to be in difficulties'. Like the ROSS COMMISSION REPORT, Shawcross offered no radical solution to the problems his Committee had delineated, trusting, as Ross had done, in the free market, albeit reluctantly: 'there is no acceptable legislative or fiscal way of regulating the competitive and economic forces so as to ensure a sufficient diversity of newspapers.'

The Report put forward an idea for a press amalgamations court which should scrutinize proposed mergers of all daily or Sunday papers with sales over three million, and to give the go-ahead only if the court considered such mergers to be no threat to public interest. In 1965 the Monopolies Commission was created by the Labour government under Harold Wilson, by means of the Monopolies and Mergers Act, which ruled that ISSUES were to be decided by government, not the courts.

Shawcross also successfully recommended the strengthening of the Press Council: a year later, in January 1964, a lay chairman (retired judge, Lord Devlin) was appointed; five lay members out of 25 became the rule, and the title of General Council of the Press was changed to Press Council. See COMMISSIONS/COMMITTEES ON THE MEDIA.

Shortfall signals In interpersonal contact, a shortfall signal is, for example, a smile of greeting that disappears too soon; in other words, it fails to carry conviction as a true smile of greeting. In the main, shortfall signals consist of simulated warmth in salutation. The evasive glance, the pulled-away glance, the frozen smile, the smile of mouth without eyes − all of these and many more are INDICATORS of personal unease about the encounter. The explanation may be because the person you greet is someone you dislike or fear, though the shortfall signal may have as much to do with personal mood − and preoccupation − as anything else. Conversely, there is the so-called **overkill signal**, where the greeting is too friendly, too effusive, the handshake too forcible. The overkill signal may be a simulation of sincere greeting; on the other hand, when people of different cultures or nations meet one person's shortfall may be another's overkill. See GESTURE.

Shot In FILM making, the shot is the equivalent, in writerly terms, of a word, a phrase, a sentence or a paragraph. The director of a movie *shoots* film; each shot is the length at which a camera works continuously from a still or moving position. A 'take' may constitute a series of shots or a continuous shot. It is visually defined by the use of the *clapperboard* held in front of the camera. The board has the title of the film written on it, and the number of the take; the clapper is extended and then closed at the moment of the take. A correspondent on the function of the clapperboard, Peter Heinze, writing from the European Institute for the Media, says its prime function is to give the editor 'a synchronous point both on the picture and the sound track, without which it is difficult − sometimes impossible − to match the picture to the sound, and thus have words mouthed "in sync".' Heinze adds that it is true that on optical tracks (both variable area and variable density) it is possible to match the two by sight, the standard way is to listen for the 'clap'.

There are many types of shot: low and high angle, tilted; tracking, where the camera rests on a *crab and track* device and follows the action into or across the picture. The zoom lens allows the CU (Close Up), MCU (Medium Close Up) and the BCU (Big Close Up). There is the wide-angle shot and the pan where the camera swings across the scene; there is the still shot and the SLOW MOTION shot. Final decisions about how long a shot will be, which shots will be used and in what order come at the editing stage of film-making. See MONTAGE.

Shotgun approach (to news coverage)
Term used by Terry Ann Knopf in 'Media myths on violence' in *Columbia Journalism Review* (Spring 1970) to describe the over-reporting – large headlines, large pictures and EMOTIVE LANGUAGE – by the media of certain types of events, usually crimes, political protests and racial conflict. See TABLOIDESE.

Showbusiness, age of The present age of advancing communications technology has been given many titles – the Age of Information, the Telecommunications Age, the Age of the Global Village. Neil Postman in *Amusing Ourselves to Death* (UK: Methuen, 1986), calls it the Age of Showbusiness, a period in which TELEVISION dominates the lives of the community, turning people – in his view – into a population 'amusing ourselves to death'. In the Age of Showbusiness, Postman argues, all discourses are rewritten in terms of entertainment; substance is translated into IMAGE and the present is emphasized to the detriment of historical perspectives.

Postman's criticism is targeted upon the COMMERCIAL TELEVISION of his native America but his points are worth examining in a British context at a time when PUBLIC SERVICE BROADCASTING looks nervously to its own future. According to Postman, TV 'does everything possible to encourage us to watch continuously. But what we watch is a medium which presents information in a form that renders it simplistic, non-substantive, non-historical and non-contextual; that is to say, information packaged as entertainment'. See CONSUMER SOVEREIGNTY; EFFECTS OF THE MASS MEDIA; MAINSTREAMING; PILKINGTON COMMITTEE REPORT ON BROADCASTING, 1962; PSEUDO-CONTEXT; TELEVISION.

Sign In communication studies, a little word which triggers complex explanations. Father of SEMIOLOGY/SEMIOTICS, Swiss linguist Ferdinand de Saussure (1857–1913) regarded LANGUAGE as a 'deposit of signs'; he viewed the sign as a phenomenon comprising an 'acoustic image' and a concept (the thing signified). A word or combina-

tion of words in a language refers to, is an indicator of, some externally existing object or idea. Charles Peirce (1834–1914), the American philosopher and logician, posed a triangular relationship involving the activation of the sign:

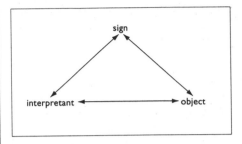

The object is that which is described by the sign, but the sign only signifies – has MEANING – in the process of it becoming a mental concept (INTERPRETANT), or what de Saussure named the *signified*. The point to emphasize here is that the sign depends for its meaning on the context in which it is communicated.

Edmund Leach in *Culture and Communication* (UK: Cambridge University Press, 1976) says signs do not occur in isolation; 'a sign is always a member of a set of contrasting signs which function within a specific cultural context'. Also, a sign only conveys information when it is combined with other signs and symbols from the same context. 'Signs signal', writes Donis A. Dondis in R. Williams, ed., *Contact: Human Communication and its History* (UK: Thames & Hudson, 1981), 'they are specific to a task or circumstance'.

Of course there are not only different kinds or levels of meaning (or SIGNIFICATION), there are many different kinds of sign. Peirce divided signs into three categories: the *icon, index* and *symbol*. These, like the triangular sign-object-interpretant are interactive, and they are overlapping. The icon is a resemblance or a representation of the object – a photograph or a map would constitute an ICONIC sign. An index is a sign connected or associated with its object – an indicator: smoke is an index of fire, for example. The SYMBOL may have no resemblance whatever to the object or idea. It is arbitrary. It comes about by choice, it exists by convention, rule or assent. It means something beyond itself. As Dondis neatly points out, 'Signs can be understood by animals as well as humans; symbols cannot'. They 'are broader in meaning, less concrete'.

Raymond Firth, in *Symbols, Public and Private* (UK: Allen & Unwin, 1973), adds a fourth sign type to Peirce's three – *signal*, a sign with an emphasis on 'consequential action', a stimulus requiring some response.

Signs combine to form systems, or CODES, from the basic MORSE CODE or Highway Code to, for example, the complex codes of musical notation. See ASSIGN; LANGUE AND PAROLE; JAKOBSON'S MODEL OF COMMUNICATION; TRIGGERS.

Signal The physical manifestation of a MESSAGE which allows it to be conveyed. See SHANNON AND WEAVER MODEL OF COMMUNICATION, 1949.

Significant others The analysis of the effects of a media message, of its impact, relies on the response not only of the direct respondent, but of those persons close to, influential upon the respondent – relatives, friends, work colleagues. These are 'significant others'. In the case of a child watching TV commercials, his/her response may be conditioned and modified by parents, brothers and sisters, friends. See INTERVENING VARIABLES.

Significant symbolizers G.H. Mead in *Mind, Self and Society* (US: University of Chicago Press, 1934), uses this term to indicate how the social organization of a society, human or animal, needs the support of reliable, regular and predictable patterns or signs if it is not to be destroyed by accumulating discrepancy and misinformation. The SYMBOL or symbolizer, whether vocal sound, GESTURE or SIGN, achieves meaningful definition only when it has the 'same effect on the individual making it as on the individual to whom it is addressed'. Thus, according to Mead, a person defines him/herself by 'talking to himself in terms of the community to which he belongs'. Through contact with 'significant' (meaningful) objects of the social world a person develops a coherent view of him/herself and of his/her relations

with others. See INTERPERSONAL COMMUNICATION; INTRAPERSONAL COMMUNICATION.

Signification One of the most valuable contributions made by Swiss linguist Ferdinand de Saussure (1857–1913) to the study of LANGUAGE was his idea of differentiating between the name, the naming and the MEANING of what has been named. This process enabled the linguist more effectively to examine the structural elements of communication. Saussure contrasted the *significant* (or **signifier**) with *signifié* (or that which is **signified**). The relationship between these, the physical existence of the sign, and the mental concept it represents, becomes *signification* which, for Saussure, is the manifestation of external reality or meaning. Signification, it is important to realize, is culture-specific as is the linguistic form of the signifier in each language. Saussure terms the relationship of signs to others in the sign system, *valeur*, and it is valeur which primarily determines meaning. Thus meaning is an active force, subject to constant change, the result of dynamic interaction. See SEMIOLOGY/SEMIOTICS.

Signification spiral Stuart Hall *et al.* in *Policing the Crisis: Mugging, The State and Law & Order* (UK: Macmillan, 1978) use this term for the process by which discrete, local problems and occurrences are pulled together by the media into a framework of news coverage which links these together in such a way as to suggest the existence of a more widespread and serious social problem. They argue that, for example, during the 1970s there emerged a signification spiral in which problems previously presented as atypical or parochial – such as student protest, industrial unrest, and mugging – were presented by the media as part of a wider concern: the breakdown in law and order. See SENSITIZATION.

Significs Enquiry into questions of MEANING, expression and interpretation, and the influence of LANGUAGE upon thought.

Silence Silence can of course communicate just as effectively as speech, as Gail and Michele Myers explain in *The Dynamics of Human Communication* (US: McGraw-Hill, 1985): 'Silences . . . are not to be equated with the absence of communication. Silences are a natural and fundamental aspect of communication, often ignored because misunderstood.' Silences are used to give meaning to verbal communication but can also communicate a range of information in their own right such as feelings of anger, a state of mourning or preoccupation with one's own thoughts. There are many kinds of silence and we often need other non-verbal or verbal cues to help us identify what is meant when someone is silent.

Being aware of the range of meanings which silence may convey, and the ability to accurately interpret them and react sensitively to them, is an important communicative skill as in the ability to fill an embarrassing gap in a conversation. There is a tendency in our culture to perceive silence caused by lapses during a conversation as awkward. Myers and Myers point out that *masking behaviours* which includes coughing, whistling and sighing are often employed to cover up such lapses until someone thinks of something to say. The use and acceptability of silence does vary from one culture to another. See APACHE SILENCE; COMMUNICATION, NON-VERBAL.

Silence, spiral of See NOELLE-NEUMANN'S SPIRAL OF SILENCE MODEL OF PUBLIC OPINION, 1974.

Silence: strategic silence In NEWS selection, that which is omitted. R. Lenz in 'The search for strategic silence: discovering what journalism leaves out' in *American Journalism* 8 (1) (1991), perceives the working of IDEOLOGY in reportorial omission and that such omission often says more about the selection process, and those who do the selecting, than what is included in news bulletins. That version of reality constructed by journalists, writes Lentz, 'relies upon the production of meanings based not only upon published content but upon ways in which some things are not "seen", or if seen, not recorded, as part of the social transaction between readers and creators of editorial matter'.

Silent majority In the briefcase of every OPINION LEADER – be he/she politician, editor or TV guru – lies a hidden weapon, the 'Silent Majority'. The opinion leader claims access to the thoughts, attitudes and beliefs of those who, having no voice of their own so the story goes – are grateful to the politicians or the PRESS for putting words and opinions into their silent mouths. They are invariably moderates; they have bags of common sense; what is more, they are impossible to identify. If it were possible to locate them in persons (no research has yet elicited the degree to which the silent are a majority or the majority silent) they might be perceived as, above all things, up-holders of the STATUS QUO, inalienably opposed to activists, do-gooders and change agents of every type and hue.

Sincerity test (by the media) Some commentators claim that a by-product of political BROADCASTING is the way TV appearances by influential public figures are assessed by audiences for honesty and sincerity. Equally, the skilled public figure can use TV to project the desired image of honesty and sincerity in order to gain public support.

Sins of omission In discussing the effects of TV on audiences, the PILKINGTON REPORT uses this phrase to balance the major criticism which was of 'sins of commission' – the capacity of TV to misuse its power to influence people. The sins of omission arise from the fact that many of the best potentialities of TV 'were simply not being realized', that is, programmes were relentlessly going for the largest possible audience and thus 'nearly always' appealing to 'a low level of public taste'. See BALANCED PROGRAMMING.

Sit-com Situation comedy on TELEVISION – the comedy growing out of context and recurringly generated or fuelled by amiable antagonism of one kind or another. Where the SOAP OPERA demands a substantial range of characters the sit-com generally focuses upon narrow circles of acquaintance and relationship such as families or groups of friends. Rarely does the narrative of one instalment of a sit-com continue from the previous one or continue to the next, again contrasting with the soap whose narrative key is balancing a number of ongoing stories and spinning these along over days and weeks. Each instalment of a sit-com begins with a situation which is resolved within a single timescale. Characters may be rounded, even complex, but rarely do they, or the situations they are involved in, develop or change. This does not mean that they are sealed against the events of the real world; indeed they often reflect real-world conditions and make use of current issues and trends. For example the UK sit-com *Men Behaving Badly* explores, amusingly and wittily, the 'gender war' of the 1990s in which men have had to adjust to the threat to their traditional dominance by women confident that the future is theirs. Writers of sit-coms have succeeded in creating diverse themes, from comedy in prison – *Porridge* – to comedy in space – *The Red Dwarf* – to aliens on earth – *Third Rock from the Sun*. The Korean War was the setting for one of the best and most incisive sit-coms, *MASH*, starring Alan Alda.

The best sit-coms prove to have a long, and recurring screen life – *The Phil Silvers Show* and *Dad's Army* have been introduced and reintroduced to succeeding generations of audience.

Notable sit-coms from the UK stable have been *Till Death Us Do Part*, *Steptoe and Son*, *The Likely Lads*, *Rising Damp*, *The Good Life*, *Fawlty Towers*, *Last of the Summer Wine*, *Birds of a Feather*, *Kiss Me Kate* and *Goodness Gracious Me*; from the US, a few of many notable sit-coms have been *Bewitched*, *Rhoda*, *Taxi*, *Cheers!*, *Cybill*, *Roseanne*, *Friends*, *Frazier* and *Ellen*.

Site The theoretical or physical space where a struggle over MEANING and the power to reinforce a particular meaning occurs.

Situational proprieties Erving Goffman in *Behaviour in Public Places* (US: Free Press, 1963) employed this phrase to describe rules of behaviour common to interpersonal and group situations which oblige participants to 'fit in'; to accept the particular normative behaviour suitable for a successful, DISSONANCE-free interaction. Such properties might be to avoid making a scene or causing a disturbance; refrain from talking too loudly or too assertively; hold back from attempting to dominate proceedings or, in contrast, to check oneself from withdrawing from what is going on.

S-IV-R model of communication Derives from general theories of learning/communication, where the relationship between stimulus (S) and response (R) is regarded as providing the key to both learning and communication. Actually it is a *teaching*-orientated model rather than learner-centred, and implies a predominantly one-way traffic of information from teacher to pupil. The IV stands for INTERVENING VARIABLES, those factors in the communication situation which help, hinder or modify the response to the intended MESSAGE. These variables are innumerable: NOISE (technical or semantic), lack of motivation or concentration, personal problems and, very importantly, the influence of other people – peer GROUPS, friends, parents, etc. See COMMUNICATION MODELS; MEDIATION; SIGNIFICANT OTHERS.

Slander A false or malicious report by the spoken word or by SIGN or GESTURE. In law, slander may constitute DEFAMATION – of character or reputation – and may be subject to heavy fines. However, no legal aid is granted in the UK for defamation cases. LIBEL is the written or printed equivalent of slander.

Slang Colloquial LANGUAGE, whose words and usages are not generally acceptable within formal modes of expression. The word was not used till about 1756. Prior to that it was called *cant*, and referred to the secret language of the underworld, of thieves and rogues; also termed *argot*. Slang usually begins as in-group language, then moves into popular use. For example, the criminal world's slang nouns for policeman (*coppers, rozzers, bluebottles, the fuzz*), for magistrates (*beaks*), for prison (*stir time, bird* and *porridge*) have achieved broad currency.

Rhyming slang, associated with London cockneys and subsequently Australians, uses slang words that rhyme with the intended word. Thus *apples and pears* means stairs, *trouble and strife* means wife. The point of rhyming slang is to conceal the MEANING of the language used from unwanted listeners. See COLLOQUIALISM; DIALECT; JARGON.

SLAPPS Strategic Lawsuits against Public Participation, a practice originating in the US but spreading globally, in which big corporations put legal frighteners on critics of their activities. Wherever corporate interests – whether in the environment, in foodstuffs, in publicizing information – are deemed at risk, out come the lawsuits, focusing on accusations of DEFAMATION, invasion of PRIVACY and interference with business. Julian Petley in an article 'SLAPPS and Chills' in *Index on Censorship*, 1 (1999), writes, 'These cases . . . are a form of strategic legal intimidation or gamesmanship, designed to frighten, harass and distract actual critics, and to discourage potential ones from even voicing their views in the first place'. Most cases do not reach court, and they are not intended to do.

However, for Helen Steel and Dave Morris, distributors of a leaflet entitled 'What's Wrong With McDonald's?' there was to be no escape from libel proceedings. Their trial was the longest in British history. It took every penny the defendants possessed (defendants are ineligible for legal aid in defamation cases). They squared up to a company which spends an estimated 2 billion dollars a year on advertising (See John Vidal's *McLibel: Burger Culture on Trial*, UK: Macmillan, 1997). In June 1997 it was revealed that a documentary made by Franny Armstrong, *McLibel: Two Worlds Collide* had been rejected by both the BBC and Channel 4 – because of the risk of libel action. Existing, well-established programmes such as the BBC's *Newsnight*, *Panorama* and *Watchdog* have stirred up snarling choruses of protest (to the Programme Complaints Unit and the BROADCASTING STANDARDS COMMISSION) from multinationals such as British Aerospace, Ford, Dixons, Hotpoint and Proctor and Gamble.

Curiously, while public authorities in the UK cannot, since 1993, bring libel actions against critics who publicize critical views, big business suffers no such restrictions. 'It could convincingly be argued', writes Petley, 'that the major political forces in the world today are no longer national governments but transnational corporations.' He states that it is high time to put to an end 'their much-abused ability to exploit our oppressive and archaic libel wars'. See CENSORSHIP; McDONALDIZATION.

Sleeper effect Researchers into the responses of audiences to messages have noted how these responses can be *delayed* and only become manifest some time after exposure. This is the 'sleeper' effect. See EFFECTS OF THE MASS MEDIA.

Slider Many experiments have been conducted to investigate the effect of group pressure upon the individual and the manner in which such pressure manifests itself in the INTERPERSONAL COMMUNICATION of the group. In a typical experiment one member of the group may take on the role of slider, that is he/she will initially disagree with the majority of the group on a matter but is persuaded to agree with them. The member of the group who takes on the role of DEVIANT, however, consistently disagrees with the majority. Of those in the experimental situation some may be *naïve*, that is, unaware of what is to take place in the experiment and some members may be *confederates*, that is, in league with the experimenters.

Slow-drip Term sometimes used to describe the regular, long-term coverage of certain ISSUES by the media with a view to influencing the formation of opinion; a softening-up process that builds evidence and feelings in preferred directions. The policy of appeasement towards Germany prior to the 2nd World War (1939–45) has been cited as an example. See EFFECTS OF THE MASS MEDIA.

Slow motion Has been used varyingly in the cinema to convey dream-like or fantasy situations, to emphasize reactions such as grief, bewilderment or to concentrate attention upon happenings which in real life would be here and gone before the full visual impact has been made. In contrast, **accelerated motion** has been generally used for comic effects, especially by the early silent movie comedians whose own actors' timing was rendered even more remarkable by the speeded-up action.

Reverse motion is another technique by which the cinema defies time: that which can happen can unhappen. In *October* (1927), for instance, Sergei Eisenstein (1898–1948) uses the magic of reverse motion to show a statue of the Tzar, previously smashed to pieces, miraculously restored, thus showing with impressive symbolism the restoration of the *ancien régime*, the old order.

Lastly, there is **stopped motion**, using either still photographs or stopping the action of an otherwise moving sequence by repeating the same frame when editing the film. The freezing of action may signal transition from one time zone to another, or may be used for special emphasis – like a fixed state – or sometimes to underscore comic effects or impressions. See SHOT.

Small World Media Founded in 1993; UK-based, non-profit making alternative media operation, originally producing under the general title *Undercurrents*. The newsvideos were aimed at bringing about social change – *Time Out* called the series, 'the news you don't see on the news'. Campaigning by video ended after 10 editions of *Undercurrents* (Number 7 was a Tokyo Video Festival Winner) and a revamped umbrella organization (February 2000) re-emerged with *Undercurrents* as its title, with global aims and a switch to chiefly INTERNET operations The organization manages a substantial archive of direct action images as well as having available a training manual, *The Video Activist Handbook* (published by Pluto Press). Contact: www.undercurrents.org.

SMCR model of communication See BERLO'S SMC MODEL OF COMMUNICATION, 1960.

Smiling professions Namely, the media; at least those parts of them dedicated to smile and keep audiences smiling. John Hartley in *The Politics of Pictures: The Creation of the Public in the Age of Popular Media* (UK: Routledge, 1992) writes that smiling 'has become one of the most public virtues of our times, a uniform that must be worn on the lips of those whose social function is to create, sustain, tutor, represent and make images of the public'. Hartley asserts that 'Smiling, in fact, is now the "dominant ideology" of the "public domain", the mouthpiece of the politics of pictures'.

Snap-shot Term invented by astronomer Sir John Herschel (1792–1871), writing in 1860 of 'the possibility of taking a photograph as it were a snap shot'. He may well have

been referring to Thomas Skaife's *Pistolgraph* of 1858. See CAMERA; PHOTOGRAPHY, ORIGINS.

Soap opera Radio or TV domestic drama series; the term emanates from the US where such programmes have often been sponsored by big soap companies who had the housewife viewer in mind. Of the long-running soap opera in the UK, *Coronation Street*, poet laureate John Betjeman once announced, 'At half-past seven tonight I shall be in paradise.' TV's appetite for soap opera is insatiable. The TV audience for the shooting of JR in the American series *Dallas* exceeded that for the FA Cup Final in the UK. Traditionally soaps have been characterized by an immediately identifiable set-up, a stereotypical cast of characters and a distancing from contemporary reality and anxieties. However, the end of the 1980s saw the arrival of soaps exploiting social problems for all they were worth. From the BBC, *EastEnders*, featuring abortion, rape, illegitimacy, murder, robbery, incest and unemployment; from Channel 4, *Brookside*, demonstrating that Merseyside can vie problem for problem with London's East End, featuring rape, stabbings, euthanasia, homosexuality and, of course, unemployment. The BBC's import from Australia, *Neighbours*, proved it could do more than hold its own – with beatings-up, meningitis, divorce *et al*.

In a sense, soaps have become a paradigm for television itself. In terms of *texts* they take up a staggeringly large amount of viewing time and occupy centre-stage in the minds of vast and international audiences. Critical theory has located in soaps rich seams for investigation, especially in an age when audience *reaction* to TV, the way meaning is read into texts by audience, the ways that audiences use media, have come to dominate critical thinking.

Essentially soaps are less concerned with action that with *interaction*, primarily between the characters on the broad socio-cultural canvas but also, in a proactive way, between the characters and the viewers (See PARASOCIAL INTERACTION). That is, the gap between one episode of a soap and the next may be used by members of the audience to mull over latest developments, talk about these to members of the family, fellow workers, friends, thus heightening anticipation and enjoyment and making the viewer a more active 'reader' of the text.

Because most soaps distribute interest among numerous characters, no single character is indispensable. Of key importance is the community of characters in their situation. As Robert C. Allen writes in 'Reader-orientated criticism', Allen, ed., *Channels of Discourse: Television and Contemporary Criticism* (UK: Methuen, 1987; Routledge, 1990), 'Anything might happen to an individual character, but, in the long run, it will not affect the community of characters as a whole'.

Soap operas, classically, both in terms of text and audience, concentrate on women, their relationships and their experiences especially within the home and neighbourhood environment. As such they have become a significant focus of feminist analysis of the media.

In a *European Journal of Communication* article, June 1998, 'European Soap Operas: The Diversification of the Genre', Tamar Liebes and Sonia Livingstone identify three types, or models, of soap opera – the *Dynastic*, the *Community* and the *Dyadic*. The first focuses on one powerful family with a number of satellite outsiders. The American soap *Dynasty* is an example of this model, while the UK soaps *Coronation Street* and *East-Enders* typify the community model. These are characterized by a number of interconnecting and interrelating families 'all living within one geographical neighbourhood and belonging to one community'.

The dyadic model concerns a 'destabilized network of a number of young people, densely interconnected, mostly unigenerational, interchanging couples, with past, present and future romantic ties, continually absorbed in the process of reinventing kinship relations'. The authors cite the American soap *The Young and the Restless* as a prime example of the dyadic model; to this we might add *This Life* which won something of a cult status in the UK until in 1998 the BBC decided not to commission further episodes.

Community soaps, Liebes and Livingstone

say, 'have been produced in the spirit of public broadcasting, indicating certain pedagogic aims' and 'constitute a type of public for debating social issues'. See FEMINISM; GENDER; GENDERED GENRE; GOSSIP NETWORKS; IDEOLOGY OF ROMANCE; MELODRAMA; PLAY THEORY OF MASS COMMUNICATION; PLEASURE: ACTIVE AND REACTIVE; RHYTHMS OF RECEPTION.

* David Morley, *Family Television: Cultural Power and Domestic Leisure* (UK: Comedia, 1986); Yvonne Tasker, 'Having it all: feminism and the pleasures of the popular' in Sarah Franklin, Celia Lury and Jackie Stacey eds., *Off-Centre: Feminism and Cultural Studies* (UK: HarperCollins Academic, 1991). Ian Ang, *Watching Dallas: Soap Operas and the Melodramatic Imagination* (UK: Methuen, 1985); David Buckingham, *Public Secrets: Eastenders and its Audience* (UK: BFI, 1987); Mary Ellen Brown, *Soap Opera and Women's Talk* (UK: Sage, 1994); Robert C. Allen, *To Be Continued: Soap Operas Around the World* (UK: Routledge, 1995); Charlotte Brunsdon, *Screen Tastes: Soap Opera to Satellite Dish* (UK: Routledge, 1997).

Soaps: docu-soaps Fashion in TELEVISION in the late 1990s of presenting documentary series as though they were soaps – with the same emphasis on characters the audience can readily identify with, real-life situations intercut with parallel situations in the typical manner of soaps. Examples in the UK have been *Airport*, *Driving School* and *Hotel*. Such programmes have tended to supplant serious, probing documentaries and are largely the result of the intense pressures of competition. Their fascination lies in the *actuality* of the mini-dramas and their sense of immediacy. Where docu-soaps are different from fictional soaps is in the freedom the 'characters' are given to comment on the mini-dramas that fill their working days.

Social action (mode of media analysis) Stresses the role of the individual as a potent force within a dynamic social system. It sees *conflict* as central to the process of change, in particular conflict between GROUPS seeking influence, power and status. Social action analysis concentrates on the media as a special group both reflecting and involved in the conflicts which concern social change, or resistance to it. A *pluralist* society, of competing ideologies and varying, changing definitions of truth and MEAN-ING, is acknowledged by social action analysis as are the complex influences at work upon media and media audiences and the interaction between them. See FUNCTIONAL-IST/MARXIST (MODES OF MEDIA ANALYSIS); PLURALISM.

Social action broadcasting A broad term describing RADIO and TELEVISION programming which sets out not only to analyse current social problems and ISSUES and bring them to public attention, but to encourage people to take action in response to what they have heard or seen. Programmes range from the BBC's adult literacy series *On the Move* or *Crimewatch UK* to Capital Radio's *Helpline*. Information on social action BROADCASTING is disseminated by the National Volunteer Centre in its publication *Media Project News* which produces a twice-yearly Directory of Social Action Programmes.

Social anthropology The study of the evolution of human communities and cultures.

Social class See CLASS.

Social influence theory See IDENTIFICATION.

Socialization The shaping of human behaviour through experience in and knowledge of certain social situations: the process by which individuals are made aware of the EXPECTATIONS others have of their behaviour; by which they acquire the NORMS, MORES, VALUES and beliefs of a social group or society; and by which the CULTURE of a social group or society is transmitted. Socialization continues throughout life as individuals change their roles and membership of social GROUPS.

There exist what are commonly known as *agents* of socialization. In modern industrial societies, the family, school and friendship groups are thought to be the most significant agents in shaping the behaviour of the individual. The mass media are also agents of socialization and are considered to be particularly influential in transmitting awareness and expectations concerning a wide range of societal behaviour.

Individuals and societies may undergo radical change, if so *re-socialization* may occur – the peeling away of learned patterns of behaviour and their replacement with quite different ones. There is interest as to the media's potential role in this process – its potential as a disseminator of PROPA-GANDA, for example, could be of significance. Additionally, media organizations are themselves social INSTITUTIONS and as such have their own patterns of behaviour, attitudes and beliefs into which their members are socialized. The degree to which the culture of media organizations affects their output is a considerable source of interest.

Social lubricators Richard Hoggart in *Speaking to Each Other* (UK: Chatto & Windus, 1970), uses this term to describe those people involved in the research, design and presentation of material aimed at aiding the smooth running of a technologically advanced society: communications experts, public relations officers and ADVER-TISING executives, for example. See PR: PUBLIC RELATIONS.

Socially unattached intelligentsia See IMPARTIALITY.

Social perception See PERCEPTION.

Social steerage Process whereby promotional practices, in origin essentially commercial in character, are re-aligned to promote other aspects of cultural life, such as politics.

Social system Consists of a collective of people who undertake different types of tasks in order to achieve common goals and solve common problems. The term can be applied to a group of two or more individuals, complex organizations or whole societies. For the members of a social system to cooperate, there must be a shared LANGUAGE and some cultural similarities between them, although within the overall system there may be a variety of sub-cultures and language CODES, as well as other individual differences.

All social systems are liable to undergo social change: a process by which the structures and functions are altered. One focus for research has been the role of the communication of innovation in the process of social change. See SOCIALIZATION.

Societally conscious See VALS TYPOLOGY.

Societally conscious achievers See VALS TYPOLOGY.

Sociolinguistics The study of the way in which an individual's linguistic behaviour might be influenced by the social groups to which he/she belongs. It investigates also the linguistic variations found between groups and their explanation.

Sociology French philosopher Auguste Comte (1798–1857) was the first to use the word 'sociology'. The discipline attempts a scientific and systematic study of society, employing precise and controlled methods of enquiry. It is concerned with social structure; social systems; social action; the various GROUPS, INSTITUTIONS, categories and classes which go to make up a society or SOCIAL SYSTEM; the CULTURE and lifestyle of a society and the groups of which it is composed; the processes of SOCIALIZATION by which such cultures are communicated and maintained; and the types and allocation of social ROLES.

Social groups, their inter-relationships and INTERACTION, and their conditioning of individual behaviour could be seen as the building blocks of the discipline.

Sociometrics (and media analysis) Sociometrics is the analysis of small GROUPS, their coherence and the interpersonal relationships and communication within them. This mode of analysis has been extended and applied within media studies to ascertain the nature of the relationships between owners of media organizations and owners of other industrial or commercial concerns and the degree to which they are interlocking. The purpose of such a sociometric *map of capitalism* is to discover whether or not shared positions in and patterns of social and economic life produce recognized shared interests and a common cluster of beliefs, VALUES and perspectives which feed back into and influence media organizations and their products.

Recent evidence suggests some overlapping points of contact. Increasingly, owners of communications concerns are also owners of other businesses, and these contacts are reinforced by overlapping directorships.

Board members of top media corporations have been found to hold membership of ELITE London clubs also favoured by directors of leading financial institutions and some business corporations. Of course evidence of points of contact does not necessarily constitute evidence of shared values, beliefs and perspectives, or deliberate influence of media products.

Software See COMPUTER LANGUAGE.

'Somme, The Battle of the' First-ever film DOCUMENTARY of war; records the first day of the battle of the Somme, 1 July 1916, during which the British army suffered 57,000 casualties, almost a third of these killed. *The Battle of the Somme* was not filmed secretly but was produced with permission of the Secretary of State for War, David Lloyd George, whose words were read out at the first screening of the film on 10 August 1916 – scarcely more than a month after the events the film so tellingly describes. Lloyd George's breathtaking openness (to us now) was based upon a belief that to tell the public the truth would reinforce support for the war: 'You are invited,' he wrote, 'to witness by far the most imposing picture of the war that our staff has yet procured.' It was true that the film was popular. Shot by Geoffrey Malins and J. B. McDowell, *The Battle of the Somme* was seen by over 20 million people in the UK, practically half the population. Perceived as PROPAGANDA by the British Army, the film had the opposite effect to what was intended. People were horrified by what they saw, and government immediately learnt that in times of war truth is better concealed than revealed.

Rarely again did countries at war permit such frank revelations of the harrowing experiences of conflict to be shown, uncensored, to the public. The exception was the Vietnam War in which film and reports of carnage eventually turned public opinion in the US against the war. In succeeding 20th-century wars – the Falklands and Gulf Wars in particular – censorship was resolutely applied. Where censorship has proved less easy to impose, as in the wars in Bosnia and Kosovo, documentary footage has had a profound effect on public opinion world-wide.

A video, *The Battle of the Somme: Official Pictures of the Army in France* is available from the Imperial War Museum.

Sound-bite Term originally derives from RADIO but has come to apply equally to TELE-VISION; describes a film or tape segment within a news story, in which a reporter talks to a source – such as a politician or an eyewitness. With the advent of more sophisticated technology for handling news reports, the use of jump-cutting has added to the complexity and the drama of the sound-bite. The *ellipsis jump-cut* splices two or more segments of the same person speaking in the same setting: these are classified as single sound-bites. The *juxtaposition jump-cut* places together contrasting segments, usually from different settings, in such a way as to make evident the discontinuity. These tend to be treated as separate sound-bites.

Research into the nature and degree of sound-bites in news broadcasting in the US indicates that contemporary news employs far more, and far shorter sound-bites, than in the past. In 'Sound-bite news: television coverage of elections, 1968–1988' in *Journal of Communication* (Spring, 1992), Daniel C. Hallin reports that the average sound-bite has been shrinking, from more than 40 seconds in length in 1968 to less than 10 seconds in the 1980s. The conclusion Hallin draws from this is that the news is much more *mediated* than the TV news of the 1960s and 1970s. He writes, 'Today's television journalist displays a sharply different attitude towards the words of candidates and other newsmakers. Today, those words, rather than simply being reproduced and transmitted to the audiences, are treated as raw material to be taken apart, combined with other sounds and images, and reintegrated into a new narrative'.

Hallin cites three reasons for the sound-bite revolution: the technological one already mentioned, the weakening in political CONSENSUS and authority following Vietnam and WATERGATE, and the discovery by the TV industry in the States that news was big business if, that is, presentation was

'punchy' enough to attract and retain audience attention. Ironically, the approach derives from the very people journalists often accuse of manipulating the media – political campaign managers – so-called 'spin doctors' whose techniques of packaging candidates have centred around sound-biting images, one-liners, the use of triumphalist music etc.

Dan Hallin acknowledges that modern news is far more 'professional', far more varied, slicker than in the past, but he identifies serious worries. 'First and simplest, it is disturbing that the public never has the chance to hear a candidate – or anyone else – speak for more than 20 seconds', especially as showing 'humans speaking is something television does very effectively'. Also the modern pace of exposition raises questions concerning audience comprehension – the ability of viewers to understand what is coming at them at such speed. Not the least concern is that sound-bite journalism emphasizes techniques over substance: the very sin the journalist accuses the spin doctor of committing. See NEWS MANAGEMENT.

Sound broadcasting See RADIO BROADCAST-ING.

Sound Broadcasting Act, 1972 Gave the go-ahead to COMMERCIAL RADIO in the UK. The name Independent Television Authority (ITA) was changed to Independent Broadcasting Authority (IBA), and the IBA was empowered to create a new group of contractors in up to 50 British cities to run local commercial RADIO stations and collect ADVERTISING revenue in a manner similar to that of the TV programme companies. The first commercial radio stations went on the air in October 1973. See TELEVISION ACT, 1954.

Sound, synchronous See SYNCHRONOUS SOUND.

Source An individual, GROUP or INSTITUTION that originates a message. See EVENT.

Source domination See PRIMARY, SECONDARY DEFINERS.

Soviet Manifesto, 1928 Probably written by Sergei Eisenstein (1898–1948), and signed by him, Vsevolod Pudovkin and

Grigori Alexandrov, the Manifesto was a declaration of faith in the artistic importance of cinema. It detailed the attitudes of the named directors to the processes of cinema, chiefly the commitment to MONTAGE in the light of the development of SYNCHRONOUS SOUND: 'The first experimental work with sound must be directed along the line of its distinct non-synchronization with the visual images.' See FILM.

Sovkino Organization formed after the Russian Revolution (1917) to control the new cinema of art and PROPAGANDA. In 1925, one of Sovkino's administrators tried to ban the foreign distribution of Sergei Eisenstein's *The Battleship Potemkin* completed that year, though the poet Vladimir Mayakovsky (1893–1930) had influence enough to get the decision reversed. In 1927 Mayakovsky publicly berated Sovkino for its conservatism. The battle against the Soviet bureaucrats was to be lost. Mayakovsky committed suicide in 1930, perhaps in presentiment of the Stalinist purges to come, and the end of all aesthetic freedom.

Spaghetti Westerns Made in Europe, usually Spain, by Italian directors such as Serge Leone whose *A Fistful of Dollars* (1967) starring Clint Eastwood was the first to be imported into the US. All spaghetti Westerns contain large amounts of explicit violence. See GENRE; WESTERN.

Spatial behaviour See ORIENTATION; PROXEMICS.

Spatial zones Those areas and distances which individuals maintain between each other, depending on the nature of the relationship between them. Edward T. Hall, 'inventor' of PROXEMICS (See *The Silent Language*, US: Anchor Books, 1973), has specified four of these spatial zones: *intimate, personal, social* and *public* (each with a near and far phase). See INTERPERSONAL COMMUNICATION.

Special effects The 'real' gorilla in *King Kong* (1933) was just 18 inches high – that is special effects. Simulations of earthquakes, explosions, floods, fires, storms, of the interior of Hell, of war in space or 40 fathoms deep is the job of the special effects wizards who today command fees as great as FILM stars. Special effects can, by dazzling defiance of the possible, make the success of a film. *Star Wars* (1977), directed by George Lucas, was raised from the humdrum and the banal to the spectacular by special effects; and COMPUTER GRAPHICS have provided an exciting new dimension to the art, with, first in the field, Walt Disney's $18 million *Tron* (1982). The financial success of such movies as *Jurassic Park* (1993) and *Titanic* (1997) owed much to their special effects.

Speech-recognition technology In the words of George Cole reporting in the *Observer*, 4 December 1994, in an article, 'Sound bytes', 'Speech-recognition systems – which allow computers to analyse, interpret and respond to human speech – have long been the Holy Grail of designers of man/machine interfaces'. These operate by converting what we say by using complex mathematical codes called algorithms to analyse speech content; basically reducing human speech to communication free of nuance, individuality and idiosyncracy, but the computers are learning fast.

Personal computers can now be told to 'open file' or 'delete'. DragonDictate of America is a speech-recognition system with a 30,000-word vocabulary. The user trains the system from scratch, repeating the words until they are recognized. Philip Dictation Systems allow the user to speak normally, with a 50,000-word recognition. Telephones too are being operated by voice signals. Voice Dialling was introduced by the telephone company US West in 1993 to residents in Colorado. Such systems may not be the liveliest or most articulate companions but, says Cole, 'Supporters of the new generation of interactive phone services say they are reliable, cost-effective, don't get tired, allow staff to carry out more important tasks and won't get upset if you swear at them'.

Speed photography See HIGH-SPEED PHOTOGRAPHY.

Spin doctor See SOUND-BITE.

Spinning top In Russian, 'Dziga Vertov', the nickname taken by one of the most influential directors and theorists in cinema history, Denis Kaufman (1896–1954), in order to proclaim his allegiance to the idea of movement. More than anyone else, Vertov challenged the studio-bound theatrical conception of film-making. He plunged into the Russian Civil War (1917–21) with both camera and rifle. The camera he saw as an eye, but more wonderful, more all-seeing: 'We cannot make our eyes better than they are', he writes, 'but the movie camera we can perfect for ever.' See DOCUMENTARY.

Spiral of silence See NOELLE-NEUMANN'S SPIRAL OF SILENCE MODEL OF PUBLIC OPINION, 1974.

Spiral model of communication See DANCE'S HELICAL MODEL OF COMMUNICATION.

Spoiler FLEET STREET parlance for a tactic used to detract from a rival newspaper's scoop story, usually by running a different version of the story as told by lesser characters.

Sponsorship There is scarcely any field of the arts, sport, entertainment or media which is not to a greater or lesser extent dependent on sponsorship; and this sponsorship originates for the most part from industry, business and commerce. However, it could be said that sponsorship is as old as the pyramids; indeed the pyramids constitute one of the most impactful examples of *state* sponsorship. Tombs, yes, but also symbols of the pharaohs' will to dominate the lives of their subjects. The pyramids were a constant reminder to the Egyptians that 'We are here'. Similarly, sponsorship of the arts by monarchs and the church was at base born of a desire to enthrone the sponsor in the minds of the people.

Some powers of monarchy and the church have been inherited by big business, as well as certain duties within the community. A company or corporation will sponsor a major art exhibition designed to give pleasure and illumination to thousands. And those thousands will in turn, so it is hoped, acknowledge the *communal benefit* made possible by the sponsoring company. Thus culture comes to us through the arch of sponsorship. At the same time the company will benefit by *association*. To sponsor Mozart or Rembrandt is somehow to be

touched by their greatness. Their quality rubs off on the sponsor.

The danger is for Mozart to be hi-jacked from the public domain and transformed into yet another device for selling goods – processed, packaged and 'profitized'. Such is the awareness in public bodies of this danger that codes are written to regulate the degree of sponsorship and its nature. See SPONSORSHIP: ITC CODE OF PROGRAMME SPONSORSHIP.

Sponsorship: ITC Code of Programme Sponsorship The Independent Television Commission in the UK was required by the BROADCASTING ACT, 1990 to draw up and from time to time review a code which sets standards and practice in the sponsoring of programmes and identifies criteria for sponsorship. Compliance with the Code is a condition of an ITC licence. The Code makes this definition: 'A programme is deemed to be sponsored if any part of its costs of production or transmission is met by an organization or person other than a broadcaster or television producer, with a view to prompting its own or another's name, trademark, image, activities, or other direct or indirect commercial interests.' The Code permits any programme to be sponsored, with the exception of News and Current Affairs programmes. Thus, 'Programmes and news flashes, comprising local, national or international news items must not be sponsored', and 'Current affairs programmes containing explanation or analysis of current events must not be sponsored'.

The following Principles form the basis of the Code: no sponsor is permitted any influence on either the content or the scheduling of a programme; any sponsorship must be clearly identified at the beginning and/or end of the programme; no promotional reference to the sponsor, or to his product or service, is permitted within the programme he has sponsored; no sponsored programme may contain within it any promotional reference to any other product or service; no programme may, without the previous approval of the Commission, be sponsored by any person whose business consists, wholly or mainly, in the manufacture or supply of a product, or in the provision of a service, which is not acceptable for television advertising under the CODE OF ADVERTISING STANDARDS AND PRACTICE (ITC). The Code of Programme Sponsorship prohibits PRODUCT PLACEMENT. The Code does not permit sponsorship of credits *within* programmes, with the exception of game shows, where there may be two factual aural references to the sponsor's provision of the prize(s) only. Credits must not suggest that a programme has been made by the sponsor and on-screen presenters as part of the sponsor credit are not acceptable. In trailers there may be only one reference to the programme's sponsor, which can be aural and/or visual, lasting not more than five seconds.

Sponsorship is denied to political parties or pressure groups whose aim may be defined as largely political. It is also denied to manufacturers of tobacco and pharmaceuticals only available on prescription. Though PRODUCT PLACEMENT is prohibited, 'When a product or service is an essential element within a programme, the programme-maker may, exceptionally, acquire that product or service at no, or less than full, cost. This is not product placement. It is acceptable providing no undue prominence is given to the product or service in question'.

Spontaneous activity Alfred Schutz promoted the concept of the communicative act as being one of spontaneity. 'Every action', writes Schutz in *Phenomenology of the Social World* (UK: Heinemann, 1972) 'is a spontaneous activity orientated towards the future'. We communicate to achieve future ends, Schutz argues, and to participate in social life; to handle the world of experience. See INTERPERSONAL COMMUNICATIONS.

Spot news Term used to describe unexpected or unplanned news events, such as natural disasters, aircrashes, murders or assassinations. These are distinguished from *diary stories* which are known well in advance and can be planned for by the newspaper, RADIO or TELEVISION news team – such as news conferences, state visits, elections or budgets. The *running story* is that which is on-going and may stretch over

several days or weeks, such as strikes, wars and famines; all stories that transcend the newsday cycle.

Sputnik First artificial satellite launched into space, by the Russians in 1957. See SATELLITE TRANSMISSION.

Spycatcher case A book by former British secret service employee Peter Wright, first published in the US in 1987, and banned from publication in the UK, became the centre of the most celebrated case of attempted government CENSORSHIP in the 1980s. *Spycatcher: The Candid Autobiography of a Senior Intelligence Officer* (US: Viking-Penguin, 1987) was not dissimilar in its revelations about the activities of MI5 to other books which had been permitted to appear, but Wright, having signed the OFFICIAL SECRETS ACT, was deemed to have breached confidence and arguably set a precedent for other secret agents to 'spill the beans' on security. The government was determined not only to prevent publication of *Spycatcher* in the UK but to block the intentions of newspapers such as the *Guardian*, the *Observer*, the *Independent* and the *Sunday Times* to publish extracts from Wright's book. At the same time, government law officers pursued the book across the world to the courts in Australia and Hong Kong. The publicity given to the pursuit of *Spycatcher* made it a world best seller; extracts from the book were published in the world's PRESS. Only the British people were to remain in the dark about Wright's revelations.

The government did not prosecute under the Official Secrets Act but pushed their case on the grounds of *confidentiality*, that members of the secret service, having sworn never to divulge information about their work, must – in law – be held for ever to that allegiance.

In seemingly innumerable court hearings, the case for the publication of *Spycatcher* made some advances and suffered rebuffs. In December 1987, High Court judge, Mr Justice Scott lifted the injunction on the *Guardian* and the *Observer* preventing them publishing extracts from the book, with the declaration that 'The ability of the press freely to report allegations of scandals in government is one of the bulwarks of our democratic society'. Bulwark or no, the government appealed against Justice Scott's ruling, ignoring his comment that 'I found myself unable to escape the reflection that the absolute protection of the security service that Sir Robert Armstrong, Secretary to the Cabinet, was contending for could not be achieved this side of the Iron Curtain'. The Law Lords deliberated on the saga of *Spycatcher* and in October 1988 rejected government demands for a blanket injunction against the publishing in the UK of extracts from Wright's book. 'In a free society', said Lord Goff, one of the five Law Lords, 'there is a continuing public interest that the workings of government should be open to scrutiny and criticism.' The Law Lords attacked the Government's conduct of the litigation and its claims that it is for Government alone to judge what information must remain confidential. An estimated £3m was spent by the Government on court proceedings. This triumph for free speech was followed by government measures to revise the Official Secrets Act to achieve the kind of censorship which had been so conspicuously rejected in the Lords' judgment. See SCOTT REPORT, 1996.

Stages in audience fragmentation See AUDIENCE: FRAGMENTATION OF.

Stamp Duty A government tax in late 18th and 19th c. Britain on newspapers, with the express intention of controlling the numbers of papers and access to them by the general public. With news of the French Revolution (1789) across the water, Stamp Duty was raised to two pence per newspaper copy, with an additional Advertising Tax at three shillings per advertisement. In 1797 Stamp Duty was raised to three and a half pence, and the hiring out of papers was forbidden. In the year of the Battle of Waterloo, 1815, the duty went up to four pence and the Advertising Tax was also raised.

The attitude of the ESTABLISHMENT to the rapid growth of newspapers had been summarized in the Tory *Anti-Jacobin Review* in 1801: 'We have long considered the establishment of newspapers in this country as a misfortune to be regretted; but, since their influence has become predominant by the universality of their circulation, we regard it as a calamity most deeply to be deplored.' Not only were heavy TAXES ON KNOWLEDGE imposed throughout the period, but subsidies or bribes became commonplace, including direct payments to journalists – to those, of course, amenable to government policies.

These measures eventually provoked what has been described as the 'War of the Unstamped', the struggle of papers unable or unwilling to pay the duties. William Cobbett (1763–1835) in his *Political Register* dropped news so as to evade tax and concentrated on *opinion*. Unstamped, and costing two pence, Cobbett's periodical achieved a sale of 44,000. 'Here, in these critical years', writes Raymond Williams in *The Long Revolution* (UK: Penguin, 1965) 'a popular press of a new kind was emerging, wholly independent in spirit, and reaching new classes of readers.'

Two of the six Acts of 1819 were directed against the PRESS and the 1820s and early 1830s featured clashes, fines, imprisonments and heroic defiance. In 1836 Stamp Duty was reduced from four pence to one penny, three years after the Advertisement Tax had been reduced from three shillings and sixpence to one shilling and sixpence per insertion. In 1853 the Advertising Tax was finally abolished; in 1855 the last penny of the Stamp Duty was removed and in 1860 the duty imposed on paper was abandoned. 'The era of democratic journalism had formally arrived', writes Joel H. Wiener in *The War of the Unstamped* (US: Cornell, 1969) 'and the daily newspaper became the cultural staple of the social classes.' See NEWSPAPERS, ORIGINS; PRESS BARONS; UNDERGROUND PRESS.

Standard and practice in advertising See CODE OF ADVERTISING STANDARDS AND PRACTICE (ITC).

Status The concept of status derives from the work of the sociologist Max Weber, who argued that status, though linked to CLASS, is a distinct dimension of social stratification. Status is the social evaluation of an individual or group, the degree of prestige or honour that society accords him, her or it.

Wealth and high income may confer status but do not necessarily do so. The reasons why individuals or GROUPS may enjoy considerable status within a community or society are complex, subject to change and derive from many sources: such as the degree of POWER or authority a person or group may have, the perceived social usefulness of the abilities of an individual or group or the level of education an individual has.

Occupation or the ownership of property may bestow status or require attributes, such as a high level of education, which themselves confer status. Hence the link between status and class.

Status may be *ascribed*, that is, based on fixed criteria over which a person may have no control – such as ancestry, ethnic affiliation, sex – or *achieved*, that is gained by endeavour or luck. Status given may not coincide with an individual's PERCEPTION of his or her status.

Status must normally be endorsed by behaviour: such as the possession of objects status symbols, accent, manners, and social skills consistent with the status position. Much communicative behaviour is involved in the display of status, the use of accent and dress for example. The mass media carry many images of status. Advertisers in particular appeal to status-consciousness as a way of selling a wide range of products from soap to newspapers.

Status quo As things are: the way in which things are done or were done in a period of time under discussion. Within the social science disciplines the term is often used to mean the prevailing or recent social, economic or political system and its attributes. There is some controversy within media studies as to whether or not the mass media generally play an important role in reinforcing the status quo by presenting it as the 'natural' or 'real' state of things, and by rarely, in their presentation of aspects of human life, calling it into question.

Richard Hoggart in *Speaking to Each Other* (UK: Chatto & Windus, 1970) argues that the tendency to accept the status quo results in the mass media concentrating on entertaining people at the expense of

exploring the nature of human existence – an exploration which might disturb the status quo. See COMMON SENSE; CONSENSUS; ESTABLISHMENT; HEGEMONY.

Stereophonic sound See GRAMOPHONE.

Stereoscopy The creation of the visual illusion of relief or three-dimensions. The stereoscope was invented by Sir Charles Wheatstone (1802–75) in 1838. The process has had many applications. In photography, two separate photographs, taken from minimally different angles corresponding to the position of two human eyes are mounted side by side on a card. Viewed through the angled prisms of the stereoscope, they interact to give the appearance of depth or solidity.

In the cinema experimental processes of stereoscopy were demonstrated as early as the 1930s. It was developed as Natural Vision, or 3-D, in the early 1950s but never caught on, mainly perhaps because members of the audience had to wear special glasses. Only in Russia has a stereoscopic process which does not require the wearing of glasses been developed, yet even there it does not appear to have been widely adopted. However, 3-D (with glasses) was brought experimentally to UK TV screens by ITV in 1982–83. See HOLOGRAPHY.

Stereotype Oversimplified definition of a person or type of person, INSTITUTION, STYLE or event; to stereotype is to pigeon-hole, to thrust into tight slots of definition which allow of little adjustment or change. Stereotyping is widespread because it is convenient – unions are like this, blacks are like this, Jews are like this, teenagers, women, Scots, foreigners are like this. Stereotyping is often – though not always – the result of or accompaniment to prejudice. It serves the media well because they are in the business of instant recognition and ready cues. It is very rare that we actually *know* any stereotypes: we only read of them, hear of them or have them 'framed' for us on TV. See HALO EFFECT; LABELLING PROCESS.

Stopwatch culture See IMMEDIACY.

Story appeal In ADVERTISING the hook which catches the viewer's, listener's or reader's attention; the angle or theme, which basically comes down to the posing of Who, What, Why, Where and How questions and answering them imaginatively.

Storyboard Sequence of sketches or photographs used by the director or the producer of a FILM to sketch out, scene by scene, and sometimes frame by frame, the film's progression, its sight and sound.

Storyness See NARRATIVE.

Strategic bargaining involves the news *gatherers* and the news *providers*. Between the subject of media interest, for example politicians, and the media, there is an interaction in which one gives to the other in return for a service. As Ralph Negrine says in *Politics and the Mass Media in Britain* (UK: Routledge, 1989), 'Each feeds off the other, each informs the other and the subsequent reactions are reciprocal and continuous . . . The product of the interaction or bargaining is the media content to which the public at large attend'. See CULTURE OF DEFERENCE; REGULATORY FAVOURS.

Strategic silence See SILENCE: STRATEGIC SILENCE.

Strategy A term sometimes used to describe a communicative act which has been planned to some extent beforehand, which is deliberate and which has a clear purpose. Strategies can become a matter of habit. An example here might be the strategy used by a door-to-door salesperson.

There are many different kinds of strategies used in INTERPERSONAL COMMUNICATION and we learn to use them through experience. Some, like the greetings strategy, are commonly used by many people, some we invent for ourselves to deal with particular situations and some may be specific to certain GROUPS or circumstances.

Stringer Name given in the news reporting business for a non-staff reporter.

Structuralism A 20th c. term of wide definition to describe certain traditions of analysing a range of studies – LINGUISTICS, literary criticism, psychoanalysis, social anthropology, Marxist theory and social his-

tory. Swiss scholar Ferdinand de Saussure's *Cours de Linguistique Générale* (1916), translated *Course in General Linguistics* (1954), is probably the initial key work in this movement, later developed and diversified by Claude Lévi-Strauss and Roland Barthes. Structuralism is something of an umbrella term linked with the study of SIGN systems or SEMIOLOGY/SEMIOTICS.

Structuralists would argue that LANGUAGE has both a natural and a cultural SOURCE. The natural source refers to language as a genetic endowment of the human race, and this is framed within a NETWORK of meanings derived from the CULTURE of society. Structuralism explores the deep and often unconscious assumptions about social reality which underlie language and its use. In particular, it examines the way language is employed to construct MEANING from social events. However, assumptions about social reality are themselves also a product of social conditioning. Thus different cultures and sub-cultures – and indeed individuals – may generate different patterns of meaning from the same objective event or situation. Structuralist analysis is equally applicable to other modes of communication, such as FILM. See POSTMODERNISM.

Style A means by which the individual or GROUP expresses identity, attitudes and VALUES, about self, about others and about society. Style takes many forms – hair style, dress style, aesthetic style, or a complete pattern of living – lifestyle. A teenager may adopt the style of a teenage SUB-CULTURE, in dress, LANGUAGE, behaviour for several linked reasons: to secure a sense of personal identity, to acquire a sense of belonging, of being 'in' with a favoured group, as a GESTURE of rebellion (against the *conventional* style of parents, for example, or the older generation in all shapes and forms) and to achieve *status* – that is, a status awarded him/her by others in the favoured group, and peers generally.

Defiance of society at large is often cited as a reason why certain styles are adopted; this may or may not be true in all cases, but what is certain is that society often *interprets* such styles as acts or defiance or rejection, and the arbiters in this process of interpretation (or MEDIATION) are the mass media. Coverage by the media, researchers have found, tends to overdramatize the significance of style, to create stereotypes and summon up exaggerated fears in the community (See FOLK DEVILS; LABEL LIBEL; LABELLING PROCESS; STEREOTYPE).

In the world of the arts style is that particular set of characteristics – of approach and treatment – which gives a work its identity. As with styles in hair or dress, styles are first created, then imitated. In painting, the style of Paul Cézanne (1839–1906) is highly distinctive and instantly recognizable by anyone with a particular interest in art. However, it took Cézanne many years to develop that style which was a visible manifestation of everything he believed about visual art; thus style represents the outer part of a whole structure which is made up of personality, experience, learning, theory, belief - and fused, if the style is successful.

Those coming after may slavishly imitate the style of the master or, like the cubists in the case of Cézanne, assimilate the style and then recreate it, thrusting it in new and exciting directions. See CULTURE; YOUTH CULTURE.

Sub-culture Alternatives to the dominant CULTURE in society, sub-cultures have their own systems of VALUES, NORMS and beliefs and in some cases their own language CODES. Such systems are often expressions of rejection of or resistance to the dominant culture. Members of sub-cultures are often those to whom the dominant culture awards low, subordinate and/or dependent status: youth, for example. Each sub-culture represents the reactions of a particular social group to its experience of society. Some sub-cultures and their members may be labelled DEVIANT by others in society.

It has been argued that because of the fragmented social nature of modern society, the mass media play an increasingly important role in relaying images of such sub-cultures both to their own members and to members of the dominant culture. Dick Hebdige in *Subculture: The Meaning of Style* (UK: Methuen, 1979), states that in doing

so the media tend to accommodate the sub-cultures within the framework of the dominant culture, thus preserving the CONSENSUS – a procedure which he calls the 'process of recuperation'. See COUNTER-CULTURE; YOUTH CULTURE.

Subliminal Signals which act below the threshold of conscious reception. Most familiarly we use the word in reference to *subliminal advertising*, the trick of flashing up on the screen, or recording on tape, messages so rapid that they are not consciously recorded but which may subsequently affect future attitudes or behaviour.

In the UK subliminal ADVERTISING is illegal and its use in other media is banned by the Institute of Practitioners in Advertising. In the US there is no such control. Many department stores use subliminal seduction to counteract shop-lifting. Messages such as 'I am honest, I will not steal' are mixed with background music and continually repeated. One retail chain reported a drop of a third in thefts in nine months as a result of its subliminal conscience coaxing. Computer games escape rules concerning subliminal messages. The *Sunday Times* published a major story 'Children "drugged" by computer games' (8 October 1995), concerning the Time Warner game *Endorfun*. The messages are there, admit the manufacturers, but they are positive, one message being 'I forgive myself completely'. Randeep Ramesh, author of the article, quotes the opinion of Howard Shevrin, Professor of Psychology at the University of Michigan: 'It does not pay to fool around with subliminal messages. The results may not be good if you are the wrong person for the wrong message.' See CODE OF ADVERTISING STANDARDS AND PRACTICE (ITC); SLEEPER EFFECT.

Subtitle Or striptitle, a text near the bottom of the projected image, usually providing a translation of foreign language dialogue. These days it is possible with foreign language films screened on TV to generate subtitles electronically so that the words are not actually on the film itself. In some multilingual areas, such as Cairo, where three or more titles in different languages and scripts are required, subtitles are projected on to separate screens at the sides and bottom of the main screen.

Succeeders See ADVERTISING: MAINSTREAMERS, ASPIRERS, SUCCEEDERS AND REFORMERS.

Super density (SD) discs Successors to the Compact Disc (CD), with more than twenty-five times the capacity of current CD-ROMs. As with the old rivalry between different VIDEO systems (VHS and Betamax) there is global rivalry between the SD format (SDI-DVD – Digital Video Disc) favoured by Time Warner and MGM/UA and that of the co-inventors of the CD, Sony and Philips, called the MultiMedia Compact Disc. Both systems are in most respects identical without being compatible.

Supervening social necessity Notion that social or cultural pressures give the impetus to technological development, serving as *accelerators* in the process of change. Brian Winston suggests this feature in 'How are media born?' in *Questioning the Media: A Critical Introduction* (UK: Sage, 1990), edited by John Downing, Ali Mohammadi and Annabelle Sreberny-Mohammadi. He cites the arrival of TV in the US as being accelerated by the 'rise of the home, the dominance of the nuclear family, and the political and economic need to maintain full employment' after the 2nd World War. Winston argues that 'Supervening social necessities are at the interface between society and technology'. They may operate as a result of the needs of corporations or because of new or rival technologies.

As well as accelerators, social necessities may serve as *brakes* upon technological developments, which 'work to slow the disruptive impact of new technology. I describe the operation of these brakes as the "law" *of the suppression of radical potential*, using "law" in the standard social science sense to denote a regular and powerful general tendency'. In this case, new technology, though available, is resisted, checked or even suppressed. Says Winston, 'The brakes ensure that a technology's introduction does not disrupt the social or corporate status quo'.

Winston is of the view that while TV had been 'accelerated' after 1945, it had been 'braked' prior to the war: 'Thus in the case of TV, the existence of facsimile systems, the rise of radio . . . and the need not to destroy the film industry all acted to suppress the speed at which the new medium was introduced, to minimize disruption.' See TECHNOLOGICAL DETERMINISM.

Surveillance Keeping watch; used in a media sense, the word indicates the way that listeners, viewers or readers employ the media with the aim of gleaning information from them: 'TV news provides food for thought' or 'I like to see how big issues are sorted out.' See USES AND GRATIFICATIONS THEORY.

Surveillance society The last quarter of the twentieth century was termed the Age of Information, chiefly because the technology of communication, from the computer to the satellite, multiplied the means of expression and reception. It vastly increased and speeded up access to personal data by those in authority or those individuals or organizations involved in financial, administrative or commercial transactions with members of the public. Each time we use a switch card; each time we dial a telephone number we offer notification of our activities, our whereabouts, and our lifestyle.

The concept of a surveillance society is not new. The English philosopher, social and legal reformer, Jeremy Bentham (1748–1832), in a proposal for the humanitarian treatment of prisoners, suggested the construction of what he called a Panopticon. This was a circular building of cells with a central watchtower from which constant surveillance of the prisoners would take place, without their being certain at any given time that they were being directly observed. They would be well aware, of course, of the presence of surveillance and this knowledge would, without coercion, rule their behaviour until, so Bentham theorized, their good behaviour would become self-regulating.

For several commentators the Panopticon has become a metaphor for our own times. In particular, the French philosopher Michel Foucault (1926–84) has focused on the 'all-seeing' Panopticon. In *Discipline and Punish* (UK: Penguin, 1977) he likens the

Panopticon to the Christian God's infinite knowledge and with computer monitoring of individuals in advanced capitalism. He argues that surveillance as represented by the contemporary Panopticon creates subjects responsible for their own subjection. See PRIVACY.

We are subject to surveillance not only as citizens but as AUDIENCE for media. In an article entitled 'Tracking the Audience', in *Questioning Media: A Critical Introduction* (US: Sage, 1990), edited by John Downing, Ali Mohammadi and Annabelle Srebemy-Mohammadi, Oscar Gandy Jr remarks how the fragmentation of audience for media, rendered possible by new technology, has resulted in a desperation among programme-makers which has led to two strategies aimed at survival. These Gandy identifies as *rationalization*, that is 'the pursuit of efficiency in the production, distribution, and sale of goods and services'; and *surveillance* which 'provides the information necessary for greater control'. Increasingly, says Gandy, 'the surveillance of audiences resembles police surveillance of suspected criminals' and people are less and less aware that their behaviour as audience is being measured.

Gandy argues that 'Perhaps the greatest threat these computer-based systems for audience assessment represent is their potential to worsen the balance of power between individuals and bureaucratic organizations. Personal information streams out of the lives of individuals much like blood out of an open wound, and it collects in pools in the computers of corporations and government bureacracies'. Resistance to such powers is, in Gandy's view, 'almost nonexistent, and what little there is may be seen as passive and defeatist'. While recognizing that a 'nearly invisible minority simply refuses to enter the system of records, giving up the convenience of credit cards and acquiring goods and services under assumed names or aliases', Gandy fears that 'to escape the information net means to become a nonperson'. It is a high risk, for one 'maintains privacy through the loss of all else'. See INTERNET: MONITORING OF CONTENT.

Survivors and the media A research report by Ann Shearer, 'Survivors of the media' (UK: John Libbey, 1991), commissioned by the BROADCASTING STANDARDS COUNCIL, found that insensitive media coverage adds to the distress of survivors of disasters and their bereaved relatives. Intrusions by media into PRIVACY, harassment, distortion and distasteful detail in what was reported, were identified by a sample of 54 people who had lost loved ones, as damaging and hurtful. Many comments placed the worst blame at the doors of the PRESS.

Sweetheart deals Term used to describe the informal practice by commissioning editors of broadcasting organizations, of awarding ex-employees with a favoured status when commissioning programmes from the independent production sector. A significant number of those formerly employed in broadcasting organizations entered the independent production sector when broadcasting organizations progressively downsized their labour force from the late 1980s to the mid-1990s. See CASUALIZATION; INDEPENDENT PRODUCERS.

Sykes Committee Report on Broadcasting, 1923 See BBC, ORIGINS.

Symbol Any object, person, or event to which a generally agreed, shared MEANING has been given and which individuals have learned to accept as representing something other than itself: a national flag represents feelings of patriotism and national unity, for example. Symbols are almost always CULTURE-bound. See ICONIC; METAPHOR; MYTH; SEMIOLOGY/SEMIOTICS; SIGN; SIGNIFICATION.

'Symbolic annihilation of women' (by the media) See NORMS.

Symbolic code See CODES OF NARRATIVE.

Symbolic convergence theory Professor Ernest G. Bormann in his article 'Symbolic convergence theory: a communication formulation' in the *Journal of Communication* (Autumn 1985), writes of 'shared fantasies' which 'provide group members with comprehensible forms for explaining the past and thinking about the future – a basis for communal and group consciousness' (See NARRATIVE PARADIGM).

Bormann posits a three-part structure to the theory: (1) the part which deals with the discovery and arrangement of recurring communicative forms and patterns that indicate the evolution and presence of a shared group consciousness; (2) the part which consists of a description of the dynamic tendencies within communication systems 'that explain why group consensuses arise, continue, decline, and disappear' and the effects such group consensus has in terms of MEANINGS, motives and communication within the group: the basic communication process is the dynamic of people sharing group fantasies; (3) that part of the theory which consists of the factors which explain why people share the fantasies they do and when they do.

By 'fantasy' Bormann means the creative and imaginative shared interpretation of events 'that fulfil a group psychological or rhetorical need'. What the author terms 'rhetorical fantasies' are the result of '*homo narrans* in collectives sharing narratives that account for their experiences and their hopes and fears'. Such rhetorical fantasies may include 'fanciful and fictitious scripts of imaginary characters, but they often deal with things that have actually happened to members of the group or that are reported in authenticated works of history, in the news media, or in the oral history and folklore of other groups and communities'. The sharing of fantasies brings a 'convergence of appropriate feelings among participants . . . when members of a mass audience share a fantasy they jointly experience the same emotions, develop common heroes and villains, celebrate certain actions as laudable, and interpret some aspect of their common experience in the same way'. This Bormann names *symbolic convergence*.

While the 'rational world paradigm' claims that there *is* an objective truth that speakers can mirror in their communication and against which its logic and argument can be tested and evaluated (and therefore regards MYTH and fantasy as untrue, as the recounting of falsehoods), for those giving credence to shared fantasies, 'the stories of myths or fantasy themes are central'. An underlying assumption of the theory seems to be that fantasies are not only creative but

benign. It would be interesting to apply symbolic convergence theory, the notion of HOMO NARRANS, to fantasies entertained about racial superiority, where fantasy becomes a nightmare.

* E.G. Boormann, *Communicative Theory* (US: Holt, Rinehart & Winston, 1980); *The Force of Fantasy: Restoring the American Dream* (US: Illinois University Press, 1985).

Symbolic interactionism Term associated with the ideas of American scholar Herbert Blumer and crystallized in his book *Symbolic Interactionism: Perspective and Method* (US: University of California Press, 1969; first paperback edition, 1986). Blumer sees 'meaning as arising in a process of interaction between people'. The meaning of an object or a phenomenon for one person 'grows out of the ways in which other persons act towards the person with regard to the thing', that is, the thing's *symbolic value*. Symbolic interactionism sees MEANING as a social product, as a creation 'formed in and through the defining activities of people as they interact. All meanings, emphasizes Blumer, are subject to a constant and recurring 'interpretative process'; and this is a 'formative process in which meanings are used and revised as instruments for the guidance and formation of action'.

Symmetry, strain towards Concept posed by Theodore Newcomb in 'An approach to the study of communicative acts', *Psychological Review*, 63 (1953). The act of communication is characterized, believes Newcomb, by a 'strain towards symmetry', that is towards balance and CONSISTENCY. See CONGRUENCE THEORY; INTERPERSONAL COMMUNICATION; NEWCOMB'S ABX MODEL OF COMMUNICATION, 1953.

Synchronic linguistics See LINGUISTICS.

Synchronous sound In FILM, sound effects synchronized with the visual image were first used commercially in 1926, in *Don Juan*, but it was *The Jazz Singer* in November 1927 which caused the sensation among audiences and marks the birth of the Talkies. Warner Brothers had been heading for oblivion in the cut-throat world of the HOLLYWOOD studios when the company adopted a system developed by the Bell

Telephones Laboratories which reproduced sound from large discs, matching sound and picture by mechanical linkage. Nothing in the cinema was ever the same again. The Talkies marked the end of many careers made in the silent era but created new opportunities for actors from the theatre, writers, musicians, vaudeville and RADIO stars.

As a technical possibility, synchronous sound had been inviting interest from movie makers from as early as 1902. In that year Monsieur Gaumont gave an address to the Société Française de la Photographie, on film and employing synchronous sound. Indeed two years earlier Herr Ruhmer demonstrated what he called 'light telephony' to record sound directly on to the film itself – the first *soundtrack*. Following the inventions of the thermionic valve by John Fleming in 1904 and the audion vacuum tube by Lee De Forest in 1907, amplification of sound by comparatively simple electric methods was feasible: the studios were simply not interested, fearing, perhaps, the impact language differences might have on the universal appeal of film as *mime*, whose only verbal language was easily translatable titling.

Though Lee De Forest's *Phonofilm* of 1923 demonstrated how light waves could synchronize sound and image, and though the Germans had developed the finest early sound system of all, *Tri-Ergon*, the continuing profitability of the silent movie blinded the studios to two significant facts: the potential of silent film had practically been exhausted; and audiences were becoming bored. *Lights of New York* (1928) was the first all-talking picture and within a year thousands of cinemas had been equipped for sound.

Warner's VITAPHONE disc was soon replaced by optical sound systems where images and sound were put together on the same film, to make the *married print* where sound synchronization with the picture could not be lost. As sound recording techniques developed, dialogue, sound effects and music were recorded separately, using a magnetic sound process, and then mixed at a later stage, thus allowing latitude for changes and creative editing.

The introduction of sound did not rescue the cinema from the general economic slump that followed the Wall Street Crash of 1929. During 1931, cinema attendances in the US dropped by 40% and in 1932 the movie business lost between $4 and 5m. However, it was probably the new dimension of sound in the cinema that enabled the industry to rally so quickly.

The Talkies interacted substantially with radio, the one drawing technical and creative ideas as well as talented personnel from the other. By 1937, 90% of US sponsored national radio programmes in the US were transmitted from Hollywood.

Synergy The establishment of relationships between differing areas and/or organizations within the cultural and media industries which allow for greater efficiency in the production and promotion of two or more cultural/media artefacts. An example of synergy is when the launching of a new film is accompanied by the promotion of a wide range of related merchandise. CONGLOMERATES are in an enviable position to take advantage of the benefits of synergies.

Syntactics A branch of SEMIOLOGY/SEMIOTICS; the study of the signs and rules relating to signs, without reference to MEANING.

Syntagm See PARADIGM.

Syntax The combination of words into significant patterns; the grammatical structure in sentences.

System X A computerized TELEPHONE exchange system developed by the UK Post Office in 1971. Involved in the marketing of System X are major companies in the private sector. According to Patrick Fitzgerald and Mark Leopold (a former British Telecom employee) in their book *Stranger on the Line: The Secret History of Phone Tapping* (UK: Bodley Head, 1987) System X permits the government and its agencies to monitor individual calls secretly and more easily. The INTERCEPTION OF COMMUNICATIONS ACT, 1985 does not cover the 'automatic call tracing' provided by the system: 'the [digital] tap leaves no physical presence anywhere', state the authors.

.T

Tabloid, tablodese, tabloidization In '"Tabloidization" of News: A Comparative Analysis of Anglo-American and German Press Journalism' (*European Journal of Communication*, September 1999) Frank Esser writes that the term 'tabloid' orginally referred to a pharmaceutical trademark for the concentrated form of medicines as pill or tablet: 'This narcotic tabloid effect and the fact that it is easy to swallow have been readily transferred to the media'. The term, in the UK, is used to refer to the *size* of a newspaper (in comparison with the *broadsheet* format), but in general 'tabloidese' describes the nature of news content and style. Esser quotes Marvin Kalb, director of the Shorenstein Centre on the Press, Politics and Public Affairs at Harvard University: tabloidese is characterized by 'a downgrading of hard news and upgrading of sex, scandal and infotainment'. At the micro level, states Esser, tabloidization 'can be seen as a media phenomenon involving the revision of traditional newspaper and other media formats driven by reader preferences and commercial requirements' while on the macro level it 'can be seen as a social phenomenon both instigating and symbolizing major changes to the constitution of society'.

Esser's study focuses on the micro level of the tabloidization process, meaning 'a change in the range of topics being covered (more entertainment, less information), in the form of presentation (fewer longer stories, more shorter ones with pictures and illustrations) and a change in the mode of address (more street talk when addressing readers)'.

Esser argues that the nature, evolution and relative predominance of tabloidization varies between America, the UK and Germany; thus it is an 'extremely problematic term' and can 'therefore only be analysed with reference to the respective media cultures and journalistic traditions' of the countries in question.

For example, tabloidization has never taken hold in Germany to the extent that it has in the UK; in part because – as far as sex scandals are concerned – Germany has a strong privacy law that 'also protects public figures'. He cites research evidence showing that extensive coverage of scandals can increase public disillusionment with public life, hence the fears which many commentators have 'that a shift towards sensation, emotion and scandal may have some negative effects on democracy'.

Tactics and strategies Term used by Michel de Certeau in *The Practice of Everyday Life* (US: University of California Press, 1984) when analysing everyday cultural consumption, to draw the distinction between the strategies of the powerful controllers of the cultural industries and the tactics of the relatively powerless ordinary consumers in finding their own space for creating MEANING, uses and adaptations of the cultural artefacts produced by the powerful. Some of these tactics subvert or resist the intentions and intended messages of the powerful. De Certeau's distinction, whilst acknowledging that audiences/consumers may be active in their consumption, does not imply that they have by any means the degree of power over cultural consumption exercised by those who own and control the cultural industries. See AUDIENCE: ACTIVE AUDIENCE; SEMIOTIC POWER.

Tag questions The addition of phrases such as 'Isn't it?' or 'Don't you think?' at the end of a statement as tag questions, according to some linguists, suggests tentativeness on behalf of the speaker, and weakens the impact of what is said. However, there is some debate here. Tag questions can serve a range of functions, some relating to the content of speech, others relating to the facilitation of interaction and the relationships and attitudes of the participants to one another. When used to facilitate interaction, tag questions do not seem to be associated with tentativeness, indeed, the tendency here is for tags to be associated with powerful speakers. Several studies suggest that women use more tag questions than men when acting as facilitators in an interaction.
* Jennifer Coates, *Women, Men and Language* (UK: Longman, 1993, 2nd edition).

Take See SHOT.

Talkies See SYNCHRONOUS SOUND.

Talloires Declaration, 1981 Concerned at the attempts by Unesco seemingly to impose upon world information systems a 'New Order' which would be characterized by far-reaching controls, representatives from news organizations of 20 countries met in the French village of Talloires in May 1981. They issued a declaration which insisted that journalists sought no special protected status – as it was planning to create – and that they were united in a 'joint declaration to the freest, most accurate and impartial information that is within our professional capacity to produce'. The declaration asserted that there could be no double standards of freedom for rich and poor countries. See MacBRIDE COMMISSION; MEDIA IMPERIALISM; NEW WORLD INFORMATION ORDER.

Tamizdat See SAMIZDAT.

Taste In a media sense, the notion of good or bad taste relates less to aesthetic judgment than to decisions about how *much* and how *far*; the answers to these questions depend upon audience EXPECTATIONS and readiness, and the degree of access and immediacy. A photograph of an execution, reproduced in a newspaper or magazine, is sufficiently controlled by the frame of print and the fact that the event took place in the past, to escape the accusation of bad taste. However, vigorous protests went up when, on TV news, a Vietcong prisoner had a pistol put to his head, and the trigger pulled. This was bringing, as it were, too much reality into the sitting room. It may have been the truth, ran the argument, but somehow the reproduction and presentation turned reality into theatre, indeed into macabre entertainment. As such it appeared an insult to human dignity, to that of the victim and to that of the audience cast in the role of voyeurs. See CENSORSHIP.

Taxes on knowledge Government-imposed taxes and duties on the PRESS in the late 18th and 19th centuries. STAMP DUTY was levied on every copy of a newspaper printed; the Advertising Tax upon every advertisement used. The intention of the taxes was made plain at the time by Lord Ellenborough: 'It was not against the respectable Press that the Bill (Newspaper Stamp Duties Act, 1819) was directed, but against a pauper press.' That is, the radical press as represented by such editors as William Cobbett (1763–1835), Richard Carlile, James Watson and Thomas Hetherington, in an age of turbulent unrest. See UNDERGROUND PRESS.

Technique: Ellul's theory of technique In a number of books written between the 1950s and 1990, Jacques Ellul saw contemporary society as being dominated by technological advances each aiding the MEDIATING power of mass communication; and together leading to a society in which *efficiency* and consequently *conformity* become the key determinants of human affairs. Ellul uses the term *technique* to suggest the generality of attitudes to, and uses of, machines in everyday life, applying equally to social production as to material production. His view is a bleak one, seeing efficiency, brought about by the wholesale adoption by those who rule and those who are ruled, as being being both authoritarian in tendency and beyond the control of governments: 'Technical advance', says Ellul in *The Technological Society* (US: Knopf, 1964), 'gradually invades the state, which in turn is compelled to assume forms favourable to this advance.' Politicians Ellul sees as 'impotent satellites of the machine, which with all its parts and techniques, apparently functions as well without them'. However, the politicians do not step down. Instead they create an illusion of politics and political leadership.

Ellul anticipates the response that the information age has brought about a more involved public in the political process. For him the sheer volume of information works to reinforce the technological society by overwhelming the citizen.

In a detailed analysis of Ellul's theory of technique in 'Hegemony, agency, and dialectical tension in Ellul's technological society' in the *Journal of Communication* (Summer 1998), Rick Clifton Moore writes, 'This is not to say that all of the blame for the political illusion must be laid at the feet of the state and the media. Ellul's orientation suggests the complicity of the citizens themselves . . . The modern citizen is much too willing to accept the comfortable route of technique, rather than make difficult choices that would require humanness'. The public, in Ellul's view, is subject to, and in thrall to, the 'spectacle-orientated society' in which everything is 'subordinated to visualization' and 'nothing has meaning out of it'. In today's society, Ellul says, there are many, and powerful, deterrents of human freedom, and a key question is, in societies where 'covetousness and the desire for power' are human constants across all cultural boundaries, whether there is sufficient *agency* among citizens to achieve freedom. See HEGEMONY; IDEOLOGICAL STATE APPARATUSES; IDEOLOGY.

Technological determinism The view that if something is technically feasible then it is both desirable and bound to be realized in practice. In many quarters in the so-called WIRED WORLD of CABLE TELEVISION, SATELLITE TRANSMISSION and VIDEO there is a degree of fatalism that these things must come to pass (even if we don't want them, even if they are likely to be socially and culturally harmful). Evidence points to the fact that such determinism is only partly convincing. Much technology usage is a by-product of technology devised for other purposes. Radio became an 'inevitability', for example, largely because its determinant was radar, required to fulfil military needs, while satellites had a long record of military/political functions before they began to beam sporting events to the peoples of the world.

Set counter to notions of technological determinism is a second theory, *Symptomatic technology*, which argues that technology is a by-product of a social process which itself has been otherwise determined. In *Television: Technology and Cultural Form* (UK: Fontana, 1974), Raymond Williams says that basically both theories are in error because in different ways they have 'abstracted technology from society' instead of examining the crucial interaction between them. Of course part of that interaction is the *belief* in technological determinism, and the risk of it becoming a

self-fulfilling prophecy. See SUPERVENING SOCIAL NECESSITY.

Dwayne Winseck in 'Pursuing the Holy Grail: information highways and media reconvergence in Britain and Canada' in the *European Journal of Communication* (September 1998), argues that contrary to 'the belief that technological factors determine how media are organized', the primary drivers of media evolution 'are machinations between governments and industries, visions of how markets should evolve, and ideas about whether communication constitutes just another commodity or is something more imbued with cultural consideration and public service values'.

Winseck notes two negative factors which might be impeding the determinism of the information superhighway – a 'decline in the telecommunications infrastructure' and a 'lack of interest' on the part of the public, raising questions as to 'whether or not information highways will ever be built'. He writes of the possibility of 'information suburbs' located in 'areas with sufficient demands and ability to pay for the new media'. Such a model, Winseck fears, 'would reinforce class divisions in society and lead to electronic-gated communities'.

Technology of the media See CABLE TELEVISION; CAMERA; CEEFAX; CELLULAR RADIO; CD – COMPACT DISC; CELLULOID; CINEMASCOPE; CINEMATOGRAPHY, ORIGINS; COMPUTER GRAPHICS; CYLINDER OR ROTARY PRESS; DIGITALIZATION; DIGITAL RETOUCHING; DIGITAL TELEVISION; DIGITAL VIDEO DISC (DVD); EARLY-BIRD SATELLITE; FACSIMILE; FIBRE-OPTIC TECHNOLOGY; FILMLESS CAMERA; GRAMOPHONE; FLAT-SCREEN TECHNOLOGY; HIGH-SPEED PHOTOGRAPHY; HOLOGRAPHY; INFORMATION TECHNOLOGY; INFRA-RED PHOTOGRAPHY; IN-TELSAT; INTERACTIVE TELEVISION; LAN; LINOTYPE PRINTING; MONOTYPE PRINTING; OMNIMAX; PHONO-DISC; PHOTOTYPESETTING; PRINTING; PROJECTION OF PICTURES; SATELLITE TRANSMISSION; STEREOSCOPY; SUPER DENSITY (SD) DISCS; SUPERVENING SOCIAL NECESSITY; TECHNIQUE: ELLUL'S THEORY OF TECHNIQUE; TECHNOLOGICAL DETERMINISM; TELEGRAPHY; TELEPHONE; TELETEXT; TELEX; TELEVISION BROADCASTING; TELSTAR; TYPEWRITER; ULTRAVIOLET/FLUORESCENT PHOTOGRAPHY; VIDEO; WIRELESS

TELEGRAPHY; XEROGRAPHY; ZOETROPE; ZOOM LENS; ZOOPRAXOGRAPHY.

Teenagers and media use See CHILDREN, YOUNG PEOPLE AND THE CHANGING MEDIA ENVIRONMENT.

Telecommunication *Tele* means far off, at a distance; a telecommunication is communication by TELEGRAPH or TELEPHONE, with or without wires or cables. In telephony and telegraphy signals are transmitted as electric impulses along wires. In RADIO and TV the signals are transmitted through space as modulations of carrier waves of electromagnetic radiation. See TECHNOLOGY OF THE MEDIA; TELETEXT; WIRELESS TELEGRAPHY.

Teledemocracy Term used to describe theories that telecommunications serve to advance democracy by extending information and widening access to information; by counteracting through the use of computers and modems, the advantages of the *information-rich* over the *information-poor*. Local networks, using computers whose capacities have advanced as the prices have dropped, demonstrate the potential to link up nationally and internationally, favouring access to individuals and communities.

As evidence of teledemocracy the work of such alliances as PeaceNet, founded in San Francisco in 1986, EcoNet, London's GreenNet and the computer-communication project Public Data Access (PDA) is cited. PDA was responsible in the US for the dissemination of research into the exceptionally high correlation between toxic-waste sites and the location of minority communities. Sceptics, however, hold to the view that in an age when information has become increasingly commoditized, it is the all-powerful agencies of information – governments, multi-national corporations – who control the 'electronic highways' and that such highways are less public than private roads.

Telegenic Looking good on TV – a factor that has had particular significance in the domain of politics. There is no proof that it does not help to be handsome. See LOOKISM.

Telegram A communication by TELEGRAPH; now only available for international purposes. The old inland telegram was superseded in 1982 by the **telemessage**, which is delivered with the post but transmitted to the local post office by TELEX.

Telegraphy Only after the discovery of the magnetic effect of electric current was telegraphy possible. The first **telegraph** consisted of a compass needle which was deflected by the magnetic field produced by electric currents which flowed through the circuit whenever the transmitting key was depressed and contact established. The first patent for an electric telegraph was taken out by William Fothergill Cooke and Charles Wheatstone in June 1837 and later in the same year they demonstrated a five-needle telegraph to the directors of the London and Birmingham railway. A year later the Great Western Railway connected Paddington and West Drayton by telegraph line which soon gave a considerable boost of publicity to telegraphy: in 1845 a suspected murderer was spotted boarding a London-bound train at Slough; the news was telegraphed to Paddington and the man was arrested on arrival and later found guilty and hanged.

In the US, Samuel Morse's first working telegraph of 1837 depended on the making and breaking of an electric current: an electromagnetically operated stylus recorded the long and short dashes of MORSE CODE on a moving strip of paper. After much persuasion, the US Congress, in 1843, voted to pay Morse (1791–1872) to build the first telegraph line in America, from Baltimore to Washington. It was in the following year, using the Morse Code, that Morse transmitted his famous message – 'What hath God wrought!' – on this line.

Development of telegraphy was swift. By 1862 the world's telegraph system covered some 150,000 miles, including 15,000 in the UK. A method of printing the coded telegraph messages had been invented in 1845 and was developed in the US as 'House's Printing Telegraph'. In 1850 a telegraph cable had been laid across the English Channel. In 1858 the Atlantic was spanned by telegraph cable. The **duplex telegraphy** of

Thomas Alva Edison (1847–1931) made it possible to transmit two messages simultaneously over the same line. Soon, four and five-message systems followed, and ultimately the teleprinter. Picture transmission by telegraphy resulted from the development work of English physicist Shelford Bidwell, the first such transmissions taking place in 1881. See TELEX.

'The significance of telegraphy,' writes James W. Carey in *Communication as Culture* (UK: Routledge, 1992) 'is that it led to the selective control and transmission of information. The telegraph operator was able to monopolize knowledge, if only for a few moments, along a route; and this brought a selective advantage in trading and speculation.' It also ushered in a new LANGUAGE of JOURNALISM, what Ernest Hemingway called 'the lingo of the cable' – terse, precise; as Carey puts it, 'a form of language stripped of the local, the regional, and colloquial . . . something closer to a "scientific" language, a language of strict denotation in which the connotative featurers of utterance were under rigid control'.

Telegraphy continues to be widely used – by news services, the Stock Exchange telex service, public message services, certain police and fire alarm systems and private-line companies for data transmission. See MORSE CODE; TECHNOLOGY OF THE MEDIA; TELEPHONE; WIRELESS TELEGRAPHY.
* Brian Winston, *Media, Technology and Society: A History: From the Telegraph to the Internet* (UK: Routledge, 1998).

Telematics Term referring to the merging of telecommunications and computers, brought about by DIGILITALIZATION. The 1s and 0s of the computer are converted into tones relayed over telephone lines and then reconverted at the other end of the line by another computer. Thus information can be held centrally, dispatched rapidly, updated easily and networked internationally. This trans-border data flow (TBDF) is enhanced by SATELLITES, the advantage of whose use is that transmission costs do not rise in relation to the distance being covered (as is the case with microwaves and cables); so long,

that is, as the communication falls within the 'footprint' of the same satellite.

Telemessage See TELEGRAM.

Telephone In his early years, a Scotsman Alexander Graham Bell (1857–1922) knew Charles Wheatstone (1802–75), co-inventor of TELEGRAPHY, and also Alexander John Ellis, an expert in sound. Ellis showed Bell that the vibration of a tuning fork could be influenced by an electric current. He was able to produce sounds very like those of a human voice. Bell, teaching deaf-mutes in Boston, Massachusetts, experimented on a musical telegraph (1872). He produced artificial 'ear-drums' from sheets of metal and linked these with electric wire. In 1876 Bell succeeded in passing a vocal message along a wire to an assistant in another room. The first telephone switching system was installed in New Haven, Connecticut, in 1878. 100 years later, the US telephone system, largely the monopoly of the company Bell founded, was handling an average of over 240m phone conversations a day and, as Maurice Richards points out in *The World Communicates* (UK: Longman, 1972), the telephone system had 'developed into a communications network infinitely more versatile than could have been envisaged by the pioneers'. Now telephone lines serve complex computer data systems; documents are transmitted via telephone – a scanning head records the light and shade of the document as it turns on a rotating drum, translating intensity of tone into electrical impulses for transmission over the wire to be re-translated at the receiving end. Telephone lines also carry TELEX services.

Microwave transmission techniques now allow telephone calls through air, free of wires, poles or underground conduits. Transmitting from point to point, tall towers now beam as many as 1500 calls on a single carrier wave. The London Post Office Tower has potential load capacity of 150,000 telephone calls and capacity to transmit 100 TV channels. See NETWORK.

Telephone conferencing A facility available both on many private TELEPHONE exchanges and, via the operator, on the public NETWORK; it enables the interlinking of more than two parties in a single call, each person being able to hear and address the others. A single telephone may be used at any site, or a group of people can use a loud-speaking phone. Pushbutton-activated light signals can be used to indicate to the chairperson of the conference or meeting a request to speak. It is also possible to combine telephone conferencing with a VIDEO link so that participants can see one another.

Telephone tapping See PHONE-TAPPING.

Telephoto lens Long focal length camera lens used in photographing distant objects and scenes by enlarging the image on the film. Telephoto is a loosely applied term for all long lenses.

Telerecording Introduced in 1947, the first telerecording equipment consisted of a special 35mm film camera pointed at the screen. Picture quality was poor as a result of incompatibility between the camera shutter and TV's scanning process. The Ampex Corporation of America produced a definitive answer using a 'quadruplex' technique: a two-inch wide tape travelled at normal speed while a rapidly spinning drum carrying four heads recorded tracks across the tape rather than along it, thus achieving the high and constant speed required.

The Ampex machine was in service in the US in 1956 and in May of the following year Associated Rediffusion in the UK installed the first pair of recording machines in Europe. The BBC followed suit shortly afterwards.

Helical scan recorders were an advance upon the quadruplex machines. Instead of recording across the tapes, the spinning head-drum laid down tracks almost parallel to its length. Gradually, in the late 1970s, these machines took over from quadruplex though there were problems over product compatibility. Ampex and Sony agreed a common standard, known as C-format, and helical scan became the norm.

Teletext Data in textual or graphic form transmitted via the TV screen; the BROAD-CASTING version of viewdata which is TELE-PHONE-linked. In the UK, the BBC provides its CEEFAX information service; the COMMER-CIAL TV equivalent was, until 1993, the Oracle service. In the auction for such services, empowered by the BROADCASTING ACT, 1990, the licence-winner was Teletext UK, a consortium headed by Associated Newspapers and Philips, the electronics company. The name of the new service from 1993 is Teleview.

Telethon A live TV discussion or entertainment programme, often lasting for several hours, during which the public may ring in with questions and comments, and guest stars appear – all in aid of charity.

Television See BBC, ORIGINS; BREAKFAST-TIME TELEVISION; BROADCASTING ACT, 1980; BROADCASTING ACT, 1990; CABLE TELEVISION; CHANNEL FOUR; COMMERCIAL TELEVISION; DIGITALIZATION; DIGITAL TELEVISION; PUBLIC SERVICE BROADCASTING; SATELLITE TRANSMISSION; TELETEXT; TELEVISION BROADCASTING; TELEVISION DRAMA; TELEVISION NEWS: INHERENT LIMITATIONS; VIDEO.

See also: ACCELERATION FACTOR; ADVERTISING; AGENDA SETTING; ANNAN COMMISSION REPORT ON BROADCASTING, 1977; AUDIENCE DIFFERENTIATION; AUDIENCE MEASUREMENT; AUTOCUE; BBC: GOVERNMENT WHITE PAPER, 1994; BALANCED PROGRAMMING; BARB; BEVERIDGE COMMITTEE REPORT ON BROADCASTING, 1950; BROADCASTING COMPLAINTS COMMISSION; BROADCASTING LEGISLATION; BUTTON APATHY; CAMERA CUE; CAMPAIGN FOR PRESS AND BROADCASTING FREEDOM; CATHARIS HYPOTHESIS; CEEFAX; 'CLEAN-UP TV' MOVEMENT; CODES; COLOUR TV; COMMERCIAL TELEVISION; CONSENSUS; CONSPIRACY OF SILENCE; CULTIVATION; CULTIVATION DIFFERENTIAL; DEVOLUTION; DRY-RUN; DUOPOLY; FLY ON THE WALL; GLASGOW UNIVERSITY MEDIA GROUP; HANKEY COMMITTEE REPORT ON TELEVISION, 1943; HIGH-DEFINITION TV; HUNT COMMITTEE REPORT ON CABLE EXPANSION AND BROADCASTING POLICY, 1982; INDEPENDENT PRODUCERS; INHERITANCE FACTOR; INTERACTIVE TELEVISION; INTER-CULTURAL INVASION (AND THE MASS MEDIA); INTERNATIONAL BROADCASTING TRUST; LITTLE MASTERPIECES LASTING ONE MINUTE; MAINSTREAMING; McLUHANISM; MEAN WORLD SYNDROME; MINORITY REPORT OF MR SELWYN LLOYD; MONOPOLY, FOUR SCANDALS OF; NATURALISTIC ILLUSION (OF TELEVISION); NEWS VALUES; PACKAGING; PAPER TIGER TV; PARAPROXEMICS; PILKINGTON COMMITTEE REPORT ON BROADCASTING, 1962; PROGRAMME FLOW; QUOTAS; SECONDARY VIEWING; SELSDON COMMITTEE REPORT ON TELEVISION, 1935; S4C; SHOWBUSINESS, AGE OF; SINCERITY TEST (BY

THE MEDIA); SINS OF OMISSION; SIT-COM; SOAP OPERA; SOCIAL ACTION BROADCASTING; SOUND-BITE; SYKES COMMITTEE REPORT ON BROADCASTING, 1923; TELEGENIC; TELERECORDING; TELEVISION ACT, 1954; TERRORISM AS COMMUNICATION; THESIS JOURNALISM; TIE-SIGNS; TIME-SHIFT VIEWING; ULLSWATER COMMITTEE REPORT ON BROADCASTING, 1936; VISUAL DISPLAY UNIT (VDU); WESTMINSTER VIEW.

Television Act, 1954 Gave birth to COMMERCIAL TELEVISION in the UK; the Act set up the Independent Television Authority (later to be named the Independent Broadcasting Authority with the coming of COMMERCIAL RADIO). A rigorous set of controlling rules was imposed on the Authority which required 'that nothing is included in the programmes which offends against good taste or decency or is likely to encourage or incite to crime or to lead to disorder or to be offensive to public feelings or which contains any offensive representation of or reference to a living person'.

A proper *balance* was required in subject matter and a high general standard of *quality*. Due 'accuracy and impartiality' were required for the presentation of any news given in programmes, in whatever form. There were also to be 'proper proportions' in terms of British productions and performance in order to safeguard against the dumping of American material.

Of vital significance in the Act were the elaborate precautions which were made to prevent advertisers gaining control of programme content. The governing body of ITV set up by the Act was similar in size and function to that of the BBC, with seven to ten governors each serving for five years and dismissible at the behest of the Post-master-General. Like the BBC, the ITA was to have a limited period of existence, followed by parliamentary review and renewal. See SOUND BROADCASTING ACT, 1972.

Television broadcasting Technical developments in the UK, the Soviet Union and the US combined to make TV a feasibility by 1931 when a research group was set up in Britain under Isaac Shoenberg, who had had considerable experience in RADIO transmission technology in the Soviet Union. He furthered the evolution of a practical system of TV broadcasting based on a camera tube known as the *Emitrion* and an improved cathode-ray tube for the receiver. Shoenberg elected to develop a system of electronic scanning which proved far superior to the mechanical scanning method pioneered by Scotsman John Logie Baird (1889–1946) who had first demonstrated his system publicly in 1926.

The BBC was authorized by government to adopt Shoenberg's standards (405 lines) for the world's first high-definition service which was launched in 1936 – a system that proved sufficiently successful to continue in the UK until 1962, when the European continental 625 line system was introduced. In the US, TV was slower to develop. It was not until 30 April 1939, at the opening of the New York World's Fair, that a public demonstration was made by the National Broadcasting Company (NBC).

The BBC's nascent TV service closed down during the 2nd World War (1939–45) which also hampered TV development in America, though by 1949, there were a million receivers in the US and by 1951, 10 million. In the UK, TV transmission resumed in June 1946.

* Anthony Smith, ed., and Richard Patterson, associate ed., *Television: An International History* (UK: Oxford University Press, 1998).

Television drama In an interview printed in *The New Priesthood: British Television Today* (UK: Allen Lane, 1970) edited by J. Bakewell and N. Garnham, TV playwright Dennis Potter (1935–95) said of TV, 'It's the biggest platform in the world's history and writers who don't want to kick and elbow their way on to it must be disowning something in themselves'. While the PILKINGTON COMMITTEE REPORT ON BROADCASTING, 1962, found that the chief 'crime' of TV was *triviality*, much of TV drama (from the very first drama production on experimental TV, the BBC's *The Man with a Flower in his Mouth* by Luigi Pirandello on 14 July 1930) has been a striking exception to that judgment. In fact few might argue with the claim that TV's most substantial achievement has been to encourage generations of quality dramatists working specially for the medium, and a canon of plays, from both the BBC and COMMERCIAL TV companies, to rival anything produced in the live theatre during the same post-2nd World War period.

In the early days of TV drama, plays were stage-bound, or more accurately, studio-bound, both in concept and execution, taking for their model the theatre rather than the cinema, but the ideas of young directors making their mark during the 1960s, excited by the possibility of FILM drama, prevailed. Nell Dunn's *Up the Junction* (BBC, 1965) marked the first occasion when virtually the whole story was done on film. The camera was seen to be as important as the pen; indeed the camera in many ways *became* the pen. The social – and sometimes political – themes favoured by many writers and directors took the cameras more and more out of the studio and into 'real life', and many plays looked like, and had the impact of, DOCU-MENTARY.

Produced by Tony Garnett, written by Jeremy Sandford and directed by Ken Loach, *Cathy Come Home* (BBC, 1966) detailed the decline into tragedy of a homeless family in affluent Britain. The sense of reality was almost unbearable: the camera was often hand-held, the scenes staged so realistically that the audience was tempted to forget it was watching something *constructed*, not something happening before their very eyes.

The intimacy, the close-scrutiny of humans under stress at which film and TV can excel, has rarely been used to more disturbing effect than with John Hopkin's quartet of plays *Talking to a Stranger* (BBC, 1966), described as the first authentic masterpiece of television. The *immediacy* of the medium was stunningly demonstrated in Colin Welland's epic *Leeds United!* (BBC, 1974) about Leeds clothing workers who struck spontaneously in 1970 for an extra 10 pence an hour: the camera became part of the ongoing action to such an extent that it was impossible to detect what had been *scripted* and what was happening for real.

Much of this kind of drama obviously grew from the opportunities of the moment, and from improvisation – a method used most notably by Mike Leigh, who works with actors for long periods before filming, encouraging them to *become* the characters and eventually invent or improvise their speech and actions. Examples of Leigh's improvised drama are *Abigail's Party* (BBC, 1976) and *Home Sweet Home* (BBC, 1982).

It is a hard task to select the outstanding TV dramas of recent years, but any comprehensive list would very probably contain David Mercer's *A Suitable Case for Treatment* (BBC, 1962), Potter's *Stand up, Nigel Barton* (BBC, 1965), his six-part musical play *Pennies from Heaven* (BBC, 1978) and *Cream in My Coffee* (London Weekend TV, 1980), Tom Clarke's *Stopper's Copper* (BBC, 1972), Garnett and Loach's four-film drama of events in Britain seen through the lives of poor people, *Days of Hope* (BBC, 1976), written by Jim Allen, and Brian Clark's *Whose Life Is It Anyway?* (BBC, 1972) about a paralysed hospital patient demanding the right to die – not a theme, or treatment, that could in any way be accused of trivialization.

In *Television and Radio, 1982* (IBA), David Cunliffe, Head of Drama at Yorkshire TV, writes 'The inescapable fact is that over the last few years the television single play has spiralled in production costs and plummeted in popularity'. Having moved from the studio to location, plays have become 'nearly Hollywood-size movies'. He cites dramas such as Potter's LWT series, *Rain on the Roof, Blade on the Feather* and *Cream in My Coffee* as works which though expensive and polished appeal to 'relatively small sections of viewers'. One such play costs as much as half-a-dozen produced, years ago, in the studio – even allowing for inflation. Increasingly in the 1980s, dramatists turned to writing TV serials, which have more over-time impact and are more saleable commodities on the international programme market. Distinguished examples of serial writing are Alan Bleasdale's *Boys from the Blackstuff* (1982), Troy Kennedy Martin's *Edge of Darkness* (1985) and Potter's *The Singing Detective* (1987), all from the BBC and Alan Plater's *A Very British Coup* (1988), from Channel 4. Adaptations of the classics have continued to be notable for lavish investment with an eye to world distribution, the genius of Jane Austen never being better served than in Andrew Davies' adaptation in six parts of *Pride And Prejudice*, directed by Simon Langton, with music by Carl Davis and an exemplary cast.

In 'modern' idiom TV drama has in the 1990s been dominated by cops/crime series such as Lynda Le Plant's *Prime Suspect* (ITV), featuring Helen Mirren, striving for a new edge in realism while at the same time focusing on the stress and ambiguities of personal and professional relationships. In 1996 the traditionally marginal (though vitally significant) role of the forensic scientist was brought centre-stage, with Amanda Burton starring as Dr Sam Ryan in BBC1's *Silent Witness* adding the gruesome to the dramatic; in its sombreness and earnestness reflecting in Burton's performance, and the depressing if intriguing narratives, something of the mood of disillusion in the late 1990s in the UK. Outstanding among the 'actuality' police series in the 1990s,. at least in terms of its popularity, was ITV's *Cracker*, with Robbie Coltrane as Fitz, the police psychologist whose sharp-edged perception brought illumination to everything but his own marital situation.

Also from ITV came Kay Mellor's tough drama on prostitutes, *Band of Gold*. From the BBC and Channel 4 in 1996 (in rare cooperation) came Dennis Potter's final plays, bequeathed on his death, *Karaoke* and *Cold Lazarus* ; and as if to remind the public that the drama of getting a play produced on the BBC has itself become a bureaucratic and monetarist melodrama, Channel 4 came up with Alan Plater's *Domino Effect*.

* John Tulloch, *Television Drama: Agency, Audience and Myth* (UK: Routledge, 1990); David Paget, *No Other Way to Tell It: Dramadoc/Docudrama on Television* (UK: Manchester University Press, 1998).

Television news: inherent limitations In analysing the degree of 'informedness' between viewers of TV news and readers of newspapers, two American researchers found that TV makes for less effective retention than the printed page. John P. Robinson and Dennis K. Davis in 'Television news and the informed public: An information-processing approach', *Journal of Communication* (Summer 1990) found that in none of their studies 'do viewers of TV news programs emerge as more informed than newspaper readers'. They identify seven inherent limitations of TV as an information medium: (1) a TV newscast has fewer words and ideas per news story than appear in a front-page story in a quality newspaper; (2) attention to a newscast is distracted and fragmented compared to attention when reading; (3) TV newscasts provide little of the repetition of information, or REDUNDANCY, necessary for comprehension; (4) TV viewers cannot 'turn back' to, or review, information they do not understand or that they need to know to understand subsequent information; (5) print news stories are more clearly delineated, with headlines, columns etc; (6) TV news programmes fail to coordinate pictures and text; and (7) TV has more limited opportunity to review and develop an entire story. It is the authors' view that 'while TV has the power to evoke EMPATHY and interest, time and other constraints prevent this power from being exercised'.

'Television without frontiers' See EUROPEAN COMMUNITY AND MEDIA: TELEVISION WITHOUT FRONTIERS.

Telex World-wide link-up system providing a rapid means of communicating written messages, via teleprinter among subscribers, combining the speed of the TELEPHONE with the accuracy and authority of the printed word. A printed copy of the MESSAGE is available at both the sending and receiving teleprinters. Calls can be made to any telex subscriber in the UK and overseas 24 hours a day and messages may be transmitted to a subscriber even though his/her machine is unattached, provided it remains switched on. A TELEMESSAGE (inland) and a telegram (overseas) can also be sent from a telex teleprinter to a Post Office telegraph office or to Cable & Wireless Telegraph offices for onward transmission at normal telephone rates, and incoming telemessages can be accepted directly on the teleprinter.

Telstar Communications satellite launched on 10 July 1962; transmitted the first live TV pictures between the US and Europe. See SATELLITE TRANSMISSION.

Ten commandments for media consumers In 'Ethics for media user' published in the *European Journal of Communication*, December 1995, Cees J. Hamelink discusses the role the viewer, reader and listener should adopt in relation to the 'quest for freedom, quality and responsibility in media performance', arguing that the consumer must not only beware of the nature of media messages but be proactive in responding to them. The ten 'commandments' Hamelink suggests to assist the consumer with moral choices concerning the media are: Thou shalt – 1. be an alert and discriminating media consumer; 2. actively fight all forms of censorship; 3. not unduly interfere with editorial independence; 4. guard against racism and sexist stereotyping in the media; 5. seek alternative sources of information; 6. demand a pluralist supply of information; 7. protect thine own privacy; 8. be a reliable source of information; 9. not participate in chequebook journalism and 10. demand accountability from media producers.

The author, however, cautions against over-reliance on such a code of user response, for moral issues and dilemmas ought to be addressed according to situation and context, a point well made when we take a global view of the 'commandments'. A pre-existing code must not be imposed on a situation, rather, the situation must be examined in the light of evolving and changing approaches to moral dilemmas. See COMPLICITY OF USERS; CONSENSUS; DISCOURSE; FATWA; PUBLIC SERVICE BROADCASTING (PSB); PUBLIC SPHERE.

Tenth art See VIDEO GAMES.

Terrestrial broadcasting That which is transmitted from the ground and not via SATELLITE.

Territoriality The need in humans and animals to establish and maintain private territory. Several elements of SPATIAL BEHAVIOUR may be employed by both individuals and groups to mark and defend territory. For example, the use of furniture and belongings to signify claim to a particular space.

Terrorism as communication The main aim of terrorist activity in liberal democracies is publicity. The existence of a free PRESS, and TV and RADIO companies independent of government authority within societies which subscribe to the sanctity of the individual's right to life, provides fertile ground for headline seeking by acts of terror such as hi-jacks and abductions. 'The modern terrorist makes maximum use of mass media', writes Dan van der Vat in *Index on Censorship*, 2 (1982). 'Little more than a century ago, before the invention of the rotary press, he would have been inconceivable; he came into his own only in the last 15 years or even less, when television became an instantaneous medium, capable of sending live pictures round the globe by satellite.' See CONTAGION EFFECT.

Tertiary text The primary text is that which is produced and transmitted – the painting, the poem, the poster, the film; the secondary text is that which members of an AUDIENCE receive, what is *perceived* as the text. The tertiary text results when the first two texts are translated into conversation between members of the audience, their families and friends. John Fiske uses the term in *Television Culture* (UK: Methuen, 1987) to denote the many uses media messages can be put to, interpretative, analytical, affirmative or rejective. The existence of the tertiary text indicates that audience has within its capacity the potential to be independent of the PREFERRED READING residing in the primary text. See ACTIVE-AUDIENCE THESIS; EMPOWERMENT; RESPONSE CODES.

A more general use of the terms *primary* and *secondary* is current. The primary text is that which is produced – the novel, the film, the TV soap. Secondary texts arise out of the first, and these may take many forms – publicity, trailers, critiques, interviews with the author or director, documentaries, translations into other creative forms (a novel into a movie or a TV series). Secondary texts at least begin as dependants upon the primary text; they are its satellites. However these may become more and more divorced from connection with the original until, arguably, they become primary texts in their own right. Where texts interact, interconnect and are interdependent we have what is termed *intertextuality*. See TEXT.

Text According to Tim O'Sullivan, John Hartley, Danny Saunders, and John Fiske in *Key Concepts in Communication* (UK: Methuen, 1983) text refers to '. . . a signifying structure composed of signs and codes which is essential to communication'. This structure can take a variety of forms: FILM, speech, writing, painting, records, for example. O'Sullivan *et al.* argue that the word text usually '. . . refers to a message that has a physical existence of its own, independent of its sender and receiver and thus composed of representational codes'.

Text is the focal point of study in SEMIOLOGY/SEMIOTICS. Texts are not normally seen as being unproblematic but as capable of being interpreted in a variety of ways, depending on the socio-cultural background and experience of the reader. The central concern of semiology is to discover the ways in which given texts can generate a range of meanings.

Occupying the special attention of analysts in recent years is the relationship *between* texts, the way they interconnect, interweave and interact upon one another. *Intertextuality* operates essentially in the perception and experience of AUDIENCE; a TV movie tells the story of a serial killer; TV news reports carnage caused by a madman loose with a machine-gun; on the way to work the viewer sees a massive poster advertising *Silence of the Lambs: the Sequel*. What does he or she make of all this, and how does one text influence another in the mind's eye? Of course intertextuality works at the level of simple publicity and promotion. A film may be writ large in our consciousness, but perhaps not only because of the power of the individual text: there will have been trailers, publicity material, interviews with the stars on TV; there will have been conversation about it.

The power of intertextuality is to blur the boundaries between individual texts. For example, which is the *text* in a promovideo – the chart-busting song of the rock group, the video of the performance, the presentation of that video on *Top of the Pops* or all of these as a *package* of texts which themselves link in with previous songs/videos by the group and by other groups, and features in fan magazines or celebrity appearances in support of AIDS research?

Roland Barthes, the French media philosopher, was of the view that culture is a web of intertextuality and that texts tend to refer to one another rather than anchor their referral in reality.

See CODES; DECODER; ENCODER; MESSAGE; EXPECTATION, HORIZONS OF; NARRATIVE; SENDER/RECEIVER.

Text: integrity of the text With the coming of the INTERNET, two major ISSUES concern the producers of texts – books, articles, scripts, photographs, music, etc. – the questions of *integrity* of the text and of *paternity*. Copyright laws have until now protected the work of an author. While a book can be quoted from, it cannot be reprinted, reproduced in any way or altered without due permission. The Net, as yet an open space for the communication of items of all kinds, uncontrolled by traditional regulation and so far evasive of what controls, legal and technical, might be applied, threatens to rob texts of integrity and to ignore their paternity (that is, the right of the author, composer, artist or performer to command 'ownership' of the text). In short, networking is open to the abuse of SOURCE; indeed texts often soar through CYBERSPACE with little or no acknowledgement of source. Released from the tie of ownership, possibly doctored in whole or in part for whatever reason – are texts reliable any more? Does authorship continue to have any meaning?

The *moral rights* of paternity and integrity are enshrined in the Berne Convention. They are central to the UK's Copyright Designs and Patents Act (1988). The right of paternity is the right to be identified as the author of a copyright work, and that includes adaptations, film rights, etc. The major exception in the Berne Convention is authorship of the 'news of the day'. The UK Copyright Act also excludes from protection all work made for the reporting of current events, and this includes articles in newspapers and journals.

Texts See OPEN, CLOSED TEXTS.

Thalidomide Case The drug Thalidomide was a tranquillizer taken by women in pregnancy. It was discovered to cause acute malformation in many newborn children. The *Sunday Times* intended to publish a series of articles based upon investigations into the Thalidomide issue, but the Distillers' Company, manufacturers of the drug in the UK, sought a court injunction preventing the newspaper making its disclosures.

It was not until 1976 that the High Court agreed to the Attorney General's submission that the *Sunday Times* now be free to publish its investigation into the Thalidomide tragedy, and the amount of compensation being considered. Thus the injunction, first granted in November 1972, waived on Appeal in February 1973, and restored by the House of Lords in July 1973, demonstrated the degree to which the courts – in this case contempt of court laws were operated – could obstruct the PRESS in matters of grave public interest and concern.

The *Sunday Times* took the case to the European Court of Human Rights which found the British government in breach of Article 10 of the European Convention on Human Rights, which guarantees freedom of the press and the right of the public to be properly informed. See COMMERCIAL CONFIDENTIALITY.

Thaumatrope Or 'wonder-turner'; a small cardboard disc, having different images on each surface, threaded on two pieces of silk or string which, when twisted, creates a joining of images, thus illustrating the phenomenon of PERSISTENCE OF VISION. The device was first produced by English doctor J.A. Paris in 1826. See ZOETROPE.

Theatre censorship See LORD CHAMBERLAIN.

Theatres Act, 1968 See LORD CHAMBERLAIN.

Theories and concepts of communication See ATTENTION MODEL OF MASS COMMUNICATION; ATTRIBUTION THEORY; CENTRALITY; CONGRUENCE THEORY; CONSPIRACY THEORY; CULTIVATION; DEPENDENCY THEORY; DESENSITIZATION; DEVIANCE AMPLIFICATION; DISPLACEMENT EFFECT; DOMINANT, SUBORDINATE, RADICAL; HYPHENIZED ABRIDGMENT; IDENTIFICATION; IDEOLOGICAL STATE APPARATUS; INOCULATION EFFECT; J-CURVE; JOHARI WINDOW; LOOKISM; MAINSTREAMING; MASLOW'S HIERARCHY OF NEEDS; MEDIASPHERE; MEDIATION; NARCOTICIZING DYSFUNCTION; NARRATIVE PARADIGM; NEWS VALUES; NORMATIVE THEORIES OF MASS MEDIA; PARA-SOCIAL INTERACTION; PLAY THEORY OF MASS COMMUNICATION; POSTULATES OF COMMUNICATION; PREFERRED READING; PROJECT OF SELF; REFLECTIVE-PROJECTIVE THEORY OF BROADCASTING AND MASS COMMUNICATION; REINFORCEMENT; SALIENCE; SAPIR-WHORF LINGUISTIC RELATIVITY HYPOTHESIS; SEMANTIC DIFFERENTIAL; SEMIOLOGY/SEMIOTICS; SENSITIZATION; SIGNIFICATION; SIGNIFICATION SPIRAL; SOCIALIZATION; SPONTANEOUS ACTIVITY; SYMBOLIC CONVERGENCE THEORY; SYMMETRY, STRAIN TOWARDS; TECHNIQUE: ELLUL'S THEORY OF TECHNIQUE; TECHNOLOGICAL DETERMINISM; TERRORISM AS COMMUNICATION; TRANSACTIONAL ANALYSIS; USES AND GRATIFICATIONS THEORY; VALUES.
* Denis McQuail, *Mass Communication Theory: An Introduction* (UK: Sage, 3rd edition, 1994); David Crowley and David Mitchell, eds., *Communication Theory Today* (UK: Polity Press, 1994); James Watson, *Media Communication: An Introduction to Theory and Process* (UK: Macmillan, 1998).

Thesis journalism Term most often used critically for TV programme making as well as newspaper work which sets out with a thesis or theory to prove and then shapes the material to support the theory. See PRESS.

Thought reform A EUPHEMISM for BRAINWASHING.

3-D The technique of filming and projecting movie pictures that gives the illusion of being three-dimensional. See STEREOSCOPY.

Tie-signs Any action – GESTURE or posture – which indicates the existence of a personal relationship is termed a tie-sign: linked arms, held hands, body closeness (or proximity), comfortable silence between two people, instinctive reciprocal movements. *Symbolic* tie-signs are wedding rings, lovers' tree engravings, etc. See COMMUNICATION, NON-VERBAL; PROXEMICS.

Time-lapse photography See HIGH-SPEED PHOTOGRAPHY.

Time-shift viewing Made possible by the introduction of the video recorder. By recording TV programmes, the viewer is released from the schedules of the BROAD-CASTING companies to watch his/her programmes whenever and as often as desired.

Titleness Allan Bell in *The Language of News Media* (UK: Blackwell, 1991) says that 'titleness' comes about through the practice of deleting the determinant of references to people mentioned in the NEWS. For example, instead of Kylie Minogue being referred to as 'the star of *Neighbours*' she will be described as '*Neighbours*' star Kylie Minogue'. This practice, says Bell, 'brings a subtle but definite semantic change' and the person referred to 'takes on a status akin to titles such as *President* this or *Lord* that'. It elevates a description to the rank of a quasi-title, implying that this person belongs to a class as exclusive as heads of state or the nobility: 'For the media a title embodies a person's claim to news value.'

Tokenism Support without true conviction; making a GESTURE towards a principle of free speech and debate, equality of the sexes or the races (e.g. 'token woman' or 'token black' where males and whites dominate). The term is used by commentators to describe semi-commitment to radical standpoints in the PRESS.

Touch Not the least important of the five senses, though often the most neglected. H.F. Harlow in *Learning to Love* (US: Albion, 1971) writes of his now famous experiments with baby monkeys. He had found that the deprivation of physical contact resulted in a failure to learn necessary responses to their own society. They became non-sociable, were unable to mate successfully or to rear their young.

Touch is an important ingredient in the transmitting of information, especially in the young when other channels of communication such as speech are undeveloped. In Western society the incidence of touching between people begins to diminish when a child reaches the age of five or six, with males being touched less than females; it increases again in the teenage period, where touching and sex become equated to such an extent that touch becomes a sexual indi-cator unless applied by validated 'touchers' such as doctors, tailors or hairdressers.

CLASS, status and ROLES are inextricably involved in touch-permission or touch-prohibition: a nurse may touch a patient, but it is not usual for a patient to touch the nurse, where it constitutes a trespass. Self-touching is acceptable, unless it becomes socially offensive (like nose-picking), as a form of substitution for the touch of others – face and head touching, hair stroking or hand wringing, for example.

Where we cannot touch other humans we substitute pets, stroking them and cuddling them, receiving (and perhaps giving) sensations of comfort. In illness and stress, in times of grief or great happiness, touching becomes more necessary and more acceptable. Touching can communicate reassurance, affection, friendship, courage-giving, support, sharing, understanding, invitation, desire, etc. as well as on occasions, hostility and aggression. The practice varies considerably from class to class, CULTURE to culture and country to country and from hemisphere to hemisphere. See COMMUNICATION, NON-VERBAL; EYE CONTACT; GESTURE; INTERPERSONAL COMMUNICATION; NON-VERBAL BEHAVIOUR: REPERTOIRE; PROXEMICS.

Tracks In FILM making, tracks are the portable 'railway lines' along which the camera, mounted on a DOLLY, moves. The term is also used to identify separate sound reels accompanying a film. These are harmonized into one at the *dubbing stage* of film production.

Traditional transmission US linguist Charles Hockett defined 16 design features characteristic of human LANGUAGE, of which *Traditional transmission* is one, described in Hockett's 'The origin of speech', *Scientific American*, 203 (1960). This design feature refers to the passing on of language from one generation to the next. 'Human genes', Hockett writes, 'carry the capacity to acquire a language, and probably also a strong drive towards its acquisition, the detailed conventions of any one language are transmitted extra-genetically by learning and teaching.'

Transactional analysis Originally an

approach to psychotherapy introduced by Eric Berne, transactional analysis is now more widely used as a technique for improving INTERPERSONAL COMMUNICATION and social skills. In essence it aims to increase the individual's awareness of the intent behind both his or her own and others' communication, and to expose and eliminate, or deal with, subterfuge and dishonesty.

The details of the framework are fairly complex and readers are referred to the works recommended below for an introduction to this area. Basically, however, transactional analysis investigates any act of interpersonal communication by considering what are called the 'ego states' of the communicators.

The hypothesis is that we are all able to function out of three 'ego states' which Berne identified as the Parent, the Adult and the Child. The states are produced by a playback of recorded data of events in the past involving real people; real times, places and decisions; and real feelings. Everyone is seen as carrying these voices inside them. We interact out of these 'ego states'.

The Parent is much influenced by the pronouncements of and examples set by our own parents and other authority figures, early in our life. It is concerned with our responsibility towards ourselves and others. It can be critical and set standards but it can also be protective and caring. The Adult within us is the part of us which rationally analyses reality. It collects information and thinks it through in order to solve problems, reach conclusions and judgments, and make decisions. The Adult develops throughout life and can arbitrate between the Parent and the Child. The Child is one of our most powerful states; it contains our feelings and carries our ability to play and act creatively. It can be spontaneous and risk-taking. It can also be rebellious or alternatively compliant or servile.

A transaction is a two-person INTER-ACTION in which an ego state of one person stimulates an ego state of another. Transactions are analysed by assessing out of which 'ego state' people are speaking. We can distinguish these states in ourselves and others by such non-verbal cues as tone of voice or facial expression, as well as by the verbal content of the transactions. One of the chief values of Transactional Analysis is that it has the capacity to help clarify communication problems.

Other concepts popular in transactional analysis which are useful in analysing interactions are GAMES, LIFE POSITIONS and SCRIPTS.
* Eric Berne, *Games People Play*, (US: Grove Press, 1964); E. Berne, *What Do You Say After You Say Hello?* (UK: Corgi Books, 1975); T.A. Harris, *I'm O.K. You're O.K.* (US: Harper & Row, 1969); Ian Stewart and Vann Joines, *TA Today* (UK: Lifespace, 1987); Amy and Thomas Harris, *Staying O.K.* (UK: Arrow Books, 1995).

Transculturation The movement of cultural forms across geographical boundaries and periods of time resulting in cross-cultural interaction which may give rise to new cultural forms. See HYBRIDIZATION.

Transferability of cues See BARNLUND'S TRANSACTIONAL MODEL OF COMMUNICATION.

Transmission model of mass communication See ATTENTION MODEL OF MASS COMMUNICATION.

Triggers Words or pictures used by the media to evoke desired responses without lengthy explanation; signs in the vocabulary of those Vance Packard has described as 'symbol manipulators'. Packard was, of course, referring to product marketing but in the age of TV – of trials by TV, of elections by TV – politicians and ideologies lend themselves to product marketing and presentational packaging as much as soft drinks, motor cars or soap powders. See PREFERRED READING; SEMIOLOGY/SEMIOTICS.

Truth, visualization of See VISIONS OF ORDER.

Two-step flow model of communication See ONE-STEP, TWO-STEP, MULTI-STEP FLOW MODEL OF COMMUNICATION.

Typewriter A patent for an 'Artificial Machine or Method for Impressing or Transcribing of Letters Singly or Progressively one after another, as in Writing, whereby all Writing Whatever may be Engrossed in Paper or Parchment so Neat and Exact as not to be distinguished from Print' was taken out in the UK as early as 1714, but the first practical typewriter working faster than handwriting was probably that of American Christopher Latham Sholes (1868) who, after several improvements to his machine, signed up with E. Remington & Sons, gunsmiths of New York. The first Remington machines were marketed in 1874.

1878 saw the introduction of the shift-key typewriter, followed by machines which for the first time allowed the typist to actually *see* what he/she was typing (1883). That jack-of-all-trades among inventors, Thomas Alva Edison (1847–1931) produced an electrically operated machine containing a printing wheel, in 1872, though it was many years before a commercially viable electric machine was produced (by James Smathes in 1920).

IBM introduced the famous 'golf-ball' electric typewriter in 1961, allowing for different type faces and type sizes to be used with the same machine. Today electronic typewriters – or word-processors – possess the mind and memory of the computer; they self-correct, they work silently, they can bank text which is recalled at the press of a button and they can print out at considerable speed. See TECHNOLOGY OF THE MEDIA.

U

U-certificate See CERTIFICATION OF FILMS.

UK Gold Launched on 1st November 1992, UK Gold is a satellite channel run jointly by BBC Enterprises and Thames Television based on their combined programme libraries. Among the 'classics' as Thames and the BBC prefer to call these repeats of repeats, are *Dr. Who, Neighbours, EastEnders, The Bill* and *The Benny Hill Show*, all available five nights a week.

Ullswater Committee Report on Broadcasting, 1936 This government-appointed committee under the chairmanship of Viscount Ullswater was given the task of making recommendations on the future of the BBC once its first charter expired on 31 December 1936. The report praised the BBC for its impartiality and catholicity but chided it for the heaviness

of its Sunday entertainment. The Charter of the BBC was renewed following the report for another 10 years; the number of governors was increased from five to seven and the ban on advertisements was to continue – though sponsorship was to be permitted in the case of TV (a right the BBC only seldom exploited).

Like reports before and after it, Ullswater made clear the very serious public responsibility of BROADCASTING: 'The influence of broadcasting upon the mind and speech of the nation' made it an 'urgent necessity in the national interest that the broadcasting service should at all times be conducted in the best possible manner and to the best possible advantage of the people.' Two other matters elicited concern. The first related to criticisms of the monolithic nature of the BBC (under the rigorous direction of Lord Reith) and the Committee recommended more internal decentralization of control, especially towards the national regions. The second concern, published in a Reservation written by Clement Attlee (1883–1967), future Labour Prime Minister, called into question the BBC's 'impartiality' at the time of the General Strike (1926): 'I think,' wrote Attlee, 'that even in war-time the BBC must be allowed to broadcast opinions other than those of the Government.' See COMMISSIONS/COMMITTEES ON THE MEDIA; PUBLIC SERVICE BROADCASTING.

Ultra-violet/fluorescent photography Used in the examination of forged or altered documents, identifying certain chemical compounds, and in the examination of bacterial colonies. See HOLOGRAPHY; INFRA-RED PHOTOGRAPHY.

Underground press Or radical, alternative or SAMIZDAT; those newspapers which are committedly anti-ESTABLISHMENT, opposing in part or entirely the political and cultural conventions of the time; often publishing information or views seen as threatening by those in authority, and likely to incur CENSORSHIP.

In the UK the so-called 'pauper press' of the 19th c., finding its readership in the increasingly literate working CLASS, was subject to harshly repressive measures by government. Editors such as William Cobbett,

Henry Hetherington, William Sherwin and Richard Carlile courted arrest and imprisonment and the shutting down of their presses as a routine professional hazard. Wooler's *Black Dwarf* stirred the government to wrath with its criticism of the authorities in their handling of the Peterloo Massacre (1819). Wooler escaped LIBEL action on the plea that he could not be said to have written articles which he set up in type without the interventions of a *pen*.

Cobbett's *Weekly Political Register* had a substantial circulation despite the crippling STAMP DUTY which forced him to charge one shilling and a halfpenny per copy. Carlile's *Republican* was both republican and atheist; the Chartist *Oracle of Reason* incurred blasphemy prosecutions while Bradlaugh's *National Reformer* declared itself 'Published in Defiance of Her Majesty's Government'. So long as radical newspapers could fight off the need to win ADVERTISING, they could prosper, despite prosecutions. They were edited by people close to the working class and they reflected the chief perspectives of the vanguard of the working class movement and directed themselves to its increased politicization.

Survival, however, depended on the ability of the radical PRESS to pay its way through circulation.

The costs of publishing and the reliance upon advertising have proved formidable barriers to underground, radical or alternative newspapers and periodicals in the post-2nd World War period (from 1945). In the 1960s they abounded – *Oz, IT, Frendz* and *Ink* – all in one way or another getting up the nose of Authority, the *Oz Schoolkids Issue* earning for itself the longest-ever obscenity trial (See OZ TRIAL).

Distribution has proved yet another hazard for the small radical press. In the UK this is practically a DUOPOLY of W.H. Smith and Menzies whose hesitancy over providing the radical press with distribution outlets has been rather more to do with a view that radicals are just not good business rather than for ideological reasons.

In the March/April edition 1994 of *Free Press*, the news-sheet of the Campaign for Press and Broadcasting Freedom, Tony Harcup mourns the decline in the Thatcher–Major years of the radical regional press. In 'Northern Star silenced', an obituary for the *Leeds Other Paper/Northern Star*, he points out that where in 1980 there had been more than 70 local alternative papers covering towns and cities in the UK, there were now only two, *Peninsula Voice* covering Cornwall west of Truro and Penzance, and the *West Highland Free Press*. The *LOP/Northern Star*, having survived 20 years, went into liquidation after 820 issues on 20 January 1994. It had been, in Harcup's words, 'a beacon of radical journalism . . . a thorn in the side of the local establishment'. Ironically the paper had made as many enemies on the Left as the Right in local politics: 'The paper was too anarchistic for some Labour party members; too rank and filist for some union officials; too male dominated for some feminists; too pro-feminist for many men.'

Perhaps the future for radical journalism lies not in print and paper but in the relatively cost-free 'pages' of CYBERSPACE and the INTERNET, where the political readership is both local and global.

* Stanley Harrison, *Poor Men's Guardians: A Survey of the Struggles for a Democratic Newspaper Press, 1763–1973* (UK: Lawrence & Wishart, 1974); Patricia Hollis, *The Pauper Press* (UK: Oxford University Press, 1970); Stephen Koss, *The Rise and Fall of the Political Press in Britain* (UK: Collins 1990).

Unitary, pluralist, core-periphery, breakup models of audience fragmentation See AUDIENCE: FRAGMENTATION OF.

United state of media See CONVERGENCE.

Use of media by the young See CHILDREN, YOUNG PEOPLE AND THE CHANGING MEDIA ENVIRONMENT.

Uses and gratifications theory View that mass media audiences make active use of what the media have to offer arising from a complex set of *needs* which the media in one form or another gratify. Broadly similar uses have been categorized by researchers based on questionnaires or interviews. An example is the *compensatory* use of the media – to make up for lack of education, perhaps, lack of status or social success.

Where the media have a *supplementing* use, the audience may be applying what they see, hear and read in social situations – as subject-matter for conversation, for example.

In 'The television audience: a revised perspective' in D. McQuail, ed., *Sociology of the Mass Media* (UK: Penguin, 1972) Denis McQuail, Jay G. Blumler and J.R. Brown define four major categories of need which the media serve to gratify: (1) *Diversion* (escape from constraints of routine; escape from the burdens of problems; emotional release). (2) *Personal relationships* (companionship; social utility). (3) *Personal identity* (personal reference; reality exploration; value reinforcement). (4) *Surveillance* (need for information in our complex world – 'Television news helps me to make up my mind about things').

Blumler and Elihu Katz in the book of which they are editors, *The Uses of Mass Communication* (US: Sage, 1974) emphasize the social origin of the needs which the media purport to gratify. Thus where a social situation causes tension and conflict, the media may provide easement, or where the social situation gives rise to questions about VALUES, the media provide affirmation and REINFORCEMENT.

Uses and gratifications theory is in alliance with the grand process of analysing human *motivation* contributed to by organizational theorists, psychologists and educationalists, and concerning lower and higher orders; cognitive (intellectual) and affective (emotional) dimensions; activity and passivity and external and internal responses. See COGNITIVE (AND AFFECTIVE); COMMUNICATION MODELS; EFFECTS OF THE MASS MEDIA; IDENTIFICATION; MASLOW'S HIERARCHY OF NEEDS; SURVEILLANCE.

Utterance meaning See SENTENCE MEANING, UTTERANCE MEANING.

V

Validity effect Carole Wade and Carol Tavris in *Psychology* (US: HarperCollins, 1993) discuss the findings of studies conducted by Hal Arkes (1991) in which he demonstrated that people had a tendency to believe a statement was true, was valid, if it were repeated frequently enough; no other means of persuasion was necessary. This is phenomenon known as the validity effect.

VALS Typology Arnold Mitchell's *Nine American Lifestyles: Who We Are And Where We're Going* (US: Macmillan, 1983) describes a landmark in the documentation of human needs – a massive research project funded and carried out in America in 1980 by SRI International. The principle on which the research was based and which Mitchell's influential book articulates is that humans demonstrate their needs in their *lifestyle* and that both needs and lifestyle fluctuate according to circumstance and 'drive'. VALS stands for Values and Lifestyle.

The VALS approach, and its typology of categories of lifestyle, pigeon-holes people on an all-embracing scale. It has given a significant boost to marketing trends which have increasingly been preoccupied with SEGMENTING people into consumer categories. VALS links the pursuit of lifestyle with personal growth: 'With this growth comes change, so that new goals emerge, and in support of these new goals come new beliefs, new dreams, and a new constellation of values,' writes Mitchell.

Though the main focus of research – ongoing rather than a one-off exercise – was upon the population of the United States, what Mitchell terms 'side spurs' of research explored VALS in five European countries – France, Sweden, Italy, West Germany and Britain. The Vals Typology to a considerable degree reflects Abraham Maslow's notion of hierarchy (See MASLOW'S HIERARCHY OF NEEDS) and gives support to his categorization. There are those for example at the bottom of the social pile, called Survivors, 'whose existence has shrivelled to the bleak reality of the moment and the fantasy world of television'.

Higher up the pecking order of lifestyle are the Achievers. They 'are at the top . . . the driving and the driven people who have built "the system" and are now at the helm'. More than anything else 'Achievers have learned to live the comfortable, affluent, affable, outer-directed life, and in so doing they have set the standard for much of the nation'.

The typology identifies lifestyles as they are, or are becoming, and consequently has offered a model for change. Arnold Mitchell claims that VALS aids the 'eminently worthwhile' endeavour of *choosing* the kind of lifestyle 'a person, or a society of persons, would like in future'. At the same time he warns that the future holds a number of possible 'scenarios', some of brighter promise than others. The *Hard Times* scenario, for example, would produce a very different VALS Typology than the one Mitchell terms 'Bouncy Prosperity'.

Each scenario would favour lifestyle types in different ways, advantaging some, disadvantaging others. The Need-Driven in the scenario of bouncy prosperity would rise up the hierarchy of opportunity, adding to the ranks of the Belongers (usually the comfortably-off, . middle-of-the-roaders with conservative tastes to match). On the other hand, VALS research seems to indicate 'the Societally Conscious segment would shrink' for many of their causes would have been addressed because there had been resources to deal with them.

With the Hard Times scenario 'There would be an increase in basic fear, insecurity, anxiety, dependence, rigidity, compulsiveness, and the desire for forceful leadership and for law and order'. See ADVERTISING: MAINSTREAMERS, ASPIRERS, SUCCEEDERS AND REFORMERS; iSOCIETY; MEDIA SPECIES.

Values Each society, social group or individual has certain ideas, beliefs, ways of behaving, upon which is placed a *value*. A collection of these values, the criteria for judgment of one often acting as REINFORCEMENT for others, may amount to a *system* of values. Such a system, if it is not to cause DISSONANCE in a person, has either to be generally consistent, or be perceived as generally consistent.

Values are not merely systems of personal belief: they represent shared attitudes within social GROUPS and society at large, of approval and disapproval, of judgments favourable and unfavourable, towards other individuals, ideas, objects (such as the value

placed on *property*), social action and events. Like NORMS, values vary from one social group or society to another; and they change over time and in different circumstances.

An individual's perception and interpretation of reality will be influenced by the values of the social groups or society to which he/she belongs. The pervasiveness of such values ensures that they are enmeshed in all aspects of communication processes. The images and codes which are the stock-in-trade of the mass media are *shaped* by value systems; and their intention is to support and reinforce the value systems that shape them.

In his Introduction to J. Tunstall ed., *Mass Sociology* (UK: Constable, 1970), Jeremy Tunstall remarks that 'The media are saturated with social values of every kind'. These values come to the fore, achieve clearest definition, at times of crisis and conflict.

See CULTURE; IDEOLOGY; MALE-AS-NORM; MYTH; NEWS VALUES; SEMIOLOGY/SEMIOTICS; STRUCTURALISM.

Vamp Early word for sex-star in the movies. In 1914 producer William Fox (1879–1952) created a star by going to the farthest extreme away from screen-idol Mary Pickford, SYMBOL of purity and innocence, by imposing a parody of sensuality and eroticism on Theda Bara in the FILM adaptation of the Kipling poem *A Fool There Was*. The word 'vamp' was used in the publicity for the film whose financial success helped Fox set up his own studio, among the most important of the 1920s.

V-chip See CLIPPER CHIP.

V-discs In 1943, during the 2nd World War (1939–45), record companies and musicians agreed to waive fees and contractual rights to a series of very high-quality musical offerings to the US forces. Such recordings, many of them by giants of the jazz world – Benny Goodman, Louis Armstrong, Duke Ellington – are now prized by collectors.

Verbal devices in speech-making Max Atkinson in his illuminating study of the speech-making techniques of politicians and other well-known contemporary orators, *Our Masters' Voices: The Language and Body Language of Politics* (UK: Methuen, 1984), analyses various forms of what the Shorter Oxford English Dictionary terms *claptraps* – linguistic or non-verbal devices to catch applause. Particularly successful, says the author, is the *list of three*, which stimulates audience response, reinforces that stimulus and then pushes it to the climax. *Antithesis* is also an effective claptrap ('I come to bury Caesar, not to praise him'). Atkinson cautions the would-be orator that these devices require skill, timing and judgment to be effective and claptrap 'always involves the use of more than one technique at a time'.

Victim funds These were organized by the UNDERGROUND PRESS in the 19th c. to help out fellow papers subjected to heavy government fines for evading the TAXES ON KNOWLEDGE – STAMP DUTY, Advertising Tax, Paper Duty and State Security System Tax. Between 1830 and 1836 at least 1130 cases of selling 'unstamped' papers were prosecuted in London alone. See NEWSPAPERS, ORIGINS.

Video The process whereby TV programmes can be recorded on a cassette tape proved to be one of the most popular technical developments in the late 1970s and the 1980s.

Video permits TIME-SHIFT VIEWING, that is, recording TV programmes off air for later viewing. Also, it can be completely independent of the TV channels, being able to play mass-produced cassette programmes of all kinds, especially feature films. Where, in the past, for example, it would have been difficult for a TV viewer to avoid at some time seeing the BBC or Independent Television News, the occasional DOCUMENTARY programme such as *Panorama* or *TV Eye*, a play by Dennis Potter, a programme on ethnic minorities on CHANNEL 4 or an in-depth science programme such as BBC2's *Horizon*, video enables him or her to by-pass even the most casual or accidental TV encounter with communal, national or international ISSUES dealt with on PUBLIC SERVICE BROADCASTING channels. On the other hand, video enables the viewer to unburden his or her viewing life entirely from quiz shows, party political broadcasts and adverts for dog and cat food.

The video CAMERA has given film makers as much freedom as the video recorder has given the TV viewer. It is lighter than traditional film cameras, cheaper both to buy and to operate and allows immediate playback. Film-making need no longer be the preserve of those with multi-million pound backing. The field is wide open to individuals, cooperatives, pressure groups, clubs, schools, media studies students in particular – anyone with a case to urge, beliefs or feelings to express – to counter, at least at the level of a local community, the dominant voices of the national broadcasters or mass media communicators generally. See CAMCORDER; INTERACTIVE VIDEO; VIDEO GAMES.
* Sean Cubbitt, *Timeshift: On Video Culture* (UK: Comedia/Routledge, 1992).

Video games Like so many examples of popular CULTURE, the video game has incurred condemnation for being anti-social, a threat to the minds and mentality of the young – who are seen to be the main players – and loaded with harmful features. However, games have also achieved cultural status and have been claimed by some critics as amounting to an important art form, while 'cult status' is awarded to some of the protagonists of such games, the formidable Laura Croft, star of the Tomb Raider series, being the most notable. In *L'Univers Des Jeux Video/The Universe of Video Games* (France: Editions La Dcouverte, 1998), Alain and Frederic Le Diberder see video games as 'the 10th art' (cinema being the seventh, TV the eighth and cartoons or 'graphic novels' the ninth). The authors point to the following distinctive pleasures derived from video-game playing: competition, accomplishment, mastery of a system and spectacle. General concern is expressed about the long-term impact of playing games in which the central actions generally focus on violence and the destruction of enemies, and the subliminal enculturalization into what might be described as 'samurai mode', arising from the Japanese origin of most games.

Some 'classics' of the history of video games have been *Spacewar* (1962), *Space*

Invaders (1978), *Tetris* (1989), *Mortal Kombat* (1992), *Doom* (1993), *WipEout 2097* (1996) and *Rainbow Six* (1998) in which the player employs six SAS warriors to save the world from deadly international terrorists. In the same year the UK's BAFTA award for best electronic entertainment went to Nintendo's *Goldeneye*, based upon the James Bond movie of the same title.

This cross-pollination between films and games has become a key trend in marketing, while players of some new games can also read 'the novel of the game'.

A highly readable commentator on the game scene, Steven Poole, in a *Guardian* article 'The new game plan' (27 November 1998) spotlights the worrying ideologies which lurk behind so many video games. He refers to 'the increasingly subterranean political messages of video games', citing Sid Meier's city-building game, *Civilization*, 'in which capitalism is king and no matter how hard the player tries, it is impossible to run a hippy commune'. It might be said that video games had come of age when the news was announced that *Tomb Raider 3* was officially classified by the UK government as a Millennium Product.

* Steven Poole, *The Prometheus Engine* (UK: Fourth Estate, 1999).

Videogram Machine which translates pictures from TELEVISION into newspaper colour pictures, first used in the UK by Eddie Shah whose all-colour electronically produced *Today* newspaper was first published on 4 March 1986. The paper passed into the ownership of Australian PRESS BARON Rupert Murdoch a year later only eventually to close down in 1995.

Video nasties A market that developed in the 1980s of specially-made-for-video films of a singularly nasty, brutal and sexist nature. Court action in the UK in 1982 against several of these films led to their enforced withdrawal from circulation but, to the considerable disgust of Mary Whitehouse and the National Viewers' and Listeners' Association – among many others – there was no order made for their destruction. However, the Conservative government brought in rigorous controls of video nasties with the VIDEO RECORDING ACT, 1984.

In 1994 there was dramatically renewed interest in the possible effects of video nasties on behaviour following the Jamie Bulger trial in which two 11-year-old boys were convicted of murdering a small boy they had abducted. The judge in the trial, Mr Justice Morland, conjectured that the boys may have been influenced by seeing *Child's Play 3* whose plot paralleled, to a degree, the real actions of the killers. Though this connection was dismissed by many in the TV and film industry, there was support from child psychologists, in particular from Elizabeth Newson, Professor of Development Psychology at the University of Nottingham, who spoke of the need for special concern when children – or, indeed, adults – are repeatedly exposed to images of cruelty in the context of entertainment.

Video Recording Act, 1984 Passed through Parliament in the UK with all-Party support, MP Graham Bright's measure was designed to restrict the access of young persons to VIDEO NASTIES, many of which eluded the usual vetting process of the BRITISH BOARD OF FILM CENSORS.

The Act established by statute an Authority (initially the BBFC) whose purpose was to classify VIDEO cassettes as suitable for home viewing and to censor those deemed unsuitable. Fines of up to £20,000 are liable for dealers and distributors breaking the law. All videoworks must be submitted for scrutiny, classification and certification unless they are educational or concerned with sport, religion or music.

However, if such videos 'to any extent' portray 'Human sexual activity' or 'Mutilation, torture or other acts of gross violence' or show 'human genital organs' they also have to be submitted to the censors. See CENSORSHIP; MORAL PANIC.

Viewers: light, medium and heavy Research into the amount and nature of TELEVISION viewing discriminates between the light viewer, generally classified as watching TV for two hours or less a day; the medium viewer, watching for between two and three hours a day and the heavy viewer watching for four hours or more a day. In the analysis of viewer response, special attention has been paid to the differences of attitude to issues and controversies which can be detected between light and heavy viewers, and thus the influence TV programmes may have on attitude formation and attitude change. See MAINSTREAMING; MEAN WORLD SYNDROME; RESONANCE.

Violence and the media See BROADCAST-ING STANDARDS COUNCIL; CENSORSHIP; 'CLEAN-UP TV' MOVEMENT; CRIME AND THE MEDIA; CRIME: TYPES OF CRIME ON SCREEN; DESENSITIZATION; EFFECTS OF THE MASS MEDIA; ITC: PROGRAMME CODE; LONG-FORD COMMITTEE REPORT ON PORNOGRAPHY, 1972; PORNOGRAPHY; RADIO AUTHORITY PROGRAMME CODES 1 AND 2; REINFORCEMENT; SENSITIZATION; SHOTGUN APPROACH (TO NEWS COVERAGE); SIGNIFI-CATION SPIRAL; SLEEPER EFFECT; TERRORISM AS COM-MUNICATION; VALUES; VIOLENCE ON TV: CODES OF PRACTICE; WILLIAMS COMMITTEE REPORT ON OBSCEN-ITY AND FILM CENSORSHIP, 1979.

Violence on TV: codes of practice Although the BROADCASTING ACT, 1990 pur-ported to exchange the 'firm' hand of reg-ulation as represented by the Independent Broadcasting Authority (IBA) for a 'lighter touch' regulatory body, the Independent Television Commission (ITC), the code of practice concerning screen violence remains rigorous (see ITC: PROGRAMME CODE). Indeed the tradition of British broadcasting indi-cates a greater caution over the amount and degree of violence permitted on our screens than many other countries. 1980 saw the publication of *The Portrayal of Vio-lence on Television: BBC and IBA Guidelines.* They offered the following criteria for pro-gramme-makers. (1) They must ask them-selves, is violent action essential to the story? (2) If essential, how much detail is necessary for the sake of clarity? (3) Is a violent act being shown in a way that may encourage dangerous imitation by the young and immature? (4) Is violence being used to create excitement and to hold atten-tion?

The ITC Code included in part two of *The Portrayal of Violence on Television* declares 'Violence is not only physical: it can be verbal, psychological and even meta-physical or super-natural. Whatever form the violence in a programme may take its inclusion can only be justified by the dra-matic or informational context in which it is seen, and the skill, insight and sensitivity of the portrayal'. Programme-makers are reminded that people seldom view just one programme and 'An acceptable minimum of violence in each individual programme may add up to an intolerable level over a period'.

A substantial amount of this Code reap-pears in the ITC Programme Code and the RADIO AUTHORITY programme codes, operat-ing from 1991.

A report by the Department of Journal-ism Studies at Sheffield University brought comfort to both the BBC and commercial channels in 1995. Report authors Barrie Gunter and Jackie Harrison summarized research findings based upon the monitor-ing of 4,715 hours of programmes. They identified a drop in the featuring of violence on the terrestrial channels, BBC1, BBC2, ITV and Channel 4, from 1.1 per cent of total output in 1966 to 0.61 per cent in 1994/5. There was marginally more violence (1.53 per cent) on satellite channels, Sky One, Sky Movies, the Movie Channel and UK Gold. Of the programmes sampled, a third contained some violence, with 21,000 separate violent acts catalogued, though most of this occurred after the 9 p.m. watershed.

The authors of the Sheffield study, costing £93,000 and jointly commissioned by the BBC and the ITC, believed that it 'would be very easy to misconstrue the level of violence on television by reference only to the gross figures . . . Violence represents only a tiny proportion of the total programme output'. See BROADCASTING STANDARDS COUNCIL.

* Barrie Gunter and Jackie Harrison, *Violence on Television. An Analysis of Amount, Nature, Loca-tion and Origin of Violence in British Programmes* (UK: Routledge, 1998).

Virgin 1215 Radio Commercial rock music radio station founded by Richard Branson; started life at 12.15 p.m. on 30 April 1993.

Virtual reality Simulation of the real by technological means, using multi-media inputs – head-mounted display, data gloves, three-dimensional audio system and mag-netic position tracker (to name the basics);

what has been termed a 'technological cluster'. Generally, the simulation of the real exists in that 'window of realities', the TV monitor. In a paper 'The ultimate display' for the Proceedings of the IFIPS Congress 2, published as early as 1965, Ivan Sutherland defined the VR dream: 'The screen is a window through which one sees a virtual world. The challenge is to make that world look real, act real, sound real and feel real.'

Virtual reality technology is three-dimensional and interactive. It is extensively used in engineering and architectural design, in medicine and telecommunications. It is potentially a vital component in reconstructing the past. At the first Virtual Reality Heritage conference in Bath, UK, November 1995, IBM's Brian Collins described the VR reconstruction of a church which no longer·exists, the Frauenkirche in Dresden 50 years after its destruction by bombing. Using the few drawings and plans and colour photographs taken by the Nazis, VR technology is providing a detailed reconstruction which will enable the original to be rebuilt. Reporting the conference for the *Guardian* ('Virtual reality's saving graces', 23 November), Maev Kennedy quotes Professor Bob Stone, director of the UK National Centre for Virtual Environments who considers VR's primary use should be for education.

Though Stone was preparing a VR reconstruction of Stonehenge for English Heritage, he was cautious about substituting VR experiences for the real thing: 'If virtual reality replaces access to real heritage sites for real people, it would be a very sad day.'

VR's employment in entertainment, in games which create new and often physically impossible worlds needs no elaboration. Ivan Sutherland believes that 'A display connected to a digital computer gives us a chance to gain familiarity with concepts not realizable in the physical world . . . The ultimate display would, of course, be a room within which the computer can control the existence of matter'. Key to the pursuit of this 'ultimate display' is the notion of *presence*, of being there, with perceptions and cognition heightened; our senses extended to the point where the user can manipulate the simulated 'reality'. As Frank Biocca points out in 'Virtual Reality technology: a tutorial' in the *Journal of Communication*, Autumn 1992, 'The goal is a computer interface that is fully responsive to actions of the user'. In another article in the same edition of the *Journal* – given over entirely to the scrutiny of VR and the claims made for it – Jonathan Stuer ('Defining Virtual Reality: dimensions determining telepresence') cautions against 'device-driven' definitions of virtual reality, preferring to call it 'a particular type of experience, rather than a collection of hardware'.

While many commentators deplore the loss of reality to the virtual, Manuel Castells shifts critical ground by discussing what he terms 'real virtuality'. He believes that all CULTURE is an interactive symbolic system now centred on CONTEXT which is essentially audio-visual. It follows, argues Castells in 'Citizens, movements, information and analysis. An interview with Manuel Castells' in *City* 7 (May 1997) that 'virtuality, the coded representation in an interactive electronic system . . . is our reality'. The real and the virtual become increasingly blurred. See CYBERSPACE.

* Mark Slouka, *War of the Worlds: The Assault on Reality* (UK: Abacus, 1996).

Virus: computer virus See COMPUTERS IN COMMUNICATION.

Visibility See GLOBAL SCRUTINY; PRIVACY.

Visions of order A notion long associated with the role and function of the journalist is that of 'bringer-of-light', of enlightenment. The French writer Jacques Derrida in *Writing and Difference* (UK: Routledge & Kegan Paul, 1978) poses the 'heliological metaphor', describing the journalist as a human version of the heliograph, recorder and transmitter of light – of revelation to AUDIENCE. The process is one of *envisioning*, that is, offering a vision of the world: light for others to see by. In *The Politics of Pictures: The Creation of the Public in the Age of Popular Media* (UK: Routledge, 1992) John Hartley takes up this theme in a chapter entitled 'Heliography: Journalism, and the visualization of truth'. What journalism brings to light, what it renders visible are,

Hartley argues, 'distant visions of order'. It is not so much the actual truth which is brought to light as the vision of truth as visualized in terms of order.

The reader might raise the objection that journalism is really all about *disorder* rather than order; and this is exactly Hartley's point: what he calls 'a process of photographic negativization' takes place, 'where the image of order is actually recorded as its negative, in stories of disorder'. The 'distant vision of order' is not, however, of 'oneness'; rather, Hartley believes, ordering works on a basis of what the author terms WEDOM and THEYDOM – Us (good) and Them (bad). See JOURNALISM..

* Richard V. Ericson, Patricia M. Baraneh and Janet B.L. Chan, *Representing Order: Crime, Law And Justice in the News Media* (UK: Open University, 1991).

Vistavision Paramount's response to 20th Century Fox's CINEMASCOPE in the 1950s. The negative was made on 70mm stock and reduced to 35mm during printing, to reduce graininess.

Visual display unit (VDU) The cathode ray tube or TV screen on which the data of a computer are displayed. Information can be summoned through a keyboard or worked on directly with a light pen.

Vitaphone Trade name of the first successful synchronous movie sound, introduced in 1926 by Warner Brothers. On 6 August at the Warner Theatre in New York, John Barrymore starred in *Don Juan*, to the accompaniment of a Vitaphone 16-inch $33\frac{1}{2}$ r.p.m. disc recording of voice and music. Curiously *Don Juan* caused less audience excitement than the Vitaphone shorts that accompanied it, such as the New York Philharmonic playing Wagner's Tannhauser Overture. The real sensation of the Talkies was Warners' next picture, *The Jazz Singer* (1927) starring Al Jolson. There were, in fact, only 281 words spoken in the FILM, all of them ad-libbed by Jolson. See SYNCHRONOUS SOUND.

Vocal cues All the oral aspects of speech except the words themselves; *pitch* – the highness or lowness of voice; *rate* – rapidity of expression; *volume*; *quality* – the pleasantness or unpleasantness of voice tone or delivery, and *enunciation* – pronunciation and articulation. See PARALANGUAGE.

Vocalics Focuses on the use of the voice in communicating a MESSAGE. It is not so much concerned with what is said as the way in which it is said and how this contributes to the meaning of the message. See NON-VERBAL VOCALIZATIONS.

Voiceover In FILM and TELEVISION film production, voiceover accompanies what the audience is seeing with comment – explanation and analysis – without the commentator being on view. In feature films voiceover is often that of the chief character in a story though the DOCUMENTARY approach of an unidentified narrator is also common. Voiceover plays a significant role in shaping the MEANING of a film TEXT. It signals the way that audience is expected to read what is seen and heard in a programme. In this sense, voiceover closes down a text to a prescribed meaning, allowing the viewer little room for interpretation. See NARRATIVE; OPEN, CLOSED TEXTS.

Vox popping Collecting the opinions of large numbers of the general public (*vox populi* is Latin for 'voice of the people') in order to broadcast public reaction to a current issue or topic.

W

'War of the Worlds' Title of the American CBS network radio adaptation by Howard Koch, produced and narrated by Orson Welles (1938), of H.G. Wells's famous story. Conveying the immediacy of a combat report from a war correspondent, the production actually convinced many listeners that an interplanetary war had broken out. However, reports to the effect that Orson Welles's radio 'hype' had caused panic in the streets have taken on the magic of legend, and become somewhat exaggerated in the tellings. See IDENTIFICATION; PARASOCIAL INTERACTION; RADIO DRAMA.

War of the Unstamped See STAMP DUTY; TAXES ON KNOWLEDGE; VICTIM FUNDS.

Watchdogs Newspapers pride themselves on their ROLE as watchdogs of injustice, abuse and corruption. Research tends to point to the media being rather less than wholly effective in this capacity; generally to follow rather than lead in the investigation of abuse and to be guilty of omission as much as commission (see GUARD DOG METAPHOR).

True 'watchdoggery' can only come about through genuine media independence – from ADVERTISING and sales revenue, from the influence of capital or institutional control. And yet, subject to all the usual constraints, the *Sunday Times* pressed on with its revelation of the THALIDOMIDE CASE and the *Washington Post*, by uncovering WATERGATE, contributed towards the toppling of a president. See NEWS VALUES.

Watergate Scene of one of history's most famous break-ins, and source of one of modern history's most dramatic scandals which eventually led to the resignation of the US president. The apartment block called Watergate in Washington DC was the 1972 election campaign headquarters of the National Committee of the Democratic Party. It was broken into in June by agents of the rival Republican Party's Committee to Re-elect President Richard Nixon. They were caught in the act as they were removing electronic bugging devices.

The ensuing cover-up was penetrated and revealed by two reporters on the *Washington Post*, Bob Woodward and Carl Bernstein, fed with significant information by a mysterious DEEP THROAT within government, possibly close to the president. A Senate investigation committee pushed fearlessly against presidential closed doors. Eventually the Supreme Court forced the White House to give access to tape recordings made, at Nixon's command, over a long period in the president's office. The tapes proved Nixon's complicity in the Watergate Affair.

He was the first president of the US to resign; if he had not resigned, he would have been impeached by Congress. His successor, President Ford, extended a blanket pardon to Nixon, but not to his associates, several of whom ended up in jail (and most of whom

wrote successful books on their experiences). Watergate is varyingly cited as a supreme example of investigative JOURNALISM; a classic case study of official corruption and an alarming illustration of the paranoia that sometimes comes with power and authority. However, it is perhaps most importantly a breathtaking glimpse of the nature of open government and the potential of the democratic process. No Watergate revelations could possibly take place in the UK: the OFFICIAL SECRETS ACT would have brought down the steel curtain of censorship long before the tide of proof of corruption swirled around the feet of a British prime minister. See SPYCATCHER CASE.

Wedom, Theydom Version of 'Them-and-Us'. John Hartley uses the term in *The Politics of Pictures: The Creation of the Public in the Age of Popular Media* ((UK: Routledge, 1992) to describe the *binary* nature of popular JOURNALISM and image-creation in the turn-of-the century press and beyond. Hartley sees the practices of popular journalism as being determinedly adversarial in nature, defining the world in terms of opposites – private and public, reality and illusion, allies and enemies – and arising out of a process in which media is integrated into social policy. Wedom incorporated not only the British but the Empire while excluding foreigners, though Theydom was soon conferred upon those elements of Wedom who stepped out of line – trade unions, pacifists or communist sympathizers.

Hartley speaks of a tradition of 'foe creation' which is related to notions of order – the upholding of it. What the press does, he argues, is operate a 'process of photographic negativization, where the image of order is actually recorded as its own negative, in stories of disorder'. In *Visualizing Deviance: A Study of News Organizations* (UK: Open University Press, 1989) Richard Ericson, Patricia Baraneh and Janet Chan had come to the same conclusion, but with regard to the modern journalist. 'In sum,' they argue, 'journalists are central agents in the reproduction of order.'

Wesley and MacLean's model of communication, 1957 In their article 'A conceptual model for communications

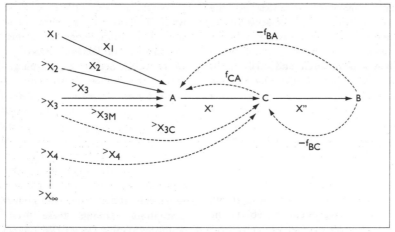

Wesley and MacLean's model of communication, 1957

research' in *Journalism Quarterly*, 34, B.H. Wesley and M.S. MacLean develop NEWCOMB'S ABX MODEL OF COMMUNICATION, 1953 with the aim of encapsulating the overall mass communication process. To Newcomb's A (communicator) B (communicator) X (any event or object in the environment of A, B which is the subject of communication), Wesley and MacLean add a fourth element, C. This represents the editorial communicating functions – the process of deciding what and how to communicate.

Newcomb's model represented chiefly interpersonal communication; it was a triangular formation, with A, B and X interacting equilaterally. Wesley and MacLean indicate that the mass media process crucially shifts the balance, bringing A (in this case the would-be communicator) and C (the mass communication organization and its agents who control the CHANNEL) closer together. C is both channel and mediator of A's transmission of X to B (now classifiable as audience), and B's contact with X is more remote than in the Newcomb model, if it exists at all save through the combined 'processing' of AC. FEEDBACK is represented by f.

It can be seen from the model that X need not go through to B via A and C but via C alone. The role of C as intermediary has a dual character, *purposive* when the process involves conveying a MESSAGE through C from an 'advocate' – a politician, for example, and *non-purposive* when it is a matter of conveying the unplanned events of the world to an audience.

The main thrust of the model appears to be emphasizing the *dependency* of B upon A and C. What is missing from the model, and what later thinking about mass media processes insists upon, are the numerous message *sources* and *influences* which work upon B other than AC, and counter-balance the influence of AC – such as the family, friends, members of peer GROUPS, workmates, colleagues, or wider influences such as school, church, trade unions, etc. See COMMUNICATION MODELS; SIGNIFICANT OTHERS.

Western Hollywood's most popularly successful transformation of the past into MYTH, with the enshrining of heroic VALUES – self-help, individualism, the legitimization of violence in the name of timeless (though rarely analysed) notions of Law and Order, and of human rights equated with access to and possession of the earth. The Western has held a firm grip on the imagination of every generation of FILM-goer since 1903 when Edwin S. Porter's *The Great Train Robbery* set the GENRE off to a brisk and colourful gallop.

Much of the fascination in studying the genre of the Western lies in relating its ideological changes to cultural and political changes taking place in America. Several commentators see the Western as a metaphor for American values, or 'Americanness': configurations of the lone hero, the community threatened by lawlessness, the appeal of the frontier and the sense of old values and lifestyles being overtaken by the urban and the corporate, continue to prompt serious research and analysis. In *Six Guns and Society: A Structural Study of the Western* (US: University of California Press, 1985) Will Wright classifies four types of Western: the *Classic*, the *Vengeance Variation*, the *Transitional Theme* and the *Professional* western. Each is characterized by the nature of its plot-line. George Stevens' *Shane* (1953), for example, is a classic Western: a lone hero enters a social group; he is revealed to have exceptional ability; the villains are stronger than society and threaten that society; the hero fights the villains; society is safe. This classical form is taken up again and again and we find Clint Eastwood re-working the form in *Pale Rider* (1985).

Fred Zinnemann's *High Noon*, directed a year earlier than *Shane* is nevertheless seen by Wright as a transitional Western, because the community, while being every bit as much at risk as that in *Shane* betrays the hero in its, and his own, hour of need.

Nicholas Ray's *Johnny Guitar* (1954) takes this theme a step further by portraying the rush-to-judgment frontier community as the real villain of the piece. The Vengeance theme has regularly been returned to, from Anthony Mann's *The Man from Laramie* (1955) via Marlon Brando's *One-Eyed Jacks* (1961) to Eastwood's *High Plains Drifter* (1972) and *The Unforgiven* (1993).

With the Professionals format the lone hero gives way to the team – a reflection, Wright argues, of changes in American business values in the 'real' world. The professionals have usually emerged from a past of crime. They undertake a job for money; society is ineffective, incapable of defending itself; the heroes all have special abilities; as a group they are independent of society; they defeat the villains (often 'respectable' citizens exploiting the community) and they either stay together or die together. The following films can be placed in this category: Howard Hawks' *Rio Bravo* (1959), Richard Brooks' *The Professionals* (1966) and Sam Peckinpah's *The Wild Bunch* (1969).

Wright says very little about Westerns in which Indians play a central part in the story, but Philip French gives this theme special focus in *Westerns: Aspects of Movie Genre* (UK: Secker & Warburg, 1973). During the chilliest days of the Cold War between west and east, the US and Russia, the Red Indian was often seen as surrogate for Red Communists – the ultimate enemy, a scenario exemplified in Charles Marquis Warren's anti-Indian movie, *Arrowhead* (1953). However, there have been many films dealing with conflicts between white settlers and Indian tribes with sympathy and perception. Among these have been Anthony Mann's *Devil's Doorway* and Delmer Davis' *Broken Arrow* both of 1950, Robert Aldritch's *Apache* (1954), John Huston's *The Unforgiven* (1960), Elliot Silverstein's *A Man Called Horse* (1970) and latterly Kevin Costner's award-winning *Dances with Wolves* (1990).

Like Wright, French draws parallels between the western and American history, seeing, for example, the Mai Lai massacre during the Vietnam War reflected in Ralph Nelson's *Soldier Blue* and Arthur Penn's *Little Big Man* (1970). The Western is, believes French, among the most didactic of film genres; as he memorably puts is, 'For every Showdown at Wichita there's a little Teach-In in Dodge City'.

Westerståhl and Johansson model of news factors in foreign news, 1994 A

useful complement to GALTUNG AND RUGE'S MODEL OF SELECTIVE GATEKEEPING, 1965 and the ROGERS AND DEARING AGENDA SETTING MODEL, 1987, this model is featured in an article 'Foreign news: news values and ideologies' by Jörgen Westerståhl and Folke Johansson, published in the *European Journal of Communication*, March 1994. Just as the *environment* or context is the centre and axis from which communicative action springs in the ANDERSCH, STAATS AND BOSTROM MODEL OF COMMUNICATION, 1969, IDEOLOGY is the central 'generator' of NEWS coverage according to Westerståhl and Johansson. As reporting of news is coloured by a prevailing ideology of *national interest*, proximity and importance constitute two of four major criteria for news selection; proximity in the sense of

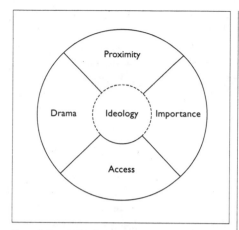

News factors in foreign news

geographic, cultural, political, linguistic or cultural closeness, affecting and being affected by another country's importance to 'us'. While the US is distant geographically from the UK it is nevertheless important – an elite nation. The Netherlands, in contrast, while being geographically close, is less 'important'. Events occurring in the US are therefore more likely to be reported than events in The Netherlands, unless those events have a direct relevance to the UK.

We recognize the NEWS VALUES as identified by Galtung and Ruge here – ethnocentrism and elitism in particular. The notion of drama is obvious enough but *access* is a welcome criterion: where reporting is possible, where reporters have access, there is greater likelihood that foreign events will be covered. The nature of that access is also critical. There was massive coverage of the Gulf War of 1991, but access to the kind of information reporters wanted if a full picture of events was to be transmitted was severely curtailed by NEWS MANAGEMENT on the part of the military authorities and by ideological pressures requiring the activities of the 'home team' to be presented in the best light.

Westerståhl and Johansson use their model to illustrate how coverage might run counter to traditional news values. They cite the case of the West's interest in Poland during strikes and protests in the 1980s mounted by the trade union Solidarity. The events were dramatic, yet Poland was neither near nor 'important'. The key

to this special attention was, in the view of the authors, ideology. Solidarity's actions threatened the chief ideological rival to capitalism – communism. If performed in the West, Solidarity's actions would have incurred critical media attention: strikes are bad for business. However, such strike action taking place in an Iron Curtain country, and in the context of the Cold War, led to Solidarity's trade unionists being cast as heroes fighting for freedom against Soviet socialist totalitarianism.

'In our view,' writes Westerståhl and Johansson, 'ideologies are the main source of deviation in news reporting from a standard based on more or less objectified news values.' See DISCOURSE OF POWER.

Westminster view Opinion that the media in the UK take their cue from and align their perspectives to the standpoint of the activities of parliament. This produces the simplistic equation – politics equals parliament, and can result in a less than adequate coverage of political events which take place away from Westminster. See POLITICS OF ACCOMMODATION.

Whistle-blowing A whistle-blower is usually an individual within an organization – industrial, commercial, governmental, etc. – who can no longer keep silent about practices in that organization; perhaps because he/she perceives them as unsafe, corrupt, dishonest or misleading. Almost invariably whistle-blowers act out of conscience. Their need for security is outweighed by a higher-order need, to square behaviour with a sense of VALUES (See MASLOW'S HIERARCHY OF NEEDS): they must speak out against the perceived abuse, even though their 'going public', by leaking information to the media, may result in dismissal. In the UK a degree of protection was offered to whistle-blowers in a private member's bill, supported by the Labour government, introduced in 1998 and becoming law as the Public Interest Disclosure Act of 1999. In future, victimization of whistle-blowers for raising concerns about financial malpractices, breaches of contract, or coverups generally will be entitled to substantial compensation. In March 1999 Trade and Industry Secretary Stephen Byers in an amendment to the government's

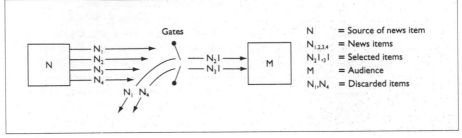

White's gatekeeper model, 1950

Employment Relations Bill raised the maximum award for unfair dismissal from £15,000 to £50,000. This put victimization of whistle-blowers on a par with victims of racial and sexual discrimination.

White's gatekeeper model, 1950 The existence of 'gate areas' along channels of communication was identified by Kurt Lewin in 'Channels of group life' in *Human Relations*, 1 (1947). At such points, decisions are made to select out information passing through the gate (See GATEKEEPING). Lewin's particular study was concerned with decisions about household food purchases, but he drew a comparison with the flow of news in MASS COMMUNICATION. David M. White in an article entitled 'The "Gatekeepers": a case study in the selection of news', in *Journalism Quarterly*, 27 (1950), applied Lewin's idea in a study of the telegraph wire editor of an American non-metropolitan newspaper.

Today the model is only acceptable as a starting point for analysis of the gatekeeping process; indeed it is a useful exercise for the student to build on the model by adding important factors which White does not include – such as the organizational elements of the mass communication process which constrain and direct it. The model also indicates only a single gate and a single gatekeeper, where in practice news passes through many gatekeepers, official and unofficial, direct and indirect. White's model should be studied in relation to McNELLY'S MODEL OF NEWS FLOW, 1959 and GALTUNG AND RUGE'S MODEL OF SELECTIVE GATEKEEPING, 1965.

Williams Committee Report on Obscenity and Film Censorship, 1979

Under the chairmanship of Bernard Williams, philosopher and then Provost of King's College, Cambridge, the Committee was set up in July 1977 by the Labour Home Secretary Merlyn Rees and reported in October 1979. The task of the Committee was 'to review the laws concerning obscenity, indecency and violence in publications, displays and entertainments in England and Wales, except in the field of broadcasting, and to review the arrangements for film censorship in England and Wales; and to make recommendations'.

After exhaustive analysis of often conflicting data, evidence and opinion on the effects of pornography, the Report concluded that 'the role of pornography in influencing the state of society is a minor one. To think anything else, and in particular to regard pornography as having a crucial or even a significant effect on essential social values, is to get the problem of pornography out of proportion with the many other problems that face our society today'.

The publication of the Williams Committee recommendations coincided with a change of government in the UK. No direct or immediate legislation resulted from the Report. See LONGFORD COMMITTEE REPORT ON PORNOGRAPHY, 1972.

* Bernard Williams, ed., *Obscenity and Film Censorship: An Abridgement of the Williams Report* (UK: Cambridge University Press, 1981).

Windlesham/Rampton Report See DEATH ON THE ROCK.

Wipe An optical effect in cinema and TV in which an image appears to wipe off the previous image. Very widely used in films in the 1930s.

Wired world Or wired society; term used

to describe the new, post-industrial economy – a telecommunications NETWORK bringing to the home multi-CHANNEL cable and satellite TV, electronic mail, push-button business transactions, all, theoretically, on a universal scale. See CYBERSPACE; INFORMATION TECHNOLOGY; INTERNET; VIRTUAL REALITY.

Wireless telegraphy In the 1870s, James Clark Maxwell (1831–79), first professor of experimental physics at the University of Cambridge, argued that wireless TELEGRAPHY would be possible by employing electromagnetic waves. In 1885, Welsh electrical engineer Sir William Preece (1834–1913) sent currents between two insulated squares of wire a quarter of a mile apart. Two years later Heinrich Rudolf Hertz (1857–94), German physicist, proved the existence of radio waves and in 1894 English physicist Sir Oliver Lodge demonstrated how messages could be transmitted and received without wires.

Similar pioneer work had been conducted by Italian Guglielmo Marconi (1874–1937) who arrived in England to further his ideas. Supported by Preece – then engineer-in-chief of the Post Office telegraphs – Marconi filed an application for a wireless patent (1896) and he was soon sending long-distance messages by Morse Code, first across the Bristol and then the English Channel. His telegraph was used to save a ship in distress in the North Sea and it was rapidly accepted that RADIO equipment was essential on board all ships. The British Admiralty paid Marconi £20,000 a year for the use of his system in the Royal Navy.

By 1901, wireless messages were being transmitted from Cornwall to Newfoundland, tapped out in morse. A year later R.A. Fissenden of the University of Pittsburg transmitted the sound of a human voice over a distance of a mile. Further progress was made possible by the invention of the thermionic valve or electron tube, by English electrical engineer John Ambrose Fleming (1904). This device served to change the minute alternating current of a radio signal into a direct current, capable of actuating a TELEPHONE receiver or the needle of a meter. American physicist Lee De Forest improved the valve by making amplification possible.

In 1910 De Forest fitted what he named a 'radio-phone' on the roof of the Metropolitan Opera House in New York, enabling listeners to hear the voices of the singers 100 miles away.

The 1st World War (1914–18) accelerated developments in radio, where it received baptism as a weapon of PROPAGANDA – by the Germans. The future possibilities for radio were encapsulated by American engineer David Sarnoff when in 1916, he declared, 'I have in mind a plan of development which would make a radio a "household utility" like the piano or electricity. The idea is to bring music into the house by wireless'.

Wireless Telegraphy Act, 1904 The result of a meeting of the major international powers held in Berlin in 1903 to prepare an international plan for the regulation of WIRELESS TELEGRAPHY at sea. The UK government required legislation in order to sign the ensuing agreements which enforced uniform rules of working. The Act established universal wireless licensing in Britain, shore and sea, granted by the Postmaster-General with the consent of the Admiralty and Army Council and the Board of Trade.

World Press Freedom Committee Formed in May 1976 to unify the free world media for major threats that develop'; consists of over 30 journalistic organizations ranging from the American Newspaper Publishers Association (ANPA), and international PRESS agencies to the INTERNATIONAL FEDERATION OF JOURNALISTS. See MacBRIDE COMMISSION; MEDIA IMPERIALISM.

X

X-certificate See CERTIFICATION OF FILMS.

Xerography Reprographic process using a photoelectric surface which converts light into an electronic charge. Documents can be reproduced in black and white and in colour to a very high standard, reduced in size or enlarged. The electrostatic image of a document attracts charged ink powder which in turn is attracted to charged paper. A visible image is formed and fixed permanently by heating.

Yamousoukrou declaration Issued by African leaders in 1985, the declaration states 'One of the main keys to solving Africa's development problems lies in mastering the national management of information in all its forms'. The text of the declaration which appeared in an International Bureau of Information report (1986) argued that information management and control are 'not only a positive force for regional and continental integration but also an essential condition for the survival of Africa within the community of nations in the 21st century'. See CORE NATIONS, PERIPHERAL NATIONS; DEVELOPMENTAL NEWS; INFORMATION GAPS; MAC-BRIDE COMMISSION; MEDIA IMPERIALISM; NEW WORLD INFORMATION ORDER; NON-ALIGNED NEWS POOL; TALLOIRES DECLARATION, 1981; WORLD PRESS FREE-DOM COMMITTEE.

Yellow journalism Phrase used in the US to describe newspapers involved in the internecine (dog-eat-dog) warfare of the popular metropolitan press empires of the late 19th c.; a battle which has continued to the present day with mass-circulation tabloids competing for readership with all sorts of exploitative offers, lurid revelations and blockbuster bingo.

Yellow Kid Newspaper cartoon character, the possession of whose widely popular image – and the use of that image – was fought over by New York's PRESS BARONS, Joseph Pulitzer (1847–1911) and William Randolph Hearst (1863–1951). The pictorial image was fast dominating the pages of newspapers at the turn of the nineteenth and twentieth centuries, proving a circulation-booster and a marketing device. Pulitzer's *New York World* first featured Richard B. Outcault's cartoon, *Shantytown* (renamed *Hogan's Alley*). Hearst 'raided' the *World's* Sunday edition, buying in the entire production team of the paper for his own, newly-purchased *Journal*. The gap-toothed Kid in his yellow smock, whose grin was recognized throughout the city on billboards and sandwich boards, joined the *Journal* as cartoon and promotional image. Soon Hearst was organizing the Yellow

Fellow Transcontinental Bicycle Relay followed by a bike carnival in New York's Central Park.

In response, Pulitzer hired Richard Buks to continue the original cartoon strip and in 1895 two Yellow Kids were in competition. 'For contemporaries,' writes Andrew Wernick in *Promotional Culture: Advertising, Ideology and Symbolic Expression* (UK: Sage, 1991), 'the Kid's colour became emblematic of the effects of intensified consumerization on the whole character of the popular press'.

No press entrepreneur was to be content with the colour yellow. Visual appeal had become central to the process of promotion. When Hearst followed Pulitzer in issuing a full colour Sunday supplement, the *Journal* announced its own 'eight pages of irridescent polychromous effulgence that makes the rainbow look like a lead pipe'.

Youth and Media See CHILDREN, YOUNG PEOPLE AND THE CHANGING MEDIA ENVIRONMENT.

Youth Culture Since the 2nd World War (1939–45) considerable attention has been paid to the cultures and sub-cultures of young people – to their symbols, signs, philosophies, MORES, NORMS, LANGUAGE, and music. Music is an essential part of all youth cultures and subcultures although the different GROUPS tend to favour different musical styles and use music in different ways.

Youth cultures and sub-cultures differ not only over time but can also differ between CLASS, sex and racial groups. Whilst they manifest significant differences there are some links between them and individuals may move from one to another. They adopt and adapt aspects of each other's cultural STYLE and those of past youth cultures and sub-cultures. The more dramatic sub-cultures have attracted attention from the media and academics. Their often spectacular modes of expression offer contrast and challenge to society, usually communicated by style – the hairstyle of the Punks for example. The media have been a notable *mediator* of society's reaction to such challenges, and this role has been a focus of media research. See COUNTER-CULTURE; FOLK DEVILS; MORAL PANIC; SENSITIZATION.

Z

Zapping The practice of TELEVISION channel-switching, especially when the commercials come on; made worryingly easy – as far as the advertisers are concerned – with the arrival of remote control. In France, an anti-zapping strategy designed to keep viewers glued to the commercials was introduced in the late 1980s: individual numbers placed in the corner of the screen offer viewers bingo-style competition. A full line of numbers wins a cash prize.

Zinoviev letter, 1924 Probably forged by Russian émigrés and used as a 'Red scare' tactic by the *Daily Mail* to put the frights on the electorate immediately before the 1924 election. Labour lost the election and the Zinoviev letter probably made some difference if not a substantial one. It was a 1200 word document marked Very Secret, bearing the address of the 3rd Communist International, the organization in Moscow responsible for international communist tactics. The letter was addressed to the Central Committee of the British Communist Party and its tenor was the need to stir the British proletariat to revolutionary action against their capitalist masters. Among other recommendations, the letter urged the formation of cells in the armed forces – the 'future directors of the British Red Army'.

The impact of the forged letter was due to its *timing*. It was 'intercepted' by the Conservative *Daily Mail* just a few days before the election of October 1924 and published four days before Polling Day. The *Mail* used a seven-deck (or lines) headline, topping the deck with 'Civil War Plot By Socialists' Masters'. With the exception of the *Daily Herald*, the entire British press swallowed and regurgitated the story. *The Times* discovered 'Another Red Plot in Germany' and on voting day the *Daily Express* warned, in red ink, 'Do Not Vote Red Today'. Labour lost 50 seats – but gained more than a million votes. See DISINFORMATION.

The truth will out and in February 1999 Gill Bennett, chief historian at the UK Foreign Office, produced a 126-page report, commissioned by Foreign Secretary Robin Cook, pointing a sure finger of accusation at Desmond Morton, an MI6 officer and friend of Winston Churchill, as the official who supplied the *Mail* with its sensational disclosure. Also named is Major Joseph Ball, an MI5 officer who joined the Conservative Central Office in 1926. Bennett reported that the forged letter was 'probably leaked from SIS [the Secret Intelligence Service, alias MI6] by somebody to the Conservative Party Central Office'. MI6 was at the centre of the scandal but Bennett could not be sure at this distance in time whether Admiral Hugh Sinclair, head of MI6, was party to the conspiracy. In a *Guardian* article 'The Hidden Hand' (4 February 1999) Robin Cook took the fullest opportunity to celebrate a 'remarkable exercise in openness' 75 years after the event, at the same time exonerating the Foreign Office from any blame, insisting that there was no institutional conspiracy and admitting that important questions remain unanswered, 'such as who forged the letter'. See FREEDOM OF INFORMATION.

Zipping Fast-forwarding through VCR programmes, most generally to zip through the commercial.

Zircon affair *New Statesman* journalist Duncan Campbell in 1986, made a series of six TELEVISION programmes for the BBC entitled *Secret Society*. The first of these was about a Ministry of Defence project – Zircon – to put a spy satellite into space, at an estimated cost of £5m. On 15 January 1987, Alisdair Milne, the BBC's soon-to-be-dismissed director-general, banned the Zircon programme on grounds of national security, a decision the *Observer* made public on 18 January.

The most notorious aspect of the Zircon affair was the police raids. Special Branch descended upon the *New Statesman* offices; upon Campbell's home as well as the homes of two *Statesman* journalists and finally there was a raid on the Glasgow offices of BBC Scotland, where all six of the *Secret Society* films were seized. Two days before, Milne had been sacked as the BBC's director-general.

The irony of the case is that Zircon (the

project was later cancelled) was not really a closely guarded state secret; indeed the position of the proposed satellite was filed by the Ministry of Defence at the International Communications Union, an institution of which the former USSR was a member. Eventually the Zircon programme was transmitted by the BBC in September 1988.

Zoetrope Or 'wheel of life'. Early 19th c. 'toy' in which pictures inside a spinning drum, viewed from the outside through slits, appear to be in motion. Invented in 1834 by Englishman W.G. Horner, the zoetrope simply but effectively demonstrated the phenomenon of PERSISTENCE OF VISION, the realization of which opened the way for the birth of cinema.

Zones In *The Hidden Dimension: Man's Use of Space in Public and Private* (UK: Bodley Head, 1966) Edward T. Hall identifies four distinct zones, or territorial spaces, in which most men and women operate. These are intimate distance; personal distance; social distance and public distance, each with its *close* and *far* phases. See PROXEMICS.

Zoom lens On a movie camera, a lens which can be adjusted automatically to give the effect of movement away from or towards the stationary camera; on a still camera, the zoom simply brings an object much closer.

Zoopraxography Pioneer photographer Eadward Muybridge (1830–1904) was not the inventor of cine-FILM but he made the first photographic moving pictures – a process he called Zoopraxography – 15 years before Lumière's first films. Muybridge described his Zoopraxiscope as being 'the first apparatus ever used, or constructed, for synthetically demonstrating movements analytically photographed from life'. In 1878 he set up an experiment at Palo Alto, California, to ascertain by photography, whether all four hooves of a galloping horse were ever simultaneously clear of the ground. 24 cameras were aligned along the running track, each triggered off by the horse as it galloped past.

The Zoopraxiscope consisted basically of a spinning glass disc bearing the photographs in sequence of movement. The disc, when attached to a central shaft, revolved in front of the condensing lens of a projecting lantern parallel to and close to another disc fixed to a tubular shaft which encircled the other, and round which it rotated in the opposite direction.

By 1885 Muybridge had produced an encyclopaedia of motion: men and women, clothed and unclothed, performed simple actions such as running, drinking cups of tea or shoeing horses; and a massive and varied study of animals and birds in movement. His carefully catalogued work was published in 1887.

Appendix: a chronology of media events

The Chronology is drawn from many sources but our best thanks go to Patrick Robertson whose *The New Shell Book of Firsts* (UK: Headline, 1994), a remarkable piece of historical detective work, has been immensely helpful. *UK* is used in a generalized sense as a composite reference to England, Britain and the United Kingdom.

AD 105   Paper produced from pulp; invention attributed to Ts'ai Lun, China.

AD 704   First printed book, the *Dharani Sutra*, created in Korea from woodblocks on a scroll, and discovered in the foundations of the Pulguk Sa pagoda in Kyongju, South Korea, October 1966.

1174   First evidence of woodblock printing in Europe, by Benedictine monks at Engelberg, Switzerland, used to print capital letters in illuminated manuscripts.

1234   ·*Compendium of Rites and Rituals*, first book printed using movable type comprising 50 chapters, 28 copies of which were published in Korea. The type was made using a sand-moulding technique developed in 1102 for casting coins.

1258   First document in English bound in leather – the Oxford Provision of Henry 111.

1287   Probable date of the first pair of spectacles, Italy. Earliest authenticated reference to spectacles as an aid to reading dates from 1289 manuscript of Sandro di Popozo.

1384   John Wycliffe makes the first English translation of the Bible.

1451   *Donatis Latin Grammar*, two leaves of a 27-line publication, the first evidence of the use of movable type in Europe, possibly the same type as that used by Johann Gutenberg in his 42-line Bible believed to have been printed at Mainz between 1451 and 1454, 48 copies of which survive, 36 printed on paper, 12 on vellum.

1454   Gutenberg prints the first calendar.

1461   Albrecht Pfister of Bamberg publishes the first books in the vernacular, Ulrich Boner's *Edelstein*, Johann von Tepl's *Ackermann aus Böhmen*.

1474   In Bruges, the Englishman William Caxton publishes *The Recuyell of the Histories of Troye*, a translation from original French text. Caxton moved to London where he printed in 1477 *The Dictes and Sayengis of the Philosophres*, a work of 74 leaves 'drawn out of frensche into our Englisshe tonge' by Anthony Earl Rivers.

1475   Jodocus Pflanzmann of Augsburg prints the first illustrated Bible.

1484   Caxton prints *Morte D'Arthur.*

1494   John Tate of Stevenage is the first to manufacture paper in England. Tate produced the first known watermark in the UK – a star and circle.

1503	Leonardo da Vinci paints *The Mona Lisa*, a year before Michelangelo carves the statue of *David*, and five years before Michelangelo starts work on the Sistine Chapel ceiling.
1513	Florence, Italy: Niccolo Machiavelli writes much of *The Prince*.
1517	Martin Luther nails his 95 Theses, protesting against the sale of indulgences, on the church door at Wittenberg. The printing and distribution of his works ignites the Reformation, and the division of Europe between Roman Catholic and Protestant faiths.
1519	Ferdinand Magellan circumnavigates the globe.
1526	William Tyndale's translation of the New Testament into English is published by Peter Schoeffer in Worms, Germany.
1536	Myles Coverdale's complete translation of the Bible into English published, probably in Cologne. This was printed in London by James Nicholson the following year.
1559	Roman Catholic church promulgates the Index Librorum Prohibitorum, a list of prohibited books; and in 1571 the Index Expurgatoris, of books permitted after censorship.
1564	Birth of William Shakespeare at Stratford Upon Avon.
1588	Dr Timothy Bright introduces the first recorded system of shorthand. His system appeared under the title *Characterie; the art of short, swift, and secret writing*. Many other systems followed. However, the first practical shorthand system, Phonographic shorthand, was devised in 1837 by Isaac Pitman, a Gloucestershire schoolteacher. His system was published by Samuel Bagster, and entitled *Stenographic Sound-hand*. The first classes in shorthand began in Bath in 1939.
1602	Printing Act, UK, includes licensing regulations which survived till 1695.
1608	The civil authorities of Norwich open the first municipal public library, chiefly for 'the use of preachers'. In 1656 Chetham's Library in Manchester became the first to employ a librarian. Chetham's was open to all. As late as 1849 it remained the only substantial collection of books fully accessible to the public. Manchester also took the lead with the lending of books. In 1852 the Manchester Free Library instituted a lending system, issuing over 70,000 books in its first year. This followed the Public Libraries Act of 1850.
1611	Issue in the UK of the Authorized Version of the Bible, the composite work of 46 translators and revisers.
1613	Publication in London of a play by Lady Elizabeth Carew the Younger, *Tragedie of Marian the Faire Queene of Iewry*. It was never performed.
1619	State of Weimar becomes the first to introduce compulsory education for all between the ages of 6 and 13. In the UK similar legislation had to wait until 1870.
1621	First *Corantos* published in London, followed in same year by first Proclamation against Corantos.
1637	Star Chamber Decree regulating printing, followed in 1643 with Ordinance for regulating printing, and in 1649 the first Printing Act.
1642	The *Mayflower* arrives in America from Plymouth, England, with a printing press on board.

1644   Publication of John Milton's *Areopagitica* presenting the case for the freedom of the press.

1649   UK: Charles I beheaded. During the period in power of the Lord Protector, Oliver Cromwell, and until the restoration of the monarchy in 1660, under Charles II, England becomes a hotbed of radical, chiefly religious publications. John Lilburne issues *England's New Chaines Discovered*.

1650   At Leipzig, the first daily newspaper, the *Einkommenden Zeitungen*, is published by Timotheus Ritzsch. In the UK the *Perfect Diurnall* was published daily, except Sunday, between February and March 1660, though British readers had to wait till 1702 for the first successful daily, the *Daily Courant*.

1651   Publication of Thomas Hobbes' *Leviathan*.

1657   First classified advertisement in a UK paper printed in Thomas Newcombe's *Publick Advertiser*, the first English paper devoted entirely to advertising.

1660   Declaration of Breda, 4 April, in which Charles II promises to grant 'liberty to tender consciences' prior to the restoration of the English monarchy.

1660–1   Parliament prohibits publication of its proceedings.

1680   Royal Proclamation suppressing all newsbooks except those under licence from the authorities.

1687   Aphra Behn, considered the first woman novelist and the first woman to earn her living from writing, publishes three works of fiction – *The Unfortunate Bride*, *The Dumb Virgin* and *The Unhappy Mistake*. She eventually produced 11 novels and between 1670 and 1687, 19 plays. *Oroonoko* (1688), an attack on slavery, was her most successful novel.

1689   Increase Mather in the US publishes *Present State of New England Affairs*, followed in the next year by Benjamin Harris's *Publick Occurrences Both Foreign and Domestick*; both were one-issue papers.

1693   In UK, the *City Mercury* is the first giveaway newspaper.

      London bookseller John Dunton issues the first women's magazine, the *Ladies' Mercury*.

1695   Parliament does not renew the Licensing Act.

1701   First provincial newspaper in the UK, the *Norwich Post*, a weekly, with an approximate circulation of 400–500 copies.

1702   First daily newspaper in Britain, the *Daily Courant*, is published in London.

1704   John Campbell publishes *Boston Newsletter*, first newspaper in the US not to be a one-issue failure.

1709   English Copyright Act, the first enactment to secure the rights of authors and publishers by offering legal protection against 'pirating' of texts. A similar act was passed in France in 1793 and in the Grand Duchy of Saxe-Weimar in 1839 (the first to employ the 30-year term of protection after an author's death). The principle of international reciprocity of rights was established in the Berne Convention of 1886.

      Under the pseudonym of 'Mrs Crackenthorpe' Mary de la Rivière Manley becomes first woman editor of a woman's magazine, the *Female Tatler*. In October she was arrested for libel for her *Secret Memoirs of Several Persons of Quality*. A grand jury indicted Mrs C. and her magazine as a 'nuisance' for similar revelations, successfully tempering the nuisance value of the periodical.

1712	In Britain, first 'Taxes on Knowledge' introduced – duties on newspapers and advertising and excise duty on paper.
1720s	Benjamin Franklin begins successful publishing career with *Pennsylvania Gazette*.
1725	Stamp Act in Britain applies 1712 regulations to all newspapers, whatever their size or format.
1739	Scotsman William Ged devises method of preserving pages of type for future reprints, using a mould made from plaster of Paris from which metal plates were made. In fear of their livelihoods, Scottish printers wrecked the invention. Sixty years later it was revived by Firmin Didot who reversed the process by creating the metal plate from sunken surfaces. Eventually stereotyping, as the process came to be known, was made a commercial proposition by amateur inventor Lord Stanhope, in 1805, at the Clarendon Press, Oxford.
	In 1829 the plaster and metal plates gave way to papier mâché, reducing time, weight and bulk – innovations happening at virtually the same time in Italy, France and England. Stanhope also improved the printing press by replacing the wooden press by an iron structure and by increasing the bed of the machine in order to produce one-pull larger scale sheets.
1741	First magazines, in US, Andrew Bradford's *American Magazine*, followed by Benjamin Franklin's *General Magazine*.
1757	UK: increases on taxes on newspapers; increased again in 1776, 1780, 1789 (the year of the French Revolution), 1797 and 1815.
1762	January: Anna Maria Smart, aged 29, becomes editor and publisher of her home-town *Reading Mercury*, a weekly. When she died in 1808 Anna was succeeded in the editorial chair by her daughter Marianne. In August of 1762, in Newport, Rhode Island, Ann Franklin, sister-in-law of Benjamin Franklin, became editor of the *Newport Mercury*.
1764	London: prosecution of firebrand editor/journalist John Wilkes for seditious libel published in the *North Briton*.
1765	Stamp Duty introduced by English government and affecting its American colonies.
1768	Publication of *Encyclopaedia Britannica*.
1770s	Thomas Paine in America. His *Common Sense* (1776), arguing powerfully for the separation of the States from English rule, proves an immensely influential bestseller.
1771	Press permitted to report the proceedings of the House of Commons, followed by those of the House of Lords (in 1775).
	The *Morning Post* published in London.
1773	London: first publication in English by a black writer – Phillis Wheatley, a slave, of Boston, US – *Poems on Various Subjects, Religious and Moral*.
1776	America wins its war of independence from English sovereignty: Declaration of Human Rights signed.
	Publication of Adam Smith's *An Inquiry into the Nature and Causes of the Wealth of Nations*.
1780	James Watt, inventor of the steam engine, takes out a patent for a duplicating

machine, to be manufactured by the firm of James Watt & Co. supported by an energetic marketing campaign run by Watt's business partner, Matthew Boulton.

UK: first Sunday newspaper published – the *British Gazette and Sunday Monitor.*

1785   Founding of *The Times* newspaper followed by the *Observer* in 1791.

Paris: fortnightly *Le Cabinet des Modes* is published, the first fashion magazine. In 1794 a German artist, Nicolaus von Heidoloff, issues in London the *Gallery of Fashion*, a monthly.

1787   First recorded advertising agency formed in London by William Tayler, who for a handling fee booked advertisements in the provincial press.

1788   UK: publication of first daily evening newspaper – *Star and Evening Advertiser.*

1789   Revolution in France: the Declaration of the Rights of Man and Citizens is promulgated 27 July; the key to this being the notion of popular sovereignty. The principles of the Revolution were to be an inspiration to radicalism in Britain and a guiding light of the Radical press.

In turn events in France provoked the authorities in Britain to take repressive measures against the Radicals and the causes they advocated.

1790   Orator and conservative theorist Edmund Burke publishes *Reflections on the Revolution in France* condemning the uprising of the common people.

1791   Tom Paine's *The Rights of Man* Part 1 published, a stirringly eloquent riposte to Burke's *Reflections.*

English philosopher Jeremy Bentham designs a 'panopticon', (the all-seeing one) for the central inspection of convicts; an idea given new life in the 20th c. in an age of electronic surveillance.

First Amendment to the American Bill of Rights guarantees the freedom of the press.

1792   First Libel Act becomes law in Britain.

Part 2 of Tom Paine's *Rights of Man* published. Also Mary Wollstonecraft's *Vindication of the Rights of Women*, demanding equal educational opportunities for women.

The French government adopts Claude Chappe's system of semaphore.

1793   Publication of William Godwin's *The Inquiry Concerning Political Justice.*

John Bell, Yorkshire-born founder of the *Oracle or Bell's New World* becomes the first-ever foreign correspondent, reporting to his own paper the fighting between the British and French in the Low Countries. He chose to march with the French rather than with the forces of the Duke of York. He reported on the British victories at Le Cateau-Cambrésis, Villiers-en-Cauche and Troixelle as well as the defeat at Tournay. His example was emulated by *The Times* in 1808 when Henry Crabb Robinson was commissioned to cover the Peninsular War.

1798   France, at the Essonne mill, Nicolas Robert introduces the first paper manufacturing machine; the first in England established at Frogmore, Hertfordshire, in 1805 by brothers Henry and Sealy Fourdriner, and at St Neots, Huntingdonshire, by John Gamble. Paper output increased tenfold.

Prime Minister William Pitt increases the tax on British newspapers from $1\frac{1}{2}$ pence to $2\frac{1}{2}$ pence and bans the import into the UK of foreign newspapers.

1800   Bavarian Alois Senefelder takes out English patent for lithographic process –

printing from the surface of a specially prepared stone. Photography is incorporated into the printed page, using lithography, from 1840.

Combination Act forbids the formation of trade unions in Britain.

1802   Founding of the *Weekly Political Register* by William Cobbett, one of the outstanding journalist/editors of the 19th c. Paper survives until 1835.

1805   Lord Stanhope's improved stereotyping machine set up at Oxford's Clarendon Press.

1806   Ralph Wedgwood in London obtains a patent for 'apparatus for producing duplicates of writing' – carbon paper – and begins successful Oxford Street business.

1807   Henry Crabbe Robinson becomes first British foreign correspondent, reporting to *The Times* under the heading 'From the Banks of the Elbe'.

1808   James Wise, son of an ex-slave who had left Nova Scotia to live in Sierra Leone, becomes the first black editor of an English-speaking newspaper, the *Sierra Leone Royal Gazette.*

1811   Thomas Bensley makes first use in the UK of the Frederick Koenig steam-driven press to print in London 3000 sheets of the *Annual Register.*

1814   *The Times* installs the Koenig press, the most significant technological advance in printing since the age of Gutenberg. The steam-driven press made mass production of newspapers a reality and, in the company of other inventions in paper manufacture and stereotyping, ushered in the first age of mass communication. The initial run was 1100 sheets per hour. The first book to be printed on the power press in the UK was Johann Blumenbach's *Physiology,* in 1817.

1820s   Publication in the US of the first black paper, *Freedom's Journal*; and in 1828, Chief Sequoyah publishes the *Cherokee Phoenix.*

1821   In Britain, the Six Acts passed, including two targeting the radical press.

        Manchester Guardian founded.

1822   Invention of the camera by Frenchman Joseph Niépce who produced the first photograph (1826). Also in 1822, William Church's letter-founding machine makes for reductions in production costs. Hand-assembly could cast between 3000 and 7000 letters a day, Church's machine between 12,000 and 20,000.

        Sunday Times founded.

1826   Leipzig publisher F.A. Brockhaus applies Koenig's steam press to the printing of books.

        First permanently fixed photograph created by Nicéphore Niépce. This was taken from an upper storey at Niépce's home at Gras, Chalon-sur-Saône.

1827   UK: *Evening Standard* founded.

1829   Four-cylinder steam press, invented by Augustus Applegarth and Edward Cowper for *The Times,* speeds the delivery of print, allowing 4000 sheets per hour. The same inventors follow this up in 1848 with the rotary press which printed 8000 sheets per hour.

        The Times carries the first full-page advertisement, 1 January, for Edmund Lodge's *Portraits and Memoirs of the most illustrious Personages of British History.*

1830   William Cobbett publishes *Rural Rides.*

US: first women's magazine published – *Godey's Lady's Book*, edited by Sara Hale.

1830s UK: the 'War of the Unstamped' waged by the radical, unstamped press against the Taxes on Knowledge.

1831–5 Publication of Henry Hetherington's *Poor Man's Guardian*, one of the outstanding radical papers of the 19th c.

1832 W.E. Weber and K.F. Gauss construct the needle telegraph in Grottingen.

The *Penny Magazine* of London becomes the first mass-circulation paper selling over 100,000 copies.

1833 Advertising Duty reduced, followed in 1836 with the reduction of Stamp Duty and Excise Duty on paper. It was not until 1853 that Advertising Duty was abolished. 1855 saw the abolition of Stamp Duty and 1861 Paper Duties.

Longman publishers issue the first book dust-jacket, to enclose *The Keepsake, 1833*, an annual publication. John Bunyan's *Pilgrim's Progress*, issued in 1860 by Longman, was encased in the first pictorial dust-jacket – a buff wrapper bearing a woodcut by Charles Bennett.

In the US, *New York Sun*, concentrating on stories of sex and violence, published by Benjamin Day. This was followed in 1835 with the *New York Herald* published by John Gordon Bennett, with specific pages dedicated to sport and finance.

1835 Henry Fox-Talbot, British pioneer in the development of photography, publishes a description in the February edition of the *Literary Gazette* of the positive-negative process which would enable the reproduction of photographs in any number.

Fox-Talbot's work coincided with that of the Frenchman Louis Daguerre who was the first to commercially exploit photography. The Daguerrotype used only the one-off positive, but it advanced exposure time from eight hours to only 15 to 30 minutes. The French government acquired the rights from Daguerre and Isidor Niépce, heir of Nicéphore Niépce (died 1833) who had gone into business with Daguerre. Thus the process became public property for all to use. Daguerre's own cameras were on sale before the end of the year.

New York Herald founded, as a 1-cent popular paper.

1836 US: Samuel Morse builds his first telegraph.

1837 Isaac Pitman invents the first practical system of shorthand, though it was not until the 20th c. that Pitman's moved ahead of rival shorthand systems in newspapers and in business.

Earliest photographic portrait image, by Louis Daguerre, of Nicholas Huet, painter and naturalist, two years before Daguerre announced his invention to the French Academy of Sciences. The picture was only brought to light, and confirmed as genuine by expert Jacques Roquencourt, in 1998.

1838 *The Times of India* founded.

Publication of the radical *Northern Star* (until 1852).

1839 In Paris, Alphonse Giroux manufactures for sale the first Daguerrotype camera.

Charles Darwin publishes *Voyage of the 'Beagle'*.

1841 First paperback book series, 'Collection of British Authors', published by Christian Bernhard Tauchnitz in Leipzig, the first title in the series being Edward Bulwer-Lytton's *Pelham*.

Voigtländer of Vienna manufacture first all-metal camera.

UK: *Jewish Chronicle* published.

1842   *Illustrated London News* is founded.

US: 27-year-old Cornelia W. Walter becomes the first woman editor of a daily newspaper – the *Boston Transcript*. She succeeded her brother, the founding editor. The two male reporters on the paper were better paid than she was. She was conservative and deeply religious and set herself, and her paper, against any scientific theories which challenged the New Testament. She was editor for 5 years but retired after her marriage.

Samuel Morse lays first submarine telegraph cable, New York Harbour.

The *Courier and West End Advertiser* prints the first full-page illustrated advertisement, for British Cornflour, 10 July.

Edward Binn's *The Anatomy of Sleep* is the first book to be set by a type-composing machine, London.

1843   Giuseppe Mazzini obtains patent for a composing machine, though the idea had originated as early as 1682 with Johann Joachim Becher, a political economist.

Though some 1500 patents had by 1900 been registered in the US for composing machines those invented by Robert Hattersley and Charles Kastenbein dominated. With each, the chief problem was the need to justify the lines by hand, a problem resolved by Linotype and Monotype machines and the punch-cutting machine of Linn Boyd Benton of Milwaukee in 1885.

Antoinette de Correvont, daguerreotypist from Paris, opens a portrait studio in Munich. Two years later, in Hull, Ann Cook opens a portrait studio. Results of the 1861 census indicated that there were 204 women photographers in the UK, approximately 8 per cent of the whole profession at this time.

A Saxon weaver, Friedrich Gottleb Keller, produces paper from wood pulp, another innovation suggested much earlier but not developed or taken up.

French physicist Reaumur in 1719 suggested the use of wood pulp in papermaking instead of rags and in 1765 naturalist Jacob Christian Schaeffer experimented with the process and wrote at length on it.

The use of esparto grass wins the interest and support of *The Times* in 1854, and is in commercial use by 1861.

The first public telegraph service is introduced following the completion of the Great Western Railway telegraph line from Paddington to Slough. William Cooke who had patented the system transferred the licence, for an annual fee, to Thomas Home and the first paid telegrams were sent by Cooke's double-needle electro-magnetic telegraph along a 20-mile wire. Eventually the Electric Telegraph Company took up the licence and pioneered nationwide telegraphy. By 1847 two systems, north and south, were in operation, linking major towns and cities. Unification of the regions took place in November.

Foundation of the *News of the World*, the *Economist* and, in Newcastle, the *Miners' Journal*.

1844   Transmission of the first press telegram, from a Congress reporter in Washington DC to the editor of the *Baltimore Patriot*, by Morse Telegraph. In the UK the first press telegraph was sent in the same year, from Windsor Castle to *The Times* via the Slough–Paddington telegraph, announcing the birth of Prince Alfred to Queen Victoria.

William Fox-Talbot's *The Pencil of Nature* is the first book in the UK to be published with photographs. This was issued by Longman's in six parts.

Society of Women Journalists founded in London.

1846   London: *Daily News* founded, with Charles Dickens (briefly) as editor.

1847   UK: publication of *Wuthering Heights* by Emily Brontë and *Jane Eyre* by her sister Charlotte, under the pseudonyms Ellis and Currer Bell.

1847–8   Karl Marx and Frederick Engels produce *The Communist Manifesto*. Having settled in the UK Marx produced his monumental work, *Das Kapital (Capital)* in 1859.

Paris, the photographic journal *Le Daguerrotype* published.

1848   In Havana, Cuba, Italian Antonio Meucci creates instrument with which he communicates between apartment floors with his invalid wife. However, it is 1860 before there is a public demonstration of the telephone, by Johann Philipp Reis of Germany, using a violin-case for a resonator, a hollowed-out beer-barrel bung for a mouthpiece and a stretched sausage skin for a diaphragm. In 1861 Reis demonstrated an improved version to the Frankfurt Physical Society, transmitting verses and songs – albeit with very poor clarity – over a 300-foot line.

The editor of the UK *Morning Chronicle* employs Eliza Lyn Linton to write features and reviews. She later became the paper's Paris correspondent. On her return to the UK she became Fleet Street's first-ever full-time woman journalist. She became known for her antipathy to women's suffrage.

1850   UK: Public Libraries Act.

Philadelphia: Frederick Langenheim patents first photographic slides.

1852   The *Englishwoman's Domestic Magazine* is first issued by 21-year-old Samuel Orchart Beeton. At 2 pence a month it soon became a mass-circulation periodical, its sales boosted by the culinary contributions of Mrs Beeton – Isabella Mayson, whom Beeton married in 1856. By the end of the decade circulation of the magazine had risen to 50,000.

J.W. Brett lays first submarine telegraph cable between Dover and Calais.

UK: House of Commons Press Gallery opens.

Surgeon John MacCosh is first British war photographer. Forty-seven studies survive of his photo-coverage of the 2nd Burma War.

1853   Liverpool: the *Northern Daily Times* becomes England's first daily provincial paper.

1854   Paris: *Le Figaro* founded.

1855   Englishman Alexander Parkes invents celluloid.

Foundation of the *Daily Telegraph*.

In UK, newspaper tax abolished.

1858   First transatlantic telegram sent by John Cash, American name-tape manufacturer, from London to his New York representative. At £1 a word, it read: 'Go to Chicago'.

1859   Mary Ann Evans under the pen name of George Eliot publishes *Adam Bede* and Charles Dickens publishes *A Tale of Two Cities*.

1861   The *Morning Star* of London commissions Jessie White Mario to write three articles a week following the unification of Italy – Jessie was a friend of both Mazzini and Garibaldi.

1863 President Abraham Lincoln proclaims abolition of slavery in the United States; Civil War follows, ending with the defeat of the Confederate states in 1865.

1865 Father Giovanni Caselli developed the first fax machine between 1857 and 1864. It was introduced for public service over the Paris–Lyons telegraph line in May 1865. However the first office fax did not become commercially available until the Xerox LDX was demonstrated in the company's showroom in New York, May 1964. The Japanese firm Sharp introduced the first colour fax in 1984.

1866 Mahloon Loomis of Washington DC, having described a system of radio signalling in a paper of July 1866, succeeds in October in broadcasting messages over a 14-mile distance.

He was granted the world's first wireless patent in 1872. Lack of funds in a period of recession prevented Loomis developing radio commercially before his death in 1886. In the UK David Edward Hughes proved a significant pioneer into the phenomenon of radio waves, but he met with little encouragement. It was left to Heinrich Hertz, the German electrical scientist, to convince the scientific community of the existence and significance of radio waves, thus making possible the development of radio telegraphy and broadcasting.

1867 Invention of the typewriter by American Christopher Sholes.

1868 London, Press Association founded.

New York: *Staats Zeitung* first newspaper to be printed on wood-pulp paper.

1870 UK: Education Act inaugurates systematic primary school education for all.

1870–1 Jessie White Mario becomes world's first woman war correspondent, covering the Franco-Prussian War for several US and British papers.

1871 Charles Darwin publishes *The Descent of Man.*

Trade unions legalized in the UK.

1872 Exchange Telegraph Company founded.

Issue of first illustrated daily newspaper, the *New York Daily Graphic.*

Although the first postcard was copyrighted by John P. Charlton of Philadelphia in 1861, and issued with a decorative border pattern, an engraving by 21-year-old Franz Rorich of Nuremberg, published in Zurich by J.H. Locher, is considered to be the first-ever picture postcard.

The first comic postcards were published in Germany in 1880. The genre was to be given its biggest boost by the prolific Donald Gill, a Scots-Canadian who produced over 12,000 different postcards from 1904. At the time of Gill's death in 1962, over 300 million of his cards had been sold.

1873 The New York *Daily Graphic* is first to publish a half-tone photograph, 2 December – an illustration of the city's Steinway Hall appeared on the back page.

1874 First Impressionist exhibition held in Paris.

American writer Mark Twain becomes the first author to possess a typewriter – made by Remington. By 1890 in the States there were 30 manufacturers producing typewriters. In the UK none were on sale until 1889, from the Maskelyne British Typewriter & Manufacturing Company.

In the same year George C. Blickensderfer's Connecticut company produced the first portable, the Blick. The introduction of the typewriter into business created new employment opportunities for women.

1876   Scotsman Alexander Graham Bell successfully initiates telephonic communication. Bell, of Edinburgh, patented the telephone on 9 March, and on 10 March, in Boston, US, the first truly coherent transmission took place – a message from Bell to his assistant, Thomas Watson: 'Come here, Watson, I want you.' The speaking telephone was demonstrated by Bell at the Centennial Exhibition, Philadelphia, 25 June. In July of the following year the first telephone line between two separate buildings was laid, in London, between the Queen's Theatre and Canterbury Hall. In the same year the first telephone exchange was created on behalf of the New England Telephone Company by Isaac D. Smith.

1877   Thomas Alva Edison of America patents the Phonograph, the first sound recording system. The prototype being completed by Edison's mechanic, John Kruesi at West Orange, New Jersey on 6 December, Edison proceeded to make history by reciting into the recording apparatus, 'Mary had a little lamb'. The Edison Speaking Phonograph Company began production in April 1879. The tin-foil cylinder provided so short a duration that public interest in the Phonograph declined.

The wax cylinder Graphaphone developed by Chichester Bell and Charles Sumner Tainter was patented in 1886, to be countered by Edison, his interest in recording renewed, with the Improved Phonograph. Edison Laboratories were the first to record music by an accredited musician, the boy pianist Josef Hofman, in 1888. There was no means of duplicating wax discs before 1892.

1878   The microphone, invented by David Edward Hughes, England and America.

1879   Dresden: Herman Krone takes first photographs using incandescent electric light.

1880   The Radiophone, devised by Charles Sumner Tainter and Alexander Graham Bell, successfully transmits speech between the top of Franklin School, Washington DC and Bell's laboratory on 14th Street.

Telephony without wires had been the invention of A.C. Brown of the Eastern Telegraph Company 2 years earlier. Reginald Fessenden produced the first conventional system of radio telephony capable of transmitting speech across distances regardless of obstacles between transmitter and receiver. He demonstrated his system for the first time over a distance of a mile, 23 December 1900. His words were addressed to his assistant, 'Is it snowing where you are, Mr Thiessen?'

In UK *Titbits* founded, followed in 1888 by *Answers* – two immensely popular weeklies.

1883   In US, Joseph Pulitzer starts up the *New York World*.

1884   Lewis Waterman in the US creates the first fountain pen.

UK: Reform Act increases electorate (excluding Ireland) from under 3 million to almost 5 million.

1885   Louis Aime Augustin Le Prince, French-born but living in the US, projects the first moving pictures – on to a wall at the Institute for the Deaf, New York, applying in November 1996 for an American patent for an 'Apparatus for producing Animated Pictures'. This was granted in January 1888 but reference to cameras and projectors was disallowed because of Dumont's British patent of

1861 (though this involved an arrangement of glass plates to form the facets of a prismatic drum and had nothing to do with the reproduction of moving images on a screen).

On the point of going into commercial production in 1890, Le Prince boarded a train in Dijon, bound for Paris where it was his intention to demonstrate his invention to the secretary of the Paris Opera. He – and his apparatus – disappeared; a mystery that remains unsolved.

1886   *New York Herald Tribune* installs the first Linotype machine, the invention of Ottmar Margenthaler.

Paris: *Le Petit Journal* becomes first paper to reach 1 million circulation.

1887   German Emile Berliner working in the US applies for a patent for the first gramophone or disc-recorder player. He demonstrated his invention at the Franklin Institute in Philadelphia in the following year. The hand-cranked gramophone was initially produced as a toy by Kammerer & Rheinhardt, Germany, using a 5-inch vulcanized rubber disc at an approximate speed of 70 r.p.m. Electrically operated machines were marketed by the United States Gramophone Company in Washington in 1894, using 7-inch records.

First overseas edition of a newspaper – *New York Herald* in Paris.

The Berliner Gramophone Company of Philadelphia produced the first shellac records in 1897. This company was also the first to create a recording studio and record shop. Double-sided discs were first manufactured in 1904 by the International Talking Machine Company, Germany, under the imprint Odeon Records.

Also in 1887, monotype printing invented in the US by Tolbert Lanston. Commercially established by 1897, the Monotype had the advantage over Linotype in that it cast each letter separately instead of in a compact line, thus making it easier to correct the text.

1888   George Eastman of Rochester, New York, produced first snapshot camera – the Kodak – for use by the general public. This used pre-loaded paper-roll film. It took 100 circular pictures 2.5 inches in diameter. Mass produced by the Eastman Company, Kodak No. 1 proved an immediate success in the US and worldwide.

In the same year John Carbutt of Philadelphia introduced celluoid film. This was made from celluloid sheets one hundredth of an inch thick, and obtained from the Celluloid Manufacturing Company. However, the first celluloid roll film to be manufactured commercially was another Eastman coup. The Eastman Dry Plate Company produced roll film for its Kodak cameras, beginning in August 1889. The first colour roll film came much later, and was invented by Robert Krayn in Germany in 1910. Amateurs had a longer wait – till Kodrachrome produced three-colour roll film in 1936.

UK: *Financial Times* founded.

1889   UK's first Official Secrets Act.

Kansas City undertaker Almon B. Stowger patents the first automatic telephone exchange. The first exchange was opened at La Porte, Indiana in November 1892. Dial telephones were introduced in 1896.

1890   Alfred Harmsworth, later Lord Northcliffe, publishes the first comic, the eight-page *Comic Cuts*, edited by Houghton Townley. Nearly 120,000 copies of the first edition were sold and this rose to 300,000 within a month. In October 1890 a rival to *Comic Cuts, Funny Cuts* appeared with the first-ever front-page strip cartoon.

Telephoto lens invented by New Zealand geologist Alexander McKay.

London evening *Star* prints the first front-page newspaper headline, 16 July. This read: MANY HAPPY RETURNS OF THE DAY – WEDDING OF PROFESSOR STUART MP.

1891 Peep-show projector, the Kinetoscope, developed by William Dickson at the instigation of his employer, Thomas Alva Edison, has first public showing in Edison's workshops in West Orange, New Jersey, to 147 representatives of the National Federation of Women's Clubs.

The first commercial showing took place at Holland Bros' Kinetoscope Parlor, Broadway, in April 1894. The films were produced by the Edison Co., which was thus the first-ever film production company. In the same year Greek showman George Trajedis installed six kinetoscopes in a converted Old Bond Street store in London, October, charging 2 pence per film.

1893 UK: first issue of the *Sketch*.

1894 The first commercially viable radio communication was the work of the Italian Guglielmo Marconi of Bologna. Experiments conducted in 1894 and 1895 led Marconi to offer his invention to Italian Ministry of Posts and Telegraphs. Failing to elicit interest, the inventor moved to England where customs officials broke open his equipment, suspecting him of being an anarchist. Undaunted, Marconi settled in London and in 1896 applied for a patent for a method by which 'electrical actions or manifestations are transmitted through air, earth or water by means of electrical oscillations of high frequency'.

The first public demonstration of Marconi's wireless took place on 12 December 1896. In the following year the Marconi Wireless Telegraph & Signal Company was formed.

1895 Brothers Auguste and Louise Lumière project the first-ever film on to a screen – *Workers Leaving the Lumière Factory*, 22 March, to members of the Société d'Encouragement a L'Industrie Nationale, at 44 rue de Rennes, Paris. On 28 December the Lumières entertained a paying audience at the Grand Café on the Boulevard des Capuchines: cinema was born.

William Randolph Hearst buys up the *New York Journal* having built up the *San Francisco Examiner*, given to him by his father, with sensational stories of gangsters and Hollywood sex scandals. The age of Yellow Journalism had dawned.

H.G. Wells publishes *The Time Machine*.

1896 First permanent cinema, the 400-seater Vitascope Hall, opened in New Orleans, 26 June, by William T. Rock. Admission was 10 cents, with another 10 to view the Edison Vitascope projector. The 5000-seater Gaumont-Palace, formerly the Hippodrome Theatre, opened in Paris in 1910. The largest cinema ever built was the Roxy Theater in New York, with 6200 seats. In Berlin 300 cinemas were opened during 1908. In the UK by 1912 there were 4000 cinemas.

J.H. Rigg of Leeds manufacture the first motorized cinema projector. An electrically powered model was demonstrated at the Royal Aquarium, London, 6 April.

Holborn-based firm Watson & Sons offers for sale the Motorgraph, the first home movie outfit, costing 12 guineas.

UK *Daily Mail* founded by Alfred Harmsworth, later Lord Northcliffe. Publication by British poet A.E. Housman of *A Shropshire Lad.*

1897   First wide-screen film on 70 mm stock introduced by Enoch J. Rector of the Veriscope Co., New York.

1898   The Telegraphone, the first magnetic recorder, is patented by Danish engineer Valdemar Poulsen employed by the Copenhagen Telephone Company. Demonstrated in public for the first time at the Paris Exposition of 1900, the Telegraphone used magnetized piano-wire running between spools at 7 feet per second.

Commercial production began in America in 1903. An improved model was used by Lee de Forest for experiments in talking-film. The use of metal tape instead of wire came in 1929 with the Blattnerphone, again used in film production, at Elstree Studios.

The use of plastic tape originated in Berlin with the Magnetophon produced by the firm AEG. This proved the archetype for all recorder developments from that time.

1900   Film: sound on disc demonstrated to a paying audience at the Paris Exposition. The first sound-on-film process was patented by French-born Eugene Lauste of Brixton in 1906. His first successful experiment in recording and reproducing speech on film came in 1910. He was ready to exploit his system commercially, only to be interrupted by the outbreak of war in 1914. He crossed the Atlantic with his idea but met with the same lack of interest as America itself entered the war.

1901   Marconi transmits messages by wireless telegraph from Cornwall to Newfoundland.

1902   Canadian-born Reginald Fessenden of the US introduces the first radiotelephone; makes the first transmission of speech by wireless.

UK: Arthur Pearson founds the *Daily Express.*

First issue of the *Times Literary Supplement.*

1903   The Telegraphone, the first telephone answering machine, invented by Danish engineer Valdemar Poulsen and patented by him in 1899, begins manufacture by the American Telegraphone Company of Springfield, Massachusetts. The machine could give a message or receive one, but could not, at this time, do both. The first machine to give and receive messages did not appear until 1943. This was designed by the Swiss firm of Buhrle and Company and manufactured as the Isophone. It was introduced into the UK in 1952.

1904   Englishman John Fleming creates the diode and in 1906 American Lee de Forest the first triode.

Alfred Harmsworth founds the *Daily Mirror.*

1906   Fessenden makes the first radio broadcast, using the 420-foot-high radio mast of the National Electric Signalling Company's radio station at Brant Rock, Massachusetts. On 24 December the programme began with Fessenden playing Gounods 'O, Holy Night' on the violin, followed by him singing and reciting from St Luke's Gospel. The first gramophone record to be broadcast came next, a recording of Handel's 'Largo'. The transmission ended with Fessenden wishing his listeners a happy Christmas. The audience for the broadcast turned out to be ships' operators within a 5-mile radius. Fessenden's second broadcast, on New

Year's Eve, in better atmospheric conditions, was received as far away as the West Indies.

In the UK the first radio broadcast came in the following year – from the radio room of *HMS Andromeda*. It was initiated by Lieutenant Quentin Crauford RN and transmitted to other ships at Chatham. News of the broadcast was not made known, for the Admiralty saw the possibilities of radio in military use, in particular as aiding communication between submarines and shore and other vessels.

1907 First regular experimental broadcasts conducted by Lee de Forest's Radio Telephone Company from the Parker Building, New York. Two years later de Forest introduced his mother-in-law Harriet Stanton Black to listeners. She gave the world's first broadcast talk; her theme was women's suffrage.

Lord Northcliffe purchases *The Times*.

In UK foundation of National Union of Journalists (NUJ).

1909 In US, National Board of Censorship of Motion Pictures established.

Sigmund Freud lectures in the US on psychoanalysis.

1911 UK Copyright Act requires copies of all British publications to be supplied to the British Museum and to five other copyright libraries.

First Hollywood studio, the Nestor Studio, opened on Sunset Boulevard by David Horsley.

UK: out of a population of approximately 40 million, 7,200,000 have the right to vote.

1912 Foundation, initially as *Herald*, of the *Daily Herald*.

1913 The British Board of Film Censors, formed in 1912 by the Kinematograph Manufacturers' Association, begins operation.

1914 Price of *The Times* reduced to one penny.

First full-length feature film in colour, *The World, the Flesh and the Devil*, shown to the trade in February, and opened at the Holborn Empire in April. Kinema-color was a two-colour system. Gaumont Chronochrome (1914) produced three colours, but three-colour processing was costly and slow in development.

Technicolor successfully produced, in 1932, the Disney cartoon *Flowers and Trees*; while the first feature-length film in Technicolor was Rouben Mamoulian's *Becky Sharp*, released in 1935.

1914–18 1st World War.

1915 UK: *Daily Express* bought by Max Aitken, Lord Beaverbrook, for £17,500.

1916 Film, *The Battle of the Somme* – first-ever war documentary.

Clydeside workers are supported in their refusal to make munitions by the Labour paper *Forward*. It is suppressed.

1918 UK: first Film Society, the Stoll Picture Theatre Club, opens with a presentation by Baroness Orczay of *The Laughing Cavalier*.

1919 UK: Arthur Mee founds the *Children's Newspaper*.

1920 The Marconi Company begins radio transmission from its Chelmsford works on 19 January. On 15 June Dame Nellie Melba gave a 30-minute recital, from Chelmsford, sponsored by Lord Northcliffe. Her fee was £1000. In November transmissions from Chelmsford were suspended on the grounds that they interfered with radio communication to aircraft and ships. Broadcasts resumed from Marconi's Station 2MT at Writtle, February 1922. 2MT was the first regular broadcasting station in the UK. Headed by Peter Eckersley, later chief engineer of the BBC, the station relied on improvisation, including that of Eckersley who proved himself an amiable broadcaster.

1922   Marconi's new station 2LO broadcasts from Marconi House in the Strand, London. Along with three other radio stations, 2LO was merged into what was to become the British Broadcasting Company. Broadcasting from Writtle remained independent until it closed down on 17 January 1923. The first BBC programme was broadcast on 14 November 1922 from 2LO – a news bulletin put out at 6 pm.

Harmsworth Newspaper Group formed, in the following year buying the Hulton chain of papers.

First play on radio, *The Wolf* by Eugene Walter, is broadcast by WGY Schenectady of New York, 3 August. In the UK *Cyrano de Bergerac* was presented by engineering staff at Marconi's experimental station 2MT Writtle, 17 October. The first play specially written for radio was Phyllis M. Twigg's *The Truth about Father Christmas*, a children's story, broadcast by the BBC 24 December.

Publication of James Joyce's *Ulysses* and of T.S. Eliot's *The Waste Land.*

First programme of sound-on-film production at Berlin's Alhambra cinema using the Tri-Ergon process developed by Joseph Engl, Joseph Massolle and Hans Voght. In the US Lee de Forest's Phonofilm process is demonstrated to the first paying audience, at the Rialto Theater in New York in April 1923.

1923   Dublin, Abbey Theatre, first production of Sean O'Casey's *Shadow of a Gunman*, followed in 1924 by *Juno and the Paycock* and in 1926 with *The Plough and the Stars.*

1924   UK: Sykes Committee Report on Broadcasting, followed in 1925 with the setting up of the Crawford Committee from which emerged the prime principles governing broadcasting in the UK until the coming of commercial TV – monopoly, funding by licence, administration by an independent public corporation.

Publication in the *Daily Mail* of the notorious Zinoviev Letter, a fake, now considered to have emanated from the UK's own secret service, MI6.

Publication of Thomas Mann's *The Magic Mountain.*

Felix the Cat becomes the first film character to be merchandized. Licences issued on behalf of Felix's creator Pat Sullivan for Felix to 'feature' on packaging and later as a soft toy.

1925   Using a mechanical scanner for transmitting and receiving, Scotsman John Logie Baird (with others) creates the first television pictures on 30 October. Baird transmitted an image with gradations of light and shade using a primitive amalgam of parts, including an empty biscuit-box for the lamphouse. For test purposes a dummy's head was used, to be replaced shortly afterwards by 15-year-old office boy William Taynton, who consented to be the first star of TV for the fee of half-a-crown.

Baird demonstrated his invention to the press on 7 January 1926, and gave a public demonstration on 27 January for members of the Royal Institution. Baird's mechanical system was soon to be overtaken by electronic TV transmission, first developed in Los Angeles by Philo T. Farnsworth in July 1929, though a more practical system developed by Russian-born Vladimir Zworykin of

Westinghouse showed the way ahead. All modern TV systems derive from Zworykin's Kinescope and the Ionoscope, the camera tube he developed in 1933.

Lionel Guest and H.O. Merriman of London apply their electrical recording process to record the burial service of the Unknown Warrior at Westminster Abbey, proving that it was possible to substitute a microphone for the studio horn, thus location recording was born. The process was not pursued commercially, but location recording was set in progress in both the US and the UK in the same year. The all-electric record player, with loudspeaker amplification instead of the usual horn, was the Brunswick Panatrope, made by the Brunswick Company of Iowa. This year also saw the introduction of the automatic record-changer, built by 20-year-old Eric Waterworth of Hobart, Tasmania.

Six records could be played in sequence. Home Recreations of Sydney bought up the idea but then went bankrupt, as did the next company Waterworth sold his patents to – Symphony Gramophone and Radio Company of London. The Gramophone Company of London launched their own machine in 1928 as the HMV Automatic Gramophone. This could play up to 20 records at a time.

First issue of the *New Yorker.*

BBC broadcast first full-length play for radio, Reginald Berkeley's *The White Chateau*, 11 November.

1925–27	Germany: Adolf Hitler writes *Mein Kampf (My Struggle).*
	Charles Chaplin's *The Gold Rush.*
1927	Kemsley Newspapers, and the Westminster Press, formed.

The Jazz Singer, using the Vitaphone synchronized disc system, opens at the Warner Theater on Broadway, 6 October. Directed by Alan Crosland and starring Al Jolson, the film is generally acknowledged to have inaugurated the age of sound-cinema and marked the death-knell of silent movies. There are only two talking sequences in the film and 354 words spoken, but the reception the film received on both sides of the Atlantic was phenomenal.

The Lights of New York, also from Warner Bros, was the first all-talking feature film. It was premièred at New York's Strand Theater, 6 July 1928. Fox Movietone's *In Old Arizona*, a Western directed by Raoul Walsh, screened in December 1928 in Los Angeles, was the first all-talking sound-on-film feature. The first all-talking colour film was Warner Bros' *On With the Show*, screened at New York's Wintergardens, 1929.

1928	On 9 February John Logie Baird makes the first international TV transmission, sending 30-line images of his own face from London by land-line to the transmitting station G2KZ at Coulsdon, Surrey and then across the Atlantic to a receiving set manned by his assistant, Ben Clapp, at Hartsdale, New York State. On 3 July Baird became the first to transmit television in colour. Employing a Nikow scanning-disc with red, blue and green filters he screened red and blue scarves, a lighted cigarette and red roses. Baird was to be the first to demonstrate high-definition colour – at the Dominion Theatre, London, on 4 February 1938.
	Lord Rothermere forms Northcliffe Newspapers.
1929	Radar invented, by Scotsman Robert Watson-Watt.
	UK: first issue of the Communist *Daily Worker.*
1931	Experiments in electronic high-definition TV transmission are carried out by an EMI research team at Hayes, Middlesex, under the direction of Russian-born

Isaac Shoenberg. The EMI system was demonstrated to the BBC in the following year – a film of the Changing of the Guard at Buckingham Palace, viewed on a 130-line cathode ray receiver with a 5-inch square screen.

RCA Victor launches the $33\frac{1}{3}$ r.p.m. long-playing record. The first recording was of Beethoven's Fifth Symphony. However, the radiograms required to play the long-player were expensive in a time of acute recession and the venture was not a success. The LP did not come into its own until 1948 when Columbia issued microgroove records developed by Peter Goldmark – vinylite discs with a playing time of 23 minutes per side, and 224–300 grooves to the inch.

1932	Stereophonic cinema sound patented by French film-makers Abel Gance and André Debrie. Gance's eight-hour silent 1927 epic *Napoléon Bonaparte* was re-edited with added dialogue and sound effects and screened at the Paramount Cinema, Paris, in 1935. Warner Bros' *House of Wax* (1953) was the first feature film with complete stereo sound.

The first stereophonic disc recordings are made by Arthur Keller of the Bell Telephone Laboratories. Made on wax masters at 78 r.p.m., they were not produced commercially but were demonstrated at the Chicago World Fair, 1933. The first stereo discs to be manufactured for sale were produced by Emory Cork of Stamford, US, in 1957.

1933   Germany: Adolf Hitler becomes Chancellor in a Nazi-Nationalist coalition, 30 January. A year later he succeeded Field Marshal Hindenberg as head of state.

Chief of the German Navy's Signals Research Department, Dr Rudoph Kühnold produces the first working radar system. Radar in the UK was the brainchild of Robert Watson-Watt, superintendent of the radio research laboratory at Ditton Park. Experiments with radar in February 1935 led to the establishment of a number of air-defence radar stations which were to prove critical in the 2nd World War (1939–45).

1934   The Emitron electronic camera is an advance on the system developed by Shoenberg in 1931. In the following year Shoenberg inaugurated the 405-line system and on 1 November 1936 the EMI-Marconi system became standard as the BBC television service began operation from Alexander Palace.

1935   UK: Selsdon Committee Report on Television.

Berlin: first television mobile unit comes into operation, employed at the opening of the Berlin TV station of the Reichs Rundfunk, 22 March. The first mobile units in the UK, designed by T.C. Macnamara, were used in the BBC's first major outside broadcast, of the Coronation, May 1937.

1936   UK: Ullswater Committee Report on Broadcasting.

1936–8   Spain: Civil War. Republican government forces eventually defeated by Fascist armies of General Franco, supported by Mussolini's Italy and Hitler's Germany.

Germany reoccupies the Rhineland.

1937   Pablo Picasso paints 'Guernica' after the destruction of the Basque town of Guernica by German planes, April 1936.

1938   Russian hypnotist, sculptor and journalist Lasalo Biro constructed a prototype ball-point pen with quick-drying ink. Having acquired British rights, Biro began manufacture in a disused RAF hangar in 1944. In 1953 Baron Bic, in France, introduced the first 'throwaway' ball-point. In the UK priced at 1 shilling, sales during 1959 totalled 53 million.

Germany annexes Austria; occupies Czechoslovakia's Sudetenland.

1939	Germany invades Poland and annexes Danzig, 1 September. Britain and France declare war on Germany, 3 September.
	US: William C. Huebner introduces photosetting of type.
	Première of *Gone with the Wind*.
1940	In UK statutory newsprint rationing introduced; ended in 1956.
1941	Release of Orson Welles' film masterpiece *Citizen Kane*, based on the life and lifestyle of American media baron William Randoph Hearst.
	USSR: Tamara Lobova becomes first woman to shoot a feature film – *Suvarov*, released in January.
	John Logie Baird demonstrates 3-D television in colour, a 500-line system, 18 December, at Sydenham.
	The Communist *Daily Worker* is suppressed.
1943	UK: Hankey Committee Report on Television.
	Germany: The *Frankfurt Zeitung* is suppressed.
1944	Automatic digital computer, by American Howard Aiken, is followed in the next year by the electronic computer invented in the US by J. Presper Eckert and John W. Mauchly.
1945	BBC launches the Light Programme, now Radio 2; and the following year, the Third Programme, now Radio 3.
	Chilean writer Gabriela Mistral is awarded the Nobel Prize for Literature.
1946	The Southwestern Bell Telephone Company of St Louis, US, offers the first commercial car phone service.
1947	Polaroid camera, by Edwin Land, US.
	Soviet Union: first 3-D colour feature film, *Robinson Crusoe*, directed by A.N. Andreyevsky. Special spectacles were not required.
1947–9	First UK Royal Commission on the Press – the Ross Commission.
1948	The Universal Declaration of Human Rights is adopted by the United Nations Assembly in Paris, 10 December.
	NBC of America screen first TV Western series, *Hopalong Cassidy*, starring Bill Boyd.
	UK: Bertrand Russell delivers first Reith Lecture, entitled *Authority and the Individual*.
1948	Bell Telephone Company scientists John Bardeen, Walter Brattain and William Shockley introduce the first transistor.
	Columbia issue first successful LP records.
	T.S. Eliot receives Nobel Prize for Literature.
1949	Xerography invented by Chester Carlson, US, the same year as Peter Goldmark of the US introduces the first long-playing record.
	CBS launch first TV thriller series, *Suspense*.
1950	UK: Beveridge Committee Report on Broadcasting.
	Yoshiro Nakamats of the Imperial University, Tokyo, develops the floppy disc.
	British philosopher Bertrand Russell is awarded Nobel Prize for Literature.

1952   First video recorder demonstration conducted in the US by John Mullin and Wayne Johnson at the Bing Crosby Enterprise laboratories in Beverly Hills, California, 11 November. A colour video was demonstrated by the same company in September of the following year. Neither was developed commercially. Ampex were the first to go into production, their initial production model being acquired by CBS.

In the UK the BBC's VERA came into operation in April 1958 with a recording of *Panorama*. Sony brought out a transistorized video recorder in 1961, while the first domestic video recorder, also from Sony, was launched in the US in July 1965. It was not until 1972 that Sony launched, in Japan, its first video cassette recorder.

In Europe Philips introduced the first domestic video cassette recorder in 1974. The VHS format was introduced in 1976 by JVC of Japan; and in the same year JVC produced the first camcorders for amateur use.

1953   Charlie Chaplin, in September, is interrogated as a suspected 'subversive' by the House Un-American Activities Committee.

American dramatist Arthur Miller writes *The Crucible.*

Winston Churchill receives the Nobel Prize for Literature.

Inauguration of the British Press Council.

BBC demonstrates colour TV. An outside broadcast of the Coronation procession was relayed by closed circuit at Great Ormond Street Hospital for Sick Children.

The first movie in Cinemascope, Twentieth Century Fox's *The Robe*, is premièred at Grauman's Chinese Theater, Hollywood and in the same month, September, *This is Cinerama* opened in New York.

1954   In the UK in July, the Television Bill is given royal assent, creating the Independent Television Authority. Commercial TV began broadcasting in Britain in September 1955.

Ernest Hemingway receives Nobel Prize for Literature.

Eurovision is inaugurated on 6 June when TV services in eight European countries linked together with a 4000-mile chain of relays. The first programme to be screened was the Festival of Flowers from Montreux, Switzerland.

Bill Haley's 'Shake, Rattle and Roll' on the Decca label tops the charts.

1955–6   First daily TV soap broadcast in Britain – *Sixpenny Corner*, running for 15 minutes daily. It failed even though it was transferred by ITV to an evening slot.

First production of *Look Back in Anger* by English playwright John Osborne, followed in 1957 by *The Entertainer.*

1957   Nobel Prize for Literature is awarded to French writer Albert Camus.

First production of *Waiting for Godot* by Irish novelist and playwright Samuel Beckett.

1958   Novelist and poet Boris Pasternak is forced by the Russian authorities to decline the Nobel Prize for Literature.

1959   Mirror Group buys Amalgamated Press.

The *Manchester Guardian* becomes the *Guardian.*

1960 Bell Telephone's Touch-Tone telephone is successfully tested and becomes commercially available in 1963.

ITVs *Coronation Street* opens its record-breaking run.

The American Telephone & Telegraph Company makes the first transatlantic satellite transmission on 11 July, from Andover, Maine to Goonhilly Downs, Cornwall, via *Telstar*.

America launches first communications satellite, Echo 1.

UK: death of the *News Chronicle*; first issue of the *Sunday Telegraph*.

UK: Harold Pinter's *The Caretaker* receives its first production.

Banned for 30 years, D.H. Lawrence's *Lady Chatterley's Lover* is ruled, at the Old Bailey, not to be obscene.

1961 UK: philosopher Bertrand Russell is jailed for anti-nuclear protest.

First issue of *Private Eye*.

1962 UK: Pilkington Committee Report on Broadcasting and the Shawcross Commission Report on the Press.

First nights on UK TV for *Z Cars*, *Steptoe and Son* and the satirical series *That Was The Week That Was*. In the following year, *Dr. Who* and *World in Action*.

Russian novelist Alexander Solzhenitsyn's *One Day in the Life of Ivan Denisovitch*, an account of prison life in the Russian labour camps, is published throughout the world, except in the USSR and the other Iron Curtain countries.

1963 US: Martin Luther King delivers his 'I have a dream . . .' speech, 28 August. On 22 November, President John F. Kennedy is assassinated in Dallas.

Founding of International Publishing Corporation (IPC); following year IPC launches the *Sun*, replacing the *Daily Herald*.

UK: BBC ends its ban on the mention of religion, politics, royalty or sex in comedy programmes.

University of Michigan scientists Emmett Leith and Juris Upatnicks develop the first hologram.

1964 BBC launches new channel, BBC2, in April.

UK starters: *Match of the Day* and *Crossroads*.

French writer Jean-Paul Sartre declines award of Nobel Prize for Literature.

1965 Via the Early Bird satellite on 2 May 300 million viewers in nine countries sample the first transatlantic programme relay. Fifteen days later America's NBC were first with a colour transatlantic satellite programme transmission.

Influential drama-documentary, *Cathy Come Home*, about Britain's homeless is broadcast by the BBC.

The Queen awards the MBE to the Beatles.

Smoking advertisements are banned from UK television.

Russian novelist Mikhail Sholokhov receives Nobel Prize for Literature.

1966 Lord Thomson buys *The Times*.

In USSR writers Andrey Sinyavsky and Yuri Daniel are found guilty of 'slandering the Soviet State' and are sent to a labour camp.

China: Chairman Mao launches the Cultural Revolution against 'reactionary bourgeois ideas in the sphere of academic work, education, art and theatre and publishing'.

Nigeria: Wole Soyinka wins Nobel Prize for Literature.

1967　First colour TV broadcast in the UK, BBC2, 1 July.

BBC Radio 1 is launched, 30 September.

The Postmaster-General, Edward Short MP, opens Radio Leicester, the first local radio station in the UK.

UK legalizes male homosexuality between consenting adults.

1968　Protest riots in many European capitals, in particular, Paris. In Vietnam US troops kill 504 villagers at My Lai. At Memphis, Martin Luther King is assassinated, 4 April. September, Soviet tanks stream into Prague. Over 300 students are killed in democracy demonstrations in Mexico.

In UK first broadcast of comedy series *Dad's Army*.

1969　First commercially produced microprocessor developed by Edward Hoff of the Intel Corporation of California.

Australian Rupert Murdoch buys the *Sun* and *News of the World*.

Denmark: film censorship is abolished.

Nobel Prize for Literature goes to Irish dramatist Samuel Beckett.

UK: York University launches first university radio station.

1970　IPC is acquired by Reed International.

London police seize Andy Warhol's film *Flesh*.

Russian novelist Alexander Solzhenitsyn is awarded Nobel Prize for Literature.

US: four Kent State University students are shot dead as they protest against America's involvement in the Vietnam War.

1971　Chilean poet Pablo Neruda is awarded Nobel Prize for Literature.

1972　UK, 30 June: 'Bloody Sunday' in Londonderry. British troops kill 13 and wound 17 Catholics during peaceful protest.

US: first pre-recorded video tapes offered for hire by Sears, Roebuck. Pre-recorded tapes were not available in the UK until 1979, supplied initially by Intervision who acquired 200 film titles from United Artists for £250,000. By the end of the year they had franchised some 150 outlets. Such was the immediate competition that Intervision soon went under despite the increase in the sales of VCRs and rental outlets.

The UK *Sunday Times* is banned on 17 November from publishing a series of articles on Thalidomide, a drug taken by expectant mothers and causing horrific deformities in babies.

Cable TV transmission starts in UK.

1973　Australian novelist Patrick White is awarded Nobel Prize for Literature.

London Broadcasting (LBC) is the first commercial radio station in mainland UK, on air 8 October.

1974　USSR: Nobel prize-winning novelist Alexander Solzhenitsyn is exiled (to America), the first deportation of a dissident from Russia since that of Leon Trotsky in 1929.

US: President Richard Nixon resigns after the Watergate inquiry.

UK: BBC inaugurates Ceefax, the UK's first teletext service.

1975   The first pop video, shown on the BBC's *Top of the Pops*, is a 7-minute film of Queen's 'Bohemian Rhapsody'. First series of BBC comedy series *Fawlty Towers*. First full colour TV service by BBC2 of tennis from Wimbledon.

1976   Czechoslovakia: members of the pop group Plastic People of the Universe, described as 'long-haired, anti-social elements', are sentenced to nine months jail for 'jeopardizing the education of youth in a socialist spirit'.

Nobel Prize for Literature goes to American writer Saul Bellow.

1977   UK: Annan Commission Report on Broadcasting and the McGregor Commission Report on the Press.

Romania: the use in the workplace of 'Mr', 'Mrs' and 'Miss' is banned, to be replaced by 'Comrade'.

1978   UK: first series of *Grange Hill*.

First video cassette recorder introduced in the UK.

US, Anaheim, California: schools are banned from studying George Eliot's *Silas Marner*.

London: Georgi Markov, exiled Bulgarian writer, is murdered on Waterloo Bridge – stabbed with a poison-tipped umbrella.

Kenya: writer Ngugi wa Thiong'o is detained for 12 months for his play *I will marry when I want*.

Japan: the Sony Walkman is launched.

1979   UK: Williams Committee Report on Obscenity and Film Censorship.

First digital recording, by Decca, of a New Year's Day concert in Vienna; recorded live by the Vienna Philharmonic Orchestra and issued in April.

Margaret Thatcher becomes first woman prime minister of the UK, 4 May.

1980   The compact disc, developed by Philips over several years, is demonstrated at the Salzburg Festival in April. By agreement with Philips, the Japanese firm Sony launched the first CD in 1982. With a playing time of 75 minutes, the CD used a grooveless miniature 12-cm disc using a laser beam to read digitally encoded information.

MacBride Commission Report for Unesco.

UK: ITV documentary *The Death of a Princess* causes offence to government of Saudi Arabia; millions of pounds in trade orders are lost as a result. The British government apologizes to the Saudis, 22 April.

1981   UK: Australian media baron Rupert Murdoch acquires the British newspapers, *The Times* and *Sunday Times*, having been exempted from a monopolies enquiry by the Conservative government, led by Margaret Thatcher.

Belfast: Bobby Sands, IRA prisoner, begins a hunger strike till death.

Spain: Pablo Picasso's Civil War masterpiece 'Guernica' is returned from New York to the Prado in Madrid.

1982   UK: Hunt Committee on Cable Expansion and Broadcasting Policy.

Poland: the sale of paper is banned in order to halt print support for the amalgamated trade union, Solidarity. In the following year the leader of Solidarity, Lech Walesa, is awarded the Nobel Prize for Peace.

Nigeria: Nobel prize-winning writer Wole Soyinka is charged with treason.

1983   West Germany: *Stern* magazine publishes alleged diaries of Adolf Hitler; soon revealed as a forgery.

British novelist William Golding receives Nobel Prize for Literature.

Breakfast TV starts on the BBC; the CD player, the pocket TV and the first cordless telephone are introduced to the UK.

1984   UK: first satellite TV channel – Rupert Murdoch's Sky Channel – begins transmission, 16 January.

Civil servant Clive Ponting is acquitted by a jury of breaking the Official Secrets Act. His relevation to the press of details concerning the British sinking of the Argentine battleship *The Belgrano* were justified in court as being in the public interest. Later the Act was redrafted to exclude public interest as a defence. The advent of a Labour government has not led to the return of the public interest clause.

Robert Maxwell takes over the *Daily Mirror* group.

1985   Rupert Murdoch buys American film company 20th Century Fox.

Citing as its reason anti-Western bias, the UK government withdraws from the United Nations Educational, Scientific and Cultural Organisation (Unesco).

Panasonic of Japan introduce to the UK the first VHS camcorder in January, and in May Sony launch the digital video recorder.

British Board of Film Censors issues age classification for videos, following the passing of the Video Recordings Act.

1986   Eddy Shah's *Today* newspaper, published in the UK, is the first to use on-the-run colour. Launched on 4 March the 44-page paper carried 16 pages in colour.

Australian TV soap *Neighbours* is introduced to UK on BBC.

USSR: Michail Gorbachev announces new policy of Glasnost, 'openness'.

Wapping, London: thousands of print workers picket Murdoch's new premises, protesting about computerization and the loss of jobs.

Northern Ireland: John Stalker's investigation into an unofficial 'shoot to kill' policy is halted as he is removed from the enquiry.

Czechoslovakia: the Jazz Union is closed down for urging the freedom of the arts.

1987   Uganda: surgeon Wilson Carswell is expelled for his *Guardian* articles on AIDS.

UK: Church of England gives the thumbs up for the ordination of women.

Sydney, Australia, September: British government is rebuffed in its courtroom appeal against the decision to permit the publication of *Spycatcher*.

Lori Miles, aged 29, becomes first woman editor of a British daily newspaper, the *Evening Standard* (Rachel Beer had been editor of both the *Observer* and the *Sunday Times*, simultaneously, in the 1890s).

1988   Poland: publication of George Orwell's *1984* (first published in English in 1949).

The first transatlantic optical fibre is laid, costing £220 million, between the US and UK/France, able to carry simultaneously 40,000 telephone calls.

1989   The Iron Curtain which divided eastern European nations – Poland, Hungary, Czechoslovakia and East Germany etc. – from the west, is drawn aside. The trade union Solidarity is permitted to contest elections in Poland; in Hungary border troops tear down the barbed-wire frontier with Austria. Most significantly, the Berlin Wall is dismantled. However, in June, freedom protests in Beijing are crushed in Tiananmen Square. The rest of the world watches events on TV.

In Iran, the Ayatollah Khomeini condemns as blasphemous the novel *Satanic Verses* by British writer Salman Rushdie and issues a fatwa or edict calling on all Muslims to strike down the offender. Despite worldwide protests, the death sentence remained active until September 1998 when the government of Iran distanced itself from, without rescinding, the Khomeini edict.

1990   UK: Broadcasting Act separates control of commercial television (ITC, Independent Television Commission) and radio (the Radio Authority).

The *Northern Echo* edited in Darlington becomes the first UK newspaper on CD-ROM.

The first tapeless answering machine, the ADAM (All-Digital Answering Machine), storing messages on a silicon chip, launched in the US by PhoneMate.

Iraq: Farzad Barzoft, journalist on the UK *Observer*, is executed in Baghdad after 'confessing' to spying.

1991   Robert Maxwell dies in a drowning accident.

1992   Los Angeles: street riots after screening of police beating up a black motorist, Rodney King.

UK: first land-based national commercial radio station – Classic FM – launched 7 September.

Canada: government Bill C-128 bans the depiction of under-18s engaging in any form of 'explicit sexual activity', including kissing.

1993   UK: carried via London Interconnect cable network, the first black TV service – Identity TV – begins, 13 July, with estimated audience of 150,000, and on 1 September BSkyB launch first women's TV channel.

Transmitting from coaches driving round London, the BBC begins first experiments in DAB (Digital Audio Broadcasting).

1994   BBC converts generalist service, Radio 5, which featured programmes for young listeners, to Radio Five Live dedicated to sports, news and chat.

Nigeria: writer Ken Saro-Wiwa is executed, with eight others, for the alleged killing of four Ogoni chiefs.

1995   Nobel Prize for Literature is awarded to Irish poet Seamus Heaney.

1997   Dario Fo, Italian dramatist, receives Nobel Prize for Literature.

1998   Bill Clinton becomes the first US president to visit Africa. In Senegal, he apologizes for the slave trade.

50th anniversary of the Universal Declaration of Human Rights (though the United Nations still spends less than 2 per cent of its budget on human rights).

UK: Sky TV launches digital television service, 1 October.

Nobel Prize for Literature is awarded to the Portuguese writer José Saramago.

1999   A jury in Oregon, US, fines anti-abortionist campaigners $107 million for publishing on their Internet website a 'wanted' list of abortion doctors, their clinics and addresses, seeing it as a thinly veiled death-threat.

February: President Bill Clinton survives Republican Party attempt to impeach him.

During the war for Kosovo, NATO bombers target TV stations in Serbia's capital, Belgrade.

UK: Greg Dyke is appointed new director-general of the BBC in succession to Sir John Birt. German novelist Günter Grass wins Nobel Prize for Literature.